NEW CENTURY BIBLE COMMENTARY

General Editors

RONALD E. CLEMENTS   MATTHEW BLACK
(Old Testament)   (New Testament)

Jeremiah

THE NEW CENTURY BIBLE COMMENTARIES

* Not yet available in paperback   *Other titles are in preparation*

8 -13 -92

Copyright © 1992 by D. R. Jones

First published 1992 in Great Britain by Marshall Pickering
and in the United States by Wm. B. Eerdmans Publishing Co.,
255 Jefferson Ave., S.E., Grand Rapids, Michigan 49503.

Marshall Pickering is an imprint of
HarperCollinsReligious,
part of the HarperCollins Publishing Group
77-85 Fulham Palace Road, London W6 8JB

Typeset by Medcalf Type Ltd, Bicester, Oxon

CONDITIONS OF SALE

Scripture quotations in this publication are from the Revised Standard
Version of the Bible, copyrighted 1946, 1952 © 1971, 1973 by the Division
of Christian Education of the National Council of the Churches of Christ
in the U.S.A., and used by permission.

Library of Congress Cataloging-in-Publication Data

Jones, Douglas Rawlinson.
Jeremiah : based on the Revised Standard Version /
Douglas Rawlinson Jones.
p.   cm.   — (New century Bible commentary)
Includes bibliographical references and index.
Eerdmans ISBN 0-8028-0490-X
1. Bible. O.T. Jeremiah — Commentaries.   I. Title.   II. Series.
BS1525.3.J66   1992
224'.207 — dc20   92-3649
                                          CIP

Marshall Pickering ISBN 0-551-02048-2

NEW CENTURY BIBLE COMMENTARY

Based on the Revised Standard Version

JEREMIAH

DOUGLAS RAWLINSON JONES

MARSHALL PICKERING
An imprint of HarperCollins *Publishing*

WILLIAM B. EERDMANS PUBLISHING COMPANY, GRAND RAPIDS

CONTENTS

PREFACE

The intention of this series of commentaries has been to provide guidance for 'students and clergy and also for the interested layman'. This is a formidable task, and few have been able to steer a safe course between the Scylla of critical complexity and the Charybdis of uncritical simplicity. The result is the gulf between the biblical scholar and the rest (including many theologians!), which is one of the characteristics of our age. I have set myself one, dominant aim: to answer the question which may be asked of any section or verse, as also of the whole text of the book of Jeremiah, viz.: what kind of material is this? The commentary represents a sustained attempt to carry out this project. This explains the preoccupation with literary problems. You have to know the genre and the structure of the book before you can legitimately draw any historical or theological conclusions from it. And this is an indispensable discipline because a book of the Bible is different in so many ways from any modern literature, and has to be read with fundamentally different presuppositions. The problem then is how to communicate such an understanding.

It is a consequence of this aim that a hypothesis has to be adopted concerning the structure and composition of the book. Without such a hypothesis no intelligible exposition of the book of Jeremiah can be undertaken. Other commentators have proceeded differently, and to them the reader must be referred, if other solutions are preferred. This is by no means an unscientific procedure. The hypothesis is tested in the course of the commentary. It is confirmed in so far as it succeeds in making sense of the whole. The reader will notice that my own hypothesis concerning the prose narratives and sermons leads to a positive estimation of our historical knowledge concerning Jeremiah. Indeed this is an important feature of this commentary. Even so this commentary differs fundamentally from many of its predecessors. The primary aim is not to strip away material identified as later than Jeremiah in order that his biography may be written. The aim is to identify each stage of the tradition, of which the ministry of Jeremiah is the first, in order that the total Jeremiah tradition may be understood.

Where textual problems have demanded solution, the Hebrew words have been indicated in transliteration. Scholars can thus discern how the resulting text has been arrived at. Others will quietly take note and pass on. For my part I am glad, again and again, to refer the Hebraist to the massive new commentary by Professor William McKane, in which justice is done to linguistic considerations, to the versions and to early Jewish interpreters.

The MS of this commentary was handed over in November 1986. In the changes and chances that befell the publishing house, it was lost, probably pulped! The loss came to light earlier this year. In the meantime major work on Jeremiah has appeared, and the opportunity has been taken to make a substantial revision. Whole sections have been re-written. That the main lines of interpretation remain the same may be put down to obstinacy or insensitivity! Or could it be that it is on sound lines? Only time will tell.

I must pay tribute to the patience of Professor Ronald Clements. Mrs Sheila Robson typed from my handwriting, and my daughter Alison took over and did the lion's share. To both I am grateful.

August 1989   Douglas R. Jones

ABBREVIATIONS

BIBLICAL

OLD TESTAMENT (*OT*)

Gen.	Jg	1 Chr.	Ps.	Lam.	Ob.	Hag.
Exod.	Ru.	2 Chr.	Prov.	Ezek.	Jon.	Zech.
Lev.	1 Sam.	Ezr.	Ec.	Dan.	Mic.	Mal.
Num.	2 Sam.	Neh.	Ca.	Hos.	Nah.	
Dt.	1 Kg.	Est.	Isa.	Jl	Hab.	
Jos.	2 Kg.	Job	Jer.	Am.	Zeph.	

APOCRYPHA (*Apoc.*)

1 Esd.	Tob.	Ad. Est.	Sir.	S. 3Ch.	Bel	1 Mac.
2 Esd.	Jdt.	Wis.	Bar.	Sus.	Man.	2 Mac.
			E. Jer.			

NEW TESTAMENT (*NT*)

Mt.	Ac.	Gal.	1 Th.	Tit.	1 Pet.	3 Jn
Mk	Rom.	Eph.	2 Th.	Phm	2 Pet.	Jude
Lk.	1 C.	Phil.	1 Tim.	Heb.	1 Jn	Rev.
Jn	2 C.	Col.	2 Tim.	Jas.	2 Jn	

GENERAL

ANET   Pritchard (ed.), J. B., *Ancient Near Eastern Texts Relating to the Old Testament*, 2nd ed. Princeton, 1969

AOTS   *Archaeology and Old Testament Study*, D. Winton Thomas (ed.), 1967

ATD   *Das Alte Testament Deutsch*

AV   *Authorised Version* (King James Version)

BDB   Brown, F., Driver, S. R., and Briggs, C. A. (eds.), *A Hebrew and English Lexicon of the Old Testament*, Oxford, 1906

BHS   *Biblica Hebraica Stuttgartensia*, K. Elliger and W. Rudolph (eds.), Stuttgart, 1977.

BJRL	*Bulletin of the John Ryland's Library*
BWANT	*Beiträge zur Wissenschaft von Alten und Neuen Testament*
BZAW	*Beihefte zur Zeitschrift für die Alttestamentliche Wissenschaft*
CD	Cairo Damascus Document
E	The Elohistic tradition in the Pentateuch
ET	English Translation
G–K	E. Kautzsch (ed.), 2nd English ed. revd by A. E. Cowley, *Gesenius' Hebrew Grammar*, London, 1910
GNB	*Good News Bible*
HAT	*Handbuch zum Alten Testament*
Heb.	Hebrew
HTOT	*The Hebrew Text of the Old Testament* (The Readings adopted by the Translators of the New English Bible), Oxford/Cambridge, 1973
J	The Jahwistic tradition in the Pentateuch
JBL	*Journal of Biblical Literature*
JSS	*Journal of Semitic Studies*
JTS	*Journal of Theological Studies*
K–B	*Hebraisches und Aramaisches Lexikon zum Alten Testament*, by L. Kohler and W. Baumgartner, 3rd ed, ed. by W. Baumgartner, 2 vols, Leiden, 1967–74
KAT	*Kommentar zum Alten Testament*
KHAT	*Kurzer Hand-Kommentar zum Alten Testament*
LXX	The Greek Septuagint Version
MT	The Massoretic Text of the *OT*
NEB	*New English Bible*
NIV	*New International Version*
NF	Neue Folge
ns	new series
P	The priestly tradition in the Pentateuch
POTT	*Peoples of Old Testament Times*, D. J. Wiseman (ed.), London, 1973
RB	*Revue Biblique*
REB	*Revised English Bible*
RSV	*Revised Standard Version*
*RV*m	Revised Version marginal note
Syr.	Syriac, the Syriac Version of the *OT*
Targ.	Targum
TB	*Theological Bücherei*
THAT	Jenni, E. and Westermann, C. (eds.), *Theologisches*

	Handwörterbuch zum Alten Testament, 2 vols, Zurich/Munich, 1971–6
TWAT	Ringgren, H. and Botterweck, G. J. (eds.) *Theologisches Wörterbuch zum Alten Testament*, Stuttgart, 1970–
VT	*Vetus Testamentum*
VT supp.	*Supplements to Vetus Testamentum*
Vulg.	Vulgate
WMANT	*Wissenschaftliche Monographien zum Alten und Neuen Testament*
ZAW	*Zeitschrift für die Alttestamentliche Wissenschaft*

Where appropriate, the divine name YHWH is rendered by LORD, as in the *RSV* and *NEB*.

SELECT BIBLIOGRAPHY

COMMENTARIES

Bright, J., *Jeremiah* (Anchor Bible), New York, 1965.

Carroll, R. P., *Jeremiah* (Old Testament Library), London, 1986.

Condamin, A., *Le livre de Jérémie* (Études Bibliques), Paris, 1936.

Duhm, B., *Das Buch Jeremia* (*KHAT* XI), Tübingen, 1901.

Giesebrecht, F., *Das Buch Jeremia* (Hand-Kommentar zum Alten Testament), Göttingen, 1907.

Harrison, R. K., *Jeremiah and Lamentations* (Tyndale Old Testament Commentaries), London, 1973.

Holladay, W. L., *Jeremiah 1 — Chapters 1–25* (Hermeneia), Philadelphia, 1986.

Hyatt, J. P., *Jeremiah* (The Interpreters' Bible V) Nashville, 1956.

Leslie, E. A., *Jeremiah*, Nashville, 1954.

McKane, W., *A Critical and Exegetical Commentary on Jeremiah Vol. I. i–xxv* (International Critical Commentary), Edinburgh, 1986.

Nicholson, E. W., *The Book of the Prophet Jeremiah* (The Cambridge Bible Commentary), 2 vols, Cambridge, 1975.

Nötscher, F., *Das Buch Jeremia* (Die Heilige Schrift des Alten Testaments), 1934.

Peake, A. S., *Jeremiah and Lamentations* (The Century Bible), 2 vols, London, 1910.

Rudolph, W., *Jeremia* (*HAT*), Tübingen, 1947, 1968.

Thompson, J. A., *The Book of Jeremiah* (The New International Commentary on the Old Testament), Grand Rapids, 1980.

Volz, P., *Der Prophet Jeremia* (*KAT*), Leipzig, 1928.

Weiser, A., *Das Buch des Propheten Jeremia* (Das Alte Testament Deutsch) 1952, 1969.

OTHER STUDIES

Baumgartner, W., *Die Klagegedichte des Jeremia* (*BZAW*), Giessen, 1917.

Berridge, J. B., *Prophet, People and the Word of Yahweh* (Basel Studies in Theology), 1970.

Bogaert, P.-M., (ed.), *Le livre de Jérémie*, Leuven, 1981.

Blank, S. H., *Jeremiah, Man and Prophet*, Cincinnati, 1961.

Carroll, R. P., *From Chaos to Covenant*, London, 1981.

Jeremiah (Old Testament Guides), Sheffield, 1989.

Diamond, A. R., *The Confessions of Jeremiah in Context*, Sheffield, 1987.

Holladay, W. L., 'Prototype and Copies', *JBL* 79, 1960.

The Architecture of Jeremiah 1–20, Lewisburg, 1976.

Janzen, J. G., *Studies in the Text of Jeremiah* (Harvard Semitic Monographs), Cambridge, Massachusetts, 1973.

Lundbom, J. R., *Jeremiah: A Study in Ancient Hebrew Rhetoric*, Missoula, 1975.

Mays, James Luther, and Achtemeier, Paul J., (eds.), *Interpreting the Prophets*, Philadelphia, 1987.

Miller, J. W., *Das Verhältnis Jeremias und Hesekiels sprachlich und theologisch untersucht mit besonderer Berücksichtigung der Prosareden Jeremias*, Assen, 1955.

Mowinckel, S., *Zur Komposition des Buches Jeremia*, Oslo, 1914.

Prophecy and Tradition, Oslo, 1946.

Nicholson, E. W., *Preaching to the Exiles*, Oxford, 1970.

Overholt, T. W., *The Threat of Falsehood*, London, 1970.

Perdue, Leo G., and Kovacs, Brian W., (eds.), *A Prophet to the Nations*, Winona Lake, Indiana, 1984.

Reventlow, H. G., *Liturgie und Prophetisches Ich bei Jeremiah*, Gütersloh, 1963.

Rietzschel, C., *Das Problem der Urrolle*, Gütersloh, 1966.

Robinson, H. W., *The Cross of Jeremiah*, London, 1925, 1955.

Skinner, J., *Prophecy and Religion*, Cambridge, 1926.

Soderlund, S., *The Greek Text of Jeremiah* (JSOTS), Sheffield, 1985.

Steinmann, J., *Le prophète Jérémie*, Paris, 1952.

Thiel, W., *Die deuteronomistische Redaktion von Jeremia 1–25 (WMANT)*, 1973.

Die deuteronomistische Redaktion von Jeremia 26–45 (WMANT), 1981.

Wanke, G., *Untersuchingen zur sogenannten Baruchschrift (BZAW)*, 1971.

Weippert, H., *Die Prosareden des Jeremiabuches (BZAW)*, 1973.

Welch, A. C., *Jeremiah, His Time and His Work*, Oxford, 1951.

Wildberger, H., *Yahwewort und prophetische Rede bei Jeremia*, Zurich, 1942.

Ziegler, J., *Beiträge zur Jeremias — Septuaginta*, Göttingen, 1958.

INTRODUCTION

to

Jeremiah

THE STRUCTURE AND COMPOSITION OF THE BOOK OF JEREMIAH

The book of Jeremiah lies open to the reader like an antique chest, full of the strange objects of a distant age, amongst which treasure is to be found. According to the received wisdom of the last century, the treasure is that which is readily accessible to our own age, the tragic life of a vivid personality, together with the uninhibited outpourings of a lonely soul, who taught mankind about individual fellowship with God. This is how the book is understood by those who describe Jeremiah as their favourite prophet. But to sort among the bric-à-brac for congenial material and virtually to ignore the rest, is to misunderstand the book, the prophet and the purpose of both.

On the other hand to try to read the book as a whole is undeniably daunting. It lacks the sequence which assists the mind to maintain attention and comprehension. At first sight it is all over the place. There is a rough, raw quality in much of the verse. We are thrown into the tragedies and sufferings of war, of defeat, of cruelty, of famine, of power struggles. We are buffeted between accusations and predictions of inescapable doom. The book is storm-ridden and only here and there does the sun break through with hope. The prophet himself seems to be no civilised philosopher, but typical of his breed, a man who speaks wild things (even to the modern ear), occasionally crude things, and behaves oddly. We have to come to terms, not with the easily received thought of a man of our own age, but with the strange, alien phenomenon of a Hebrew prophet who generated a tradition.

In the past the book of Jeremiah was served by a scholar (John Skinner), who wrote one of the most attractive books on any part of the *OT*. But everything has now changed (except, fortunately the Jeremiah text). The most extreme critics have removed the familiar landmarks and turned received opinions upside down. But if there is any way in which the modern reader can improve on the approach to be found in John Skinner's *Prophecy and Religion*, it is by understanding better the structure and composition of the book, and thereby knowing better the literary character of what he is reading. There can be no escape from this discipline, even if, for a while, it seems that secondary considerations extinguish the primary. In fact the rewards are very great for those who, with patience and faith, work for them.

POETRY AND PROSE

The first impression is of a medley of poetry and prose. This is set out more or less accurately in the *RSV* and, with some variations, in other modern versions. There are passages, like for example, the passages in chapter 50 which the *RSV* prints as prose, which can be regarded as verse. Again there are prose passages which have isolated rhythmical elements embedded in them. And there is a strong case for regarding the so-called Deuteronomic prose as prose of a special formal and enhanced kind. But whatever the reservations, the primary distinction between prose and verse stands. It is a distinction which forms the basis of all modern analysis of the book of Jeremiah. It was Bernard Duhm (1901) who confined the original utterances of Jeremiah to 280 verses of the poetry. The rest he divided between Baruch's biography and editorial additions. In 1946 Sigmund Mowinckel published his *Prophecy and Tradition*, a persuasive influence behind the thinking of this commentary. He studied the main divisions of the material, not now as 'sources' (his earlier theory), but as 'tradition complexes': A the poetry; B the prose narratives; C the prose speeches. As we shall see, in respect of language, style and thought, the distinction between B (narrative) and C (sermons) cannot be maintained. But every guide has to operate with some hypothesis or other in respect of these three types of material. Although William McKane (1986) has a different conception of the growth of the material, he too remains convinced that the poetic oracles are our principle access to the thought and message of the historical Jeremiah.

The oracle in poetic form is what we would expect from a prophet, in the light of previous prophetic collections. (See introduction to chapter 36 and especially the quotation from W. Robertson Smith.) Prophets characteristically, from the time of Amos, used the poetic form. This was the cultural form of the time. It suited both the message and the circumstances of delivery. The occasional obscurity, the allusive images, the teasing play on words, the rhythmical force of the poetic art, were what prophecy required. In an age of oral transmission, this was memorable. The first prophet who explicitly took steps to write something down was Isaiah (8.1–4, cf. 29.11). This was hardly more than a phrase on a placard, but it was done before witnesses in order that its fruition might be checked in due course. What he wrote was itself another form of prophecy, a sign in its own right to reinforce the message. There may well be a clue here as to the earliest motive for giving oracles the

permanent form of writing. Otherwise the oracles were left to the mercy
of the memory of others, and collected in due time. There is no reason
to suppose that the earliest poetic oracles of Jeremiah obeyed any other
law. Prophets did not lack fervour and the ability and will to hammer
home a message at length. But on the whole, what comes down to us
is short, sometimes tantalisingly brief. A process of the survival of the
fittest went on. We should assume that, except where there are special
reasons for the preservation of a complete oracle of artistic wholeness (eg.
Isa. 2.2–5; 5.1–7), we are faced with, so to speak, poetic concentrates.
We almost certainly have such concentrates in the early chapters of the
book of Jeremiah. The reader learns to recognise the independent units
of the prophetic tradition, and is no longer puzzled or worried by the
lack of logical sequence.

At the same time, with Jeremiah a change has taken place. The form
critics have defined the basic forms of prophetic speech as the reproach
or diatribe or indictment or ground of judgment, together with the threat
or proclamation of judgment, associated with the messenger formula. Such
clarity of analysis becomes impossible in the book of Jeremiah; the forms
are dissolved. 9.2–9 is a rare example of the classic form, and cf. 2.4–9;
22.13–19; 23.1ff. Jeremiah speaks much more frequently in the name
of God, in the first person, abandoning the clear distinction between divine
and prophetic speech. There are more laments. The forms of speech
correspond to the chaotic nature of the times. Such poetic oracles as may
be attributed to Jeremiah are mainly to be found in chapters 1–25
(Mowinckel). Other scholars have included chapters 30–31 and some even
46–51. My own approach to both these sections is complex, and the reader
is referred to the commentary. Commentators continue to differ widely.

Was Jeremiah unique in the sense that he employed two radically
different types of language? Was he like his predecessors in using the verse
form natural to prophecy, and unlike them in developing a sermon style
in Deuteronomic prose? The prose of the book of Jeremiah constitutes
one of the most serious critical problems of the book.

The B type prose is commonly identified as 19.1–20.6; 26–29; 36–45.
Some add 21.1–10; 33–34 and 52; and there are other variations. It may
be significant that the A type material stops substantially at chapter 25
(30–31 and 46–51 constituting special problems), and the B type material
at chapter 45, for both 25 and 45 have special importance for the structure
of the book.

As to the C type prose, this is commonly identified as sandwiched
between the poetic oracles (not a description I myself would use). And

although it may be anticipated in 1.1–13 and 3.6–18, it begins most clearly and characteristically at chapter 7. It includes 7.1–8.3; 11.1–4; 18.1–12; 21.1–10; 24.1–25.29; 31.23–32.44; 35.

The B and C type material are the so-called Deuteronomic prose of the book of Jeremiah. To read and use these sections, the reader has to make at least a preliminary judgment as to what kind of material it is. This is quite unavoidable. If an informed guess is not made, then an intuitional and perhaps subconscious evaluation is made. It is possible to make an error similar to that of the reader who does not understand the conventions of the historical novel, and receives it as straight history (if there is such a thing!).

The first and basic point to establish is the style of the prose. The importance of this question may be gauged from the fact that nearly all the information about the life of Jeremiah is derived from this prose. Contradictory answers have been proposed. The prose is undeniably in the style of the Deuteronomic writings. This is the most clearly recognisable style in the Old Testament, marked by a distinct vocabulary, the repetition of memorable and often sonorous phrases, simple and strong patterns of thought and sermonic structure, and devoted to a highly didactic and homiletic purpose. But the occurrence of this style does not necessarily point to a single author. It is the style of its age, the seventh/sixth century, and it is the style of learned circles during this period.

Some have thought it was also Jeremiah's style when he wrote, in recollection, the substance of his poetic oracles. To me this is overstepping the bounds of credulity. For there are characteristic themes which are not those of the poetic oracles. The difference in substance is too great, and this difference excludes the hypothesis that the main purpose of the prose was to provide, even through Baruch or others, the gist of the teaching of Jeremiah. There is no reason to doubt that whoever was responsible for the prose sermons believed that he (or they) was applying Jeremiah's teaching to his own time. But his primary interest was his preaching responsibility to his contemporaries, not an anachronistic desire to preserve the teaching of Jeremiah. Some, as hinted above, have associated both the collection of the prose sermons and the writing of narratives with Baruch. But even if he began the process (an unverifiable guess), others of a later time took on the task and left the signs of later preoccupations and problems. Whoever was responsible was motivated by a direct preaching intention, not by the concerns and disciplines of a modern historian.

The strongest tendency in recent scholarship has been to emphasise the Deuteronomic character of the prose to such an extent that it is distanced altogether from the poetry and even the time of Jeremiah. It is located in the Deuteronomic preaching circles of the early post-exilic synagogue. E. W. Nicholson here follows Enno Janssen, acknowledging that these preachers used the Jeremiah tradition, but stressing the freedom with which they preached to their own age. They deny that disciples of Jeremiah himself are responsible for these developments. They are Deuteronomists who write Deuteronomic prose and belong to the Deuteronomic tradition. Here it may be thought that these scholars are failing to admit the force of the evidence. It is true that the book of Jeremiah makes no mention of an active group of disciples, and suggests that Jeremiah worked alone, or with Baruch. It is true that the prose is Deuteronomistic. But this is only half the truth about the prose. Throughout this commentary it has been stressed that this prose is as much Jeremianic (i.e. of the specific Jeremiah tradition) as it is Deuteronomic. It has words and phrases which are common to the Deuteronomic writings; but it also has words and phrases which are peculiar to the Jeremiah tradition. A preliminary list of such words and phrases was set out by S. R. Driver in his *Introduction to the Old Testament*, 9th edition, pp. 275-7. See also the appendices in Moshe Weinfeld's *Deuteronomy and the Deuteronomic School* (1972).

McKane is critical of what he regards as narrow, lexicographical arguments. In this commentary they are used deliberately, as being the nearest we can get to an objective examination of the prose – a prose which actually lends itself to this kind of analysis, by reason of its repetitive, even monotonous character. When C. H. Dodd argued that the Fourth Gospel and the First Johannine Epistle were not written by the same author but were nevertheless closely related, he noted the usual comparisons of phrase and thought, but then he drew attention to a certain monotony in the Epistle caused by overworking a few grammatical constructions, and by using a tenth of the compound verbs found in the Gospel; and especially he noted the use of particles as being the unconscious betrayal of an author's idiosyncratic style. Greek is not Hebrew. But it is a fair extension of the argument that the author of the prose in Jeremiah betrays himself in the use of overworked, stereotyped expressions which are the nuts and bolts of his style. This does not exclude observing subtle differences of nuances in the use of expressions that are found in the Deuteronomic writings (Weippert). But there, subjective considerations are stronger. It should also be noted that the listing of phrases in this commentary has cumulative force. One or two could fall foul of the objection that they involve the argument from silence. But the total effect is overwhelming. The prose is Deuteronomistic, but it is not exactly the prose of Deuteronomy or the Deuteronomic history. It is prose of the Jeremiah tradition.

This phenomenon has not been recognised by many who speak rather glibly of Deuteronomic prose as a result of a comprehensive editing of the book of Jeremiah in Deuteronomic circles. It has been recognised by some who have then proceeded to draw wrong conclusions from it. J. W. Miller, following John Bright, analysed the difference between the prose sermons of Jeremiah and the Deuteronomic writings, and concluded that the differences were such that one could not think in terms of common authorship. But he then argued that the prose sermons were the direct work of Jeremiah. Helga Weippert fell into the same trap. She acutely drew attention to significant features of the prose which are unique to the Jeremiah tradition, but then argued for Jeremiah's personal authorship. She may be said to have made the case for a distinctive Jeremianic prose, but to have pressed her linguistic considerations beyond the evidence in attempting to prove Jeremiah's personal authorship. The conclusion does not follow from the premiss.

Nor is it sufficient to account for the peculiar vocabulary and stylistic features simply as evidence of authentic material from the prophet, which has been incorporated wholly or partly in the present sermons (Nicholson, p. 26). The features peculiar to the Jeremiah tradition are far too pervasive. They recur again and again, and they occur in different kinds of material. They are evidence not of basic source material but of the style. They point to a Jeremiah tradition, and to continuity within that tradition. Who then were these preachers? Not Deuteronomists of the post-exilic synagogue or in Babylonian exile, but representatives of the Jeremiah tradition, educated in the Deuteronomic schools. And this means they were in a real sense distant disciples of Jeremiah, forming a succession devoted to the Jeremiah tradition, preaching it relevantly to their day, extending it and preserving it, as the later redactors succeeded in doing. Jeremiah may have known only of the beginning of this prose tradition, or indeed nothing of it, nor intended it. Nevertheless the tradition, as it has come down to us, requires a Jeremiah school of preachers and redactors to account for it.

Two further conclusions may be drawn from this linguistic analysis. The first is that this analysis is relevant to both the B type and the C type material. Considered as prose of the Jeremiah tradition, the distinction

between B and C cannot be maintained. The so-called biographical prose
does not have a primarily biographical interest in the prophet. Rather does
it show the same concern as the prose sermons with Israel's disobedience
in response to the LORD's command, and the consequent threat of
judgment. This is a position cogently argued both by John Bright and
E. W. Nicholson, and there should be no retreat from it. It is confirmed
in detail in this commentary. The prose of both B and C material displays
the same phenomena of language and syntax. It is prose of the Jeremiah
prose tradition and shows the same patterns of thought.

The second conclusion has to do with the facts and episodes which are
handed down in the prose tradition. Most of our information about
Jeremiah the prophet is in fact embedded in the prose. The most recent
tendency has been to discount these facts and episodes. All is preaching.
And indeed the more it is emphasised that the prose is that of
Deuteronomic preachers of the Babylonian exile or of the putative post-
exilic synagogue, the more plausible it is to argue that they knew little
about the life of Jeremiah.

A test case is chapter 36. Here we have the story of Jeremiah, Baruch
and the writing down of Jeremiah's oracles in a scroll. It has usually been
interpreted as primarily biographical and has led to various theories as
to the identity of Baruch's scroll and the way in which the written
collection of Jeremiah's oracles came into being in the first place.
Nicholson (op.cit. pp.39–45) has compared it with 2 Kg 22, and finds
such correspondences as to confirm Deuteronomic authorship. The
underlying motive, he argues, is to contrast the reaction of Jehoiakim
to the Word of God, with the very different reaction of his father Josiah
to the newly discovered scroll of the Law. The correspondences are
notable, and we need not doubt that the one is written in the light of
the other, or that the dominating interest is Judah's rejection of the Word
of God, as spoken by Jeremiah, and the consequent judgment.

Although Nicholson calls these edifying stories (as they are), he does
not deny that they provide historical information. Robert Carroll is more
root and branch. He concludes that the chapter is entirely a literary
creation 'designed to incorporate the scribal influence into the Jeremiah
tradition . . . a story created to legitimate the role of the scribe in the
creation and transmission of the Jeremiah tradition' (*From Chaos to
Covenant*, p.15). The figure of Baruch is a Deuteronomistic invention.
So much for chapter 36. The same principle, according to Carroll, holds
for the interpretation of all the events which the prose narrative relates.
Without the prose framework, the poetic oracles are anonymous, and

they are without any hint of authorship or distinctiveness as poetry. 'It is a dogma of Jeremiah studies that the prophet is the poet of the tradition. The dogma cannot be established by argument; it can only be believed' (*Jeremiah*, p. 47). The prose framework provides a definite attribution otherwise missing. In the prose sermons Jeremiah is edited into the material. 'We should treat the character of Jeremiah as a work of fiction and recognise the impossibility of moving from the book to the real "historical" Jeremiah' (*Jeremiah*, p. 12). Thus Jeremiah disappears along with Baruch.

We may and must accept that the primary interests of the narratives and prose framework are theological, as Nicholson has demonstrated. But does this recognition entail an entirely sceptical attitude to the events and persons? There are several reasons for concluding that it does not.

First, we must insist that the prose is prose of the Jeremiah tradition, produced by men educated in the Deuteronomic schools (whether formally or informally). We are dealing with the work of men who both preached to their generation and preserved the tradition they had inherited. The mind of scholars of this age can be discerned in the Deuteronomic history, which combines a didactic purpose with a profound and unique sense of history. The Chronicler, several centuries later, shared the same insight. He had the Deuteronomic history before him. He wrote with a dominant theological intention. But he achieved his aim, not by tampering with the text before him, but by omitting what did not serve his purpose, by quoting selectively, and by adding interpretative passages. His principles and aims were not those of a modern historian, but he had such respect for the tradition that came down to him that he left it substantially intact. The beginnings of midrash stand out in contrast. For this reason his work becomes important material for the modern historian.

It was not otherwise with the men of the Jeremiah tradition. Where they referred to events in the life of Jeremiah, they accepted the tradition that had come down to them. We are worlds away from the later legendary inventions and it is vital that the modern reader should be able to see and make the distinction. Events in the ministry of Jeremiah often became the basis of the sermon, or the starting point of a collection, or both. Thus in 7.1 Jeremiah intervenes in the Temple; in chapter 11 he is commanded to preach the Law throughout Jerusalem and Judah; in chapter 14 there is a situation of drought; in 17.19 he is to stand by the Benjamin Gate; in 18.2 he goes to the potter's house; in 19.1 he is to buy the flask and break it; in chapter 20 Passhur beats him and puts him in the stocks. Both 25.1 – 14 and chapter 36 come into this category. All these are events which precipitate sermons. Then there are the sections where narrative predominates, the encounter with Hananiah and false prophets (chapters 28, 29), the buying of the family property (chapter 32), the release of slaves (chapter 34), the encounter with the Rechabites (chapter 35) and the story of the fall of Jerusalem and the flight to Egypt (chapters 37–45). Are these all didactic tales? Carroll innocently remarks, 'It is difficult to demonstrate why the Deuteronomists took up the Jeremiah poetic tradition and developed it into such a lengthy carrier of their theological outlook' (*Chaos* p. 16). Difficult indeed if you fail to acknowledge that there were men of the Jeremiah tradition who had inherited both the poetic tradition and significant stories in the prophetic ministry of Jeremiah, and who conserved, developed and proclaimed both.

This does not diminish the necessity of exercising the utmost discrimination in the use of this material. To acknowledge that we are reading about actual events and living people does not mean that the traditionists were miraculously protected from the hazards of story-telling. Even witnesses rarely give an account that is accurate and few can pass on a story without 'improving' it. As Tolstoy remarked in *War and Peace*, it requires an effort of will to tell only what happened! That being so, it is unwise to build impressive theories and hypotheses upon the basis of precise details. This seems to me the error that informs the work of William L. Holladay, who believes he can establish a coherent chronology of the life of Jeremiah ('A Coherent Chronology of Jeremiah's Early Career' 1981, and 'The Years of Jeremiah's Preaching', 1987). According to Holladay, Jeremiah was born in 627 B.C., and began to preach in 615 B.C. (at the age of twelve!). Having deduced that Deuteronomy was recited every seven years, he further deduced that the sermons of Jeremiah were preached on the same occasion in 615, 608, 601, 594 and 587. He associates a whole set of oracles and events with these dates. This is a kind of precision which the nature of the tradition does not permit us to achieve.

The second reason for not yielding to total scepticism is the existence of the prophetic succession. Are Hosea, Amos and Isaiah also the invention of editors? It might be answered that Amos and Isaiah are more involved in the text of their oracles, that the editorial framework is not as heavy as it is in the book of Jeremiah. But it is there, and Clements draws attention to 'the substantial points of connection between the redaction of Amos and Hosea and the theology of the Deuteronomic movement' (*Prophecy and Tradition*, p. 46). But if Amos and Isaiah are historical personages, then what is the phenomenological difference between Jeremiah on the one hand, and Amos and Isaiah on the other?

What in the context of the prophetic succession makes Amos and Isaiah historical personages and Jeremiah an editorial projection? And if Amos and Isaiah are said to be projections, then we have to ask questions about the historical sensibility of the person who says so. Jeremiah stands with Amos and Isaiah in being radically different from Daniel, and that difference has to do with history.

The third reason is that we have to posit an adequate explanation for the generation of the Jeremiah tradition. The oracles of the book of Jeremiah are not adequately explained as emerging anonymously, and subsequently collected together in somewhat chaotic order by editors who invented the figure of Jeremiah to link them together. Great effects have great causes. What we have in the book of Jeremiah is the intervention of a prophet, in the succession of Hosea, Amos and Isaiah, who interpreted a tragic turning-point of history in the manner of a prophet, whose ambivalent existence was itself a sign to those with eyes to see. Without Jeremiah the tradition is, to me, inexplicable, lacking the generating force to bring it into being. It is no weakening of this conviction if Jeremiah's contemporaries did not altogether see him in this light. We have the benefit of hindsight, reflection and a larger horizon. Nor can we be accused of inventing reasons for his existence. He is there, the recognised fountain-head of the tradition. Cause and effect are presented together in the tradition.

The fourth reason lies in the results of a sceptical appraisal of the Jeremiah tradition. It is remarkable how the removal of Jeremiah from the historical scene, and the interpretation of the stories as didactic legends, often weakens their character and their impact. The most striking example of this effect is the interpretation of the new covenant in 31.31–34, but there are numerous examples from the earliest chapters onwards. If the legendary status of Jeremiah were demonstrable, it would have to be accepted. But it may be said to be confirmatory of the position taken here that it opens up the full, dynamic impact of passages which are otherwise ordinary and pedestrian. Actual prophetic intervention is quite different from stories thought up subsequently. Ordinary words become charged with meaning.

There is still another aspect of the relation between the poetry and the prose which must be touched on. Allowing that Jeremiah did not have two quite different modes of communication and that, as with the prophets before him, his primary mode of communication was the poetic, was there nevertheless an inner connection between the poetry and the prose? Related answers have been proposed.

In his article 'Prototypes and Copies' (1960), William Holladay claimed to find detailed evidence that the poetry was used as a linguistic resource in the writing of the prose. And W. Thiel in his *Die Deuteronomische Redaktion von Jeremia 1–25* (1973), *26–45* (1981), proceeds on similar assumptions. Each example has to be examined on its merits. My own view is that the evidence is usually not strong enough to suggest a conscious and deliberate purpose to reinterpret or re-use the poetry. It does however support the view that the writers of the prose lived and worked in the same Jeremianic circles, were acquainted with the poetic tradition and were naturally and inevitably influenced by the vocabulary they knew well. A similar judgment is appropriate on the less convincing attempt to find a kernel of poetry in the prose. Where this is the search for the very words of Jeremiah it is doomed to failure. More formidable is the approach of William McKane, who proposes a theory which he calls 'a rolling *corpus*'. I leave him to explain his own concept.

What is meant by a rolling corpus is that small pieces of pre-existing text trigger exegesis or commentary. MT is to be understood as a commentary or commentaries built on pre-existing elements of the Jeremianic *corpus*. Where the argument is that poetry generates prose there is an assumption that the poetry which generated prose comment is attributable, for the most part, to the prophet Jeremiah. Where the thesis is that prose generates prose, the kernel may not be regarded as giving access to the period of the prophet Jeremiah and preserving the sense of words he spoke. In general, the theory is bound up with the persuasion that the rolling *corpus* rolled over a long period of time and was still rolling in the post-exilic period.

(*Jeremiah* p.1xxxiii)

McKane gives a long list of examples from chapters 1–25. There is no need to question that the process he describes sometimes happens. There is however need to question whether this is as comprehensive a process as he suggests. In individual cases other explanations may be more probable, e.g. there may be an echo from a limited reservoir of phrases held in the memory. Accident may account for some verbal connections, or another kind of editorial purpose, the putting together of observed similarities. Often it is not so much that one passage 'generates' another, as that one passage triggers the assembly of one passage with another.

McKane's theory has two great weaknesses:

(1) It overlooks the design in the putting together and assembly of complexes of originally independent oral units. This is not the logical design beloved of the modern mind. But it is compelling on its own terms

and is described in the commentary. Characteristically the design dissolves at the end of a section or complex and is completed with quotation or mosaic. Examples of mosaics may be found in 2.26-28; 33.1-13; 48.14-28, 29-47; 50.39-46. Examples of a certain kind of design in the arrangement of the material begin with chapters 1-6 and continue throughout the book. The reader is invited to examine with care the summaries given in the commentary of each main section. On chapter 2, see pp. 81f.; on 3.1-4.4 p. 96; on 4.5-6.30, p. 109; on 2-6, pp. 30, 136, 438f.; on 7-8.3, p. 158; on 8-9, pp. 158f.; on 14-15, pp. 226f.; on 14-17, p. 251; on 18-20, pp. 276f.; on 21-24, pp. 277f., 317; on 27-29, p. 346; on 26-29, pp. 358-360; on 30-31, pp. 372-376; on 37-45, pp. 448-451; on 50-51, pp. 522f. This may be described as an element of editorial homogeneity, and once criticism has done its work, it provides a way of reading the sections, as they have been finally left to us, on their own terms.

(2) The McKane theory assumes that, aside from the pre-existing poetic pieces, the whole process has to do with a written manuscript. It tends to treat the process as a vast and complicated intellectual exercise pursued at the scholar's desk. This is to underestimate the continuing oral use of sermons and stories and oracles. My own conception of the structure of the book is outlined in the next sections. It gives greater allowance for this oral tradition. On the other hand it recognises that, in the end, we are left with a literary deposit, and the literary activity becomes increasingly dominant.

BARUCH'S SCROLL

If chapter 36 may be understood to present a significant encounter in the life of Jeremiah, then further questions must be asked. There need be no retreat from the recognition of the primarily theological purpose of the presentation; nor need there be any expectation of a photographic picture of the event. But this nevertheless leaves open the interpretation of this chapter as the version of an event which the tradition did not fundamentally falsify, let alone fabricate. Then it is proper, and by no means vain, to ask whether it is possible to identify Baruch's Scroll. For this must be in the book somewhere, even if it is for ever hidden and overlaid. Some scholars identified the scroll as type C material, i.e. prose sermons or autobiographical prose. This was the view of T. H. Robinson and Eissfeldt. It has been revived by J. W. Miller. But the previous discussion must dictate an out of hand rejection. More often the scroll has been identified with part of the A material. This must be correct to the extent that the earliest collection of oracles, delivered before 605 B.C., must have been a collection of poetic oracles containing the Foe from the North poems.

Here it is appropriate to recollect the probable method of ancient redaction. Many have assumed that redactors dealt with the material that came down to them, after the image of 'scissors and paste', selecting from here and there, re-arranging to their taste. The more plausible image is that of 'nucleus and deposit'. The tendency was always to build up collections or 'complexes', and to add complex to complex. Rietzchel calls it the 'law of concentration'. At the redactoral level it is a 'rolling *corpus*'. Where a complex of traditional material is identified it is remarkable how often, both in the Isaiah tradition, and in that of Jeremiah, the last section contains mosaics of the redactor's art. This general conception leads the mind to seek the original scroll in chapters 1–6, before a series of fresh complexes begins in chapter 7. Chapters 1–6 contain mainly poetic oracles of Jeremiah's earlier ministry, and all the main oracles concerning the Foe from the North. They are all marginally subject to later expansion. Chapters 7–24 on the other hand are a collection of collections. These divide into 7–10, 11–13, 14–17, 18–20 and 21–24 (substantially the solution proposed by Claus Rietzschel. On chapters 21–24, see notes pp. 277).

In these sections, the Deuteronomic prose of the Jeremiah tradition seems to provide the structure and initiation (or generating force) of the collection. Each opens with a prose passage. 7.1; 11.1; 18.1 and 21.1 are all introduced with the formula 'the word that came to Jeremiah from the LORD'. To point the contrast, three other prose passages within the complexes (16.1–19; 17.19–27; 22.1–10) do not have this superscription. All have an event character (see pp. 24–25). If then say 1–6 is an edited form of the original scroll, the 'many like words' of 36.22 will be found in chapters 7–20. But here the redaction process is so comprehensive that it is vain to seek precise identification. It is sufficient to say that Baruch initiated a process of which the present book is the completion. See further, introduction to chapters 7–20.

The hypothesis that chapters 1–6 substantially constitute Baruch's scroll seems to me to be confirmed by the detailed exegesis of the section. If you read these chapters not as a collection of older oracles (seeking vainly for their historical context), but as a selection carefully made for its relevance to the crisis situation in 604 B.C., and intended as direct preaching to Jehoiakim as he faced the news of the Babylonian threat, then they take on an electric significance. We see Jeremiah's mind fixed, not on older controversies in the time of Josiah, but on the crisis of judgment in the time of Jehoiakim. How inevitable that this should be so! How proper to the prophetic task! What we have is what his memory sorted out as the most significant brief signals of the divine message relevant to the new situation. The importance of re-minting and newly proclaiming the old oracles was precisely to enforce that, however long the delay, the word of the LORD comes to pass in the end. There is no ultimate escape. It catches up with those to whom it is directed despite all their evasions. Although the collection represents originally separate oracles (perhaps thirty-two of them, none longer than twelve verses), the new circumstances conferred a certain homogeneity, and this is what we find.

For example, chapter 2, a collection of oracles, nevertheless presents an underlying unity of theme — the case against God's people, with the legal metaphor obtruding in vv. 9 and 29. The idea of accusation and defence runs through the whole. One senses the increase of tension as he piles oracle on oracle. No doubt Jeremiah communicated the substance of his earlier teaching, but we can be fairly sure that these verses never assumed precisely this form until he dictated them to Baruch.

Similarly, in 3.1–4.4 there is a unity of purpose dictated by the new situation. Divorce from the LORD is now inevitable. The brazenness of Israel's behaviour and worship – like the infidelity of a harlot — is stressed. Judah is warned to ponder the tragic example of her sister Israel. The section ends with a dialogue of repentance (3.19–4.4) in which the LORD sums up the conditions for avoiding the full force of the divine judgment. When the full force of divine judgment could be thought to be on the point of erupting, it is not difficult to imagine the power of these oracles and the dismay of those who witnessed their recital in 604 B.C.

The final section 4.5–6.30 contains the oracles on the Foe from the North, and so, presenting unrelenting judgment about to fall, the hitherto anonymous enemy now identified, provides a climax and a culmination for the preceding sections. The collection ends with an assertion that the work of Jeremiah as an assayer or refiner of the people has been ineffective. The Foe from the North, once teasing, uncertain, enigmatic is now committed to attack; Jeremiah cannot, the LORD will not, break his promise. There was no need to gloss these poems. They were and are irresistibly terrifying. All comes together in a unity which is not that of a modern writer, but it is intelligible and compelling in its own terms.

If this is in any respect a correct account of the composition and

structure of Baruch's Scroll, then we have confidence that we are in touch
with original oracles of Jeremiah. But also we can be certain that we do
not have them all in exactly the form of their original utterance, and that
we shall never be able to recover that form.

25.1–14

This chapter now falls to be considered, not only because it follows the
collections we have just analysed, but also because it is parallel to chapter
36 and is an oracle on the oracles of the previous twenty-three years.
Jeremiah was commanded to comment on the fact that he had exercised
his prophetic commission for all these years without response or success,
and that now judgment would fall. The commentary on chapter 25 shows
that vv. 1–14 are a model of the distinctive prose style of the Jeremiah
prose tradition. The sermon starts from an event. The event in chapter
36 is of course the specific command to Baruch to write down the oracles
'from the day I spoke to you, from the days of Josiah until now'.

Chapter 25 may be interpreted as expressing the intention behind the
writing down and reading of the oracles as narrated in chapter 36. It is
not necessary to set one against the other. The relationship between
25.1–14 and 36 has features in common with the relationship between
7.1–15 and chapter 26. Chapters 26 and 36 are more concerned with
the event; chapters 7 and 25 with the content of Jeremiah's message. None
can claim to be photographic representations either of event or message.
Thus the passages have complementary intentions, but it is a mistake
to try to harmonise them historically.

The only thing that is clear is that 25.1–14 discloses its significance
when it is read after Baruch's Scroll. Its centre of interest is not a narrative
with prophetic force (like chapter 36) but the total impact of Jeremiah's
ministry to date. In the year 604, Jeremiah was concerned with the
cumulative effect of his past prophecies in relation to the incomprehension
of the people and the judgment about to break. A preacher of the Jeremiah
tradition developed this in his characteristic way and a redactor placed
the passage, as is overwhelmingly probable, at the conclusion of a
collection of Jeremiah's oracles rather than at the beginning. The
Massoretic Text (MT) and the Septuagint (LXX) agree in placing 25.1ff.
in its present position, but their major differences begin thereafter. This
suggests that at a comparatively early stage of redaction, it was arranged
as the conclusion to chapters 1–24. At this stage we may suppose that

the fundamental deposit of the Jeremiah tradition was contained in chapters 1–25. We can be confident that this is an editorial phenomenon, since the collection contained in chapters 21–24 belonged to the reign of Zedekiah. This position for chapter 25.1–14 is not therefore likely to be the original one. It is plausible to suppose that at the earliest stage it completed Baruch's Scroll, the nucleus upon which subsequent collections were deposited. As then subsequent collections were added, it remained in its position at the end.

The commentary on 25.1–14 yields further evidence of a complex redaction process. The LXX provides the essential clues. The LXX form of the text is slightly shorter than MT. It was the view of Rudolph and others that the LXX tends to abbreviate MT. The evidence here does not support them. On the contrary, it confirms the judgment of Gerald Janzen (*Studies in the Text of Jeremiah*, 1973), that MT represents an expansion. The fragmentary Jeremiah texts from Qumran support the view that the two textual traditions existed side by side in the community's library. Two of the three Jeremiah MSS from Cave 4 follow MT; the third (4 Q Jer^b) follows LXX in chapter 10. As will appear it is not possible, nevertheless, to suppose that LXX in every case provides the original text *simpliciter*. Each case has to be examined separately and it is a complex process that emerges. When we turn to 25.1–14 we find that a series of expansions are disclosed by comparing MT with LXX. These are all by way of identifying glosses such as are familiar in the Isaiah tradition (eg. Isa. 7.8b, 17, 18, 20; 8.7b), and contain all the references to Nebuchadrezzar and the Babylonians. The whole of v. 14 is absent from LXX. The older spelling of the name Nebuchadrezzar is used in the glosses. LXX always uses the later form of Nebuchadnezzar. This means that the original text referred to 'tribes of the North' (v. 9) and did not specify the Babylonians, echoing the oracles of the Foe from the North in chapters 4–6. The wording is close to 1.15 (a double reading), and of course chapter 1 also shows the influence of the prose tradition.

In the light of these considerations it becomes plausible to treat the problem v. 13 as an addition brought in to relate the passage to the oracles against the Babylonians. 'I will bring upon *that land* all the words which I have uttered against it, everything written in this book, which Jeremiah prophesied against all the nations'. The expedient of changing 'that land' to 'this land', favoured by many, so applying the original oracle to Judah is not acceptable. But as it stands in relation to the original text, 'that land' has no antecedent and little to constitute an adequate prediction to claim fulfilment. We may suppose vv. 12–13 were added when the glosses were added and when the oracles against the nations were appended, especially those against Babylon (50–51). The LXX here shows itself adapting v. 13 perhaps clumsily to introduce the first of the oracles against the nations. 'Which Jeremiah prophesied against the nations' — becomes: 'The things which Jeremiah prophesied against the nations — Elam'. So the last words of 25.1–13 become the first words of the collection against the nations. In this respect MT is primary and LXX secondary.

The stages of transmission may be summarised thus:

1. Intervention of Jeremiah in the fourth year of Jehoiakim, *speaking* to the people concerning all his oracles of the previous twenty-three years (627–604) (25.1–7) and *writing down* his oracles and *reading* them (Baruch) on the fast day in Dec. 604 (chapter 36).

2. Baruch or another in the Jeremiah tradition writes down an account of this intervention, as in 25.1–11. This did not contain the glosses i.e. the text is that of LXX. This may well have been part of the editorial procedure when chapters 1–6 or 1–20 were set out in writing and 25.1–11 concluded them.

3. In the time of Zedekiah or later, vv. 1–11 were expanded by the addition of the prophecy of the downfall of 'that land' (v. 13), still without precise reference to Babylon. The addition of the prophecies against Babylon (chapters 50–51) made it possible to gloss the references to the nations to make the implicit reference to Nebuchadrezzar clear and to add v. 14.

4. A redactor found 25.1–13 a good place to add a prophecy concerning the nations generally. In the case of the LXX the collection of the oracles against the nations (chapters 46–51 in MT) were placed here with their own heading adapted from the last phrase of v. 13. In the MT tradition a more careful building up of 25.1–13 was achieved by the addition of v. 14 and the two sections on the. Cup of Wrath (vv. 25–29) and the Shepherds (vv. 30–38).

25.15–29 AND THE ORACLES AGAINST THE NATIONS (46–51)

In 25.15–29 also, the text as it exists has been subject to a process of transmission and amplification, particularly in relation to the list of foreign nations that are to drink the Cup of Wrath. Omit those absent from the LXX including Babylon, and it becomes intelligibly slimmed down, showing that the list was extended in the light of history. The question then arises whether the text common to MT and LXX was itself subject to such expansion. One notes that the phrase 'all the kings of . . .' occurs somewhat erratically. If these are omitted then the following are left:

Pharaoh king of Egypt, etc.
Ashkelon, Gaza (Ekron) and the remnant of Ashdod,
Edom, Moab and the Ammonites
Dedan, Tema, Buz and all who roam about on
the fringes of the desert.

It must then be significant that the list of foreign nations in chapters 46–51 corresponds to this basic fourfold division, save that Damascus and Kedar stand for the Arab element and Babylon is added:

Egypt
Philistia
Moab, Ammon, Edom,
Damascus, Kedar

Elam
Babylon

The LXX (25.14–31.44) departs from this order, and if the hypothesis above is correct, then the order retained by MT is primary, except that the literary character of the oracle against Moab raises special problems. See commentary.

As now arranged, the oracles against the nations, for reasons set out repeatedly in the commentary, must belong to the period before the rise of Cyrus. They are likely to have a liturgical or quasi-liturgical context. They exhibit clear signs of the Jeremiah tradition and it must be concluded that they owe their authorship to men of this tradition. Some are original poems (e.g. 46), some are learned mosaics (48; 50.39–46; 51.41–46). But none are likely to be the work of Jeremiah himself. In particular the oracles against Babylon, which form an independent collection, are based on a theology clean contrary to the teaching of Jeremiah himself, and yet not inappropriate to the later period and its problems. These oracles exhibit familiar signs of the redactor's skill, not only in the compilation of poems out of Jeremianic material, but also in quotation (The Song of the Creator 52.15–19), in the addition of prose comment, in arrangement and in total concept (51.59–64). Because they stand out as a unique *genre* the reader is referred to the relevant parts of the commentary where an attempt is made to work out the literary problems.

CHAPTERS 26–35 (36)

The first reason for regarding chapters 26–35 as a separate complex of material within the tradition is that chapters 37–44 (45) clearly form an independent section, with marked homogeneity. The second is that, although it contains varied material (poetry and prose, didactive narrative, prose discourses and poetic oracles of salvation), it is possible to see how the collection was built up. An attempt is made on pp. 337ff. to understand the construction of the collection, including the oracles of salvation or so-called 'book of consolation' in chapters 30–31. Chapter 36 may then be interpreted as an appropriate conclusion to the oracles of Jeremiah as they had been collected to date. The emphasis is then not on chronology (the fourth year of Jehoiakim), since material from the time of Zedekiah has been included, but on the fact that the oracles of Jeremiah had survived attempts to extinguish them and now contained the many 'similar words' with which the earlier collections had been augmented. Thus we can understand how chapter 36 performed a function rather like that of chapter 25 for an earlier collection. The position of chapter 36 is not therefore chronological but a phenomenon of the transmission process and the redactor's intention.

As to the 'book of consolation', this shows the signs of being an independent collection of oracles held within the Jeremiah tradition about the future. This is suggested by the degree of homogeneity of the subject matter, the predominantly northern affiliation of the oracles and the special superscription of 30.1–2. If this is so, it is possible to see why these oracles were placed to follow chapters 27–29. Chapters 27–29 provide yet another important study in transmission history and are so studied in the commentary. As the shorter LXX suggests, these chapters were subject to glossing (see especially 29.11–14, 22). This glossing was precisely to put a new emphasis on the hope of salvation, and it was this emphasis which prepared the way for the concentration on this hope in chapters 30–31. The collection contains prose in 31.26–34: in fact three passages each introduced with: 'Behold the days are coming . . .' as in prose passages throughout the book (see p. 397). This suggests the same sort of editorial intention as chapters 7–24 have disclosed.

CHAPTERS 37–44 (45)

Here the reader is aware of moving into a different and unique section of the book. These chapters are sustained narrative, telling the story from the siege of 586 B.C. to the flight to Egypt after the murder of Gedaliah. The story is told chronologically. There are less marks of the characteristic prose style of the tradition. There are sections, 39.1–10 and 40.7–41.15, in which Jeremiah does not occur. This alone should prevent one from thinking in terms of the 'passion' of Jeremiah. In fact the fundamental interest of the narrative is not biographical. It concerns the divine judgment which Jeremiah tries to persuade king, ministers and people to accept, first as they face the Babylonian invasion, second when Gedaliah is made governor, again when Gedaliah is murdered and finally under Johanan in Egypt. The Gedaliah tradition presents the same challenge through the Babylonian captain Nebuzaradan. It does not affect the theme therefore that Jeremiah does not figure in this section. These chapters constitute a prophetic interpretation of history in narrative form. They need to be read as a whole.

This homogeneity is achieved by means of the unity of theme. The narrator certainly used sources. He was acquainted with the Deuteronomic history as is shown in 37.1, but particularly in 39.1–2 where he abridges 2 Kg. 25.1–4a. This gave a later redactor the starting-point for the introduction of a longer section from 2 Kg., as he contrived to clarify, improve and complete the narrative. The narrator seems to know the brief passage concerning Gedaliah in 2 Kg. 25.22–26. He had access to a separate Gedaliah tradition of which 2 Kg. knows nothing.

The probability also, as is argued in the commentary, is that chapters 37 and 38 are duplicate traditions of Jeremiah's dealing with Zedekiah and his imprisonment, which the narrator has understood to be consecutive. Likewise there appears to be a duplicate account of the assignment of Jeremiah to Gedaliah in chapters 39 and 40.

We are not therefore reading the narrative of a single author, except in the sense that the editor has imposed his theme with clarity and force on the material he had at hand. The addition of these chapters performs something of the same function as the inclusion of chapters 36–39 from the Deuteronomic history in the book of Isaiah.

Why then is chapter 45 placed immediately after this narrative, reverting to the fourth year of Jehoiakim? (cf. 25.1; 36.1; 51.59). The reason why a passage concerning the fate of Baruch is placed here can have nothing to do with historical sequence. It is surely to do with the reference to the writing of 'these words in a book' and to the hint of some continued existence as 'a prize of war in all places to which you may go'. We have here a redactor's touch, using this passage to complete a collection of 'these words', much as chapters 25.1–11 and 36 had performed this function before.

APPENDIX, CHAPTER 52

The final addition of material from the Deuteronomic history has the effect of redirecting the attention of the reader to the central theme of Jeremiah's prophetic work, viz. the role and fate of Zion and the LORD's chosen people. Verses 4–13 are absent in LXX and this may be taken to indicate that there was an earlier and shorter edition of this chapter. In fact, as the commentary attempts to show, there were two layers of redaction before the chapter assumed its present form. The quotation of the passage concerning Jehoiachin's release is a final glimmer of hope. But the story is left without comment to speak for itself.

Such are the complexes which were deposited one on top of another to create the present book. Each represents the crystallisation in writing of material that was used for living purposes. All belongs to the tradition initiated by Jeremiah, the monument of an intense period of activity from the call of Jeremiah to a time shortly before the fall of Babylon, i.e. 627 B.C. to 538 B.C. And of course the LXX shows that redactoral work continued for centuries. We have to think not simply of Jeremiah the prophet but of the word of God conserved, proclaimed, re-minted and reapplied for a century, and the book of Jeremiah as written testimony of this long tradition.

B. THE HISTORY OF THE TIMES

In the early years of his ministry Jeremiah witnessed the end of Assyrian domination in the Middle East. Twenty years later he saw Babylon replace the Assyrians. Within a hundred years men of the Jeremiah school anticipated and hailed the end of Babylon. Such were the changes in the international arena. The pressure of events was intense. The decline of the power of Assyria was taking place under Asshur-bani-pal during the long and repressive reign of Manasseh (697/6–642/1) in Judah. Egypt asserted its independence and by 663 had disengaged itself from Assyrian control. Manasseh remained subservient.

It was Josiah (640/39–609/8) who made it his consistent policy to get free of Assyria, and achieved a fair degree of success, profiting by the rise of Babylon and the advance of Medes and Scythians. The so-called Chaldeans gave notice of their new domination when Nabopolassar, father of Nebuchadnezzar, became king in 625 B.C. He may be regarded as the founder of the neo-Babylonian Empire. His triumph over the Assyrians is marked by the fall of Nineveh in 612 B.C., celebrated in the prophecies of Nahum. A last attempt of the Assyrians to regain power was made possible by Egyptian help. The Egyptians were trying to wrest, out of the apparently favourable turn of events, control of Syria/Palestine. In pursuit of this objective Pharoah Necho II (610–595) arrived in Palestine and it was apparently trying to resist him that Josiah lost his life in 609/8.

Josiah's reign and policies were important for Jeremiah, who both admired the rectitude of the king and supported his reform. From the point of view of the Deuteronomic historic, Josiah's policy was essentially religious (2 Kg. 22.3–23.25, cf. 2 Chr. 34.8–35.9). It was based on a version of the Deuteronomic legal traditions discovered in the Temple in the course of routine renovations. The book of the law, or book of the covenant, has been identified with Deut. since Jerome and Chrysostom, and we regard this identification as certain. It is however a mistake to regard these traditions, or the nucleus of them, as though they were composed expressly to promote the reform. They are traditions of the north, surviving the fall of Samaria and the northern kingdom in 721, and preserved in the Temple, to which they found their way, and where, during the unfavourable climate of the reign of Manasseh, they were forgotten.

This law extends the rights of the priests, requires the purging of the state from all foreign cults, practices and emblems, enjoins a single sanctuary and a new form of the Passover. What the Deuteronomic historian does not make clear is the political side of all this. The purging of foreign cults meant eradicating the signs of Assyrian domination. The exclusive sanctuary meant that Josiah was attempting to reclaim the northern kingdom. The reformation was the basis of Josiah's policy to create a united kingdom, joining the traditions of north and south. The death of Josiah at Megiddo put a premature end to the enlightened policy of a successful king.

In the reign of Josiah's eldest son, who took the name of Jehoiakim (609/8–598/7), the real enemy became clear. The Babylonians turned their attention south and first dealt with the Egyptians whom they defeated at Carchemish in 605 B.C. This, referred to in Jer. 46.2, is now documented by the Wiseman Chronicle (see further, p. 00). The Babylonian conqueror was Nebuchadnezzar, who reigned from 605–562. In view of the importance of the year 604 B.C. in the dealings of Jeremiah with Jehoiakim, and indeed in the book of Jeremiah, it is interesting to note the events of that year. Nebuchadnezzar reached Syria, a number of petty kings submitted to him, Ashkelon fell to him. According to 2 Kg. 24.1 Jehoiakim became his servant for three years. Nebuchadnezzar then seems to have overstretched his resources and to have been defeated by the Egyptians in 600 B.C.

This may well have been the occasion which Jehoiakim exploited as the opportunity for rebellion. He mistook the power and will of the Babylonians as Jeremiah did not. Exemplary punishment was only a matter of time and, for Jehoiakim, prevented by his death in January 597. Jerusalem was occupied on the 16th March, 597 without too much difficulty. The weight of Babylonian wrath fell upon Jehoiakim's son Jehoiachin, who was taken to Babylon with his mother, his wives and ministers and all who were judged capable of exercising power in Jerusalem. (See on Jer. 52.28–30.) Ezekiel was among the exiles.

Nebuchadnezzar evidently thought that another son of Josiah, Mattaniah whom he named Zedekiah, would be more amenable (598/7–587/6). Our main documentary source for the major part of his reign is the narrative in Jer. 37–38 which, with the story of Hananiah, illustrates the difficulties of Jeremiah as he recommended submission. Zedekiah was an essentially weak leader. Temperamentally favourable to Jeremiah, he nevertheless submitted to the pressure of his leading ministers, keeping his dealings with Jeremiah secret. The rebels believed what they wanted. They wrongly judged that local disturbances had taken the heat off Babylon and that Egypt could and would help. Zedekiah declared his independence of Babylon and drew upon himself the very onslaught he sought to evade. Jerusalem was besieged to the point of starvation. The Babylonian army breached the walls in the summer of 586 and destroyed both the palace and the Temple. Zedekiah tried to escape but was caught and taken to Riblah where his sons were killed before him, and he himself blinded and taken to Babylon. The event is well attested by archaeology. The Lachish letters give evidence of the last stages of the Babylonian attack on the nearby fortresses, before resistance ceased, and speak of those (like Jeremiah?) who undermined the will to resist.

The fall of Jerusalem and the exile seemed to be the end of the chosen people. The promises made to the fathers seemed to be no longer capable of fulfilment. Henceforth the land was a wilderness and the people scattered. It is not difficult to understand the difficulties of faith for those who had been brought up on the stories of the Scriptures.

The editor of chapters 37–44 in the book of Jeremiah fortunately had the tradition of Gedaliah to enable him to tell more of the story. Gedaliah was an official whose father had been a supporter of Jeremiah in the time of Jehoiakim (2 Kg. 22.12, 14; Jer. 26.24). He set up his headquarters at Mizpah. But he was regarded as a quisling, and after his murder a group of leaders under Johanan, in fear of the Babylonians and against the advice of Jeremiah, fled to Egypt taking Jeremiah forcibly with them. We are told that they reached Tahpanhes, a border fortress.

This was the effective beginning of a substantial Jewish settlement in Egypt. It must have continued from time to time especially under the Ptolemies in the third century, until in the Christian era there were a million Jews settled in Alexandria, filling two of the five quarters of the city, and, no doubt, scattered elsewhere. It was in Egypt that the Jewish Scriptures were translated into Greek (LXX), a process that spanned several centuries. Probably Jeremiah died there. But the Jeremiah tradition remained for the most part in the home country. There is no evidence that the influential preaching activity of the tradition was carried on in Egypt and much to suggest that it was in Palestine.

The situation in Jerusalem and its environment was parlous. Archaeological evidence supports the tradition that the Babylonian conquest was total and terrible. 'There is not a single known case where a town of Judah proper was continuously occupied through the exilic period' (Albright). It was complete devastation. Such was Jerusalem's weakness that Edomite and other clans from the south pressed into the city and took advantage of its impotence. Nevertheless some worship was possible despite the destruction of the Temple, and the conditions were created for the preservation of the traditions. Laments were composed; the Deuteronomic traditions preserved and edited, and in the course of time, after an initial pause (Ps. 74.9), the voice of prophecy was heard again within the Jeremiah circle. Despite some signs of a special interest in Babylonia, it seems that the evidence is stronger for a Palestinian home for the preaching activity of this circle and for the establishment of the tradition.

Nevertheless it was in the Babylonian exile that the best of the nation now had to learn to live. The provincial organisation allowed a measure of freedom which permitted Ezekiel's prophetic ministry and later that of Second Isaiah. Jeremiah himself recommended that the earliest exiles should accommodate themselves to their new masters and it seems that his advice was heeded. Jehoiachin was held in honourable detainment. The priestly traditions were preserved there and fashioned to become the foundation document of the future priestly theocracy. The Hebrew language was preserved in its purity. Out of this community sprang the leaders of the sixth and fifth century.

The Jeremiah tradition knows nothing of the actual fall of Babylon which it expected to be bloody, but turned out to be painless, and it knows nothing of the return of the exiles, though it looks forward to both. The Babylonian oracles belong to the last decade before the emergence of Cyrus in 540 B.C. We know nothing of the history of the Jews from the flight to Egypt to the Return, except what may be deduced indirectly. It is not unlikely that in exile a period of persecution was endured under the last Babylonian king Nabonidus, from 555B.C. until the fall of Babylon. An early alliance with the Persian king Cyrus gave him temporary security. But Cyrus' rise to power was irresistible. Croesus of Lydia was defeated in 546 B.C. It was then the turn of the Medes, who had assisted in the overthrow of Assyria, to meet their own nemesis. Cyrus became king of the Medes and Persians at the behest of their own nobility and thus gained control of Iran. He attacked Nabonidus in 539. Babylon capitulated without resistance and the new conquerors were welcomed by the priests of Marduk. *Sic transit gloria.*

C. THE TEACHING OF JEREMIAH AND OF THE TRADITION

According to an editor of the book of Jeremiah, the prophet was called in the thirteenth year of Josiah i.e. 627/6 B.C., six years before the discovery of the law book in the Temple and the ensuing Deuteronomic reformation. This information, held within the Jeremiah tradition, is much more likely to be correct than the recent speculations of scholars. It is also probable that Jeremiah was young, and the divine command to be celibate (16.2), which was no doubt associated with his call, suggests that he may well have been under twenty, adding force to the complaint: 'I am only a youth' (1.6). Apparently he came of a priestly family,

Anathoth his home town, about two miles north-east of Jerusalem, being one of the Levitical cities of Benjamin. Later on he encountered hostility from his family (12.6) which owned land (32.6ff) and did not take easily to his criticism of the establishment.

Jeremiah's call was in the prophetic tradition and the account of it takes a familiar pattern (cf. Exod. 3; Jg. 6; Am. 7; Isa. 6; Ezek. 1-3). A unique feature was his strong sense of predestination — 'before you were born I consecrated you'. All those who were thus called shrank from the commission. Jeremiah's special reason is immaturity, unreadiness. But as always the LORD overcomes the objection by means of a sign and a renewal of the commission. Unique also is the explicit indication that Jeremiah will be concerned not merely with the life of God's people but with the 'nations' and so with the movements of history. An essential element in his ministry is going to be, as we would put it, the interpretation of history. The account of his call proceeds to describe the total opposition that the prophet will encounter in carrying out his ministry. Its main theme is the sovereignty of the Word of God over all nations and causes and persons. No doubt we must reckon with the amplifications of the men of the tradition; yet there is reason to suppose that Jeremiah began his ministry, with foreboding, aware of the ominous and threatening circumstances he must face. His reason for not marrying was itself a recognition of the maelstrom that lay ahead and, because of its very unusualness, a prophetic sign to those who questioned it.

If the account given above (pp. 17-37) of the structure of the book is at all correct, then we shall look for his earliest teaching in chapters 2-6. There may be other evidence elsewhere, not least in chapters 30-31, but it is now incorporated inextricably into the tradition. Even chapters 2-6 are written in the light of the circumstances of 604 B.C. and for that occasion, but some conclusions can be drawn.

Jeremiah uses his linguistic skill to enforce two simple messages. One of them is that the people of God have been and are fundamentally unfaithful to their God. He sees in their syncretism a fatal rot. All else proceeds from their infidelity. He uses a legal metaphor and a sexual metaphor to bring this home. Like Hosea he looks back to a period of innocence in her pre-Canaanite life (2.1-3). But her current plea of innocence will not hold (v. 35). She is promiscuous like an animal (vv. 26-28). Jeremiah is quite clear that moral decadence follows upon apostasy. His is essentially a religious analysis of the people's condition. And in this respect he believes the people have been ill served by their leaders, priests, the wise or educated, the statesmen and the popular prophets (v. 8). This is a theme to which he will recur. It is summed up in 5.30-31. He holds up the example of Judah's sister Israel, showing a special interest in the northern kingdom within which Anathoth was just situated. At this stage Jeremiah envisages the possibility of repentance and a turning back to the LORD, as in the 'dialogue of repentance' in 3.19-4.4.

The other clear message of this period is the warning that, without repentance, Judah will be subject to judgment in the form of a Foe from the North (45.9, 13-17, 19-21, 29-31; 5.15-17; 6.1-8, 22-26). This appears to be a theme which dominated Jeremiah's mind from the beginning. He expressed it in the prophetic signs of the almond branch and the boiling pot (chapter 1), and then in a series of vivid poetic oracles. It is altogether probable that Jeremiah did not know which nation precisely would assume this role. He believed that the LORD's judgment would materialise in the movements of predatory nations. It was because Jeremiah could not name the invader that he was not believed. But for the same reason the oracles came alive when, twenty-three years later, the foe appeared in the form of the Babylonian invader. Already Jeremiah is sensing that the people and leaders of Judah are not going to change their ways and that judgment is inevitable (chapter 5). Later on he would be precluded from interceding for them.

At some stage in his ministry Jeremiah concentrated his fire on the Temple, as the nerve-centre of Judah's falsely motivated worship. This is presented in the prose sermons of chapters 7 and 26. The memorable feature which the prose amplifies is the accusation that the Temple is used as a fetish, and appeal is made to the ruins of Shiloh. The most holy place is not immune from judgment. Chapter 26 gives Jeremiah's criticism of the Temple as the occasion of a serious attempt on his life. But although Jeremiah claimed to be alone, there were some, among the ministers of state and the elders, representatives of the community, who supported him, not least the influential Ahikam (26.24).

It has often been concluded from 7.21-26 that Jeremiah went further and denounced the whole sacrificial form of worship in principle, thus sweeping away the cult and preparing for a purely inward worship of heart and mind. This is inconceivable and incorrect. What Jeremiah stresses, even in this prose form of the tradition, is the uselessness, not the intrinsic wrongness, of a worship thus carried out. The offering of burnt-offerings is of no more avail than his own intercession! What is essential is the disposition of the heart; hence he asks for a circumcision of the heart (4.4). An enlightened Deuteronomist did the same (Dt. 10.16) in the context of a reform of the cult.

When Josiah attempted his reform of the cult, on the basis of the discovery of the 'book of the law' in the Temple, it is probable that Jeremiah supported the reform. The prose account in 11.1 – 14 enshrines the tradition of such an activity and we have learned to take these traditions, conserved within the Jeremiah tradition circles, with full seriousness as events in the life of Jeremiah. Just because the account is given in the vocabulary of the tradition, 'the words of this covenant' can hardly be other than the substance of what we call Deuteronomy. Evidently Jeremiah proclaimed it in the cities of Judah and in the streets of Jerusalem. This accords with the admiration he expressed for King Josiah (22.15–16). Did he become disenchanted with the reform? Obviously he did, judging by his denunciation of priests and scribes and by his later conviction that Judah's rebellion against her God made judgment inescapable. He thought the scribes made the law a false protection, in the same way as priests and people regarded the Temple. Their pen he denounced as false, their wisdom a lie (8.8–9). No one is safe without total obedience to God in heart and mind.

Opposition to Jeremiah became implacable as his message became the more uncompromising. The force of his prophetic signs could not be misunderstood; the pot that was worked but, being imperfect, was scrapped and re-moulded (18.1–12); the smashing of the earthenware jar in the valley of Hinnom (19.1–13); the re-naming of Pashhur, after he had beaten Jeremiah and put him in the stocks, as 'Terror on every side' (20.1–6). It is altogether comprehensible that Jeremiah should feel this opposition acutely. The combination of the international threat which became menacing in the time of Jehoiakim, and the murderous personal hatred of the king, accounts fully, according to the modern mind, for the expression of despair in the so-called Confessions (11.18–20; 12.1–13; 15.10–18, 19–21; 17.9–10, 14–18; 18.18–23; 20.7–12). Personal stress and an introvert temperament are said to be the unhappy lot of this maudlin prophet. Indeed the redactor himself associates the first two poems with the implacable hostility encountered by Jeremiah from the men of his home town. The deeper reasons are otherwise.

The poems fall into the category of psalm laments. Many of the ideas and expressions are found in psalms which Jeremiah must have known and used on fast-days and occasions of national prayer. 12.1ff. might well be interpreted as a community lament presented by an individual who in his individual 'I' incorporates the collective identity of the whole people.

Chapter 15.10–21 is not only a lament in form, but in verses 19–21 we have the divine answer to the lament, renewing the office of the prophet. In 20.13 we have a sudden change from despair to praise, expressing the so-called 'certainty of hearing', formally characteristic of the lament cf. Pss. 6.9; 22.22.

This is not to say that the Confessions of Jeremiah are liturgical pieces. It is to suggest that they are based on well-known liturgical patterns, and this may be of significance in interpreting them. It is part of the prophetic office that the prophet should not only be the spokesman of the LORD, but that he should be representative of the people in intercession. He becomes the 'I' who, in his individual character, represents the collective identity of the people. This godward office of the prophet is stressed in early prophecy, expressed in the phrase: 'call upon the name of the LORD' (1 Kg. 18.24; 2 Kg. 5.11) cf. Gen. 20.7, Am. 7.2. Nowhere is it more clearly pronounced than in the book of Jeremiah. In 7.16; 11.14; 14.11 Jeremiah is commanded to refrain from interceding for the people. In 37.1–10; 42.2, 20 he is specifically asked to intercede, in the one case by Zedekiah, in the other by Johanan and Jezaniah. In 18.18 he says: 'Remember how I stood before thee to speak good for them, to turn away thy wrath from them'. In 27.18 he attacks Hananiah and the false prophets with the challenge that, if they be the prophets they claim, 'let them now make intercession to the LORD of hosts'.

In the light of all this, 7.16 becomes suggestive: 'As for you do not pray for this people, or lift up cry or prayer for them, and do not intercede with me, for I do not hear you'. What then may the prophet do? Keep silence? Yet he still has the word of God committed to him and still represents the people to whom he is sent. The simplicity of his task is dissolved. His own soul is filled with the confusion of the situation. He expresses this confusion in the laments which are his confessions, a kind of struggling with the ruthlessness of the message with which he is charged. His utterances are the prophetic expression of the condition of the prophet and people. We evacuate them of their true significance when we turn them into the introspective heart cries of a sensitive soul. Jeremiah's sensitivity was such as to express in this way the situation of the people of God vis-à-vis their God. The confessions are prophetic signs.

This is far from individualism in the modern sense. Nor is it possible to understand Jeremiah as the creator of a new individualism which influenced the Psalms and through them passed into Christianity. The psalms in question are mostly earlier than Jeremiah and in any case Jeremiah had no wish to destroy the structure of religion upon which

Judah could properly rely. What he did understand was that all structures would disappear in the conflagration that must happen. It is in this context that one should consider the theme of the new covenant in chapter 31. This is an element in the hope which has become an integral part of the Jeremiah tradition. For the most part we cannot tell what in chapters 30–31 might go back to Jeremiah and what is the contribution of later tradition circles. Verses 31–35 do however merit special consideration, not only for their remarkable content, but also for their form. Their content is a new covenant which amounts to a revision of the old. The law will be written within and upon the heart; no longer an external requirement but inwardly accepted and absorbed by every son and daughter of God. No longer will there be a distinction between the teacher who knows God and those who do not know him. But, as in Jl 2, all will know him and will do so on the basis of the divine forgiveness.

This is an eschatological picture to be realised when God's purpose is achieved. It comes in the prose tradition. Yet the linguistic form stands out. These verses have a perfection of form and at their climax reach the rhythm of poetry. They are as much a passage inherited and collected as the poetic oracles. They raise the question, who had the authority to proclaim the new covenant but the prophet Jeremiah? And is not this kind of prose the appropriate vehicle for such proclamation? But if the force of these questions is not felt in this way, the passage is still a contribution of the Jeremiah tradition and still a high-point in that tradition.

Jeremiah's conflict with Jehoiakim comes to a climax in chapter 36 which has already received sufficient attention. His subsequent struggles and dangers in the time of Zedekiah and Gedaliah down to his enforced flight to Egypt are dealt with in the narrative chapters. The material for a biography is not provided, but just because Jeremiah is part of his message we learn more about him than about any other prophet. All is absorbed in the total tradition, with its simple strong message of divine command — disobedience — judgment. Just because this is a century-long tradition, it can admit features which Jeremiah himself could not have embraced during his ministry, at least in their present form. Such might be the passage on sabbath observance in 17.19–27. Such certainly are the emphases of the Babylonian oracles where the sin of Babylon is its destruction of the Temple and the righteousness of God's people is taken for granted.

An effort has been made to determine cautiously some of the main lines and features of the ministry of Jeremiah himself. This has been based on a reasoned approach to the literary problems and also upon the principle that great effects require an adequate cause to account for them. But the main benefit of the literary analysis is to help us to understand how the book reached its present form. It is its present canonical form, thus understood, which is finally important. Then we can leave behind the 'probably' and 'likely' and 'possibly' of critical guesswork and hypothesis and seek the theology of the Jeremiah tradition.

Five examples may serve to illustrate this. First, chapters 27–29, the end result of a complicated transmission process, deal with false prophecy. They are the product of the prose tradition and they deal with the problem not only by presenting Jeremiah's teaching, but also by presenting Jeremiah as a true prophet in conflict with the false. From the point of view of the life of Jeremiah the story tells of a vivid prophetic sign and Jeremiah's greatest conflict, according to Martin Buber, with the false prophets led by Hananiah. But when we come to the analysis of criteria by which to judge between true and false, we are surely in contact with the considered reflection of the tradition on both the incident and the problem. The answer is (a) fidelity to the prophetic succession and (b) the test of fulfilment. In chapter 29 a further consideration is suggested, but not stated, in relation to the false prophets Ahab and Zedekiah, viz. that the true prophet will be one with his message. Moral and spiritual truth are one, and reflected in a unity of moral and spiritual character. No better example can be found of the combination of witness to a crisis in the life of Jeremiah and theological elaboration using the story to prove the point. The redactor is far more than a treasurer of the life and teaching of Jeremiah; he is a theologian and a preacher in the tradition. The work of Jeremiah himself and the use made of that work in the tradition are now inextricable, illuminating as it is to try to distinguish them.

Second, the story of Jeremiah's dealings with Zedekiah highlights the predicament of Jeremiah in relation to the problems of patriotism and treason. This is anticipated in the sign of the yoke in chapter 27, but comes to a climax when he advises Zedekiah and his people to surrender to the Babylonian army (chapter 38), and is the underlying theme of chapters 37–44. On the basis of the dramatic interventions of Jeremiah, the truth is taught that submission to judgment must include a readiness to resist national pride and instinctive patriotism. This must however involve a prophetic recognition of what is divine judgment. This was Jeremiah's problem and remains ours. Who does not sympathise with Zedekiah, wishing to support the 'wet' Jeremiah, but unable to resist the pressure of strong men confident that they are right and that Jeremiah is a traitor? It is remarkable that the men of the tradition held to this truth so consistently.

Third, the commentary has given grounds for supposing that Jeremiah had something to say about the future beyond the tragedies of judgment. The redemption of his family property (chapter 32) was recognised by Jeremiah as a sign and so preserved in the tradition. It happened at the least propitious time, after the defeat of 597 and before the invasion of 586. 'Houses and fields and vineyards shall again be bought in this land', he said (v. 15). Some of the oracles in chapters 30–31 may be Jeremiah's, but we have no certainty. The idea of the seventy years' exile may be Jeremiah's. But much belongs to the tradition, and the MT contains a number of predictions of salvation which are not in LXX. Here above all we need the concept of the Jeremiah tradition, if we are to do justice to this element. In the century-long tradition it belongs to the wholeness of prophecy. Death is never the last word. Jeremiah needed his successors to provide a balanced message.

Fourth, as soon as the importance of the whole tradition and the finished book are understood, it is possible to give full attention to emphases begun by Jeremiah but developed in the tradition. Such is Jeremiah's teaching that there is no security other than in moral obedience to the LORD. It was in this sense that he taught the fundamental insecurity of the Temple (chapter 7), of sacrifice, and even the claim to possession of the Law (chapter 8). Nor could the Ark provide a Talisman, nor circumcision (9.25–26), nor even the prayer of the disobedient. These then are reinterpreted — the Ark in 3.15–18, the Torah in 30.31–34, circumcision in 4.4, the Exodus in 23.7–8. The impetus to such revolutionary teaching must come from a prophet with full authority. Its development, as in the messianic hope of 23.7–8, no doubt belongs to the tradition. But if it is sometimes difficult to disentangle the one from the other, it matters not. The tradition is as important to the book of Jeremiah as Jeremiah is to the tradition.

Fifth, the oracles against the nations, which probably owe very little to Jeremiah himself and belong mainly to the decade before the rise of Cyrus, crown the tradition with a sustained chorus on the sovereignty of the LORD the king. The whole world, they sing, is in his hand. Babylon itself is to be cut to size. The tradition understood these oracles to be fulfilment of the promise made to Jeremiah at his call that he should be a prophet to the nations. If we set our concentration exclusively on the prophet, we lose sight of them. If we study the canonical book which is the tradition, we begin to see their importance.

In a visionary way they celebrate Yahweh's ultimate control of his creation and the vindication of his people in relation to the nations. The *hubris* of the proud conquerors receives its proper reward. Judgments are made within a larger time scale than was possible to Jeremiah. If the emphasis on Israel's innocence is complacent, it was nevertheless possible to draw out some of the implications of Jeremiah's call (chapter 1) and the Cup of Wrath (chapter 25), with occasional hints of a time of redemption, e.g. 46.26, 27–28; 48.47; 49.6. All is the plan and purpose of the LORD, before whom the plans of men and nations must fail. On the vast scale of the world powers, a divine judgment is being enacted. To be crushed by Babylon was a national disaster. In Jeremiah's book, the conqueror was but an instrument of the LORD, though he himself knew it not. But the supreme irony is that when the instrument of judgment exceeds his commission, he himself comes under judgment. The LORD puts down the mighty from their seat and exalts the humble and meek.

When one considers the circumstances in which these oracles were uttered, both those of the prophet and those of the tradition — a situation of extreme weakness and hopelessness — and when one considers the inner confidence evinced in the LORD of all creation, the divine king who has a work to do alike of judgment and of vindication, this must be accounted one of the most amazing perceptions in the long saga of religion and thought.

D. THE TEXT

The Hebrew Massoretic text (MT) is the fundamental text for the book of Jeremiah. At the same time the Greek (Septuagint — LXX) text has special importance because it may be taken to witness to an alternative and shorter Hebrew text. It has over 300 words not found in MT, but MT has over 3,000 words not found in LXX. In addition the two versions arrange differently the oracles against the nations. Chapters 46–51 in MT appear as chapters 26; 29; 31; 30.17–21, 1–16, 29–33; 25.14–22; 27; 28 in LXX.

The easy conclusion would be that LXX witnesses to the primary, or at any rate more original Hebrew text, and the expansions in MT should be ignored. But the fact that the two versions held their position for a lengthy period is now shown by the existence of four fragments found among the Qumran texts. There are fragments of chapters 42–44, 46–49 in 2 Q Jer; 7–12, 14, 15, 17, 18, 19, 22 in 4 Q Jer[a]; 8, 19–22, 25–27, 30–33 in 4 Q Jer[c]. These are our earliest witness to the Hebrew text. Some have dated 4 Q Jer[a] as early as 200 B.C., and although this may be an arguable conclusion, it may nevertheless be about right. Fragments of 9, 10, 43, 50 appear in 4 Q Jer[b] and these have correspondences with LXX. Thus there is some evidence that the two Hebrew text traditions remained in existence until the second century B.C. The Syriac version (Peshitta) has minor deviations, and may be said to reflect MT. Even more so may this be said of the Targum and the Vulgate.

This statement of the facts may however be misleading. It might encourage the impression that the two versions are more independent than they are. In fact LXX must represent an earlier form of the same text. The comparison of the two has been studied in detail by Emanuel Tov ('Some aspects of the textual and literary history of the book of Jeremiah' in *Le livre de Jérémie*, ed. by P.-M. Bogaert, 1981) in terms of edition I (LXX) and edition II (MT). Beside the obvious re-arrangement of the text in MT, he analyses the additions of headings to prophecies, repetitions of sections, the addition of new verses and sections and certain changes in content. Undeniably this constitutes substantial amplification. It is essentially editorial, but includes significant variations.

J. G. Janzen, in *Studies in the Text of Jeremiah* (1973), sums up what he calls the 'secondary expansion' of MT. It includes frequent attention to names, with titles and epithets and the making explicit of what is implicit. There are many interpolations and some must be called deliberate scribal notation and harmonisation.

But now it must be emphasised that LXX itself is a heavily edited text. It witnesses both to the poetic foundation and the prose of the Jeremiah tradition, but also to the ubiquitous and sometimes clever and complex work of redactors. The LXX cannot therefore be called the original or superior text. It is simply an earlier stage in the evolution of the text. Nor is the relation between the two as simple as it seems. In particular the discussion of chapter 25, in relation to the oracles against the nations, suggests the superiority of MT. At the very least it must be acknowledged that the problem is at times exceedingly complex. It remains true that MT is the fundamental text for the book of Jeremiah.

William McKane, in the introduction to his commentary, sets out the variations for chapters 1–25 comprehensively and systematically. His commentary gives unique attention to the problems raised by these versions, and to their role in helping to solve textual riddles.

E. ANALYSIS OF THE BOOK

1.1–3   Superscription

I PROPHETIC CRITICISM AND WARNINGS AGAINST
   JUDAH AND JERUSALEM   1.4–25.38

   A THE EARLIEST COLLECTION OF THE WORDS OF
      JEREMIAH   1.4–6.30

1.1–19   THE AUTHORITY OF JEREMIAH
   1.4–10   The Call and Commission of Jeremiah
   1.11–12   The Vision of the Almond Branch
   1.13–16   The Vision of the Boiling Pot
   1.17–19   The Prophet's Strength

2.1–37   THE CASE AGAINST GOD'S PEOPLE
   2.1   Superscription
   2.2–3   The Innocence and Promise of Youth
   2.4–9   The Charge against Israel
   2.10–12   The Exchange of Gods
   2.13–19   Spring of Life and Rivers of Deception
   2.20–22   A Rebel Beyond Recovery
   2.23–25   Like Beasts
   2.26–28   A Thief Caught Out
   2.29–30   The Judge's Appeal
   2.31–37   The Lord's Response to Israel's Plea of Innocence

3.1–4.4   THE LORD'S APPEAL TO HIS PEOPLE
   3.1   Irretrievable Divorce
   3.2–5   Open Infidelity
   3.6–14   A Cautionary Example
   3.15–18   A People United
   3.19–4.4 Dialogue of Repentance

4.5–6.30   UNRELENTING JUDGMENT FROM THE NORTH
   4.5–9   The Alarm Call
   4.10   First Personal Interjection
   4.11–18   Second Announcement of Judgment
   4.19–26   Second Personal Interjection
   4.27–31   Third Warning of Judgment

(2) A COLLECTION OF ORACLES ON KINGS AND
     PROPHETS MAINLY AFTER THE TIME OF
     JEHOIAKIM   21.1–24.10

21.1–23.8   On the Kings of Judah
  21.1–10 The Fate of Judah and the End of the Monarchy
  21.11–14 The King, Guardian of Justice

  22.1–9   Reinforcement of the Preceding Oracle
  22.10–12 Mourning for Jehoahaz
  22.13–19 Contempt for Jehoiakim
  22.20–23 Zion's Dismay at the Loss of her Kings
  22.24–30 Jehoiachin Broken and Thrown Away

  23.1–8   Good Shepherds on the Throne of David

23.9–40   On the Prophets
  23.9–12 Their Offence against the LORD
  23.13–15 Their Offence against Morality
  23.16–22 Their Offence against Truth
  23.23–32 Lying Dreams and Stolen Words
  23.33–40 On the 'Burden' of the LORD

24.1–10   Vision of Good and Bad

   C CONCLUSION OF THE COMPLEX (1–25)   25.1–38

   25.1–14 Jeremiah's Oracle on his Oracles
   25.15–29 The Cup of Wrath (LXX 32.1–24)
   25.30–38 The Nations and their Leaders Sentenced (LXX 32.30–38)

II PROPHETIC NARRATIVES AND SERMONS MAINLY OF
    THE TIME OF ZEDEKIAH INCLUDING THE ORACLES
    OF HOPE   26.1–35.19 (36.32)
    A THE EXPOSURE OF FALSE PROPHECIES OF HOPE
       26.1–29.32

26.1–24   Responses to Jeremiah's Temple Sermon (LXX 33.1–24)

27.1–22   Oracles to Neighbouring Nations, to Zedekiah and to Priests
            and People to Accept the Yoke of Babylon, with Warnings
            against False Prophets (LXX 34.1–22)
  27.2–11 The Sign of the Yoke
  27.12–15 The Message to Zedekiah
  27.16–22 The Destiny of the Temple Vessels

COMMENTARY
ON
JEREMIAH

SUPERSCRIPTION **1.1–3**

How much of the book of Jeremiah are these verses intended to introduce? The discussion of chapter 25.1–14 will show that in all probability chapters 1–24 formed an early collection, and 25.1–3 links up with 1.1–3. It could be therefore that 1.1–3 was intended to introduce chapters 1–24. Others have argued that a new superscription in 40.1 suggests that chapters 1–39 was the collection introduced by these verses. All this is speculation. All we know is that the final editor meant us to understand that this is the introduction to the whole Jeremiah tradition collected in the book that bears his name.

The thirteenth year of the reign of Josiah is 627–6 B.C. The absence of any reference to Jehoahaz (609) and Jehoiachin (598/7) is not significant since they reigned only a few months. It is not necessary to assume that the editor thought the thirteenth year was the only year of Josiah's reign in which Jeremiah uttered prophecy. Plainly this is the beginning of his prophetic ministry. On the other hand the choice of language here may be deliberate, reflecting the fact that a period of silence followed Jeremiah's earliest intervention. A fresh outburst of activity occurred in the days of Jehoiakim (608/7–598/7) and continued until the fifth month of the captivity (586).

The superscription was of course written by an editor. When he did his work we cannot tell. In this case there is no shorter Greek version, though the Septuagint adopts the same type of superscription used in Hos. 1.1; Mic. 1.1; Zeph. 1.1 and Jl 1.1. It is possible, even probable, that the main task of collecting and arranging the oracles of Jeremiah, as received and interpreted in the prophetic circles that carried on his work, was not long delayed after the prophet's death (see Introduction pp. 28ff.). If this were so, these circles would retain some traditional memories of the length and circumstances of Jeremiah's ministry, and they are unlikely to be seriously mistaken. If on the other hand the editorial work was done much later, then the editor might have derived his dates mainly from those he found in his sources. Even so the circles in which the oracles were treasured may well have retained independent information. In view of the fact that the first initiative towards producing a written collection of the oracles came from the prophet himself, we may suppose that the completion of the process was not long delayed.

Some recent scholars have questioned the accuracy of the information, to the extent that they deny any prophetic ministry by Jeremiah until after the death of Josiah. Suffice it here to say (a) that none of the reasons alleged for this view is compelling, (b) that it involves a cavalier treatment of the text, and (c) that it must mean a sceptical appraisal of the Deuteronomic passages, particularly in chapter 11 (see comment). The view of the Deuteronomic passages taken in this commentary is that they must be judged seriously as for the most part the subsequent expansion and application of genuine Jeremiah tradition. The view (J. P. Hyatt, Whitley Holladay) that 626 B.C. is the date, not of the beginning of Jeremiah's ministry, but of his birth, is unverifiable speculation. At least it implies that the editor had access to correct dates though he misinterpreted them. It is easier to suppose that he knew both the dates and their correct meaning. The view (T.C. Gordon, Bardtke) that 626 is a textual error for 616 is gratuitous, open to all the objections to which unsupported conjectural emendation is susceptible.

The view that Jeremiah's apparent silence between 621 and 609 is best explained by the hypothesis that his ministry did not begin until 609 is not as convincing as it seems. For one thing it is reasonable to assume the editor was guided by his sources and the tradition, not by his imagination. For another there is early material which, in my view, is best explained if Jeremiah had a close interest, even involvement in Josiah's plans for reform. And for a third, the occurrence of the most dramatic events in the time of Jehoiakim is consistent with the acceleration of Jeremiah's prophetic activity, but does not require silence previously. Jeremiah was particularly vulnerable to the difficulties of gaining a hearing, especially when he was young and untried. The elderly and experienced do not like to be lectured by neophytes. One would expect in the early period a rather select body of prophecy concerned mainly with internal, social and religious affairs, but with a strong sense of political foreboding. And that is what we find.

A more radical view has found expression recently in the works of R.P. Carroll. This is the view that this editorial setting need not reflect any reliable historical information at all, that it is a fictional creation which may or may not reflect traditional beliefs or may indeed be imaginary. Accordingly the character of the book of Jeremiah is fiction, and it is not possible to proceed from the book to the Jeremiah of history.

The fact that it is not possible to demolish this view does not mean that it is cogent. Probability is the guide in all such judgments, and probability, in my view, leads in a more positive direction. The hypothesis which is eventually seen to make sense of all the evidence is the one that will prevail. What we have is one of the largest and most powerful collections of prophetic tradition in the prophetic corpus. Such a tradition has a pedigree in the prophetic succession and comparisons may justly be made. Adequately to account for it, there must be a creative originator who generates a particular tradition. This tradition may span a long period, according to his influence and that of his successors. The name of the prophet covers the whole tradition, both that which he said and did, and that which he did not say and do. But the historical rootedness of this tradition is an integral element of the phenomenon. To dissolve it is to fail to understand the nature of the material and the process of prophecy. This is different from the attribution of psalms to David or wisdom sayings to Solomon or later legendary traditions to Jeremiah. Not to recognise this difference is a form of academic blindness. The historical figure of Jeremiah is necessary to the facts. To dispense with him is to leave the tradition without its inspiration or its explanation, and it is gratuitous to do so.

We are left with the traditional interpretation that the editor had substantially true information, which he neither misinterpreted nor invented; and this is not a tradition-bound judgment.

1. The words of Jeremiah: The Hebrew *dibrê* can mean both 'words' and 'history' and 'deeds'. In view of the space given to the experiences of Jeremiah, the latter is not to be excluded. But the importance laid upon the 'word' in Hebrew thinking, together with its dominance as the characteristic vehicle of divine disclosure through the prophets, means that the main emphasis is probably put on the book as a collection of Jeremiah's significant words.

Possible guesses as to the meaning of the name Jeremiah are: 'Yahweh shoots or throws', and Hilkiah would have thus named his son to suggest the divine warrior. 'Yahweh loosens (the womb)' or 'Yahweh exalts' are also possible. 'May Yahweh found . . . ' is another guess.

the son of Hilkiah: if this were the high priest who found the book of the law in 621 B.C. (2 Kg. 22.4, 8–14), one would expect more than this single annalistic reference. No doubt at that time the high priest lived in Jerusalem.

of the priests who were in Anathoth: cf. 11.21, 23; 29.27; 32.7–9. A village of uncertain identification, probably about two miles north-east of Jerusalem and half a mile south-west of the traditional 'Anata, now known as Ras el-Kharrubeh. In the time of Josiah Anathoth was reckoned among the Levitical cities of Benjamin (Jos. 21.18, cf. I Chr. 6.45). It is not said that Jeremiah himself was a priest, and the impression given by the book of Jeremiah as a whole is that he was not. But he belonged to a priestly family which, until the Deuteronomic reform may well have been responsible for the local sanctuary at Anathoth. This is the best explanation of the unique expression 'of the priests'. The custom of the Jerusalem priests living outside Jerusalem and coming into the capital for their course of duty was a later one. It is probable that the family was descended from Abiathar, descendant of Eli (a Levitical family), who was banished to Anathoth by Solomon (1 Kg. 2.26). Lineages of this kind were prized and the privileges jealously guarded.

If Jeremiah had intimate experience of the orders he criticized so strongly, he was as independent of them as he was knowledgeable. Such a picture of the family background of Jeremiah provides the most convincing reason for the family plot against his life, recorded in 11.21, when as a result of the Deuteronomic reformation, the shrine had been suppressed. Every detail in this reconstruction has been contested in the interests of one theory or another. If the text is trusted, it remains the hypothesis which best accounts for all the data. Meek's view that these words are a gloss is unsupported conjecture. These observations make it proper to ask whether Jeremiah may not have represented the interconnection of Levitical and prophetic traditions, particularly if the Deuteronomic traditions were transmitted in Levitical circles. The grounds for this assumption seem stronger than those against it (see H. Weippert, op. cit. pp.13–19).

I   PROPHETIC CRITICISM AND WARNINGS AGAINST JUDAH AND JERUSALEM 1.4–25.38

A   THE EARLIEST COLLECTION OF THE WORDS OF JEREMIAH 1.4–6.30

This section may be regarded as substantially the original collection of oracles made by Jeremiah himself in obedience to divine instruction, written out by Baruch, destroyed by Jehoiakim, and then written out a second time by Baruch, as narrated in chapter 36. (See further, Introduction pp. 28–31.) It contains two complexes of oracles. Chapters 2–4.4 are most convincingly interpreted as belonging to the earliest period of Jeremiah's ministry, before the repair of the Temple and the Deuteronomic reformation. Jeremiah, strongly influenced by Hosea, dealt

with the idolatrous worship of Israel and it is at least possible that he
was concerned with Israel, the northern kingdom, with whose fate he
felt himself intimately concerned, as well as with the 'Israel' (the whole
people of God) which included Judah.

Chapters 4.5–6.30 contain the oracles concerning the Foe from the
North. If Jeremiah could not at first identify the enemy, these also would
be early oracles. If he had the strong suspicion that the Babylonians would
turn out to be the enemy, then in their present form they might date
towards the last year of king Josiah or just after. We need to explain the
ambivalent character of these chapters, both the passages which seem
to lack specific relevance to dramatic events and those which must find
their explanation in tragic national downfall. They can be understood
at two levels and the above hypothesis alone does justice to both.

THE AUTHORITY OF JEREMIAH 1.1–19

When a prophet recited the story of his call, he was in effect presenting
his credentials. We see this particularly in the case of Amos, who
recounted his experience of the divine commission in answer to the Bethel
priest's proscription of his ministry in the northern kingdom (Am.
7.10–17). It was appropriate that a first collection of Jeremiah's words
should open with the divine legitimation, and likely that he himself would
wish to introduce the collection of his oracles in this way.

On the other hand the chapter betrays unmistakeable signs of
Deuteronomistic handling. The chapter is constructed of four units: (a)
the call (vv. 4–10); (b) the vision of the almond branch (vv. 11–12); (c)
the vision of the boiling pot (vv. 13–16); (d) the re-affirmation of the
commission (vv. 17–19). The two visions have little to do with the call
and are best understood as originally independent units. This does not
mean that their presence here is arbitrary; their content suggests the
reason why (by their association with the call-narrative) they have been
given such a commanding position. Each points to a major theme of
Jeremiah's ministry, the one the vindication of the divine word, the other
the certainty of judgment in the events of history, and so provides a
programmatic opening to the book. What one might call the
Deuteronomic mind is particularly plain in vv. 9, 10, 17–19. It seems
likely therefore that the final arrangement of his opening chapter has been
carried out by one who is influenced by Deuteronomic phraseology and
ideas. This will nevertheless be within the Jeremiah tradition. As Jeremiah
sought his own legitimation in the divine call made directly to him, the

editor sought the legitimation of his preaching and teaching from the word spoken to Jeremiah.

THE CALL AND COMMISSION OF JEREMIAH 1.4–10

The call narratives conform to some kind of loose pattern (see H. Graf Reventlow, *Liturgie und prophetisches Ich bei Jeremia* (1963) and N. Habel, 'The Form and Significance of the Call Narratives', *ZAW* 77 (1965) 297–323) and a comparison of the calls of Moses (Exod. 3), Gideon (Jg. 6), Amos (Am. 7), Isaiah (Isa. 6), Jeremiah and Ezekiel (Ezek. 1–3) suggests that the particular and unique inwardness of each call is expressed in the framework of a conventional schema. The common elements of the schema are:

(a) *Confrontation with God*. (Exod. 3.1–4; Jg. 6.12–12; Isa. 6.1–4; Ezek. 1). This is not stated in this chapter, but it is presupposed and becomes explicit in 23.18:

> For who among them (the prophets) has stood in
> the council of the LORD
> to perceive and to hear his word
> or who has given heed to his word and listened?

Moreover the *ah!* in verse six is more than an interjection of surprise or remonstration. It is an expression of religious dread in the presence of the holy God. Cf: Jg. 6.22; Isa. 6.5.

(b) *The ground of the commission* (Exod. 3.7–9; Jg. 6.12–14; Ezek. 2.3). In the case of Jeremiah, the situation becomes clear only in the visions which are knit into the chapter (vv. 13–16); and vv. 18–19, which may well echo elements of the call experience, draw attention to the iron obstinacy of the people. But the weight is uniquely thrown here on the pre-natal calling of Jeremiah. He is the realisation of a divine intention determined before he was born. He has come into the world for no other purpose than this, to be the LORD's spokesman to the nations.

(c) *The commission*. This is commonly expressed in terms of sending (*šlḥ*) and going (*hlk*) (Exod. 3.10–11; Jg. 6.14; Am. 7.15; Isa. 6.8–9; Ezek. 2.3, 4), and is particularly clear in the call of Jeremiah: 'to all to whom I send you you shall go'. But it also relates to the burden of the divine word committed to the prophet: 'and whatever I command you you shall speak' (v. 6; cf. Am. 7.15–16; Isa. 6.9; Ezek. 2.7).

(d) *The objection*. The one who is called shrinks from the commission. The prominence of this feature in the call narratives suggests that it is

unwise to stress the psychological implications for Jeremiah. Moses shrinks
back three times (Exod. 3.11; 4.1, 10); Gideon stresses his powerlessness
(Jg. 6.15); Amos, by implication, his lay status (Am. 7.14–15); Isaiah
his sinfulness (Isa. 6.5) and Ezekiel his dependence (Ezek. 2.1). The form
this takes in the case of Jeremiah is the stressing of his immaturity or
unreadiness.

(e) *The reassurance.* Commonly here, or at some other point, there is
the command not to fear (unexpressed at Exod. 3.6, expressed in Jg.
6.22; Isa. 6.5; Ezek. 2.6). This is explicit in Jer. 1.8 and reinforced in
v. 17. The commission is renewed and in a number of cases, a sign is
given (Exod. 3.12; Jg. 6.17, 19 ff.; Isa. 6.6–7; Ezek. 3.2). The sign of
Jeremiah, whether corresponding to some outward action or entirely
visionary, is appropriate to the nature of his commission. The touching
of the mouth, not unfamiliar in the mouth-purification rites of
Mesopotamia and Egypt, here has clear and simple prophetic significance,
and indicates that Jeremiah is to be the LORD's spokesman, if not as
his own mouth (Jer. 15.19).

Such are the principle elements in the call-narratives of the Old
Testament. Zimmerli (*Ezechiel, Bk XIII*, (1969), pp. 15–21. See also Hans
Wildberger, *Isaiah, Bk X* (1968), pp. 235–6.) thinks that the call-narratives
which exhibit this pattern fall into two main types.

(a) The first is the kind of call which at every point is subordinated
to the controlling idea of the word of God. Examples are the call of Moses
according to J (Exod. 3.1–4a, 5, 7–8, 16–22; 4.1–9), E (Exod. 3.4b, 6,
9–15; 4.17) and P (Exod. 6.2–12; 7.1–7) and those of Gideon (Jg. 6)
and Saul (I Sam. 9). The call of Jeremiah may be regarded as the classical,
prophetic instance of this type. It is characteristic of the charismatic leaders
of Israel's early history (Moses, Gideon, Saul) and means that, in some
sense, the prophet is regarded as in the line of the early 'saviours'.

(b) The second is the call which starts from a vision of the court of
the LORD in heaven. From his throne, the LORD sends his word
through his prophet who is thus closely associated with the divine
messengers who fulfil his will. Isa. 6, which is closely parallel to the story
of Micaiah ben Imlah's vision in I Kg. 22, and Ezek. 1–3, 15, somewhat
modified, belong to this category. Jer. 23.18 shows that Jeremiah was
not unfamiliar with this imagery. Probably it is unwise to regard
Zimmerli's description as more than an aid to analysis. Certainly it should
not be exploited to underplay the visionary element which is undoubtedly
present in Jeremiah's call.

Reventlow concludes that we are reading a liturgical document, that the narrative of Jeremiah Chapter I points to an actually enacted ceremony of ordination to the prophetic office, conducted by a priest or a prophet, and that no conclusions may be drawn concerning the personal character or psychological makeup of Jeremiah.

This is not convincing, for it involves supposing that this cultic act was concealed in the form of a vision. The visionary experience is said to be only the form: the real event is the cultic act (op.cit. pp. 46, 64, 75). Speculations of this kind are too tortuous and do not do justice to the simplicity and directness of the narrative. In any case this is surely to advance too far into the realm of speculation, since there is not a single concrete piece of evidence for such a ceremony in the case of any of the prophets, and it is singularly unconvincing to read any of the other call-narratives in terms of such a liturgy.

This being so, we are free to draw some conclusions about the specific character and commission of Jeremiah. The evidence is best interpreted if we suppose that the prophet expressed his inward consciousness of mission in terms of a well known conventional pattern. We ought to be able to understand the nature of such conventional patterns. The call experience, like all the deepest experiences of human life, is strictly incapable of being put into words. That is the reason for obscurity in poetry and the stretching of language beyond the rule-governed in theology. To be communicated, that which is unspeakable is here projected in a picture, with simple narrative sequence. Once the experience is encapsulated in language, it then plays its part in determining other like experiences. The similarity of description is therefore inevitable, and is no argument for the secondary nature of the narrative. One might compare the accounts of conversion experiences, the description and understanding of them being assisted and in part determined by received patterns.

The force of this observation is not weakened by the presence of Deuteronomic touches. The unique elements of the prophet's particular use of this pattern are the direct register of his own temperament and understanding of his relationship with God. What then stands out is (a) his conviction that he has been born for this purpose according to the pre-determinate will of God; (b) that his prophetic task is going to be concerned with the vast movements of history so that he must be a prophet in relation to the nations; and (c) his heavy sense of foreboding that he must face implacable opposition. His sense of inadequacy to the task which he recognised to be so immense was matched by a faith that he must fulfil his prophetic destiny, though the odds be hopelessly weighted against him.

We may conclude that Jeremiah related a powerful visionary, or at any rate auditory experience and that it came naturally to him to clothe this experience in well known, conventional terms.

5. Before I formed you in the womb I knew you: cf. the language used by Second Isaiah of Israel, the servant of the LORD, in Isa. 44.2; 49.1, 5. The initial background of this vocabulary may well, as Reventlow argues, be the divine choice of the king. (op.cit. p.37.) But already in the Psalms (22.10–12; 76.6) it has been given a wider application. The common idea in Second Isaiah and Jeremiah is election to *office*. But it is the theological implications which are now important. 'Know' here has the same overtone of 'elect' or 'choose' as in Am. 3.2. Likewise **I consecrated you** expresses the idea of separation from worldly ambitions to the purposes and service of God. Ethical implications are not raised.

to the nations (*gôîm*): Some commentators, following Stade, have changed this to the singular; others following Rothstein have omitted it altogether. But the plural is implied also in v. 10, as also in 18.9–10; 25.15–16; 36.2, and the Hebrew does not necessarily mean that Jeremiah has a prophetic mission to the nations in exactly the same sense as he is a spokesman of the LORD to Judah ('my people'). It suffices that the universalist implications of his ministry become more and more prominent, and his office is carried out always *in relation to* the nations. On the other hand, the thought of the prophet's universal mission may be more precise. There are prophecies against the nations in all the major prophetic collections. As the king will exercise the LORD's dominion over the nations (Pss. 2, 110), and man over the natural world (Ps. 8), so the prophet utters the word whose reach cannot be less than the sovereignty of God himself.

In this sense, as Reventlow says, the prophetic office is a royal office. When this has been said it may be observed that Jeremiah, during his ministry, uniquely took steps to communicate the word of the LORD to Edom, Moab, Ammon, Tyre and Sidon, sending a message to the kings of these nations by the hands of their envoys, and refuting their prophets, diviners, dreamers, soothsayers and sorcerers in exactly the same terms as he opposed those of Judah. (See commentary on chapter 27). Verses 9–10 suggest the sovereignty of the word of God over all the nations, and this is never far from his thought. Indeed, it is precisely this scope of the prophetic interpretation of history, that makes the prophecy of the exilic period a model for the understanding of history. It is enough to conclude that this is how Jeremiah was understood in the tradition. This sovereignty is the theme of the Oracles against the Nations in chapters 46–51.

6. I do not know how to speak, for I am only a youth: The term rendered youth can describe a lad of four or a servant of forty and must not therefore be used to determine Jeremiah's age. On the other hand the prophet seems to be speaking of his unreadiness and immaturity and this is how the LXX understood it: I am too young. The command not to marry (16.1–2) also points in the same direction, since men married young and celibacy was rare, so that only in his youth would the command have its striking sign-value. It is not unreasonable to conclude with Skinner (*Prophecy and Religion* (1922), p.24 n.1.) that Jeremiah was under twenty.

The evidence is best served if it is supposed that Jeremiah received his call when he was young and, in his own opinion, immature, and that as a result he was largely ignored by the establishment until events validated his warnings. We cannot draw conclusions about Jeremiah's psychology. We can draw conclusions about his realism and the power of the divine initiative.

8. Be not afraid of them, for I am with you to deliver you: The cry 'be not afraid' has a long history in Israel and its natural context is the theophany (cf. Jg. 6.23, etc.) and the holy war (cf. Dt. 20.1–4; Jos. 10.25; Isa. 7.4; 2 Chr. 20.15, etc.). The affirmation 'I am with you' is also ubiquitous (cf. Jos. 1.1–9), and the combination of the two is not infrequent (cf. Dt. 20.1; 31.8; Isa. 41.10, etc.). Begrich argued that this belongs to the priestly oracle of salvation ('Das priesterliche heilsorakel', *ZAW* 52 (1934) 8f, 92 — *Gesammelte Studien zum Alten Testament*, *TB* (1964) 217–231). All this merely shows that the expression is commonplace and may not encourage conclusions about Jeremiah's anxious and timorous character. It is here applied to a specific threat viz.: the certain hostility of those to whom Jeremiah must deliver his message, cf. Ezek. 2.6; 3.9.

9. Then the LORD put forth his hand and touched my mouth: It does not seem necessary to look beyond Israel for the explanation of this decisive moment in the vision. The *mis pi* rites of the Accadian royal *kuppuru* ritual and the equivalent royal mouth purification rites in Egypt (Ivan Engnell, *The Call of Isaiah* (1949), pp. 40–41) merely demonstrate the widespread idea of preparing the mouth for the utterance of god-given words, (in the case of the king, laws). Israel believed that the LORD would put his words in the mouth of his chosen spokesman. This is explicit in what has been called the *magna carta* of prophecy —

Dt. 18.18; and the same expression is echoed in Num. 22.38; 23.5, 12; Isa. 51.16; 59.21.

> I will raise up for them a prophet (or prophets, if 'nabi' here is to be interpreted as 'distributive') like you from among their brethren; and I will put my words in his mouth, and he shall speak to them all that I command him. (Dt. 18.18).

Every word of Dt. 18.18b is to be found in vv. 7 and 9, but before it is suggested that the Deuteronomist had a hand in the composition, it is important to contrast the prose of Dt. 18.18b with the undeniable poetic form of v. 7b. There is insufficient ground for deducing from this verse that Jeremiah is intended to be understood as the new Moses and little to confirm the thesis in the rest of the book (see J. Muilenberg, 'Baruch the Scribe', in *Proclamation and Presence*, ed. by John I. Durham and J. Roy Porter (1970), p. 221). But there is no reason to doubt that the passage faithfully conveys the essence of Jeremiah's experience, that this experience was the consciousness that he must speak words *given* to him, and that this was reinforced by the vision of the hand of the LORD (not of a priest or prophet!) laid upon his mouth.

The hand of the LORD, as a figure of inspiration, is found in Isa. 8.11; 2 Kg. 3.15 (of Elisha), frequently in Ezekiel (1.3; 3.13, 22; 8.1; 37.1) and again in Jer. 15.17. The mystics bear their own witness to this sense of receiving something given. But so do many poets, and it may be regarded as characteristic of those gifted with poetic or prophetic sensibility. A number of them explicitly describe the sense of being used as a mouthpiece. Blake said: 'I have written this poem from immediate dictation, twelve or sometimes twenty or thirty lines at a time without premeditation and even against my will.' Goethe said: 'The songs made me, not I them: the songs had me in their power.' Dickens said on one occasion, when he sat down to his book: 'some beneficent power showed it all to me'. W. B. Yeats affirms: 'The poet becomes, as all the great mystics have believed, a vessel of the creative power of God.' A critic wrote of T. S. Eliot, 'His nervous sensibility secretes poetry as infallibly and as automatically as an oyster secretes pearls.' Similar avowals are to be found amongst musicians. Perhaps most revealing of all is the witness of the unbelieving philosopher Nietzsche:

> If one had the slightest trace of superstition left in one, it would be hardly possible to set aside the idea that one is the incarnation, mouthpiece and medium of almighty powers. The idea of revelation, in the sense that something suddenly and with unspeakable certainty and purity becomes *visible*, audible . . . simply describes the fact.

The account of Jeremiah's being possessed by the Word of God should
be taken as no less than a direct transcript of a remarkable but not unique
phenomenon. The question for people today is whether his interpretation
of this phenomenon is the correct one.

10. See, I have set you this day over nations and over kingdoms:
The Heb. suggests the idea of appointment with authority 'I give you
authority' (*NEB, REB*). This is entirely in relation to the sovereignty of
the Word of God. It is possible that 'nations and kingdoms' is a conflated
reading of alternative texts. On the other hand the whole verse is marked
by the build up of synonyms.

to destroy and to overthrow: a number of commentators, following
Volz, treat this sentence as a gloss, whose omission restores the balanced
form of the verse with two negative and two positive phrases:

> to pluck up and to break down, (*NEB* 'pull down and uproot', *REB* 'uproot
> and pull down'!) to build and to plant.

But it is doubtful if such precision should be aimed at. Elsewhere the
antithesis of build is 'overthrow' (*haras*) — Jer. 24.7; 42.10; 45.4. It could
be argued that the present text was suggested by 31.28, but in view of
the variations in these passages (cf. also 18.7), and the tendency in
prophetic poetry (particularly Isaiah) to build up a climax by the
comprehensive adding of synonyms, it is better to leave the text as it is.
Nicholson (*Preaching to the Exiles* (1970) p. 115) points out that all the other
instances of these words occur in prose passages and concludes that this
judgment — salvation terminology was intended by the Deuteronomists
as an anticipation statement of one of the central themes of the tradition.
But it is not obvious that v. 10 is prose. It may well be the word of
Jeremiah upon which the prose tradition subsequently built. See further
on 18.7–10, Weippert, and Holladay, 'Prototype and Copies.'

Many have doubted, following Duhm, whether Jeremiah could have
spoken in this way. But Jeremiah's sense of his own insignificance is
matched by an overmastering awareness of the irresistible power of the
divine word.

to build and to plant: Significantly the positive element is present in
the terms of Jeremiah's commission. It is a ground of confidence that
the element of hope is not absent from the total message of Jeremiah (see
especially on chapters 26–35 and note 31.28), and anticipated in the
beginning.

THE VISION OF THE ALMOND BRANCH **1.11-12**

It is probably a mistake to romanticise the process of prophetic inspiration here, after the manner of Skinner (p. 31) and many others:

> Thus it is midwinter, when all nature is asleep, and Jeremiah's attention is arrested by a solitary almond-branch bursting into flower. The almond, which blossoms in January, was poetically named by the Hebrews the *wakeful* tree, as the first of all the trees to wake up at the touch and promise of spring. Looking at it, the prophet is impelled to pronounce its name: *šākēd*, 'awake'. What does it signify? The answer comes unbidden: 'I am wakeful (*šōkēd*) over My word to fulfil it'.

What tells against this interpretation is the form of the vision. The apparently jejune question and answer seems to be a conventional characteristic of a certain kind of prophetic vision, in which the initial private communication between God and the prophet is thereby stressed and its meaning highlighted. A close parallel is Amos' vision of the basket of summer fruit (Am. 8.1-3, cf. 7.7-9, and Zech. 5.1-11), where there is a precisely similar play on words. It is improbable that the visions of Amos, still less those of Zechariah, were directly occasioned by the observation of physical objects; much more likely that the objects, recollected subsequently, became the material of visions in which the word of the LORD is entirely dominating.

This view is supported by the use of symbolic names unrelated to the character of the persons so named, e.g. the naming of Isaiah's sons (Isa. 7.8; 8.1-4). It is therefore unnecessary to ask whether the rod is dead (a stick) or alive (fresh twig or bough, with its blossom showing). If a decision were required, one would have to opt for the meaning 'rod' or 'stick' (cf. Gen. 32.11; Exod. 12.11; Num. 22.27; I Sam. 17.40, 43; Jer. 48.17; Exod. 39.9; Zech. 11.7, 10, 14). The weight of the prophecy is on the word, and the background of vision and word-play (almost identical sounds) is intended to throw into relief one of the major themes of Jeremiah's ministry, the power and inescapability of the divine word moving inexorably towards fulfilment. In Jeremiah there was indeed a new awakening of prophecy after a long sleep.

The same considerations tell against the view that Jeremiah was directing his polemic against particular cult practices and that the almond rod was an instrument of magic (Georg Sauer, 'Mandelzweig und Kessel in Jer. 1.11ff', *ZAW* 78 (1966) 56-61). The word *makel*, like *matteh*, means rod, and magic associations exist only if the context demands it, as in Num. 17 (esp. v. 8, Heb. 17.23). Here the meaning inherent in the word-play, not implicit hostility to magic practices, determines the vision.

It is again over-subtle to read into the passage an allusion to Aaron's rod as a symbol of Yahweh's judgment on his rebellious people, (P. S. Woods, 'Jeremiah's Figure of the Almond Rod', *JBL* 61 (1942) 99–103, J. P. Hyatt, *TB* 5 (1956) 806), at any rate as a motivating idea.

THE VISION OF THE BOILING POT 1.13–16

Since this vision has the same form as the vision of the almond branch, it is a fair presumption that it should be approached in the same way, and that the primary emphasis is on the divine word, not on the details of the vision. It is plain that there is similar word play, designed to concentrate attention on the essential communication. It comes emphatically at the end of the statement of the vision, but even more emphatically at the beginning of the subsequent interpretation of the vision. Alternative claimants for this word-play, viz. 'boiling' (*nāpûaḥ*) and 'breakforth' (*tipāṭaḥ*) are not plausible, and it is significant that some commentators feel the need to make emendations (following the LXX) in order to achieve a convincing correspondence.

It is not necessary to resort to such guess-work. The evil proceeding from the north is the dominating substance of the vision and summarizes a major theme of the prophecies for Jeremiah over several decades, until the judgment from the north could be recognised in the Babylonian threat and onslaught. (Cf. 3.12, 18; 4.6; 6.1, 22; 10.22; 13.20; 16.15; 25.9). The centre and climax therefore is the sentence: **Out of the north evil shall break forth upon all the inhabitants of the land** (v. 14). Starting from this, it is possible to see how the details of the vision are determined by it. The pot is not strictly a 'boiling' pot, but one 'blown upon'. Again, strictly it is the fire which is blown upon, so making the pot boil more fiercely. But we are dealing with poetry and vision, and it is stupid to ask too many pedestrian questions. The pot is turned, or perhaps tilted away from the north, and the steam gushes out as though driven by a northerly wind. We do not have to wonder whether Jeremiah was gazing at a pot on his own hearth! The idea of evil breaking forth from the north clothes itself, in the poet's vision, in the picture of steam belching out from a pot.

It is perhaps conceivable that the picture was rendered more ominous in Jeremiah's mind by the thought of a magic cauldron (see Sauer, op.cit.). But it is probable that if this had been in his mind he would have qualified the word *sîr*, which normally refers to the ordinary pot, such as was used either in the home or in the Temple. Moreover, *ṣapôn* (see the excursus on *ṣapôn* in A. S. Kapelrud, *Joel Studies* (1948), pp. 93–108) has sinister overtones enough. In Canaanite mythology, Baal was the 'Rider of the Clouds', enthroned on the mythological mountain in the north. There also, in the Ugaritic mythology, the struggle between the gods takes place, when Mot (death) is vanquished. Jebel el-Aqra, on the horizon of Ras Shamra, known to the Greeks as Mount Kasios, seems to have been the Canaanite Olympus, where a temple for Baal was built, though the geographical identification does not exhaust the mythological reference. The use of the term as a divine name — *baal ṣapôn* — may well be the primary use, and 'north' a secondary meaning. However that may be, it is clear that *ṣāpôn*, besides its ordinary meaning 'north', stood for the home of the Canaanite gods.

There is evidence that long before Jeremiah the myth of the home of the gods was domesticated within Israel, and certainly the description of Zion in Ps. 48.2 as 'in the far north' is as mythologically suggestive as it is geographically inappropriate. In Ps. 48 there is no hint of the hostile and threatening; quite the reverse. The mythological background is plain in Isa. 14.13. But the fact that this is Canaanite myth made it always susceptible to the hostile significance Jeremiah sees in it. The anti-Canaanite element in Jeremiah's thought, together with his affinity with the thinking of the Deuteronomists, made this use of the term 'north' natural. The element of the sinister thereafter inevitably attends it, both in Ezekiel (38.6, 15; 39.2) and Jl 2.20 (which may well be dependent on Jeremiah). Add to this the consideration that anyone alive to world politics would expect any threat to Israel to come from the north, not from Egypt, then the circumstances of Jeremiah's use of the term 'north' becomes clear. All this provides sufficient background to Jeremiah's use of the motif of the Foe from the North.

At the same time it is pertinent to observe that the idea is a widespread one. T. H. Gaster (*Myth, Legend and Custom in the Old Testament* (1969) collects examples from Indians of the Vedic period and the Iranians, from Greek magical literature and Mexican mythology, and from European folklore. It is also probable that a particular danger, brewing in the north at this time, was the Scythian invasion of western Asia (see H. H. Rowley, 'The early prophecies of Jeremiah', *BJRL* 45 (1962) 206–220), to which Herodotus refers *Hist.* i. 205f. If the historians can give us confidence in the substance of Herodotus' account, and also establish that the Scythian incursion was of a kind and at a time to form a background to Jeremiah's thought, then they may be mentioned as a relevant factor. But the material in Jeremiah cannot be used to establish the historical facts. We know of the Scythians from cuneiform sources and they shared responsibility for the downfall of Assyria. They were a marauding people from the steppe lands of southern Russia, who might well be called 'the tribes of the kingdoms of the north' (Jer. 1.15). Only Herodotus gives any information about their raids in Palestine. Though Herodotus is to be treated with caution, he is not to be dismissed, and Rowley rightly draws attention to his account of their robbing the temple at Ashkelon, an account based on specific enquiry. Rowley acutely observes that alternative views 'rest not on evidence, but on the explaining away of the only evidence we have' (Ibid. p. 217. But see R. P. Vaggione, 'All Over Asia? The Extent of the Scythian Domination in Herodotus', *JBL* 92 (1973) 523–30). If the Scythian menace first created anxiety and then faded away, this would explain why Jeremiah excited such contempt and mockery. On the other hand it is unlikely that Jeremiah was referring directly to the Scythians, still less to the Babylonians, when he referred to the Foe from the North. Verses 15 and 16, as expounded below, virtually exclude this interpretation. He expressed as much as he knew and waited on events to show who this destructive instrument of judgment would turn out to be.

15. For, lo, I am calling all the tribes of the kingdoms of the north: probably the word 'tribes' here is not original. It is lacking in the LXX and may well be an assimilation to 25.9. The construction of the sentence — *hinnēh* with the first person suffix and the participle — occurs fifty-eight times in the book of Jeremiah, and is characteristic of the prose tradition. But it is not found at all in Deuteronomy itself. It also occurs in the poetic oracles (e.g. 2.35; 5.14, 15; 8.17; 9.6) and the oracle here in vv. 15–16 is itself in unmistakeable poetic form. It is therefore unsafe to conclude that these verses are a Deuteronomistic expansion of vv. 13–14 (Nicholson, op.cit. p. 131, n.2) and these lines may be regarded as the words of Jeremiah himself. This conclusion is reinforced by the examination of the imaginative character of the image.

and they shall come and every one shall set his throne at the entrance of the gates of Jerusalem: The picture of kings (in the plural) setting up their thrones at each gate of Jerusalem is vivid but unrealistic. Of course it has a basis of realism in the story of the king of Israel and king Jehoshaphat of Judah 'sitting on their thrones . . . at the entrance of the gate of Samaria' (I Kg. 22.10), and we may assume that the idea of setting up thrones at the city gates was not therefore unfamiliar. Moreover there are a number of occasions recorded when the enemy was able to get no further than 'the entrance of the gate'. (Jg. 9.40; 2 Sam. 10.8; 11.23). To establish oneself here was to secure the city. When Jerusalem was conquered, 'all the princes of the king of Babylon came and sat in the middle gate' (39.3). But the symbolic nature of the picture is clear not only from the plural 'kingdoms . . . thrones', but also from the nearest parallel in Jer. 43.10. Here we learn that after he had been taken to Egypt, Jeremiah buried some stones in front of the government building in Tahpenhes as a prophetic sign that Nebuchadrezzar would set his throne *over them*.

against all its walls round about, and against all the cities of Judah: not therefore 'against' but 'over'. It is absurd to ask how thrones can be set over the walls of Jerusalem and the cities of Judah. This is the highly charged symbolism of poetry (missed by *NEB* but caught in the paraphrase preferred by *REB*). The symbolism is meant to convey the notion of a total subjection of Jerusalem and Judah by the foreign nations. The plural 'kingdoms . . . thrones', together with the total nature of the conquest may also be significant in relation to the well known myth of a final conflict with the nations outside Zion, in which the nations would be destroyed and Zion saved. This hope was clearly nourished in the worship of the Temple as expressed in Pss. 2; 110; 46. Ps. 48.4–8 is particularly to the point. It is an integral part of the influential Zion theology, in all probability formed an inseparable element of the pre-exilic New Year Festival, constituted a crucial feature of the hope of the Day of the Lord and received variant prophetic adaptation in Ezek. 38–39, Zech. 12, 14 and Jl 3. If this is so, Jeremiah is already, at the beginning of his ministry, setting himself against the false expectations of his contemporaries, associated with their fetish-like devotion to the Temple (see esp. chapter 7). For his hearers, the young Jeremiah created the greater impact because what he was declaring in this exaggerated, symbolic language was exactly the reverse of what their faith and their Temple worship led them to expect. The reversal of the thought of Ps. 48 is striking. The north is sinister as the source of Judgment, not benign as the home of Yahweh. The nations successfully establish their sovereignty in Jerusalem: they are not panicked into retreat.

16. And I will utter my judgments against them, for all their wickedness in forsaking me: This is the heart of the prophetic analysis of the sin of man. Cf. Hosea *passim*; Isa. 1.4. It is then illustrated in terms which are, in substance, though not in exact expression, Deuteronomistic commonplaces.

they have burned incense to other gods: occurs in I Kg. 22.17 and Jer. 19.4; 44.3, 5, 8, 15. The paucity of occurrences, together with the absence of this expression from Deuteronomy itself, makes it difficult to label it as Deuteronomic, let alone characteristic of the prose tradition. In any case it would be odd if Jeremiah did *not* incorporate some well-known Deuteronomic expressions into his poetry.

and worshipped the works of their own hands: while 'works of their own hands', as a description of other gods, is to be found in the Deuteronomic writings (Dt. 4.28; 27.15; 31.29; I Kg. 16.7; 2 Kg. 19.18; 22.17), its presence in Hos. 14.3; Mic. 5.13; Isa. 2.8 and Pss. 115.4; 135.15 means that it cannot be labelled Deuteronomic. Moreover the whole sentence, with the word 'worship', occurs otherwise only in Isa. 2.8 and Mic. 5.12! It is characteristic of Jeremiah to regard other gods as utterly lacking in reality, the projections of misplaced human imagination, and to see in the worship of them the symptoms of a radical alienation from the truth.

THE PROPHET'S STRENGTH **1.17–19**

The prophet's commission (vv. 4–10), is now amplified by the assurance that he will be fortified by overwhelming divine strength. No doubt **this day** in v. 18 refers precisely to the time and experience of the call. This does not mean that the whole of chapter 1 represents an original unity, or, as some scholars think, that an original call-narrative consisting of vv. 4–10, 17–19 has been broken up by the insertion of the two visions. Nor is it obvious that these verses can be attributed to a Deuteronomic editor. There are features in them which are best accounted for by Jeremianic authorship and there are features which suggest reflection on the prophet's later experience. It is perhaps easiest to suppose that the chapter has been built up on the basis of the fundamental call-narrative (vv. 4–10) and that in some way the prophet himself influenced the form assumed by the tradition.

17. But you, gird up your loins; arise, and say: The echo of the tradition of Elisha is unmistakeable (2 Kg. 4.29; 9.1) and suggests the activity of the prophet as messenger.

For the rest, the imagery of these verses is of the holy war, somewhat heightened by exaggeration, to describe the strength with which the prophet may stand alone against the world.

Do not be dismayed, like the **do not fear** of v. 8, is an expression
of the attitude appropriate when there is the assurance that God will strike
terror into the enemy. Cf. Dt. 7.17–26; 2 Chr. 20.15, 17.

18. The imagery is military. Jeremiah will be as a **fortified city**: this
is the only example in the *OT* of the use of this expression figuratively
to describe a person.

an iron pillar, and bronze walls: it is not clear what these can be,
literally. As poetic hyperbole they make good sense. Iron and bronze
figure together, as symbolic of strength, in Isa. 45.2; 48.4; Mic. 4.13;
Ps. 107.16; Job 6.12; 20.24; 40.18; 41.27 and Jer. 6.28 and it is probably
an error to omit the 'iron pillar' with LXX. Gates, made of wood but
decorated in bronze, and now to be seen in the Assyrian section of the
British Museum, suggest that the bronze refers to a decorative feature
of particularly strong walls. The image seems to have been used by
Thutmose III of himself in a hymn-like description of his sovereignty.
('A king is he, a hero, excellent fortress of his army, a wall of iron (?
or bronze) for Egypt'. G.A. and M.B. Reisner, 'Inscribed monument
from Gebel Barkal', *ZAS* 69 (1933) 30). The bow of brass of Job 20.24
may, as Professor G. R. Driver has argued ('Problems in the Hebrew
Text of Job', in *Wisdom in Israel and in the Ancient Near East*, ed. M. Noth
and D. Winton Thomas, — *VT* supp. 3, 1955), refer to a bronze-tipped
arrow, or it might refer to a decorative feature of the bow. But again
the reference to iron and bronze together suggests a symbolism of power,
and Ps. 18.35 is not easily interpreted of the arrow. The versions have
'wall' in the singular. But MT is better. A poetic picture is being built
up of a prophet strong as an impregnable fortress city.

**against the kings of Judah, its princes, its priests, and the people
of the land**: the reference to 'kings' in the plural suggests reflection on
the ministry of Jeremiah covering several reigns. The people of the land
may be the influential country landowners (G. von Rad, *Studies in
Deuteronomy* (1953) pp. 60–66) but the purpose of the list is to suggest
the opposition of the whole land. Cf. 2.26; 8.1; 13.13; 17.25; 25.18; 32.32;
44.17, 21.

19. for I am with you . . . to deliver you: see on v. 8.

We are thus presented in this first chapter with an uncompromising
statement of Jeremiah's authority. He does not, like the false prophets,
speak the deceit of his own mind (14.14). On the contrary, he does not
know how to speak. His word is given to him. He is the messenger of
another. The substance of this message is the sovereignty of the divine

word over all nations and causes and persons. This means inescapable judgment, particularly for the holy people who complacently hope for their own vindication.

It is altogether calculable that the utterance of this message will bring Jeremiah into total conflict with every element in the life of the nation. Paradoxically this pacific man, who was later to enjoin submission rather than resistance to the Babylonian invaders, employed the familiar language of the holy war, to describe his lonely prophetic stand against universal opposition, — not — Yahweh on the side of Israel against the nations but — Yahweh on the side of his prophet against his people. He appropriated to himself the language of assurance customary in the wars of Yahweh. He could not and would not bend the word entrusted to him a fraction of a degree to the will of the people. But the God to whose word he would be utterly true, would fight with him. Every subtlety and refinement of argument, relating to human weakness, needs of state and the interpretation of Israel's faith, was to be exploited to deter him from his course.

Jeremiah remained a model of the minister of the divine word and of faith. If we may suppose that chapters 1–6 substantially represent Baruch's scroll, then Jeremiah himself would be responsible for collecting this material together and the diversity of character in it would be explained. We can accept the call as Jeremiah's account of his own experience, but recounted with amplifying material coloured by his lonely and painful ministry through several decades. We should expect that the form of the chapter would not be uninfluenced by those who shaped the Jeremiah tradition.

THE CASE AGAINST GOD'S PEOPLE 2.1–37

The next section is a collection of short oracles arranged to constitute a solemn lawsuit in which Judas is accused, as an adulterous woman might be accused, of infidelity. There is every reason to assume that the model of the lawsuit was used by Jeremiah, among other analogies and metaphors. The power of this section, in its present form, lies in the way in which the image is sustained.

In the manner of an advocate, questions are put to the accused (2.5ff). In v. 9 the legal background becomes explicit in the word contend (*'ārîḇ*) cf. v. 29. This is what scholars sometimes call the *rîḇ* pattern. As in Isa. 1, there is an appeal to the heavens as witness (v. 12), the background to this feature being perhaps the near eastern suzerainty treaties. The accusation is summed up in v. 13. There are further questions in 2.14ff. The answering accusation of the people against Yahweh follows in v. 29. They plead innocence (vv. 35ff.), and the whole section reads like the judge's account of his efforts to persuade the accused of their guilt and bring them to repentance.

Along with this element of homogeneity are signs of the collection of a series of short oracles. Both the homogeneity and the division into a number of independent oracles are explained if we can attribute the final form of the section to Jeremiah and Baruch, Jeremiah dictating the substance or poetic concentrate of oracles long ago delivered by him, Baruch influencing arrangement and sometimes expression in ways appropriate to one who was no mere copyist but an independent literary figure of considerable attainment. The final arrangement was undoubtedly made with this legal motif in mind, as the editorial dominance of v. 9 stresses. That this is consistently in the second person singular makes the accusation direct and explicit.

All these oracles are best associated with the earliest phase of Jeremiah's ministry, when he was mainly concerned to draw attention to prevalent Baal worship and to give emphatic warning of the disaster that must come in the form of the northern peril. The absence of precise signs of contemporary events is immaterial. The attempt of Milgrom to find such evidence in the reference to Egypt and Assyria in 2.18, 36 and pre-Deuteronomic Baal worship in 2.8, so narrowing the period to 627–622 B.C., cannot be said to amount to demonstration, even if the result is probable. (See *JNES* 14 (1955) 65–69 and Rudolph, op.cit. p. 13.)

Within the section 2.1–4.4 which we have seen to be clearly distinguished from 4.5–6.30, chapter 2 itself exhibits a certain homogeneity of content. The commentary will show that it is composed of a number of originally independent oracles, but that the special circumstances of their recall and writing down permitted and encouraged the imprinting upon them of a unity of thought. With this insight into the history of the transmission, it becomes vain to ask what actual words Jeremiah uttered. On the other hand the peculiar features, the lack of logical sequence and the repetitive and stereotyped elements, which are as baffling to the modern reader, become intelligible, and the whole may be understood as a composite and meaningful set of variations on a theme.

As we have seen, the key to the unity of the chapter is the legal metaphor. Like Isaiah, Jeremiah begins at the beginning with the divine election of Israel to be his people. Like Hosea he looks back to the wilderness period as the time of youthful idealism before corruption began

(vv. 2–3). He then describes what went wrong. The indictment is that Israel turned from her loyalty to the God who had treated her as a bride, and defiled the heritage with which she had been entrusted, prophets and priests conniving at this betrayal (vv. 4–8). On this ground the Lord opens his case (v. 9) and calls the heavens to witness this unparalleled exchange of the Living God for the counterfeit (vv. 13–19). The Lord draws attention to Israel's obstinacy (vv. 20–22) and the sexual metaphor is pursued into the animal world to describe her spiritual promiscuity and infidelity (vv. 23–25). Only in time of trouble will Israel turn to the Lord, but then they will be like a thief caught in the act (vv. 26–28). For her part, Israel speciously argues her case (v. 29) and against all the evidence maintains her innocence (v. 35a). But the divine Judge's final word is that he will bring the legal process to a conclusion (v. 35b).

SUPERSCRIPTION **2.1**

The use of the first person supports the hypothesis that Jeremiah himself had some responsibility for the setting down of these oracles, and may well form a link with the narrative of chapter 36. With v. 2a, cf. 36.5ff. The address is explicitly to Jerusalem, rather than Israel (as in the oracles) and this may support the same hypothesis (Rudolph). The emission of Jerusalem in LXX and Old Latin may however indicate that the explicit linking of the oracle with Jerusalem was a relatively late stage in the redactoral process.

THE INNOCENCE AND PROMISE OF YOUTH **2.2–3**

The first of the oracles is a brief poetic statement, in lament rhythm, of Israel's lost promise as the bride of Yahweh. The thought is closely dependent upon that of Hos. both in the image employed and in the use of the wildnerness traditions, cf. Hos. 2. Note also the expression **became guilty** i.e. 'made themselves guilty' here and in Hos. 5.15. Neither Hos. nor Jer. depends upon those traditions in the form we have them in the *OT*, for the traditions emphasise more the persistent rebellion and ingratitude of God's people than their bridal joy. Deut. emphasises Israel's fundamental faithlessness and infidelity in the wilderness period (7.22–26), but also alludes to an Israel enjoying the LORD's care and bounty (32.10–14).

Both traditions were preserved, the tendency being to see the black and the white, rarely the grey. The point here is the contrast between Israel's honeymoon and the present state of the marriage (Carroll). There was truth in the contrast, as also between the protection she then enjoyed and her present vulnerability. Sinai was, so to speak, the marriage covenant between God and his people. That this covenant remained the foundation and enduring basis of Israel's life, indicates a strong and decisive acceptance of the relationship by Israel. All the greater her fall from grace.

2. the devotion of your youth: the word *ḥeseḏ*, as in Hosea, is particularly appropriate in the context of the marriage covenant. And both the history of nations and movements, and the experience of individuals, present the ever repeated pattern of bright hopes of youth, gradually extinguished by the infidelities and compromises of age, and succeeded by disillusionment and despair.

your love as a bride: contrast v. 33, q.v. The contrast between **a land not sown** and the settled agricultural life of Canaan was the contrast between relative simplicity and the relative complexity of civilisation with its corrupting allurements.

3. That **Israel was holy to the LORD** means that she was separated wholly to him, and was not driven to rival loyalties by the pressure of life among the nations.

the first fruits of his harvest implies God's sovereignty over the nations and his election of Israel, not to a private privilege, but to a task as God's servant, anticipating the turning of the other nations to the same Lord.

All who ate of it are those who attempted to obstruct the early progress of Israel towards nationhood. In those early days despite setbacks and difficulties, it seemed that none could stop the onward march of Israel to the promised land.

says the LORD emphatically ends the oracle. Although contrast between the young vigorous semi-nomad people and the settled nation corrupted by syncretism, may be overplayed and must be qualified, it remains a proper contrast which is echoed in the experience of every mature adult. Historical reservations should not distract attention from a profound truth about human nature, individual and collective.

THE CHARGE AGAINST ISRAEL **2.4–9**

The delimitation of the successive oracles in this chapter is not easy and scholars differ. The view taken here is that the second oracle ends with *nᵉʾūm Yahweh* 'says the LORD' (v. 9); like the first (v. 3), the third (v. 12), and fourth (v. 20). It is of course common, as Rendtorff has shown ('Zum Gebrauch der Formel ne'um Jahwe im Jeremiahbuch', *ZAW* 66 (1954) 27–37), to find this phrase both as part of an introductory formula and in the middle of an oracle, even between two parallel members of a verse. It is most frequently found at the end of an oracle, and this is the most likely interpretation here.

and with your children's children I will contend (v. 9), is probably a gloss written at a time when it was clear that Judah's tribulations were continuing, and illustrating the truth that the sins of the fathers are visited on the children to the third and fourth generation. This gloss is the same sort of historical comment as is found in Isa. 7.8 with the same use of *'ōd* meaning 'still' (Cf. also 2 Kg. 17.41). See also on v. 30 which strengthens this interpretation. The 'for' in v. 10, like those in vv. 12, 20 is a connecting link or suture to introduce the next oracle with its related theme.

The oracle is a *reproach* directed against the whole nation, mentioning particularly **your fathers**, the **priests**, the wise (see on v. 8), **the rulers** (Heb. 'shepherds') and **the prophets**. And the whole nation means the nation from the beginning. A remarkable solidarity is assumed between the contemporary nation and the nation of the fathers. The responsibility spans the generations. It behoves the present generation to exercise their historical memory. The substance of the indictment is the turning of the people from their primary and exclusive loyalty to the true God, who has providentially governed their history and given them their land. Jeremiah accuses them of spurning the gifts of the past, of ignorance of the divine will, of direct rebellion against their God and of falling to the allurements of vanities. He completes the oracle, with a statement that God will enter into a lawsuit with his people, beginning with the familiar 'therefore' (Heb. *lāḵēn*) of the prophetic oracle sometimes called the threat.

4. On the structure and significance of the superscription, see on 10.1.

and all the families of the house of Israel: Since Jeremiah is referring back to the history of Israel from the settlement, this could refer specifically to the northern kingdom. It is equally possible that here, as elsewhere in prophecy, 'Israel' is primarily a theological term denoting the people of God. In the light of v. 2, this is more probable.

5. and went after worthlessness, and became worthless: The word means vapour, breath, that which is insubstantial, vain, nothing. This expression is used in 2 Kg. 17.15 in the course of a passage which is often regarded as the classical Deuteronomic model of the prophetic interpretation of history. The reference is in the first instance to the syncretism that stained Israel's religious life from the time of the settlement, but in principle includes every ultimate allegiance placed otherwise than in the true God. Jeremiah states succinctly the truth that character is fashioned according to the scale of our priorities, cf. Hos. 9.10 'they became detestable like the thing they loved'. This is an aspect of the *order* of life in which judgment is inherent and inexorable.

6. They did not say, 'Where is the LORD who brought us up out of the land of Egypt? The question — Where is the LORD? — may be asked in two senses. Frequently it is on the lips of the foreigner or the scoffer who taunts the faithful Israelite with the impotence or inactivity of his God, cf. 2 Kg. 18.34 (= Isa. 36.19); Pss. 42.3, 10; 79.10; 115.2; Jer. 17.15; Jl. 2.17; Mal. 2.17; Mic. 7.10. For the Israelite himself to question the presence and activity of God is the supreme temptation as at Massah (Exod. 17.7) cf. Ps.95. But the meaning here is different. It is like the question on the lips of Elisha who, exercising the charisma of his master, seeks a divine answer: Where is the LORD, the God of Elijah? (2 Kg. 2.14). And in Job 35.10 it is the mark of the believer to cry: 'Where is God my Maker?' Jeremiah is therefore saying that the people have not been *seekers* of the God who showed his love for them in their history. The aridity of the wilderness is contrasted with the fruitfulness of Palestine, which is the heritage promised by Yahweh to his people.

7. you defiled my land and made my heritage an abomination: the language is that of the cult, familiar to Jeremiah's hearers, and much more challenging than it appears to the modern reader. The priests were responsible for cultic purity and it was their duty to pronounce authoritatively whether people or things were clean or unclean. To say that they, with the other leaders, had 'defiled my land', was therefore (so it seemed) to stand truth on its head. It was to charge them with the very uncleanness they existed to eradicate. To pronounce the land an abomination (cf. Isa. 1.13) was to say that it had become as repugnant to God as unclean practices were to the priests (cf. Dt. 13.15; 17.4; 18.9; 20.18). And this land was the LORD's 'heritage', i.e. what we have learned to call 'the promised land'. See on 3.19–4.4. The conception is dominant in Deuteronomy. The saving design of God himself is being frustrated by his own people.

8. The priests did not say, Where is the LORD? again the meaning is that the priests are not seekers of Yahweh and of his will.

Those who handle the law: This is in parallel with the priests and may be simply an alternative way of referring to them. The word for 'handle' is used elsewhere of wielding a weapon or being skilled in war and may allude to the priestly expertise in transmitting and interpreting the law. We know that this was one of the primary functions of the priesthood (Dt. 33.10; Jer. 18.18; 2 Chr. 15.3; Mal. 2.7–9). On the other hand, it is possible that this verse should be linked with 8.8–9 where the 'wise' or intellectual leaders are to be identified with the scribes who interpret the law. In Jeremiah's time the wise had comprehended the law within their interest, and indeed Deuteronomy itself was presented as a new wisdom (4.5–6). If this is right, then Jeremiah in v. 8 refers to four classes of people who are failing the nation, viz. the priests, the wise, the statesmen and the prophets. See further on 8.8–9. They do not have that personal knowledge of Yahweh which Hosea regarded as the test of genuineness (Hos. 6.6, cf. Isa. 1.3; Mal. 2.7). The condition of these 'lawyers' is exactly that of their *NT* successors to whom (according to the author of the Fourth Gospel) Jesus said: 'You search the Scriptures . . . yet you refuse to come to me that you may have life' (Jn 5.39–40).

the rulers transgressed against: Heb. shepherds,' an image of the leadership, cf. Ezek. 34; Zech. 11. Transgression, rebellion is the most characteristic of all Heb. words for sin in the prophetic literature; it indicates broken personal relationships, cf. Isa. 1.2.

the prophets prophesied by Baal: most appropriately, though not necessarily, understood of the period before the Deuteronomic reform.

9. See introduction to vv. 4–9. The 'therefore' is a characteristic introduction to the threat or announcement of judgment. Here it introduces the legal process which will end in judgment.

There is no contemporary historical allusion in this passage, such as one would expect in the dramatic events of the reign of Jehoiakim. The reference is to the wide sweep of Israel's story as God's people and to the whole leadership, comprehensively denounced. The passage is placed in a section which we have seen reason to regard as mainly early prophecies of the young prophet, acquiring a new cutting edge in the later period. If this is so, we see Jeremiah boldly attacking the whole establishment and are not surprised if, for many years, he made little headway and could not penetrate the confident dogmatism of his elders.

THE EXCHANGE OF GODS **2.10–12**

The accusation in this oracle is that the people have exchanged the true God for false, those whom Hosea earlier had called 'no-gods' (Hos. 8.6; cf. Dt. 32.21).

10. Cyprus (Heb. *kittim*) is to the west and Kedar a desert tribe to the east, i.e. look east and west.

11. my people have changed their glory: is also close to the thought

and expression of Ps. 106.20 (cf. Rom. 1.23), where the allusion is to
the golden calf (Exod. 32), the classical image of such exchange. The
rhetorical cry to the peoples of the world 'has a nation changed its gods?',
appears on the face of it somewhat naive. Was there much point in other
peoples making such an exchange? The burden of their gods was light
and there was little gain in exchange. Was not the temptation for Israel
so much the greater because Yahweh made such unique and onerous
demands? In this sense the exchange is a sign of the incomparable
character of Yahweh. To seek to escape from him, though there is no
escape, is to seek security, ease, the familiar and domestic; it is to evade
the terms of the covenant. The ironic overtones of the Hebrew suggest
barter. The exchange is the exchange of business dealings. Ironically Israel
has settled for a poor deal, for she has exchanged the invaluable for the
worthless.

their glory: the word glory is capable of a variety of related meanings.
The 'glory of the LORD' in Exod. 24.16, 17; 33.18, 22. Isa. 6.3, Ezekiel
passim, is an expression for the divine accommodation to human
apprehension in revelation. It is closely associated with the symbol of light
(Isa. 60.1), and with the moment of epiphany in temple worship (Ps.
29.9; Zech. 2.8; Ps. 73.24). Here it contrasts the splendour of the self-
disclosed God of Israel with the nonentities preferred by his people. That
this is the correct interpretation is perhaps confirmed by the fact that '*their*
glory' is one of the eighteen corrections made by the scribes. The original
was probably 'my glory', a circumlocution for Yahweh. The change from
'my' to 'their' was no doubt intended to depersonalise the expression
and make it refer to Israel's religion.

12. Be appalled, O heavens, at this: as often in the rhetoric of
prophecy, the heavens (and sometimes the earth) are regarded as impartial
witnesses. The ultimate background suggested for this in near eastern
suzerainty treaties is irrelevant to the understanding of the symbolism
here. This appeal to impartial witnesses provides the ending of the oracle.

(**13. for**: is an editorial connecting link leading on to the next oracle.)

SPRING OF LIFE AND RIVERS OF DECEPTION **2.13–19**

The overall theme of this passage is the forsaking of God (vv. 13, 17,
19), described both in the contrast between a perennial spring and a
cracked cistern (v. 13), and in the image of drinking Egyptian and
Assyrian waters (v. 18). Although vv. 14–16 appear intrusive, they are
nevertheless woven in to the theme as warning to Judah of the
consequences of this betrayal by Israel.

13. my people have committed two evils: the evil is one, viz. the enormity of forsaking the God who has taken Israel as his bride (v. 2). But it has two aspects; the rejection of God and the adoption of a substitute. The image of the fountain of living waters is suggestive, both in view of the geographical and climatic conditions of Palestine and in the light of the doctrine of the *living* God (Jos. 3.10, Pss. 42.2; 84.2; Hos. 1.10; 2 Kg. 19.4, 16; Dt. 5.23; 1 Sam. 17.26, 36; Jer. 10.10; 23.36). The term 'living' implies both the contrast between the true God and false Gods which Jeremiah is here making, and the further truth that Yahweh is the Giver of Life. In his power are the issues of life and death. The same point is made with the similar imagery in Ps. 36.10. The importance of cisterns capable of holding the rain water does not need emphasis. This passage points to the fundamental question of discernment of truth and commitment, which the prophets from Elijah onwards had asked.

14. Is Israel a slave? Is he a homeborn servant? A rhetorical question requiring the answer no. Yet Israel, son of the house has suffered as a slave might suffer and become a prey. The lions (i.e. the foreign nations) roar and the evidence is for all to see in the desolation and the uninhabited waste. Whoever forsakes God, loses the status of sonship and becomes a slave with all the consequences thereof. The tenses in this verse suggest that Jeremiah is pointing to the awful example of destruction still to be seen in the old northern kingdom.

15. See on 4.7.

16. Moreover, the men of Memphis and Tahpanhes have broken the crown of your head: This verse is a crux and the Hebrew plainly corrupt. *RSV* represents an emendation based on the Peshitta. But there is no evidence of any such humbling of Israel by Egypt in the period. In fact the hebrew verb, as revocalized according to the Peshitta, is in the imperfect tense and is so translated in *NEB*. 'Men of Noph and Tahpanhes will break your heads'. The sense is then 'Israel is so weak that even Egypt will break her!' If the past tense were preferred, the verse would have to be treated as a gloss, as many in fact treat it, noticing that it somewhat breaks the sequence between vv. 15 and 17. Interest in Memphis and Tahpanhes belongs to the period of the oracles against the nations. See on 46.14.

17. This verse links the apparently intrusive vv. 14–16 with the theme of the whole section.

when he led you in the way: probably to be omitted, as by LXX. It looks like a dittograph of verse 18a.

18. The second of the two metaphors, expressing what it means to forsake the LORD, is that of drinking the waters of the Nile and Euphrates.

the waters of the Nile: in the Heb. *šiḥôr* 'pond of Horus', i.e. probably one of the arms of the Nile, standing here for the Nile itself. The metaphor is perhaps less poetically apt than that of Isaiah in 8.6–7. Both contrast, either explicitly or implicitly, trust in the LORD with reliance on the great military powers, with all that that involves of compromise and apostasy. It is not convincing to interpret Assyria as a poetic equivalent of Babylon, as some have done, in the interest of proving a late setting for this passage. On the other hand, as a consequence of Israel's history, Egypt and Assyria had become symbols of the great powers that threatened and defeated Israel. It does however make sense to suppose that the passage has an earlier setting when Assyria was the realistic enemy, but that in Jeremiah's handling of the material in the time of Jehoiakim the enemy was clearly Babylon. The prophet would see no need to alter a symbolic name.

19. Your (own) wickedness will chasten you: the irony of judgment, whereby the people blindly bring upon themselves their own punishment, is often observed by the prophets. It is exemplified in Israel's history and will surely happen again. The rest of v. 19 summarises the theme of this section (13–19).

A REBEL BEYOND RECOVERY **2.20–22**

Three images are used in this section, all derivative and unconnected as images, but linked in respect of their application. The point of each is that Israel has obstinately rendered herself irreclaimable.

The first image (v. 20) is the composite one of the slave who, like a stubborn beast, breaks his yoke, repudiates the limitation of his service and says, **I will not serve.** Israel's rejection of her vocation to be the servant of the LORD is complete and can be traced back in her history.

The second image is that of the harlot (vv. 20, 22), **bowed down**, or, in the paraphrase of the *NEB*, *REB*, which recaptures the force of the Hebrew, 'sprawled in promiscuous vice'. So defiled she can be washed clean by no soap and **the stain** of her **guilt** is indelible.

The third image is that of the planting of vines. What was planted to produce red grapes has proved wild and worthless. As Jeremiah's use of the image of the waters of the Nile was less poetically strong than that of Isaiah, so here there is nothing of the depth and range of Isaiah's classical vineyard parable. Indeed his mind is so riveted on the *subject* of the metaphor that he loses contact with the realism of the metaphor. Thus the expression **wholly of pure seed** (v. 21) is probably dictated less by horticultural method than by the image of Israel as a seed, actually evildoers (Isa. 1.4), intended to be a holy seed, (Isa. 6.13; Ezr. 9.2). In v. 22 the prophet reverts to the theme of defilement and washing. In all these ways the prophet reinforces his accusation that Israel had rendered herself beyond recovery.

The expression **upon every high hill and under every green tree** (v. 20), indicating the practice of Canaanite fertility rites, is widely used in the *OT* in one form or another (Dt. 12.2; I Kg. 14.23; 16.4; 2 Kg. 17.10; Isa. 30.25; 57.5; 65.7; Ezek. 6.13; 20.28; 34.6; Hos. 4.13; 2 Chr. 28.4. In Jeremiah 3.6, 13; 17.2). It is argued that the form of the expression here is appropriate to its poetical context, and may be due to Jeremiah himself. (See W. L. Holladay in *VT* 11 (1961) 170–176, and *Jeremiah* p. 98). The use particularly of 'Deuteronomic' phrases elsewhere in the poetry of Jeremiah suggests that this is a view which should be considered.

LIKE BEASTS **2.23–25**

This passage has the form of a disputation, cf. 6.16–21. The behaviour of Israel is now described in terms of the uncontrollable waywardness of a young camel and the sexual urge of the female ass. An impressive weight of opinion, including the *NEB* and *REB*, is in favour of omitting the reference to the ass, and interpreting the whole passage as a description of the female camel in heat. It is alleged that otherwise the picture is spoiled, and the grammar is difficult.

Certainly the versions witness to early difficulties in translation, though they do not agree on a better text. On the other hand it can be argued that the present Heb. text is the best we have (McKane), that the grammatical difficulties are not insuperable, and that the text, as translated in *RSV*, reveals Jeremiah alive to the actual behaviour of both the camel and the ass.

For the camel here is not meant particularly to be the female camel, but the young camel. The female camel does not come into heat. It is the male that experiences rut (K. E. Bailey and W. L. Holladay, *VT* (1968) 256–260).

The young camel is the perfect illustration for all that is 'skittery' and unreliable. It is ungainly in the extreme and runs off in any direction at the slightest provocation, much to the fury of the camel-driver. To sit in a village courtyard and watch such a young camel go scooting through, with some alarmed peasant dashing madly after it, is an unforgettable experience; such a young camel never takes more than about three steps in any direction. To this day the young camel provides a dramatic illustration for anything unreliable. Thus 'interlacing her paths' is an accurate description of a young camel — it provides Jeremiah a perfect illustration for the fickleness of Israel. In contrast to the female camel, however the habits of the female ass in heat are dramatic and vulgar. She sniffs the path in front of her, trying to pick up her scent of a male (from his urine). When she finds it, she rubs her nose in the dust and then straightens her neck, and with head high, closes her nostrils and 'sniffs the wind'. What she is really doing is *sniffing* the dust which is soaked with the urine of a male ass. With her neck stretched to the utmost, she slowly draws in a long, deep breath, then lets out an earthshaking bray and doubles her pace, racing down the road in search of the male'. (ibid. pp. 258–259).

Thus Jeremiah describes the conduct of God's people giving themselves over to the popular fertility rites. The claim **I am not defiled** (v. 23) picks up the theme of vv. 7, and 22.

I have not gone after the Baals is deleted by some commentators on the ground that this claim could not be made (cf. v. 25, but also cf. v. 35). No doubt the worst excesses were committed in the name of Yahweh. The Accadian texts illustrate the custom of walking behind the deity in procession. Or it may be that the particular rites to which Jeremiah refers here were carried out in secret. The way in which the picture is worked out would support this.

23. Look at your way in the valley: the LXX translates as the place where many assemble. But probably the reference, as in 19.2, 6 (cf. Ezek. 39.11) is to Ben-Hinnom (see on chapter 19). Cf. Isa. 57.3–17 for witness to such practices here a few years later.

24. in her month they will find her: Jeremiah seems to be saying that just as there is no difficulty in finding the ass when she is in this condition, so it will be easy to track down the superstitious practices which Israel complacently thinks she can hide.

25. Keep your feet from going unshod: *NEB* 'Save your feet from stony ground'. *REB* 'Stop before your feet are bare'. **I have loved strangers**: once again the sexual metaphor is combined with the expression of ruthless headstrong obstinacy, as elsewhere in this chapter (v. 20). Indeed the apparent contradiction 'I have not gone after the baals' and 'after them I will go' may be an exact register of the fickle, untrustworthy behaviour of Israel. The sexual metaphor enables the prophet to point to a profound truth of human nature. He sees that Israel is in the grip of a passion that totally weakens her will. Her predicament is indeed hopeless, because she is the victim of her own ungovernable nature.

A THIEF CAUGHT OUT 2.26–28

This section lacks the clear identity of the previous sections and appears to be composed equally of allusions to Jeremiah's known teaching and echoes of Hosea. Thus v. 26b **they, their kings, their princes, their priests and their prophets** is a list which, in variant forms, occurs nine times. Verse 27b **they have turned their back to me, and not their face** occurs in 18.17 and 32.33. Verse 28b is identical with 11.13. **in your time of trouble**, cf. 15.11; 14.8, 11, 12. Verse 27a **who say to a tree, You are my father**, has affinity with Hos. 4.12 and verse 28a. **where are your gods that you made for yourself?** cf. Hos. 14.3; while the ironic cry **Let them arise, if they can save you** is close to Dt. 32.38.

This mosaic character the passage shares with a number of sections in Isa. (cf. esp. 10.19–26; 11.10–16) and Jer. (see p. 34). It seems to be a characteristic of the process of composition, when further material is built upon a fundamental nucleus. This does not mean that the passage has necessarily been added by an editor. As Jeremiah (or Baruch) recalls his teaching over a gap of many years, it may well be that it is in this way his mind and memory lead him. The association of ideas between the opening v. 26 and the previous passage is clear and confirms our view that Jeremiah is condemning, amongst open vices, the *secret* rites of the people. The main point of the metaphor of the thief is in fact that it is essential to his success that none finds out. The reference to the tree and the stone is probably wider than a straight allusion to the asherah and the mazzebah (cf. Hos. 3.4; 10.1–2), and symbolises the whole Canaanite cult. In the moment of testing, that cult will prove useless. Then they will openly cry to Yahweh who will make the ironic response of v. 28.

THE JUDGE'S APPEAL 2.29–30

These verses stand out from the sections that precede and follow in that they are in the second person plural. On the other hand their close relation to v. 9 which ends an oracle in the second person plural suggests that they are deliberately used to build up the image of the chapter as a whole, as distinct from the individual oracles, in the form of a lawsuit between God and his people. In v. 9 God declared that he would bring a charge. The intervening oracles illustrate Israel's contumacy in a variety of metaphors. Already Israel's unteachableness has been shown in a series of rejoinders and denial, particularly in vv. 20–25. This protestation of innocence will be explicit in the final section of the chapter. Now Yahweh makes his appeal **Why do you complain against me?** (v. 29) i.e. why argue your case? Israel's obstinacy is summed up in terms of the most characteristic expression for sin viz. rebellion.

Verse 30 has puzzled the commentators, who have resorted to emendation. In particular **your children** has been changed to 'through the prophets' or by a more modest re-arrangement 'your fathers' or 'fathers and sons'. But all miss the point. We have here, in all probability, a subsequent comment or gloss which looks at the situation from the point of view of the next generation. Upon that generation the judgment fell, but still, as Jeremiah's later experience showed, it refused to learn the lesson. The reference to 'your children' is thus of exactly the same kind as that in verse 9 (see p. 84). Probably for the same reason the third person **they took** (often changed to 'you') should remain.

In vain have I smitten your children, they took no correction: the form of words might be suggested by the undoubted Jeremiah passage 5.3.

your own sword devoured your prophets might include reference to Manasseh's probable persecution of the prophets (cf. 15.1–4). But if we are correct in interpreting the verse as a later comment, it might more pointedly refer also to the ruthlessness of Jehoiakim by whose command Uriah was put to death (Jer. 26.20ff) and who would have destroyed Jeremiah if he could. This is the ironic fulfilment of the prophecy 14.15 according to the principle of 30.16. And if the reference to the prophets is thus to be interpreted, then the smiting, as in 5.2, might well refer to the death of Josiah (see on 5.2). Emendations of the text are hypothetical and without authority.

THE LORD'S RESPONSE TO ISRAEL'S PLEA OF INNOCENCE **2.31–37**

If the interpretation of v. 30 is correct, then vv. 31–37 clearly form a distinct section and the introduction **And you, O generation, heed the word of the Lord** correctly marks the break. LXX and L both have the more usual 'hear the word of the LORD' and bear witness to some uncertainty. 'Heed' or, literally 'See' is uniquely used here of the study of prophecy and might belong to a time of reflection. Or could Jeremiah have introduced this note deliberately, as he dictated his prophecies of an earlier generation to Baruch, in order that they might be seen by the later generation as on the point of fulfilment? See on chapter 36. The omission of this expression in *NEB*, uncorrected in *REB*, is irresponsible in a version. If this is the correct interpretation, it makes good sense in a passage which recalls the earlier themes of this chapter, the early promise, the joyful bride, the promiscuity of the harlot, the threat of the great powers, and the inescapable verdict of the divine judge.

31. The LORD begins his retort with a somewhat curious metaphor, which nevertheless makes sense. **Have I been a wilderness to Israel or a land of thick darkness?** The wilderness is the land which yields nothing; it lies under a curse and there is no blessing in it. On the contrary the Lord has been the lavish bestower of nature's goods. The land of thick darkness is the land in which men grope about, distressed and wretched (v. 6), at worst the land of death. In contrast the Lord is a light and life to his people (cf. Isa. 8.22–9.2).

Why then do my people say, We are free? The Versions bear witness to uncertainty, but the probable meaning is 'free' in the sense of roaming unbridled. It is the thought of v. 20. In a similar way verse 32 echoes the thought of verse 2. Verses 32 and 33 take up again the image of the harlot, as in vv. 20, 23–25. In 33 it is taken to the limit: Israel is the teacher of all harlots!

lovers: cf. 22.20, 22 and Hos. 2.7, 9, 12, 15.

34. Also on your skirts is found the lifeblood of guiltless poor; you did not find them breaking in. Yet in spite of all these things — This is a *crux*. The first line is overloaded and it is plausible to suppose that 'poor' is a gloss which has the effect of interpreting the bloodshed in terms of judicial murder. About the second line there can be no certainty. But it seems right to translate 'find them breaking in' in the light of the similar vocabulary in Exod. 22.2. 'If a thief is found breaking in, and is struck so that he dies, there shall be no bloodguilt'. 'You did not find' can easily be translated 'I (Yahweh) did not find it (the blood)'. 'These things' can, by simple change of vowels, supported by LXX, read 'oak' or 'terebinth'. The meaning of the verse as a whole will then be:

> You have taken part in your illegitimate sacrifices and the evidence of the sacrificial blood is on your very clothes. It wasn't as though I caught you housebreaking, when the law excuses violence in self-defence and the stains of blood would be understood. The blood you shed is to be seen on every oak where you practise your profane cult.

Duhm thought there was a reference to child-sacrifice, but this was probably confined to one place (cf. 7.6). The alternative is to take the verse as referring to the sort of judicial murders which blotted the reign of Manasseh (cf. 19.4; 22.3, 17; 26.15).

35. You say, I am innocent: i.e. either a denial of guilt in respect of the miscarriage of justice; or a claim that the sacrifices have done their atoning work. This latter interpretation is perhaps supported by the expression **surely his anger has turned from me**. However this may be, this protestation of innocence, following the charges that have been laid, is the signal for the decision of the divine judge: **Behold I will bring you to judgment**: The *niphal* perhaps suggests an intensifying of the process of bringing to conviction by accusation and legal argument.

36. How lightly you gad about changing your way! The *RSV* incorporates the meaning of two different Hebrew words here. A choice has to be made. Better: 'how lightly you change . . . '. This echoes the thought of v. 11, unless as Cornhill thought, the allusion was to some unknown change of political policy.

You shall be put to shame by Egypt as you were put to shame by Assyria: this is exactly the thought of v. 16 as interpreted above. It suggests that the prophecy dates well before the defeat of Egypt at Carchemish. See p. 39.

37. With your hands upon your head: a gesture of lamentation cf. 2 Sam. 13.19.

It is impossible not to be impressed by the way this passage sums up much of the thought of the preceding oracles. Verse 31 cf. v. 30; v. 32 cf. v. 2; vv. 32–33, cf. vv. 20, 23–25; v. 36a cf. v. 11; v. 36b cf. v. 16. At the same time it brings to a head the legal process explicit in the vocabulary of vv. 9, 29, implicit in the accusation and defence that runs through the whole chapter. Israel's confident assertions: 'I will not serve' (v. 20), 'I am not defiled' (v. 23), 'We are free, we will come no more to thee' (v. 31), are now reaffirmed by the double protestation of innocence (v. 35).

Can this relation to the preceding oracles be accidental? The recognition of deliberate literary relationship is consistent with the view that this is the work of Jeremiah, once the circumstances of composition are understood. We have to imagine Jeremiah recalling the images and telling phrases he had used twenty or more years earlier. It is inconceivable that this was no more than a mechanical effort of memory. He selects those oracles which are fittest for the purpose and which survive in his memory. As he reaches a climax in his column of oracles, so the recollection of old words imperceptibly takes a new form appropriate to the purpose they are now to serve. One senses the increase of tension as he piles oracle on oracle. The content is not different, but the form is dictated by the new circumstance. Thus we may conclude that vv. 31–37 (and vv. 26–28), correctly communicate the earlier message of Jeremiah, but never assumed precisely this form until he dictated them to Baruch. Baruch too may well have influenced the expression here and there.

THE LORD'S APPEAL TO HIS PEOPLE 3.1–4.4

In the same way that we discovered a measure of homogeneity of content in chapter 2, it is possible to see a purposeful intention running through 3.1–4.4. Again this is redactional, though through Baruch it may well represent the thought of Jeremiah. The original situation of the oracles is lost. And indeed the attempt to identify an original poem of Jeremiah, with equal and balanced strophes 3.1–5, 19–20, 12b–13, and 3.21–4.2 underestimates and overlooks the power of re-presentation, as old oracles were remembered and reapplied in this new context. The mind of Jeremiah is fixed on the situation of 604 B.C. and he calls the old prophecies to mind entirely in terms of this situation. He is not concerned to remember accurately for the sake of prophetic archives but to speak the divine word to Jehoiakim and his cabinet. But not even this is the end of the process of transformation. For Baruch has his hand in it and there is evidence of subsequent amplification in terms of the way events turned out.

First, Israel is exhorted to weigh the consequences of so behaving that divorce becomes inevitable (v. 1). Then the brazenness of her infidelity is stressed — the Israel who in her worship calls the LORD 'father' (vv. 2–5). Then specifically Judah is addressed and warned to consider the example of her sister Israel who was indeed, divorced (in the disaster of 721 B.C.). Yet Judah is the more guilty. Hope still exists for Israel and she is exhorted to return to Yahweh (vv. 6–14). The hope is extended to a picture of a united people under good shepherds. Jerusalem itself, no longer the Ark, will be the focus of the divine presence and, not only will Judah and Israel be united, but Zion will be the centre of the world (vv. 15–18). So despite the threat of divorce, there is hope. The section concludes with a dialogue of repentance (3.19–4.4) which displays a number of verbal links with the earliest part of the chapter. The Lord describes his initial intentions for his people and their unfaithfulness (returning to the recurring image of the faithless wife in v. 20). But Israel is penitent and, after the manner of the lament, confesses her fault (vv. 21–25). The Lord sums up the conditions of avoiding the full force of divine judgment (4.1–4). When the full force of divine judgment could be thought to be on the point of erupting in the shape of Babylonian invasion, it is not difficult to imagine the dismay of those who witnessed the recital of these oracles in 604 B.C.

Plainly there is meaningful sequence in the oracles as they have been set down. The commentary will disclose the sometimes intricate verbal and thematic connections which serve to create this strange logic.

IRRETRIEVABLE DIVORCE **3.1**

The next section of oracles opens with a brief but pointed oracle on divorce. There can be no certainty that Jeremiah was familiar with the exact terms of the law of Dt. 24.1. Some have argued that this was a new formulation, but neither the story of David and Michal, nor Hosea's language concerning Gomer prove that the ancient laws were different from the provision of Dt. 24.1 (see J. D. Martin, 'The Forensic Background to Jeremiah III.1', *VT* 19 (1969) 82–92). The law may well therefore reflect an old and well-known provision. Nor is it significant that Jeremiah does not use the precise words of Dt. 24.1 for 'bringing sin upon the land'. Nor is the LXX, Vulg., reading 'wife' necessarily to be preferred to 'land'.

The plain fact is that this verse exactly corresponds to the *content* of Dt. 24.1 and takes its significance from the fact that the law was familiar. Two stipulations are made. The first is that a divorced woman, i.e. correctly supplied with 'a bill of divorce' (Dt. 24.2; Jer. 3.8), may not return to her first husband, even if she is subsequently divorced from her second husband or if he dies. This is Israelite society's way of saying that people shall not play fast and loose with marriage. Divorce is serious, to be undertaken only when it is sufficiently weighed; and when decided, it is irreversible. Jeremiah is thus asking his people to ponder seriously the consequences of their unfaithfulness. Let them return while there is time and before the point of no return is reached.

The second feature of the verse is the principle that unchastity defiles the whole land (Lev. 18.25, 28;19.29; Num. 5.3; Hos. 4.3). This no doubt is a reflection of ancient cultic ideas (cf. also Hag. 2), but it is also simply and directly true in a way that is dangerously ignored by individualists who assume morality to be solely the affair of the individual. This is taken up again by Jeremiah, cf. vv. 2, 9. **will he return to her?** . . . **and would you return to me**: Heb. *šûḇ*, cf. 3.7, 10, 12, 14, 22; 4.1; 5.3.

OPEN INFIDELITY **3.2–5**

The theme of this oracle is the brazenness of Israel's infidelity. It furnishes an indictment answering to the rhetorical question of v. 1. If in 2.26–28 Jeremiah was concerned with secret rites, here he emphasises the open shamelessness of her conduct.

2. Lift up your eyes to the bare heights: i.e. to the high places of idolatrous worship. The 'Arab' is here the typical robber to be seen waiting for his chance to pounce on the unwary traveller. LXX has 'raven'. God's people are as committed to their faithless way of life as a highwayman to his. The failure of the rains, as a sign of divine displeasure, is ineffective to bring them to their senses (cf. Am. 4.7-8). Then another metaphor (v. 3): **You have a harlot's brow, you refuse to be ashamed**: this is an allusion to the resolute obstinacy that appears on the face of those who habitually defy the standards of society. There is no pretence of fidelity, and no shame.

4. have you not just now called to me, My father, thou art the friend of my youth: This may be an allusion to a significant mode of address to Yahweh in an act of worship otherwise unknown to us. In old Israel, the king, who is in a special sense God's son (Ps. 2.7), is allowed to say, 'Thou art my father' (Ps. 89.26) and Hosea sees Israel as God's son (11.1-3). Later than Jeremiah the fatherhood of God is the ground of the prayer in Isa. 63.7-64.12. Otherwise the *OT* is reticent, probably because of the danger, in a Canaanite environment, of implying a natural relationship between God and people. Jeremiah may be quoting a psalm of lament not preserved in the Psalter. 'Friend' here is tantamount to 'teacher' (W. McKane, *Proverbs* (1970) p. 286) and the image is of the son undergoing discipline from his fatherly instructor.

5. all the evil that you could: better with *NEB*, *REB* 'you have done evil and gone unchallenged' i.e. you have had free course and none has prevented you.

The effect of placing this oracle to follow v. 1 is to probe the meaning of the defilement of the land. The phrase 'pollute the land' in vv. 1 and 2 provides a catchword. At the same time v. 4 contrasts with 2.27. To call a thing of wood 'my father' was more obviously deviant. To use the unexceptional language of worship to cover brazen apostasy was even more serious. The prayer of v. 4 is pathetic and tragic. It is uttered by an Israel set in infidelity, an Israel that has openly turned from the LORD to the alluring counterfeits of her Canaanite past. She hopes pathetically that some cheap lip-service will put things right without any change of heart. But everyone knows that marital relationships are not mended that way. The prophet appeals not only to the divorce law, but also to the personal experience of his audience. On these terms there is no way back. But an element of hope is introduced in the next section.

A CAUTIONARY EXAMPLE **3.6-14**

Verses 6–11 are in prose and are introduced by a brief superscription in the first person, as in 2.1. It does not, however, follow that this is the exact reproduction of the words of Jeremiah. Most recent commentators find vv. 6–18 intrusive and breaking the natural sequence of vv. 1–5 and 19–25. This may be too surgical a solution.

Indeed it may be significant that vv. 12–13, which are recognised to be in verse, contain the answer to the question of the lament in v. 5: 'I am merciful, says the LORD; I will not be angry for ever' (v. 12). Without v. 12, the question of v. 5 remains unanswered. But then v. 12 has the phrase 'faithless (i.e. backsliding or apostate) Israel', characteristic of Jeremiah, and recurring in vv. 6, 8, 11; cf. 2.19; 3.22; 5.6; 8.5; 14.7.

The term Israel may be ambiguous. Theologically it is God's people, in Jeremiah's time to be identified with Judah, and many scholars think this was the original intention in vv. 12–13. But it can also refer to Judah's northern sister Israel. That is the intention here where Judah and Israel are contrasted. The northern kingdom's fate is a cautionary example of what divorce means. This connection is explicitly drawn out in v. 8, — 'that faithless one, Israel'. In v. 9 there is also the theme of polluting the land which links with 3.2–5.

So the passage is woven subtly into the theme of the chapter as a whole. It is not likely that this is accidental. It is an example of the care with which former teaching was remembered and restructured. For Jeremiah this was not simply a memory exercise, and Baruch was more than a copyist. We may suppose that when the exact wording of a poetic oracle was not remembered, it was natural to give its substance in prose. More probably prose was the means of expression normal to Baruch and his successors as they gave the content of their master's work in their own words. There is no reason to suppose that this chapter ever existed in any other written form.

The theme is the historical example of Judah's sister Israel, whose apostasy is described in terms of adultery and whose destruction in 721 B.C. is described as divorce. This goes beyond the implication of v. 1. This is observed by Judah, but the lesson has not been learned. She, so far from abjuring such corruption, herself 'pollutes the land' by her harlotries, and therefore her guilt is the greater.

10. Yet for all this her false sister Judah did not return to me with her whole heart, but in pretence, says the LORD: Heb. *šûḇ* return

cf. vv. 1, 7, 12, 14, 22; 4.1; 5.3. The word 'in pretence', *šeqer*, occurs
with such frequency in the book of Jeremiah that it must be considered
amongst the features of his theology (see Thomas W. Overholt, *The Threat
of Falsehood*, 1970). In fact it occurs in three contexts, to denote the people's
false sense of security, the activity of false prophets and, as here, the
spurious character of idolatry. The idol is the counterfeit god. It may
be that the historical allusions of the imagery account for the
superscription, ascribing the oracles to the period of Josiah. There is no
need to doubt its accuracy.

This prose passage (vv. 6–11) completed with a solemn 'says the
LORD', leads up to a rhetorical address (vv. 12–14) to the dispersed
people of the northern kingdom. Though faithless Israel has suffered the
ultimate punishment, she is nevertheless **less guilty than false Judah**,
(v. 11, cf. 23.13–15). Therefore Jeremiah is to proclaim these words
towards the north (v. 12). This is a characteristic expression of Jeremiah,
referring most frequently to the place from which evil or invasion is to
come (see esp. on 1.14) but also, as here and 16.15; 23.8; 31.8, to the
place of Israel's banishment from which her sons and daughters will
return. In general the hope of return, as expressed in Isa. 11, 49 and
60 was an act of faith, unrealisable on any human calculation. But the
thought here is realistic. The imperative *šûbāh* in v. 12 and *šûbû* in v.
14 'return' does not, in the first instance, have the moral meaning so
clear in vv. 1, 7, 10, 22, but it is not excluded. To return from the
dispersion to Zion is to return to Yahweh in heart and mind.

14. for I am your master: cf. 31.32.

**I will take you, one from a city and two from a family, and I will
bring you to Zion**: Many commentators take this verse as showing that
the address is clearly to Judaeans. This is not necessarily so. Zion is a
theological concept as much as 'Israel'. It became the symbol of Israel's
unity and her magnetic centre. When the northern kingdom had become
a dream of the past and her shrines suppressed, Zion was both the centre
of sacrificial worship and pilgrimage, and the badge of Israel's identity.
Here was the 'house of the God of Jacob' (Isa. 2.3); here the place to
find the law and 'the word of the LORD' (Isa. 2.3). To Zion would all
dispersed Israelites and Judaeans come in the time of hope (Isa. 11.12;
35.10; 60), as also would the nations come for instruction (Isa. 2.2–3;
60.3). Zion will be 'the joy of the whole earth' (Ps. 48.3).

These ideas come to expression in v. 17 (**all nations shall gather to
it**) and v. 18 (**the house of Judah shall join the house of Israel and
together they shall come**). It is too facile to suppose (Thiel, McKane)

that vv. 6–13 refer to the northern tribes, vv. 14–17 to Judah and v. 18 a harmonising device. It seems more probable that v. 14 concludes the previous section with a climax created by the repetition of 'Return faithless . . . ', and that this verse (as interpreted above) generated vv. 15–18 (as interpreted below). This interpretation may be supported by the contrast between 'Return, faithless Israel' (i.e. the northern, ten tribes) in v. 12 and 'Return, faithless children' (i.e. Israel and Judah) in v. 14.

The ground of Jeremiah's hope is the mercy (*hesed*) of the LORD (v. 12, cf. 9.23; 16.5; 32.18; all prose passages). He uses the adjective 'merciful' here only, but the basic importance of the conception is not to be underestimated. On this basis also he appeals to Israel to acknowledge her guilt (v. 13) in a way that Judah shows no disposition to do. Nor must the possibility be ruled out that some of Jeremiah's early preaching was precisely such a warning to Judah of Israel's ill-fated behaviour. Chapters 30–31 show how deeply he felt for the northern kingdom in which he himself had been born. Was he not of the family of Eli and the priests of Anathoth? But now we are to understand these warnings and appeals in the light of the Babylonian threat to extinguish the 'people of God' altogether.

A PEOPLE UNITED **3.15–18**

There follows another prose passage. This time it appears to fall into the category of 'many similar words' (36.32) added to the complex of oracles in the light of history. Easily the horizon, already future in vv. 11–14, is extended to the ultimate future as it lies in the prophet's perspective — often ambiguously called eschatological. 'In those days . . . 'at that time' may be conventional language for this dimension. Verse 18 suggests that both Judah and Israel are in exile. The comparison with 5.18 reinforces the impression that this is an exilic compilation by an editor who sees the Day of the LORD actualised in the exile and its consequences. See on 5.18.

Every element of the thought is paralleled elsewhere in the book of Jeremiah. First, the shepherds, figure of kings (2.8; 10.21; 22.22; 23.1, 2, 4; 25.3–6; 50.6) and here of the Davidic kings who shall rule in Zion (33.14–26; 23.5; 30.9, 20). Second, the attitude envisaged to the Ark is similar to that which Jeremiah requires to the Temple itself (7.4). Third, the ingathering from the North, together with the unity of Israel and Judah, is the theme of chapter 31. There are also verbal parallels: *wehaśkēl* 'with understanding' v. 15, cf. 10.21; 23.5; and linked with 'knowledge', see especially 9.24.

16. multiplied and increased (the 'Be fruitful and multiply' of Genesis) occurs in 23.3: 'come to mind' occurs in 7.31; 19.5; 32.35; 44.2b and may be taken as characteristic of the redactor's prose, in which the Deuteronomic name theology will come as no surprise.

they shall come from the land of the north (v. 18) links the passage, according to the catchword principle, with v. 12. The balanced 'they shall not more say, "The ark . . ." At that time Jerusalem shall be called' indicates a fundamental reinterpretation of a time-honoured institution, matched by the reinterpretation of the Exodus (23.7–8) and the Torah (31.31–4) cf. also 31.29, 30.

Altogether the evidence points to the conclusion that the passage has been carefully built up in its setting, and, like vv. 6–10, never had independent written existence.

As it now stands, the passage sketches a picture of a united people, Judah and Israel as one, under ideal kings, their unity focused on Zion which will effectively be the centre of the world. The image of all the nations gathering to it is anticipated in Isa. 2.2 and repeated in varying forms in Hag. 2; Isa. 11.12; 49.6, 22; 60.3; Zech. 14.16f. If this were a significant part of the theology of Jeremiah, one would expect him to make much more dramatic use of it, though it must be admitted that the circumstances of his ministry provided little occasion for this emphasis.

On the other hand one feature of the passage stands out as unique and characteristic of Jeremiah. That is the teaching on the Ark. The term 'ark of the Covenant of the LORD' is standard Deuteronomic terminology and in Dt. the Ark is the container of the book of the Law. But older conceptions seem to be in mind here. Here the Ark is regarded as the sign of the presence of the Lord in his Temple, and in the projected time of the future it will be irrelevant and undesired. The language implies that it will have been destroyed and no attempt will be made to remake it. Instead the new symbol of the presence of the Lord will be his 'Name' (v. 17, in the *RSV* translated 'presence', a not inaccurate equivalence).

The phrase **to the presence (name) of the LORD in Jerusalem** is absent in the LXX, but it may nevertheless be accepted as an unerring pointer to the underlying thought of the passage. This is the so-called name-theology of Deuteronomy, pervasive in the Jeremiah tradition. Jerusalem itself will be the throne of the Lord. Some scholars have argued that the original significance of the Ark was precisely this, that it was the throne of Yahweh who was invisibly seated upon it, and that this text is the most unambiguous evidence for this conception.

It is, however, more likely that the original significance corresponded to the term 'ark', which means box, and this is set out with clarity in Dt. 10.1–5. It was closely associated with the presence of Yahweh, and became the symbol of his presence, by reason of its association with the cherubim and the *kapporeṭ* or mercy-seat (see R. E. Clements, *God and Temple* (1965), ch. 3). This association may well have started at the sanctuary at Shiloh where the Ark was established. In Jer. 7.12 Shiloh is regarded as the first Canaanite centre in which Yahweh vouchsafed his presence, i.e. 'where I made my name dwell at first' (cf. Ps. 78.60). The Ark survived when Shiloh was destroyed. It was transferred to Jerusalem, eventually to Mount Zion and to Solomon's temple (Ps. 132.11–14).

Jeremiah clearly saw the destruction of Shiloh as a historical sign of what might happen to the Jerusalem temple (chapter 7). Here he visualises the loss of the central cult emblem without a tremor. This is prophetic insight of the highest order and may be taken as an indication that this passage, whether written by Baruch in the light of events or enlarged by subsequent disciples, is based on the memory of a powerful saying of the master himself.

It is this negative kernel of the oracle which is the most explosive element in it. It represents the most radical criticism of the organised cult, in its sacred centre, by the assertion of its ultimate irrelevance: **it shall not come to mind, or be remembered or missed** (v. 16). In the light of the traditions which attribute a divine origin to the cult, and in the face of popular loyalty which regarded the Ark and the Temple with fetish-like devotion, this is like the shaking of the foundations. It is tantamount to the abolition of religion in its folk-character.

The essentially sacrilegious, iconoclastic character of this prophetic criticism, which no doubt drew on Jeremiah the hostility narrated later in the book, is somewhat disguised by its new setting in a glimpse of the visionary future. This is perhaps a strong pointer to the history of the tradition, and the transformation of the teaching of Jeremiah by other hands. The truth remains that the divine presence is not necessarily and essentially linked with cultic symbols, however sacred. God is free and sovereign, and cannot be mastered and controlled by those who have a vested interest in his service. To argue that this oracle merely reflects the current unimportance of the Ark is to confuse cause and effect.

17. stubbornly follow their own evil heart: the expression 'stubbornness' or 'obduracy of heart', is used eight times in Jer. in prose passages (7.24; 9.13; 11.8; 13.10; 16.12; 18.12; 23.17) and elsewhere only in Dt. 29.18 and Ps. 81.13. It could well therefore be a phrase of the tradition. Nevertheless it sums up the teaching of Jeremiah who 'traced sin to the individual perverted will' (Skinner) and taught that 'The heart is deceitful above all things and desperately corrupt' (17.9).

DIALOGUE OF REPENTANCE **3.19–4.4**

This section is built up in the form of a dialogue. It has five connections with what precedes.

(1) The word 'heritage' in 3.19 serves as a catchword, forming a link with the verb in v. 18 (cf. also 2.7). The effect of this is to say: 'The hope of the future is Israel as the worthy occupant of the Lord's inheritance. This indeed was his intention. His purpose was that Israel should be supreme in the whole world. *But* she has been as a faithless wife . . .' According to Dt., the *naḥ⁽ᵃ⁾lāh* is the supreme blessing which God promised to his people. This is a term taken from the vocabulary of land tenure and first used of Israel in this theological way by Dt. As von Rad points out, it is, as thus used, a strictly theological term (*Old Testament Theology*, vol I (ET 1962), p.224) and it comprehensively signifies the fulfilment of promise. The Deuteronomic imprint is not confined to the word alone, for **how I would set you among my sons** (3.19) is the essence, if not the language, of the Deuteronomic doctrine of election.

and give you a pleasant land, a heritage most beauteous of all nations: exactly the spirit, if not the language, of the theme as set out in Dt.

(2) The expression: **I thought you would call me, My Father**: (v. 19) cf. 2.27 and esp. 3.4, q.v.

(3) The term **faithless** (v. 20): cf. vv. 7, 8, 11 and cf. also 5.11; 12.1, 6. This serves also to link the passage with the theme of the faithless wife in 3.1.

(4) **A voice on the bare heights** (v. 21) links with v. 2. There Israel is the brazen harlot, here penitent for her sins.

(5) A **delusion** (v. 23): *šeqer*, the same word, characteristic of the book of Jeremiah, translated 'in pretence' in v. 10.

Once again this can hardly be accidental. Whatever previous history these oracles may have had as perhaps the concentrates of longer prophetic interventions in the early ministry of Jeremiah, they have been incorporated into their present literary structure with the utmost care and skill. This means that the dialogue is not a form-critical unit, let alone a 'liturgy' with a liturgical context of its own. As it now stands it is an essentially literary structure. If it is modelled on a Temple liturgy, that liturgy is not known to us, unless it be the divine answer following the people's confession in the familiar lament.

The dialogue is constructed of the following elements:

(1) Verses 19–20: The Lord speaks and describes both his initial hopes for his people and the cause of his disappointment.

(2) Verse 21: Narrative description of Israel's penitence.

(3) Verse 22a: The Lord's invitation to return, with word play on the verb *šûḇ*, cf. Hos. 14.1. See on vv. 12, 14.

(4) Verses 22b–25: Israel's confession. **the shameful thing**: one of those passages where *bôšeṯ* has been substituted for Baal, unless it has been used deliberately to make verbal link with v. 25.

25. we have not obeyed the voice of the Lord our God: this expression occurs about sixty-five times in the *OT*, eighteen times in Jeremiah, and otherwise overwhelmingly in the 'Deuteronomic history'.

(5) 4.1–2. The Lord's final word. It is possible that there is a play on the word *šûḇ*, 'return', and that later readers are meant to understand **If you return** to mean return from exile. But this is not a necessary interpretation, as is shown by 3.1. This is what it means to return to the Lord, whether from exile, or in heart and mind, or both. See on vv. 12, 14. It means uncompromisingly cutting out all **abominations**: a word used in Dan. 11.31 for Baal. Its use in Hos. 9.10 is unique before Jeremiah and the Deuteronomic writings; cf. Jer. 13.26 for the clear indication that it refers particularly to Canaanite, sexual rites. 'To return' means also positively a commitment to the Living God.

4.2 if you swear, As the Lord lives, in truth, in justice, and in uprightness: the oath is in effect a particularly strong sort of confession, and the form of the oath in Hebrew an acknowledgement that it is Yahweh who is the Living God (See on 2.13). **in truth** is the exact antithesis of the **in pretence** of 3.10 and the **delusion** of 3.23, cf. 5.2–31.

then nations shall bless themselves in him: probably a reference to the promise made to Abraham (Gen. 12.3; 22.18; 26.4; 28.14, but more particularly 18.18). *NEB*, *REB* 'like you' is a conjecture, based on the fact that it is Yahweh who is speaking and designed to avoid an apparently awkward change of person. But change of person like this is not infrequent.

(6) 4.3–4. Explication of the Lord's word. The **for** indicates an editor's effort to join this section on to what precedes. At the same time the whole section serves as a suture, both completing the Lord's summing up of the dialogue and introducing the following announcement of Judgment. Thus:

(a) The address is now specifically to **the men of Judah and the inhabitants of Jerusalem**. Though Israel's example has been cited for the attention of her sister Judah, and indeed Israel has been directly addressed (3.12, 14), with some consequential ambiguity as to what is meant by 'Israel' in chapter 2, now all ambiguity is set aside.

(b) The admonition to obedience is uttered precisely to avoid the terror of wrath and judgment which is now announced 4.5ff. It is left to the reader to draw his own conclusion. And though we cannot certainly identify the passages added subsequently in the course of tradition, we can imagine the devastating effect of this technique on those who listened to the recital of these oracles as the story is told in chapter 36.

3. Break up your fallow ground: a wisdom type of imagery, but no more than one would expect from a prophet whose eyes are open to the natural world. In any case the phrase is found in Hos. 10.12.

4. Circumcise yourselves to the LORD, remove the foreskin of your hearts: Dt. 10.16. The old cultic custom is here presupposed. Probably a sign of initiation into the clan, based on old marriage ceremonial, it may well have contained the idea of dedication or cleansing. This reinterpretation in terms of the opening of heart and mind to the Lord is common to Jer. and Dt. It is vain to ask who originated it. Deuteronomic thought so interpenetrated the most individual work of Jeremiah that one can only conclude in the most general terms that there was a profound mutual influence. The thought was certainly congenial to Jeremiah and supported his deepest intuitions concerning the basis of religion.

The rest of v. 4 corresponds exactly to 21.12b. It is composed of two commonplaces.

lest my wrath go forth like fire and burn with none to quench it: this image of the divine wrath as unquenchable fire is to be found in Jer. 7.20; 17.27; 21.12b, but previously also in Am. 5.6, and in a late compilation in Isa. 1.31.

because of the evil of your doings: Jer. 26.3; 44.22; cf. 4.18; 23.2, 22; 25.5; 17.10, etc. cf. Hos. 9.15; Isa. 1.16. Again we have a teaching which may plausibly be thought to be derived from that of the authentic Jeremiah, paralleled in Deuteronomy and associated with language which is commonplace. A reasonable conclusion would be that we have the teaching of Jeremiah mediated through less original minds who have left the imprint of well-known phrases.

Unrelenting Judgment from the North **4.5–6.30**

In this section the oracles on the Foe from the North are gathered together (4.5–9, 13–17, 19–21, 29–31; 5.15–17; 6.1–8, 22–26). They are characterised by directness and urgency. They therefore raise acutely the question of the situation to which they were relevant. Two views suggest themselves in the light of the interpretation of Jeremiah's early ministry adopted here.

(a) They were originally uttered in the early period of Jeremiah's ministry, probably soon after his call in 626 B.C. and related to the vision of the Boiling Pot (1.13–16). In this case, the Scythians may or may not have been a factor in the background, but an element of uncertainty is reflected in the fact that Jeremiah does not name the enemy (See on 1.13–16). At the time of writing the enemy is identified.

(b) The alternative is that they were originally uttered in relation to the Babylonian threat in the period immediately before the writing down of these oracles (605/4 B.C.) This is the view of, amongst others, Claus Rietzschel (*Das Problem der Urrolle*, 1966), who thinks the vision of the Boiling Pot also belongs to this period and that its introduction 'The word of the LORD came to me a second time', betrays a temporal separation from the vision of the Almond Branch which introduces the earlier oracles contained in 2.1–4.4.

The second alternative is at first attractive for giving full weight to the significance of calling the alarm, sending people away from Jerusalem, resorting to sackcloth and lament in a readily intelligible way. But on further consideration the first alternative must be adopted.

(a) There is no strong reason for dating the vision of the Boiling Pot at any other period than the one given in chapter 1. Indeed if we correctly identify Baruch's scroll with chapters 1–6, there is reason to ascribe the arrangement of this chapter to Jeremiah and Baruch, who presumably knew what they were doing. This means that one of the first themes of Jeremiah's ministry, following his call, was the threat from the North. The *presumption* is that 4.5–6.30 contain the working out of this theme in detail.

(b) The oracles are set in 4.5–6.30 in such a way as to suggest subsequent arrangement. Indeed, as we shall suggest in the comment on 4.5–9 the prophet seems to be projecting himself back into earlier circumstance from which the present crisis appears as an event of the future (v. 9). Although there is some sort of pattern in the alternating speech of Yahweh through the prophet, and response of the prophet on behalf of the people, yet there are the familiar signs of the use of old material in new connections. It is difficult to think the section would have its present form if the whole were composed *de novo* at or just before the period of writing down.

(c) If these oracles had been used first of the Babylonians in the period 605/4 B.C., it is difficult to understand why the repetition to Jehoiakim and his minister of passages very recently proclaimed at large, should have the effect they did. On the contrary, as will be explained in the commentary on chapter 36, the effect of the reading of the oracles can best be understood if the identity of the Foe from the North was not known with confidence until the Babylonian army was on the march and its intentions plain. Indeed Jeremiah may well have been driven into silence by the non-fulfilment of those early oracles, and the consequent collapse of his credibility. It was the clarification of forgotten enigmatic and ominous prophecies, in the critical events of the Babylonian invasion, which constituted the power of Baruch's reading and evoked terror in his hearers. It was when oracles, hitherto ignored, were repeated and could be seen to be on the point of fulfilment that the inevitability of divine judgment was fully apprehended. There is therefore insufficient reason to set these oracles in the time of Jehoiakim. They belong in some earlier, irrecoverable form to the years following 626 B.C.

This is not to deny that in their present form they belong to the crisis of 605/4 B.C. and are so intended to be read. They were recalled and written out for the special purpose described in chapter 36. Once again it is necessary to stress that we have to put out of our mind all modern ideas of accurate reporting and anachronistic ideas of scientific historiography. Jeremiah's mind was on the word of the Lord being spoken to Jehoiakim and his officials in the circumstances of December 604 B.C.

Baruch also influenced the form in which we now have the oracles. This means that the reader should be alert for some relation between 4.5–6.30 and the oracles that precede in 1.1–4.4. Two preparatory features may well be deliberate.

First, Jeremiah has emphasised, in the context of a trial scene, that God's people are brazen and impenitent. The whole section is in effect a witness to the divine judgment about to take effect on the basis of the careful examination of Israel's case.

Second, the example of the northern kingdom (the kingdom that perished in 721 B.C.) has been put before Judah. Yet Judah's guilt is pronounced greater. Could the punishment then be less or different? 2.1–4.4 leads up to the final exhortation to repent:

> lest my wrath go forth like fire, and burn with none to quench it, because of the evil of your doings (4.4)

Now in a series of related oracles the terrors of judgment are described as directly imminent. Jeremiah voices the alarm to flee for safety.

The passages on judgment from the north are laced with passages which, in one way or another reinforce the deadly seriousness of Israel's predicament. Thus 4.10 and 5.12–14, 31 allude to the damage done by prophets who prophesy a false peace. At the same time the true prophet (Jeremiah) is tortured by the pain of his impossible position, poised between the LORD and his people (4.14). 4.32–28 sees the coming destruction as in some sense a reversal of the process of creation. Order is giving way to chaos.

5.1–11 finds no ground of hope in the search for a righteous remnant which might be a promise of salvation. 5.20–31 affirms that every ground of mercy and escape has been examined, but has dissolved. Israel is as foolish as she is brazenly stubborn. Her leaders are false without exception, and the people like what they are given.

In 6.9–21 the prophet counters the divine command to seek and seek again for a faithful remnant with the objection that no one will listen. He is full of words, but they are words of judgment spelling universal destruction. 6.16–21 is a final warning which is spurned. And the complex ends in 6.27–30, as it began in chapter 1, affirming the divine credentials of the prophet who has the authority of the LORD himself. Such was the word of the LORD to Jeremiah on many and varied occasions, gathered and concentrated to present an explosive challenge in the time of crisis.

THE ALARM CALL **4.5–9**

It looks as if the oracle which Jeremiah here recalls is contained in vv. 5b–8. There is urgency and immediacy about it. The enemy is about to take Jerusalem. Therefore the ram's horn is to be sounded, warning the people to flee to fortified cities. The enemy from the north is likened to a lion out to destroy. The people are to lament to turn away the divine wrath.

But then v. 9 gives a different impression. It is true that the expression **in that day** is often little more than a connecting link, but here it is as though Jeremiah projects himself back into the circumstances of the utterance of the oracle (cf. also v. 11), and looks forward to the situation which has now developed (604 B.C.), and sees the discomforture of king, his officers, priests and prophets (cf. 2.26; 1.18; 8.1; 13.13; 17.25; 25.18; 32.32; 49.17, 21).

Possibly we see here therefore both the earlier oracle (vv. 5b–8) and the added element (v. 9) which relates it to the situation of chapter 36, assisting to promote the discomposure of which it speaks. Jeremiah here exercises the office of 'watchman' (cf. Ezek. 3.17; 33.1–7, where the analogy of war is explicitly used. See also Jer. 6.17), but nevertheless not in a military sense. He is primarily the messenger of Yahweh telling of the judgment of Yahweh who is using the enemy as his instrument.

Though this prophecy is in poetic form and predominantly in the *qinah* rhythm, this is not a guarantee that the very words of the earlier oracle have been accurately recalled. The poetic quality is not high. The image of the lion has already been used in 2.15, and 2.15b is identical with 4.7b. Verse 6b assembles phrases much used in the book of Jeremiah. Verse 8b is a prophetic commonplace. The imperatives — blow the trumpet, assemble, raise the standard, flee, put on sackcloth, and wail — are bald and without the assistance of the poetic imagination, in contrast with 6.1–8. This is consistent with a simple effort to recall the content, in well worn phrases, without much anxiety about the form of the early oracle. Poetic rhythm does not always guarantee the very words of the prophet.

5. Declare in Judah, and proclaim in Jerusalem: an introductory sentence which indicates that the prophet is being instructed by the LORD.

Blow the trumpet: the horn, known at Mari in the third millennium, used by the Hittites and the Egyptians in the second. It summoned men to battle (Jg. 3.27; 6.34; 1 Sam. 13.3; Jer. 6.1; 15.27). It was also used to herald the beginning of the great feast, (Num. 10.1–10) and particularly to summons the people to a day of fasting (Lev. 25.9; Jl. 2.1).

cry aloud: this represents two imperatives and is probably correct. It is possible that the second imperative *mal^e'û* means 'call up' in the sense 'declare mobilisation' (D. Winton Thomas).

7. A lion has gone up from his thicket: the image, which in 2.15 is used generally, is here applied specifically to an unnamed enemy.

a destroyer of nations: According to Welch, 'the leonine destroyer of nations was the first hint of the conception which gave rise to the figure of Antichrist'. Cf. on 51.25–26.

will be ruins without inhabitant: practically the same as 2.15b. But it is not necessary, like Duhm, to suppose an editor has added it. It would be natural for phrases to recur if chapters 1–6 are the work of Jeremiah and scribes in the way we have supposed. Cf. also Isa. 5.19; Jl. 1.6 and Jer. 2.30 'like a destroying lion'.

8. lament and wail: i.e. more specifically 'beat the breast'. 'Wail' suggests mourning rites of some violence taken over into the fasts, associated with the wearing of sackcloth. Cf. Jl. 1.5, 13; Zech. 11.1–2. **for the fierce anger of the LORD has not turned back**: cf. Isa. 5.25, cf. the complacency of 2.35. The expression is a commonplace. **9. king, princes, priests, prophets** — the list is often repeated in the prose oracles cf. 8.1; 13.13; 17.25; 25.18; 32.32; 44.17, 21. It is impossible, with W. L. Holladay (*JBL* 79 (1960) 351–367), to regard this as the genuine poetical original which is then reshaped in the prose passages. One too obviously sees the editorial hand at work in the composition of the whole section to be able to distinguish so clearly.

FIRST PERSONAL INTERJECTION **4.10**

Older commentators (e.g. Duhm, Cornill) regarded this verse as an interpolation to be excised. If it is verse, it is overloaded. Rudolph and the *NEB, REB* no doubt correctly regard it as prose. Skinner was puzzled, because he thought it must belong to the later period when Jeremiah was struggling with the problem of false prophecy. But if we are correct in our view of the way Jeremiah and Baruch set about their work, it would be natural and easy to introduce into the 604 B.C. version of the prophecies elements which had become clear only in recent years, but above all elements whose form and wording was determined by the situation now being faced. We conclude that Baruch's scroll did not exist without this important witness to the godward function of the prophet, recurring in 4.19–22, 31; 5.3; 4–6; 6.4b, 10–11a. The change proposed by some, from **Then I said** to 'then they shall say' is as poorly supported as it is misconceived.

The intercessory responsibility of the prophet is often overshadowed by his role as spokesman of God, forth-telling his will and foretelling his judgment. Nevertheless the prophet was essentially both messenger of Yahweh and representative intercessor on behalf of the people. This is to be discerned earlier in the expression 'call upon the Name of the LORD' (1 Kg. 18.24; 2 Kg. 5.11, cf. Kg. 13.6; 17.20; 18.36, 37; 2 Kg. 6.17). Israel's view of this aspect of a prophet's function comes out luminously in the Abraham story of Gen. 20 (E). For the canonical prophets, this aspect, present e.g. in Am. 7.2, 5, is most clearly seen in the book of Jeremiah. In 7.16; 11.14; 14, 11 he is commanded to refrain from interceding for the people. This assumes that he was assiduous in this prophetic responsibility of intercession. In 37.1–10; 42.2, 20 he is specifically asked to pray, in the one case by Zedekiah and in the other by Johanan and Jezaniah. In 18.20 he says, 'Remember how I stood before them to speak good for them, to turn away thy wrath from them'. In 27.18 he attacks Hananiah and the false prophets with the challenge that if they be the prophets they claim, 'let them intercede with the LORD of hosts'. No distinction can be made in this matter between the institutional prophets and the canonical prophets.

It is impossible to follow Reventlow's thesis (*Liturgie und prophetisches Ich bei Jeremiah*, 1963) that this chapter of Jer. contains an actual, literally quoted lament, in which the prophet takes his part in the changing dialogue of the ritual, first as messenger of Yahweh and then as representative of the people. It is however possible to see into the mind of Jeremiah as he dictated these oracles. He brings into relief the gravity of the situation and the imminence of judgment precisely by emphasising that the prophetic duty of prayer has been discharged. This is the cause of the anguish of which he speaks in v. 19.

In this case the prayer refers to the complacent exercise of this prophetic function by the institutional prophets (cf. 4.9; 5.13, 31; 6.13, for Jeremiah's preoccupation with the problem of false prophecy – that is, within the Baruch scroll).

Ah, Lord God: the expression is a cry of anguish, characteristic of prayer (cf. Jer. 1.6; 14.13, also concerned with false prophecy; 32.17, and especially Ezek. 9.8, where the prophet shrinks from the realities of the destruction of Jerusalem). The oracle of welfare is of course the stock in trade of the institutional prophet, as is explicit in 14.13. Behind the accusation that the Lord has **utterly deceived this people and Jerusalem** is the conception that the lying prophet is the instrument of a lying spirit as in 1 Kg. 22.22.

this people and Jerusalem: is sometimes omitted by critics but its repetition in v. 11 may well be deliberate. We have only to allow Jeremiah and Baruch a little licence as the one dictates and the other writes and re-writes.

it shall be well with you: Heb. *šālôm*. This in a word sums up the false prophets; they are expected to bring the comforting proclamation of *shalom*, and they never fail.

their very life: the Heb. *nepeš*, also means throat. This is one of the instances where the latter makes good sense, cf. *NEB, REB* 'the sword is at our throats'.

SECOND ANNOUNCEMENT OF JUDGMENT **4.11–18**

This section has a clearly defined beginning. In it Jeremiah speaks as the LORD's watchman. If in vv. 16, 17, it appears the LORD is speaking, that does not necessarily destroy the sequence of the passage, since the prophet is also the LORD's spokesman. Verse 19 begins a new section in which he speaks as representative of the people. Nevertheless vv. 11–18 are composed of at least three parts, drawn together by the purpose of Jeremiah's dictation to Baruch.

11. At that time it will be said to this people and to Jerusalem: Jeremiah, as in v. 9, projects himself into the early days of his ministry when he spoke of the Foe from the North. Now the time has come! 'to this people and to Jerusalem' links naturally with the same phrase in v. 10. Once one imagines the circumstances of writing, these literary connections become quite natural and there is no need, like the earlier commentators, to resort to emendation. Perhaps the impersonal 'it will be said' indicates that this is a saying which has been spoken before, perhaps not originally by Jeremiah, but will be spoken in circumstances which make it cruelly relevant.

A hot wind from the bare heights in the desert toward the daughter of my people, not to winnow or cleanse: this surely is the complete prophecy which Jeremiah remembers, poetic, cryptic, ejaculatory, memorable. He refers to the sirocco, the hot wind that blows in from the desert east, south-east and south, but *not* the north. But the subject of comparison here is not the direction but the character of the wind. In the desert a sudden gust can be irresistibly destructive. Elsewhere (13.24; 18.17) Jeremiah uses it as an image of the scattering of Israel; Hosea (13.15) of its power to dry, to parch and so destroy life. Other winds promote life, this one threatens life. Such now is the judgment. The alternative translations of *drk* 'towards', (a) 'is the conduct (way) of' or (b) 'it has trodden' are not convincing. The double negatives are a familiar idiom of Hebrew rhetoric suggesting the antithesis of what is named. 'Not to winnow, not to cleanse' . . . that is, to destroy! Here the brief, mysterious, oracular sentence ends.

12. a wind too full for this comes to me: or, as in *NEB*, *REB* 'a wind too strong for these will come at my bidding'. So most commentators understand the sentence as continuing v. 11, the word *rûaḥ* being translated wind in both verses. But it is well known that *rûaḥ* can also mean spirit. We can understand how Jeremiah is moved to reaffirm his divine authority and credentials. He says:

> The spirit has come to me in plenitude; now I will speak with them of the judgments.

This translation assumes that *mēʾelleh* ('for this') omitted in LXX is a dittograph of *mālê*. The emendation '(full of) curse', i.e. *mēʾālāh* for *mēʾelleh*, is again not convincing. The LXX interprets *rûaḥ* in both verses, the first wrongly, as 'spirit', but may be taken as a witness to the correct meaning of the second. The Vulg. translates the first as *ventus*, the second as *spiritus plenus*. The divine 'judgments' (*mišpāṭîm*) introduces once again the language of the lawsuit. It is not difficult to understand that Jeremiah would naturally take up the thought of 2.9, 35b. He has indeed brought Israel to judgment and his decisions are to be seen in imminent events.

This provides an appropriate basis for the announcement that follows, in vv. 13–17, beginning with **Behold**, and ending with **says the LORD**. The demonstrative particle 'behold' presents the prophet's picture of disaster to the mind and so describes the sudden divine intervention. (See K. Koch, *The Growth of the Biblical Tradition* (ET 1969), pp. 211–212).

The section, vv. 13–17, which is the second of the oracles dealing with the enemy from the North, describes the oncoming army in terms which had already in part been used of the Assyrian (cf. Isa. 5.26–29 and see on v. 7).

13. his chariots like the whirlwind: cf. Isa. 5.28b.

his horses are swifter than eagles: cf. Hab. 1.8 which, also has the 'from a distant land' of v. 16 and the wolves of 5.16. The emphasis on swiftness is also marked in Isa. 5.26, cf. also 'the distant land' in v. 16 and Isa. 5.26. There is plainly common ground here, though it is perhaps unwise to attempt more than to define themes shared by Jeremiah with others. If the language was already known to his hearers, the effect would be to announce an invading enemy as terrible and destructive as the Assyrian, on the point of effecting the divine judgment.

14. O Jerusalem, wash your heart from wickedness: the word used for wash here and in 2.22, is used primarily of the ritual washing of things; only in poetry of persons. Probably this extended use in a context which makes the moral meaning clear has the effect of heightening the effect. In 2.22 it was said the stain was indelible. Realism and the hope of repentance to the last nevertheless go together in prophecy.

15. Dan is in northernmost Israel, **Mount Ephrain** in the centre of the old kingdom of the north. They give advanced warning to Jerusalem, as messengers tell of the invader's progress.

17. Like keepers of a field: probably we are meant to think of men protecting crops from beasts or thieves. They make a tight circle, closing all gaps. So is the enemy from the North.

18. Probably the oracle ends with **says the Lord** (v. 17), and this verse is the pointing of the moral by Jeremiah as he dictates, with Jehoiakim, his ministers and the temple crowd in mind. If so, he may intend word play in the comparison between **because she has rebelled** (*mārāṭāh* (v. 17) and **is bitter** (*mār*). **It has reached your very heart**: i.e. the evil has affected the springs of action, or, has now caught up with her at the centre of her being. The heart was regarded as what we should call the seat of the will or the mind.

SECOND PERSONAL INTERJECTION 4.19–26

Again the prophet speaks as the representative of the people. This is the key to understanding the passage which, on the face of it, seems intensely personal. See especially pp. 44f. Without abandoning his primary responsibility to deliver the LORD's word of warning and judgment, at the same time the prophet feels the pain of his people, because he is one of them, and because he represents them before the LORD. He is torn in two between the LORD and his people. Thus this anguish is not a means of gaining insight into his soul; it is itself prophecy. An anguished prophet is a sign which no one can ignore.

Verses 23–26 are often taken as a separate prophecy. So it may be. But our understanding of the composition of the whole section leads us to discern how closely its theme belongs to vv. 19–22. The form of the passage is as appropriate to a climax as it is to a separate prophecy. The repeated emphasis on *seeing* follows well the declaration of anguish, as also it is the consequence of the inspiration of v. 12. It is quite unnecessary to label these verses as later apocalyptic.

19. My anguish, my anguish! I writhe in pain: literally, 'my bowels, my bowels, let me writhe'. The *NEB* neatly combines nouns and verb with, 'Oh, the writhing of my bowels'. The bowels were of course regarded as the instrument of feeling. Jeremiah feels the pain of Israel's plight as his own. That he goes further and feels her guilt is suggested by **Oh, the walls of my heart! My heart is beating wildly**. By association of ideas, Jeremiah is led from the announcement that the evil has reached the very heart of Israel (v. 18), to feel as Israel's representative the threat to his own heart. This is some way in the direction of an Old Testament counterpart to St Paul's insight: 'For our sake he made him to be sin who knew no sin' (2 C. 5.21). It is possible that Jeremiah refers to the walls of his heart, not because this was normal Hebraic anatomy, but because Jerusalem was the heart of Israel, her walls were to be breached, and Jeremiah sympathetically felt this in himself.

I cannot keep silent: See esp. 20.9 and 6.11; also the Psalmist (39.3-4). Amos expresses this classically of prophetic inspiration (3.8) and St Paul of Christian preaching (1 Cr. 9.16). There are parallels in Islam and among the poets. See further, on 20.7-9.

for I hear the sound of the trumpet, the alarm of war: here above all we see how Jeremiah can change his personal viewpoint as he now acts, not as the Lord's spokesman, but as the people's representative. For in vv. 5-8 it was he who had commanded, in the Lord's name, that the trumpets be blown. Now he is as one of the people listening to the dread alarm call. With typical prophetic insight, he anticipates the **disaster . . . on disaster**.

20. Suddenly my tents are destroyed: either a glimpse of Jeremiah's own simple way of life, or a symbolic picture of Israel made homeless. For the figure of the tent and its curtains, cf. Isa. 54.2.

21. How long must I see the standard? (cf. v. 14). The question 'how long' belongs characteristically to the lament, particularly when Israel is suffering oppression (cf. Pss. 74.10; 79.5; 90.13; 94.3). The implication of the question is that judgment and destruction are not the Lord's last word to his people. No doubt the question was actually put to a prophet in this formula and an oracle of welfare (*šālôm*) would be expected. The canonical prophets could offer no comfortable answer. Cf. Isa. 6.11.

the standard: as in v. 6.

22. Here Jeremiah or perhaps Baruch interrupts this personal *cri de coeur* with an explanatory comment. Yahweh now speaks of **my people**, and the vocabulary is that which, for convenience of distinction, we call wisdom vocabulary. **Foolish**: i.e. those (in Prov.) who despise wisdom; **stupid**: used in Ecc. and Jer.

have no understanding: with *hªkāmîm* in Gen. 41.33, 39 (the story of Joseph) Dt. 1.13; 4.6; 1 Kg. 3.12 (of Solomon).

skilled: *hªkāmîm*, i.e. 'wise.

But none of this vocabulary is exclusive to wisdom passages, and it is difficult to know what other vocabulary could be used to say this sort of thing. Such wisdom passages occur with sufficient frequency and naturalness in the book of Jeremiah to suggest that we do not need to look further than the scribe (*sōp̄ēr*) with his scribal-Deuteronomic background and training. How naturally this vocabulary is assimilated into prophetic oracles, is illustrated by Isa. 1.16c, 17a; 5.20, 21. It is convenient to identify the vocabulary, but it may be unwise to draw conclusions about composite authorship. Verses 23-26 revert to the experience of the prophet but now present the vision of destruction which he anticipates and which causes his agony, in so far as he experiences solidarity with the people. The skilled artistry of the form matches the content.

23. I looked on the earth: better 'I saw', like the statement of prophetic vision in 1 Kg. 22.17; Zech. 1.8 **and lo, it was waste and void; and to the heavens, and they had no light**: the picture is explicitly a return to the chaos before creation, cf. Gen. 1.1–2.4. In the LXX 'and void' is missing, and it could be that it has been added in MT precisely to complete the allusion to Genesis.

Indeed the oracle seems to be composed in relation to the sequence of creation in Gen. 1, perhaps freely recollected. The order of waste, light and heavens, earth (here in the process of being disturbed), man and birds is close enough to stir the listener to remember the well known story of creation, and to understand the oracle as pointing to the reversal of creation. No doubt the main lines of this story were known long before the Priestly account was definitely set down. If this is so, then the 'fierce anger' of v. 26 may well be the deliberate alternative to the sabbath rest after creation (Fishbane). The idea of the return to chaos, usually in terms of the 'many waters' is so well known in the Psalms and elsewhere in prophecy that it is difficult to find in the *content* a reason for denying the passage to Jeremiah. The argument that the term *r'š* ('quaking') became a technical term 'within the language used to depict a return of chaos' (B. S. Childs, *JBL*. 78 (1959) 187–189) is also difficult to maintain in view of the wider usage of the word. However the association is to be noted in Isa. 13.13; 24.18f, Hag. 2.6, 7, 21; Jl. 2.1. The meaning of the imagery is clear: it denotes the ultimate in destructive, divine intervention.

25. there was no man: repeatedly predicted, cf. 2.15; 4.7, 29.

26. The fruitful land: *karmel*, not here the mountain of that name, but an eppellative as in 2.7 and elsewhere. This is the reversal of the heritage described in 2.7.

THIRD WARNING OF JUDGMENT **4.27–31**

This section falls into three parts. First, vv. 27–28 declare the irrevocability of the divine purpose of judgment.

27. yet I will not make a full end: this, as a parenthesis, might be right, as a modification of the threat of total destruction. But it is odd in this context where the stress is on the unalterability of the Lord's purpose and where the parallel **I have not relented nor will I turn back** (v. 28) seems thereby weakened. Despite the absence of help from the

Versions, it seems best, either to omit the 'not' as an addition made to
modify the judgment as in 5.10 and 5.18, q.v., or to follow Soggin (*Biblica*
1965, pp. 56ff) in reading *lō* as an emphatic *lamed*, or Rudolph who for
lō' (not) reads *lāh*, i.e. 'I will make a full end in relation to her'. *kālāh*
seems to have more the sense of 'completion' than annihilation (cf. Isa.
10.23), though the latter cannot be excluded.

28. I have spoken, I have purposed: Response to this declaration
depends upon how seriously the word of God is taken, and that means
the word of God spoken through his prophets. Jehoiakim's ministers took
it seriously. Jehoiakim did not. Those who came after took it very seriously
indeed. This is the basis of the care with which the prophecies of Jeremiah
were preserved.

Second, v. 29 describes once more the flight before the sound of
horsemen and archers.

29. they enter thickets; they climb among rocks: cf. Isaiah's classic
description of the Day of the Lord (2.19, 21) and the ubiquitous 'fly'
and 'bee' (7.18–19). **all the cities are forsaken**: so the LXX. MT has
'the whole city' referring to Jerusalem, but the plural **no man dwells
in them** probably indicates that LXX is right. MT's alteration was no
doubt suggested by the image of the daughter of Zion now following.

Thirdly, vv. 30–31 contain a rhetorical address to Jerusalem in the
familiar image of a woman (see on 15.4–9). She who had been called
a harlot (cf. v. 30) is now desolate (LXX omits, but the fact that it is
masculine in Hebrew makes it the more difficult reading). The despairing,
perhaps brazen attempt to behave as though all is well is described in
terms of the extravagant dress and alluring artifice of the paramour.

30. that you enlarge your eyes with paint: like Jezebel before she
was thrown to her death (2 Kg. 9.30). The prophet has already heard
in anticipation Zion's cry of pain, as of one bringing forth her first child.
There are reasonable grounds for translating *ṣārāh* not as 'anguish' but
as 'sharp cry' (*NEB, REB*). The image of the woman in childbirth to
express the time of affliction starts with Hosea (13.13, cf. Isa. 13.8). In
later Jewish thought the implications of the image are accepted. The pain
is the prelude to the gift of the child and 'when she is delivered of the
child, she no long remembers the anguish, for joy that a child is born
into the world' (Jn. 16.21). The time of affliction is the essential condition
of the promised redemption (Mk. 13.8; Mt. 24.8). Jewish teachers after
the time of Bar-Cochba used the term 'birth-pangs of Messiah' to denote
this time of distress (See J. Klausner, *The Messianic Idea in Israel*, 1956,
pp. 440–450). But the message of hope, though integral to the image,

is not here drawn out, and is indeed partly cancelled by the last line **Woe is me! I am fainting before murderers** (v. 31). One understands more and more the terror of Jehoiakim's ministers.

ONE FORLORN HOPE, WITH FOURTH WARNING **5.1-11**

The one hope for a people such as Jeremiah has described is the existence of a righteous 'remnant', a nucleus of the faithful leavening the lump. Jeremiah obviously shrank with all his being from the consequences of his own prophecy of judgment. The judgments of history, as he knew, and as Ezekiel knew (9.5-6), are apt to be indiscriminate and ruthless. He looked for every possibility of mitigation from the God he knew to be forgiving. The question had arisen in Israel: When does a community become so corrupt that there is not enough righteousness within it to save it? The answer given in Gen. 18.23-33 was that for the sake of ten righteous men, the wicked city will be spared. Isaiah taught explicitly: 'If the LORD of hosts had not left us a few survivors, we should have been like Sodom, and become like Gomorrah' (1.9) and saw the judgment as a purging. Jeremiah came to the grim conclusion that there were not now enough righteous in Jerusalem to save it. Cf. Ps. 14.2-3; Rom. 3.10-12. That is the subject of this section.

Whether vv. 1-11 formed a homogeneous whole from the beginning is difficult to say. Some divide the passage into 1-6 and 7-11. Verse 9a ends with the formula 'says the LORD', and is itself in the nature of a refrain repeated in v. 29 and 9.9. Verses 10-11 introduce a new metaphor. Against this, commentators have remarked on the smooth connections running through the whole chapter. For reasons that will appear (see especially on vv. 12 and 20ff.), it seems nevertheless that the chapter is built up of units and that the connections are sufficiently accounted for by the single-minded purpose of Jeremiah and Baruch. This means that this section has an earlier purpose in the ministry of Jeremiah.

It is going too far to speculate with Duhm that this represents Jeremiah's disillusionment with the capital when he moved from Anathoth to Jerusalem, or with Skinner that this first impression of social conditions in Jerusalem is a clue to our understanding of Jeremiah's spiritual development (*Prophecy and Religion*, pp. 138-164), or with Holladay that it accompanied the seasonal reading of the deuteronomic law in the autumn of 601. Jeremiah's positive appreciation of Josiah, who did justice and righteousness, and judged the poor and needy so that then it was well and he knew the LORD (22.15-16), makes it at least questionable whether Jeremiah would have uttered this judgment in these terms until after Josiah was dead (608 B.C.). Undeniably the situation following the death of Josiah, a time of confusion, when the brightest hope of political and social salvation was extinguished, provides a background which fits this passage. This is our best guess.

1. Run to and fro through the streets of Jerusalem: Who is speaking? The second person plural suggests the prophet speaking rhetorically. But then it is Yahweh who says **Search her squares to see if you can find a man, one who does justice and seeks truth; that I may pardon her**. It is unnecessary to excise this latter phrase in order to maintain consistency. The LORD speaks through his prophet. Changes of emphasis and person of this kind are frequent. The deepest truth about God is that he forgives. *mišpāt* here the manner of life (cf. vv. 4.7; 8.7; 2 Kg. 17.26) which the LORD requires.

2. Though they say, As the LORD lives: the test of integrity and of commitment to the Living God, as already made plain in 4.2 (q.v.) cf. 12.16.

yet they swear falsely: *laššeqer*, meaning here to 'swear by Baal' (12.16), the resort to the spurious. See on 3.10. The moral and the spiritual allegiance are inseparable.

3. Thou hast smitten them, but they felt no anguish; thou hast consumed them, but they refused to take correction: If the passage belongs to the early ministry of Jeremiah, then this can be interpreted in two ways. One might, with Duhm and Skinner, allow the imagination to create a picture of the individual dealer with unscrupulous methods, who supports his confidence tricks with oaths in the name of Yahweh, but suffers chastisement in the form of say a broken leg and yet remains as obstinately insensitive to truth as ever. The verse then refers to the typical individual, as Jeremiah has his eyes open to the lower orders of society in Jerusalem. This interpretation must be judged fanciful and out of keeping both with the immediate context and with other similar passages in Jeremiah. More plausibly the 'smiting' would refer to the tragic judgments of history upon the nation. Rudolph refers to 2.30. But this is not directly realistic at the end of Manasseh's reign. We have already had reason independently to refer the context of 2.30 to the period of Jehoiakim. And if we correctly attribute this whole passage to the situation that followed the death of Josiah, then this verse becomes brutally relevant. The 'smiting' is the death of Josiah on the fields of Megiddo, an event, wrapped in mystery, but unquestionably a tragedy for Judah. All we know of the reaction of kings and people afterwards suggests precisely the obdurate refusal to take correction. They would not read the writing on the wall. **take correction**: 2.30; 7.28; 32.33; 35.13. **They have made their faces harder than rock**: cf. 3.3; 2.27. **they have refused to repent**: i.e. *šûb* 'turn', cf. the repeated use of this term in 3.1, 7, 10, 12,14,22; 4.1. The translation 'repent' is dynamic rather than literal.

In vv. 4–5 the theme is developed. The search for the man of integrity is widened so that the whole community, the poor and the great, is combed. The 'great' are in all probability the leaders of society, such as are listed by Isaiah in 3.2; in Jer. more often referred to as kings, princes, priests and prophets (cf. 2 Kg. 10.6). The 'poor' are the rest. Jeremiah allows diminished responsibility to the common people, cf. Mat. 23.13–15. This is in effect a third personal intervention by the prophet as representative of the people. His search for the man of integrity is the effort of a prophet to discover some ground for pleading mercy on behalf of the people. Alas! He cannot make the case.

4. the law of their God: here *mišpāṭ*, better with *NEB*, *REB* 'ordinances' to distinguish from *tôrāh*. See on v. 1.

5. But they all alike had broken the yoke: cf. 2.20, where the image is used to describe how Israel had made herself a rebel beyond recovery.

6. The punishment is re-affirmed in a picture of predatory animals preying upon Judah, developing somewhat the image of 4.7, 'the leonine destroyer of nations' to add the wolf from the plains and the leopards. Cf. Hab. 1.8, and the different image of Jer. 4.13ff. This, much briefer than the other descriptions, is in effect a fourth announcement of the Foe from the North.

7. The answer to the question implied in v. 1 has already been given. Now the full dimension of the divine reaction is spelled out. The LORD speaks, addressing Zion the mother.

How can I pardon you? answering to v. 1. **and have sworn by those who are no gods**: see on 2.11. Jeremiah reaffirms the analysis of chapter 2 by using again the image of the harlot (v. 7), and of animals, in their season, uncontrollable and promiscuous (v. 18). If we are correct in attributing chapter 2 to the period following the death of Josiah, and if also we allow for a certain freedom in the process of dictating and editing, then we can detect the intention to reaffirm for the society of Jehoiakim the criticism made two decades earlier. The question remains however whether vv. 7–8 in their original form may represent a criticism of the morals of the upper classes, whether Jeremiah was speaking literally and then drew out the extended meaning only when he used the words in their present context. The question cannot be settled. The translation remains problematical.

When I fed them to the full: MT is supported by LXX, Targ., Pesh., Vulg. Some MSS support a reading 'when I made an oath with them' or 'I made them swear allegiance to me' (McKane), involving the change of *š* for *ś*. The essential meaning is not different. In the one case Jeremiah refers to the promise of the land and the danger of plenty and surfeit envisaged in Deuteronomy (8.11–20; 32.15, cf. Hos. 13.6; Neh. 9.25). Their turning to no-gods is adultery, as it is a breaking of the covenant inherent in the promise. In the other case Jeremiah refers to the divine oath which is the promise inherent in the covenant.

and trooped to the houses of harlots: MT reads literally 'they gashed themselves in the harlot-houses'. If this is right, it refers to orgiastic practices of Canaanite religion such as continued to be practised even after the Deuteronomic reformation, and the harlot-house could be a way of describing the sanctuary itself. All the English Versions including *RSV* and *NEB* and most commentators but not McKane, follow the LXX.

8. They were well-fed lusty stallions: This is the most convincing translation of two uncertain Heb. words (both *hapax legomena*) which have probably been obscured by attempts to euphemise, cf. 2.13–25. LXX and Old Latin have 'mad about women'! But the words probably refer to the genitals. **each neighing for his neighbour's wife**: the pun is not in the Hebrew! 'neighing' has the same overtones as in 13.27.

9. Shall I not punish them for these things? Heb. *pāqad* which can mean visit, either graciously or for punishment. It is a characteristic expression of Jeremiah's, as also the noun 'visitation', which sometimes carries with it the suggestion of the Day of the LORD.

and shall I not avenge myself: not necessarily 'entertain vengeful feelings'. But the thought is anthropomorphic as is shown by Isa. 1.24. The LORD can, so to speak, breathe easily when justice has been achieved. 'Vengeance is not so much a claim of honour as a claim of justice, resting in God before whom all are small'; 'no one can arrogantly make himself great and take the law into his own hands' (Pedersen). Hence it is to be left to God — Rom. 12.19. Verse 9 is repeated, like a bell tolling, in v. 29 and 9.8. Who is to say where it is original? This is another indication that the chapter is a compilation and not initially a composition.

Verses 10–11 introduce a new metaphor but with vocabulary that links it with its context.

10. Go up through her vine-rows: not of course literally. This is an allusive use of the metaphor of the vineyard, applied to Israel classically in Isa. 5.1–7.

but make not a full end: the 'not', as in 4.27, is probably a subsequent modification to assimilate the passage to 30.11 and its dependent 5.18. As in 4.27 the sense demands the idea that Yahweh complete his punishment for Israel. Her branches are to be stripped away, the vineyard destroyed. See on 5.18.

11. For the house of Israel and the house of Judah have been utterly faithless to me: a summarising comment going beyond the theme of the passage, but taking up the more comprehensive horizon of 3.6–18, and employing the word *bāgaḏ*, 'deal treacherously', 'be faithless' which was there repeatedly used 3.8, 11, 20; cf. also 9.2.

FALSE AND TRUE WORDS **5.12–14**

This appears to be an independent section about false prophets.

12. They have spoken falsely of the LORD: logically the antecedent should be 'the house of Israel and the house of Judah'. But that which 'they' are alleged to say in 12b is precisely what in so many words is ascribed to the false prophets in 23.17 and 14.13, 15, and otherwise the prophets are introduced abruptly in v. 13. 'They' then are the prophets, and the fact that the pronoun lacks its antecedent is a pointer to the independence of the unit. Nevertheless it is possible to discern the underlying connection of theme which led to this order of compilation. The prophets are the spokesmen of treachery and faithlessness referred to in v. 11, the conscience of the whole community in which the man of integrity cannot be found. (The *NEB* translates: 'They have denied the LORD, saying, "He does not exist".' This misleadingly suggests a modern-type atheism. The verb indicates deception rather than negative confession cf. verse 31. The *REB* has the improved rendering: 'He does not matter.')

He will do nothing: literally 'not he'. Commentators have found this difficult, but probably, like a number of ambiguous expressions, it is deliberately brief, ejaculatory, enigmatic. Jeremiah's message is: 'I bring evil from the north' (4.6). 'Shall I not punish (visit) them?' (5.9) 'Behold I am bringing upon you a nation from afar' (5.15). The prophets reply, 'Not he! no evil will come upon us' (23.17) nor shall we see sword and famine' (cf. 14.13, 15).

13. The prophets will become wind: i.e. *rûaḥ*. The men whose very claim implies that they are activated by the spirit of the LORD (*rûaḥ*), will become a mere breath (*rûaḥ*). With this play on the term Jeremiah pours contempt on their pretension.

the word is not in them: for more extended treatment of this theme, see chapter 23 especially vv. 18, 21, 30. This is close to the central nerve of the *OT*. It stands or falls by the claim that the LORD has spoken, and discrimination between true and false claims to speak his word is vital.

Thus shall it be done to them: overloads the line. This is not a proof of a gloss, but the character of the expression, not in fact saying *what* shall be done, strongly suggests a gloss. It says allusively what is explicit in the prose passage 14.13–16, particularly v. 15.

14. In contrast to these professional 'windbags', Jeremiah will speak words which are genuine and therefore not the soothing deception of those who cry peace (6.14), but powerful and effective, cf. Heb. 4.12. Fire is one of the images consistently used to describe the Day of the LORD as judgment.

Because they have spoken this word: this translation represents an unsupported conjectural emendation of the Heb. which reads 'Because you have spoken . . .'. Here *NEB* against all recent commentators is surely right: 'Because you talk in this way, these are the words of the LORD to me'. *REB* unnecessarily changes 'you' to 'they'. The passage becomes illuminating when the reader understands how Jeremiah has his attention riveted on Jehoiakim and his ministers. For a moment he addresses them directly as those for whom he is recalling his earlier oracles. The earlier oracles are directly applicable.

FIFTH WARNING OF THE NORTHERN ENEMY **5.15–17**
Though it is not explicitly said that the destroying nation will come from the north, there can be no doubt that this prophecy belongs to the same category as 4.5–9 and the related passages about the Foe from the North. What distinguishes this form of the warning is its association with Deuteronomic passages as detailed in the comment below. This would not be significant if the passage in Dt. (28.49–53) were dependent upon Jer. But such a position rests on a literary and anachronistic interpretation of Dt. Even if some of the material is actually written down in the exilic period, it still represents the tradition of older material.

It is likely therefore that Jeremiah is deliberately using language which is familiar to at least some of his hearers, and particularly the leaders. Descriptions of invasion which they have complacently taken for granted are now invested with terrifying relevance and urgency. The nation that was remote both in miles and in mind is now threatening. The foreignness of their tongue increases the sense of a terror of unknown magnitude. They are a recrudescence of Babel. They will consume the produce of their fields and vineyards (like locusts?), but also the people and their flocks. The picture is of a comprehensive, all enveloping avalanche of destruction, against which their fortified cities, in which they have so much trust, will be useless. The threat is being rammed home a fifth time like a curse. He who has ears to hear, let him hear.

15. Behold, I am bringing upon you a nation from afar: The expression — 'behold I bring' with the participle — is frequent in Jer. (6.19; 11.11; 19.3, 15; 31.8; 35.17; 39.16; 45.5; 49.5). 'from afar' as in 4.16 and Isa. 10.3, cf. 5.26. Isaiah thus referred in equally allusive terms to the Assyrians, cf. also Dt. 28.49.

It is an enduring nation, it is an ancient nation, a nation whose language you do not know: It has been argued that Jeremiah would not so describe the Scythians, whom Herodotus described as the youngest of the nations (*Hist.* iv.5). It is of course impossible for us to know what impression Jeremiah had of the national history of the Scythian nor indeed whether he had them directly or only indirectly in mind. But this passage raises again the Deuteronomic character of some of the poetic passages in Jer.

The closeness of this passage to Dt. 28.49–53 has often been noticed: 'the nation from afar' (v. 49), 'as swift as the eagle' (v. 49, cf. Jer. 4.13), whose language (*lāšôn*) you do not understand (v. 49, cf. Jer. 5.15), 'and shall eat the offspring of your cattle and the fruit of your ground . . .' (vv. 51, 53, cf. Jer. 5.17), 'they shall besiege you in all your towns until your high and fortified walls, in which you trusted, come down' (v. 52, cf. Jer. 5.17c). The thought and much of the vocabulary is clearly related. Some (Giesebrecht, Rudolph, Hyatt) see a literary dependence of Deuteronomy on Jeremiah, in view of the probably exilic date of the relevant section of Dt. 28, which goes beyond the statement of blessings and curses, and seems to announce details of disaster in what Westermann calls one of the most unnerving documents of the Old Testament. The argument is not strong when hypothesis is built on hypothesis. Moreover many of the phrases are in any case commonplaces. It is sufficient to note the strong Deuteronomic flavour, probably introduced by the scribe, into some of the poetry as well as into the prose.

16. Their quiver is like an open tomb: sense *can* and probably should be made of this (their arrows are deadly), but the image is strained. LXX omits. Following Vulg. many have amended 'their quiver' (*'ašpāṭô*) to 'whose mouth' *ᵃšer pîhu*) *NEB*, *REB* 'jaws, as might be suggested by Ps. 5.10. If emendation is necessary, more likely is *ᵃšer śᵉpāṭo* (whose lips). This is nearer to MT and links tongue and lips as in Isa. 28. 11; 33.19; Prov. 17.4, cf. Ps. 81.6. For lips in the sense of 'language' see also Gen. 11.1, 6, 9; Isa. 19.18.

they are all mighty men (*gibbôrîm*) cf. 'the mighty men that were of old' in Gen. 6.4.

17. The repetition reads like a summary, whereas Dt. 28.47–53 is more detailed and imaginative.

with the sword: looks like an explanatory addition, stuck awkwardly on the end of the sentence.

Jeremiah now announces the destruction of the **fortified cities**, to which in 4.5 he had bidden the people escape. The picture of destruction which was represented in the Deuteronomic tradition as a curse on disobedience, Jeremiah now sees as imminent in the historical crisis of his day. The nation from afar is identified. The divine judgment is inescapable.

EXILE **5.18–19**

18. Just because the previous passage presents a picture of unmitigated destruction, this verse must be understood as part of the build-up of the tradition, modifying the judgment and so making sense of the fact that Judah did survive, though in exile. Undoubtedly also features of Jeremiah's later teaching, embracing a positive hope, would give justification to the editor. In particular the phrase 'I will not make a full end of you' may well be taken from the poetic piece in 30.11 where it firmly belongs to its context. No doubt the same scribe would be responsible for the modifications we have noticed in 4.27 and 5.10. This might well be subsequent to Baruch's final work. The first scroll ends in 6.27–30 with the explicit denial that there can be any remnant.

in those days: cf. 3.16,18; 31.29; 33.15, 16; 50.4,20. This seems to betray an exilic editor who sees in the exile the actualization of the Day of the LORD.

19. This is the question why? — which haunts Jeremiah throughout his ministry. Here it is on the lips probably of the exiles who, we know from Second Isaiah and Ezekiel, were deeply disturbed by the problems of faith, cf. Isa. 40.27; Ezek. 18.25. See in Jeremiah especially 12.14. The tense, **Why *has* the LORD our God done all these things to us?** — is to be taken seriously. The exile to the speaker is a present experience. The answer here given in terms of forsaking Yahweh and serving other gods (cf. Dt. 28.64) is true to the teaching of Jeremiah (see esp. chapter 3).

you shall serve strangers: cf. the reversal of this in 30.8 which must represent a still later modification.

A FOOLISH AND SENSELESS PEOPLE 5.20–31

This section stands out from the rest of the chapter. There is no cogent reason to deny it to Jeremiah, but some reason for seeing the heart of it (vv. 21–25) as belonging to a situation at the beginning of his ministry, and the rest of it as carefully built up in relation to the theme of the chapter as a whole and the purpose of Jeremiah in 605/4 B.C. Thus:

(a) it has a separate introduction (v. 20) which harks back to the vocabulary of 2.4 and differs from the precise address of 5.1.

(b) It seems to envisage a situation of drought (vv. 24–25), not the peril from the north.

(c) It contains some hymn-like verses celebrating the sovereignty of Yahweh as creator (vv. 22, 24) together with an emphasis on the fear of Yahweh which is not otherwise found in chapters 1–6.

(d) There is more than the usually acceptable change of persons; and this is the longest Yahweh speech in the complex.

On the other hand the links with other teaching of Jeremiah are marked:

(a) The emphasis on the rebellious *heart* (vv. 23–24) was the theme of 4.4, 14, 18, 19 qv, cf. 3.17.

(b) The theme of the earlier part of the chapter, that there are no men of integrity, is confirmed by the judgment that there are wicked men trapping the people (v. 26).

(c) Verse 29 = v. 9a, and v. 29b = v. 9b, cf. 9.8. This acts as a sort of refrain and links up with the question 'Why?' — asked in v. 19.

(d) Verses 30–31 bring the chapter to a thunderous close. This sums up the prophet's judgment on the whole people disastrously guided by their prophets and priests.

When all this has been said, the section is now to be read as part of Jeremiah's case to Jehoiakim and his ministers. What he had said about the people years ago is true now. The vicissitudes of the natural life had not forced them to their senses. He reaffirms his social criticism (v. 28). This is the character of Judah. Every ground for mercy or escape has been examined. So in chapter 6 he repeats his announcement of doom from the north.

20. Declare this in the house of Jacob, proclaim it in Judah: As in 2.4, this could be a theological way of referring to Jerusalem and Judah. Or it may be that in the earlier part of his ministry this man from the north still addressed remnants of the old northern kingdom of Israel (Jacob). 21. **Hear this, O foolish and senseless people**: cf. 4.22b, q.v. **who have eyes, but see not, who have ears, but hear not**: language used of idols in Ps. 115.5–8. The people are like the objects of their illegitimate worship. But the more relevant comparison is perhaps with Isa. 6.10. The people are referred to in the third person. 22. **Do you not fear me?** The fear which is the beginning of wisdom. **Do you not tremble before me?** (*tāḥîlû*). There is possibly a play on words, which the *NEB* attempts to suggest as follows: 'will you not shiver before me, before me who made the shivering sand (*hôl*) to bound the sea'. The thought of the limits of natural life, ordained by God, and not to be overstepped by man, is a recurring one in the Old Testament which encourages an attitude of reverence for the natural order. (Cf. Am. 6.12; Job 26.10; 38.10, 11; Ps. 104.9.) 23. **this people has a stubborn and rebellious heart**: The expression 'stubborn and rebellious' (*sôrēr ûmôreh*) occurs otherwise only in Ps. 78.8, of the next generation of Israelites who are exhorted not to be like their fathers, and Dt. 21.18, where the case of the rebellious son is dealt with and the punishment is death by stoning. It is possible therefore that this somewhat striking phrase was well known and applied particularly to the hopelessly recalcitrant child. If so, its use by Jeremiah has added sting. It is already becoming clear that for Jeremiah what constitutes the reason for the brazen stubbornness which he has so frequently described is the perverted will. See on 3.17. The location of Israel's trouble in the heart has been a recurring theme of chapter 4. See vv. 4, 14, 18–19. 24. The question of v. 22 is answered. The people do not have the proper awe of their Maker. The description of the goodness of God in dispensing his life-giving gifts begins with a participle after the manner of the participial sentence in what Westermann calls the 'descriptive' song of praise. Jeremiah does not necessarily quote. 'Weeks' (*šebu'ôt*) is probably a gloss by someone who wishes to identify the fixed seasons of harvest with the Feast of Weeks, i.e. a later name for the corn harvest, earlier known simply as harvest (*qāṣîr*) cf. Exod. 34.22. Jeremiah himself refers not to the feast but to the divine provision of harvest, which the LORD keeps unfailingly for us, as another fixed feature of the natural order. Only one thing can upset this order; and Israel's sin has done precisely this. 25. **Your iniquities have turned these away, and your sins have kept good from you**: *NEB*. *REB* correctly paraphrase 'your wrong-doing has upset nature's order'. No doubt Jeremiah saw a connection between sin and the withholding of rain and harvest, closer than the modern mind is able to recognise. Indeed Jesus perceived clearly that the sun and the rain provide their life-giving boons for the evil and the good alike (Mt. 5.45). Conversely a widespread famine, killing good and evil indiscriminately, cannot be attributed to the direct intervention of a loving Creator. On the other hand, the contemporary world understands better how soil erosion and pollution are the result of ruthless exploitation, how also the unwillingness of the rich to share with the poor turns local famines into cruel disasters. Thus understood, Jeremiah's statement stands. See on 26.19.

26. For wicked men are found among my people: the word 'found' echoes v. 1. A man of integrity cannot be found, but the wicked are not lacking.

they lurk like fowlers lying in wait: this is the best that can be done with Heb. that defies explanation. Its absence from LXX is an indication that the difficulty is a very early one in the transmission of the text. It is of course possible that the word *šak* is an unknown Heb. word rather than a corruption of the text, perhaps meaning 'net', or better 'as in a hide' (J. A. Emerton).

They set a trap; they catch men: cf. Isa. 8.14–15; Am. 3.5; Ps. 124.7; Prov. 1.11. These men are the leaders who should have been expected to preserve justice and defend the needy (v. 28).

27–28. Instead, they feed and enrich themselves, like the prosperous wicked vividly described in Ps. 73.4–9 and the false shepherds in Ezek. 34.8. Jeremiah is describing not simply the rich, but those who, having the responsibility of leadership, exploit their position and use people for their own ends.

29. The question, asked already in v. 9, q.v., and again in 9.8, does not need to be answered.

30–31. These verses provide a summarising conclusion to the chapter, describing the condition of the people in a nutshell and drawing together the strands of the chapter. The **appalling and horrible thing** (cf. 23.14, also of the prophets prophesying falsely), is the pretence of the false prophets to speak in the LORD's name together with the connivance of the priests.

The priests rule at their direction: this is the most probable translation of MT. A simple change of pointing makes possible the *NEB* rendering 'go hand in hand with them' (*REB* 'in league with'). But it must be emphasised that changes in pointing cannot be lightly made, since the

Massoretic vocalization represents a long tradition of reading. The translation 'teach' (Cornhill, followed by Rudolph and others) is a conjectural emendation. Holladay (*VT* 15 (1965) 111–113 and *Jeremiah*, p. 201) prefers the second meaning of *rādāh*, 'scrape out' and thinks of this as a sort of imaginative play on the idea of consecration in the expression 'Fill the hand'. Here we have the opposite: 'the priests deconsecrate themselves'. But it is doubtful whether the expression 'fill the hand' naturally evoked any literal picture of this kind. The interpretation is fanciful. G. R. Driver interpreted 'rule' in the sense of the Accadian *ridu* and extracted the meaning 'the priests ran beside them', i.e. imitated them.

Undeniably the Heb. is difficult, perhaps only because of our inadequate knowledge, and certainly the versions (especially LXX, Vulg., Pesh. and Targ.) had difficulty with it. Nevertheless the difficulty may have lain more with the idea of the subservience of the priests than with the Heb. verb. The translation 'at their direction' for the Heb. which means literally 'on or at their hands', is supported by Jer. 33.13, but particularly by 1 Chr. 25.2, 3, 6. Cf. also 2 Chr. 23.18; 26.13; Ezr. 3.10. We may therefore take this verse as evidence of the power of the false prophets over other sections of the leadership and especially the priests. (See A. R. Johnson, *The Cultic Prophet in Ancient Israel* (1961) pp. 63–5). We see the priests looking to these prophets for guidance, as also in a later development of the crisis, the prophets gave a message of particular comfort to the priests (27.16). Zech. 7.1–3 is probably to be interpreted as meaning that the representatives of the sanctuary at Bethel sent to ask Zechariah whether they should continue the fasts. Cf. also 1 Mac. 4.46.

But though Jeremiah ascribes special responsibility to the leadership and locates the primary blame in those who give false advice, yet he cannot acquit the ordinary people, a foolish and senseless people, since **my people love to have it so.** This is an acute observation to be pondered by those who secretly glory in the success of dictators and tyrants, so long as they are successful. There are times when the support of the masses should be cause of suspicion.

This then is the answer to the question implied in v. 1. Is there a man of integrity whose influence is such that he can confer a righteous character upon this community? There is none. They are false (v. 2). They refuse to learn from experience (v. 3). All strata of society exhibit the same obtuseness (vv. 4–5). Though the LORD wills to forgive (v. 1), he cannot (vv. 7–9). The prophets who should have been the conscience of the nation, have proved blind leaders of the blind and their word is going to blow up in their faces (vv. 12–14). Judgment is re-affirmed (vv. 15–17) for this foolish and senseless people (v. 21) who cannot understand that they must adjust themselves to the natural order established by God (vv. 22, 24–25). Their brazen stubbornness proceeds from a perversion of the will which is the spring of action (v. 23). Not men of integrity conveying integrity but wicked men are to be found in the places of influence (vv. 26–28). This is the situation summed up so penetratingly in vv. 30–31.

SIXTH WARNING: ALARM CALL 6.1–8

The alarm call of 4.5–9 rings out again in similar terms. There is the command to sound the ram's horn, to raise a signal, the advice to flee, the statement that evil looms out of the north and great destruction (v. 1c,cf. 4.6b), the threat of an uninhabited desolation (v. 8,cf. 4.7b). But whereas in 4.5–9 the themes are barely stated, here there is much more elaboration. The trumpet is to be blown in Tekoa, the address is to the Benjaminites, the signal is to be set up at Beth-hakkerem. There is a dramatic picture of the beginnings of the siege of Jerusalem. There is literary play on the word *blow* (v. 1, cf. vv. 3b, 8a). This perhaps confirms the preliminary impression that 4.5–9 represents the assembly of these themes from elsewhere for the purpose of the build-up of the scroll. In 6.1–8 we have the repetition of Jeremiah's alarm call, forming now the climax of the scroll.

Why should the address be to the people of Benjamin, the trumpet be blown in Tekoa and the beacon lit on Beth-hakkerem? The play on words might suggest that the reference to Tekoa is determined by poetic licence. The assonance suggests that we are not to imagine that Jeremiah is making precise military recommendations! On the other hand the concreteness of the language, typical of poetry and prophecy, is also suggested by the circumstances of invasion. If the enemy is coming from the north, then the flight would most likely be to the south. Tekoa, the home of Amos, was in fact twelve miles due south of Jerusalem, and Beth-hakkerem is plausible identified with Ramat Rahel, now a suburb of Jerusalem, on high ground lying between Jerusalem and Bethlehem.

On the other hand the proposal of some, including McKane, that these verses reflect the movements of the Babylonians in 587 B.C. and a movement from the south, seems to be standing probability on its head. The main drift of the passage is clear, and with stereotyped images, presents the single idea of an invasion from the north threatening Jerusalem. The address to the people of Benjamin is difficult to explain.

It may be that Jeremiah thereby drew attention once again to the impenetrable obstinacy of the people of Jerusalem, bent on the destruction which was the consequence of their faithlessness. He does not now waste time even in addressing them. He himself was of the tribe of Benjamin. He seems to be saying, 'Let the people of Benjamin who are in Jerusalem at least show their belief and their sense, and escape while they can'.

1. a signal: the word *maś'ēt* occurs in the Lachish Letter IV.10 and means a fire-beacon. Cf. on 34.7.

2–3. The comely and delicately bred I will destroy, the daughter of Zion. Shepherds with their flocks shall come against her: These verses defy satisfactory translation. There seems to be two possibilities:

(a) The one involves the emending of *dāmîtî* 'cease' (probably the transitive 'I destroy') to *dām⁻tā*, giving the sense: 'The comely and delicate daughter of Zion has come to her end' (cf. LXX, Targ., Rashi and *NEB*). It is then possible to interpret v. 3 as a dependent clause, describing Zion's delightfulness. She is the centre, around whom the shepherds pasture their flocks and pitch their tents. The picture is not hostile as in *RSV*, but highlights the dreadful contrast with the warlike preparations (v. 4) which will shortly shatter her peace.

(b) The alternative is to adopt the second meaning of *dāmāh* 'resemble', repointing in the pi'el *dimmîtî*, 'I liken (cf. Vulg.). The meaning would then be: 'Lovely and delicate — I have likened the daughter of Zion to such a one' (Kimchi). The contrast between her loveliness and the threat of war is then made at once in the picture of hostile shepherds coming to pitch their tents against her. That this is the correct interpretation is suggested by the word-play. The *tiḳ⁻'û* 'blow' of v. 2. already suggestive of *bit⁻kôa'* (in Tekoa), now suggests *tāḳ⁻'û* (pitch). The word-play would be pointless if the pitching of tents were merely an aspect of pastoral peace. Similarly the *rā'āh* (evil) of v. 1 suggests here the *rō'îm* shepherds (v. 3), with the unmistakeable implication that they are instruments of the evil. There is no etymological relation between the two words, but that never deters the Old Testament poets from word-play. The shepherd is frequently a figure of the ruler.

4. Prepare war: lit. 'sanctify war', with an allusion no doubt to the cultic preparations once appropriate to what has been called 'holy war', (cf. Jl. 4.9; Jer. 22.7; 51.27, 28) and involving sacrifices (1 Sam. 7.8–9) and the consecration of the soldiers. The imperative is rhetorical, but accords with the prophetic insight that it is the LORD who commands the enemy, so that even the great imperialist powers become the unwitting instruments of judgment and salvation (cf. Isa. 10.5–7; 45.1–4). This is a reversal of the fundamental principle of the holy war that the LORD fights for his people and gives them salvation. The prophet sees that the LORD's war has to be against his people and the end must be judgment, cf. notes on 21.4–7.

against her: *'ālehā*, as also the shepherds pitched their tents against her.

let us attack at noon: In this rhetorical passage, the speaker is now the enemy, the 'destroyer at noonday' (15.8) who attacks when people are feeling secure. We overhear his council of war. The next sentence makes good sense if it can be supposed that the enemy misses his chance of attack. For **Woe to us!** the *NEB, REB* have 'Too late!' and understand the speaker to be the enemy who decides anew to attack at night (v. 5). But it is doubtful whether the Heb. *'ôi lānû* can bear this attenuated meaning. In 4.13; 10.19; 15.10 and elsewhere it expresses the strongest emotions of forboding and despair. The speaker therefore is Jerusalem expressing helplessness before the enemy, and the oracle is in the form of imaginary dialogue.

6. cast up a siege mound: for the phrase see 2 Kg. 19.32; Ezek. 4.2; 26.8. This was a regular method of siege warfare cf. 2 Sam. 20.15. The mound was of earth and served as a ramp.

This is the city which must be punished; there is nothing but oppression within her: The Heb. *hopqad* (punished) looks grammatically odd but may be right all the same. LXX has 'woe to the city of falsehood' (*šeqer*). Both the term falsehood *šeqer* and the term *pāqad* used of the Lord's visitation in punishment are frequent in Jeremiah. But LXX has the advantage of providing a thought parallel to 'nothing but oppression within her'. *NEB* paraphrases (with a little licence!) 'the city whose name is Licence'. Clever, but unverifiable and *REB* withdraws the suggestion.

Jeremiah states anew the ground of judgment in the condition of Jerusalem. It is not a question simply of particular sins but of her total condition. There is 'nothing but oppression within her'. Isaiah had spoken similarly of the sickness of the whole people in the eighth century, developing the metaphor of illness (Isa. 1.4–9) with more poetic detail, and using the words 'sickness' and 'wounds'. The prophets were united in judging that it is possible for a whole people to be mortally sick. It is notoriously difficult to date passages like these. This description is especially applicable before the Deuteronomic reformation; but if so, Jeremiah re-applied it in the time of Jehoiakim. Cf. Lk. 19.41.

8. The poem ends rhetorically as it begins, with another pun on *tiḳ'û* (v. 1). **lest I be alienated from you**: Heb. *tēḳa'*. The appeal seems something of an anti-climax in the context of the announcement of an irreversible judgment about to fall any moment. But the linguistic connection is against any theory of subsequent addition. We have to adjust to the plain fact that the prophets uttered certain doom and yet never ceased to exhort to repentance. See also on 4.14.

THIRD PERSONAL INTERJECTION 6.9–15

In 4.10 Jeremiah expressed distress that the people were deceived by false prophets; in 4.19ff. he is shown feeling the anguish of a sinful people under judgment and unable to keep silent. Here the identification is not so much with the people as with the word he is given to utter. He is full of it and cannot hold back. There is a marked verbal relationship with 20.7ff, q.v. In particular, v. 10a is close to 20.8a; v. 10c to 20.8b and v. 11a to 20.9c. 20.7–12 can hardly be secondary. Perhaps the language of 6.9–11 is best explained if we imagine that Jeremiah exercised a certain freedom in the compilation of that first scroll of his oracles. Jeremiah is here facing the unwillingness of his people to listen to his message, even to the point of contempt, as anticipated at his call. His response is according to the explicit requirement of his call.

9. Glean thoroughly as a vine the remnant of Israel: The metaphor, as in 5.10, might suggest the removal of all the people leaving the land uninhabited like stripped trees, as had been stated explicitly in v. 8. On the other hand there seems here to be an unexpressed assumption that the LORD's instruction is to look for a faithful remnant. The prophet replies that no one will respond.

10. To whom shall I speak? This is the problem of communication, anticipated in 1.17–19, faced notably by Isaiah particularly in his call-vision in chapter 6, a continuing problem for the disciples of Jesus (Mk. 4.10–13), and never answered by Jeremiah except by the affirmation that the word he speaks is inescapable judgment. What people will not understand they will nevertheless suffer.

Behold, their ears are closed: Heb. 'uncircumcised'. See on 4.4.

11. Therefore I am full of the wrath of the LORD: which is not different from 'The spirit has come to me in plenitude; now I will speak with them of the judgments' in 4.12 qv., cf. 15.17.

Pour it out upon the children in the street: The prophets who speak like this (cf. Ezek. 9.5–6) must not be accused of callous disregard for the preciousness of human life. They are recognising the brute fact of the indiscriminate nature of all such historical judgments (cf. 11c). This is what has happened in all ages: it is what happens in this age. The difference for us is that we properly shrink from the simple, unqualified attribution of these consequences to the direct will of God and are compelled to find more refined modes of describing the same truth.

12. Their houses shall be turned over to others: a familiar consequence of war and therefore a commonplace in descriptions of judgment (cf. Dt. 28.30).

their fields and wives together: i.e. their wives treated as disposable property. See on 8.10a.

The personal thrust in this oracle serves to draw attention, not to the emotional involvement of Jeremiah, but to the horror of the content of the message with which he is entrusted. He is himself a signal of the divine judgment. It is therefore by an inner logic that the speech of the prophet (vv. 10, 11) becomes the speech of the Lord (v. 12b).

for I will stretch out my hand: To omit 12b, as many commentators do, on the ground that the sudden change to Yahweh-speech is harsh, is to underestimate the identity of the prophet with his God.

13–15. Verse 12b becomes the occasion for the introduction of an independent passage which is identical with 8.10b–12. It is vain to ask whether the passage is original to the one context or to the other, since we are dealing with the phenomenon of the editorial composition of independent units. On the other hand, if we are correct in regarding chapters 1–6 as the Baruch Scroll, the presumption is that it found written fixation here first, and this is supported by the fact that this is marginally the more natural context (Rudolph). The passage now serves to rehearse both the reason for the judgment of the whole people (v. 13, cf. v. 11) and the special responsibility of the professional mentors of Judah (v. 14, 15, cf. 5.31). It is introduced with the suture **For**.

from the least to the greatest: this restates the affirmation of v. 11 that it is the whole people who are under judgment and that prophets and priests are mentioned as being the most important cultic officials. No distinction is made between prophets and others. All are guilty of unjust gain and dealing falsely (*šeqer*). See on 3.10.

14. They have healed the wound of my people lightly: This is one of the classical descriptions of false prophecy, with application far beyond its original context. It is the mark of the un-genuine leader to bend his message to the will of the people and to connive at their own designs. They are essentially prophets of peace (shalom) when there is no peace. It is the mark of the authentic prophet to express the will and purpose of his Lord 'a purpose rising above the current ideas of his worshippers, and a will directed with steady consistency to a moral aim'. (Cf. Ezek. 13.10, 16.)

15. they committed abomination: this expression which is found both in Deuteronomy and in the prose sections of Jeremiah (7.10; 32.35; 44.4, 22), normally refers to Canaanite cult practices, which are the symbol of apostasy. Here it bears an extended meaning and refers comprehensively to the unacceptable behaviour of the whole people.

at the time that I punish them: a characteristic Jeremianic expression for the crisis of judgment, cf. 8.12; 10.15; 11 23; 23.12; 46.21; 48.44; 50.27; 51.18. See also in the Qumran literature, I QS III.18, IV.19, 4Qp. Is[b].

FINAL DISPUTATION **6.16–21**

This section has the form of a disputation between the LORD and his people, bringing to a close the process of investigation and appeal. The LORD invites his people to return to the ancient ways, but they reply: 'We will not walk therein' (v. 16). He reminds them that he provided them with watchmen (i.e. prophets). They reply: 'We will not listen' (v. 17) The LORD then, before the witness of the whole earth, re-affirms his verdict. The punishment must fall (v. 19). Assiduous and costly worship will avail nothing (v. 20). The final word is 'they will perish'.

Though there is no specifically legal vocabulary, it is impossible not to recognise here the climax of a process of judgment the description of which owes much to legal patterns. This pattern is first detected in chapter 2, where also questions are put to the accused in the manner of an advocate (2.5ff). 2.9 has well known legal vocabulary. In 2.12, the heavens are witness, as is the earth in 6.19. There are replies of a peremptory kind like those of 6.16, 17. 'I am not defiled' (2.23) and 'After them I will go' (2.25). They return to the attack against the Lord himself (2.29) and plead innocence in 2.35 'I am innocent . . . I have not sinned'. In the same verse the LORD declares that he will bring the legal process to a decision. The whole of 3.1–4.4 is built up to suggest a powerful plea of the divine judge, in 3.13, that Israel may acknowledge her guilt, and reaching a climax in the dialogue of repentance in 3.19–4.4. In chapter 5 the judge seeks the least possible ground for clemency (vv. 1, 7), but finds no alternative to punishment (vv. 9, 29). In 6.16–21 the decision is given and there is no appeal.

The legal theme is not the only one running through chapters 1–6 and it must not be over-emphasised. The basic prophetic oracle is the giving of grounds for judgment (reproach) and the announcement of judgment (threat). The very word 'judgment' implies the legal metaphor which is as inevitable as it is natural.

16. Stand by the roads, and look: by a plausible but entirely conjectural emendation, often changed to either: 'Stand by the ways of old' (Driver — parallel with **ask for the ancient paths**) or 'Stop at the cross-roads' (*NEB, REB*). But it is doubtful whether emendation is necessary. The metaphor of the way has been described as the central figure of biblical ethics. To interpret as the ways of Moses is not wrong but too precise.

17. I set watchmen over you: i.e. to anticipate what would happen and give warning, cf. Ezek. 3.17ff; 33.7ff; Isa. 62.6–7. **Give heed to the sound of the trumpet**: as Jeremiah himself had given warning in 4.5, 19, 21 and 6.1. This image is the implication of 1.15–19.

18. know, O congregation: i.e. in the sense of those who witness what is happening (*'ēḏāh*). Emendation is not necessary.

19. behold, I am bringing evil: cf. esp. 4.6; 11.11; 18.11; 19.3, 15; 23.12; 32.42; 35.17; 36.31; 45.5; 49.37; but also 1.14; 6.1 descriptive of the northern enemy. The expression occurs both in poetry and in prose and cannot be denied to Jeremiah. It is vocabulary of the Jeremiah tradition. The appeal here to **my law** (*tôrāh*, parallel with **my words**), is unique in the poetry of Jeremiah. It is of course frequent in the prose tradition, cf. 9.13; 32.23; 44.10, 23; 16.11.

20. To what purpose . . . .: echoing the question asked by Isaiah also concerning contemporary religion, cf. Isa. 1.11. This is the most direct witness to Jeremiah's view of sacrificial worship, though the simple unqualified disapproval here expressed may be elaborated from chapter 7.

frankincense . . . from Sheba: i.e. the area now at the heart of Saudi Arabia and in biblical times a source of trade (Job 6.19; Jl. 4.8) with Tyre (Ezek. 27.22) as well as with Judah. It was famed in the past for the queen who visited Solomon (1 Kg. 10.1–13), and it was expected in the future to bring gold and frankincense to Zion (Isa. 60.6) **or sweet cane from a distant land**: i.e. some aromatic spices.

Your burnt offerings are not acceptable, nor your sacrifices pleasing to me: as in Isa. 1.10–17, these two sacrifices comprehensively describe the main animal sacrifices of the monarchical period. The burnt-offering or holocaust was the principal offering of tribute and therefore of atonement, being offered by fire entirely to God. The sacrifice or peace-offering was the principal communion sacrifice in which the worshipper shared. The Heb. *l⁽rāṣôn* 'acceptable' is regularly used to indicate what, in worship, is legitimate or, as we might say, valid. Cf. Exod. 28.38; Lev. 1.3; 19.5; 22.19, 20, 21, 29; 23.11; Isa. 49.8; 61.2; and also 2 Sam. 24.23; Hos. 8.13; Mic. 6.7; Jer. 14.10, 12; Ezek. 20.40ff; 43.27; Mal.

1.10, 13; Ps. 51.18. Jeremiah with uncompromising simplicity states that contemporary worship is unacceptable and cannot therefore affect judgment that is imminent. The sacrament is useless if the word is disobeyed. *NEB, REB* set out this passage as prose. But there is sufficient indication of poetic parallelism and rhythm to prove that, whatever modifications the passage received in transmission, it is based on a poetic utterance. This interpretation entirely accounts for signs of Deuteronomic vocabulary in vv. 16, 19, 21. All is within the Jeremiah tradition. The reader's mind should be directed to the way in which the last excuses are being dismissed, the last expedients exposed, the last stance of self-righteousness swept aside, before the last terrible warning is given.

FINAL WARNING OF THE NORTHERN ENEMY **6.22-26**

Yet again Jeremiah hammers home the message that the enemy from the north is coming, again using the demonstrative **Behold** (v. 22) with the participle (as in v. 18 and elsewhere) to bring the picture of the enemy vividly to the imagination. The description is recognisably of the same enemy that is presented in 4.5-9, 11-18, 27-31; 5.15-17; 6.1-8. At the same time the items of the picture are conceptually, if not verbally, those of Isa. 5.26-30. In both passages the enemy appears with vigour, armed with offensive weapons, roars like the sea, is borne upon horses, and is fully prepared for action. The description may therefore be said to be conventional, applicable to Assyria (as in Isaiah) and to any imperial aggressor. Jeremiah is not reporting a contemporary invasion, but foretelling what he sees about to happen. By the same token he sees present to his imagination, the response of distress as the news of the invasion comes to the people (v. 24), and commands the people to stay indoors and to resort to the only expedient left to them — bitter lamentation. Thus understood, the passage forms a not ineffective climax to Baruch's Scroll. The conventional is about to take on a new dimension of realism.

23. They lay hold on bow and spear: the *kîdôn* is the sabre, as in 1 QM 7-14, 6.5.

they are cruel: cf. Dt. 28.49-50.

set in array as a man for battle: perhaps better, omitting the *kaph* as a dittograph: 'each one in a position for battle'.

against you, O daughter of Zion! the vocative betrays the rhetoric. Jeremiah does not for a moment lose sight of his real aim and audience.

24. Zion's response is simulated in a metaphor which, on the basis of Hos. 13.13, gave rise to the rabbinic conception of the birthpangs of

Messiah. There is no escape from pain either in judgment or in the attainment of the salvation which is the yonder side of judgment. **our hands fall helpless**: cf. 30.6. **as of a woman in travail**: cf. 13.21; 22.23. **25. terror is on every side**: Heb. *māgôr missābîb*, a striking expression which becomes a sort of slogan, 20.3, 10; 46.5; 49.29; and for Plashhur, who had Jeremiah beaten and put in the stocks, a symbolic name of grim appropriateness (20.3). **26. mourning as for an only son**: cf. Zech. 12.10. The uninhibited nature of early mourning customs makes them an eloquent sign of the judgment, which is now nothing less than the death of the nation. **suddenly the destroyer will come upon us**: cf. the destroyer at noonday in 15.8 who causes sudden anguish and terror. Cf. also 6.4–5, and especially 48.8, 18, 32; 51.48, 56; 12.12.

THE USELESS WORK OF JEREMIAH **6.27–30**

The scroll which Jeremiah was commanded to dictate in 604 B.C. ends with a statement of the complete failure of his prophetic mission. The passage is significant in three respects.

First it presents judgment under the image of a refining process, as in Isa. 1.22–25. Isaiah is able to look forward to the effective operation of the process so that judgment is the *saving* activity of God. But Jeremiah cannot hold out any hope of separating the precious metal from the base. All are stubbornly rebellious. This is the summing up of the fruitless effort, described in 5.1–11, to discover if there are any righteous who might provide ground for a plea for mercy. It is not even possible to separate out the wicked. The whole people are refuse silver.

It is possible that Jeremiah has the teaching of Isaiah in mind. The word **rebellious** (v. 28) *sôrᵉrîm* occurs in Isa. 1.23 and the word **stubbornly** represents a doubtful Heb. word *sārê* which may either be omitted as a dittograph of *sôrᵉrîm* or, with a number of the Versions, read as *śārê* or *śārîm* and thus close to the *śarayik* of Isa. 1.23 and meaning perhaps 'all of them are rebellious rulers'. Or perhaps the *NEB* has hit on the right idea with the expression 'arch-rebels'. Then unmistakeably reminiscent of Isa. 1.4 is the expression **all of them act corruptly** (v. 28). The Hebrew participle is *hiphil*. One would not therefore expect an intransitive meaning, but the context in both passages shows that it is correct. Isaiah uses the verb *srp* refine, as Jeremiah also uses it and each refers in particular to the refining of silver. The case for Jeremiah's awareness of Isaiah's oracle cannot be final, but it is suggestive. If Jeremiah was thus influenced by the known teaching of Isaiah, what is startling is the utter independence of Jeremiah. It is as though he says, Isaiah saw a vision of a *new* Zion, purged by the refining process. This has not happened. There is no hope for *this* Zion. Judgment must mean, not the production of the pure metal, but death.

Second, Jeremiah sees his own prophetic task as a process of refining the pure metal. He is an assayer of the Lord's people, who tests their conduct. In this respect the rebellion of the people of God is the failure of the prophet. This brings to a climax the prophet's personal involvement in his message.

Third, two expressions indicate a linking of the end with the beginning. **I have made you** . . . (v.27) is similar in form to 1.18 'and I make you this day a fortified city'. The word **and tester** represents a repointing of the word *mibṣār* 'fortified city' as in 1.18. This is surely the touch of a redactor who correctly saw the relation with 1.18 and pointed it up in this way. Jeremiah's mission may have been a failure, but he remained the tower of strength he was commissioned to be at his call. No doubt the same editor added the phrase **they are bronze and iron** (v. 28) from 1.18 where Jeremiah is described as 'an iron pillar and bronze walls'. Somehow this marginal gloss has been attached inappropriately to the description of the rebellious people. It seems highly speculative to transpose the phrase, with *NEB, REB* to v. 29 and work it into the description of the refining process. Rather is it a second touch of the redactor who correctly saw the connection with 1.18. The second expression is **the bellows blow fiercely** (v. 29). The word for bellows *mappuaḥ* is closely related to the verb *nāpuaḥ*, translated 'boiling' in 1.13 and meaning 'blown upon'. The 'closure' is unmistakeable.

30. Refuse silver are they called: a descriptive name of a kind beloved by Third Isaiah and employed with measured care by Jeremiah, cf. 20.3.

Thus the first complex of oracles in the book of Jeremiah, a complex which we have identified as substantially Baruch's scroll, ends as it began declaring the credentials of the prophet. The reader starts to read, reckoning with the claim that the prophet has received the LORD's call and that his word is the LORD's word. What he then reads is a catalogue of unremitting criticism and warning of inescapable judgment. As he inclines to rationalize and distance himself from the excesses of an ancient prophet, he is faced once again with the affirmation that Jeremiah was divinely authorised to do what he had done. The scroll is an exercise in excuse stripping. We begin to understand why it received so hostile a reception.

B THE MANY SIMILAR WORDS OF JEREMIAH

(1) Mainly of the Time of Jehoiakim 7.1–20.18

In all probability this block of tradition complexes contains material which falls under the category of the 'many similar words' referred to in 36.22, as being added to the original, re-written Baruch scroll. One would expect that the type of content would be similar. In general, this is true, with this reservation that while in 2.1–4.4 there were oracles which were plausibly interpreted of the early part of Jeremiah's ministry, in chapters 7–20 there is nothing which may not as plausibly be interpreted of the period of the reign of Jehoiakim.

The great difference is that we now encounter the prose sections in Deuteronomic style (7.1–8.4; 9.12–16, 23–26; 11.1–14, 21–23; 12.14–17; 13.1–14; 14.11–16; 16.1–19; 17.19–27; 18.1–12; 19.1–20.6). These may well furnish our main clues to the identity of the separate complexes within the section. For 7.1; 11.1 and 18.1 (also 21.1) are introduced with the formula **The word that came to Jeremiah from the LORD**, followed. in each case by a specific commission and a note of the prophet's obedience. Chapter 14 is an exception and opens what may well be a separate complex (14.1–15.4). In contrast there are three prose passages which do not have this introduction (16.1–19; 17.19–27; 22.1–10). It looks therefore as if the introductory formula marks the beginning in each case of a tradition complex. The block 1–20 thus divides into chapters 1–6 (the Baruch Scroll), 7–10, 11–13, 14–17, 18–20. 21–24 is another complex which will however require separate consideration as it belongs to the period of Zedekiah. Claus Rietzschel has argued that the formula is a pointer to the reading or preaching of the material in the synagogue of the exilic period. We have seen reason in the Introduction (pp. 21,23) to reject this hypothesis. The formula has to do with the editing of the complexes within the tradition circles that grew up around the work of Jeremiah. Indeed, since, with the exception of chapter 14, a prose passage in every case provides the foundation for the complex, we must assume that the author of the prose had responsibility for the collection of the poetical material as well.

The most probable hypothesis is that Baruch initiated this process, though no doubt others carried it on. This would fit in well with the observation of Deuteronomic touches in chapters 1–6 and with the liberties there taken with the oracles of Jeremiah. It would suggest that when 'many similar words' were added to the original scroll, Baruch took the opportunity to introduce his own version of important features of Jeremiah's teaching. May it not be that the accomplished and dedicated Baruch overstepped the mark and that Jeremiah saw in him a certain ambition to which he referred in 45.5, when he asked, 'Do you seek great things for yourself?'

It is perhaps significant that many of the prose passages betray an interest in events in Jeremiah's life or contain prophecies with a specially marked event character. In 7.1, Jeremiah intervenes in the Temple at the time of worship. In chapter 11 he is commanded to proclaim 'the words of this covenant throughout Jerusalem and Judah'. The liturgy in chapter 14 seems to imply a situation of drought and leads to a restraint on Jeremiah from exercising the normal prophetic function of intercession in such a situation. In 17.19, Jeremiah is to stand in the Benjamin Gate. In 18.2, he is commanded to go down to the potter's house. In 19.1, he is commanded to buy a potter's flask and to break it at the entry of the Potsherd Gate. In chapter 20, Pashhur beats Jeremiah and puts him in the stocks. See also on chapters 32–35. The conclusion is irresistible. It was left to Baruch to record those oracles and that teaching which arose out of incidents and prophetic signs. Baruch, as his temperament required, used a good deal of freedom and the Deuteronomic style is substantially his. That this material coming from Baruch, was put together with other material by later editors is suggested at once by the structure of 7.1–8.3. See especially on 7.27–8.3.

It would however be an error to conclude precipitately that the whole of chapters 7–20 is sufficiently explained as a phenomenon of editing and desk work. Each complex will have had its own history, answering to the needs created by new situations, and each unit will have had its own history, sometimes in the ministry of Jeremiah, often re-appointed and re-applied. Once a remembered prophecy was recognised as the LORD's word it had a dynamic quality. We are not dealing with dead oracles recollected, but with live oracles working out their potential. It is often more important to recognise this truth than to trace out the process in obscurity and uncertainty.

FIRST SUPPLEMENTARY COLLECTION OF ORACLES 7.1–10.25

THE TEMPLE SERMON 7.1–15

There can be little doubt that this version of the Temple Sermon (whether by Baruch or another) is confined to vv. 1–15 and that vv. 16–20, 21–26,

27–34 are a series of supplementary accounts of Jeremiah's teaching, linked to the sermon by common features and catch words (W. L. Holladay, *The Architecture of Jeremiah 1–20*; Isbell and Jackson *VT* 30 (1980) 20–26). Thus vv. 1–15 are related to chapter 26 in a way that the rest of the chapter is not. A comparison of 7.2 with 26.2; 7.3, 5 with 26.3, 13; 7.12–14 with 26.6 shows that both traditions are dealing with the same event. Chapter 26 is more interested in the event itself and its consequences for Jeremiah who faces a threat to his life. Chapter 7 concentrates on Jeremiah's speech. As Reventlow has shown, the summary of the speech in chapter 26 is given in Deuteronomic commonplaces, and if either tradition were dependent upon the other, chapter 26 would be the dependent version. But so different are the purposes of the variant traditions that the conclusion is precarious. Both are in the prose style of the Jeremiah tradition. Support for this view of 7.1–15, against those who would regard it as late Deuteronomic interpretation, is now given by Helga Weippert (op.cit. p. 48).

In view of the widespread tendency to regard the prose speeches in the book of Jeremiah as *Deuteronomic* elaboration or preaching, it is important to establish clearly the literary character of the first of them. So far from being Deuteronomic, it is difficult to find more than one or two unambiguously Deuteronomic phrases in the whole section.

1. Verse 12: 'where I made my name to dwell at the first'. This is central to the Deuteronomic name-theology, cf. Dt. 12.11; 14.23; 16.2, 6, 11; 26.2. But it appears to be quoted in a somewhat different sense from its developed theological meaning in Deuteronomy. Here the primary idea is that of the divine *ownership* or protection of the Temple, expressed in the thrice repeated 'which is called by my name' (vv. 10, 11, 14). This phrase means more precisely 'over which my name is called' (see on 25.29 and cf. 32.34; 34.15; Isa. 4.1; Ps. 49.12). It occurs also in 2 Sam. 6.2 and 1 Kg. 8.43 and may be regarded as ancient (Weinfeld), not specifically Deuteronomic.

The thrust of Jeremiah's teaching is that, though the Temple belongs to the Lord so that he may call it 'my Temple' (11.15) it is not in itself the object in which people should repose their trust (vv. 4, 8, 14), giving them confidence of deliverance (v. 10). He will do what he wills with his own, and when it becomes a fetish he will destroy it as he destroyed Shiloh. In Deuteronomy the accent appears to be on the idea of the divine dwelling. It is not the LORD himself who lives in the Temple. Indeed his dwelling-place is in heaven. But he permits himself to be known here (the Jerusalem Temple) rather than there (other Israelite or Canaanite shrines) by means of his name upon which men and women may call. Thus although Jeremiah here uses the same phrase, the context of his thought is subtly and substantially different.

2. 'and go after other gods' is a Deuteronomic commonplace. With the addition of 'that you have not known' (v. 8) it is found in Dt. 11.28; 13.13. With the addition of 'to your hurt' (v. 6), it is unique.

3. 'burn incense to Baal', in so many words, is found in 2 Kg. 23.5, but more significantly in Hos. 2.15. Neither the verb $q \, t \, r$ nor the noun Baal occur in Deuteronomy, though they are separately common enough in the Deuteronomic writings.

4. 'in the land that I gave to your fathers for ever' (v. 7) is a Deuteronomic commonplace, but in exactly this form is found only in Jeremiah 25.5, q.v.

Other significant expressions, some of them in Jeremiah *suggestively*, and therefore only superficially Deuteronomic, are in fact characteristic of the Jeremianic prose tradition.

5. 'the alien, the fatherless or the widow' (v. 6): certainly Deuteronomic, but also taken up in the prophetic tradition (Isa. 1.17).

6. 'And I will cast you out of my sight' (v. 15). Variations of this — dismiss, cast, remove, cast off — are found sporadically in the Deuteronomic history and each of them once in Jeremiah (15.1; 32.31; 23.39).

7. 'Amend your ways and your doings' (v. 3) — the thought may be regarded as Deuteronomic, the expression is found only in Jer. 7.3, 5; 18.11; 26.13; cf, 35.15; more often the Jeremiah prose has 'return from . . .', cf. Hos. 4.9; 12.3.

8. The association of 'justice' with 'oppress' (vv. 5–6) occurs in Jer. 21.12; 22.3.

9. 'Do not trust in these deceptive words' (v. 4) i.e. 'words of falsehood' *šeqer*. (Three times in this passage alone, in vv. 4 and 8 with *bāṭaḥ* — trust). See on 3.10 for the view that this word is a feature of the distinctive theology of Jeremiah himself and of the prose tradition (3.23; 5.2, 31; 6.13; 7.4, 8, 9; 8.8, 10; 9.2, 4; 10.14; 13. 25; 14.14; 16.19; 20.6; 23.14, 25, 26, 32; 27.10, 14, 15, 16; 28.15; 29.9, 21, 23, 31; 37.14; 40.16; 43.2; 51.17).

10. 'all these abominations': the term *tô'ēḇâ* is used in Deuteronomy of idolatrous rites, magic and divination, of immorality and commercial injustice. The most characteristic use of it is the singular 'an abomination to Yahweh' (Dt. 7.25, etc). In the plural it is usually 'the abominations of the nations' (Dt. 18.9, etc, 1 Kg. 14.24, etc) and refers to their

idolatrous practices. Here the plural term is used comprehensively of the offences, both moral and idolatrous, named in v. 9, and this is in accord with the meaning of the term in the poetic passage 6.15, which may be attributed to Jeremiah himself; cf. 2.7; 8.12; 16.18; 32.35; 44.4, 22.

Other expressions belong more or less exclusively to the Jeremiah tradition and particularly to the prose tradition.

11. 'Do not trust in these deceptive words' (v. 4) . . .

12. 'and when I spoke to you persistently you did not listen (v. 13). This is a striking idiomatic phrase, literally 'rising up early' and . . . speaking (7.13; 25.3; 35.14), sending (7.25; 25.4; 26.5; 29.19; 35.15; 44.4), warning (11.7), teaching (32.33). It belongs to the Jeremiah prose tradition.

Then there are two expressions which represent the specificity of this version of the Temple Sermon.

13. 'This is the temple of the Lord . . .' (v. 4).

14. 'Has this house . . . become a den of robbers?' (v. 11).

When we turn from the analysis of the language to the structure of the passage, we find that here also claims have been made for the Deuteronomic character of the 'sermon'. The framework of the passage may be understood thus:

(a) Introduction (vv. 1–2)

(b) The Lord's command and call to obedience (vv. 3–7)

(c) Description of Judah's apostasy and rejection of the Word (vv. 8–12)

(d) Announcement of judgment (vv. 13–15).

This may be compared with a similar pattern in chapters 11, 17, 25, 34, 35 in Jeremiah and chapters 6, 7, 8 in Deut., together with other passages in the Deuteronomic history. This, it has been argued, is a Deuteronomic covenant pattern, and along with the language and content, supports the view that the prose is that of the preachers in the synagogues of the Babylonian exile. Suffice it here to say that the structure observed in the prose passages does not seem to have the significance placed upon it. The reason is simple and obvious. In the period with which we are dealing, anyone giving an account of prophetic preaching, Jeremiah, Baruch, or any unknown editors or interpreters, would most likely have used this pattern. The structure tells us something about the conventions of the day: it says nothing precise about authorship. It is a well understood stereotype.

When these observations are weighed along with similar findings from the analysis of the other prose speeches, the conclusion is irresistible. The prose is influenced by the well-known Deuteronomic style but it is not

Deuteronomic. When Deuteronomic phrases are used they not only exhibit a literary independence but they are often given a significant shift of meaning. Some phrases look Deuteronomic superficially but belong exclusively to the Jeremiah prose tradition. There are also the striking phrases which look like memories of the actual event and speech. This is a version of Jeremiah's speech which has been written in the specifically Jeremiah tradition. It is more reasonable, if guesses are permitted, to think of Baruch and/or a school of later followers of Jeremiah than of Deuteronomic preachers in the Babylonian exile.

1. Verse 1 is absent from LXX and we may therefore conclude that it is an amplification based on 17.20; 22.2; cf. 26.2. Nevertheless it may well gloss the situation correctly. The occasion, when **all you men of Judah . . . enter these gates** to worship the Lord, is probably one of the three annual pilgrimage feasts. 26.1 dates the event in the beginning of the reign of Jehoiakim. If 'the beginning of the reign' (*rēʾšît mamlʿkût*) is to be understood like the Babylonian *res šarruti*, then it refers to the period between the death of the previous king and the enthronement at the ensuing New Year's Festival, from which his reign is counted. Thus Jehoiakim's reign dates from the New Year Festival 608 to 598 B.C. Jeremiah exploited the opportunity when the Temple precincts were crowded.

Chapter 7.1 records the command **Stand in the gate of the LORD's house**. Chapter 26.2 refers more explicitly to the 'court of the LORD's house'. Probably Jeremiah stood at the gate between the inner and outer court, where he would have a vantage point to address the assembled crowd.

It is widely held that worshippers were prepared for the liturgy of the Temple by means of a specific dialogue with the 'keepers of the threshold'. Psalms 15 and 24 are examples of the entrance-liturgy in which the conditions of fellowship with God are set out. It is plausible to suppose that this suggested the pattern of Jeremiah's sermon. This is not to say that Jeremiah was simply imitating the entrance-liturgy. His purpose is too specific. He is concerned with the false sense of security which lulls the people. He breaks out with prophetic sternness into a prediction of the destruction of the Temple. In Chapter 26 this is the dominating theme, which leads to a demand for Jeremiah's life. He speaks not like a liturgist, but like a prophet. But the conventional pattern lent thrust to his speech.

Jeremiah was, so to speak, presenting himself as an unexpected barrier between the people and their God. What was normally an easily compassed form of words, became a life and death challenge. The gates were opened ceremonially as a matter of course: Jeremiah was suggesting that the liturgical action should correspond with reality. They could revert to their former complacency only by ignoring the prophet, and some felt his intervention so strongly that they would have killed him. On the structure and character of the superscription in vv. 2–3, see on 10.1.

3. Amend your ways and your doings, and I will let you dwell in this place: The exhortation, amplified in vv. 5–6, is in line with the requirements of the entrance-liturgies (Pss. 15 and 24, cf. also Isa. 1.16–17; Am. 5.14–15; Mic. 6.6–8). It would then be logical to follow a simple and widely adopted re-vocalisation of the Heb. words (supported by Vulg.) and read 'and I will dwell with you in this place'. The massoretic vocalisation would then be explained as motivated by reverential considerations. However the identification of *māqôm* (place) with the sanctuary cannot be maintained throughout the passage. The explanation in v. 7b interprets it of the land, and the Temple is described as the LORD's 'house'. It is probably better to leave MT with the recognition that land and Temple are both the LORD's gift, just as the sacred mountain in Jerusalem was a symbol of the whole land. Certainly the interpretation of *māqôm* as 'land' is as early as the present form of the tradition (see R. E. Clements, *God and Temple* (1965), p. 85 n. 1).

4. Do not trust in these deceptive (*haššeqer*) **words**: for this characteristic expression, here repeated three times, see on 3.10.

This is the temple of the LORD, the temple of the LORD, the temple of the LORD: it is often assumed now that the Heb. *hēmmâ* (those, translated 'this') is really an abbreviation for 'this place' (so *NEB* and *REB*). Ingenious as this explanation is, it is not convincing. Why should the abbreviation be confined to this one instance of the expression out of four in the same passage? And why this sentence, which is a phrase in the cryptic, ejaculatory language of the people, expressing their passionate attachment to a fetish? Above all here a scholar's abbreviation is unlikely. The Temple was a complex of several buildings and the plural was not inappropriate. The *RSV* translation above may be preferred. The repetition constituted a word of protective power.

It is this verse which pinpoints succinctly the attitude with which Jeremiah is in conflict. It is the confidence (the word 'trust' is used three times in vv. 4, 8, 14) no doubt encouraged by the long liturgical tradition, that the LORD's house can never be destroyed and therefore the people are safe. This conviction was strengthened by the theology of the Zion psalms, the events of 701 B.C. and by a complacent understanding of the teaching of Isaiah. Isaiah had predicted that, in his day, Zion *would* not fall. He had not taught that Zion *could* not fall. The dogma of the inviolability of Zion is not taught by Isaiah: it is popular. How painful the nerve was that Jeremiah touched is shown by the reaction narrated in chapter 26.

5. The ordinary covenant demands with which the people were familiar. **execute justice**: cf. Isa. 1.17; Am. 5.15; Mic. 6.8; Dt. 10.18.

6. if you do not oppress the alien, the fatherless or the widow: cf. Is. 1.17; Zech. 7.10; Dt. 10.18; 16.11, 14; 24. 19, 20, 21; Jer. 22.3. These are the people without rights. To be without country, father or husband was to be deprived of responsible protection. How they are treated is a test of inner disobedience.

or shed innocent blood in this place: cf. Isa. 1.15; 59.3, 7; Dt. 19.10; 21.8; Jer. 22.3, 17. In a society where the death penalty was frequent, the miscarriage of justice easily led to the ultimate perversion.

and if you do not go after other gods: summing up what the earlier oracles have shown to be a central theme of Jeremiah, as of Deuteronomy. The prophet recognised the connection between conduct and ultimate belief, cf. 11.10; 16.11; 25.6; 35.15; Dt. 6.14, etc.

7. then I will let you dwell in this place: See on v. 3

in the land that I gave of old to your fathers for ever: this is the fundamental promise, made to Abraham, and a charter of Israel's existence as the People of God. It is this which is threatened by Jeremiah's property. The place (*maqôm*) is defined as the land.

9. Will you steal, murder, commit adultery, swear falsely: directly from the Ten Commandments, fundamental obligations for all members of the covenant community, and, in one way or another, set before worshippers as the condition of entrance into the Temple court. Cf. Ps. 24.4, and especially the covenant psalms 50.18–20; 81.9. Hence the gates are 'gates of righteousness' (Ps. 118.19) 'This is the gate of the LORD. the righteous shall enter through it' (118.20) Exod. 20, followed here by LXX, has 'murder' first.

burn incense unto Baal and go after other gods: cf. Ps. 81.9. See on v. 6.

10. in this house, which is called by my name: hinting at the Deuteronomic name-theology, but not precisely quoting. Deuteronomy thinks in terms of choosing 'to put his name and make his habitation there' (Dt. 12.5, cf. v. 12 below). The expression here used is particularly characteristic of this chapter, cf. vv. 11, 14, 30, and 32.34; 34.15; and in effect affirms that the LORD is the real *owner* of the Temple. The irony is scarcely veiled. See also on 25.29.

and say, we are delivered!: (cf. 2.28), this expresses in general the theme of the passage. See on v. 4. But in particular it suggests the thought of the Temple as an asylum from contemporary dangers (and judgment), and so prompts Jeremiah's description of it as 'a den of robbers' i.e. the base in which they imagine themselves to be secure, and from which they perpetrate their outrages.

Behold, I myself have seen it, says the LORD: in the Heb., brief, cryptic, introduced by *hinnê* and completed by the enigmatic *n^e'ūm Yahweh*, appropriate to the rhythmic prose. These two Heb. expressions occur together sufficiently to suggest a strong emphasis on the mysterious divine disclosure. What gives point to the oracle is that many believed Yahweh did not see. These were the practical atheists of the day, cf. Ps. 73.11; Job 22.13. It is probable therefore that *n^e'ūm Yahweh* simply ends the short, exclamatory oracle beginning 'behold', rather than the whole section vv. 9–11 as Rendtorff thinks. (*ZAW* 66 (1954) 32.) But Rendtorff correctly points out that vv. 9–11 contain what is peculiar to chapter 7, as compared with chapter 26. Verses 12–15 contain the theme which is common to both chapters.

12. Go now to my place that was in Shiloh: The archaeological investigation at *Seilum* suggests that the site was occupied in the period 1200–1000 B.C., and then lay in ruins for centuries. This judgment may stand, despite attempts, on the basis of Danish archaeological excavations, to date the destruction of Shiloh in the eighth century. (See John Day, 'The destruction of the Shiloh sanctuary and Jeremiah VII 12, 14' *Studies in the Historical Books of the Old Testament, VT* supp. 30 ed. J. A. Emerton (1979)). The story of Samuel indicates that there was a sanctuary there, housing the Ark (1 Sam. 1.9) and that this was a centre of pilgrimage. It is consistent with the evidence both of 1 Sam. and of archaeology to assume that Shiloh was destroyed by the Philistines about 1050 B.C. It is a reasonable hypothesis of modern scholarship that the sanctuary which both housed the Ark and became a centre of pilgrimage was the focal point of the confederation of tribes (as many as were effectively united in that period).

This verse (with 26.5–6, 9) is the evidence that Shiloh remained in ruins until the time of Jeremiah. The prophet's purpose is to demonstrate that a sacred place, in which the LORD covenanted to make his name dwell (i.e. in the same terms as the divine tabernacling presence was affirmed of Zion in Dt. 12.5) had been destroyed, and this was proof that the Jerusalem Temple was not immune. The cry 'go' was more than rhetorical, since Shiloh was only nine miles north of Bethel and twenty-one from Jerusalem. This forms the natural climax to the section and to Jeremiah's speech; and it is not difficult to understand that it was the clinching argument which led to the murderous uproar described in chapter 26.

13. when I spoke to you persistently: lit 'rising up and speaking'. The sense of the Heb. expression is to do a thing eagerly or do it repeatedly. This is shorthand for the fuller picture of the activity of the prophets, cf. v. 25 and 25.4; 26.5; 29.19; 35.15; 44.4; and cf. 25.3; 11.7; 32. 33; 35.4. Characteristic of the prose passages in Jer.

14. and to the place which I gave to you and your fathers: the *māqôm* here is plainly the land. Only by arbitrary surgery can this theme be removed from the Temple sermon so as to achieve a tidy, unified oracle without reference to either the land or the threat of exile. See on v. 3. Even if the Temple sermon is a Deuteronomic rewriting (which is not obvious) or Baruch's own account (which is possible) written after the events, it remains likely that the passage registers the mind of Jeremiah closely. Exile was as inevitable a result of the northern enemy's advance as the destruction of the Temple. Certainty is neither possible nor necessary. But the grounds for leaving the text as it is, as a representation of the thought of Jeremiah, are far stronger than the grounds for peeling away alleged secondary elements in order to identify putative *ipsissima verba*.

15. For the threat of exile in the book of Jeremiah, see 9.16; 15.2, 12; 16.13; 17.4; 20.5; 21.7, 11f; 22.22, 24–27, etc. There is no such explicit threat in the passages which we have attributed to Jeremiah's earliest ministry in chapters 1–6. See on 5.18–19. On the other hand, 3.6–14 contains what we have understood as a version of Jeremiah's comparison of the guilt and fate of the northern and southern kingdoms. In view also of the predictions of exile in Amos, Hosea and Isaiah of Jerusalem, it is precarious to follow those commentators who deny the theme of v. 15 to Jeremiah. He did not in the early years stress it, but he knew it was the inevitable result of conquest by an imperial power.

The central affirmation of the Temple Sermon is that the conditions of health and stability in church and state are *moral*. In Israel church and state were one. Life was simpler, the canvas much smaller than that with which we have to deal, and therefore it was easier to see the relationship between the quality of a people's life and the fate of their institutions. And because the conditions are moral, there is no substitute, not even the covenanted presence of the LORD in his House. This represents the highest conceivable spiritual privilege. But when the moral conditions are broken, it is a privilege which the LORD himself repudiates. The principle is of universal application. It undermines all attempts to create an ultimate religious *security*. The most monolithic, time-honoured, powerful religious institution stands under the possibility of the fate of Shiloh.

A PEOPLE PAST PRAYING FOR **7.16–20**

This passage is linked with the Temple Sermon by its general theme of idolatrous worship. It describes what is going on among the people of Judah and Jerusalem and implies that this is what makes the divine judgment inevitable. It is linked also by the use of the term *māqôm*. Here the 'place' is explicitly the whole land, **man and beast, . . . trees of the field and the fruit of the ground** (v. 20). There is in fact no reference to the Temple at all. But the redactor who has placed the passage here has thus given to it the character of an elucidation of the charge made in vv. 1–15.

The distinctive note of the passage is twofold:

First, it refers particularly to the intercessory function of the prophet (see on 4.10 and cf. Moses and Samuel in 15.1). The explicit divine prohibition on this activity is eloquent evidence of the hopelessness of the people's condition (cf. similar prohibitions in 11.14 and 14.11). The time when the prophet might avert the judgment by his prayer on their behalf is past.

Second, v. 18 describes the extreme of superstition which is the reason for the prohibition. Such is the urgency with which the people reach after supernatural protection that whole families co-operate, children and fathers helping to make the fire, the women making cakes (*kawwānîm*) to accompany the libations they offered to **the queen of heaven** (v. 18). That the women were the natural leaders in this form of worship is perhaps implicit here: it is explicit in 44.15–19.

The expression 'queen of heaven' is used of the Babylonian-Assyrian Ishtar, goddess of the planet Venus. It is probable that this cult was introduced into Judah during the reign of Manasseh. The references to it in Jer. suggest that it became popular in the dangerous period following the death of Josiah. Its devotees, according to 44.15–19, attributed the disasters that followed to neglect of this cult, much as prophets associated disasters with the neglect of the LORD (cf. 44.20–23). The cakes are described in 44.19 as 'bearing her image': this might be the figure of a star. As described here, the cult seems to have been practised among the people in their villages, not in the Temple. After the first attack on Jerusalem in 597, the related cult of Tammuz, brother-consort of Ishtar, is to be found practised, again by the women, in the heart of the Temple precincts (see Ezek. 8.14–15).

No doubt, whatever the precise Babylonian or Canaanite origin of this cult, the queen of heaven was understood as the consort of Yahweh. If as Jung maintained, this worship of the queen of heaven corresponds to a profound need of the human psyche, to which the Jewish and Protestant traditions are insensitive, it remains true that it could be admitted at this time only at the cost of the betrayal of Mosaism. The essential character of the obedience and faith for which the LORD looks in his servants was at stake.

18. to provoke me to anger: a commonplace of the Deuteronomic tradition and Jer. (8.19; 11.17; 25.6; 32.30, 32; 44.3, 8. See introductory note on 25.1–14).

WORSHIP LEGITIMATE AND FALSE **7.21–26**

The editor now brings into the context of the Temple Sermon some enigmatic but centrally important words concerning the accepted and legitimate cult of the Jerusalem Temple. There is no doubt that there will continue to be different and even contradictory interpretations of Jeremiah's teaching. He seems to be not only denouncing sacrificial worship comprehensively, and affirming that the Lord's true requirement is obedience to his commands, but even denying the Mosaic institution of the Levitical system, to be excluding the ritual from the basis of the covenant. Three interpretations are possible:

(1) It is possible to resort to the hypothesis of prophetic exaggeration. On this view Jeremiah is really commanding judicious reform. When he says no to this and yes to that, he means that that is more important than this. If this is so, it must be admitted that Jeremiah has none of the clarity we find in Hosea 6.6

(2) It is possible to suppose that Jeremiah already knew the results of modern scholarship that the sacrificial system as a whole was *Canaanite* and borrowed. This is often coupled with the observation that the priestly traditions had not yet been codified. But we now know that the priestly traditions contained material far older than their final codification. Moreover Jeremiah was almost certainly familiar with Deuteronomic traditions, and must have been aware of the convention which associated all law with Moses.

(3) Part of the difficulty lies in the nature of the passage. It lacks a context. We have seen reason to conclude that chapter 7 contains three and possibly four independent units which have been brought together

editorially. The immediate context does not therefore help us to penetrate
to the fundamental meaning of the oracle. On the other hand, for this
very reason we may be confident that this uncompromising judgment
was uttered by Jeremiah himself. However the theme has been developed
in vv. 23ff, it is clear that vv. 21–22 are unlikely to be the invention of
a Deuteronomist editor or a post-exilic preacher! The only safe guidance
for interpretation lies in the words themselves.

21. Add your burnt offerings to your sacrifices, and eat the flesh:
Here the word 'burnt offerings' comes first in the Heb. sentence in a
position of emphasis. It seems reasonable to infer that Jeremiah had
particular reason to stress these; and the reason might be precisely their
ostensibly exemplary character. These were the solemn tribute to the
LORD, not eaten by the people but etherealised to the LORD. In the
pre-exilic period they not only provided the main morning and evening
offering at the sanctuaries (2 Kg. 1.20; 1 Kg. 18, 29) but also served
as the principal atoning sacrifices. And of course they were legitimate.
It is really inconceivable that Jeremiah should deny that these had been
commanded by the LORD *at some time*. For some reason Jeremiah is now
maintaining that not merely the illegitimate Babylonian cult and the
excesses of vv. 31–32 are to be rejected, but also the normally accepted
and central sacrifices of Mosaism are useless. He does not say that the
burnt offerings are wrong; he does say that they are vain. They might
just as well be eaten, like the 'sacrifices' (i.e. the communion *z^ebāḥîm*,
otherwise called peace-offerings), by the people. Both 'burnt offerings'
and 'sacrifices' are no more than 'flesh'. The offering of 'burnt offerings'
is of no more avail than the prophet's intercession. Thus it is unnecessary
to try to wriggle out of the problem by making a distinction between the
public *tāmîd* which Jeremiah leaves untouched, and the voluntary sacrifices
which he repudiated.

**22. For in the day that I brought them out of the land of Egypt,
I did not speak to your fathers or command them concerning burnt
offerings and sacrifices**: If Jeremiah knew of the association of the cultic
law with Moses, what can this verse mean? Perhaps we should note that
what is being referred to is the great act of redemption which was the
model of all subsequent redemptive acts, not precisely the legislative work
of Moses. This is followed by the wandering in the wilderness (the 'way'
cf. v. 23).

Jeremiah may well have understood, as in Dt., that Moses made a
complete legislative provision for the life of the people of God, in

anticipation of the time when they would receive their land and their sanctuary. He can have separated this from the fundamental covenanted conditions of becoming the People of God on the basis of the liberation from Egypt. Jeremiah has it in mind that the judgment now to be experienced, or perhaps already in part experienced, is nothing less than a return to an Egyptian bondage, and nothing short of a new display of divine redemptive power will achieve liberation.

It may be that the prophets are not so far from one another as might seem to be the case. Hosea envisages a period when sacrifice will not be offered because the life of the nation will be disrupted (Hos. 3.4). Amos also seems to think of sacrifice as belonging to settled sanctuaries and not to nomadic existence (Am. 5.25), and therefore impossible when Israel is exiled from her land (5.27). Jeremiah is in this tradition. He is not repudiating what he must have known to be a divine provision of worship. He is envisaging or witnessing a historical situation in which the Lord deliberately strips Judah of the great gifts of the promises. History is God speaking. No Temple, no land, but exile (cf. 8.3). She must pack up her sacrificial worship. Now her sights must be set on one hope only — a new redemption. And as once her 'way' was through the wilderness to the land of promise, now her way must be **all the way that I command you**, a way of obedience to 'walk' in. See also on 29.12–14a.

23. Obey my voice, and I will be your God, and you shall be my people: an expressive summary of the covenant relationship, found in Lev. 26.12 and Ezek. 11.20; 14.11; 37.23; 36.28, but otherwise mainly in the prose sections of Jer. 11.4; 13.11; 24.7; 32.38. Cf. also Zech. 8.8. It is entirely consistent with the view that the section contains some striking and original teaching of Jeremiah to detect here the hand either of Baruch or of some other exponent of Jeremiah's teaching.

that it may be well with you: mainly characteristic of the introductory chapters of Dt. (4.40; 5.16, 26; 6.3, 18; 12.25, 28; 22.7) cf. Jer. 42.6.

24. incline their ear: cf. 7.26; 11.8; 17.23; 25.4; 34.14; 35.15; 44.5. This expression, characteristic of the prose of Jer., is not found in Dt. or in any prophetic book save Isa. 55.3. It is set alongside the theme of persistently sending the prophets (as in v. 25 here), also in 25.4; 35.15; 44.4, and of speaking (as in v. 13) also in 25.3; 35.14; and occurs with the theme of **stubbornness of their evil hearts** in 11.8 (cf. 3.17; 9.13; 13.10; 16.12; 18.12; 23.17).

This verse is sometimes contrasted with the picture in 2.2–3 of the wilderness period as the time of Israel's youthful devotion. If there is a contradiction, it would be explained by the fact that the teaching of

Jeremiah is here being freely handled and developed. But it is doubtful whether the contradiction really exists. Jeremiah is simply stating what the traditions plainly tell. Hosea and Ezekiel share the belief that there was a short honeymoon period which very quickly gave way to unfaithfulness and degeneracy (**backward and not forward**).

25. I have persistently sent all my servants the prophets: as in 25.4; 26.5; 29.19; 35.15; 44.4; 2 Chr. 36.15, cf. Zech. 1.2-7. See on v. 24. 'persistently': literally 'rising early'. The character of the prophets as messengers is thus vividly depicted. The main signal of the care and instruction of the Eternal God is his word spoken through the prophets. To disregard this word is to disobey God himself.

THE EXTREME OF CORRUPT WORSHIP **7.27-8.3**

This section does not form an integrated unit like the previous two sections, for three reasons:

(a) It is by no means certain that it begins at v. 27, which might just as easily be read as a continuation of v. 26.

(b) Verse 29 is a verse fragment in which Judah is addressed in the second person feminine, i.e. as mother Zion.

(c) Verses 30-33 are related closely to 19.7, suggesting that the theme was used freely by the editor (or preacher) in different contexts. All this suggests compilation.

Whatever the previous history of the Temple Sermon tradition, it looks as if the Sermon formed the basis of the chapter, vv. 21-26 introducing one amplification of the judgment, and vv. 27ff, bringing it to completion with the quotation of a memorable verse fragment of Jeremiah's (v. 29 and the description of another feature of the people's corruption in v. 31). All this leads to a vision of frightful nemesis which includes both the violation of corpses and exile (8.3).

27. So you shall speak these words to them, but they will not listen to you: a return to the second person singular as in v. 16. The prophet may not intercede further for the people; but he must declare their sin and pronounce the punishment.

28. and did not accept discipline: (*mûsār*) this expression is characteristic of Jer., and occurs elsewhere only in Zech. 3.2, 7 and Prov. 1.3; 8.10; 24.32. It occurs in 2.30 and 5.3, i.e. in poetic passages belonging to Baruch's Scroll and in the prose passages 17.23; 32.33; 35.13. The most straightforward conclusion is that this is a judgment made by Jeremiah and echoed by those who proclaimed his teaching. 'Discipline' (*mûsār*) is sometimes 'chastisement', but also moral discipline and so 'correction' or 'instruction' or even 'culture'. It is a word which belongs to the sphere of education and occurs frequently in Proverbs.

truth has perished: *ʾemûnāh* i.e. faithfulness, trustworthiness.

29. Cut off your hair and cast it away; raise a lamentation on the bare heights: the word for 'hair' is literally 'consecration', meaning here consecrated and therefore uncut hair. The oracle is ironic. The expression of grief by cutting or shaving the hair and mutilating the body is found widely among the peoples both of antiquity and of the contemporary world. Cf. 16.6; 48.37, (see T. H. Gaster, *Myth, Legend and Custom in the Old Testament*, 1969, pp. 590–602). It is possible only to guess at the reason. The most plausible explanation is that these were thought to be means of giving strength to the dead. But customs long survive their original rationale. So much had the precise signification of the ritual passed into oblivion that the command is easily attributed to the LORD himself. On **bare heights** or paths, see on 3.2.

Verses 30–31 are virtually identical with 32.34–35, see notes.

30. abominations in the house: the word 'abomination' is used contemptuously of heathen deities and idols and occurs most frequently in Jeremiah and Ezekiel. What is meant concretely is shown in Ezek. 8. This verse links the section editorially with the Temple Sermon. The main point of the rest of the section is however what is happening *outside* the Temple.

31. the high place of Topheth, which is in the valley of the son of Hinnom: the valley is situated west, south-west and south of old Jerusalem. With the special name Topheth, this seems to be the local centre of a specific cult, connected with Molech. (32.35, cf. 2 Kg. 23.10; Lev, 18.21; 20.2–5.) According to chapter 19 Jeremiah made a special expedition to prophesy in the valley, and to reinforce his oracle with a prophetic sign. Topheth has been given the vowel points of the word 'shame' (cf. 3.24) to indicate the loathsomeness of the object. LXX *tapheth* is perhaps nearer the mark. It probably means 'fireplace' or 'roaster'.

Molech is either the god worshipped (no doubt identified with Yahweh), described as *melek* or king, again with the vowel points of the word 'shame'; or as in Punic, a designation of the kind of sacrifice. This would then be a sacrificial term denoting a *mlk* sacrifice. However this may be, Molech was understood as the title of a foreign god.

When these passages, together with Isa, 57.5, 9, are put together, it becomes clear that the cult involved child sacrifice. Archaeological investigation shows that such sacrifice was practised in pre-Israelite

Canaan. The first mention of such practice in Israel is in the time of Ahaz
(2 Kg. 16.3). This was under the threat of the Syro-Ephraimite war. Again
it occurred in the time of Manasseh (2 Kg. 17.31) under the threat of
Assyria. In both cases the country was subject to foreign influence, though
it is also plausible to think of an upsurgence of dormant Canaanite customs
in these times of special stress. Condemnation by prophets, Deuteronomist
and Leviticus must be evidence of the seriousness of the apostasy. Verse
31 makes it clear that this was a local cult practised in a particular valley,
that 'high places' (*bāmôt*) were built for the purpose (cf. 19.5) and
unrelated to the ordinary Israelite worship connected with the *bāmôt*, and
that the sacrifice was by fire (cf. 2 Kg. 23.10).

32. the valley of Slaughter: the giving of significant descriptive names
is an aspect of prophetic symbolism (cf. Isa. 1.26; 56.7; 58.12; 60.14,
17f.; 61.3, 6; 62.4, 12). The pronouncing of this name was itself prophetic
of what would be, and is part of Jeremiah's intervention, as narrated
in 19.6. The breaking of the flask is not mentioned here (cf. 19.1, 10ff.).
The narrative itself is not relevant to the latter part of this chapter, which
is concerned with the amplification of the reasons for judgment on the
Temple and its worship. For further use of descriptive names by Jeremiah
see 6.25; 20.3, 10; 44.25; 46.5.

33. Some scholars have found the rest of this section intrusive, and
contradictory. In v. 32 the dead will be buried in Topheth because there
is no room elsewhere. In v. 33 the dead will not be buried at all. In 8.1
dead kings will be disinterred. But Reuss, Condamin and Rudolph are
surely right to see here a horrifying climax. First there will be so many
dead that, in place of ordinary tombs, an unclean place like the valley
of Hinnom (origin of the *NT* term Gehenna) will have to be used. More
than that, there will be so many that corpses will be left to the carrion
birds. More even than that, the tombs of kings and others will be looted
for treasure and their bodies scattered on the ground. In this judgment
even the dead, who might be thought to be sacrosanct, will be violated.

34. The voice of mirth and the voice of gladness: characteristic of
the prose material, cf. 16.9; 25.10; 33.11.

8.1 kings, princes, priests, prophets, inhabitants of Jerusalem —
a list repeated in 1.18; 4.9; 13.13.

2. the host of heaven, which they have loved and served: The irony
of judgment so often observed by the prophets, followed by powerful
rhetorical repetition — loved, served, gone after, sought, worshipped.
On 'the host of heaven' see on 19.13.

they shall not be gathered or buried; they shall be as dung on the

surface of the ground: a stereotyped expression of the prose sermons, cf. 16.4; 25.33.

3. in all the places where I have driven them: i.e. banished them into exile, cf. 5.18–19; 9.16; 15.2, 14; 17.4; 16.13; 20.5; 21.7; 22.11f; 22.24–27. Although some passages may be subsequent 'preaching', it is foolish to deny this prediction to Jeremiah. Exile was involved in the terrible judgment he proclaimed, and he knew it. He did not need to be more explicit.

Note on 7.1–8.3

It has become clear that this section, the first part of the complex 7–10, has redactional unity. All the sub-sections, 7.16–20, 21–26; 7.27–8.3 are brought together because they may be regarded as elucidating the fundamental judgment of the Temple Sermon. Upon this nucleus the rest has been deposited with recognisable design. Jeremiah, Baruch, other interpreters of Jeremiah's teaching, and the redactor have all played their part in the production of this witness to the word of the LORD concerning the worship of Judah before her final collapse.

CULPABLE FOOLISHNESS **8.4–13**

Chapters 8 and 9 are another remarkable example of the way in which the oracular and other material has been meaningfully built up into complexes. Here the outer structure is determined by wisdom considerations and vocabulary. The wisdom note is struck in v. 4, with the quotation of a no doubt wellknown wisdom saying.

> When men fall, do they not rise again?
> If one turns away, does he not return?

The interrogative form is that which occurs in the quotation of wisdom sayings by Amos (6.12) and by Isaiah (10.15), and was plainly a feature of international wisdom, as is shown, for example, by the Accadian proverb:

> Has she become pregnant without intercourse?
> Has she become fat without eating?

(See McKane, *Proverbs*, 1970, pp. 189–190).

Sometimes the double rhetorical questions demand a negative, sometimes a positive answer. The point of the proverb is its obvious commonsense, capable of immediate application to a variety of cases, and here to the condition of Judah. But then comes the twist. Judah has not risen up after her fall, or returned to the LORD. She is going against the natural order of things; her backsliding is perpetual, she refuses to return. (On this theme see esp. on 31–4.4) The sense of the proverb is reflected in the confidence of Mic. 7.8.

The wisdom theme continues with the criticism of those who claim to be the embodiment of wisdom (vv. 8–9); it is taken up again in the prose passage (9.12–16); and it reaches a climax in the summary of the faithful's duty in 10.23–24, which magisterially associates the true wisdom with the knowledge of God.

6. no man repents: See on chapters 5 and 6.

like a horse plunging into battle: again reminiscent of known teaching in Jer., cf. 2.23–24; 5.8.

7. Even the stork in the heavens knows her times; . . . **but my people know not**: again the form of the passage provides the vivid particularity with universal meaning, typical of proverbial wisdom and is echoed elsewhere in prophecy. Cf. Isa. 1.3. 'The ox knows its owner, and the ass its master's crib; but Israel does not know, my people does not understand.'

turtledove, swallow, and crane: these are not certainly identified. They are migratory birds. 'Crane' is not in LXX and may be an early attempt at identification. Read perhaps 'dove' and 'swift', but there can be no certainty.

8. In the light of this wisdom vocabulary, it is not surprising that Jeremiah now explicitly refers to 'the wise men' and to their responsibility in misleading the people. This verse is notoriously difficult to interpret, and some have argued that there is no reference here to a class of men at all, that the word 'wise' is simply adjectival. Such a conclusion hardly accounts for all the facts. On the whole, sense is best achieved if it is supposed that the principle teachers in Israel were scribes (*sōp͏erîm*), amongst whom the ministers of state (*śārîm*) were normally recruited, that it was in these intellectual and literary circles (where literacy was mainly found) that wisdom traditions were preserved and propagated, that these were also the circles in which the Deuteronomists of this period were located. This explains why Dt. itself was commended as 'your wisdom and your understanding in the sight of the peoples' (Dt. 4.7), why it is emphasised that Baruch was a *sōpēr*, with his strongly Deuteronomic manner of writing, why here the *sōp͏erim* are associated with **the law of the LORD**.

In this context the law is probably the Deuteronomic law in which they had taken so much pride. The meaning of the verse is then something like this: people or scribes (we are not told which) arrogate to themselves the title 'wise' and therewith the authority of the intellectual tradition. As people made a fetish of the Temple and regarded it as a guarantee of safety, so do these pretenders to wisdom take refuge under the protection of the law. They think that because they have the law, teach it and propagate it and determine policy on the basis of it, they are safe. On the contrary, the pen of the scribes is false (*šeqer*). They manipulate it to their own ends, so that they have made it into a lie (*šeqer*).

9. So far from achieving inviolability, the **wise men shall be put to shame, they shall be dismayed and taken.** The word 'taken', as we shall see, is used as a catchword.

what wisdom is in them?: It is reasonable to deduce that the class of men in question were scribes (*sōpᵉrîm*). They were the repositories and exponents of the wisdom tradition. Therefore although the term 'wise' was not precisely the title of a class, it became the identifying mark of the literary scribes. Some became *śārîm*, and although some were both, the tendency was for a distinction between them to be maintained and widened. The overlapping of *śārîm* and *sōpᵉrîm* is probably to be detected in Jer. 18.18 (qv). What you expected from wise ministers was good 'counsel'.

Verses 10–12 are now introduced, as in 6.12–15, to state the reason for the judgment of the whole people. All are guilty from the least to the greatest. But also to stress the special responsibility of those who are the professional leaders of Judah. In this case the passage describes the *sōpᵉrîm*. In chapter 6 it has no such specific reference, and this illustrates how redaction may subtly change the precise meaning of the passage. Verse 10a is close enough in both sense and vocabulary to 6.12a to indicate that this also was part of the oracle that has been used both in Baruch's scroll and in this later complex. For further comment on the section see on 6.12–15. The new use of this passage is strong confirmation of the view that we are dealing with a build-up of material.

The purpose of the redactor may also be seen in the last line. As so often in the process of redaction, we are able to find not only an appropriateness of theme, but also a linguistic link. **Therefore they shall fall among the fallen** (v. 12) provides a verbal echo of v. 4: **When men fall, do they not rise again?** More than that, the redactor found in this passage not only a catchword connection but also a paradoxical answer to the proverbial question. Men expected the answer, Yes, and faith might confirm it (Mic. 7.8). The answer in these circumstances for this people is, No! Again the 'they shall be taken' of v. 9 is reinforced by **they shall be overthrown** of v. 12 (i.e. made to stumble). The Heb. words are often found together, as in Isa. 8.15.

13. The section is summed up with the image of a barren fruit harvest, (see on v. 20), sign of the curse about to fall on the people.

When I would gather them: The Hebrew suggests that, as in Zeph. 1.2–3, there is a play on the idea of Ingathering. When the LORD should be able to gather the fruits of his own people, there are none. But the attempt to prove a dependence on Zeph. 1.2–3 from the similar structures of the two passages is vain.

the leaves are withered: verbally close to Isa. 1.30, a late passage in Isaiah.

and what I gave them has passed away from them: this is absent from the LXX and may be the corruption of a dittograph, to be omitted as in *NEB*, *REB*. On the other hand a simple change of vocalisation, proposed by Houbigant, gives the sense: 'those whom I give to them shall make them go away' i.e. into exile. There can be no confident reconstruction of the text. *RSV* represents the literal translation of obscure Hebrew.

PROPHETIC LAMENT **8.14–9.1**

This section has the general character of a lament. This does not mean that this is a liturgical piece. It does mean that Jeremiah found the liturgical pattern to his purpose, as he now assumes the representative mantle implicit in the prophetic 'we' and 'I'. As he identified himself with the people and with the LORD, the lament is the appropriate form of indirect prophecy. At the same time the originality and creativity of Jeremiah is in no way inhibited by the form. Indeed this is a lament with a difference, as will become clear. It is difficult to be certain of the correct limits of the lament. Some begin the section with verse 13. But on the whole this verse is best understood as the completion of the previous section, particularly as there is clearly a redactoral building up of the parts to make a climax of judgment. The thematic link between the barren vines and fig trees of v. 13 and the passing of harvest in v. 20 is entirely in keeping with the frequently observed arrangement of redactors and would simply indicate one of the reasons why 8.14–9.1 is placed to follow 8.4–13.

The lament character of the section explains the change of person and the dialogue element in the structure.

(a) In vv. 14–15 the prophet speaks in the first person plural for the people, and expresses their terror in the face of invasion.

(b) In vv. 16–17 the herald-like announcement of the enemy coming from Dan leads into the word of the LORD in the first person, warning of the Foe from the North in the image of serpents.

(c) In 18–9.1 the first person oscillates between the speech of the prophet (8.18, 21; 9.1, 11) and that of the LORD (8.19, 21, 22), in such a way that one is not quite sure whether the lament is that of the prophet or of the LORD himself. The distinction between this lament and others in which the prophet identifies himself particularly with the people, is rendered the more vivid by the quotation of the people's complaint in vv. 19, 20. At the point where one would expect the strongest representative expression (v. 21), Jeremiah turns the lament into a channel of the suffering of God.

Moreover, the lament character pervades the whole section so that it is impossible to follow those commentators who distinguish an announcement of the northern enemy in vv. 14–18 from the lament proper in 8.18–9.3.

14. Why do we sit still? The question 'Why?' in one form or another is the ever recurring question of the lament.

Gather together, let us go into the fortified cities: the rhetorical call is identical with 4.5c, which is the introduction to an oracle (4.5–9) raising the alarm concerning the enemy from the north. That oracle leads up to an explicit call to lament (4.8). Where no doubt worshippers expected a conventional call to lament and fast, Jeremiah introduces an unexpected and urgent alarm-call.

for the LORD our God has doomed us to perish: the irony of the perplexed cry is that this is exactly what Jeremiah has been teaching.

and has given us poisoned water to drink: cf. 23.15. = 9.14. The idea of the cup of the wrath of the LORD may lie behind this expression. More particularly Weiser draws attention to the story of the golden calf which Moses burned, then ground to powder, scattered upon the water and made the people drink (Exod. 32.20).

15. = 14.19b, where it seems more naturally at home. This however does not mean that it is inappropriate here. The redactor knew what he was doing! **peace**: the substance of the comfort offered by false prophets cf. v. 11. **healing**: cf. verse 22. It is possible that somewhere along the line of the cult, the people were accustomed to hear the affirmation of Exod. 15.26: 'I am the LORD your healer'.

16. The snorting of their horses is heard from Dan: again the theme of the enemy from the north, cf. 4.13–17 the second of the oracles on this theme. For Dan see 4.15. Cf. also 6.22–23.

17. behold, I am sending among you serpents, adders which cannot be charmed, and they shall bite you: the reason for this unique description of the northern invader would be obvious to those who listened to the prophet. It is not simply that the viper is insidious and dangerous, but also that the Heb. word *ṣipᵉʿōn* is a pun on *ṣāpôn* (north).

18. My grief is beyond healing: this translation represents perhaps the best that can be done with unintelligible Hebrew: it has the support of LXX and Old Latin. Now there is change of person appropriate to the dialogue of the lament. The prophet speaks, and no doubt the grief is his own. As the LORD's messenger, and one who knows the inner counsel of the LORD, he expresses the lament of the people.

19. Is the LORD not in Zion? Is her King not in her?: not from their point of view but from the standpoint of heaven. For this, the supreme test of their faith, see on 2.6. Their faithless question is set in ironical contrast with their apostasy and brazen provocation of the LORD. The formulation of these questions in terms of the presence of the divine *King* in *Zion* becomes significant in the exposition of v. 20.

Why have they provoked me . . .?: naturally many commentators are driven to regard this obtrusion of the direct speech of the LORD as an addition. Those who give weight to the method of compilation will be slow to remove it. Moreover dialogue is of the essence of the lament.

20. The harvest is past, the summer is ended and we are not saved: again the lament of the people is quoted. The logic of this, not obvious to us, was clear to the people. The summer (*qayiṣ*) was, according to the Gezer Calendar (tenth century B.C.) the last of the months of the year and the new year began in the autumn. The new year feast (later Tabernacles) was in a special sense *the* liturgical observance of the year, celebrating the kingship of the LORD (cf. v. 19), and guaranteeing both the crops and victory of the nation for another year. Plainly a trust was reposed in this observance comparable to the fetish-like trust in the presence of the LORD in his Temple. The observance was central to the 'Zion theology'. When the observance was over and there was no safety for the nation, no sign that the danger had passed, then superstitious people began to question the observance. Probably the Babylonian system of a year beginning in the spring was adopted about this time; but this did not affect the arrangement of the agricultural feasts or diminish the importance of the autumn festival.

21. For the wound of the daughter of my people is my heart wounded: 'heart' is not mentioned in the Heb., though the translation is not objectionable. Better *NEB*: 'I am wounded at the sight of my people's wound'. Again the lament compounds the feelings of the prophet and those of the LORD who alone can speak of 'my people'. The hinted anthropomorphism is bold. Here is Jeremiah's witness to 'the suffering of God'.

22. Is there no balm in Gilead? Is there no physician there?: Coverdale's 'Great Bible' of 1539 had 'There is no more treacle in Gilead'. Hence it was popularly known as the Treacle Bible. The balm is a medicinal resin from either the Storax tree or mastic (cf. 46.11; 51.8). Gilead was apparently wellknown for it and exported it (Gen. 37.25; Ezek. 27.17).

Why then has the health of the daughter of my people not been restored?: the word 'health' or 'healing' is properly the making of new skin. The particular image of the Hebrew is recaptured in *NEB, REB*: 'Why has no new skin grown over their wound?'

9.1 O that my head were waters: again the prophet speaks, but in such a way ('the daughter of my people') as to suggest that he expresses the divine grief through his own.

A DECEITFUL AND UNTRUSTWORTHY PEOPLE **9.2-9**

The build-up of oracles continues with a section which has a questionable beginning but a certain homogeneity of content. A case can be made for linking v. 2 with the previous section. Verses 1 and 2 begin with the same idiomatic phrase, which introduces a desiderative clause. Moreover, there is the same ambiguity between the speech of the prophet and the expression of the mind of the LORD ('the daughter of my people' v. 1; 'that I might leave my people' in v. 2; cf. 'they do not know me' in v. 3).

On the other hand the connection between vv. 1 and 2 can be that of the catchword, observed and exploited editorially. And certainly vv. 2-9 introduce an indictment of Judah in respect particularly of treachery, falsehood, slander, deception and lies. The tongue is like a bow in v. 3, like an arrow in v. 8. Again v. 3 concludes 'they do not know me, says the LORD' and v. 6 'they refuse to know me, says the LORD'. 'Falsehood' (*šeqer*) reigns, in vv. 3 and 5. Formally also vv. 2-9 constitute a cohesive unit. Verses 2-6 are in effect a statement of the ground of judgment (the reproach). Verses 7-9 are the judgment itself (the threat) beginning with 'Therefore (*lākēn*) thus says the LORD' (the old messenger formula) and a participial phrase to introduce the judgment. It is not often that the exemplary form-critical unit of the earlier prophetic books turns up so clearly in the book of Jeremiah.

2. O that I had in the desert a wayfarer's lodging place: The mind at once thinks of Elijah's flight into the wilderness and his lament: 'It is enough: now, O LORD, take away my life'. As Elijah fled from Jezebel, the prophet would flee from the people, a sign of the LORD leaving his people.

For they are all adulterers: it is not clear whether the prophet refers to the moral offence of adultery, as in 5.7; 7.9; 23.14 or the spiritual treachery of apostasy as in 3.8–9. It is remarkable how he links adultery with lies in 23.4 in the case of prophets (cf. also 29.23). Moral and spiritual decadence go together, and it may be that we are not meant to make a rigid distinction.

4. The first consequence of a disregard for truth is the destruction of confidence between one man and another, and the creation of suspicion. The prophet is prepared even to question the validity of the cleverness of Jacob. There is *sub voce* approval of Jacob's cunning in the narratives of Genesis. But **every brother is a supplanter** plays on the name of Jacob in such a way as to suggest that such compromise with truth is unacceptable. The Heb. *'āqôb ya'ᵉqōḇ* might be paraphrased 'every brother stoops to Jacob's trickery'.

5. everyone deceives his neighbour: perhaps more accurately with *NEB* 'they make game of their friends'. Cf. Zech. 8/16.

they have taught their tongue to speak lies (*šeqer*): the stress on teaching, here and in vv. 13 and 19, links these next sections with the wisdom theme of 8.4–13. So also the false (*šeqer*) pen of the scribes has turned the 'law' into a lie (*šeqer*).

they commit iniquity and are too weary to repent: represent a rearrangement and repointing of the Heb. text, which has much to be said for it. 'Repent' is possible here, though the same verb in Exod. 7.18 must mean 'to be unable'. (So LXX, Vulg.) Moreover *šûb* can mean either 'return' or 'repent'; hence *NEB* 'they cannot retrace their steps'. In view of the use of this term in chapter 3, it is probable that the meaning is substantially the same, i.e. 'repent'. See on 3.1, 10, 12. *REB*, on the basis of an unamended text; has 'weary themselves going astray'.

6. they refuse to know me: there is inadequate reason for changing this, as some wish to do. Though Jeremiah speaks, he easily passes into the direct speech of the LORD. Nor should **says the LORD**, here and in v. 2, be omitted on the strength of its omission in LXX.

7. Therefore: as so often introducing the threat of judgment. The judgment, as in Isa. 1.20–27, is to refine them and test them; but the hope of finding good metal proves vain (cf. 6.29–30).

9. = 5.9 and 29, and, as there, is probably a sign of the activity of the redactor who has placed this section here to illustrate the full consequences of the betrayal of truth.

Thus this section gives out two signals, the one indicating editorial build-up, the other the homogeneity of a powerful theme. It seems quite inadequate to leave it as simply the product of desk work. The followers of Jeremiah have taken hold of their master's memorable teaching and shaken it into a powerful new preaching instrument, first as part of the 'many similar words' (36.32), but also as the constant witness to the word of the LORD in their midst.

THE CALL TO LAMENT **9.10–22**

It is convenient to consider this section as a whole, because the theme of the call to make lamentation runs through vv. 10–11 and 17–22, and because the prose vv. 12–16 are clearly built on vv. 10–11 (see on v. 12). But the section is not altogether homogeneous and, with v. 22, shows ample signs of a redactor's structural techniques. The point of the lament hardly needs explanation. It implies death, the death of the nation — the end, as in Amos, who also anticipated the professional mourners (Am. 5.16). What is not quite clear is whether the disaster has taken place, or whether Jeremiah is employing a particularly vivid mode of prophecy. The latter seems to consort much more convincingly with the mind and purpose of Jeremiah. When the disaster had happened, would he not leave the mourning to the course of events? Would there be prophetic mileage in exhorting the women to do what they would do anyway? The power of the call to lament as prophecy lies precisely in the fact that the prophet was anticipating events. The prophecy was remembered and retained its power because the events happened.

10. Take up weeping: the imperative is the reading of LXX and Pesh. MT reads 'I take up weeping'. It is probable that MT is to be preferred, that this begins as a speech of the prophet and that LXX represents an effort to reconcile v. 10 with v. 11, where Yahweh is the speaker. But such repairs are unnecessary.

10. for the mountains . . . for the pastures: the translation is possible, but it is more likely that the prophet envisages a lamentation which takes place on the mountains, *concerning* the mountains. The word 'over' captures the ambivalence. The absence of cattle, birds

and human inhabitants is a sign of the desolation.
11. Reaffirms the prophecy of Micah quoted in 26.18. **a lair of jackals**:
cf. Ps. 40.20, and applied to Babylon in 51.37, but also in 10.22, 49.33.
Verses 12–16, in prose, read like a catechetical expansion of the
previous section. At the same time the reappearance of wisdom vocabulary
suggests that this is part of the framework in which the call to lament
has been incorporated.
12. Who is the man so wise that he can understand this? Cf. the
proverb in 8.4, followed by the question in 8.5; the question in 8.8 'How
can you say, "we are wise, and the law of the LORD is with us"'; the
judgment on the wise in 8.8–9.
Why is the land ruined? Cf. 8.5 and see on 16.10–13. No doubt it
makes sense, in the context of a prediction of mourning for the end of
the nation, to anticipate the questions which judgment would raise in
the minds of the suffering people; and it would be foolish to deny that
Jeremiah himself might forestall the questions as part of his prophecy.
But the build-up of the complex of traditional material suggests a different
solution. It suggests that the question is the actual question asked by the
people who suffer the judgment Jeremiah had predicted. Then those who
worked on the tradition of Jeremiah's oracles sought to answer these
questions from their memory of the teaching of Jeremiah, but in their
own language. That appears to be the character of the Deuteronomic
prose in vv. 12–16.

This explains both the unmistakeable Deuteronomic style, the threefold
structure (see on 16.10–13), and the echoes of Jeremiah's teaching, or
perhaps the turns of phrase characteristic of Baruch. Such echoes are the
phrase 'stubbornly followed their own hearts' (see on 3.17); v. 15 which
equals 23.15 and is anticipated in 8.14. At the same time the section is
editorially knit into the context of 8.4–10.25 by the contrast of 13a ('they
have forsaken my law') with 8.8 ('the law of the LORD is with us'); the
contrast of 13b ('as their fathers taught them') with 10.2 (learn not the
way of the nations') cf. also 9.4; but particularly and primarily by the
way the question of v. 12 ('Why is the land ruined and laid waste like
a wilderness so that no one passes through?') puts a 'Why' to the lament
of v. 10, using the same expressions.

Altogether this is a remarkable example of the redactor's art. We are
not dealing with the simple and clumsy process of setting one traditional
piece alongside another, but with a sensitive building upon the known
teaching of Jeremiah in order to answer live questions in new situations.
To whom has the mouth of the LORD spoken . . .?: i.e. a reference

to a prophet. There is no wise man who can explain the disaster, and no prophet who has received a genuine 'word' from the LORD.

16. I will scatter them among the nations: the scattering which, over centuries, led to the situation which was later called the diaspora, and was to be answered by the prophecies of ingathering cf. Isa. 11.12, 49, 60; Jer. 23.3; 29.14; 31.8, 10.

17. The reversion to poetry (vv. 17–22) is also the renewal of the theme of lament (as in vv. 10–11). Probably omit (with LXX and Pesh) **consider, and**; but problems of the text here fortunately do not materially affect the sense. The mourning women are, so to speak, professionals, cf. Am. 5.16. The word 'skilful' is $h^a k\bar{a}m\hat{o}t$ (wise). In the light of the wisdom vocabulary of the section, and the scathing reference to the 'wise' in 8.8, 9, it is difficult not to detect an element of irony. 'In the judgment that is coming, this is the only use you will be able to put your wisdom to — wailing!'

18. that our eyes may run down with tears, and our eyelids gush with water: the way in which the wish of 9.1 will be realised.

19. How we are ruined! The Heb. '*ēk* is the familiar opening word of the elegy, cf. Isa. 1.21; Lam. 1.1; 2.1; 4.1. The elegy or dirge (*qînâh*) is explicitly referred to in v. 20.

20. teach to your daughters: the irony is continued. 'And if you teach any more, it will be to teach how to wail!' On teaching, cf. 9.5, 14; 10.2. All the women will learn how to lament, such will be the time of necessity. So Jeremiah attempts to breach complacency and communicate the certainty of judgment which the optimism of the people persistently shrugs off.

21. Omit **For**. It is simply a mark of direct speech. **death has come up into our windows**: a unique personification of death making his awesome visitation. More usually in the Old Testament one descends to the realm of death. The most direct comparison occurs in the Ugaritic texts (Baal II v 60–65), where Baal, discussing the building of his house, says: 'Put not a lattice in (the mansion) a window in the midst of the palace.'

The reason is assumed to be to prevent Mot (death) from entering and carrying off his daughters. The sixfold occurrence of the parallel lattice window in the Ugaritic texts makes one wonder whether lattices should be read here for palaces ($^{a}rub\bar{o}t\hat{e}n\hat{u}$ for '$arm^e n\bar{o}t\hat{e}n\hat{u}$).

22. The dead bodies of men shall fall like dung upon the open field: In the light of 2 Kg. 9.37 and Jer. 8.2 it is unlikely that 'dung' should be omitted for the sake of the metre. Of course it would be tidy to have the familiar 3:2 metre in a verse which is set out as the substance of the

women's lament. But were the Hebrew poets always so metrically exact?
and none shall gather them: cf. that less poetical 8.2.

THE TRUE WISDOM **9.23-24**

On the wisdom theme pervading chapters 8-9, see on 8.4-13. Verses
23-24 read like a comprehensive comment on what has so far been said.
The expedient of summing up and appraising a section of teaching is
sufficiently attested in the wisdom literature to encourage the view that
it is a recognised procedure. (See B. S. Childs, *Isaiah and the Assyrian Crisis*,
1967, Excursus I).
Significantly the stamp of wisdom traditions is clear in Isa. 14.24-27
and 10.5-15, where the theme is the plan (*ʿeṣah*) of the LORD. Isa. 10.15
is a wisdom saying (cf. 28.29). So here, although there is little formal
similarity in the section itself, the wisdom theme is obvious, and the
function of the section in summarising what has gone before it and
appraising the situation in a comprehensive statement can be easily
discerned by the reader. If there is a trace of formal identity it is in the
expression *bᵉzoʾṭ* ('in this') which corresponds to the *zeh* or *zōʾṭ* of Isa.
14.26, 17.14, 28, 29; Job. 20.29, 27.13; Ec. 7.23, etc.
The passage thus makes good sense in terms of the redactor's purpose.
It does not fit with Jeremiah's intense effort to bring home the complete
collapse of Judah, when neither wealth nor military strength has any more
relevance. This is a characteristic generalisation in the wisdom style.
Significantly the complex also opens in 8.4 with a wisdom saying. It is
difficult to be patient with those who still quote Duhm's view that this
is 'a harmless unimportant saying' of later piety. It is not the only time
he confuses the classic and the commonplace.

23. Let not the wise man glory in his wisdom: links with the mention
of the wise in 8.8, 9; 9.12, and the wise women in 9.16. Cf. also 10.7.
The secular, utilitarian character of some wisdom traditions has often
been noted. The wisdom of men may have little to do with the knowledge
of God.
24. that he understands and knows me: this combination of wisdom
vocabulary has been met already in 3.15, a prose passage which could
well owe its origin to a redactor's instinct for the essence of Jeremiah's
teaching.
**I am the LORD who practise steadfast love, justice and
righteousness**: the form is that of the Ten Words (cf. Exod. 20.5-6) with
the strong divine self-affirmation (or self-predication) which occurs in the

Psalter (Pss. 50.7; 81.10) associated with the proclamation of the saving deeds of the LORD, and is taken up powerfully in Second Isaiah (esp. 44.24-45.25). But not only has this verse a cultic echo; it also suggests the influence of Hosea (as elsewhere in Jeremiah), whose 'I delight in steadfast love not sacrifice, the knowledge of God, rather than burnt offerings' (6.6) is surely reflected in 'and knows me, that I am the LORD who practise steadfast love, justice and righteousness; for in these things I delight'. On the knowledge of God, cf. Hos. 4.1, 6; 5.4; 6.6; 8.2; Jer. 2.8; 4.22; 9.3, 6; 22.16; 24.7; 31.34 and cf. Isa. 1.3). The passage starts therefore by bringing the previous section to a summarising conclusion: it ends by summarising the essence of the biblical understanding of God.

AN ULTIMATE JUDGMENT **9.25-26**

It is first necessary to establish the meaning of the text, with which *RSV* has struggled not too happily!

25. those who are circumcised but yet uncircumcised: is literally 'those who are circumcised in the foreskin'. There is no need for the paradox.

26. that cut the corners of the hair: may be right (cf. Jer. 25.23; 49.23). Reference is usually made to Herodotus (III.8), who speaks of those who shave off the hair on their temples, apparently as a religious rite. There is no doubt that in Hebrew this is a possible translation. It would refer to certain desert tribes known by this mark. But equally possible, is the rendering of *NEB*, *REB* 'all who haunt the fringes of the desert'. The edge is thus the edge of the cultivated land rather than the edge of the hair. Such tribes constituted a substantial and important element in the geography of the area.

all these nations are uncircumcised: this is patently untrue, particularly when glossed by the words 'in the flesh', as by LXX and Targ. It is best to suppose that 'are uncircumcised' has been ambiguously introduced here and, omitting it, to translate: 'all these nations and the house of Israel are uncircumcised in heart' (cf. 4.4). The passage then reads: 'Behold the days are coming, says the LORD, when I will punish all the circumcised: Egypt, Judah, Edom, Ammon, Moab and all who live on the fringes of the desert, for all the nations and the whole house of Israel are uncircumcised in heart.'

But when the translation is established, the difficulties are not at an end. The nations specified are not the only ones which practised circumcision. It may be that those named have entered into an alliance with Egypt, but even then the selection seems restricted. It is more likely

that the list is rhetorical, and belongs to a time when these nations, which
practised circumcision, were friendly enough to be linked together for
the purpose of the preacher. And the preacher's purpose must be to add
another example to the principle enunciated in chapter 7, that the outward
expressions of religion are no guarantee either of the people's health or
of their salvation.

The opening formula **Behold, the days are coming, says the LORD,
and I will** . . . (v. 25) is found frequently in mainly prose passages, often
introducing messianic prophecies, always referring to the ultimate hope
of the future (cf. 7.32; 16.14; 19.6; 23.5, 7; 30.3; 31.27, 31, 38; 33.14;
48.12; 49.2; 51.47, 52), and it is one of the characteristic expressions
of the book of Jeremiah, characteristic, moreover, of an interpreter of
Jeremiah rather than of the prophet himself. If then one asks, why this
section has been added to 8.4–9.24, with its apparent lack of connection,
the answer must lie in the underlying theme. As there is no ultimate
security in the Ark (3.15–18) nor in the Temple itself (7.1–15), nor in
the activity of the wise men (8.8–9), so there is no security in circumcision.
The only genuine test is the circumcision of the heart (4.4).

The prose expression may be that of an interpreter. But to deny that
this teaching is pervaded with the influence of Jeremiah seems to betray
insensitivity. Here once again we encounter another example of the most
characteristic teaching of Jeremiah, which rests upon the conviction that
all rites and religious customs and symbols have a precarious validity. They
are the work of men and are acceptable only so far as men allow them to
be the vehicle of the word of God. And the word of God 'is not the
expression of a familiar deity, with whom man comes into regular contact
in fixed placed and at fixed times. He, who speaks, is incomprehensible,
irregular, surprising, overwhelming, sovereign' (Martin Buber).

FALSE GODS AND THE TRUE **10.1–16**

Appended to chapters 7–9 is a section in which a later prophet, no doubt
a follower of Jeremiah, attacks idols in the manner of Second Isaiah and
contrasts the incomparable majesty of the LORD to whom alone
allegiance is due. If there is any work of Jeremiah himself in this, it is
now impossible and unnecessary to recover it. As it stands, a totally
different situation from that encountered by Jeremiah is implied. The
laments and oracles of chapters 8–9 are directed precisely to the
hopelessness of the situation and the certainty of judgment. Here it is
assumed that Israel has the time and opportunity to learn the lesson (v.
1); still more significantly that Israel is 'the tribe of his inheritance' or

as *NEB* aptly paraphrases: 'the people he claims as his own' (v. 10). The relation of this passage to the anti-idol polemic of Second Isaiah is close enough to suggest a relationship in time and situation, though it is vain to speculate more precisely. This may well be 'preaching to the exiles'. See especially Isa. 40.19–20; 41.6–7; 44.9–20; 46.5–7. There are other features which suggest that this passage has been the subject of perhaps a complicated history of transmission. Thus the Greek version omits vv. 6–8, 10 and places v. 9 between vv. 4 and 5. This has the effect of removing the 'praise' sections from the main anti-idol poem and leaving the praise of the creator at the end. But this latter praise section (vv. 12–16, including a passage on idols in vv. 14–15) is identical with 51.15–19 where it has been deliberately used by the exilic editor of chapters 50–51. This tends to confirm our hypothesis that this chapter was built up into its present form in the exilic period.

Verse 11 is an unusual and puzzling intrusion of Aramaic, incorporated into the text. This was already present in the Hebrew text which came into the hands of the Greek translator, but as will be seen it makes best sense as a comment on v. 10 which is absent in the Greek. We may conclude, with McKane, that the LXX has already been subject to addition, that it should be regarded as a stage on the way to our present text (MT), that the Qumran fragments (4 Q Jer.) show that LXX is a shorter and earlier, not an abbreviated and later text. Superficially it is easier to explain the praise sections as expansions of the original. But what is now clear is that the full text makes sense, that there is a sort of liturgical coherence in the alternating pattern of vv. 1–16.

The passage is therefore a fascinating example of the way in which an irrecoverable element in the teaching of Jeremiah has been developed, subject to other influences, to provide appropriate teaching in the face of later, exilic challenges. This cathedral-like edifice of prophetic teaching may well be thought to involve every bit as remarkable a phenomenon of inspiration as the poetry of an original genius. These conclusions do not rule out the possibility that both Second Isaiah and the exilic preacher in the school of Jeremiah use a common oral cult tradition. Cf. Isa. 2.8, 18, 20; Pss. 97.6–9; 96.4–6).

Thus accepting the passage in its completeness, it is possible to see why the redactor placed it here. His theme has been the futility and deception (*šeqer*) of Ark, Temple, sacrifice, wise men and their Torah, and circumcision. How much more obvious the futility of idols which are the most blatant substitute for the 'living God'. Chapters 8–9 had their own summarising conclusion. But chapter 10 takes the total sweep

of the complex towards a new climax. The wisdom theme of chapters
8–9 is present in 'learn not' i.e. 'do not be disciples' (v. 2), 'the wise
ones of the nations' (v. 7), 'the work of skilled men' (lit. 'wise men')
(v. 9), 'who established the world by his wisdom, and by his
understanding stretched out the heavens' (v. 12). The stamp of
characteristic Jeremianic vocabulary is to be found in the 'false' (*šeqer*)
of v. 14 and 'at the time of their punishment (visitation)' (v. 15). Despite
therefore the signs of a history of tradition later than Jeremiah, confirmed
by the separate superscription of v. 1, the passage is thematically and,
to some extent linguistically knit into the complex of chapters 7–10 by
the skill and subtlety of the redactor's art.

1. The superscription is of the same general type as is found in 2.4;
7.2; 11.2; 17.20; 19.3; 21.11; 22.2; 29.20; 31.10; 34.4; 42.15; 44.24,
26; generally but not exclusively in prose sections. It includes (a) the
imperative 'hear', (b) 'the object', the word of the LORD, (c) the people
addressed in the vocative: 'O house of Israel' and (d) the messenger
formula 'Thus says the LORD'. The lengthened form of (b) is not
precisely found elsewhere. That this is the addition of the redactor is shown
by the logical unsuitability of the superscription; for the passage that
follows is not directly a word of the LORD but a word of the prophet,
including the praise of the LORD. The superscription belongs therefore
to the time when every collected word, of whatever form, is recognised
as in some sense the word of the LORD, and the tradition of Jeremiah
is the object of preaching to the congregation.
   the signs of the heavens: that which may be innocent (Isa. 7.11;
38.7–8; Mk. 13.4; 24–25; Ac. 2.9, etc.) may become the stock-in-trade
of a pernicious astrology (Am. 5.26). There is little evidence that astrology
was a problem in ancient Israel. But it was common enough among the
Assyrians and Babylonians, and this passage is evidence that it was
constituting a temptation to the superstitious in the period of the exile.
It was 'the way of the nations'.
   3–4. The same technical terms — craftsman, axe, nails — as in Isa.
44.12, where the picture is filled out with more detail.
   5. a cucumber field: cf. Isa. 1.8. Scarecrow or shed in such a field,
presented an image of vulnerable isolation. Somewhat obscure, but the
best that can be done.
   they have to be carried, for they cannot walk: cf. Isa. 46.1–4. In
Babylon the captives had seen the processions of Bel-Marduk and Nebo
his son, god of wisdom. In contrast the LORD carries his people from

birth to old age. The effect of vv. 4–5 is to emphasise the essentially passive character of idols. The tree 'is cut down', 'worked' 'decked' 'fastened' by man. The idols are speechless, are 'carried', impotent to do either good or evil. All this is contrasted with 'the living God' (v. 10) who acted to create, whose speech issues in action (vv. 12–13). Indeed it must be said that if vv. 12–16 were originally independent, they fell to the redactor's purpose aptly.

6. There is none like thee: the theme of the incomparability of God as in Isa. 40.18.

7. King of the nations: this as a comprehensive expression is unique, although near to it are Pss. 22.28; 47.8; 96.10; Zech. 14.9, 16; Mal. 1.14. The worldwide sovereignty of the LORD over the nations was already implicit in the Zion-Theology and in the faith, enshrined in cultic observance, that the LORD would give his people victory over the nations. But as explicit monotheism was only slowly formulated, and most clearly in Second Isaiah, so also the implications of Israel's faith in the cosmic sovereignty of her God were slowly drawn out. Here that faith comes to clear and unambiguous expression. It is the theme of the Oracles against the Nations. See also on vv. 12–16.

9. Tarshish: this place, and 'ships of Tarshish' are usually mentioned in connection with metal. Cf. Ezek. 27.12 where it is the source of iron, tin and lead. Sometimes identified with Tartessus on the Guadalquiver in Spain, it seems to stand for the western Mediterranean, as the source of this luxury trade. **Uphaz** cf. Dan. 10.5 where also it is the source of gold. Targ. and Pesh. understand this as Ophir, whence Solomon sought his gold (1 Kg. 9.28; Job 28.16). This has been located variously in S. Arabia, Africa and India.

10. But the LORD is the true God; he is the living God and the everlasting King: further descriptive titles which sum up the revelation of the character of God over against all substitutes (idols). 'True' (*'emet*) is probably adverbial here — the LORD is God in truth, i.e. over against all false and hollow claims for ineffective idols. 'Truth' is the co-relative of falsehood (*šeqer*, v. 14, and occurs thirty-six times in the book of Jeremiah).

the living God: cf. 2.13 where the same contrast between the true and the false Gods is implied, together with the same affirmation that in his power is life and death. The occurrences of this term, though comparatively few, are determinative for the theology of the Old Testament. Here the preacher is calling into play an expression which has had a long history, already embodied in the oath 'as the LORD lives', i.e. 'Yahweh is living' (cf. 1 Kg. 17.1). Otherwise see Jos. 3.10; Pss. 42.2; 84.2; Hos. 1.10; 2 Kg. 19.4, 16; Dt. 5.26; 1 Sam. 17.26, 36; Jer. 23.36. This is not an exilic invention to counter the claims of false gods. It springs fundamentally from the experience of life as power encountering man personally, of life not merely as existence but as vitality and well-being, of life as more powerful than death. It sums up the encounter between Elijah and the prophets of Baal. It involves a whole series of related ideas: the path of life, the way of life (Jer. 21.8), the book of life, the land of life (Jer. 11.19), the light of life, all expressions occurring in the psalms and the prophets. It comprehends both the beginning and the end of true religion. Here we touch the pulse of the Bible.

the everlasting King: the general meaning of 'everlasting' (*'ōlām*) is long duration, perpetuity, a period of time whose beginning or end are out of sight. The word can therefore refer to ancient time or to the future time or to both. As God is king of the nations, and creator of the cosmos, so also he is lord of the ages. The word is probably adverbial here, though Isa. 40.28 shows that this is not necessarily so. As all other kings are temporary, the LORD alone transcends time. His kingship is, as we say, for ever (cf. Ps. 145.13), as also is his covenant, his word or promise and the messianic age. This is a theological refinement of the 'everlasting God' once worshipped at Beersheba (Gen. 21.33). In Daniel we have the combination: 'he who lives for ever' (12.19). When these descriptive titles are put together, the following is the emphasis of the passage; in contrast to all delusive substitutes, it is the LORD

> who alone is God in truth (the rest are empty pretension),
> who alone is living and the source and giver of life
> (the rest are projections and constructions of men),
> who alone is permanent, the lord of time itself.

So much for the wisdom of men (v. 9)

the earthquakes: see on 10.22 where the noun is translated 'commotion'.

11. This Aramaic verse creates a number of problems. It is surely a gloss, and not an original element in the text. Thus the hymn of praise, beginning in v. 12 with a participle, hardly follows the statement about idol-gods in v. 11, whereas it follows excellently the affirmation that the LORD is the true God in v. 10. If v. 11 is a gloss, it makes sense as a comment on v. 10, the **them** of v. 11 finding its antecedent in 'the nations' of v. 10. The comment is sparked off by the descriptive titles of v. 10 in the context of a discussion of idols. In contrast with the true God who is **living** and **ever-lasting**, the idol gods will perish. Moreover it looks forward to the picture of the creator in v. 12, stating that these idol-gods are they who did not make the heavens and the earth. But it going too far to see in v. 11 an Aramaic summary of vv. 12–16. The undoubted affinity simply explains why it was placed in its present position.

We are left with the enigma of a unique appearance of a verse in Aramaic. We have to find an explanation for the careful preservation of the Aramaic form. Some have assumed that the verse is the beginning of something longer. This is to build guess upon guess. We must deal with what we have and look for a reason why there was a desire to preserve this short Aramaic piece. The best explanation is that it was an incantation, the verb being a jussive: 'Let the gods who did not make the heavens and the earth perish from the earth and from under the heavens.' If this were so, there would be a strong impulse to retain the very words in the language used. Compare the Aramaic words of Jesus preserved in the accounts of several of his healing miracles. Once the verse was incorporated in its present context, its original context would naturally be forgotten. It now makes the required contrast with the true God of v. 10, the Creator of vv. 12–16, and suits well the wider context of a section in which the idol gods are lampooned.

As to the Aramaic, it certainly contains some word-play *ʿbdw* (make) — *yʾbdw* (perish). Some find rhyme and therefore verse. There is certainly some sort of chiasmus. Whether, as Cornill argued, it is possible to find Aramaic forms characteristic of Eastern Aramaic (Babylonian) of the fifth century, is not certain.

12–16. This passage is identical with 51.15–19, where it fits into an oracle of the period of the Babylonian exile. At the same time it is entirely appropriate here, following the affirmation of v. 10 concerning the true, living, permanent God. There is no difficulty in this, once we clearly recognise the way such traditional complexes are built up. The participial opening and the content identify this as psalm-like descriptive praise. On the other hand its derivative character is perhaps betrayed by the fact that **and he makes the mist . . . from his storehouses** is an exact quotation of Ps. 135.7. Psalm 135 is a hymn. It is also one of the psalms which contains a scathing comment on 'the idols of the nations' made of silver and gold, and the work of men's hands. Clearly the whole psalm was in the mind of the redactor. As the section now stands, it offers signs that it belongs to the work of the Jeremiah circle. Thus the 'is stupid' of v. 14 echoes 'they are stupid' of v. 8, and we have already noted the word false (*šeqer*) and punishment (visitation) in v. 14, both characteristic expressions of the tradition. Notable also is the way in which this section fits into the wisdom theme of chapters 8–10. Altogether it looks like the work of an editor in the Jeremiah tradition; and if it is an independent piece it has been incorporated here with great sensitivity. It has been noted above that the theme of the LORD's kingship (sovereignty) over the nations in 10.1–16 is also the theme of the Oracles against the Nations (46–51). The occurrence of these verses in both sections confirms that there is a relationship between them.

12. who established the world by his wisdom, and by his understanding stretched out the heavens. Cf. Prov. 8; Job 28; Ps. 104.24; Wis. 9.2. The *OT* as easily thinks of creation by the *word* of God, (Gen. 1; Ps. 33.6; Isa. 55), or by his spirit (Gen. 1.1; 2.7; Pss. 33.6; 104.30; Job 33.4; Ezek. 37, Wis. 7). Here we have an emphasis characteristic predominantly of the post-exilic wisdom schools; this verse reflects a theological tendency. In this context the creative wisdom of God is implicitly contrasted with the ineffective wisdom of men.

13. When he utters his voice: this translation involves reversing the order of two Heb. words, but it is perhaps the best that can be done with a perplexing text. Word and wisdom are one. **and he makes the mist . . . from his storehouses** = Ps. 135.7. The idea of rain and wind being stored up beyond the sky-vault is part of the accepted cosmology.

14. Every man is stupid and without knowledge: cf. vv. 8, 21, the plain opposite of the true wisdom. This is close to the theme of the whole complex, and the statement that fabricated images are false (*šeqer*) is one of the recurring themes of the whole book.

there is no breath in them: the giving of breath is the creative act of God, cf. Is. 42.5.

15. at the time of their punishment: the divine visitation as a punishment is a characteristic idea in Jeremiah. Cf. 8.12; 46.21; 50.27; 6.15; 49.8; 50.31; 11.23; 23.12; 48.44. It occurs both in poetry and in prose; in what might be thought both early and late passages.

16. The incomparability of the LORD is re-affirmed in language probably derived from the Psalter. For in Pss. 73.26; 119.57; 16.5; Lam. 3.24, the LORD is addressed as 'my portion' or 'possession', often parallel with 'inheritance'. The same combination of the transcendent otherness of God and his close relationship with his people Israel is found in Second Isaiah.

the LORD of hosts is his name: this expression also forms the conclusion of three participial hymns of praise in Amos (4.13; 5.8; 9.6). These three passages are convincingly regarded as post-exilic touches to the Amos tradition from a liturgical source. Here the formal similarity to this passage is strong and suggests a similar liturgical background. Jer. 31.35, (= Isa. 51.15), Jer. 32.28; 33.2; are also participial praise (however brief) with this same ending. Three examples of the phrase in Second Isaiah (47.4; 54.5; 48.2) do not have the participial form, but underline the observation that it has its natural context in an alien situation where confession of the name of Yahweh is necessary. It is reasonable to infer that this hymn type originated in Israel's encounter with the faith of surrounding peoples and in the challenges of the exilic period.

THE PROPHET ARTICULATES THE PEOPLE'S DESPAIR **10.17–25**

The last section of the complex of chapters 7–10 reverts to one of the dominant themes of the material originating in the prophetic work of Jeremiah. There is a reiteration of the alarm-call (vv. 17–18, cf. 4.5–9, 13–17; 8.14); this is followed as in 8.18; 4.10, 19; 6.9, by a prophetic utterance on behalf of the people (vv. 19–21, cf. 4.10, 19–26; 6.9–15; 8.18–9.2) and a renewal of the warning of the Foe from the North (v. 22, cf. 1.14; 4.5–9, 13–17, 29–31; 5.15–17; 6:1–8, 22–26); in v. 23 there is what amounts to a confession of sin; and the section concludes with a prayer for judgment upon the nations (v. 25). This is certainly in keeping with the psalm lament-form on which the whole section is clearly based. We are brought back to the situation of hopelessness and imminent judgment which was rigorously stressed in chapter 9, but which was notably absent in the more didactic chapter 10. There is the verbal connection with chapter 10 in the word 'stupid' (v. 21, cf. vv. 8, 14) but it is doubtful if the catchword principle is the reason for the placing of the section in its present position. It is more likely that 10.1–16 is an exilic redactor's insertion into a complex which represents the first part of the 'many similar words' provided by Baruch.

The section (vv. 17–25) is probably homogeneous. Plainly the sequence of alarm-call followed by lament is too frequent to be simply an editorial device. It must belong to a situation in the activity of Jeremiah. Moreover the personal outcry, as in all previous and subsequent cases, is not a personal grief of the prophet. Here the expression of lament by a representative individual on behalf of the people becomes clear. Thus the situation itself is not a private one, as the image of sickness in v. 19 superficially suggests, but tragically public. The people are under seige, about to be uprooted. The image of the tent in v. 20 is not that of a private

property, but of Israel as a people, like the picture of Mother Zion in
Isa. 54; hence the reference to 'my children'. This is confirmed by the
use of the same image within a similar lament in 4.20. The enemies are
not private enemies but both the stupid shepherds, i.e. the rulers of Judah
(v. 21), and the nations whose turn for judgment must come (v. 25).
Significantly v. 25 = Ps. 79.6–7, unmistakeably a lament of the
community. The threat is not an individual danger but the Foe from the
North (v. 22). Accordingly the confession of sin in vv. 23–24 must also
be on behalf of the people.

At the same time this lament is not of general application like the
laments of the psalter. It is everywhere applied to the particular situation.
Perhaps the most convincing hypothesis is that there were moments in
the ritual of the fasts when a representative individual (in old Israel often
the king, perhaps in post-exilic Israel the high-priest) would express before
the LORD the lament of the people. What Jeremiah did was to seize
these moments creatively and utter the response of the people in such
a way as to reinforce his prophetic message. This hypothesis would explain
both the pattern running through Jeremiah's laments and the number
and variety of them. It would explain also their similarity to the psalm
laments in their general features, and their difference from them in
particular application.

The lament belongs to the actual invasion: it is not simply an
anticipation of it.

(a) The alarm call 10.17–18

Gather up your bundle from the ground: the word 'bundle' is otherwise
not found in Hebrew. It means a bundle of 'goods' and the whole sentence
is a pregnant construction aptly paraphrased in *NEB* 'Put your goods
together and carry them out of the country'. Perhaps 'baggage', i.e. the
situation is similar to that envisaged in Ezekiel's acted sign (Ezek.
12.1–16), miming the consequences of siege. In the first of these alarm-
calls (4.5) Jeremiah had said: 'Go into the fortified cities'. In the second
(8.14): 'Gather together, let us go into the fortified cities and perish there'.
Here he counsels escape to those under siege.

18. I am slinging out: more accurately 'uprooting'.

that they may feel it: the Heb. is literally 'that they may find'. *NEB*
seeks a consistent metaphor 'I will press them hard and squeeze them
dry'. This involves reversing some Heb. letters and is highly dubious.
The best solution is suggested by the Syriac and involves the addition
of the suffix 'me'. The LORD says: 'I will bring distress on them that

they may find me'. This fundamentally is the purpose of his judgments, cf. Isa. 1.18–20.

(b) The suffering of God's people 10.19–21

19. Woe is me because of . . .: for the form, cf. Jer. 4.13, 31; 6.4; (13.27); 15.10; 45.3; (48.46); Isa. 6.5; but never in the Psalms.

my hurt . . . **My wound is grievous**: as in 14.17, where, in the context of lament, the same vocabulary is used of 'the virgin daughter of my people'.

20. My tent . . . **my children**: the prophet makes himself the voice of Zion, considered as the mother, a frequent image in both prophecy and psalms. Cf. 4.20. For the picture of Jerusalem as a tent, whose stakes will never be plucked up, nor its cords broken, see Isa. 33.20.

21. For the shepherds are stupid: 'shepherds' as a figure for kings or rulers is characteristic of Jeremiah. Cf. 2.8; 3.15; 22.22; 23.1, 2, 4; 25.34–36; 50.6.

(c) Renewed warning 10.22

22. Hark, a rumour! Behold, it comes! — a great commotion out of the north country: the word 'rumour' has more elusive overtones than the Heb. They receive a report of the enemy. The Foe from the North has materialised! 'Commotion' is often used in contexts which suggest a return to chaos. It is unwise to read this idea into every occurrence of the word, though the continuation of the verse suggests something very like it. In this instance, cf. 10.10.

a lair of jackals: again a characteristic expression. See on 9.11.

(d) Confession 10.23–24

23. the way of man is not in himself: i.e. it is not in his own power to determine his life. A wisdom-type comment, like Isa. 2.22, but in character with the psalm pattern of the whole. Cf. Pss. 8.4; 143.2; 144.3, etc. It is quoted in IQS XI.10 and IQH XV.12–13.

24. in just measure: perhaps too limited a translation of *mišpāṭ*, which suggests the just judgment of God.

(e) Concluding prayer 10.25

Commentators often deny this to Jeremiah and dissociate it from the section, vv. 17–24; and it is, apart from the addition of 'they have devoured and consumed him' (probably a dittograph to be omitted), identical with Ps. 79.6–7. But the prayer belongs to the liturgical pattern of the whole, with its dialogue character. Jeremiah may well be quoting a well known formula, which was also used in the exilic Ps. 79. No certainty is possible, least of all the certainty that the verse is intrusive.

SECOND SUPPLEMENTARY COLLECTION OF ORACLES 11.1–13.27

THE PREACHING OF THE DEUTERONOMIC LAW 11.1–14

The new complex, like the last, begins with a prose section, in which the teaching is based on a significant event in the life or ministry of Jeremiah. See introduction to chapters 7–20. Whether the author is Baruch or another, the emphasis in all these prose passages is such that certain similarities of Deuteronomic style and theme must not draw attention away from the historical events. These events are all different, and all the springboard for sermons. We have therefore to take seriously the tradition that, at a time unspecified, Jeremiah commended 'the words of this covenant' (v. 2) and himself proclaimed it 'in the cities of Judah and in the streets of Jerusalem' (v. 6).

There ought to be little hesitation in accepting the widespread view that 'the words of this covenant' are to be identified with the substance of the book of Deuteronomy, found in the Temple during repairs in 621 B.C., and the basis of Josiah's reform of the kingdom. It is true that v. 7 refers to the Exodus, and v. 10 to the Sinai covenant, but this is part of the preaching based on the incident. The truth is that the 'words of the covenant' is an expression which occurs, outside Jeremiah, only in Dt. 29.1, 9 and in the account of the Deuteronomic reformation (2 Kg. 23.3). 2 Kg. 23.3 explicitly identifies 'the words of the covenant' with 'the book of the covenant which had been found in the house of the LORD'. Dt. 29.1 explicitly associates these words with the Sinai (Horeb) covenant, and places them in the context of the great redemptive act.

Those who think that Jos. — 2 Kg. constitute a Deuteronomic history compiled in the sixth century on the basis of Dt., can have no doubt that this historian himself identified 'the book of the covenant which had been found in the house of the LORD' (2 Kg. 23.2) with the law of Deuteronomy. When to these considerations it is added that the writer of Jer. 11.1–14 was saturated with Deuteronomic language and ideas, there should be no reasonable doubt that, whatever hesitations of modern scholars, he believed that 'the words of this covenant', preached by Jeremiah, was this same book, viz.: the inner substance of Dt. It is interesting to note how the developments of modern scholarship have rendered cogent an argument which, for John Skinner (*Prophecy and*

Religion, pp. 98–99) was weak, though he came to the same general conclusion. And what he believed is more likely to be correct than the sceptical hypotheses of some of our contemporaries.

No other hypothesis remotely satisfies all the facts and clues as this one does. It is reasonable to conclude that the young prophet, in his early twenties, saw such hope in the promulgation of Dt. (621 B.C.) that he espoused it. The interpretation of Dt. was a scribal task. Clearly Baruch the scribe was educated in this school and learned its characteristic mode of writing. The congruence between Jeremiah's teaching and many of the features of Dt. is already demonstrated. On the other hand 8.8 (q.v.) shows that Jeremiah saw through the activity of many of the scribes whose responsibility was to interpret Dt. but who exploited it and so 'made it into a lie' (*šeqer*).

1. The superscription as in 7.1; 18.1; 21.1.

2. the men of Judah and the inhabitants of Jerusalem: a way of speaking of the whole people of God, as now restricted. See on 4.4. This has become a stereotyped, if not a technical expression, though the precise form here is mainly confined to Jer. (17.25; 18.11; 32.32; 35.13; 36.31).

3. Cursed be the man who does not heed the words of this covenant: the place of cursings and blessings in the idea of covenant is now commonplace. In Dt. see 28.15–68; 30.

this: some have argued that the demonstrative pronoun must have a known antecedent, and since Dt. has not been mentioned, the reference must therefore be to the Sinai covenant. The argument belongs to the study. From the earliest days until now, and in most languages, the demonstrative pronoun is used to conjure up that which is vivid in the narrator's imagination.

4. which I commanded your fathers when I brought them out of the land of Egypt: even so, Dt. was nothing if not the drawing out of the Sinai covenant. Cf. Dt. 4.44–45. 'This is the law which Moses set before the children of Israel; these are the testimonies, the statues, and the ordinances, which Moses spoke to the children of Israel when they came out of Egypt'. The references back to Horeb and the Exodus are frequent.

from the iron furnace: Dt. 4.20; I Kg. 8.51.

So shall you be my people, and I will be your God: a standard expression of the covenant relationship. Cf. Dt. 4.20; 7.6; 27.9; 29.12–13; Jer. 7.23; 24.7; 30.22; 31.1; 32.18; etc.

the oath which I swore to your fathers: cf. Dt. 7.8, 12.

a land flowing with milk and honey: Dt. 6.3; 11.9.

as at this day: Dt. 2.30; 4.20, 38; 6.24; 8.18; 10.15; 29.27; and in the prose sermons Jer. 25.18; 32.20; 44.6, 22, 23.

So be it: cf. the response to the cursings in Dt. 27.15–26.

6. Hear . . . and do them: cf. Dt. 4.1; 5.1; 6.3. The addition of 'do them' is a characteristic Deuteronomic touch.

7. warning them persistently: characteristic of Jeremiah. See on 7.24–25.

8. incline their ear: characteristic of the prose of Jeremiah. See on 7.24. **the stubbornness of his evil heart**: also see on 7.24.

What these comments show is there is some vocabulary very close to, if not identical with, that of the Deuteronomists who provided the introduction and setting of the Deuteronomic law, but that the rest of the vocabulary is characteristic of the prose sections of Jer. We are not at liberty to think simply of a Deuteronomic editing of the Jeremiah tradition; we have a handling of the tradition which is heavily influenced by Dt., but which has its own stamp and purpose.

9. There is a revolt: better 'conspiracy' (*NEB, REB*) cf. Isa. 8.12–15. This may well have double reference, both to the brazen refusal of the people to obey the Deuteronomic requirements, and to the conspiracy of the men at Anathoth against the LORD, but also in all probability connected with the reformation.

10. they have gone after other gods: cf. Dt. 6.14; 8.19; 11.28; 13.3; 28.14 and in the prose of Jer. 7.6, 9; 13.10; 16.11; 25.6; 35.15.

11. Behold, I am bringing evil upon them: see on 5.15 and 6.19, characteristic of Jeremiah.

I will not listen to them: cf. 14.12. This is reinforced by the command to Jeremiah in v. 14 not to intercede.

13.: This describes the situation which the Deuteronomic reformation was intended to remedy. It is reasonable to suppose that this aspect of the reform appealed to Jeremiah as wholly right and necessary.

altars you have set up to shame: both the somewhat clumsy repetition and the absence of this phrase in LXX suggest that this is a familiar comment on the character of Baal. It became a not infrequent pious expedient to substitute the word 'shame' for Baal. See also on Topheth in 7.31. The comparison of vv. 11–13 with the poetic 2.27c–28 has led Holladay to conclude that the prose writer is here using the vocabulary of the poet. Indeed he thinks v. 13 is a secondary insertion from 2.28. We may speak of a reservoir of vocabulary, but not more.

14. do not pray for this people: see on 7.16.

Thus we have established the character of this section. It is akin to the Temple Sermon in chapter 7. It starts from an event in Jeremiah's prophetic activity, but freely develops teaching from this starting-point in the Deuteronomic style. The style is strongly related to that of the editor of the Deuteronomic history (or at least the introductory setting of the Deuteronomic law), but it has sufficient features peculiar to the book of Jeremiah to indicate that the redactor here is a follower of Jeremiah. Baruch in every respect fulfils the conditions, but this must remain hypothesis however attractive.

What then was Baruch, or the preacher (whoever he was) in the school of Jeremiah, intent to say? He wished to make it clear that Israel was under the divine law from the moment of her election, and that the divine will was presently expressed in the law which Jeremiah was commending. The relationship of God with his people depended on obedience to it, and the divine curse hung over those who disobeyed (v. 3). He reminded his hearers that Israel had been constantly reminded of this law throughout her history (v. 7), had as constantly gone her own way and received the consequences in the tragedies of her history (v. 8). Indeed the Deuteronomists wrote the history of Israel (Jos.–2Kg.) to illustrate just this point. Then he turned to his contemporaries. Their repudiation of the divine law was like a conspiracy (v. 9). If one thing stood out in the Deuteronomic law it was the denunciation of apostasy. Yet to other gods the people had turned. So far from destroying altars, they had set them up (v. 13) to Baal. For this reason the full sanctions of the Deuteronomic law must inexorably come upon them (v. 11); and so extreme is the situation that the time for exercise of the prophetic task of intercession is past (v. 14). This sermon is a powerful enforcement upon Israel of her covenant obligations.

EXTERNAL WORSHIP NO PROPHYLACTIC **11.15–17**

The redactor adds a poem to the sermon on the Deuteronomic law, and assimilates it to the context by adding v. 17 which is in the unmistakeable Deuteronomic prose style. In particular he speaks of the people's 'provoking me to anger by burning incense to Baal'. 'provoke' is a Deuteronomic commonplace (Dt. 4.25; 9.18; 31.29; 32.16, 21), occurring nineteen times in the Deuteronomic history and 11 times in the book of Jeremiah. 'burn incense to Baal' is mentioned as a factor in the Deuteronomic reformation (2 Kg. 23.5) and occurs in Jer. 7.9; 11.13, 17; 19.13; 32.29. Thus he links this section explicitly with v. 13 of the previous section. But this is a somewhat forced expedient. For the substance of the poem is not about worship of false gods, but about the uselessness of the normal sacrificial worship of the Temple. In this it is close to the theme of 7.21–26.

The text is unusually corrupt and incomplete; but it may well represent what is left of the actual words of Jeremiah.

15. What right has my beloved in my house: Some change 'beloved' to 'basket' and refer to 24.1. This is an arbitrary and unnecessary conjecture. LXX has 'beloved' in the feminine, and may thereby capture the spirit of the poem. Cf. Isa. 5.1. Jeremiah is saying that Israel has forfeited the privilege of entering the house of God, because of her shameless conduct.

when she has done vile deeds: the Heb. is obscure. Perhaps this correctly expresses the sense demanded by the context. Strictly not 'vile' deeds, but 'adroit', 'clever'.

Can vows and sacrificial flesh avert your doom? For 'vows' Heb. has 'many', which does not make sense. LXX has 'prayers' and to that extent supports 'vows' which is as near as can be found to the Heb. Old Latin has 'fat', preferred by *NEB* which paraphrases: 'Can the flesh of fat things upon the altar . . .' In either case the reference is to the proper worship of the Temple. This worship may be legitimate, but it has ceased to be of any avail.

Can you then exult? Here one feels that the text has been irrecoverably damaged. The *NEB* (but not *REB*) transposes in such a way as to diminish the force of v. 16. Others offer conjectures. It is best to make sense of what is left of the text as in *RSV* above.

16. A green olive tree: an appropriate image because there was apparently an olive tree or perhaps several, along with palms and perhaps myrtles, in the Temple courts. Cf. Ps. 52.8. 'I am like a green olive tree in the house of God', Ps. 92.12–13, Zech. 1.8. The luxuriant tree is a symbol of health. So Israel was meant to be but is no longer.

set fire to it: fire, of course, an image of judgment. The flames will make a great roar. The imagery expresses the central point of the poem.

17. who planted you: the image of the LORD planting his people links this verse with the theme of v. 16. Cf. 2.21, and 24.6 with the converse 'uprooting'. Here the fire imagery of v. 16 must be assumed to apply. Cf. Zech. 11.1.

PERSECUTION OF THE LORD'S SPOKESMAN **11.18–12.6**

This section consists of two laments, 11.18–20 and 12.1–6, which are
linked together and interpreted specifically of Jeremiah's experience at
Anathoth by the redactor. The redactor achieves his purpose by the
addition of the prose passage 11.21–23.

Some interpreters, including McKane, regard vv. 18–19 as prose.
Then it is proper to observe that the prose verses 18–19 and 21–23
are separated by the intrusive poetic lines of v. 20. And this view,
it is claimed, finds confirmation in the observation that v. 20 is
substantially the same as 20.12 from which it could have been borrowed.
But I believe this analysis to be incorrect. Verses 18–19 are a poetic
piece (as set out in *RSV*) though perhaps disturbed, and v. 20,
appropriate in both its homes (both laments), has a refrain-like character
which makes its repeated use intelligible. If then vv. 18–19 are poetry
and linked with v. 20, then we have a lament-like piece, and a second
lament in 12.1–6, separated by the prose vv. 21–23, which interpret
a feature of vv. 18–20.

Jeremiah's use of the lament is significant and needs analysis. Gunkel
distinguished between individual and communal laments. But despite the
obvious distinction between the 'I' and the 'We' form, the distinction
cannot be maintained in any absolute way. Often the 'I' and the 'We'
are interchanged (Pss. 44, 74, 83, 123). Sometimes the 'I' appears in
a psalm which is obviously communal (e.g. Ps. 129). Particularly in the
royal psalms the enemy is a national, not an individual enemy. In fact
the only essential distinction between the 'I' laments and the obvious
national laments is the use of 'I' and 'We'. The conclusion must be that
these psalms are for the most part dealing with similar national situations,
but that those in the 'I' form look at them from the point of view of the
representative individual (often the king), while those in the 'We' form
look at them from the point of view of the people.

There is then no difficulty in interpreting the first of these psalms along
these lines, if it is taken out of context. The 'I' is the representative
individual who experiences as an attack on his own person the threat to
the community. There is frequent reference in the Psalter to the
machinations of opponents (21.11; 35; 41.8; 56.6–9; 64; 140). The image
of the sheep led to slaughter is found in Pss. 44.11, 22 (a communal
lament); the idea of trying the heart or mind in Pss. 7.9; 17.3; 26.2; cf.
also Pss. 66.10; 81.7. This creates a link with 12.3. Indeed v. 20 is
identical with 20.12 and might well be a quotation from a psalm. It

introduces the metaphor of the legal case (*rîb*) which provides another link with 12.1, (cf. 2.9, 29). The prayer for vengeance upon the enemies is entirely in keeping with the *genre* (11.20, 12.3). That the natural reference of these psalms is not in the first instance to a personal and individual problem is confirmed by 12.4, where the land itself seems to be under the curse which its inhabitants have brought upon it.

There is therefore every reason to explain the form and language of these psalms in terms of the lament of the Psalter. At the same time it must be clear that Jeremiah gives to the familiar vocabulary a new and unwonted application. The enemies cannot be national enemies, because Jeremiah believes the defeat of Judah by them is the inevitable judgment. He is forbidden to intercede on Judah's behalf. At the same time the national reference remains (12.4).

The explanation lies in the special use of this language made by Jeremiah. If the enemies are not national enemies, they are the enemies of Jeremiah; but they are the enemies of Jeremiah considered as the LORD's representative. In as much as the wicked do these things unto Jeremiah, they do them unto the LORD. Jeremiah is in this situation a 'sign' to the LORD's people, as Isaiah (8.18) and Ezekiel (24.24) were. It is in this sense that the so-called individualism of these psalms should be understood.

Interpretation is eased if we suppose that, particularly with 12.1–4, Jeremiah is using a known psalm rather than composing afresh. His point is perhaps more pointedly made if he can apply to himself language which would normally be applied to the royal representative of the people. Possibly vv. 5–6, the LORD's answer to the prayer, are such an application of the psalm, though even this language has echoes in the Psalter. The enemies of the LORD have become the LORD's people and they can no longer be called the righteous. The redactor, for the avoidance of all doubt, makes clear what is the new application of these psalms by adding 11.21–23.

The redactor interprets these poems of Jeremiah's encounter with the leaders of the community in his own native village. If the poems are read on their own, they could as easily refer to the time of Zedekiah when attempts were made on Jeremiah's life. Even 12.6 has suggestive parallels in the Psalms (55.12–13; 41.9). But if we are correct in regarding the complexes following chapter 6 as the 'similar words' collected by Baruch and other, then we may expect him to know the correct application of these psalms in the experience of Jeremiah. We may also justly infer that he intended the natural conclusion to be drawn from the fact that he places these poems to follow the preaching of the Deuteronomic law.

From this standpoint we approach the popular view that the persecution of Jeremiah at Anathoth was a consequence of his preaching the Deuteronomic law, or perhaps more correctly, a consequence of his support of the implementation of that law. If there was a sanctuary at Anathoth, it was closed. Henceforth the Jerusalem sanctuary was to be the only place of sacrifice. Priests were unemployed (2 Kg. 23.9). The reformation involved a frontal attack on vested priestly interests. This was part of the anti-Canaanite spirit of Dt. But of course this worship was offered in the name of Yahweh. Priests and scribes defended it (8.8). Their complacency and conservatism were the ground of Jeremiah's continuing polemic against them. No other explanation so convincingly accounts for the hostile reaction of Jeremiah's own people to their gifted son. And if in this matter they regarded him as a false prophet, they were bound by the Deuteronomic law to proceed against him.

These laments form the beginning of those outbursts which collectively have been called the 'confessions' of Jeremiah (11.18–12.6; 15.10–12, 15–21; 17.9–10, 14–18; 18.18–23; 20.7–12, 14–18). This is not an apt term, because only allusively are they a key to the inner consciousness of the prophet. They are from first to last, prophecy in the sense that they register the phenomenon of a prophet poised painfully between the twin prophetic duty of uttering the divine word and representing God's people in prayer and solidarity. Inspired by the psalm laments, these passages have been precipitated by his tortured situation and so become themselves a phenomenon of prophecy. Thus understood they belong to a number of situations in the ministry of Jeremiah. Theoretically the Anathoth connection could be an editorial identification. Equally it could be a true one.

19. if we are to take the language of the psalm literally, Jeremiah for a time remained innocent of the plot against him. He regarded the opening of his eyes as part of the divine communication to him as a prophet (v. 18). He draws out therefore the full implications of the image of the **gentle lamb led to the slaughter**. In Ps. 44 the image is used of Israel's defeated armies! **Let us destroy the tree with its fruit**: we know Jeremiah did not marry. But the Heb. *lehem* probably has the meaning 'sap' here — 'destroy the tree while its sap is in it' (*NEB, REB*).

20. let me see thy vengeance upon them: modern people, to whom the idea of vengeance is anathema, must come to terms with this. It is quite simply the satisfaction of strict justice (v. 20a) such as the

Lord alone knows. Cf. Rom. 12.19. This is typical psalm language, cf. 20.12.

my cause: *rîḇ* i.e. the image of the courts.

21–23. The prose makes the situation explicit and moves into an announcement of the divine judgment (vv. 22–23), which sees the people of Anathoth suffering the punishment of the whole nation.

21. Do not prophesy in the name of the LORD, or you will die by our hand: No doubt the men of Anathoth were sincerely threatening to bring into force the provision of Deuteronomy that a false prophet shall be put to death (Dt. 13.1–15), and that, even if he be a close relative, he is to be publicly stoned (Dt. 13.6–11; cf. Zech. 13.1–6).

22. Behold, I will punish them . . . .: the expression, with participle, is characteristic of the prose style of the book of Jeremiah, as also is the expression **the year of their punishment** (visitation), cf. 8.10; 10.15 q.v., 23.12; 46.21; 48.44; 50.27.

12.1 Righteous art thou: cf. 11.20. This is both the ground of the prophet's hope for justice and the reason for his perplexity that the wicked prosper.

plead my case: cf. 11.20 (*rîḇ*), again the image of the courts.

Why does the way of the wicked prosper? Some scholars think this the earliest expression of fundamental questioning concerning the fortune of the godless in the Old Testament literature. This may be so. But of course such a view begs the question of the date of Pss. 37, 49, 73. Certainly the question became an urgent question in the exilic period as a result of the sufferings involved in the downfall of Judah and the problem it posed for faith. It appeared that the divine promises were no longer of any validity. Not only was the question asked by the faithful, as here and in the book of Job, but the people at large asked it (Isa. 40.27; Ezek. 18.25). The problem here is the way in which the question is formulated. It is stated in the most general terms, as in the wisdom psalms and the discussions of the book of Job. One might expect Jeremiah to formulate it in terms of the hostility of the men of Anathoth, particularly as he is apparently stating his case. It is possible that Jeremiah deliberately subordinates his own situation to the general problem. But it is not likely, since the acid of the problem he faced was connected with the fact that he was a prophet, the LORD's man. It is more likely that Jeremiah is using a known psalm, relating the general situation envisaged in the psalm to his own predicament, and letting the divine answer be spoken to his own predicament in vv. 5–6, so as to give the poem its particular force.

2. they grow: LXX and Old Latin 'they have children'. It is possible that the Heb. 'they go', as in Hos. 14.7, bears the sense 'develop (shoots)' or 'grow'. Cf. 11.19.

3.a. Cf. 11.20b. **3.b.** Cf. 11.19 and 11.20c.

4. The words 'mourn' and 'wither' are words that turn up in the ritual used in time of drought. Cf. Lev. 26; Dt. 28; Jer. 14.

How long: a technical term of the lament, cf. 4.14, 21 q.v.

He will not see our latter end: LXX has 'God will not see our ways', cf. Ps. 73.11. The least disturbance of the Heb. involves the interchange of two Heb. letters and revocalisation to read 'He (Jeremiah or Yahweh?) will not see our ways'.

5–6. These verses provide the divine answer within the lament, and we have suggested that it is here the originality and the main point of Jeremiah's intervention is to be found. And yet again the originality lies partly in the use, at the appropriate moment, of what is already known. For v. 5 looks like a piece of proverbial wisdom:

> **If you have raced with men on foot, and they have wearied you,**
> **how will you compete with horses?**
> **And if in a safe land you fall down,**
> **how will you do in the jungle of the Jordan?**

Here are two sayings, with the same form and the same meaning. If you are unable to cope with a small task, how will you face a really difficult one? If small challenges defeat you, you will not be able to rise to the great ones. As with the wisdom saying quoted in 8.4, it is meant to be self-evident. Anyone can see the truth as stated in the saying. This would be true also of the saying about Jordan's difficult terrain. Though not obvious to us, the point was easily taken by those living in the region.

The truth, thus obvious, is then applicable to a variety of particular situations. We have to ask what this was intended to mean to Jeremiah in his situation. No doubt it was intended even so to have a certain openness of meaning. Nevertheless we may tentatively suggest that Jeremiah is being warned that what he suffers now is as nothing to the terrors he will have to face subsequently. He is having a taste of opposition, which is a foretaste of things to come. Therefore let him face the problem of the prosperity of the wicked by all means. But do not let him over-dramatise the present situation. If he falters now he is not going to be able to endure the man-size tribulations that are on their way.

Thus interpreted the passage fits very well into the sketch of Jeremiah's life that we have assumed. This is an early experience of Jeremiah's. The telling of it is all the more vivid in the reign of Jehoiakim, when the situation is not simply opposition to reform but the dissolution of the kingdom, and the threat to his life comes not from relatives from whom he can escape, but from the king and his ministers who are far more formidable. Indeed the oracle is seen as a prophecy of the judgment to come.

5. you fall down: this may be the right translation if the Heb. *bôṭēaḥ*, normally 'trust', can be regarded as a homonym meaning 'fall flat on the belly'. There are plausible grounds for this meaning, though it is not certain that the more common meaning fails to make sense. *NEB, REB* 'fall headlong'.

Translate: 'If it is only in easy country that you feel safe, what will you do in Jordan's jungle?'. Cf. Targ.

the jungle of the Jordan: lit. 'the pride of Jordan', the fertile, inner valley of the Jordan was an almost impenetrable jungle, associated in 49.19 (= 50.44) and Zech. 11.3 with lions. Cf. Jer. 4.7 and 25.38.

6. Finally the persecutors of Jeremiah are identified as **your brothers and the house of your father**. That the issue between them was a matter of the interpretation of the will of God, and therefore of true and false prophecy, is confirmed by the LORD's injunction to Jeremiah: **believe them not, though they speak fair words to you.** No doubt every effort was made to persuade Jeremiah that he was wrong, that he was not true to the tradition, that he was overthrowing the legitimate order. But Jeremiah has been given his instructions by the LORD, and he is not to believe them or their persuasive arguments. If Jeremiah had proved weak in this preliminary test, he would have had no stomach for the situation that arose fifteen years later. He would have had no independent message. The threat of his family to see 'that his name be remembered no more' (11.19) would have been achieved paradoxically by submission to them.

THE LORD ABANDONS HIS MOST PRECIOUS POSSESSION **12.7–13**

The probability is that the smaller complexes containing 'the similar words' were originally contained in separate scrolls, and that the basic oracles contained in them formed a nucleus upon which other oracles were later deposited. 11.1–12.6 forms such a nucleus, and it is possible to guess the reasons why the succeeding oracles were deposited in their present position. This section (12.7–13) clearly belongs to the period when a foreign army was either about to devastate the land, or had already done so. Its connection with the preceding oracles is thematic, in line with the observed practice of redactors, and not chronological.

The section must first be examined independently of its context. It is a self-contained poem, in varied rhythm with at least five lines in the 3:2 *qinah* metre. It is a lament without accustomed lament vocabulary, on the lips of the LORD, concerning the abandonment and desolation of his most cherished possession, his own people. This, the general character of the poem, sufficiently decides the question of the tenses. They are not prophetic perfects, predicting a future invasion. They describe what has already happened from the standpoint of the LORD himself. Many commentators identify the event with the invasion by neighbouring peoples described in 2 Kg. 24.2. In 602 B.C. Nebuchadnezzar sent against Judah, as a punishment, 'bands' of Syrians (or Edomites), Moabites and Ammonites. It is thought that these better fit the description of **birds of prey** (v. 9) and **many shepherds** (v. 10) than do the Chaldeans alone. But it is impossible to be sure. It is always unwise to press metaphors too precisely, and if the poem were composed after the Babylonian invasion, it could well be a comprehensive description of the series of onslaughts. On the other hand, the redactor who set vv. 14–17 to follow this section, probably thought in terms of Israel's neighbours.

What stands out in this poem is the set of descriptions of God's people. They are 'my house' (v. 7) unless this refers to the Temple; 'my heritage' (vv. 7, 8, 9); 'my vineyard' (v. 10); 'my pleasant portion' (v. 10). All these expressions have strong overtones (see below), and the possessive adjective stresses that God's people are his special and cherished possession. It is this cherished child of his own that he is forsaking. Thus Jeremiah underlines indirectly the enormity of her offence.

7. I have forsaken my house, I have abandoned my heritage: 'heritage' in the Deuteronomic writings is a regular description of Canaan, the promised land, and of Israel as the subject of the promises. This makes it marginally more likely that 'house' here refers to Israel rather than to the Temple. On the other hand 'house' and **beloved** act as catchwords associating the section with 11.15 where the 'house' is clearly the Temple. Some uncertainty must remain, which the redactor felt no need to clarify.

my soul: here a strong way of expressing the *personal* relationship. Translate simply 'my beloved'. There is no suggestion that the LORD has a *nephesh*!

therefore I hate her: probably we ought not squeamishly to underestimate the personal disposition thus described. On the other hand love and hate are used to indicate election and rejection. (Mal. 1.3; Rom. 9.13).

9. like a speckled bird of prey: as the Heb. stands, this must be the translation. The meaning then is that Judah is like a splendid bird encircled and set upon by other birds of prey. It is a case of the biter bit. However, some scholars think that the past participle is really a noun meaning 'hyena'. The LXX reads 'hyena's lair' and the rendering hyena is suggested if not confirmed by cognate words in Ethiopic and Syriac. Hence *NEB, REB* 'Is this land of mine a hyena's lair?' This involves the omission of the first bird of prey as added by suggestion of the second. The image is then slightly different, though the meaning is not significantly changed.

bring them to devour: with a slight change found in some MSS and implied in Vulg. and LXX: 'come to the feast'.

10. Many shepherds have destroyed my vineyard: it is characteristic of the book of Jeremiah to refer to kings as shepherds. 'Vineyard' the image of God's people, skilfully used by Isaiah (3.14; 5.1-7; cf. Jer. 2.21; 5.10).

11. it mourns to me: better, 'to my sorrow'.

12. no flesh has peace: exactly the form of the redactoral comment in Isa. 48.22 'there is no peace to the wicked'. 'No flesh' means 'nobody'.

the sword of the LORD: no doubt a much used, ancient cry, usually suggesting triumph over Israel's enemies, but here, ironically, the opposite. See 47.6 and cf. Jg. 7.20. Duhm, Volz, Rudolph and others have omitted the phrase, for the sake of the metre. This is unnecessary and to be resisted.

13. The change of image here has worried commentators from Duhm onwards. But if this were a passage which belonged to a situation of drought and not military disaster, who would put it here rather than with one of the drought oracles? The truth is that the image is totally appropriate. The passage in which Yahweh declares he has abandoned his most beloved possession to destruction ends with the summary judgment that his people have reaped what they have sown!

THE FUTURE OF ISRAEL'S NEIGHBOURS **12.14-17**

This section is in prose, with sufficient echoes of familiar expressions from the book of Jeremiah to suggest that it is in the nature of a late tidying up operation. Thus the word **heritage** in v. 14 links it with the previous section, and provides a catchword connection. The **Behold** with participle to express future judgment in v. 14 has been noted as a characteristic idiom. The 'plucking up' and 'building' harks back to 1.10, q.v. 'Swear by my name, as the LORD lives', links with 4.2; 5.2, 7; 7.9.

Though the language has these links with the context, the theme is new and strange. In the previous sections, the neighbours, or the all powerful Foe from the North, are called upon to be the agents of judgment upon an evil Judah. Here it is the neighbours who are evil, who are themselves to be blocked out of their land, and subsequently, on condition of obedience, to be restored. Cf. the oracles on these neighbours in Chapter 47–49 and the hint of the restoration of Moab in 48.47 and of Ammon in 49.6.

It is very difficult to imagine Jeremiah himself proposing the condition that these neighbours shall **diligently learn the ways of my people** (v.16), when he has so ruthlessly exposed these ways as false. Much more probably a redactor, meditating upon the total work of Jeremiah, when the judgment is past, completes the teaching of Jeremiah for his own time, in terms of Jeremiah's vocabulary. Thus the exhortation that the nations shall 'learn the ways of my people' is in conscious contrast with the exhortation to Judah: 'Learn not the way of the nations' (10.2). But few would deny that the redactor, in anticipating the conversion of foreigners (cf. 3.17, q.v.), is drawing out the inner logic of Jeremiah's understanding of the nature and purpose of God.

14. **my people Israel**: i.e. the people of God, not exclusively the northern kingdom.

I will pluck them up from their land . . . :i.e. exile.

15. **and I will bring them again**: 'I will cause them to return', i.e. restoration from exile.

16. **The ways of my people**: i.e. the faith of Israel, to be contrasted with 'the way of the nations' (10.2).

they shall be built up in the midst of my people: the future Israel will consist of Jews and proselytes. It seems clear that the section belongs to the post-exilic era when these questions were matters of urgent decision.

THE SIGN OF THE WAISTCLOTH **13.1–11**

At first sight this section appears to be a straightforward description, written by Jeremiah in the first person, of a typical piece of prophetic symbolism. Closer scrutiny reveals difficulties which have led to a variety of interpretations. The vocabulary contains sufficient elements characteristic of the Jeremiah corpus to suggest that this is not a free Deuteronomic sermon: e.g. 'who stubbornly follow their own heart'. In fact the only strongly Deuteronomic cliché is in v. 10: 'have gone after other gods to serve them and worship them'. (Cf. 11.10, q.v.) All this is consistent with the authorship of Baruch or someone like him, whose Deuteronomic touches we have often observed in material otherwise coming from Jeremiah or composed by himself. It is sometimes argued that this section can owe nothing to Baruch because it is in the first person. This is by no means certain. If Baruch could transmit and round off poetic oracles of the prophet, he could also transmit and doctor to their new purpose narratives in the first person, cf. 1.7, 12, 13; 12.9; 11.6; etc. The first person of the formula may be suggested by the first person in the narrative itself. We may therefore regard this section as the free transcript of a narrative going back to an account given by Jeremiah of a prophetic sign whose significance lies not in the event but in the prophecy.

But then a new difficulty arises. Is this something which Jeremiah actually performed? Or is it something which he saw in a vision (like Zechariah) and then recounted? If this is an act performed by Jeremiah, then we have to make sense of the action itself. He is commanded to buy a linen waistcloth and to wear it. The subsequent interpretation informs us that this denotes the closeness of the LORD to his people (v. 11). It is not to be dipped in water. Probably this emphasises that, to begin with, it is fresh, new and unspoilt, like the earliest relation of the LORD with his people (cf. 2.2; Hos. 2.15; Ezek. 16.7–14), and is intended to be contrasted with its later spoiling. Then Jeremiah is ordered to go to Perath, which is the usual term in the Old Testament for the river Euphrates. There he hides the waistcloth in 'a cleft of the rock'. After an indefinite period he is ordered to go to Perath again and dig it up. He finds it ruined and useless.

In vv. 8–11 the people of Judah and Jerusalem are likened to the waistcloth; but whereas the significance of the waistcloth is explained, no other details of the sign are interpreted. Perath, for instance, must have some meaning; otherwise the sign could have been performed without any mention of Perath. Usually this is thought to be a crucial element in the sign. If Euphrates is meant, then Jeremiah is saying either that the people will be taken to exile, and there they will deteriorate, or that they will be corrupted by political and religious alliances with Babylon. When they are, so to speak, dug up, they will be no use.

Some interpreters think that Jeremiah really did go to the Euphrates, perhaps in the time of Jehoiakim, and bury the waistcloth there; then, after a period he returned there and dug it up. But this defies credulity. The journey took Ezra (7.9) nearly four months. This would be an odd sign to the people of Judah who would not see what Jeremiah did. And seeing is of the essence of the prophetic sign. Moreover there is no other hint of such a journey by Jeremiah. Is it conceivable that the observant and sensitive Jeremiah would be so untouched by the experience that not a suspicion of direct knowledge would enter into his prophecies concerning the Babylonian invasion and the exile? It seems that the idea of a prophetic sign enacted in Babylon must be firmly ruled out of court.

Two alternatives are normally canvassed. The first is that there was a river Perath or a place called Perath in Palestine. Some point to the present Khirbet el-Farah, mentioned in Jos. 18.23, about four miles northeast of Anathoth. The objection to this interpretation is that the choice of Perath becomes meaningless, and contributes nothing to the sign. It might then have been performed anywhere. Moreover Perath, linked with the word 'river' in every other instance, refers to the Euphrates.

The second expedient is to regard the whole episode as a vision of a sign performed in Babylon. But this too does not seem to be a sound answer to the problem. The visions of Zechariah are explicitly called visions and are never prophetic signs enacted in vision by the prophet. If this were a vision, there would be every reason to call it such, particularly as a series of prophetic signs are recorded, in exactly similar terms, which are plainly not visions but signs enacted by Jeremiah.

Of course it is possible that a wady in Palestine had ironically been given the name of Euphrates. There are numerous British villages and cities whose names are repeated in the United States and former African colonies like Sierra Leone. But the best solution is the most obvious, and being at the end of our noses, has eluded us. Just as Jeremiah took a loincloth and put upon it (for the purpose of the sign) the meaning of the intimacy between the LORD and his people; so (for the purpose of the sign) he selected a wady and designated it Euphrates so that it might stand for the place of exile, or at least the Babylon with whom the complacent in Judah thought alliance was possible.

On this interpretation it is not necessary to suppose that Jeremiah was speaking differently in chapter 29. Then he hid the cloth in a cleft of the rock. This expression occurs in Isa. 7.9 (cf. also Jer. 16.16) of the clefts found in the typical precipitous ravines of the wildest terrain in Palestine. It there (and in the other instances also) describes the most withdrawn and grim, inaccessible places. This is essentially the geography of Palestine and not of the Euphrates. Jeremiah went to one of the rocky valleys whose wady ran down into the fertile country. He took people with him. He said in effect, 'Let this be Euphrates. Now I will bury this cloth. Observe that it is unspoilt. Come back with me later and see what happens to it.' What happened to it signified the corruption of the people by the Babylonian contagion (cf. 2.18). This then is essentially a prophetic sign, performed in Palestine, probably in the reign of Jehoiakim, either predicting the exile and its effect on the people of Judah, or enforcing the corrupting influence of Babylon on Jewish policies.

1. a linen waistcloth: this is the right translation. It is more than a girdle. Cf. the cloth worn by Elijah (2 Kg. 1.8). Elijah's was made of skin. Priests wore linen cloths (Lev. 16.4), no doubt because they were cool.

10-11. It is possible that these verses represent an undatable but subsequent interpretation of an otherwise immaterial element in the symbolism of the narrative. Its Deuteronomic character is shown by a comparison of the last line with Dt. 26.19. That is merely to guess how the complete section came to be what it is.

11. that they might be for me a people, a name, a praise and a glory: the language of election.

THE WINE OF WRATH **13.12-14**

Again this section has no clear connection with what precedes or follows. It is prose, without any Deuteronomic phraseology, but with some elements of the prose style characteristic of this book, e.g. 'Behold' with participle to express threat of judgment; the list of kings, priests, prophets and people (cf. 1.18; 2.26; 4.9; 8.1; 18.17, 25. This list occurs both in prose and poetry). The expression 'sit on David's throne' (17.25; 22.2, 4.30; 29.16; 33.17; 26.30; also recurs in prose and poetry. This occurs in the Deuteronomic history, but also in Isa. 9.7). 'I will not pity, or spare, or have compassion', (cf. 21.7). This section is associated with the previous one by means of the word 'destroy them': *mēhašḥîtām*, cf. vv. 7, 9 'was spoiled' (*nišḥat*) and 'so will I spoil' (*'ašḥît*), on the catchword principle.

The most popular explanation of the passage is that Jeremiah takes up a proverb: **Every jar shall be filled with wine** (v. 12) which, it is imagined, was used by tipplers as a sort of drinker's wisecrack. But it is by no means easy to see where the wisecrack is, or what might be the meaning of the proverb, even if it is admitted that it is a banal one. The explanation may well be more obvious and more urgent. Is it not plausible to associate the saying with a good vintage? Jeremiah observes the pleasure of the people and their complacency (cf. 8.20). He publicly declares that 'every jar shall be filled with wine'. So good will be the vintage that there will not be any empty jars left over. It now makes sense that it is Jeremiah who first makes the observation. The reaction of his hearers is 'We know that, so what?' This now gives Jeremiah his lead. He reaffirms the judgment that is to come in terms of drinking the cup of wrath.

Of course the vintage festival, which we know as the autumn feast of Tabernacles and which was in all probability the New Year Festival, involved drunkenness. And it is possible that Jeremiah had these drunken orgies in mind, as Isaiah did in Isa. 28.7–8. But it is much more likely, in view of his development of the prophecy in v. 14, that he was using a theme already known, 'the cup of the wine of wrath'. Indeed he uses this theme perhaps more classically in 25.15–29, q.v. Cf. The cup of reeling in Ps. 60.3 ('Thou hast given us wine to drink that made us reel'); Ps. 75.8; Hab. 2.16 ('Drink. . .and stagger'), Nah. 3.11; Lam. 4.21; Isa. 51.22 ('the cup of staggering, the bowl of my wrath'); Zech. 12.2. So what Jeremiah does is to turn an observation about the prospect of a splendid wine harvest into a prophecy that the whole nation will indeed drink wine plentifully, but it will be the wine of the wrath of the LORD, and their drunken staggering will be the chaos of judgment. All this is part of the image of the 'cup' as it is received in the New Testament (Mk. 10.38; 14.36). Such a prophecy might belong to any period in Jeremiah's ministry before the Babylonian invasion.

12. Jar: a storage jar, the largest of which (as so far found) might hold up to ten gallons.

14. I will dash them one against another, fathers and sons together: no doubt as jars might be broken into pieces. The destruction of family relationships is a familiar theme in the prophetic pictures of judgment. The reference to 'fathers and sons' might be a reason, in the mind of the redactor, for setting this section in the context of the laments concerning the family at Anathoth. Our guides have made heavy weather of this verse, doubting whether the images of intoxication (v. 13) and shattering (v. 14) can be credibly combined. But as so often the unity is in the thought. The interpretation above makes complete sense. The shattering is the inexorable consequence of drinking the cup of wrath.

FOUR BRIEF ORACLES **13.15–27**

The complex of chapters 11–13 is now brought to completion by the addition of four brief oracles. Increasingly we see that the normal method of compilation is not that of scissors and paste, but of building upon a nucleus. The redactor arranges the material with great care, according to his own principles; but tends to put together at the end material which has either come to hand subsequently or has not obviously fallen to his purpose. This expedient is particularly clear in the first half of the book of Isaiah, where such additions are fragmentary or sometimes pastiches, composed of verses and expressions from the prophet's known teaching.

In this case the four oracles appear, on the face of it, to be complete, though they are short. They also seem to be independent, though related by their implicit background situation. Verses 15-17 seem to have the character of a last warning before disaster, spoken by the prophet to the people whom he addresses in the second person plural. Verses 18-19 are addressed to Jehoiachin and Nehushta while Jerusalem was besieged and shortly before its fall in 597 BC. Verses 20-22 are addressed to Zion the mother in the moment of her anguish, when the Foe from the North is coming.

Verses 23-27 are variously addressed, but amount to a last despairing appeal to Jerusalem to turn from her uncleanness. All are in poetic form, with varied metre, all with some element of the *qinah* rhythm. The first poem particularly appears to be of high poetic quality.

(a) Final Warning (13.15-17)

The warning is against complacency in the face of the disaster that is now inevitable. The disaster is depicted in the image of darkness and prompts the compelling picture of stumbling 'on the mountains of twilight'. In place of the daylight for which the people expectantly wait, the LORD will bring gloom and deep darkness. The 'gloom' (*ṣalmāwet*, v. 16) is literally 'the shadow of death'. This may be a Hebraic mode of expressing the superlative, but it always retains the overtone of death. (Cf. Ps. 23.4; Job 38.17). The gloom is that of death, and modern translations often miss the suggestiveness of the language. For a similar use of these terms and of the imagery, but in terms of the hope of salvation, see Isa. 8.22-9.2.

17. my soul: i.e. 'I myself'. The prophet speaks of his own anguish, as he is torn between the horror he feels for the people he represents (cf. 9.18) and the grief he feels in the heart of the LORD for whom he speaks (cf. 8.18; 9.1).

my eyes . . . run down with tears: as 9.18; 14.17.

Because the LORD's flock has been taken captive: this must be a prophetic perfect and might be translated 'will have been taken captive'. Otherwise the warning of the darkness to come is meaningless and the suggestion that it might be avoided is superfluous. If there is any significance in the placing of this section before vv. 18-19, it would be best explained as belonging to the period immediately before Jehoiachin was taken into captivity in 597 B.C. If not, the oracle is too general to be dated. Too much should not be made of the word 'flock', as though it provides the clue to the whole section, indicating that we are to think of 'shepherds' on the mountains. The key thought is not shepherds, but the onset of darkness, when light is expected, at dawn.

(b) The exile of Jehoiachin and Nehushta (13.18–19)

These verses are capable of two interpretations. The one takes the perfects as referring to an event which has happened. Jehoiakim died in 598 B.C., probably during Nebuchadnezzar's siege of Jerusalem. He was succeeded by his eighteen year old son Jehoiachin. Perhaps because of his youth, the queen mother, who is mentioned by name in 2 Kg. 24.8, exercised powerful influence. That she is referred to here does not mean that Jehoiachin was not married. After only three months, Jerusalem was taken, and Jehoiachin, with his family and leading officials, was deported to Babylon, where he continued to live as deposed king. Presumably Jeremiah refers to this humiliation when he counsels:

18. Take a lowly seat. Certainly, on this interpretation Jehoiachin must be in Babylon, since v. 9 declares that 'all Judah is taken into exile'; and if one perfect is to be taken in this way, all must be interpreted in the same way.

But this interpretation tends to make the oracle otiose. What is the point of saying to or concerning a king who has suffered Jehoiachin's fate, 'Take a lowly seat'? Where is the power of a prophecy which shouts after the horse when the stable door is unlocked? Observe how the oracle immeasurably gains in power and penetration when the perfects are interpreted as prophetic perfects. Observe also how the theme comes closer to that of vv. 15–17. Verses 15–17 are addressed to the complacency of the people; vv. 18–19 to the pride of the royal house.

First, it makes sense that Jeremiah is to **say to the king and the queen mother.** They were *there*, in the besieged city, to be spoken to!

Second, **Take a lowly seat** is seen to contain forceful irony. The Hebrew is literally: 'Make low and sit', the second imperative has adverbial force, i.e. 'sit humbly' (the opposite of 'walk tall'). The word 'sit', in association with royalty, means sit *upon a throne*. 'One who sits', with elipse of 'on a throne', is sometimes used in poetry to mean 'king', e.g. Am. 1.5. Jeremiah is therefore addressing Jehoiachin in full possession of his royal throne, and he is saying: 'You who enjoy all the pride of sovereignty,

begin to sit with the humility of a man who is going to lose everything
and be banished from his kingdom.'

your beautiful crown *will have been* taken from your head. Judah will
have been taken into exile!

Jeremiah sees it all in his mind's eye as having happened. To say this
to Jehoiachin before it happens is prophecy. To say it afterwards is beating
the man when he is down. At one point only does Jeremiah refer to what
has already happened—**The cities of the Negeb are shut up, with none
to open them** (v. 19). The meaning is not obvious. It could mean that
they have closed their gates for protection, realising perhaps that they
can count on no assistance from outside. But the composite phrase 'shut
up . . . and open', occurs frequently enough to suggest it has idiomatic
meaning, cf. Job 12.14; Isa. 22.22. To have the right or the power to
open the doors is to have sovereign authority. Cf. also the power given
to Cyrus 'to open doors before him, that gates may not be closed' (Isa.
45.1).

The suggestion may therefore be that the cities of the Negeb have
already lost their independence. Jerusalem's turn is coming. Martin Noth
remarks, 'It may be inferred from this that the Negeb was lost to the
kingdom of Judah at this time and the southern frontier running north
to the latitude of Hebron established, which is well known to us as the
southern frontier of the later province of Judah in Persian times' (*The
History of Israel*, 1959, p.283). The Edomites no doubt took over the lost
territory: hence their special unpopularity, in Judaean eyes, in this period.

(c) The tribulation of unclean Zion (13.20–22)

This poem contains some difficult Hebrew which in part defies solution.
But the overall meaning is clear. Although 'your eyes' is in the second
person plural, the oracle as a whole is addressed to someone in the second
person singular feminine. Some have supposed that the queen mother
is the object of the oracle. But analogy suggests that the sexual imagery
of v. 22 is more likely to be applied to Jerusalem. Certainly the LXX
understood Zion to be addressed, and added the vocative 'Jerusalem'
in v. 20. Verses 26–27 take up the same imagery, and there the application
is unmistakeably to Zion. As so often in prophecy, therefore, Zion is
addressed as the mother. This explains the easy change to 'your eyes'
in the plural, for this kind of transition often occurs as the poet thinks
now of Zion the mother, now of the individual members of the
community.

20. those who come from the north: Literally 'see them (unspecified) coming from the north'. On the significance of the north, see on 1.13–16. This is best interpreted, like the previous section, of that brief and terrible three months when Jehoiachin was king. The enigmatic, ominous prophecies of the Foe from the North are now being fulfilled. Jeremiah does not have to identify the foe, only to point to 'them' coming.

Where is the flock that was given you: the image of the shepherd as king implies that his people are his flock. (cf. Isa. 40.11; Zech. 10.3). Here the metaphors are mixed. The flock has been entrusted to Zion the mother. Always the prophets are intent on the meaning, not on the consistency of their images.

21. The first part of this verse is corrupt beyond recovery. No convincing emendations have been proposed. But it is just possible to make sense of the verse without resort to the arbitrary transpositions of *NEB, REB,* and others. Translate: 'What will you say when they appoint over you (and you taught them) teachers to be head over you'. The difficulty then is to know what 'and you taught them' can mean. Could this be an ironical reference to the rebellion against Babylonian sovereignty which made Nebuchadnezzar send troops against Judah? Jeremiah has already counselled Judah not to learn the way of the nations (10.2). A later preacher thought of Israel's neighbours diligently learning her ways (12.16). Jeremiah implies that what Judah has to teach has come like a boomerang on her own head. Caution is necessary because there can be no certainty about the correctness of the text.

friends to you: here 'teachers'. For this translation of *'allupîm* cf. Prov. 2.17 and Jer. 3.4 *NEB* has 'leaders'—'What will you say when you suffer because your leaders cannot be found?' This involves not only arbitrary transposition but also the stretching of the meaning of *pāqad* which normally had the meaning 'to be missing' only in the *niphal.*

a woman in travail: this metaphor of suffering and travail (cf. Mic. 4.9, 10; Isa. 13.8; 21.3; 42.14; Jer. 6.24; 22.23; 30.6; 49.24; 50.43; Ps. 48.7) is of course particularly appropriate here.

22. Why have these things come upon me?: the question of faith which is increasingly asked in this period. See on 12.1.

the greatness of your iniquity: the Heb. *'āwōn* is, of the many terms for sin, the one which comes nearest to our notion of guilt.

your skirts are lifted up, and you suffer violence: literally 'your heels be made to suffer violence'! A notable example where a cognate language comes to the rescue, to establish a homonym here and in Job 15.33, the word *hamas* having the meaning 'strip, make bare'. Translate therefore:

'your skirts are torn from you and your heels (limbs) laid bare'. The image is a sexual one, indicating extreme public humiliation.

(d) Can the Ethiopian change his skin? (13.23–27)

This poem has a proverb-like opening and seems to develop by association of ideas from this point. The rhetorical question, addressed to the people of Judah in the second person plural, is intended to be so obvious that it answers the subsequent implied question: Is it possible for the people of Judah to do good when they are accustomed to do evil? This is of course poetry, and the image is not to be pressed to the extreme. Jeremiah is not saying that Judah is born to be evil and that repentance and cleansing are intrinsically impossible. Otherwise it is the LORD who addresses Judah, because it is he who in v. 24 makes the threat of judgment. In v. 25 it is the LORD who continues to speak, but he now addresses Judah in the second person singular, i.e. as Zion the mother. The accusation is the now familiar one of trusting in lies (*šeqer*); the punishment a repetition of the sexual metaphor of the previous poem.

Some scholars (Rudolph, Weiser, Bright, Nicholson) have accordingly transposed this verse to the previous poem, but this is a most unimaginative procedure. It is much more likely that the existence of the same metaphor in the two poems helped the redactor to decide to set them together. The poem ends with a despairing cry, addressed to Jerusalem, asking how long it will be before she will become clean. This artistically rounds off the poem, since it draws out further the implications of the proverbial opening, and links with the metaphor of shame in v. 26. The poem does not communicate the sense of imminent judgment, or judgment now in process of its terrible fulfilment, like the previous oracles. It may well belong to a slightly earlier period. But it does read like a despairing reflection on the obdurate character of Judah, perhaps prompted by the previous oracles. We can therefore see what the redactor was about when he closed this complex of oracles (chapters 11–13) on this note.

24. I will scatter you like chaff: a commonplace image cf. Isa. 40.24; 41.2; Ps. 83.13; cf. also Isa. 5.24; 33.11.

25. This is your lot, the portion I have measured out to you. LXX has 'the portion of your disobedience to me'. This would be explained if the Heb. read *miryēk* instead of *middayik*. It appears to be more straightforward Heb. and marginally better sense.

26. I myself will lift up your skirts over your face: cf. v. 22; Ezek. 16.8; Lam. 1.9; and almost the same expression in Nah. 3.5.

27. neighings: a metaphor of animal sexuality, cf. 5.8.

How long will it be before you are made clean?: literally, 'Will you not be made clean? after how long yet?' It is not certain that the Heb. is translatable as it stands. *mātai 'ōd* is surely the *'ad mātai* 'how long?' of the lament. *'aḥ°re* 'before' may be the remains of *t°'aḥ°rî*, so yielding the translation: 'how long will you delay?' (*NEB*). Or there may be dittography. Translate simply: 'will you be made clean? How long?' Through the uncertainties, the prophet's profound and despairing desire for Zion's return to her LORD, even at the last moment, finds expression.

THIRD SUPPLEMENTARY COLLECTION OF ORACLES 14.1–17.27

The new complex begins with a superscription which betrays the hand of an editor. **The word of the LORD which came to Jeremiah** (14.1) is appropriate to what follows, only on the basis of what might be called a word of God theology. The LORD is not predominantly the speaker in these oracles; but all is now recognised as the word of the LORD. Thereafter we encounter the familiar build-up of oracles on the foundation of a nucleus.

The nucleus in this case concerns drought. Almost certainly, as in Joel, the drought was the occasion of a national fast day and expression of penitence. It is possible that it was on such an occasion that Jeremiah found his audience crowded in the Temple and seized the opportunity to transform the expected and uniform prophetic assurances into warnings and predictions of judgment. This would explain his refusal to intercede (vv. 11–12; 15.1) his polemic against the prophets (vv. 13–16) and his lament (vv. 19, 22).

None of these is explicable as liturgy. They are explicable as Jeremiah's intervention in a liturgy. When the moment comes to record this intervention, it is Jeremiah's prophetic contribution, not the details of well known fast-day order, which are set out. And as Baruch or another sets out Jeremiah's words, he also builds upon them, using the nucleus so as to deposit upon it 'similar words'. The result is that we are now unable to identify precisely what Jeremiah said on the occasion of the drought and what was added subsequently, still less identify a liturgy.

After two complexes containing oracles anticipating the very moment of judgment, we are here taken back probably to an earlier period in the ministry of Jeremiah. The occasion is a drought, which is regarded as a sign of judgment to come, in much the same way as Joel saw the plague of locusts as a sign of the Day of the LORD. The associated oracle,

14.11–16, speaks in general terms of sword and famine; and the working out of judgment, of which the drought is a sign, seems very much in the future. There is in 15.19–21 a reaffirmation of Jeremiah's call. Chapter 16 also opens with an episode which must belong to the very beginning of Jeremiah's ministry. Certainly in this complex, there is a setting together of some oracles appropriate to an early period in Jeremiah's life.

LAMENT OF THE PEOPLE IN TIME OF DROUGHT **14.1–10**

Verses 1–6 describe a situation of drought such as occurred not infrequently in the climatic conditions of Palestine. Occasionally a drought would reach extreme proportions, as in the time of Elijah (1 Kg. 17.1), and again in the time of Elisha (2 Kg. 8.1). In all probability a national fast would be proclaimed. (See Gunkel, *Einleitung in die Psalmen* (1933), pp.117–121.) That fasts were called in times of national emergency is clear from Jer. 36.9. Jehoiakim proclaimed such a fast in the desperate circumstances of December 604 B.C.; Jeremiah used the occasion as the opportunity to have his collected oracles read to the assembled people. According to the book of Jonah, when Nineveh was threatened with destruction, the people proclaimed a fast (Jon. 3.5), a story which no doubt reflects Jewish practice. Cf. also 1 Sam. 7.6.

The nearest parallel to the calling of a fast in time of natural disaster is in the book of Joel. This offers a number of parallels of practice and vocabulary with Jer. 14.1–10. The locust plague has the same effect as drought in destroying all the vegetation, and imperilling life. There is a similar description of the disaster, though in the setting of exhortation to fast. The equivalent of the confession of vv. 7–9 is an invitation to repentance (Jl. 2.12–14). In Jl. there follows the representative intercession of the priests (Jl. 2.17), in terms close to those of Psalm laments. In Jer. 14 the prophet is explicitly commanded not to intercede (vv. 11–12; cf. 15.1). Here the comparison ends. In Jl. there is assurance of restoration (2.18–27):

> Be glad, O sons of Zion and rejoice in the LORD, your God;
> for he has given the early rain for your vindication,
> he has poured down for you abundant rain,
> the early and the latter rain, as before. (Jl 2.23)

This is precisely the assurance that the people expected to get from Jeremiah, but which he refused and, in his time, only false prophets would give. The fact that fasting is mentioned in v. 12 may confirm the probability that the context of Jeremiah's lament is such a fast publicly proclaimed. It is however premature to conclude that the lament and what follows is a liturgical document. Oddly enough there is no single psalm in the *OT* book of Psalms which belongs to such a situation of famine, nor any comparable to this lament of Jeremiah's. Hymns celebrate the power and goodness of the LORD who gives the rain (Ps. 65.9–10), and there is evidence that the autumn (New Year) feast of Tabernacles was believed to be the supreme means of guaranteeing the rain for another year (Zech. 14.17).

Perhaps the most we can conclude is that chapters 14–15 contain material which was the subject of Jeremiah's prophetic intervention on the fast day, together with some exposition written up with some freedom perhaps long after the event, in the conviction that all was the word of the LORD through Jeremiah to his people. This is essentially a lament of the people, expressed on their behalf, by the prophet in his capacity as their representative before the LORD.

There is clear evidence that confession of sin accompanied fasting. When Samuel called the people to Mizpah, we read that 'they fasted on that day', and said: 'We have sinned against the LORD' (1 Sam. 7.6). David's repentance was accompanied by fasting (2 Sam. 12.16). Lev. 26, which sets out the consequences of breaking the covenant, and includes among them famine, pestilence and the sword (as in Jer. 14.12; 15.2), enjoins confession as the condition of restoration (26.40–42). Accordingly, in terms of the thought of the *OT*, the confession of vv. 7–9 follows with perfect naturalness the lament of vv. 1–6, and does not have the abruptness which some scholars have found.

1. concerning the drought: cf. 17.8. The drought is referred to as though familiar. General considerations above make it likely that this occurred in the early period of Jeremiah's ministry, cf. the equally allusive reference to the earthquake in Am. 1.1.

2. Judah mourns and her gates languish: the verbs as in Jl 1.10. 'gates' stands for 'cities'.

lament: as in Jl 2.10; 4.15. Literally 'become dark', like the sun, and therefore 'sink to the ground'.

Her nobles send their servants: the terms indicate social status, cf. 25.36 where the 'mighty ones' are clearly 'masters of the flocks'. The servants are 'boys'.

they are ashamed and confounded and cover their heads: omitted by LXX and probably to be deleted on the ground that it is dittography, virtually a repetition of 4b, overloading the metre.

4. Because of the ground which is dismayed: the versions obviously had difficulty with obscure Heb. LXX has 'because the works (i.e. produce) of the land have failed'. But this may be as much a guess as the modern conjectural emendation: 'because of scorched ground' (cf. 17.6). The Heb. is lit. 'because of the ground (which) is dismayed (*ḥattā*)'. Possibly this verb has an extension of meaning not otherwise familiar in the comparatively small amount of Heb. that has come down to us from biblical times; or perhaps the modern academic mind is inclined to underestimate the degree to which the poetic mind can ascribe human responses to the natural world. Cf. Jl 1.18; 2.22. The conjecture involving least change is to read a plural verb: 'they (i.e. the boys searching for water) are dismayed'. So Symmachus.

there is no rain: see general comment above.

the farmers are ashamed: the same Heb. words translated: 'Be confounded, O tillers of the soil' in Jl 1.11.

6. they pant for air: not quite! Lit. 'they sniff the wind', i.e. for signs of moisture.

7. our iniquities testify against us: 2.19; cf. Isa. 59.12.

our backslidings: cf. 3.6, 22; 5.6; 8.5; a characteristic expression.

act, O LORD, for thy name's sake: for this element in the lament, cf. Pss. 25.11; 31.3; 79.9; 109.21; 115.1; 143.11.

we have sinned against thee: cf. 1 Sam. 7.6; Pss. 79.8–9; 106.6; Lam. 1.18, 20; 3.42. It is remarkable that there is so little of this direct confession of sin in the Psalms. It is more fully represented in prophecy (Isa. 59.12–13; 64.5b–7; Mic. 7.9) and in exilic and post-exilic writings (1 Kg. 8.47; Ezr. 9.6.15; Neh. 9.16–38; Bar. 1.15–3.8). If there was a tendency to claim fidelity to the covenant as a ground for salvation (Pss. 22.4–5; 44.17–22; 74.20), it seems that the experience of the destruction of the covenant people led to a more radical questioning. Remarkably Jeremiah anticipated the sense of guilt before the events which alone could bring it home to the great majority of the people. Although it is true that, by and large, every misfortune involved a measure of guilt, Judah questioned her condition only after the misfortune. Jeremiah saw it in advance.

8. O thou hope of Israel: cf. 17.13; Ezr. 10.2.

its saviour in time of trouble: sums up Israel's history as succinctly expressed in Ps. 22.4–5. Cf. Pss. 7.1; 17.7; 106.21. Cf. also 'beside me there is no saviour' in Hos. 13.4; Isa. 43.11. Here only in Jer., but as in Isa. (43.3; 45.15, 21; 49.26, 60.16, 63.8) the term saviour has become almost a proper noun (Volz).

Why? the double 'Why' here and in v. 9 is characteristic of the lament, cf. Pss. 10.1, 13; 44.24; 74.1, 11; 79.10; 80.12; Lam. 5.20, and similar passages in prophecy, Jl 2.17; Mic. 7.10; Hab. 1.13; Isa. 58.13; 63.17.

9. confused: LXX seems to have read 'sleeping'.

Like a mighty man: on the face of it, a natural enough metaphor. But the word *gibbôr* is employed of the LORD and of his anointed king in significant contexts, e.g. Ps. 24.8; Dt. 10.17; Neh. 9.32; Isa. 9.5; 10.21; Jer. 32.18. 'The LORD, your God, is in your midst a warrior (*gibbôr*) who gives victory', in Zeph. 3.17, is so similar to this passage as to suggest that Jeremiah alludes to a well known theme. Thus Jeremiah seems to adopt the accepted form of the lament, to express confession of sin where it would be normally expected in the ritual of the fast, and to use perhaps well known expressions of faith.

At the same time, the use of the word 'backslidings', combined with the poetic images of v. 8, support the view that this is Jeremiah's free adaptation of conventional modes. The question comes near to the ultimate scepticism, typically represented in 'the temptation in the wilderness', that is the putting the LORD to the test, as at Massah, with the reproach, 'Is the LORD among us or not?' (Exod. 17.7). But at this point, Jeremiah stands firm in the affirmation of v. 9. Here again Jeremiah conforms to the pattern of the lament in which the confession of trust (implicit in the 'thou hope of Israel') forms a constituent part.

10. Following the lament and the confession of trust, the people would expect a divine answer through prophet or priest. They would expect an oracle of salvation and normally would get one, as in 2 Chr. 20, where the prayer of Jehoshaphat (vv. 5–12) is followed by the oracle of Jahaziel (vv. 15–17). In Joel also the lament of the priests (v. 17) is followed by the LORD's reply through the prophet (vv. 19–27). The absence of such an answer is a feature of prophecy (see Gunkel, op. cit. pp.137–138).

McKane concludes that vv. 2–10 'are connected with later, perhaps exilic, reflections on the failure of Jeremiah, acknowledged to be a true prophet, to prevail with Jahweh as an intercessor'. If this were so, it would seem to me to be an odd and convoluted way to go about it. The interpretation offered above seems much closer to the evidence. And the explanation of the interdict on Jeremiah's role as intercessor, viz. that it is itself a vital part of the prophecy, seems totally convincing. What is striking about this verse is that after lament and confession of sin (in which the prophet speaks representatively), together with expression of trust, the divine answer is not the expected word of salvation but a threat of judgment. Such an intervention on a fast day at the beginning of his ministry indicates a remarkable insight into the condition of the people, a remarkable independence of customary forms.

This no doubt explains the fact that the oracle is in the third person. What the people hear is not the direct word of the LORD, but what the LORD has communicated to his own man. The third person emphasises the event character of the divine answer and the mediatorial role of the prophet. Moreover it enables Jeremiah to speak, as he thought it important ot speak (29.8–9), in the tradition of authentic prophecy (so Volz). For v. 10b exactly corresponds to Hos. 8.13b. Of course one has to be open to the possibility that Hos. 8.13b is a gloss from Jer. 14.10b. But it is not represented in LXX and v. 10 looks like poetry that has been disturbed in transmission. *NEB* and *REB* wrongly print as prose.

They have loved to wander thus: a description of their indiscipline and promiscuity, as in 2.18, 23–25; 3.2, not of processions, as some think.

the LORD does not accept them: a recognised form of declaratory judgment used by the priests. Cf. Lev. 1.4; 7.18; 19.7; 22.25, 27.

TRUE AND FALSE PROPHETIC RESPONSE **14.11–16**

This section is in prose and is set out as a dialogue in the Deuteronomic style. It begins **The LORD said to me.** Jeremiah replies in v. 13, and the LORD answers in vv. 14–16. The expression 'the LORD said to me', so often in prose passages, cannot be taken as evidence of the direct writing of Jeremiah. At the same time the structure of the whole complex conforms to what we might expect from the ritual of the fast-day. Petition was part of the lament. The fast was itself a reinforcing of the prayer. But just when the prophet would be expected to carry out his mediatorial function by interceding on behalf of the people, he announced the LORD's prohibition against his doing this (vv. 11–12). If also we correctly infer that a prophet would be expected to give an oracle of salvation on the occasion of the fast, and that Jeremiah created a stir and shock by giving an oracle of doom instead, then we may suppose that the question of false prophecy was triggered directly by the events of this day, and became an issue at an early stage of his ministry. It is of course possible that his own family regarded *him* as a false prophet. (see on chapter 11). Later he came into direct and open collision with the prophets (chapters 27–29).

There is therefore every likelihood that the issue discussed here became a contentious issue on the fast-day, even if the discussion is here narrated in stereotyped language and in the light of later experience. It makes sense to think of a redactor who knows the structure of the fast-ritual, who knows in general terms what Jeremiah did on that occasion and indeed has access to Jeremiah's poetic oracles (vv. 1–10), but who also develops the themes on a wider scale in terms of the Deuteronomic and Levitical traditions, in relation not to the famine but to the invasion with its consequences of famine. The whole dialogue looks *forward* to this event. It would therefore fulfil all the conditions to think of Baruch or another scribe assembling the 'similar words' and adding his own preaching after 604 B.C. This would also explain why vv. 11–16 with their Deuteronomic prose are *separate* from verses 1–10, but in over-all structure are integrally related.

11. Do not pray for the welfare of this people: Integral to the divine answer, given through the prophet, is the command to exercise his mediatorial role of intercession. See on 4.10; 7.16. The phenomenon of a prophet declining, on orders received from the LORD, to exercise his expected ministry of intercession, is itself a *sign* to the people. But see on 14.21.

12. Though they fast: this is the only explicit reference to a fast. The ground for supposing such a context for these oracles, is general probability, making sense of every part of the chapter, in the light of our knowledge of contemporary custom.

though they offer burnt offering and cereal offering: not here a repudiation of sacrifice in principle.

I will consume them by the sword, by famine, and by pestilence: three standard punishments, occurring eighteen times in Jeremiah, mainly in prose, but at least twice in poetic passages. Cf. also Lev. 26.14–20; 2 Sam. 24.12–13; 2 Chr. 20.9. Thus the horizon is wider than that of a famine. It concerns the ultimate punishments promised for disobedience, including the defeat of the nation in war.

13. the prophets say to them, You shall not see the sword, nor shall you have famine: This is formally just what prophets might say when an oracle was required of them. But it is as inappropriate to the particular fast-day as it is typical in principle. What answer was this in the actual circumstances of the famine described in vv. 2–6? This shows clearly that the theme has been developed beyond the circumstances of its origin into a warning of the final judgment on Judah.

I will give you assured peace in this place: peace when there is no peace. Cf. 6.14; 8.11. 'this place' must here be the land, not the sanctuary. See on 7.1–20. LXX has 'land' and 'temple'.

14–16, The style is Deuteronomic prose, but the kind which is characteristic of the book of Jeremiah. Thus the prophets prophecy lies (*šeqer*). The combination (or parts thereof) of sending, commanding, speaking is found in 7.22; 19.5; 26.2; cf. 1.7; and in passages on false prophecy 23.21, 32; 29.9, 31. On the punishment of prophets cf. 29.21–23. The punishment does not include exile, which suggests that the passage is not likely to be post-exilic preaching.

with none to bury them: the fate of Jezebel (cf. 2 Kg. 9.10; cf. Jer. 8.2; 16.4, 6; 25.33; Ps. Sol. 2.27).

LAMENT OF THE PROPHET IN TIME OF WAR **14.17–22**

There now follows a second lament. The first (vv. 2–10) had to do with a drought probably at an early period in Jeremiah's ministry, and it was a lament of the people, uttered by the prophet. But as the dialogue (vv. 11–16), probably of the period following 604 B.C., has widened the theme so that the divine judgment of the nation in war has become the issue, so the second lament has to do with war and its consequences of famine and exile (see on v. 18). This time it is the lament of the prophet, in personal terms, speaking representatively on behalf of the people. The difference is one of emphasis only. It is difficult to know whether the lament is a prophetic anticipation of disaster or whether it describes the disaster actually happening. Some scholars think the lament ends at v. 18 and that vv. 19–22 are a second piece dealing with drought. This is unlikely, since vv. 19–21 with confession of sin (v. 20) and petition (v. 21) are integral to the lament form. Verse 22 refers to the LORD as the giver of rain. This does not narrow the issue again to famine. The appeal is to the God who alone has power over nature and who *a fortiori* can deliver from the present distress. This is of course one of the great arguments of Second Isaiah.

The lament includes prayer, the very petition which Jeremiah has been forbidden to make. This is another reason why the second lament cannot belong to the original context of 14.1–16. At the same time the reference to the sword and famine in v. 18 suggest the motive for placing the lament to follow vv. 11–16, while the reference to rain in v. 22, no doubt initially suggested a connection with the drought theme. Once again we see the complex motives which led to the depositing of traditional material upon the nucleus.

17. Let my eyes run down with tears: the first person is that of the prophet speaking representatively for the people. Cf. 9.1, 18; 13.17. There is no need to drive a wedge between the psychology of the prophet and the form of the lament. Again and again we see that the prophet feels both the grief of the people and the grief of the LORD as his own.

the virgin daughter of my people is smitten with a great wound:
the prophet, speaking of 'my people' (which cannot be explained as the
LORD speaking), stands for a moment in the place of the LORD. Cf.
8.21 q.v. where there is the same terminology and the same ambivalence.
The Heb. *šeḇer* is more than a wound: it is 'shattering' 'crushing'. Judah
is broken in pieces.

a very grievous blow: superfluous metrically, and perhaps added from
10.19. But we cannot be sure, and the phrase is entirely appropriate.

18. If I go out into the field: it is difficult to think that all this is
happening in the mind of the prophet. But that may well be a modern
point of view. Either the perfects are prophetic perfects and after 604
B.C., and Jeremiah *anticipates* the terrible events of 597 and 586. Or the
perfects are *descriptive* of what has happened, and the lament belongs to
the circumstances of the fall of Jerusalem. But see on verse 21.

both prophet and priest ply their trade through the land, and have
no knowledge: the Heb. *sāḥǎrû* can certainly mean 'go about buying and
selling', even 'go begging' as in *NEB*. But it can also mean simply 'go
about'. *REB* has 'wander without rest'. In all probability the 'and' ought
to be omitted. Translate therefore 'both prophet and priest have gone
(to be sold!) to a land they do not know'. The 'nation you do not know'
is a feature of the curse in Dt. 28.33, 35; promising exile to disobedient
Israel. Cf. Jer. 5.15. The phrase 'a land you do not know' occurs in Jer.
15.15; 16.13; 17.4; 22.28. This translation is supported by both LXX
and Vulg. And it adds to pestilence, sword and famine, the fourth
punishment which is present in 15.2.

19. The LORD has rejected (cf. 6.30) those who have rejected him—
a familiar theme of the lament. Cf. Pss. 44.9–19; 74.1; 79.5; 89.38–39.

Does thy soul loathe Zion?: the violent language of Lev. 26.11, 30,
44. See further on v. 21.

Why? See on vv. 8–9

We looked for peace, but no good came; for a time of healing, but
behold, terror: = 8.15. This verse belongs naturally to this lament, from
which it has probably been taken by the redactor for his own purposes
in 8.15.

20. The acknowledgment of not only our own wickedness, but also
that of our fathers is an important feature of the lament (Pss. 79.8–9;
106.6; Lev. 26.40). It is Israel, both past and present, considered in the
same way that one considers the life of an individual, which has failed
to obey the LORD and to heed explicit warnings. The linking of
contemporary Jews with the fathers is a persistent theme of the prose

sections. The promise of the land was made to 'you and your father'. The warnings were given. And now the responsibility and the guilt belong to both. Cf. 3.24; 7.26; 11.10; 16.12–13.

we have sinned against thee: as also in v. 7.

21. thy glorious throne: in 3.7, a late passage, a figure for Jerusalem. But in 17.12, in a passage which refers to the LORD as the hope of Israel, as in v. 8, it is a figure for the sanctuary. Cf. Ps. Sol. 2.19. Is it possible to believe that Jeremiah himself composed this lament, with the prayer 'do not dishonour thy glorious throne' (i.e. the sanctuary)? Is such a prayer in the aftermath of the seige of Jerusalem consistent with either the prohibition of intercession or the Temple sermon? Or could it be that Jeremiah was free to speak and to pray after the judgment as he was not free before, much as the whole tone and content of the work of Ezekiel radically changes? If this is so, then a redactor has suppressed the story of destruction by adding this lament, for the reasons suggested above, to a complex of material mainly belonging to the early period of his ministry. The alternative is that a lament, having nothing to do with Jeremiah, has subsequently been added to the complex. These ambiguities do not of course affect the authenticity of the lament considered in its own right.

remember and do not break thy covenant with us: this again is the theme of Lev. 26.40–55 which reads like the *basis* of this lament. There must be some relationship, though it is difficult to know how to establish it precisely. Probably Lev. 26 represents a traditional statement of sanctions, comparable to Dt. 28, made at the annual covenant festival. If so it would be well known. The lament is an expression of known principles. Cf. also Pss. 44.17; 74.20. Would the author of 31.31 express himself in these terms? This is only to insist that the book of Jeremiah, spanning many years and varied transmission, exposition and application, contains different traditions which may claim their own validity.

22. can the heavens give showers?: i.e. by their own power. This verse cannot mean that the lament belongs simply to a situation of drought. Its imagery and its urgency too strongly depict the extremities of war and invasion. This is the appeal to the only God, who is creator of heaven and earth, the Living God who is the sole Lord of nature (cf. 2.13) and *therefore* the only saviour.

We set our hopes on thee: links with the descriptive title of the LORD as the hope of Israel in v. 8, cf. 17.13.

Two views of this lament have been set forth in the course of these comments; that Jeremiah uttered the lament after the fall of Jerusalem when he was free to intercede, as he had not been free to intercede before; or that the lament is a traditional piece by another hand added subsequently. A third view deserves consideration. Was it part of the prophetic art of Jeremiah to express the conventional and expected thoughts of the people in a lament form with which they would be familiar, in order to provide the basis and context of a divine answer such as follows in chapter 15? Was this the way he relentlessly drove home his terrible message? Even an apparently unexceptionable expression of intercession like this is no use! Then the lament has to be understood in the light of what follows.

INTERCESSION OF THE RIGHTEOUS UNAVAILING 15.1-4

This passage which combines the theme of vicarious intercession with the motif of the four classes of punishment, is closely similar to Ezek. 14.12–23. In Ezekiel the problem is posed in relation to the behaviour of any land or country, and the question of salvation in relation to the existence within the land of three exemplary righteous men, Noah, Daniel and Job. The four classes of punishment are sword, famine, evil beasts and pestilence. The existence of the righteous cannot now prevent the judgment, as survivors join them in exile. Since there is other evidence of Ezekiel's acquaintance with the prophecy of Jeremiah, it is not implausible to suppose that Ezek. 14.12–23 is dependent upon Jer. 15.1–4. At the same time there seems to be some confusion in the identification of the four kinds of destroyer in Jer. 15.3, and this suggests that Jer. 15 is itself dependent upon a traditional motif which is common to both prophets.

As the lament in 14.2–10 is followed by the command not to intercede for the people, together with the insistence that they would be consumed by sword, famine and pestilence, so the lament of 14.17–22 (in which there is both confession of sin and earnest prayer) is followed by the insistence that the intercession of the most righteous intercessors will be of no avail. Moses and Samuel are given as examples. Both are represented as intercessors in the tradition: Moses in Exod. 32.11–14; Num. 14.13–24; Samuel in I Sam. 7.8–9; 12.19; and the tradition of their successful intercession is referred to in Ps. 99.6–8. In Dt. 18.15, 18, it is implied that Moses is the exemplary prophet. If Jeremiah allowed himself to utter the representative prayer of the people, as in 14.21, then 15.1 follows as an appropriate answer. 'Do not suppose that Jeremiah's prayer will do you any good, prophet as he is. Intercession on your behalf would be useless, even if it were uttered by the greatest and most powerful intercessors of Israel's whole history. Not even Moses and Samuel could avert the judgment that is coming upon you.'

There then follows a dialogue which is probably a conventional way of giving the interpretation of prophetic signs, as in Ezek. 12.9; 24.19; 37.18.

The answer to the question, **Where shall we go?** in v.2 is a laconic statement of the four punishments, in terms of a traditional motif. The first: **Those who are for pestilence, to pestilence,** is literally 'those who are for death to death'. Cf. 43.11. 'Death' can mean 'plague' as in Ps. Sol. 15.7; 18.21; Lam. 1.20; as also *thanatos* in Rev. 2.23; 6.1; 18.8. Cf. the Black Death in sixteenth-century England. The succinct Heb. *ᵃšer lammāwẹt lammāwẹt* is probably the quotation of a well known formula. The last: **and those who are for captivity, to captivity,** adds to the three which figure so frequently in Jer. (see on 14.12). It is altogether probable that at some stage Jeremiah added this element into his predictions, and unlikely that every allusion to exile is prophecy after the event. (See pp. 48, 326f.) The punishment of exile (scattering) is already present in Lev. 26 where the first statement of the motif corresponds to this order. (Cf. Lev. 26.14–20.)

This is not however to argue that this passage is directly the work of Jeremiah. It belongs firmly, by content, to the Jeremiah-Deuteronomic tradition. It is vain then, with Thiel, to try to identify a fragment of a genuine Jeremiah saying, upon which the passage might have been based. The tradition believed that the whole passage was the thought of Jeremiah.

It is impossible to avoid the impression that with v. 3, some confusion is introduced into the otherwise clear motif of the four classes of judgment. One would expect, sword, pestilence, famine and captivity. For captivity, Ezek. has 'evil beasts' (cf. Lev. 26.22) in a context which assumes captivity. The 'evil beasts' might well be suggested by this passage or by Lev. 26.22. It seems that 15.3–4 is a confusion of the motif of the four classes of judgment with the description of judgment in Dt. 28.25–26. Dt. 28, like Lev. 26, is a statement of the divine sanctions, appropriate to a covenant ceremony. It seems clear that Jer. 15.2 is dependent upon Lev. 26 and Jer. 15.3–4 upon Dt. 28. The phrase **I will make them a horror to all the kingdoms of the earth** in v. 4 is closely similar to Dt. 28.25. The word 'horror' (*zᵉwā'āh*) is rare, but occurs in Jer. 24.9; 29.18; 34.17; (and Ezek. 23.46) in contexts where Judah is seen as 'a proverb and a byword among all the peoples where the LORD will lead you away' (Dt. 28.37). It looks as if Dt. 28.28 is behind this usage in Jeremiah. But in Dt. the horror will be that 'your dead body shall be food for all birds of the air, and for the beasts of the earth'. We are dealing here and in Ezek. with variants of traditional motifs. The four horsemen of the Apocalypse (Rev. 6) and in particular the fourth horse with its fourfold role are a variant of the motif, based on Ezek. 14. Cf. Ec. 40.9; and Test. Benj. 7.

3. four kinds: the Heb. *mišpāḥôt* can mean clan or 'family' in both the sense of kinship and of classification. Here the latter.

4. because of what Manasseh the son of Hezekiah, king of Judah, did in Jerusalem: this corresponds exactly to the judgment of the Deuteronomic historian, as in 2 Kg. 21.11, 46; 23.26; 24.3–4; and may be regarded as a typical Deuteronomistic judgment. The analyses of Jeremiah are altogether more profound. The whole phrase looks like a gloss of a kind that not infrequently occurs in the prophetic books, particularly in Isaiah. The glossator likes to make historical identifications.

LAMENT OF THE LORD IN TIME OF WAR **15.5–9**

The third lament in this series is an expression of the mind of the LORD himself. Whereas the first two laments have their formal parallels in the familiar worship of Israel, this is the kind of utterance which is possible only on the lips of the prophet in his capacity as the LORD's representative to his people. It is linked with the preceding section by the word 'for'. Still more strongly than in the second lament, the perfects seem to be descriptive of an event that has taken place, rather than prophetic perfects describing the prophet's vision of what is yet to take place.

The events of both 597 and 587 could fit the conditions. Perhaps the earlier date is the more likely for reasons connected with the mode of redaction. McKane quotes Skinner, who sees here the language of prophetic anticipation. Undeniably this is possible. We have ventured to identify Baruch's scroll. This was followed by the setting down of 'similar words'. The process seems to have involved the building up of complexes of traditional material after the year 604. We may suppose that the early material tended to belong to the reign of Jehoiakim and might well take us up to the fall of Jerusalem in 604 B.C. The tendency is for the material belonging to the reign of Zedekiah to be set together in the later complexes. On the other hand certainty is unobtainable, and the early complexes may, as some clearly do, contain material which has been added subsequently. The terms of the description also favour the earlier date. The 587 invasion involved the actual destruction of

Jerusalem, going beyond the defeat of the army and the killing of men which is the theme of this lament.

5. The situation in which Judah has become friendless and alone is that also described in Lam. 1.1–2. The motif is the pitiless gloating of the surrounding world, cf. Ps. 69.20, where also the verb *nûd* is used (bemoan).

6. You keep going backward: cf. Isa. 1.4 (*RSV* 'they are utterly estranged').

I am weary of relenting: the relenting which marked the LORD's response to the great intercessors; cf. Exod. 32.14; Num. 14.20; 1 Sam. 7.10; and promised in Lev. 26.42–45. On the weariness of God, cf. Isa. 1.14; 7.13; and felt by the prophet, cf. Jer. 6.11.

7. in the gates of the land: 'gates' for cities as in 14.2, cf. Dt. 5.14 = Exod. 20.10 and throughout Deut. and the Deuteronomic history. It is sometimes thought that here and Nah. 3.13 the 'gates' indicate the entrance to the land. But this is not really likely. The 'winnowing' was not confined to the entrance to the land; it did take place in the cities.

they did not turn from their ways: cf. the refrain in Am. 4.6–11.

8. I have brought against the mothers of young men a destroyer at noonday: the theme is clear enough. The verse describes the suffering of wives and mothers, as the men perish in war. But the Heb. of the above sentence is obscure: literally, 'I have brought for them against the mother of the youth'. *RSV* follows LXX in omitting 'for them', but the solution is deceptively simple and still leaves the problematic *'al ēm bāhûr.* Syr. and Targ. witness to an underlying *'alēhem*, which leaves the object uncertain. *l³'ōm maḥ³rîb* is a plausible but conjectural emendation: 'a marauding people'. Translate then: 'I have brought upon them a destroying people' (*NEB* 'horde of raiders'). But see notes on next section for the reason to suppose that the word 'mother' existed in the text as it was first put together. *REB* restores it.

The 'destroyer at noonday' is probably a traditional idea, and the adverbial phrase is not to be taken with the main verb as in *NEB* 'to plunder at high noon'. The midday destroyer might be sunstroke, but more personally a demon, whom Theocritus thought was Pan. This 'sort of dangerous Pan, whose time of activity is in the heat of the sun at its highest point, was perhaps a personification of the fever and discomfort which makes itself felt in the hour of the day's greatest heat' (L. Kohler, *Hebrew Man* (1956), p.135). Pliny knew of the noon-tide demon and the idea is alive in Greek, German and Slavonic popular lore (T.H. Gaster, op.cit. pp.770–771). This figure is used here of the Foe from the North.

anguish and terror: the Heb. *ʿr*, a rediscovered homonym of *ʿr* 'city', means 'invasion'. Translate 'invasion and terror' or 'terror of invasion' (*NEB, REB*).

9. She who bore seven: the ideal of fruitfulness. Cf. the seven sons of Job (42.13), the seven sone of Jesse, in addition to David (1 Sam. 16.10), the mother and her seven martyred sons in 2 Mac. 7, the seven brothers in the story told to Jesus by the Sadducee (Mk. 12.18–27). The word 'languished', used in laments for famine, is appropriate to describe this waste of human life.

she has swooned away: lit. 'her throat (*nepeš*) 'gasps' before their enemies: as in the two sanctions statements, Lev. 26.17, 37; Dt. 28.25; cf. Jer. 18.17; 19.7; 49.37; and several times in the Deuteronomic history.

Behind the varied images and motifs contained in the poem is the idea of Zion as mother, addressed in the second person feminine, centred in Jerusalem but standing for the whole people of God. The poet passes easily therefore from Jerusalem to the daughter cities (v.7) and as easily to the mothers and daughters who lose their men. The same flexibility is found in the redactional handling of Isa. 3.16–4.6 and Lamentations. The effect of this is to concentrate attention wonderfully upon the pathos of Zion's fate.

RENEWAL OF THE DISCONSOLATE PROPHET **15.10–21**

There follows a carefully built up section in the form of a dialogue between the prophet and the LORD. The depth of suffering as a result of fidelity to the message intrusted to him, is of such an order that the situation must be the invasion of the country. It is most probable that the particular historical situation will be as for the preceding lament, i.e. 598 B.C. It is attractive to use these 'confessions' of Jeremiah to supply authentic material relating to the actual conflicts of the prophet narrated of the reign of Zedekiah. But undeniably the sign is most potent at the time of the earlier crisis.

At the same time it is important to recognise that exact historical reconstruction was not the motive of the redactor. Indeed it is not improbable that the immediate suggestion which led to the placing of vv. 10–12 to follow vv. 5–9 was the recognition of two catchwords. **my mother** (v. 10) links with 'the mothers' of v. 8; **you bore me** (v. 10) links with 'She who bore' in v. 9. But catchwords are rarely mere mechanical associations. They stand for wider, sometimes theological connections.

Here the sorrows of mother Zion are answered by the sorrow of her most representative son. Perhaps when Jeremiah first uttered these despairing words he was referring to his mother after the flesh (cf. 20.14–21; Job 3.3–12). As the passage now stands the word 'mother' is ambivalent. The prophet's expression of despair and his reply to those who curse him is followed by a divine oracle reaffirming the LORD's intention of judgment, despite his prayers and laments (vv. 13–14). Then the prophet expresses once more, and at greater length, the pain involved in hearing and transmitting the divine word (vv. 15–18). The section concludes with a word of the LORD to the prophet renewing him in his prophetic office in the terms of his call and promising him the divine strength and salvation.

There is no doubt that this sequence makes good sense. It is impossible however to think of the actual structure of the chapter corresponding to a liturgical piece. The signs of redactoral activity are too obvious. The redactor has used material that has come to him and built it up on his own principles. This does not exclude the probability that, in building up the section in this way, he was aware of the kind of dialogues that took place between Jeremiah and the LORD, aware also of the pattern of dialogue involved when Jeremiah intervened as a prophet in the Temple worship, and that he naturally conformed his structure to known and observed patterns. Just so the word of the LORD has been transmitted to us.

Other commentators take a less favourable view of the unity of the section. Some omit vv. 13–14 as being an intrusive gloss derived from 17.3–4. NEB irresponsibly omits these verses, thus imposing a critical hypothesis on the text. Responsibly REB restores them. Some take out vv. 11–14 on the ground that they are marked by textual obscurities and obscure the clarity of vv. 10, 15ff. McKane treats vv. 10–12 as a separate unit consisting of Jeremiah's complaint (v. 10) and the LORD's answer (vv. 11–12), vv. 15–18 as a separate unit ('a personal and private anguish of the prophet Jeremiah'), and vv. 19–21 as a supplementary divine answer. Holladay thinks that vv. 20–21 are the supplement, leaving vv. 15–19 as the main unit. All these observations have their force. It may however be concluded that their value is to point to the varied material the redactor used to build up this section. That includes vv. 13–14. The true scepticism is the critical scepticism whether it is possible to dissolve the unity created by the redactor.

The key then to the interpretation of the section lies in the recognition that it is inappropriate to apply tidy minded modern logic. The anguish of the prophet at the trap the LORD has put him in, is not separable

from the anguish of the nation. The ease with which the thought passes
from the personal to the communal is no reason for critical dissection,
but an integral part of the prophet's role in the crisis.

10–11. Already there has been a considerable build-up of material to
illustrate the conflict which overwhelmed Jeremiah. He is emerging as
a lonely figure (v. 17) charged with a word from the LORD which is
unrelieved tragedy. At the same time his business as a prophet is to
represent the people, to intercede for them and to express their desolation
and yearning. All this he does without compromise. But there is no
reconciliation between the LORD and the people. Jeremiah therefore
feels in his own person this unresolved alienation. He is a man of strife
(*rîb*) in this sense. There is no reason whatever to deny that these
'confessions' of Jeremiah register his own psychological and sympathetic
reactions. They are not liturgical pieces behind which the prophet himself
is entirely hidden. But neither are they the extravagant effusions of an
introvert soul. They express the exact situation of the prophet, caught
in a dangerous and ineluctable dilemma. They reveal him as a
phenomenon of his time, a sign to the people. Jeremiah's grief, his
desolation, his sense of betrayal by them and even by the LORD himself
is precisely the word of the LORD to his contemporaries. The LORD
speaks not in detachable verbal symbols but in this total human
occurrence.

10. On the legal significance of **strife** (*rîb*) see on 11.20; 12.1.

I have not lent, nor have I borrowed: Dt. 23.19 prohibits all lending
on interest to a fellow Hebrew, though not to a foreigner. But why the
abrupt introduction of this moral and social consideration, as though
Jeremiah's acceptance depends upon obedience to this one requirement
out of so many? The answer must surely be that this was one of the
requirements asked of worshippers in the entrance liturgy in the Temple
(see also on 7.1–15), and can therefore be used as a symbol for the divine
demand as a whole. Ps. 15.1 provides the background:

> O LORD, who shall sojourn in thy tent?
> Who shall dwell on thy holy hill?

There follow in Ps. 15 a list of conditions of which the last but one is
'He who does not put out his money at interest' (Ps. 15.5). Jeremiah
is in effect saying that , in terms of the liturgical order, he has fulfilled
all the conditions for being with God. And yet he is the object of hostility

and contention—**yet all of them curse me.** The curse was probably normally pronounced on those who failed to fulfil the conditions.
11. This is a *crux interpretum* and no certain solution is possible. But there are some guidelines. Following the last word of v. 10 'all of them curse me', it is perhaps significant that v. 11 is in the familiar Heb. idiomatic oath-formula. Jeremiah replies to the curse with an oath. Moreover the claim, **I have . . . entreated thee,** must be taken as a fixed point. Although the verb *pgʿ* can mean 'to light upon', it is used in Jer. (7.16; 27.18) only of prophetic intercession (cf. also 36.25). What therefore Jeremiah is saying in answer to the curse, is that he has not only fulfilled the conditions of entering the Temple, but he has also fulfilled his prophetic task of intercession on behalf of the people. MT has 'the LORD said', a divine answer to Jeremiah. It is more likely that the true text is witnessed by LXX, Old Latin: 'Amen' *ʾāmēn*), for 'he said (*ʾāmar*), aptly introducing the oath and avoiding the inappropriate introduction to a divine speech, when it is the prophet who is speaking. *RSV* is right, *NEB* and *REB* wrong. It then becomes necessary to offer some explanation of the *šārôtîkā* (ketib) 'I have strengthened you', or 'I have set you free', *šērîtîkā* (qere). The most favoured suggestion is *šērattîkā* 'I have served you'. But the parallelism with *hipgaʿtî* ('I have entreated') is more adequately achieved by the suggestion *śārîtîkā*, which is the verb used of Jacob's wrestling with the angel in Gen. 32.29, and vividly catches the note of Jeremiah's intercessory strugglings. *RSV*. has settled for this solution but without satisfactorily translating it. Translate: 'Truly, as God is my witness, I have wrestled in prayer for your good and pleaded on your behalf.' To this probably belongs the 'thou knowest' of v. 15.
on behalf of the enemy: this is not good sense. The *ʾet hāʾōyēb* is either taken as an accusative or altered to *ʾel* 'concerning'. But the phrase occurs awkwardly at the end of the sentence. More probably the *ʾet* is the sign of an identifying gloss, as often in Isa. Omit altogether, as an effort by a glossator to make sense, when the text was already corrupt and perplexing.
12. Can one break iron, iron from the north, and bronze? So *RSV*. correctly translates the present Hebrew text. Alternatively the *NEB* and *REB* render it: 'can iron break steel from the north?' Then the addition of bronze appears somewhat otiose, and may be omitted as an addition from v. 20. The sense of either rendering is: Can you, with your poor military strength, hope to resist the juggernaut that is going to crush you to pieces? This is the text we have received from the redactor's hand and

so we now interpret it. But it is hard to overcome the suspicion that this verse is the manful attempt to make sense of a mutilated test. Verses 13–14 are almost identical with 17.3–4 and, with minor variations, represent the same material. That being so, the suggestion of relationship between 15.12 and 17.1 is, if not proven, at least uncanny:

(1) Compare $h^a y\bar{a}r\bar{o}{}^{\varsigma}a$ 'break' (which on the basis of strong MS and Version evidence should read $h^a y\bar{o}dia^{\varsigma}$, with the meaning, according to D. Winton Thomas 'can iron subdue iron?') with 17.1 $y^e h\hat{u}d\bar{a}h$ 'Judah'.

(2) Compare $barzel$ 'iron' with 17.1 $barzel$.

(3) Compare $missāp\hat{o}n$ 'from the north' with 17.1. $b^e sipp\bar{o}reh$ 'with a stylus', 'point of diamond'.

(4) Compare $n^e h\bar{o}set$ 'bronze' with 17.1 $h^a r\hat{u}s\bar{a}h$ 'engraved'.

It looks as if the redactor originally placed the section now in 17.1–4 at this point. It became mutilated. Verses 13–14 remained intact (i.e. 17.3–4); but only four words of the first part of the oracle remained. A later redactor made sense of these four words in the form of the present v. 12. It is a compelling part of the argument that the four words now contained in v. 12 are in the same *order* that they (or their variants) occur in 17.1, q.v.

If this were so, then the words of 17.1, following 15.11, would make a powerful sequence of thought. In reply to the cursing of the people, Jeremiah replies that he has wrestled and pleaded for them in the days of crisis, God knows. Then the LORD speaks, 'tell the people that their sin is indelibly engraved upon them'. This is the reason why Jeremiah has to be a figure of strife. Then the judgment is reaffirmed (vv. 13–14).

13. Without price: i.e. for no payment. If the text of 17.3 is a guide, this should read 'as the price of your sins'.

in a land you do not know: the Deuteronomic formulation, e.g. Dt. 28.33, 36; and see on 14.18.

15–21. The redactor now introduces a fourth lament which seems to have a rounded completeness of its own. It contains the essential components of the lament—petition (vv. 15–16), lament (vv. 17–18), basis of trust and assurance of help (vv. 19–21). It has no *direct* concern with the terrible events which are mirrored in the previous laments. It has to do with the prophet's experience of isolation and even persecution, as he tries to communicate the message with which he is charged. It therefore follows appropriately the expression of desolation in v. 10.

It is characteristic of the redactor's art that he builds up his complexes on a sort of association of ideas. A couple of catchwords, and the connection between the sorrows of mother Zion and those of her representative son, were the reasons for setting vv. 10–12 to follow vv. 5–9. The experience of strife in fidelity to his divine office in vv. 10–12 suggests the placing of the lament (vv. 15–21) in its present position. The sequence of thought shows through. The prophet, whose conscience is clear, nevertheless encounters the curses of the people. He claims that he has wrestled and interceded for them. In the lament, he turns to the LORD to remind Him how he accepted His word as his own, and accepted with it the isolation. He asks why there seems to be no remedy for his situation, and hints that the LORD has not kept faith with his servant. The divine answer is given in a reaffirmation of the terms of his call, a renewal of the promise to protect him in the holy war he must fight against his own people (See on 1.17–19).

Much in the lament is of a kind we might expect in the *OT* Psalms, the prayer for remembrance and vengeance, the delight in the words (usually in Ps. 119 'word') of the LORD, the loneliness and pain. But two features prevent us from supposing that the redactor has simply used a suitable lament which came to hand. First, the questioning of the faithfulness of God in v. 18 presupposes an unusually bold and independent spirit who has suffered unusual persecution and grief. Second, the reaffirmation of the call is in terms which we have already seen to be uniquely applicable to Jeremiah. All in all this lament bears the stamp of Jeremiah upon it.

15. O LORD, thou knowest: omitted by LXX and Old Latin; probably concludes the oath in v. 11 where it makes powerful sense. It is not a good introduction to the lament. Cf. Ps. 40.10.

remember me: Cf. Pss. 25.7; 89.50; 106.4; **and visit me:** Ps. 106.4.

take vengeance for me on my persecutors: this is familiar sentiment in the psalms of Israel. See on 11.18–12.6 and particularly on 11.20.

In thy forbearance take me not away: this is the best that can be done with the Hebrew and involves only a slight chance of vocalisation. It is followed by *NEB (REB* misses the point). But the text early created difficulties, as is shown by LXX which read 'in thy forbearance' but omitted the rest. Certainly the verb *lqḥ* can bear most of the meanings of the English 'take'. But, as Von Rad (*The Problem of the Hexateuch and Other Essays* (1966), p.263), has shown, with God as its subject and a human being as its object, it is practically a technical term. When it has the sense 'take away', it means to be with God, as in the story of the ascension of Elijah (2 Kg. 2.3,5) Cf. Gen. 5.4. Elsewhere it means 'receive' as in Pss. 49.15; 73.24 (critical emendations of this verse are unsatisfactory). The likelihood is therefore that here the meaning is not the unfavourable: 'take me not away', i.e. 'banish me', but the favourable: 'receive me'. This is the more probable because there seems to be a notable case of dittography in this verse, and once this has happened it can lead to complications, in the effort to provide an intelligible text. Either omit the negative *ʿal*, giving the rendering: 'with forbearance receive me'; or omit *lᵉereḳ*, leaving *ʿal bᵉappᵉkā*, exactly as in 10.24. As there he cried: 'correct me . . . not in thy anger,' so here he says: 'not in thy anger . . . receive me', or 'do not receive me in anger; know that it is for thy sake that I bear reproach'.

16. The LXX and Old Latin represents a variant text which reads: 'I bear the reproach of those who despise thy words. Destroy them, and thy words will become the joy and delight of my heart'. A number of commentators have preferred this text, and it lies behind the rendering of *NEB* (rejected by *REB*), but it is the easier text and provides no explanation of the variations of MT. Indeed MT is best explained as the correct but difficult text. For despite the comparable picture of Ezek. 2.8–3.3, the idea of Jeremiah eating the words of God and finding them a delight is not likely to have been readily comprehensible. Neither version is easy to arrange in metrical lines; and yet this is emphatically poetry. *nimṣᵉ'û* 'were found' is characteristic of Jer., and in various contexts occurs in the niphal in all thirteen examples. Lam. 2.9 has the verb in a similar context: 'the prophets find (obtain) no vision from the LORD'. Here lit. 'There were found thy words', i.e. 'Thy words came to me and I ate them'. As in the case of Ezekiel, these words were 'lamentation and mourning and woe', and in v. 17 Jeremiah says: **thou hadst filled me with indignation.** If then we ask how such words can be **a joy and the delight of my heart**, the answer is not that Jeremiah took a sadistic delight in inflicting painful tidings, but that joy lay in fidelity to the LORD himself, in receiving truth rather than lies. This is what he seems to be saying when he adds: **for I am called by thy name.**

17. The prophet now expresses the isolation which his office involved, in terms familiar in the Psalms; cf. Pss. 1.1; 26.4–5.

the company of merry makers . . . rejoices: both terms, not necessarily, but as determined by the context, may have a pejorative sense 'rejoice maliciously', 'exult over'. This is probably the case here. These 'merrymakers' are the enemies of the LORD, who mock at his prophet and deride his message.

because thy hand was upon me: a figure of inspiration. Cf. 1 Kg. 18.46; 2 Kg. 3.15; Isa. 8.11; Ezek. 1.3; 3.14, 22; 8.1; 33.21ff; 37.1. 'Hand' here is a figurative synonym of 'spirit'. Here the metaphor of the 'hand' is particularly apt because of the suggestion that it is heavy. (See J.J.M. Roberts, *VT 21* (1971) 244–251.) In the non-biblical literature, there seems to be an association of the hand of God with illness. If the expression was applied to prophetic inspiration because there seemed to be some similarity between the symptoms of illness and ecstatic inspiration, then its use here is doubly significant.

thou hadst filled me with indignation: i.e. he is possessed with the message of doom he is charged to deliver. Cf. 6.11 and see on 4.12.

18. my wound incurable: for the image, cf. Mic. 1.9; Isa. 17.11; Job 34.6. But the classic passage, where the image is developed, is in Jer. 30.12–17. Cf. also 8.18, 21–22.

Wilt thou be to me like a deceitful brook, like waters that fail?: the opening *hāyô* should no doubt read as *hôi* 'alas!' or 'ah!', not easily translatable in modern English. 'brook' is the reading of LXX, Old Latin and Pesh. and is surely right. The figure is of a wady where water might be expected, but none is found. Such is the appearance of the divine dealings with Jeremiah, who had described the LORD as 'the fountain of living waters' (2.13). 'fail' is *lō' neʾmānû*, the word used of faith in Gen. 15.6; Isa. 7.9, i.e. waters that are not reliable. This is a remarkable accusation, characteristic of the utterly direct and honest approach of the prophet. He is as sensitive to the features of his situation which contradict his faith, as he is to the gracious word of God which evokes it. It is this which makes him a trustworthy witness. Cf. 20.7.

19. The LORD's answer to the prophet's lament begins with the familiar formula. No doubt the reassurance of the prophet is meant to allay his own disquiet, but the reaffirmation of his call is also a public act designed to interpret the role of the prophet to the people. This is the reason, no doubt, why the opening words of the divine reply are as suitable to the people as they are to Jeremiah:

If you return, I will restore you, and you shall stand before me. This could mean: 'If you will abandon your self-concern and your revulsion, and turn again to me, then I will reestablish you and once more you shall stand before me as my trusted servant.' The expression **stand before me** is one used of the service of God (1Kg. 17.1; 18.15; 2 Kg. 3.14; 5.16; and in the Temple, Dt. 10.8; Ezek. 44.15; 2 Chr. 29.11). But the play on the verb *šûḇ* is so similar to that in chapter 3 where it is applied to the alienation and restoration of Israel, that it is hard to resist these overtones. Jeremiah sees himself as representative of the people in this also.

18. like waters that fail: this, said of the LORD himself, threatens to contradict the very nature of God as the Living God, 'the fountain of living waters' (2.13; 17.13), the source of all vitality.

If you utter what is precious, and not what is worthless, you shall be as my mouth: 'precious' is that which is costly, rare, splendid, like gold or precious stones, applied here to speech which is noble, lofty and true. The idea of the prophet as the mouthpiece of God is vividly portrayed in Exod. 4.11–16 and particularly v.16: 'he shall be a mouth for you, and you shall be to him as God'. Hence the touching of Jeremiah's mouth at his call (see on 1.9). This lament thus acts as a sort of catalyst in his confusion and distress, restoring to him his integrity as the LORD's man, a purification strengthening him for renewed conflict with his hostile and sceptical people.

They shall turn to you, but you shall not turn to them: again a play on the verb *šûb* as above. This expresses the fundamental character of *OT* prophecy. The strength of the Old Testament is that within it the LORD reveals himself as the true God by maintaining throughout the long history of his people a purpose that rises consistently above the current ideas of his worshippers. It is impossible to see in prophetic religion simply the register of the people's humanity or the projection of their subconscious hopes and fears, let alone a mythological explanation of the world and their place in it. The principle characteristic of the prophets is that they do not bend to the will of the people; that is the way of the false prophets. On the contrary, they expect the people to rise up and respond to a higher way and standard which is inexplicable in terms of their own heredity and environment.

20. a fortified wall of bronze: see on 1.18.

they will fight against you, etc.: practically the repetition of 1.10., qv, with the addition of 'to save you'.

21. This expands the previous verse, to describe the enemy and so to relate the renewal of the call to the situation of the lament. It is this background of conflict which supplies the terminology of salvation. The word **redeem** is derived from a different background and suggests release from slavery by payment of ransom-money. Thus the addition of v. 21 shows that the author's mind is on wider notions of salvation—we might say, freedom from all external threats to do the LORD's will.

The section chapters 14–15 has emerged as a significant example of the redactor's art. The more subtle connections and associations have been suggested in the commentary above. The effect of the whole is a simple alternation of laments with consequential directions for the prophet in the exercise of his office.

The first lament, in which the drought is taken as a sign of the more serious judgment to come, in which the prophet both makes confession on behalf of the people and prays for salvation (14.2–10), is followed by the divine embargo on intercession, with a denunciation of the false prophets who deny the radical and imminent judgment. (vv. 11–16). The second lament, in which the prophet describes the judgment (in the form of invasion), and reiterates the confession and the prayer (vv. 17–22), is followed by the insistence that the intercession of the most effective saints in Israel's history would not now avail (15.1–2) and a repetition of the threat of judgment.

The third lament, in which the prophet now speaks for the LORD and expresses his mind on the desolation of mother Zion (15.5–9), is followed by the prophet's outburst of pain that he is caught between the LORD and his people. He declares on oath, in reply to the curse of the people, that he has faithfully fulfilled his prophetic task of intercession (vv. 10–12).

The fourth lament is his own, declaring how he has indeed made the words of the LORD his own. But this has caused him unceasing and incurable pain. The climax is reached when he accuses the LORD of failing to stand by him, of unreliability (vv. 15–18). The conclusion of the matter is the renewal of his office in terms of his call with reassurance of the divine help. There is a symphonic character in the structure of these two chapters; four movements with similarities and variations, a climax and a finale. Is it all in the mind of the beholder? Or, having analysed for so long the constituent elements of prophecy, must we begin to take seriously the shape of the tradition in its final form, as it has come down to us, shaped by the R., whom Franz Rosenzweig tells us we must learn to call, not redactor, but Rabbenu 'our master'?

JEREMIAH'S CELIBACY: A SIGN OF JUDGMENT **16.1–9**

The rest of the material in this complex of oracles (i.e. chapters 14–17) betrays little of the careful, artistic arrangement we have found in chapters 14–15. This suggests that chapters 14–15 are the nucleus of the collection, and that the rest of the complex represents a deposit placed here for various reasons. Verses 1–9 are a prose section. The attempt to find poetry here, by looking for either poetic metre or a poetic kernel, is not convincing. The signs of heightened language are best explained as signs of the source used by the writer, the exact nature of his source being for ever lost. The signs of the Jeremianic-Deuteronomic prose style are more substantial, though sporadic. See on vv. 4, 6, 9.

This is not Jeremiah's own work, not is it possible to identify a core which is his work. The narrative is by an exponent of his teaching who starts from a significant incident in his life which serves as a sign of the LORD's message to his people. In this respect it is similar to 7.1–15; 11.1–13; 13.1–11; and other sections to follow.

This view is not without its challengers. Carroll regards it as a complicated piece of editing which, stripped down, tells us nothing about the prophet. Rather it is about the community and, apart from vv. 1–2, shows no interest in any putative symbolic action. But this view has its own difficulties:

(1) It is odd to complain that the symbolism is not sustained when its whole point is to act as a trigger for a message to the community. The silences of the text are entirely explicable.

(2) The prose passages with an event character must stand or fall together. The argument that the link to an event in the life of the prophet is secondary wears thin when it is repeated again and again.

(3) What we are left with is emasculated and unconvincing. What does it signify to tell the community not to marry and have children, when everyone knows that they will do this, even in time of crisis? It does however make sense to accept the text as it is and to understand the command as delivered to Jeremiah himself, who then becomes in himself a sign to the community, whether they believe him or not. Moreover it is intelligible that the narrator should indicate the further implications in respect of funerals and mourning rites (vv. 4–7). It seems to me that the traditional interpretation, which assumes that the narrator knew what he was talking about, does justice to the passage, and modern sceptical interpretations do not.

Similarly this passage does not fit the hypothesis that the prose passages are the work of Deuteronomist preachers of the exilic period in Babylon. Not only does this hypothesis fail to explain the exclusive preoccupation of those preachers with the tradition of Jeremiah, but again the passage loses its power in terms of this background. As preaching it becomes totally indirect. It requires the exilic congregation to listen as though they were in Judah before the disaster. It refers to 'this place', and 'this land', meaning Judah. It is questionable whether preaching of this kind to *exiles* is sympathetically consistent with the known teaching of Jeremiah to the exiles concerning marriage and bearing children (29.6). If it were an exilic passage, its point from the point of view of the exiles would be *explanation*

of the judgment, which one might think would be better done by telling
the story in the manner of the Deuteronomic historian. Nor is it clear
that a convincing way of offering explanation to the later exiled Jews is
to start from Jeremiah's celibacy. But if we are correct in attributing these
passages either to Baruch or to a similar figure, who preaches this message
before the final disasters of 598 and 586 B.C. then the passage takes on
a new relevance and urgency.

The scribe, who assembled some of Jeremiah's teaching in the crisis
of 604 B.C. and collected 'similar words', here expounds the meaning
of the sign. He was a scribe trained in the Deuteronomic schools. He
both transmitted the oracles of Jeremiah and took a hand in arranging
them so that they were not just a collection of past oracles but living words
for the situation of 604 and afterwards. It would be odd if another or
others did not assist in this work. That is not to deny that further material
might well be deposited, as seemed fitting, in the exilic period. Indeed
vv. 14–15, which seem to presuppose the exile and look forward to a new
redemption and ingathering, might well come under this category.

It is not difficult to see why the redactor has deposited the section to
follow chapter 15. It illustrates the isolation of Jeremiah's life as described
in 15.10–18, and might even be considered as an extended comment on
15.17. At the same time the exposition of the meaning of Jeremiah's
celibacy, in the situation of pestilence, sword and famine (16.4), links
the passage with the same theme in 14.11–16 and 15.1–4. Like chapter
14, it starts from an event in the early ministry of Jeremiah and expounds
this as a sign of the disaster to follow. Such was the drought (14.2–10);
such was the command to celibacy.

**16.2 You shall not take a wife, nor shall you have sons or daughters
in this place:** the command takes its significance from the representative
role of the prophet, so that, as in the lives of Hosea, Isaiah and Ezekiel
(the death of his wife, Ezek. 24.15–24), events of their lives make them
signs of the LORD's word to his people; but also from the fact that celibacy
was rare and exceptional, if not unheard of in Israel. If Jeremiah had
a conviction on this matter before the normal age of marriage, then he
would be little more than 18 years of age; and this awareness must be
associated with the very beginnings of his ministry. We may safely assume
that Baruch (or whoever related the tradition) correctly drew out the
meaning of Jeremiah's celibacy. It was not simply that Jeremiah believed
the demands of his ministry to be inconsistent with family cares, or that
he did not have time for the joys and comforts of family life. This is an
implausible, calculating notion. Rather was it that the denial of marriage

expressed the word he was commissioned to give. It turned him into a living 'sign and wonder' to the people. He became a visible proclamation for all to read of the deprivation all must face. They might forget his words, but they could never escape the challenge of his person. To separate v. 2 from the exposition of its meaning is to isolate the personality of Jeremiah from his prophetic function, and interpret him in our terms rather than his. There can be little doubt that the exponent knew not only the story of Jeremiah's early life but also the meaning he attached to it. For this reason also we must presuppose an exponent of his teaching who was close to him.

If this is so, then we have a remarkable insight into the mind of the young prophet which confirms the grim account of his call, confirms also our conclusion that from the moment of his call Jeremiah uttered prophecies of doom focused on the Foe from the North. For it means that he started his ministry with heavy foreboding. It has been remarked that Jeremiah's defiance of custom implied extraordinary strength of individuality. It also implied a vivid intimation of the fate reserved for the people, children then born, destined for terrible deaths, and a moratorium on all the happy functions of family life, universal grief taking the place of joy.

3. who are born in this place: some have supposed this means Anathoth. Of course, in the light of chapter 7, it means the land.

4. They shall die of deadly diseases: the word in 14.18 'the disease of famine'.

They shall not be lamented, nor shall they be buried; they shall be as dung on the surface of the ground: the whole v. recurs in 8.2; 25.33. For the latter half cf. 9.22; 2 Kg. 9.37; a freer practical expression, contrasting with the stereotyped formulation cf. Isa. 5.25.

their dead bodies shall be food for the birds of the air and for the beasts of the earth: for the motif, see on 15.3. This is the curse of the sanctions document, Dt. 28 (v. 26). What the prophet is saying is that disobedience will bring the consequences stated in the conditions of the covenant. The phrase, which is a stereotype of the prose sermons (cf. 7.33; 19.7; 34.20), stands for the whole set of sanctions of which it is a descriptive part.

5. Do not enter the house of mourning: 'mourning' here, *marzeaḥ*, as in Aramaic and late Heb. 'mourning-feast'. This no doubt is meant to be a scandalous command, offending the sensibilities of the people! Who would not at least carry out the proper mourning rites for the dead? No doubt the prophet means to illustrate the character of the holocaust in which there will be no time or place for the civilities of life. Again the command is itself prophecy in having significance as a word of God to the people, like the command to Ezekiel to refrain from mourning for his wife so that he might be a sign of the fall of Jerusalem in 586 (Ezek. 24.15–27). All individual deaths will be as nothing compared with the death of the people of God.

6. they shall not be buried: a recurring theme cf. 14.16 q.v. **or cut himself or make himself bald for him:** see on 7.29. As the note there indicates, these are widespread mourning customs; in origin the blood was probably intended to refresh the ghost, and the hair was a means of communicating strength. No doubt just because of this kind of superstitious background, the practice is explicitly forbidden in Deut.: 'You shall not cut yourselves or make any baldness on your foreheads for the dead' (14.1). Lev. 19.28 also prohibits these two practices associated with augury and witchcraft. Despite the prohibitions, the custom was obviously normal, and the prophet refers to it, without explicit censure, as what people do. The events of the future will put an end to it all, good or bad.

7. No one shall break bread for the mourner: the word *prs* is used in Isa. 58.7 of breaking bread; it describes an ordinary meal, and in Lam. 4.4, it is a figure of offering food to starving children. The kind of meal is therefore determined by the context.

bread is the reading of two MSS and LXX. It is however possible that *prs* may be used with ellipsis of 'bread'. In that case the translation would run: 'No one shall break (bread) for them' (*lāhem* being the reading of the Heb.). **for the mourner** might well be a gloss to make sure the idea of giving food to the dead was excluded. The fourfold repetition of *'al* suggests that there has been some doctoring of the original Heb. It is best to keep the translation of *RSV.*, but to recognise that there may have been some underlying reference to the feeding of the dead. This then makes all the more pertinent the evidence assembled by T.H. Gaster (op.cit. pp.602–604) illustrating the widespread custom of serving and partaking of funeral meats. Eating 'the sacrifices of the dead' is referred to in Ps. 106.28 as an abhorrent Canaanite practice.

cup of consolation: cf. the cup of salvation (Ps. 116.13; cf. Ps.23.5) and its opposite the cup of wrath (Isa. 51.17, 22; Lam. 4.21, 32, 33.

8. the house of feasting: no doubt a description of the 'house of mourning' (v. 5) and not a reference to an inn or a meal-house, an anachronistic idea!

9. The whole verse is a cliché of the sermon style. Cf. 7.34; 25.10;

33.11. Its appropriateness here is to be noted, for the exposition starts from the command that Jeremiah refrain from marriage, and goes on to indicate the ghoulish darkness which will shroud all the elemental moments of human life: birth (v. 3), death (vv. 5–8), and marriage (v. 9).

HOW TO EXPLAIN THE DISASTERS 16.10–13

The 'Deuteronomic' structure of these verses is similar to that found in Jer. 5.18–19; 9.12–16; 22.18–19; and also in Dt. 29.21–27 and 1 Kg. 9.8–9. (a) A question is asked concerning the disaster. Sometimes this takes the form of an enunciation of the divine demand, particularly as expressed in the repeated warnings of the prophets (cf. 7.25); (b) the explanatory answer (vv. 11–12); (c) a restatement of the judgment which has caused the question to be raised (v. 13). Most of these passages belong to the aftermath of disaster when people gaze at the desolation and ask, 'Why?' In this passage the question is phrased differently. It formulates the questions the people might ask, not in terms of the disaster that has come upon them, but in terms of the punishment that has been *pronounced* upon them: **Why has the LORD pronounced all this great evil against us?** (v. 10). At the same time the vocabulary is a combination of familiar Deuteronomic phrases and phrases characteristic of the prose of Jeremiah. Verse 11 comes under the former category; but the Jeremianic stamp is predominant. Thus 'have not kept my law' occurs in this form only here. Dt. prefers the longer 'keep all the words of this law'. The accusation that the people have done worse than their fathers is found in Jer. 7.26, though the idea is present in the judgment on kings in the Deuteronomic history.

12. Follows his stubborn evil will is Jeremianic (see on 3.17; 7.24; 9.23; 11.8; and cf. Dt. 29.18).

13. 'a land which neither you nor your fathers have known' is also Jeremianic (14.18; 15.14; 17.4). Dt. 28.33, 36 has 'a nation you do not know'. All this shows the same circle of ideas and some common vocabulary, but the individuality of the prose sections of Jeremiah. It fits all the facts to suppose that this section is the work of a scribe of the Jeremiah tradition, expounding the message of Jeremiah to the questioning people, when they begin to take his threats seriously as the word of the LORD, in the face of the movement of events. The situation might be the eve of invasion, i.e. the same general background as vv. 1–9, or it might be later.

THREE ADDITIONS CONCERNING THE FUTURE **16.14–21**

(a) Redemption from northern exile (16.14–15)
When we turn to the next two verses, the situation is entirely different. The promise of a new redemption like the classic redemption of Israel from Egypt, presupposes the fall of kingdoms and the Babylonian exile. The 'people of Israel' is clearly here a theological term referring to the people of God, and does not bear its narrower meaning as a description of the northern kingdom. This is shown by the quotation of the oath formula in v. 14 where the narrower connotation would not make sense. The passage belongs to the exilic period. It occurs also in 23.7–8 where it is associated with the hope of a righteous king in David's line.

We may conclude then that the passage was deposited here in the exilic period on the original nucleus of this complex. The motive would be the proper desire to complete the balance of teaching within the Jeremiah tradition in a section where the historical retrospect needed to be complemented by the future hope. The passage is one of a number of indications that within the Jeremiah circle the hope of a great ingathering of God's people had its place, as especially in the Isaiah circle (especially chapters 11, 49 and 60). However great the individual prophet, other contributors are needed to create the total harmony. At the same time it is unwise dogmatically to deny the thought to Jeremiah. See on 23.1–8.

14. Therefore: normally introduces an announcement of judgment or threat; here a promise of salvation. Form-critical analyses become less useful, even misleading in the course of time.

15, the north country: what began, in the prophecies of Jeremiah, as an enigmatic and ominous threat, has now become a new 'Egyptian bondage', as envisaged in Dt. 28.27, 60, 68. The theme of the new Exodus is dominant in Second Isaiah, and in the thought of the redactor who arranged Isa. 1–12, probably in the same exilic period.

(b) Cleaning out the last pockets of evil (16.16–18)
At first sight it seems strange that the redactor has placed this oracle of judgment to follow the oracle of hope in vv. 14–15. It might seem that vv. 16–18 follow more naturally vv. 10–13. This together with the fact that vv. 14–15 are identical with 23.7–8, where it can be argued that they occur more appropriately, has led a number of scholars to conclude that the passage is intrusive here and should be omitted. This may be a premature judgment. It is more likely that in the circles which handled Jeremiah's oracles in the exilic or post-exilic period, it was felt important

to add to oracles concerning the redemption of Israel a note of warning that the glorious age to come must include the cleaning out of the last pockets of evil.

To express this purpose, two images are used. First that of the fisherman. The image of catching men as though they were fish is found otherwise only in Am. 4.2 and in Ec. 9.12, cf. Hab. 1.14. Second that of the hunter, who hunts out the evil doer from his hiding places. Here once again **the clefts of rocks** (v. 16, as in 13.4) are an example of the inaccessible. So the Day of the LORD will fall and men shall be humbled, though they 'shall enter into the caves of the rocks and the holes of the ground' (Isa. 2.19) and they will cast their idols to the moles and bats 'to enter the caverns of the rocks and the clefts of the cliffs' (Isa. 2.21, cf. 7.19). There is therefore some reason to suppose that the redactor introduced this passage, not as further description of the completeness of the destruction of Judah in 586, but as a picture of the final future as it lay within his perspective. When the LORD would fulfil his promise for Israel, there would be not only a final salvation, but also a final purification. The assaying which Jeremiah could not achieve (6.29), would be carried out, the base metal removed, the wicked rooted out.

17. The all-seeing eye of God: cf. Pss. 10.14; 11.4; 33.13–15; Jer. 23.24; Ezek. 1.18; Am. 9.24; Zech. 4.10; Mt. 10.26; Mk. 4.22.

18. The branding of idols and the emblems of heathen worship as **detestable** things occurs in Dt. 29.17, also in Jer. 7.30; 32.44; as **abominations**: Frequently in Dt., also in Jer. 2.7; 6.15; 7.10; 8.12; 32.35; 44.4, 22. But these two words, which by the time of the exilic and post-exilic period, had become common currency, are insufficient to establish a Deuteronomic character of the passage. Indeed none of the three passages in vv. 14–21 is Deuteronomic. Within the limits of this chapter this is significant. The so-called Deuteronomic material in vv. 1–13 has the stamp peculiar to the prose material in Jeremiah and seemed to belong to the period of Jeremiah himself. The best explanation seems to be that it is the work of a scribe explaining and expounding. When we turn to this material which is plainly exilic or later, it patently lacks this stamp and cannot be called Deuteronomic in any sense at all.

(c) The turning of the nations to the LORD (16.19–21)
The last of these three additions concerning the future is in poetic form with some features of the lament. The hope of a glorious second Exodus from the northern exile (vv. 14–15), and the cleaning out of the last

pockets of evil in the land (vv. 16–18), will make it possible for the LORD
to make Zion the centre to which all the nations will turn (vv. 19–21).
Zion is not mentioned, but the meaning is unmistakeable. Some
commentators, impressed by some features which the passage has in
common with Isa. 45.20–25, think this an extraneous exilic piece, and
v. 21 thereby cut off from v. 18 which it completes. Verse 21 refers then
to the wicked in Israel who will feel the might of the LORD's hand. Arthur
Weiser has, on the other hand, rightly stressed that the central idea of
this passage is by no means confined to Isa. 45 and that the poem contains
a set of expressions taken from the book of Jeremiah. It firmly belongs
to the Jeremiah circle, if not to Jeremiah himself.

The motif is the turning of the nations to the LORD. This is already
strongly expressed in Isa. 2.2–4; Mic. 4.1–4, which is widely regarded
as a manifesto of eighth-century belief concerning the centrality of Zion.
But in the light of our knowledge of the transmission and redaction of
the prophetic tradition, confidence is out of the question. It is notoriously
difficult to date the passage. It is full of traditional Zion themes. On the
other hand, whereas the traditional Zion theology, expressed in the
Psalms, looks for the defeat of the nations, here we have the nations
streaming to Zion for the LORD's instruction. All other similar passages
are exilic or post-exilic.

Isa. 11.10 sees the nations seeking 'the root of Jesse'. Isa. 49 the nations
bring back the exiled Israelites. In Isa. 60, they contribute wealth and
labour for the rebuilding of Zion (cf. Hag. 2.7). In Zech. 14.16–19 they
will go up to Jerusalem at Tabernacles to worship the king. There are
differences of emphasis in these pictures, but a common basis. Cf. Gen.
12.3; Isa. 19.21–25; Mat. 1.11; Ps. 117 'Praise the LORD, all nations'.
It becomes clear that the motif is widespread in the exilic period, but
we cannot be sure how far it is already present before this period. Perhaps
the strongest pre-exilic evidence is in the Psalms, which provide some
evidence that non-Israelites were admitted to the worship of the LORD
(Pss. 47.9; 87; 102.22; Jg. 5.23; cf. Jos. 9).

When we examine the passage for literary echoes, we are on much
surer ground. **O LORD, my strength and my stronghold** (v. 19) is
familiar psalm language ('my strength' cf. Pss. 46.1; 59.9, 17; 81.1; 89.17;
118.14 = Isa. 12.2 = Exod. 15.2; 140.7, 'my stronghold', cf. Pss. 27.1;
31.4; 43.2; 52/7; and both together in Ps. 28.8). **my refuge in the day
of trouble** is close to Ps. 37.39. The repudiation of foreign gods is an
important feature of the cult (Pss. 16.4; 31.6; 40.4; 58.1; 82; 96.5; 97.7;
115.4; cf. Exod. 20.3; Jos. 24.24–18) and by no means confined to the

Deuteronomic writings. Once v. 21, which should be set out in verse form as in *NEB* and *REB*, is understood to belong to the section, it presents the picture of the nations coming to know the power and might and name of the LORD. The nearest parallel to this is in Solomon's prayer in 1 Kg. 8.41–43. This envisages a foreigner coming from a far country and praying towards the Temple. 'Hear thou in heaven . . . in order that all the peoples of the earth may know thy name'. But again the name theology is not confined to the Deuteronomic writings and is so pervasive in the psalms that it must have been, as Weiser has argued (*The Psalms (1959)*, pp. 30–32, 41.42), a feature of the covenant liturgy. Altogether this section seems to have a marked psalm background, beginning as it does in the style of the laments.

At the same time this is indirect prophecy, and in the form of a prayer to the LORD, it formulates the hope of the nations coming from the ends of the earth to the LORD (and that must mean to Jerusalem, where he covenants to dwell), repudiating their gods, experiencing his power and acknowledging his sacred name. The power of the worship of the universal God has proved stronger than the limiting influence of its racial instrument.

Could this be a prophecy of Jeremiah himself? On grounds of general probability it is difficult to be confident. It does not consort well with his bitter preoccupations right up to the fall of Jerusalem. What of his later period? There is a looking forward to the future in Jeremiah. We cannot rule out the possibility that he included such a hope as this in his faith-vision of the future. It would provide the final hint of the fulfilment of his call to be a prophet to the nations (1.5). But we cannot be sure. If this is an exilic oracle from the Jeremiah school, this we *can* say, that the unknown prophet believed himself to be speaking in the spirit of Jeremiah, if not in the letter. For there are distinct echoes of the known words and teachings of Jeremiah. While 'my refuge in the day of trouble' echoes Ps. 37.39, it is also close to Jer. 17.17. Lies (*šeqer*) is a commonplace of all sections of Jeremiah.

19. Worthless things: cf. Jer. 2.5; 8.19; 10.8; 14.22.
   in which there is no profit: cf. 2.8.
   20. such are no gods: cf. 2.11.
   It is more likely that the poet has deeply imbibed the Jeremiah tradition than that he has included these features eclectically from elsewhere. The author is probably an exilic successor. It is a remarkable passage, often ignored on account of the widespread and mischievous assumption that

if there is a doubt about the authorship of a passage there is a shadow over its authenticity. It ought to be obvious that some of the LORD's most effective servants have had no concern to obtrude themselves and are content to retire into anonymity behind the word, which, in their view, alone had any importance.

It is possible that the word 'inherited' in v.9 provided a catchword to link the passage with 'my inheritance' in v. 18; more likely that the association was thematic as suggested above. But once these two verbal links existed, they may have suggested the placing of 17.1-4 to follow. This also in v. 4 has the same word 'heritage', practically a technical term for the promised land (see on 12.14-17, where also it is a catchword).

THE INDELIBLE SIN OF JUDAH 17.1-4

Reasons for regarding this as the complete form of the damaged oracle in 15.12-14 have been given above (see on 15.12). Here the oracle stands unconnected with what immediately precedes or follows, except that the catchword 'heritage' in v. 4 may provide a simple ground of association (cf. 16.18, 19). The end of this small scroll (chapters 14-17) provides a place for a few independent pieces which do not demand a place elsewhere. The section (17.1-4) is entirely omitted by LXX. It is precarious to conclude that LXX represents the earlier text, particularly because the LXX does not seem to have the complete and correct text of the passage in chapter 15, and because it is possible to see a redactional reason for placing the passage here. It may be that the general congruence of this section with 16.1-13 led to its present position. It is also possible that the LXX omitted the passage through homoioteleuton, cf. 'the LORD' in 16.21 and 17.5. Since the section is quite independent, a decision on this matter is in any case secondary.

The main thrust of the oracle is in the figure of V. 1. In an age when speaking face to face and oral transmission took precedence over literary activity as the principle means of communication, writing implied unusual immutability and permanence. The phrase **written with a pen of iron; with a point of diamond . . . engraved** (v.1) shows also what it meant to have the word of the LORD written. Here it is the sin of Judah which is engraved upon **the tablet of their heart** and is therefore indelible. But the prophet is concerned with more than a generalised denunciation of indelible sin. He specifies, with a characteristic mixture of metaphors, that their sin is engraved not only upon the heart, but also **on the horns of their altars.** The horns were the four protuberances at the corners of the altar, miniature 'high-places' upon which the blood was poured (cf. Exod. 27.2; 29.12; Lev. 4.7; 16.18). The pouring of blood on the horns of the altar was the action which more than any other signified the quintessence of sacrificial worship.

The prophet's words are highly ironic, for here on the Day of Atonement the people believed their sins were washed away. The prophet says that so far from being obliterated they are engraven on the very symbols of their cleansing. This is a radical criticism of the sacrificial system (cf. 6.20; 7.21–26; 11.15; 14.12), and its effectiveness as used by the people, without being a demand for its abolition. It corresponds to Jeremiah's view of the unchangeability of Zion herself (13.23). The judgment will be not only the loss of her wealth (i.e. by invasion), but also exile. This is in accordance with the sanctions laid down in both Lev. 26 and Dt. 28.

There are Deuteronomic touches in this passage. But we shall give reasons for supposing that the Deuteronomic sentence in v. 2 is a gloss. 'A land which you do not know' occurs in 14.18; 15.14; 16.13; and is sufficiently different from ' a nation you do not know' in Dt. 28.33, 36 to suggest therefore the passage is not Deuteronomic and once the Deuteronomic addition has been removed, appears to have been in poetic form, though the regularity of the metre has been disturbed. This being so, one has to be open to the possibility that this is an utterance of Jeremiah himself (Rudolph, McKane), and probably belonging to the earlier part of his ministry. The intense irony of the accusation would be heightened still more, if one could follow Volz in supposing that Jeremiah uttered this oracle on the Day of Atonement.

1. With a pen of iron; with a point of diamond: cf. Job 19.24: 'Oh that with an iron pen and lead they were graven in the rock for ever', where it is not clear what was the function of lead. Here presumably the pen had a diamond tip capable of cutting rock. There is no archaeological support for this in Palestine; Pliny attests the use of diamonds by sculptors in his day.

their altars: if the plural is correct, it must refer either to the period before the Deuteronomic reform, i.e. before 621 B.C., or to the period when the reform was ignored, i.e. under the pressure of invasion. MT has 'your altars'.

2. while their children remember: this is the meaning of the Heb., but it is not altogether intelligible. A simple transposition of two letters and a change of the preposition gives the emendation: *lᵉzikkaron bahem* 'as a memorial against them', i.e. the sin on their altars bears witness against them. So *NEB* and *REB*. This is an attractive proposal since the word 'memorial' is used in sacrificial contexts. God remembers sin. It is perhaps wise to give it a provisional acceptance in order to make sense of the passage. Certainty is impossible on the basis of a text which has clearly been disturbed at a very early stage.

2–3. their altars and their Asherim, beside every green tree, and on the high hills, on the mountains in the open country: See on 2.20 for other references, and for the 'mountains in the open country' cf. 13.17. But although some of these phrases are found elsewhere in Jer., one has the impression that this is a prose expansion based on a passage link like Dt. 12.2–3. This is the characteristic condemnation of Baal worship. It is not inconsistent with the view expressed above that v. 1 refers to a central feature of Yahweh worship. For such a people they were indistinguishable. For Jeremiah both were the vehicle of disobedience.

3. as the price of your sin: *RSV* and *REB* wisely correct the text from 15.13. MT has 'your high places for sin' or 'with sin'.

4. you shall loosen your hand' again *RSV* adopts an emendation (*yāḏᵉka* for MT *ûḇᵉka*) which goes back to J.D. Michaelis in the eighteenth century. It is suggested by the use elsewhere of the verb *šmṭ* with 'hand' and makes good sense. The LORD will disengage himself from the 'heritage' which has been the object of his covenant promises.

REB imports the idea of the hand into its translation of 'heritage' — 'You will lose possession of the holding which I gave you'. This is no doubt idiomatic but makes it impossible for the English reader to link up the passages in which the important word 'heritage' occurs. Moreover the overtones of 'heritage' are different from those of 'holding'. *RSV* maybe literal, but it is better.

Here we have precisely the complacent error which Jeremiah sought to combat—the confidence that the relationship between the LORD and his people is indissoluble. This line is absent in the version in 15.12–14. Its presence here is important not only for the powerful image it contains, but also for the catchword 'heritage' which links it with the two previous sections.

THREE REFLECTIONS IN WISDOM STYLE **17.5–11**

To call these three passages (vv. 5–8, 9–10, 11) reflections is both to represent their general character and to misrepresent their particular energy. The first contrasts the man who trusts in man with the man who trust in God, rather in the manner of Ps. 1. The second ponders the deviousness of the human heart. The third considers the foolishness of the man who seizes that to which he has no right. The wisdom character is plain in the reflective generalisations as in the simile of v. 11, and the contrasts of opposites.

But what are such generalisations doing in the book of Jeremiah where every word has had to do with penetrating criticism and critical situations? What have the calm reflections of the wise to do with the passionate outcries of the prophet? But suppose the prophet uses these calm reflections in circumstances where their application becomes obvious? Do we not find that these innocent looking affirmations hide the energy of prophecy?

First we notice that whereas in Ps. 1 the beatitude begins, 'O the happiness of the man who . . . ', here the word 'blessed' is *bārûḵ* which is explicitly contrasted with **cursed**, and the curse clause comes first. This is the same contrast that is found in Dt. 27 and 28. It is the supreme and all important contrast between salvation and damnation.

Second, we observe the closeness of the theme of v. 5 to Isa. 31.3, where Isaiah denounces recourse to military alliance with Egypt against Assyria. For, he says: 'The Egyptians are men, and not God and their horses are *flesh* and not spirit'. Notice **and makes flesh his arm** i.e. 'support' in v. 5 of this passage. It is altogether probable that Jeremiah intended the vivid images of this reflection to be a criticism of those who, in his day, turned to rely on foreign alliances. There were several candidates: Josiah opposing Pharoah Necho at Megiddo in 608 B.C. (R. Davidson, 'The interpretation of Jeremiah XVII.5–8', *VT 9* (1959) 202–205), with fatal consequences, Jehoiakim revolting against Babylon probably encouraged by promises of help from Egypt, Zedekiah adopting a frankly pro-Egyptian policy. Whoever the cap fits, let him wear it!

We have no means of knowing with what circumstances in mind the poem was composed. Perhaps Jeremiah drew on already existing material. Perhaps he used it and detonated its charge on more than one occasion. We cannot know precisely. Unquestionable these become powerful pieces when understood as contrasting the true and false conduct of the leadership. If this is so, it might be asked why passages referring to the conduct of kings are not placed in the complex of chapters 21–24, a section devoted to criticism of the kings of Judah. The reason why the redactor has placed this section here will be suggested below.

For the moment note that comparison of 22.13–17 with 17.11 provides a third example of the prophetic energising of these reflections. For the figure of the partridge effectively makes the point which is expressed more directly in 22.13–15 in a comparison of Jehoiakim and Josiah. Jehoiakim is the example of the man who rejects the strict principles of justice for his own ends 'and at his end he will be a fool'. Again we must not assume that this is the only application of the passage. Wisdom sayings are designed to be of wide relevance. It is possible that in Jeremiah's mouth the effect of these sayings would be all the greater if he was understood by his hearers to be quoting from the proverbial wisdom of the past. All we need to know is the general character of these wisdom sayings and the possibilities of use to which Jeremiah may have put them.

Why then did the redactor place vv. 5–11 in their present position? Some detect no obvious reason. Others see it as illustrating the reasons for the punishment of exile pronounced in v. 4. A more probable reason arises from the hypothesis we have adopted that chapters 14–17 form a separate complex of oracles. These are headed: 'The word of the LORD . . . concerning the drought'—The first lament 14.2–10 alone directly illustrated this theme, but it appeared sporadically (e.g. 14.22; 15.18), and attracted passages on the traditional scheme of punishment by sword, famine and pestilence. Now the first of these wisdom reflections reintroduces the theme of drought. The faithless man will be **like a shrub in the desert:** He will **dwell in the parched places . . ., in an uninhabited salt land** (v. 6). In contrast, the man who trusts the LORD, **is not anxious in the year of drought** (v. 8 *baṣṣōreṯ*, cf. *baṣṣārôṯ* in 14.1). The theme of drought is also implied in the contrast between the curse and the blessing. Blessing in the *OT* is fruitfulness, all things realising their potentialities, fulfilling the purpose of creation. The opposite is the curse, and the symbol of the curse is the desert where no green thing grows, cf. (Dt. 28). This wisdom poem then attracted the other two to it. This is a significant example of the way in which a hypothesis concerning the structure of a book suggests a convincing answer to a redactional problem and so strengthens the validity of the hypothesis. See further the note at the end of this complex.

(a) Trust in God (17.5–8)
5. **Thus says the LORD:** as in 14.1, this is inappropriate as a direct introduction to what follows, and implies a developed word-of-God theology. The word of God is more than divine speeches in the first person; it is the collected words of Jeremiah.
    cursed: cf. 11.3; 20.14–15; 48.10. see above.
    6. shrub: thought to be the juniper.
    8. He is like a tree planted by water: cf. Ps. 1.3, cf. also the leaves and fruit in both passages. The general similarity with Ps. 1 is striking

enough to raise questions of relationship. If the exposition above is correct, then the reasons for denying at least the use of this passage to Jeremiah are weak. In that case Ps. 1 is the dependent piece. For Ps. 1 is not only recognised to be an introduction to the Psalter, placed in position when the other collections were already assembled; it also represents an approach to religion which belongs to the late post-exilic period. Its approval of separation from sinners is pharisaic, its torah-piety characteristic of Judaism. Reasons of this kind never amount to a demonstration of chronology, but in this case the probability is strong. What is certain is that the Jer. version of the Psalm touches on the depths of trust in God in time of distress. Drought is here the concrete idea which is capable of the widest application according to the circumstances: to the leaders in crisis, to the people, to the prophet himself.

(b) The seat of our problem (17.9–10)
This reads like a divine answer to the objection which the previous section might well give rise. Does the man who trusts in the LORD really get what he deserves? The answer is that man cannot judge because he cannot see deeply enough. Only the LORD can penetrate the depths and deviousness of the human heart; and therefore his righteousness is not to be questioned, his dealings are fair. It may be that such considerations gave rise to this observation. However that may be, it now represents a remarkable psychological and theological perception. Sin is here traced back to the perverted will. For 'it is as the seat or instrument of (man's) intellectual and volitional activity that (the heart) figures most prominently in Israelite thinking' (A.R. Johnson, op.cit, p.77).

9. deceitful: *ʿāqōḇ,* cf. 9.4 like the duplicity of Jacob! LXX has 'deep', no doubt in the sense of Shakespeare's 'deep, hollow, treacherous, and full of guile'.

desperately corrupt: Better 'sick' or 'weak'. So *NEB* and *REB*.

(c) The ultimate futility of injustice (17.11)
The third reflection is in the form of a proverb *(māšāl)*.

Like the partridge that gathers a brood which she did not hatch: This appears to be the 'rock-partridge' *(caccabis chukar)* of the eastern Mediterranean. Its Heb. name *qōrēʾ*, derived from the verb 'call', may be onomatopoeic. This verse does not accurately describe the bird's habit. The chukar lays two clutches of eggs for its mate. But the verse does fit the popular belief, recounted by an Arab writer, that the hen visits a neighbour's nest and adopts the eggs, that as soon as the chicks can fly they return to their mother. In fact, this behaviour is exactly described in 'in the midst of his days they will leave him'. The Arabic *yaqubu* 'black partridge' is a play on the name Jacob and appears to have been his totem-name. Could it be that a knowledge of this tradition led to the placing of this proverb next to a passage which speaks of Jacob-like deviousness? (See on v. 9.) Perhaps this is too subtle, but the coincidence is tantalising. Whatever the difficulties in the identification of the bird, the sense of the proverb is clear and conforms to a theme which is to be found in both the Egyptian and the Israelite proverbial traditions. Wealth based on injustice will eventually leave its unscrupulous owner. For the applicability of this proverb to the conduct of Jehoiakim, see on 22.13–17 and above.

but not by right: the same phrase 'by injustice' occurs in 22.13.

and at his end: the Heb. *ʾaḥᵃrît* indicates the 'final period of the future so far as it falls within the range of the speaker's perspective' (S. R. Driver). Here it means a man's final destination.

THE VINDICATION OF THE PROPHET **17.12–18**

Details of this prayer, composed in the style of the lament, are perplexing. The general meaning is unambiguous. The sovereign LORD, enthroned on the praises of Israel, is implored to vindicate his prophet who is suffering humiliation at the hands of those who are forsaking the LORD himself. The prophet claims that the words he has uttered had the divine approval. It is only right that the terror should fall not upon the prophet but upon those who persecute him.

The prophet speaks in the first person, using both the framework and some of the vocabulary of the familiar lament. But those who would see here nothing more than a liturgical piece, have not reckoned with the intense personal force of the poem. It fits nothing so well as the situation of Jeremiah in the face of the persecution of Jehoiakim. The traditional form has been moulded to be the expression of Jeremiah's most searing experience of hostility and persecution.

At the same time Jeremiah's grief is more than a personal grief, as in the other so called 'confessions'. He is a phenomenon of prophecy. The persecution of Jeremiah focuses on one individual, Israel's betrayal of her LORD. Jeremiah's grief is a public sign of the LORD's grief. The prayer is not simply a glimpse of the inner conflicts of a prophet. It is itself prophecy, publicly uttered, probably in the Temple, replacing with shocking, convicting petitions, the conventional utterances which people expected from a prophet in time of national distress. When Jeremiah, standing among the people in the Temple, cries, 'Heal *me*', he is not resorting to a new individualism, he is speaking as the LORD's spokesman, whose vindication is necessary to the effective communication of his message. When in their presence he refers to 'them', in prayer, in the third person, he is emphasising his role as the LORD's representative. Nevertheless it is as their representative that he prays at all. He is torn asunder between the LORD and his people.

But details of the passage admit of no certain solution. The first question is the relation of verses 12–13 to the body of the lament. It is the view of most scholars that these verses are inconceivable on the lips of Jeremiah, and that his prayer begins in v. 14. It is said that the psalm introduction (v. 12), addressing the LORD on his glorious throne in the sanctuary, is inconsistent with the known teaching of Jeremiah on the Temple and its worship. It is suggested that these verses were added by a redactor for whom there was no difficulty in thinking of the restored Temple as centre of true worship, to contrast the authentic praise of the LORD with the counterfeit worship denounced in 17.1–4; or perhaps the phrase 'the hope of Israel', already occurring at the beginning of this collection in 14.8, was as good a reason as any for placing the verses somewhere in the same collection.

But, from the literary point of view, vv. 12–18 belong together. There is a link between vv. 13 and 18 in the phrase 'put to shame'. But more important, vv. 12–13 provide an introduction of a kind that has a parallel, for example, in Ps. 80. They express Israel's trust in the LORD who makes himself known in the worship of the Temple. The introduction to the prophetic call in Isaiah 6 also comes to mind. Proof is impossible and no doubt scholars will continue to be divided. One has therefore to fall back on personal judgment. My own judgment is that the separation of vv. 12–13 from 14–16 divides what belongs together. The reasons for dividing them is the precarious opinion as to what the prophet could have or could not have said (but cf. on 14.21!) or the view that vv. 12–13 are a patchwork drawn from other passages. Neither view holds up.

There are two interesting possible solutions.

(a) Assuming that vv. 12–13 refer to the sanctuary in Jerusalem, it is possible that Jeremiah deliberately begins his lament by quoting an introduction known to his audience in the familiar Zion liturgy. This would not be double-talk, for although Jeremiah predicted the destruction of the Temple, and taught that the people's worship could give them no security, he nowhere denied the presence of the LORD in his Temple, not least when speaking through himself. If our hypothesis is correct, Jeremiah took a prophet's part in that worship. The LORD made himself known to his people. But instead of uttering the comforting words of salvation they expected, he spoke of judgment and disaster. If Jeremiah is here quoting a typical psalm introduction or speaking in the familiar style, this would explain the first person plural **our sanctuary** (v. 12), which some have found difficult. And if this is the mode of Jeremiah's introduction in which **all who forsake thee** (v. 13) would be interpreted by his hearers as the enemies of Judah, or at least obvious apostates, then all the greater the trauma when the prayer that followed identified themselves as the objects of judgment in the day of disaster. Did Jeremiah indicate with a gesture who he meant as he cried (v. 15), **Behold, they say to me, where is the word of the LORD?** The use of the terms 'throne' and 'on high' in Ugaritic mythology for the throne where Baal sits (the mountain being identified with Mount Zion) can be adduced to support this view, but it is ambivalent evidence.

(b) Is it possible that interpreters (not Duhm) too easily assumed that vv. 12–13 refer to the Jerusalem sanctuary? Or rather is it possible that the sanctuary is meant to be the pointer to him whose home is in heaven and who vouchsafes to make himself known in Zion? Plainly there is some flexibility in the use of the term 'throne', since in 14.21 it is used of Jerusalem; in Isa. 66.1 'heaven is my throne'. The term 'place of our sanctuary' (cf. Isa. 60.13) is consistent in Third Isaiah with a strong sense of the heavenly being of God. Prayer is directed to the Father in heaven. The term 'set on high' (based on an emendation suggested by the LXX) is the Heb. *mārôm* 'height', and is often a figure of heaven (cf. Pss. 18.16; 93.4; 10.19; 144.7; Lam. 1.13; Jer. 25.30), though it is also used of Zion (Jer. 31.12; Ezek. 17.23; 20.40). Perhaps the tension in the thought of the Old Testament is neatly expressed in Ps. 11.4

> The LORD is in his holy temple,
> the LORD'S throne is in heaven.

Most significant of all, the Deuteronomists repeatedly affirmed that the LORD dwells in heaven (Dt. 4.36) and the adequacy of the Temple as his dwelling-place is explicitly denied (1 Kg. 8.31–40). In view of the strong association of Jeremiah and Baruch with Dt., it would not be unreasonable to assume that when Jeremiah used the language of the Zion theology, as in verses 12–13, he should interpret it in the sense familiar in the Deuteronomic writings. Whether Jeremiah was saying, like Ps. 11 and Isa. 66, that the LORD's throne was on high (in heaven) from the beginning, or whether he was pointing through the earthly sanctuary to the LORD on high, he was saying nothing inconsistent with his view that the LORD would treat the Temple with the utmost detachment.

12. The *NEB* (rejected by *REB!*) may be right in translating these expressions as vocatives. 'O sovereign throne, on high from the beginning'. Is 'the place of our sanctuary' a subsequent gloss identifying the heavenly throne with the Temple? In that case it is easier to restore the rhythm of the Heb. parallelism in verse 13.

13. those who turn away from thee: Heb. 'from me'. Perhaps a better answer is to understand *yᵉsûrai* (*sûrê*) *bᵉ'āreṣ* as construct before preposition, as in Isa. 5.11; 9.2, i.e. 'those in the land who turn away'.

shall be written in the earth: most interpreters think the figure is of inscribing the names of the guilty in the dust. But the Heb. would then more probably be *ᵃdāmāh*. The idea of the book of life, in which the destiny of the blessed is written down (cf. Isa. 4.3; Exod. 32.32–33; Mal. 3.16; Ps. 69.28; Enoch 47.3; 104.1; Lk. 10.20; Heb. 12.23; Rev. 3.5; 13.8; 20.12–15; 21.27) may be thought to imply also the record of the wicked, though normally it is said that the name of the wicked is blotted out from the book of life. However it is not necessary to suppose that the book of life is in mind. As in 17.1, the writing is meant to indicate the permanence of the decision. Translate: 'The names of those in the land who turn away shall be written down'. The proposal that 'earth' here means the underworld, on the basis of alleged Ugaritic usage, is unnecessary.

the fountain of living water: cf. 2.13, q.v. Here the expression is taken out of its poetic context and becomes a descriptive title.

14. Heal me, O LORD: the terminology which no doubt originally referred literally to healing from sickness has here, as elsewhere, a wider meaning. It is synonymous with 'save me', cf. Pss. 6.2; 30.2; 60.2; Jer. 3.22; 30.17; 33.6; 9.22; 14.19.

thou art my praise: this forms a natural link with the introduction, and there is no need to emend it.

15. Where is the word of the LORD? Let it come!: clearly a typical taunt of the faithless who demand instant proof, cf. Isa. 5.19, 'Let him make haste, let him speed his work that we may see it; let the purpose of the Holy One of Israel draw near, and let it come, that we may know it' and the popular proverb quoted by Ezek.: 'The days grow long and every vision comes to naught' (12.22). This is a special form of the taunt characteristic of the lament: 'Where is your God?' cf. Pss. 42.3, 10; 56.4, 10.

16. I have not pressed thee to send evil: this rendering implies *l³ra⁽ah* ('for evil'), in place of *mero⁽eh*('from grazing'), and is partly supported by Aquila, Symmachus and Pesh. Its strength is that it preserves the parallelism and corresponds to 18.20 and particularly 15.11 as interpreted above. It is not however certain that this is right. LXX understood the text to mean 'I have not tired of following after you', and it is at least possible that the Heb. yields this translation without emendation. *'us* would be capable of meaning 'to press or hasten or work to the point of tiredness'. The participle would have to denote the action or abstract idea of the verb, equivalent to the infinitive construct, and the verb *r⁽h* means 'graze', as a sheep follows the shepherd. For many examples of such close association of participle and infinitive, see P. Wernberg-Møller, 'Observations on the Hebrew Participle', *ZAW 71* (1959) 54–67; on this passage, p. 64.

the day of disaster: *'ānûš*, literally 'incurable' without healing, i.e. without salvation, cf. 15.18; 17.9. A theme of this collection (chapters 14–17), otherwise only in 30.12, 15. There is surely no connotation of magic in this word, as has been suggested.

thou knowest: the metre becomes clearer if this phrase is added to what follows. Thus: 'thou knowest all that has come out of my lips' (*REB*).

was before thy face: i.e. 'it had thy approval'. 'You are fully aware of it' (*REB*).

17. the day of evil: cf. v. 16. Behind these expressions is the traditional conception of the Day of the LORD, as expounded in Am. 5 and Isa. 2. There the LORD's day, expected to bring salvation to Israel, was reinterpreted as a day of judgments. Here the expression 'day of evil' is an accepted symbol of this prophetic teaching. But pronounced on the LORD's day, that is, in the course of Israel's worship, it has ironic and disturbing force.

THE TEST OF SABBATH OBSERVANCE **17.19–27**

The third collection of oracles ends with a section on obedience to the sabbath law. It is the familiar Deuteronomic style of Jer. Its structure also is on the same lines as we have already encountered:

(a) The sabbath law stated (vv. 21–22);
(b) The disobedience of the forefathers (v. 23);
(c) The benign consequences of obedience (vv. 24–26);
(d) The fatal consequences of disobedience (v. 27).

This in a general way corresponds to the threefold pattern of divine word or warning, story of rejection, judgment, which is to be discerned in

Deuteronomy, the Deuteronomic history and in Jer. At the same time there are features peculiar to the latter.

(a) The passage starts with what purports to be the specific preaching activity of Jeremiah in a specific place, as also in 7.1; 11.6; 13.1–11; 18.1–5; 19.1–2; (22.1–2).

(b) The expressions 'enter by these gates' (v. 20), cf. 7.2; 22.2, 4; 'receive instruction' (v. 23), cf. 2.30; 5.3; 7.28; 32.33; 35.13; otherwise in Zeph. 3.2, 7 and Prov. 1.3, 8; 8.10; 24.32; 'incline their ear (v. 23), cf. 7.24, 26; 11.8; 25.4; 34.14; 35.15; 44.5, see on 7.24.

(c) The picture of kings 'who sit on the throne of David', entering by the gates, seems to be composed in conscious contrast to the picture of foreign kings setting their thrones at the entrance of the gates of Jerusalem (1.15).

This passage belongs clearly to the traditional exposition so characteristic of the book of Jeremiah, and is therefore by no means the composition of Jeremiah. Here there is substantial agreement. It is the work of a Deuteronomist of the Jeremiah tradition, expounding in terms of the issues of his day. When that day was and what the relation of this teaching is to anything Jeremiah may have said are more difficult questions.

It has been cogently argued by E.W. Nicholson (*Preaching to the Exiles*, 1970), that this is the work of Deuteronomists, within an active preaching tradition carried on in the exilic synagogue. Here, it is argued, the observance of the sabbath had become a confessional mark of the Jews and a test of their faith. It is in exilic texts that the sabbath becomes a living issue. Cf. Lev. 23; Ezek. 20.12, 16, 21, 24; 22.8, 26; 23.38; 44.24; 46.1, 3, 4, 12. Cf. Also Isa. 56.1–8; 58.13–14. The sermon, it is thought, does not represent the thought of Jeremiah, but rather the teaching of men who deliberately represented Jeremiah as proclaiming the law, no doubt to give their preaching (not the law itself) an authoritative backing. No doubt for the best of reasons they invented the connection with Jeremiah.

Underlying this view is the assumption that this teaching contradicts the known teaching of Jeremiah. Certainly in its totality it has deviated from his teaching. For it seems to teach security for the Jews in the possession of the divine blessings. And it was precisely this sense of security in the outward performance of religious rites that Jeremiah was most concerned to destroy. See particularly on 7.1–15 and 7.21–27. Moreover the divine blessing itself is elaborated in the picture of people flocking in from all directions to Zion bringing their sacrificial offerings.

On the other hand, those features of the section which link it with the Jeremiah tradition prevent us from dissociating it completely from Jeremiah. It does not make sense to suppose that the preachers were simply exilic Deuteronomists. The evidence is better satisfied when we suppose that these preachers operated within the Jeremiah tradition. They were the heirs of his teaching and the guardians of the collected oracles. His known teaching and deeds provided the text of their sermons, however free the exposition. They believed they were expounding the word of God as delivered to him. The analogy of other passages, particularly 7.1–15 and 11.1–14, suggests that when they assert Jeremiah did something, he really did it! When they elaborate his teaching, they fall naturally into their Deuteronomic patterns and vocabulary.

It is entirely in keeping with this understanding of the Deuteronomic prose of Jeremiah to conclude that Jeremiah did on some occasion remind his hearers of their obligation to keep the sabbath law as a test of obedience, but that in expounding it his later disciples deviated from the known teaching of Jeremiah in the way the passage shows. Certainly the exile or the immediate post-exilic period would be a plausible occasion for this, not only because the observance of the sabbath was an issue, but also because, the judgment being past and the Temple rebuilt and restored, it would seem natural to look for the proper use of the sanctuary by a people enjoying the LORD's blessing.

Then one must ask, what kind of reference might Jeremiah himself have made to the sabbath law? The answer is that he might well have used it as a particular test of obedience to the law of God in general. Indeed, it is probable that Jeremiah would discern an objectionable hypocrisy in those who made the Temple a fetish (7.1–15) and yet put their business and commercial interests above the observance of the sabbath. The argument would be similar to that implied in his commendation of the Rechabites, whom he set up as an example not for their total abstinence but for their obedience (chapter 35). The profanation of the sabbath was a symptom of disobedience.

The passage then has a distant but substantial link with the teaching of Jeremiah, but in its elaborated form belongs to the exilic or post-exilic period. It is understandable that such a passage should be appended on some remaining space at the end of the third scroll of the Jeremiah tradition. The knowledge that this was based on the tradition of Jeremiah's work would be sufficient reason for adding it. Conceivably it might have been thought to illustrate the meaning of the obedience required of the fathers but not given, expressed in 16.11.

19. the Benjamin Gate: the Heb. has 'gate of the sons of the people', i.e. 'the People's gate'. No such gate is known. But one of the gates may well have been referred to thus, because it was used by the laity, as distinct form the officiants at the cult. There is no need, with *RSV NEB* and *REB* to change to Benjamin. This gate was well known (cf. 37.13; 38.7) yet none of the Versions read it here. Follow *RV, GNB* and *NIV.*

kings of Judah: the plural here and especially in v. 20, shows the oratorical character of the sermon, altered perhaps when there was no particular king to refer to or to address, and when there was hope of the restoration of the Davidic king. Always the preacher thinks in terms of the history of Israel's apostasy, as explicitly in verse 22.

21. do not bear a burden on the sabbath day or bring it in by the gates of Jerusalem: the best illustration of this sort of violation of the sabbath is in Neh. 13.15–22. But there is no reason to assume that the practice was not common in early post-exilic times. Cf. Am. 8.5. It has been suggested that there was a law, no longer preserved, forbidding the carrying of burdens on the sabbath.

24. And do no work: quotes sufficiently accurately the covenant law as set forth in Exod. 20.10; Dt. 5.14. **but keep the sabbath day holy:** cf. Exod. 20.8, 11; Dt. 5.12. Thus the sermon is in part an exposition of the sabbath law in the decalogue. Jeremiah and his later interpreter have this in common that they held the people up to their covenant obligations.

25. kings: MT had 'kings and princes' (*śārîm*). The *śārîm* were the ministers of state and did not sit on thrones. Probably dittography suggested by the next line. The picture is rhetorical and designed to contrast with 1.15. See also 22.3.

26. This verse describes the whole of the post-exilic territory of Judah, first on the basis of the political divisions and then from the geographical point of view.

bringing burnt offerings and sacrifices: implies the fully restored Temple and the resumption of sacrificial worship after 538 or 516 B.C. After 586 it is probable that sacrifice ceased. The eighty men from Schechem, journeying to Jerusalem the day after the murder of Gedaliah, brought only cereal offerings and frankincense (41.4).

27. then I will kindle a fire in its gates: cf. 21.14. The fire imagery so often used of the day of judgment, the more terrifying to those who had memories of the events of 586 B.C.

The theme of the final form of the tradition—chapters 14–17

On pp. 226f. we reviewed chapters 14–15 as an example of the redactor's art. It is now expedient to review chapters 14–17 as a whole, and to discern such homogeneity as the redactor has conferred upon them. What must stand out at once is the theme of drought. This theme appears to be more pervasive than first impressions encourage. The heading in 14.1 refers to 'the drought', and 14.2–10 is a lament appropriate to drought, but with an answering oracle in v. 10, not of salvation, but of judgment to come. This leads into a prose section (vv. 11–15) on false prophets, built around the prediction of sword, famine and plague, the three standard punishments. The false prophets say there will be no famine. Verses 17–22 contain a lament, this time centred on the grief of the prophet at the fate of 'my people' under judgment. This judgment is clearly wider than drought, and it anticipates Judah's rejection by her Lord, but it includes 'the diseases of famine' (v. 18), and ends with the affirmation that it is not the false gods, but only the LORD, who can bring rain (v. 22), symbol of salvation.

Chapter 15 returns to the theme of the standard punishments, including famine, and makes the threat explicit. If the 'destroyer at noonday' (v. 8) is correctly understood as, at one level the mythological personification of fever and the destroying sun, at another the destroying enemy, then the association of drought and the wider judgment is subtly continued. In the fourth lament (vv. 15–18) Jeremiah's food, in time of drought, is the words of the LORD (v. 16). These he had joyfully consumed. And yet (v. 18), it seemed to the prophet, stranded between obedience to the LORD and solidarity with his people, that the LORD's provision disappeared, like a waterless brook. The command to Jeremiah not to marry (in 16.2) is given in the context of the warning of death by 'deadly diseases' ('diseases of famine', 14.18), sword and famine (v. 4). He is to be in his own person a symbol of famine and death.

The complex ends with a number of passages deposited on the main collection. These include three passages concerning the future (16.14–21), by an exilic successor and three reflections in wisdom style (17.5–11). The first of these (17.5-8) reverts to the theme of drought and contrasts the tree planted by water as proof against drought, and symbol of the person who trusts in the LORD. Verse 13 reaffirms that the LORD is 'the fountain of living water'.

FOURTH SUPPLEMENTARY COLLECTION OF ORACLES **18.1–20.18**

This section has many of the characteristics of the previous collections. Like chapters 7–10 and 11–13, it is introduced by the formula **The word**

that came to Jeremiah from the LORD, and a prose passage (18.1–12) provides the foundation of the collection.

Like all the collections it contains varied material, including poetic oracles probably of various periods. 18.13–17 seem to have connection with the early oracles of Jeremiah; 20.7–17 belongs probably to the experience of persecution in the time of Jehoiakim. The theme of Jeremiah's intercessory function recurs in 18.18–23, and 20.7–18 contains some of his bitterest laments. The section seems to be built up, like the previous collections, on the principle of nucleus and deposit, with inner collections sometimes difficult to discern with confidence. The encounter with Pashhur (20.1–6) is perhaps most convincingly assigned to the period before the compilation of Baruch's scroll narrated in chapter 36. Nothing need be later than the reign of Jehoiakim. At the same time there is no hint of the desperately urgent warning of imminent judgment, as in chapters 1–6; 8.16–17; 9.10–11, 17–22; 10.22; 12.7–13; 13.20–27; 14.17–22; 15.1–9.

There is no theme or teaching or emphasis which we have not met before. The main structure is based on the prose narrative of three prophetic signs:

  (a) the potter (18.1–11)
  (b) the breaking of the earthenware jar (19.1–13)
  (c) the encounter with Pashhur (20.1–6).

Cf. the prophetic sign narrated in 13.1–11. Each of these narratives suggests what follows. Thus 18.12 is a suture connecting 18.1–11 with the poem in vv. 13–17. This leads to the theme of the fate of the prophet himself, who becomes the target of the rebellious people's hostility, as in 11.18–23; 12.6; 15.16, 20. In the poem 18.19–23 he declares once again how he interceded for the people, as is implied in 7.16; 11.14; 14.11; 15.1, cf. 4.10.

The alternation of oracles (or here, prophetic signs) with personal utterances of the prophet is characteristic of all the collections and therefore a significant pointer to the mind of the redactor. The expression of personal discomforture (itself a form of prophetic sign) in 20.7–18 is similar in principle to the personal poems in 4.10, 19–26; 6.9–15; 10.19–21; 14.17–22; 15.10–21; 17.14–18. It is plainly foreign to the purpose of the redactor to arrange these passages together; he thinks much more in terms of challenge and response. The challenge of the prophetic word is followed by the response of people or prophet, usually in a form owing something to the lament. Occasionally the combination may reflect a liturgical background. More often the liturgical sequence has been in

the background of the redactor's mind, determining the way he arranges
the material.

THE SIGN OF THE POTTER 18.1–12

This account has the double character so often observed in the prose of
the book of Jeremiah. It has Deuteronomic features and it has features
unique to the Jeremiah prose tradition. The tendency has been to discover
unambiguous Deuteronomic material in vv. 7–10, the evidence being
partly literary and partly thematic. The phrase 'not listening to my voice'
(v. 9) has been labelled Deuteronomic together with other phrases, and
so has the projection of the fundamental choice between good and evil
(vv. 7–10). The commentary below will show how the principal affiliation
of the rest of this passage is with the Jeremiah prose tradition.

Verses 7–10 are not however so unambiguously Deuteronomic that
they can be attributed to a preacher of the school, offering forgiveness
and blessing to Judah after the disaster of 586 B.C. on condition that they
'turn again' and repent. The word *regaʿ*, translated 'if' in vv. 7 and 9,
and meaning literally 'at one moment . . . at another moment' occurs
in Jer. 4.20 and nineteen times in the *OT*, but never in the Deuteronomic
literature. 'turn again' in vv. 8–11 is completed by 'from its evil' and
though 'turn again' in various combinations is a Deuteronomic
commonplace, this precise form is never found in the Deuteronomic
literature. 'listen to (my) voice' is so found, but is so common elsewhere
that it cannot be regarded as Deuteronomic. (For a full study of this
phrase, see A.K. Fenz, *Auf Jahwes Stimme hören, Wiener Beiträge zur Theologie*
6, 1964.)

There is thus a Deuteronomic appearance about this passage which
partly dissolves on close inspection.

If one then turns to the theme of choice between good and evil, this
also cannot with confidence be denied to Jeremiah or to his followers and
attributed to a Deuteronomist. Even the contrast between evil (*rāʿāh*) in
v. 8 and good (*ṭôḇāh*) in v. 10 may be sought in a prophetic tradition
rather than a Deuteronomic. (See Helga Weippert, op.cit. pp. 203–209.)

Although the presentation of the alternatives of conduct and its
consequences is undeniably Deuteronomic, it is also to be found elsewhere,
particularly in Isa. 1.19–20 where it is in my view integral to the approach
of Isaiah (see D.R. Jones, 'Exposition of Isaiah 1.18–20', *SJT* 19 (1966)
319–327). It is also present in the poetry of Jeremiah (13.15–17; 17.5–8)
as well as in the prose (21.8–10).

In the light of this ambiguity, it is the more striking that the passage

(vv. 7–10) shows the marks of elevated speech. It is not necessarily poetry, but it contains parallelism and the use of synonyms and antonyms. It may be set out thus:

> At any moment (*rega*ʿ) I may threaten
>   a nation (*gôi*) or a kingdom (*mamlākāh*)
> to uproot it, pull it up and destroy it. (cf. Jer. 1.10)
> But if the nation which I have threatened
>   turns back from its evil,
> then I will repent of the evil I intended to do it.
> Or at any moment (*rega*ʿ) I may decide
>   concerning a nation or a kingdom
> to build it and plant it. (cf. Jer. 1.10)
> But if it does evil in my sight,
>   not listening to my voice,
> then I will repent of the good that I had intended to do it.

Next it is to be observed that some of these word pairs and triads are also to be found in 1.10 where the form of poetry or elevated prose was similarly discerned, and that word pairs and parallelism are also to be identified in v. 11:

> Now therefore (*wᵉʿattah*) tell the men of Judah (*ʾîš yᵉhûdāh*)
>   and the inhabitants of Jerusalem (*yôšᵉbê yᵉrûšālaim*)
> Thus says the LORD,
> Behold, I am shaping (*yôšēr*) evil against you
>   and devising (*ḥōšēḥ*) plans (*maḥᵃšābāh*) against you
> Turn again everyone from his evil way (*derek*)
>   and amend your ways (*darkêkem*) and your doings (*maʿalᵉlêkem*) (cf. 7.3, 5)

We also note that v. 12 takes up the theme of 'plans' from v. 11 and in 'that is vain' (*nôʾaš*), cf. 2.25, and particularly 'stubbornness' (*šᵉrîrût*) uses words belonging to the Jeremiah tradition.

The use of 'behold' with a participle in V. 11 is also a characteristic idiom of the Jeremiah prose tradition.

It is not easy to draw precise conclusions from all this. At least authorship by an independent Deuteronomist is excluded, and the framework belongs firmly to the prose tradition. The elevated prose and parallelism is best explained as a form held in the memory and therefore going back either to Jeremiah or one close to him, and this is supported by the relation to 1.10. In general we conclude that this passage confirms the view that when we speak of the Deuteronomic prose of the book of Jeremiah, we are referring to disciples of Jeremiah who, because they lived in that age, were influenced by the dominant intellectual and literary (i.e. Deuteronomic) tradition. It does not appear easy to follow those who divide this section into two or three parts of varied authorship, or who, with McKane, attribute vv. 1–6 to Jeremiah and vv. 7–10 to later theorizing.

Jeremiah is instructed to go down to the potter's house. Every movement lies under the divine providence. There, as is the intention, he derives a message from observing the potter at work. When the potter finds that the pot being moulded under his hands is unsatisfactory, he starts again and fashions the clay to a shape that pleases him. Even so the LORD finds the people he has formed to be his servant marred, and even so will he strip them down and start again.

The lesson, up to v. 6, implies both judgment and hope, though the implications are radical and uncomfortable. There are unquestionably genuine theological conclusions to be drawn concerning the sovereignty of God (cf. esp. Rom. 9.20–24, which owes more to Isa. 29.16), but Jeremiah does not draw them. The emphasis here is not so much on the complete power of the potter, as on the possibility of scrapping the first effort and starting again. The narrative has more in common with a parable than an allegory, and the pictorial details are not to be pressed beyond the central requirement of the narrative. Strictly this is not a prophetic sign in the sense of 13.1–7 or 28.10. That is to say, Jeremiah does not create the sign. He recognises a divine word in a familiar process. Of course, it amounts to the same thing. Whether Jeremiah saw an object in a vision, or whether he mimed his message, or whether he interpreted a familiar event as here, the emphasis in every case is on the divine word thus communicated.

Whoever was responsible for the exposition of the sign in vv. 7–10 pressed home one part of its meaning. Indeed it is often the case that a sign has such a wide field of application that one may say, if the cap fits, wear it. Here the emphasis is upon the element of discretion which the divine potter claims. His decision to destroy depends on the quality of the vessel. Let the vessel therefore make sure it is worth keeping. Thus the expositor postulates a choice between obedience and disobedience with consequences of life and death.

If this interpretation goes beyond the strict limits of the sign itself, that is a prophetic licence which we might expect. It is of course perfectly true that after 586 B.C. such preaching would offer an explanation of why

Judah had suffered judgment. That would be true whatever the origin
of the passage. But there is nothing to indicate that it originated in post-
exilic explanatory preaching and much suggestive of an earlier date. It
makes sense to suppose that it was the presentation of a genuine choice
anticipating the judgment, expressed as it is in terms of plucking up,
breaking down and destroying on the one hand and building and planting
on the other. For the view that this terminology originates in a poetic
oracle of Jeremiah in connection with his call, (however it is subsequently
developed in the prose tradition), see notes on 1.10.

1. Jeremiah does not have witnesses as is essential to the effectiveness
of the normal sign. He is simply telling of the circumstances of his
apprehension of the divine word. This word does not stand on its own,
but has to be understood as an interpretation of the work of the potter.
Jeremiah must therefore tell both the experience and its interpretation,
and it is in the combination of these that the truth is seen. This disposes
us to entertain the possibility, particularly in the light of the above
discussion, that the interpretation of vv. 7–10 goes back ultimately to
Jeremiah.

2. the potter's house: probably a workshop in a place where water
was available (Siloam?). The importance of the industry is shown by
the fact that one of the gates of the city was named 'the Potsherd Gate'
(19.2).

3. he was working at his wheel: the Heb. word is dual; probably there
were two wheels, the lower one turned by the feet, cf. Ec. 38.29–30.

6. The given interpretation likens Israel to the clay in the hands of
the potter.

7–10. The exposition of the meaning of this combination of image and
interpretative word takes an unexpected turn. Two alternative situations
are posited, in the manner of case law, and in general terms, applying
the principle to any nation or kingdom. This way of envisaging contrary
responses is akin to the technique adopted by Ezekiel (chapter 18) and
it is more in line with prophetic than with Deuteronomic methods of
persuasion (cf. Isa. 1.18–20). The implication is the utter sovereignty
of the LORD over all nations and kingdoms. Whatever licence Baruch
or another has allowed himself, he has in no way distorted the teaching
of Jeremiah whose call was to be a prophet to the nations. See the general
discussion above.

pluck up and break down and destroy . . . build and plant: cf. 1.10
and comment, and see above. This is entirely in keeping with Jeremiah's

emphatic teaching that there is no security in received positions and attitudes. Possession of the Temple, or Ark, the practice of sacrifice or prayer do not in themselves confer immunity from judgment. Nor does righteousness build up a treasury of merit. The sentiment of the divine potter will change according to the way the pot turns out. Like all images, this one is suggestive of a number of interpretations. It is the power of images that they continue to be capable of extended meanings. They remain in the imagination stimulating fresh thought. We have therefore a combination of image and interpretation, a combination also of the imaginative inspiration of Jeremiah himself and the exposition of Baruch or another. The lines between each cannot be definitively drawn. It is enough that in the dialectic between the one and the other the word of God is spoken.

11. the men of Judah and the inhabitants of Jerusalem: cf. 11.2, 9; 17.25; 32.32; 35.13. See on 4.4 and 11.2.

Behold, I am shaping evil against you: The form, 'behold' with the participle and the first person is characteristic of the prose tradition in Jeremiah. See on 5.15. Moreover the participle *yôṣēr* corresponds with the noun *yôṣēr* (potter) in the same way that the participle *šōqēd* (I am watching) corresponds with the noun *šāqēd* (almond branch) in 1.11ff. As we have seen, this is not the only link with chapter 1.

Return, every one from his evil way: again, particularly the individualism of the expression, characteristic of the book of Jeremiah, cf. 25.5; 26.3; 35.15; 36.3, 7; 44.5; cf. also 15.7 and 23.14.

amend your ways and your doings: cf. 7.3, 5; 26.13; 35.15.

12. That is in vain!: cf. 2.25 where this expression also occurs in a rhetorical response of the people, but there in a poetical oracle.

our own plans: In contrast with the plan the LORD is devising against them (v. 11).

according to the stubbornness of his heart: as in 11.8; 16.12.

BREAKING THE NATURAL LAW **18.13–17**

The editor of this collection now chooses to illustrate what is wrong with God's people by introducing a neat and striking oracle in poetic form. Its central point is that their desertion of their LORD is unnatural. It is as unnatural as it is to break the observed uniformities of the natural world. The rhetorical question of v. 14 contains problems of translation; but there is no doubt about its drift. It speaks of reliable elements in our environment, of rock, snow and water. In certain places these never fail. In contrast the people of God have forgotten their God. Their unreliability

is notorious and the punishment will be ignominious. The appeal is similar
to that of Am. 6.12:

> Do horses run upon rocks?
> Does one plough the sea with oxen?
> But you have turned justice into poison.

See the similar theme, in terms of birds, in Jer. 8.7
Isaiah (Isa. 1.3) points the same contrast:

> The ox knows its owner, and the ass its master's crib;
> but Israel does not know, my people does not understand.

and in 28.23–24 voices a similar question implying that the farmer's
obedience to the laws of the soil and the seasons, should be matched by
a like obedience to the will of God on the part of his people. Both the
natural and the moral laws are aspects of the same universe and its wise
governance (Isa. 28.29). Of course it is going beyond the philosophical
intentions of the prophets to call this a theology of natural law; yet the
inference is near at hand.

13. a very horrible thing: cf. 5.30; 23.14; Hos. 6.10.
14. Does the snow of Lebanon leave the crags of Sirion?
Do the mountain waters run dry, the cold flowing streams?
This is the essential sentence of the oracle which gives it both its
character and its point. Fortunately the over-all meaning is clear on any
translation, but it is unfortunate that in detail there are insoluble
problems. The conjectural emendation 'Syrion' (Heb. *śiryôn* for MT *saday*
'field') is too uncertain to be accepted. It lacks any support in the Versions
and neither the constant repetition of Cornhill's guess in commentaries
nor its acceptance in *RSV* and *NEB* increase its remote statistical chance
of being correct.

Is it possible that *śạdaÿ* should be pointed *śadday*, meaning 'mountain',
and that the use of this word as a divine name (Gen. 49.29, etc) obscured
its earlier meaning? (cf. Assyr. *sadu* 'to be high'). In that case the
translation would run 'Does the snow of Lebanon leave the mountain
crags?' cf. The Jerusalem Bible and *REB*.

Alternatively it might be appropriate to observe the stylistic device,
in this oracle, of placing two nouns or nominal phrases in apposition.
This occurs in vv. 14b, 15b, 15c and 16a. In that case one might favour

Albright's ingenious suggestion which involves dropping the mem and repointing ṣûr as ṣôr, meaning 'flint', giving the translation: 'Do flints depart from the fields or snow from Lebanon?' This accords with the facts, the northern plains of Palestine being strewn with flints. The former of these two proposals seems preferable. **Mountain waters** involves too arbitrary an emendation. The reading mimiṣraim for mayîm zārîm, yielding: 'Will the flowing streams from Egypt run dry?' is again too hypothetical to inspire confidence. Here the emphasis seems to be on the two participles, and if we can follow Dahood (JTS 74 (1962) 208) in postulating a meaning 'flow' for zûr, the difficulty largely disappears. There is no need to translate qārîm 'cold', since qôrîm may well mean 'source', 'spring' (see Dahood). Nor is there need to follow Dahood in tracing behind naṭaš the word nāšāh 'forget'. This does not adequately maintain the metaphor. More likely is naṭaš a slip for našaṭ 'dry up' (metathesis?). The translation of the whole verse would thus be: 'Does the snow of Lebanon leave the mountain crags? Do flowing waters, running streams dry up?' Of course in certain places and circumstances they do, cf. Job 6.15 where the treacherous are likened to mountain streams that run dry. But the accent here is on the participles.

The interrogative form of this sentence is characteristic of a type to be found scattered throughout the OT (cf. Am. 6.12; Isa. 28.24; Prov. 6.27–28; Job 8.11). It is possible that this form is derived from teaching techniques and that these may be called 'school questions'. If so, this would accord with the wisdom affiliation of significant sections of Jeremiah, and throw light on the techniques employed by the prophet to communicate his message.

15. But my people have forgotten me: cf. 2.32; 3.21; 8.7; 13.25; Hos. 2.18; 8.14; 13.6.

to false gods: literally 'to emptiness, vanity' cf. 11.13 'to burn incense to Baal'. Usually in Jer., the expression is adverbial, 'in vain' (2.30; 4.30; 6.29).

they have stumbled in their ways' the Heb. has 'they have caused them to stumble'. This introduces a 'they' without an antecedent. The emendation is trivial.

not the highway: i.e. on unmade roads.

16. The image here is characteristic of the lament (cf. Pss. 44.13–16; 79.4, 10, 12; 80.6; 89.41, 50; 123.3–4; Lam. 2.15–16; Joel 2.17). It was part of the Deuteronomic curse that disobedient Israel should become a byword among the nations (Deut. 28.37), a threat literally taken up in Jer. 24.9.

and shakes his head: cf. 15.5; Pss. 22.7; 109.25; Lam. 2.15; Zeph. 2.15. This verse in the Heb. contrives to suggest the hissing contempt of the nations by the use of assonance.

17. the east wind: often a symbol of the appearance of the LORD in judgment. Cf. 4.11; 13.24; Pss. 48.7; 50.3; 83.13.

I will show them my back: the reverse of 2.27.

A PLOT AGAINST JEREMIAH AND HIS RETALIATION **18.18-23**

Verse 18 tells of a plot against Jeremiah, without clarifying whether the threat is against his life, as in 11.18–12.6, or against his message, as in 15.15–21. If the lament of vv. 19–23 belongs originally to v. 18, this will determine that the plot is against his life. But it looks as if, by placing the poem here, the redactor wished to illustrate the enormity of Israel's sin by describing her reaction to the LORD's representative among them. More particularly the catchword 'plots' (*maḥᵃšāḇôṯ*) falls to his purpose, since the plot against Jeremiah can be presented as a contrast to 'our own plans' (*maḥᵃsᵉḇoṯênû*, v. 12) which the people are intent to pursue, regardless of the 'plan' (*maḥᵃšāḇāh*, v. 11) which the LORD is devising against them.

Then they said is without an antecedent. The identity of the plotters is of little importance. What is stressed is their confidence that, in the recognised leaders, they have all the divine guidance they need. The inference is that Jeremiah is out of line with every official spokesman and his intervention is as totally superfluous as it is unacceptable. The confidence of the people in these spokesmen is similar in principle to the confidence they repose in the Temple, the Ark and in their sacrificial offerings. The inference must also be drawn that the three named types of leader represent the three principle ways by which it might be expected that the LORD would communicate his will. This means that **the wise** cannot be a term simply denoting what we should call secular office-holders, nor can it denote less than a distinct type of leader, comparable in some way with priest or prophet. This is not to deny that the term 'wise' was capable of much more comprehensive meaning than either 'priest' or 'prophet'. For further discussion see below.

Verses 19–23 are a prayer of Jeremiah in which, having reminded the LORD how he had previously interceded for the people, he now prayed for the LORD's judgment to be loosed against them. On the face of it this is a prayer for personal vengeance of a vicious kind. The prayer that the enemy's children shall be given over to famine, their wives childless and widowed, their young men cut down in battle, sounds like a malicious and disproportionate personal vendetta. But of course this is the point, it is not a personal vendetta.

Here, as elsewhere, Jeremiah is not simply a persecuted individual, he is a representative figure pulled apart in two directions. His intercession on behalf of the people was the exercise of the proper function of the prophet drawing God's people back to himself. Their rejection of him was a rejection of the LORD and therefore draws upon them the LORD's judgment, which is customarily worked out in the vicissitudes and tragedies of human life. The thinkers of Israel did not always allow for mediate causes. All was personal and direct. The unspeakable suffering and tragedy which Jeremiah knows to be coming, he identifies as judgment. As the LORD's man he cannot but be the spokesman of the LORD's plan and hail it into effect. His word is grim and harsh, but it exactly corresponds to the reality.

18. the law shall not perish from the priest, nor counsel from the wise, nor the word from the prophet: the pairs of words provide an exact correspondence between the office-holders and their characteristic form of utterance. One of the main functions of the priest was the conservation and promulgation of law, particularly the rules relating to worship, the holy and the sanctuary. The teaching office of the priest is stressed in Dt. 33.10: 'They shall teach Jacob thy ordinances and Israel thy law', Mal. 2.7: 'the lips of a priest should guard knowledge, and men should seek instruction from his mouth', and 2 Chr. 15.3. Cf. also Hag. 2.10–14. It is plain that while the law was a codified corpus of practice, the word *torah* included the wider sense of 'instruction' and that priests were consulted on matters of greater importance than ritual niceties. The establishment which they existed to uphold was threatened with extinction, if Jeremiah was right. The association of 'word' with the activity of the prophets is one of the central features of the *OT*. The incipient problem here is of the kind of prophet whose word is clean contrary to the word of Jeremiah himself, a problem to be faced squarely in chapters 27–28.

The alliance of priests and prophets has already been stressed in 5.30–31. There it appeared that the prophets were the principle inspiration of false teaching, and the priests the main day to day contact with the people. The new feature here is the 'counsel from the wise'. We have already argued that the term 'wise' here must indicate a type of leader in some way comparable with priest and prophet, and like them, in some sense a spokesman of the LORD's will. At the same time the term lacks the same precision as 'priest' and 'prophet', and must now be elucidated.

It is probable that wisdom in Israel was nourished from two sources. First there were circles of native wisdom, such as in the time of David were represented by the people of Abel-beth-Maacah (2 Sam. 20.18–19), and the wise woman of Tekoah (2 Sam. 14.1–21), such as also conferred upon Edom a reputation for wisdom (Jer. 49.7; Ob. 8; Bar. 3.22–23). From such circles emerged the proverbial sentences collected in the wisdom literature. Second, there were the schools, probably attached to the Temple in Jerusalem, which trained young men to become statesmen, so that they might give 'counsel'.

The importance of 'counsel' is most vividly illustrated in the story of Ahithophel of whom it was said: 'The counsel of Ahithophel which he gave in those days was as if one should ask concerning the word of God. Thus was all the counsel which Ahithophel gave to both David and Absalom'. Training in statecraft involved writing. A wise statesman (*śār*), who might take one of the offices of state, was therefore a scribe (*sōpēr*) cf. 8.8. It was in these circles that the Deuteronomic writings were preserved and developed, introducing a more comprehensive didactic function to their work.

From a modern point of view the wise man had a secular function. From Israel's standpoint, this was not so. 'Counsel' offered to the king affected the ideals and conduct of the people of God. It was important therefore that 'counsel' should be in line with the 'word' of God. It was a cardinal element in the teaching of Isaiah, who taught that the 'counsel' of men fails (Isa. 7.7; 8.10; 19.11) and the 'counsel' of the LORD alone stands (Isa. 5.19; 11.2; 14.26; 19.17; 44.26; 46.10). The word 'counsel' in these prophecies is equivalent to what we should call the providential purpose of God. In a similar passage, Ezekiel links the counsel of the 'elders' with the vision of the prophet and the *torah* of the priest. In post-exilic Israel the rulers were the effective rulers of the community and Ezek. 7.26 thus confirms the general sketch of 'counsel' which we have drawn. Probably then to speak of a *sōpēr* who was 'wise', was to speak of a professional adviser to the elders and to the king above them.

It has been suggested that when Jeremiah said, 'the law shall not perish . . .', he was describing pejoratively three classes of people who would not stop talking. This is to trivialise the sentence, which is a rhetorical quotation placed on the lips of the classes concerned. When full weight is given to the balance and detail of the verse, then it becomes clear that the wise are professionals as much as prophets and priests and that their task is to advise the king and those in authority under him.

Come, let us smite him with the tongue: this is a literal translation, paraphrased correctly in *NEB* and *REB* 'let us invent some charges against him'. Pesh. implies a slight change of text: 'let us smite his tongue', but this is less likely.

let us not heed any of his words: LXX omits 'not', but can hardly be right. Those who wish to accept the reading of Pesh. and LXX here have missed the sense of the verse as a whole. The enemies of Jeremiah are claiming that they *have* torah, counsel and word of God. They therefore have confidence to speak and to drive Jeremiah to silence.

19–23. The psalm which now follows has two characteristics. It is in all respects in the style of the laments of the Psalter, often echoing the phrases as well as the sentiments of these psalms. At the same time, at a crucial point, it is particularly applicable to the ministry of Jeremiah, and refers in v. 20 to his ministry of intercession, now to cease. While it is possible to think of a previously existing psalm, used by other prophetic leaders in the cult, it is not plausible to do so. Here the psalm language is used by Jeremiah to express his own unique situation, between the upper and nether millstones of God and man. It is also verbally fashioned to fit the language of v. 18. 'let us not *heed* any of his words', say his opponents: 'Give *heed* to me, O LORD', prays Jeremiah. They speak of the *counsel* of the wise; he affirms that the LORD knows all their *plotting* (lit. their *counsel*) to slay me'. It is therefore the most straightforward response to the hostility expressed in v. 18. Verbal links with the laments of the Psalter are as follows:

(1)   **19. Give heed to me, O LORD:** Pss. 5.3; 10.17; 17.1; 55.3; 61.1; 66.19; 86.6; 142.6.

(2)   **my plea** (Heb. *rîb*, *NEB* 'what my opponents are saying against me' cf. introduction to chapter 2 and 11.18–12.6): Pss. 18.43; 31.20; 35.23; 43.1; 55.9; 74.22; 119.154.

(3)   **20. Is evil a recompense for good?:** Pss. 35.12; 38.21, cf. 109.5.

(4)   **I stood before thee:** this expression regularly describes a servant, as Elisha in 2 Kg. 3.14 refers to his own place in the service of the LORD: in Ps. 106.23 it is used of Moses intercession, turning the wrath of the LORD from the Israelites in the wilderness.

(5)   **21. deliver up their children to famine . . . let their wives become childless and widowed:** The vituperative elements in the Psalm are well-known, cf. 5.10; 7.6, 9; 10.15; 28.4; 31.17; 35.4–6, 26; 40.14; 55.15; 59.11–13; 69.22–28; 139.19; 140.9–10; 143.12. These are all cast in general terms. For the more precise mention of children and wives, one has to turn to Pss. 137.8–9 and 109.6–19. Jeremiah is as circumstantial, from the point of view of Christian sensitivity, as the most violent of the Psalms. The reason is clear. Jeremiah describes the terror which he now

knows to be inescapable and which he identifies as retribution. It is therefore misleading to contrast the **forgive not** of v. 23 with the 'Father forgive them' of the crucifixion, without a serious attempt to understand the context and the motive.

(6)   **22. the marauder:** Ps. 18.29.

(7)   **they have dug a pit to take me:** this hunting metaphor is to be found in Pss. 7.15; 9.16; 35.7–8; 140.5; often with the thought that the wicked will fall into the trap they have laid for others. The exact expression occurs in 57.6; 119.85.

(8)   **23. yet thou, O LORD, knowest:** Pss. 40.9; 69.5, 19; 139.2, 4; 142.3, cf. 44.21.

(9)   **Forgive** (*kippēr*): Pss. 65.4; 78.38; 79.9, (with *ʿal*).

(10)   **nor blot out their sin:** Ps. 109.14.

deal with them: i.e. *ʿāśāh* used absolutely, cf. Ps. 109.21. All this firmly establishes the poem in the psalm tradition with which Jeremiah was profoundly familiar.

Verse 20 takes up the theme of Jeremiah's intercessory task, which has been a recurring motif. See on 7.16–20; 10.17–25; 11.18–12.6; 14.17–22; 15.1–4.

THE SIGN OF THE BREAKING OF THE EARTHENWARE JAR
19.1–13 (14–15)

This is the second of the three prose narratives, describing prophetic signs, upon which the structure of chapters 18–20 is based. As in the sketch of the potter (18.1–11), there are features of didactic amplification. When we are told (19.1) that Jeremiah buys an earthenware jar and takes with him some elders and senior priests and goes out through the Gate of the Potsherds, we naturally expect him to perform a sign under the eyes of his companions who fulfil the role of witnesses. Instead, we are given a sermon on the Topheth ritual in the valley of Hinnom (already denounced in 7.27–8.3), and containing its own significant sign—the renaming of v. 6. Not until v. 10 is there mention of the breaking of the jar.

Accordingly most scholars regard the original narrative as contained in vv. 1–2, 10–12 and the rest, either as a secondary narrative knit into it, or as a subsequent hortatory development. McKane believes he can detect three stages in this complicated development: (a) 1, 2a, 10, 11, (b) 2b, 3f, 7–9 referring to Jerusalem, (c) the application to Topheth and Ben Hinnom. This of course is theoretically possible, but in the light of the interpretation favoured here, over-confident.

There is of course some force in this view. It is thought to be supported by the fact that the sermon is addressed to the kings of Judah and the inhabitants of Jerusalem (v. 3), rather than to the elders and priests. The similar and more convincing example of this kind of treatment of the text in chapter 18 increases the probability, and there are signs of such amplification in the interests of preaching elsewhere in the book of Jeremiah. Nevertheless it is wise to be cautious. If the elders and priests are present to be witnesses of the sign, there is no reason why they should not witness the sermon also, addressed rhetorically (cf. 1.18; 17.19–20) to the kings of Judah and inhabitants of Jerusalem. If the sign is a portent of the destruction of the nation because of its corruption, it would be not unreasonable to give some idea of the nature of the corruption. Moreover, though the mention of the Gate of the Potsherds perhaps gains significance if the sign was performed at this spot, it also heightens the solemnity of the narrative to name this Gate as the direction Jeremiah took on this grave prophetic errand. Note the narrative of his return in v. 14. Altogether it is wiser to interpret the narrative as a single whole, holding the theory of didactic amplification in the back of one's mind as a possible but by no means certain explanation of the present form of the narrative.

1. flask: Heb. *baqbuq*, a pitcher to contain water, those known being from 4″ to 10″ high with narrow necks. There is word-play in the 'I will make void' (*baqqōtî*) of v. 7. It would be in the spirit of redactors and preachers to make this sort of allusion; but equally it would be in the spirit of the prophet himself.

take some of the elders: 'take' is not in MT but, supported by LXX, Pesh. and Targ., is necessary to the sense.

2. valley of the son of Hinnom: see on 7.31.

the entry of the Potsherd Gate: the exact location is not known. It is enough that it should be the most direct way from the Temple to the valley of Hinnom.

3. O kings of Judah and inhabitants of Jerusalem: cf. 1.18–19 and notes, 13.13, but especially 17.19–20 and notes. The judgment is not against a particular king, but against the whole nation and its line of kings. From this point to v. 9 the language is thoroughly Deuteronomic, a pastiche of well known phrases and yet a meaningful sequence of thought. As always there is a centre which is most convincingly attributed to the prophet himself (the renaming in v. 6, cf. 7.32). And there are Jeremianic phrases in v. 8. The effect of the Deuteronomic phrases, particularly v. 9 taking up Dt. 28, is to declare that the judgment is the implementation of a clear warning already given.

Behold, I am bringing such evil . . .: a characteristic expression. See 5.15 and references there cited; but in this case cf. 2 Kg. 21.12.

this place: on the ambiguity of this term (*māqôm*), see on 7.3. Probably the meaning here is 'Jerusalem and Judah' as in 2 Kg. 21.12. But see also vv. 4, 6 below.

the ears of every one who hears of it will tingle: cf. 1 Sam. 3.11, and particularly 2 Kg. 21.12, where the whole verse occurs, save only that 'Jerusalem and Judah' replaces 'this place'. The generalised judgment on Manasseh at the hands of the LORD's 'servants the prophets', together with the characteristic vocabulary there, betrays the Deuteronomic historian, in contrast to this passage.

4. Because the people have forsaken me: cf. 16.11 where the Deuteronomic language has a Jeremianic stamp and was attributed to a scribe of the Jeremiah tradition.

have profaned this place: the verb, used in this sense, is found here only. The 'place' would be most naturally the sanctuary, though in the previous verse it is Jerusalem and Judah and later in the same verse and in v. 6 it is Hinnom.

by burning incense in it to other gods: cf. 2 Kg. 22.17; Jer. 1.16; 44.5, 8, 15. As noted on 1.16, it may be premature to call this Deuteronomic, but it is characteristic of the prose sermon style in Jer. The specific reference here may be to the prevalent astral cult. See on v. 13 below.

whom neither they nor their fathers nor the kings of Judah have known: cf. Dt. 11.28; 13.3, 7, 14; 28.64; 29.26; Jer. 7.9; 44.3. Here the Deuteronomic language is more precisely a quotation and stresses that the behaviour of God's people is the direct disobeying of an explicit command and must bring upon them the punishment spelled out in Dt. 28. 'nor the kings of Judah' is an addition peculiar to this chapter, fitting the sermon to the audience addressed in v. 3.

and because they have filled this place with the blood of innocents: the shedding of innocent blood, in the *OT*, refers usually to the miscarriage of justice, and particularly to the wrongful application of the law of vengeance, where the avenger of blood killed an innocent person in error. The Deuteronomic law was particularly concerned to control this area of violence (Dt. 19.10; 21.8; 27.25; cf. Jer. 7.6; 22.3; 26.15). But here the use of the plural shows that the familiar language is applied to the innocents who were the victims of the child sacrifice practised in Hinnom (see on 7.31); 'this place' is therefore Hinnom.

5. and they have built the high places of Baal: in 7.31 more accurately

Topheth (q.v.), referred to in v. 6. There is no indication that child sacrifice was practised on *bāmôṯ* generally; it was localised in this single horrifying place where 'they built the high place of Topheth' (7.31).

to burn their sons in the fire as burnt offerings: cf. 7.31 and Dt. 12.31 where the sacrifice is made 'to their gods'. Baal here serves as an umbrella for any false deity.

which I did not command or decree, nor did it come into my mind: practically equals 7.31 and 32.35, in both cases in connection with the Molech cult.

6. = 7.32a. See on 7.31–32.

7. I will make void the plans' the Heb. *baqqōṯî* is word-play on the *baqbuq* (jar) of v. 1 and so makes a catchword connection between the passage on the Molech cult and the prophetic sign. See on v. 1. 'plans', i.e. *'ēṣāh*, see on 18.18.

8. a horror, a thing to be hissed at: always together—Jer. 18.16; Jer. 25.9, 18; 29.18; 51.37; cf. Mic. 6.16; 2 Chr. 29.8. Once again we encounter an expression which occurs in the poetry but mainly in the prose of Jer., but not in any of the Deuteronomic writings.

9. And I will make them eat the flesh of their sons and their daughters: one of the most gruesome and bloodcurdling consequences of ancient warfare, vividly exemplified in the story of 2 Kg. 6.24–7.20. Josephus tells how, in the siege of Jerusalem, a rich woman by the name of Mary roasted her own baby *BJ* vi. 3,4). Similar stories are told of Ashurbanipal's siege of Babylon, cf. Ezek. 5.10; Lam. 2.20; 4.10. But the main point here is that this, when it happens, will be the fulfilment of the warning given in Dt. 28.53, for the Deuteronomic curse is explicitly quoted. Cf. Bar. 2.3. See also on v. 4.

10. Then you shall break the flask in the sight of the men who go with you: the prophetic sign which was the object of the journey. Although its meaning, spelt out in v. 11, is simple and almost self-explanatory, nevertheless there are witnesses whose task is to hold the event in their memories and testify in the destruction of Jerusalem that this was the fulfilment of the word of the LORD as spoken by his prophet Jeremiah. Cf. Isa. 8.1–4, 16–18. Isaiah made provision for the writing down of the name of his child and then of his prophecies, and this led to the further preservation in writing of all that was recognised as word of God. In all probability the witnesses here exercised a like function. This is an argument for regarding this section as having been preserved within a Jeremiah circle, rather than as the free composition of Deuteronomic preachers. We may expect the witnesses to have fulfilled their function, and may take this passage as evidence that they did.

11. Men shall bury in Topheth because there will be no place else to bury: in 7.32, these words follow the symbolic naming of Topheth, i.e. we should expect them in v. 6. Yet they make sense here, following the prediction of the destruction of the people and the city like an unrepairable potter's vessel. This suggests that chapter 19 is not the combination of a narrative and a Deuteronomic sermon, joined together by 'scissors and paste', but a careful rewriting intended to come to us in its present form and not to be broken down into separate parts.

12. this place . . . its inhabitants: here Jerusalem, which rather than Topheth, is the direct object of the prophetic sign.

13. The reference to the houses of the kings is to the buildings which constitute the royal palace, and links with the address of v. 3.

upon whose roofs incense has been burned: cf. 32.29. The reference here is to the Assyrio-Babylonian astral cult, the worship of 'the sun, and the moon, and the constellations, and all the host of heaven' favoured by Manasseh (2 Kg. 21.3), repudiated by Josiah (2 Kg. 23.5, 12), but flourishing as the state was threatened and the people became desperate. (Cf. Jer. 8.2; Zeph. 1.5.)

14. Then Jeremiah came from Topheth: usually emended to 'from the entry of the gate'. This is plausible because the words tōpeṭ and peṭaḥ have a similarity in Heb., and it is necessary if the thesis of a composite structure is to be maintained. But it is unsupported in the Versions and if the chapter is, as we have maintained, a unified amplification of the narrative, which never existed in another written form, then v. 14, as it stands, is necessary to the sense of the whole.

15. Behold, I am bringing upon this city . . . all the evil: see on v. 3.

because they have stiffened their neck, refusing to hear my words: cf. 7.26; 17.23. Cf. Dt. 10.16; 2 Kg. 17.14, but the expression in Jeremiah may be regarded as a minting of the Jeremiah tradition.

THE SIGN OF PASHHUR **20.1–6**

The event here narrated took place in all probability before the opposition to Jeremiah became so intense that he was compelled to hide (chapter 36—604 B.C.). It represents the reaction of the establishment to the way Jeremiah was fulfilling his prophetic commission (cf. Am. 7.10–17). Pashhur was discharging his responsibility for discipline as 'overseer' in the Temple. He is often said to be head of the Temple police. This perhaps conveys too modern an image, though unquestionably he had police-like functions. But he had prophetic responsibilities too. When he is accused of prophesying falsely (v. 6), this is not simply a rhetorical or an analogical way of speaking. We now know that many prophets were closely attached to the cult and that some priests, like Ezekiel, were prophets. Pashhur was a priest who ventured to claim that he could speak the word of the LORD. This is what made him dangerous, not his authority in the establishment.

Jeremiah took the opportunity to turn the encounter with Pashhur into a prophetic sign, by giving him a name significant of the judgment about to come. The editor of the fourth collection of oracles has used it as the third of the three prose narratives upon which the structure of the collection is based. But the passage has this difference from the other two, that it tells of the response to Jeremiah's presence and preaching and turns this response itself into a sign. Cf. 18.18, 19–21. On the meaning of the sign see, below.

1. Pashhur . . . son of Immer: another Pashhur, son of Malchiah, is mentioned in 21.1 and Gedaliah son of Pashhur in 38.1. In later times it was the name of a priestly house, cf. Ezr. 2.37. For the disciplinary function of the chief officer, where Zephaniah is called into action against Jeremiah, see 29.26–27. The name Pashhur is usually understood to be of Egyptian origin.

2. Then Pashhur beat Jeremiah: for thrashing as a regular means of administering punishment in criminal law, see Dt. 25.2–3; 2 Cor. 11.24.

the stocks: cf. Job 13.27; 33.11; Ac. 16.24.

3. The LORD does not call your name Pashhur, but Terror on every side: thus Jeremiah makes Pashhur himself a sign to the people. He who both prophesied in the name of the LORD and attempted to suppress the true prophet will henceforth bear a name which openly declares the judgment which he and the people must bear. In a general sense there is no ambiguity. In precise detail, there are two difficulties:

(1) It is not altogether certain how we should determine the text. The LXX did not have the words 'on every side'. Since the interpretation of the expression in v. 4 makes no use of these words, it is thought by many that the fuller phrase is an assimilation to what had become a favourite slogan in the Jeremiah corpus (cf. especially v. 10 and 6.25; 46.5; 49.29; cf. Ps. 31.14; Lam. 2.22).

(2) The translation 'terror' is disputed. In none of the passages listed above does the LXX render 'terror'. Here it translates *metoikos*, 'sojourner' or 'alien' and it is plain that the addition of 'on every side'

would not make good sense. Isa.31.9, where the meaning 'terror' might seem to be confirmed by the parallelism, suggests that the LXX translators did not know this meaning. It is also alleged that the name 'terror', or more accurately 'cause of terror', is inappropriate of Pashhur and applies rather to the Babylonian army. The sense 'destruction all round' is proposed, as supported by the LXX of Jer. 49.29 and the Targum.

None of these arguments is conclusive. In particular it is a mistake to assume that the name given to Pashhur must somehow suit the man himself. When Isaiah gave his son the name Shear-jashub, it had no bearing on the nature or situation of the boy (Isa. 7.3). Isaiah was simply adopting a means of placarding the name, and indeed, in the case of Maher-shalal-hash-baz he did just that (Isa. 8.1). 'Horror' (MT), 'dread' (Vulg.) or 'destruction'—are therefore all possible translations to the extent that they make sense in the context. On the whole this tips the balance in favour of the meaning 'horror' (active) or 'terror' (active or passive) which is sufficiently attested in Heb. This conclusion weakens the argument for omitting the words 'on every side'. Indeed, where certainty is impossible most readers will feel that there is inadequate reason for disturbing the received English translation.

Nor are attempts to find word-play on the words 'from every side' convincing. How devious to depend for the force of the sign on a word-play which is in fact tacitly assumed and never expressed. This is not a sign, but esoteric mumbo-jumbo. The suggestion is too clever and must be rejected.

This leaves us with a simple solution. Jeremiah gives Pashhur a name 'Terror on every side', which means that he will walk about as a living proclamation of the horror that is to come on God's people and their land. This will be very different from the lies (*šeqer*) which he proclaimed when he thought he had the authority to speak God's word! This interpretation consorts well with the use of the expression for the Foe from the North in 6.25.

4. Behold, I will make you a terror to yourself and to all your friends: probably this is a misleading translation. In no sense is Pashhur the cause of the terror or even the instrument of it, and the fact that **they shall fall by the sword of their enemies while you look on** cannot be laid at his account. Rather is he the living sign that the 'terror' is a judgment, not a passing incident. While he is around, his friends cannot forget that their terrible plight is the implementation of the word of God. The sense is: 'Behold I am delivering you up to be *Magor* in respect of yourself and your friends. As they fall by the sword of their enemies, there you will be at hand, watching it all, your new name the inescapable sign to them that their fate is according to the determinate counsel of God, warning having been duly given in prophecy'.

The clear prophecy in vv. 4 and 5 that the people will be taken into exile corresponds to the time when Jeremiah can identify the foe as the Babylonian invader. Not all the predictions of exile can safely be ascribed to Jeremiah (see on 5.18–19), but it is probable that he came to amplify his earlier predictions of total destruction as events unfolded.

6. We may take it as historical fact that Pashhur was among the leaders taken into exile, whether this is prophecy or whether it is prophecy after the event.

DOOM-LADEN SUFFERING **20.7–18**

These verses contain the last and most bitter of all the personal expressions of grief and suffering ascribed to Jeremiah (cf. 11.18–12.6; 15.10–21; 17.9–10, 14–18; 18.18–23). They reach a new depth of desolation and reproach. If in 15.18 he had asked the question concerning the LORD's reliability in the figure of the deceitful wady, here he plainly accuses the LORD of duping him, as false prophets are duped. And if in 15.10 he protested that he had been born to be a man of strife, here he acknowledges a curse on the day of his birth with all the power of the book of Job (chapter 3).

The section is set to follow Jeremiah's encounter with Pashhur. It is doubtful whether the editor knew precisely that this outburst was sparked off by Jeremiah's experience of the stocks; more likely that, in the building up of his material, he saw this as a suitable context in the whole situation of Jeremiah's prophetic activity during those years. At the same time Pashhur is a symbol of the general hostile reaction to the word of God.

Many scholars emphasise the differences within vv. 7–18 and see here at last three separate units of tradition. In particular the expression of confidence and hope in vv. 11–12 and the song of deliverance in v. 13 have appeared to them incongruous in the midst of such strong expression of despair. The fact that, according to the prevailing critical theory of the composition of Jeremiah, (rejected in this commentary), 19.1–20.6 and 20.7–18 were thought to belong to different literary sources, supported this view.

It is more probable however that verses 7–13 at least belong together. The argument that the order of vv. 11 and 12 should be reversed (Weiser, Bright), and the further argument that vv. 7–9 should be considered separately from vv. 10–13 (Volz, Rudolph, McKane), seems to me to be based on an anachronistic view of what is possible in the free prophetic use of the lament form. The psalms of lament commonly included not only a petition for deliverance (as in v. 12) but also some sort of anticipation of that deliverance in the form of a declaration of trust (as in v.11) or a vow of praise (as in v. 13).

Whether vv. 14–18 can be interpreted in this way, so that they can be seen as part of a single psalm, is more difficult. D.A. Clines and D.M. Gunn *ZAW* 1976, pp. 390–409) argue for original separateness. One is inclined to see the editor appending comparable material because of the general suitability of the context, and ending this collection deliberately on the note of the curse and of the tragic contradiction of the life of Jeremiah, as the hideous future now unfolds. The climax is not in the assurance of deliverance but in the inevitability of doom. Verses 14–18 bring this collection to an end in a theme comparable to that of 6.27–30 completing the first collection (Baruch's scroll). Jeremiah is not simply wishing himself out of life like a potential suicide. He is using the strongest possible terms to express the truth that he did not wish to deliver the terrible message that was given to him. He would prefer not to have lived. He ends with the question, 'Why did I come forth from the womb to see toil and sorrow, and spend my days in shame?' The unspoken answer is that he had to speak as he was commanded and the consequences had to be what they would be. This answer was in fact spoken in vv. 8–9. This was the destiny of Jeremiah. His life gives the lie to those who dismiss religion as comfort, wishful thinking, opium. His medicine he would have given his life not to have to administer. But he did what he had to do. Verses 14–18 are treated here with vv. 7–13, not necessarily because they form a single poem, but because they have been editorially united.

As will be seen below, the evidence is against the view that the lament is lifted into this context from elsewhere. It is the unique utterance of Jeremiah. At the same time it uses the lament tradition and leans heavily on Ps. 31.

7. O LORD, thou hast deceived me, and I was deceived: the verb is used in Exod. 22.16 and Sir. 42.10 of seducing a virgin. But the more significant usage is of the deception wrought by a lying spirit, as in 1 Kg. 22.20–22, or by the LORD himself in Ezek. 14.9: 'if the prophet be deceived and speak a word, I, the LORD, have deceived the prophet, and I will stretch out my hand against him, and will destroy him'. D.J.A. Clines and D.M. Gunn in *VT* 28 (1978) 20–27 argue for the meaning 'entice'.

It is quite impossible to interpret this as meaning that in a black mood Jeremiah believed his message to be false. Nowhere does he betray any doubt that it was the word of the LORD he was speaking, and he never ceases to denounce the false prophets. He was not saying that he himself was in some sense a false prophet. In the very next breath (v. 8), he made it clear that it is the word of the LORD which causes his trouble, not a lying word. It is because, as in Ezek. 14.9, all inspiration, true and false, was attributed to the LORD, that Jeremiah can use words deliberately ambivalent. A false prophet is deceived as to the message itself. Jeremiah is deceived, not as to the message, but as to the personal reception he encounters for delivering the message. Speaking the truth, he is greeted as a liar. The LORD's spokesman, he is persecuted as a criminal. Deeply concerned for his people, he is treated as their enemy. His love and devotion to the LORD is unswerving against every enticement to seek peace, but the LORD treats him as though he hates him. This is the predicament of the prophet of the LORD in times like these. The words are not too strong.

I have become a laughingstock all the day; every one mocks me: the idea is familiar in the psalms of lament e.g. 22.7; 40.14–15; 35.16; 44.13–16, etc.

8. I shout, Violence and destruction: a slogan-type combination. Cf. 6.7; Am. 3.10; Hab. 1.3; Isa. 60.18. Clines and Gunn (op.cit.) interpret the phrase as a cry of protest against the LORD. This is linked with the argument that 'shout' means the cry of the innocent for justice (as in Isa. 42.2). But not always. Context has to be the arbiter. Context suggests that the slogan serves as a summary of Jeremiah's message, from which he cannot escape, and 'shout' expresses the force with which he utters it. It is, of course, absurd to worry what this could have meant in Jeremiah's experience of opposition. It is prophecy, and sums up the total situation of judgment and disaster.

For the word of the LORD has become for me a reproach and derision all day long: here is the unmistakeable sign that Jeremiah has applied the familiar lament language to his own unique situation. It is commonplace in the laments for the representative person (king?) or Israel to be described in these terms (Pss. 22.6; 31.11; 39.8; 44.13–14; 69.10–11; 79.4; 89.41). It is unique to describe the word of the LORD so, but this is exactly the prophetic point of Jeremiah's lament.

9. If I say, I will not mention him, or speak any more in his name: again the same theme is found in Ps. 39, but of the psalmist's silence before the wickedness of the ungodly and the transitoriness of life. When his heart becomes hot within him and he is driven to speak, he prays for a divine hearing in face of the vanity of human existence. The point of Jeremiah's silence is that he has no desire to speak his terrible message. He has none of the secret delight in judgmental attitudes, characteristic of the pharisee of all ages. He has to obey intentions deeper than conscious desires. He is in touch with a reality that claims and controls him.

shut up in my bones: the bones form the structure of the body, so to speak the building within which the fire burns and generates its heat. 'Shut up' is sometimes used of ceremonial taboo (Neh. 6.10), sometimes more generally of constraint and the reverse of 'free' (cf. 2 Kg. 17.4; Dt. 32.36; I Kg. 14.10, etc., cf. also Jer. 36.35). The image therefore suggests both the hiddenness of his inspiration and its power over him.

10. For I hear many whispering. Terror is on every side!: This line is identical in Heb. with Ps. 31.1a. The terror is created by the enemies who 'scheme together against me, as they plot to take my life'. At first sight this seems far from the meaning attached to this slogan when Jeremiah renamed Pashhur. But in all probability the 'I' of the psalmist is the representative person, the king; and the king's enemies are Israel's enemies. Even so one might be inclined to think that this lament was drawn into the context of Jer. 20 editorially, by reason of the catchword 'Terror on every side', were it not that such uniquely prophetic use is made of the lament. The most satisfactory hypothesis is that Jeremiah quotes this lament language precisely because of its familiarity. Its new application to his own prophetic role thus becomes all the more striking and effective. The slogan is, of course, ambivalent, and no doubt intended to be ironic. The enemies of the prophet utter the slogan without realising that they are making themselves unwitting vehicles of prophecy.

say all my familiar friends: cf. 41.9 where the equivalent Heb. expression occurs in the context of the psalmist's lament that his enemies are maliciously waiting for his death (v. 5).

11. But the LORD is with me as a dread warrior: this image is taken even further in Isa. 10.21; Ps. 24.8 and the Magnificat.

my persecutors: cf. 15.15; 17.18; Pss. 7.1; 31.15. This verse expresses the assurance which is a feature of the laments. Jeremiah believes the LORD will both save him from the final snatch of his enemies and bring upon them a just retribution, even the shame and dishonour that they have wished upon Jeremiah.

12. This verse is practically identical with 11.20. It comes appropriately in both places. This appropriateness is seen once the structure of the lament is understood. There is therefore no profit in asking which passage is original and which is secondary. Its refrain-like character may be an indication that Jeremiah repeated it more than once.

13. The sudden affirmation that the LORD has delivered the life of the needy from the hand of evildoers is difficult for the modern mind. Nevertheless it is typical of the lament form, cf. the 'certainty of hearing' in 6.9; 22.22. In the Psalms, the 'needy' or, literally 'poor' are usually faithful Israel contrasted with the 'evildoers' who are her national enemies. But these words are capable of wider and more particular application. Here Jeremiah himself is the sole representative of God's 'poor' and the evildoers are those who, in setting themselves against him, have identified themselves as the enemies of God.

14. The sudden reversion to the theme of lament is undeniably inappropriate if vv. 7–18 are to be interpreted on the lines of a single lament form. It is perhaps better to understand the placing of vv. 14–18, which constitute a completely formed lament, as due to an editorial arrangement, providing a conclusion to the collection, similar to 6.27–30. The cursing of the day of his birth has affinities with the outcry of Job in 3.3–16. But the underlying reasons are different. Job was protesting against the undeserved suffering he was called upon to endure. Jeremiah is not simply resisting persecution and pain. He is resisting the compulsion to utter his message of doom. Would that he had not been born to this destiny! This consciousness of destiny was with him from the beginning of his ministry and found expression in his call (1.5). Herein lies the appropriateness of this section at the very end of a collection of oracles. It is the strongest possible way of saying that his message is not his own. The only way to have avoided it would be not to have been born!

cursed be the day: This can as easily be translated 'cursed is the day'. See below on v. 15.

The day when my mother bore me: this way of referring to elemental human life, in terms of the 'mother', is repeatedly found in the laments. Cf. Pss. 22.9–10; 35.14; 51.5; 71.6; 109.14; 131.2; 139.13. This language may easily extend to refer to the origins of Israel herself, as in Isa. 44.1–2; 49.1, 5; 48.8.

15. Cursed be the man who brought the news to my father: It is usual to contrast this gruesome response to the messenger with the usual custom of rewarding him for good news, and to suggest that the curse on the messenger is, in a sense, a softening of the curse which might be expected most appropriately upon the prophet's father and mother. Such a curse, it is said, is unthinkable, but the messenger provides a convenient substitute! But the Heb. can easily be translated 'cursed is the man', i.e.

this is not so much the pronouncement of a curse upon him as the recognition that the curse of the divine judgment *is* upon him. If this is correct it makes good sense. The man who announced Jeremiah's birth was the first, so to speak, to encounter the man who was born to be a prophet. He is representative of all those who later encountered his message and are the objects of the judgment. In this context the language of v. 16 becomes fully intelligible.

16. Let that man be like the cities which the LORD overthrew without pity: i.e. like Sodom and Gomorrah in Gen. 18.23–33, types of the community which has become so corrupt that no redemption is possible. Cf. Isa. 1.7–9.

let him hear a cry in the morning and an alarm at noon: It was probably at dawn, with the rising sun, that the LORD was believed to bring help to his people, as celebrated in the cult (Ps. 46.5). Likewise the normal security of noon will be broken by the 'noonday destroyer', cf. 6.4 and, with mythical overtones, 15.8, q.v. This echo of the Foe from the North poems indicates the substance of the word that has become a reproach, the occasion of Jeremiah's prophetic suffering and consequent lament. This is the symbol of the LORD's judgment in this crisis of history.

Theme of the final form of the tradition—chapters 18–20
It is now necessary to give chapters 18–20, as they have come down to us from the redactor, the same kind of scrutiny we gave to chapters 14–17. Here the pervasive theme is quite different, though some of the material overlaps. The theme seems to be the mortal conflict between the LORD and the leaders of Israel who, because they reject the LORD's plan, are therefore ruthlessly hostile to the LORD's man. Between them Jeremiah is crushed, and anguished.

The LORD's sovereign purpose is declared in the signs and their interpretation in 18.1–11, 19. The hostile response of the leadership is described in 18.12 'We will follow our own plans'; 18.18 'Come, let us make plots against Jeremiah . . . and let us not heed any of his words'; and comes to a climax in the person of Pashhur, who beats Jeremiah and puts him in the stocks (20.1–6). Jeremiah's position is that of a target for the abuse and machinations of the leadership. His representative status is fully implied in the elucidation of the sign of the potter (18.7–10), for this is worked out in the terms of Jeremiah's call ('I will pluck up and breakdown . . . I will build and plant').

What Jeremiah is saying is precisely what the LORD called him to say. Therefore to reject the LORD's will and plan is to reject Jeremiah, and to reject Jeremiah is to reject the LORD. When Jeremiah says, 'Remember how I stood before thee to speak good for them', (v.20) he alludes to the other side of his prophetic office. He is the LORD's voice but also represents the LORD's people in intercession. His anguish is caused by the irony that the people whom he represents and serves 'dig a pit to take (him)' and 'plot to slay him' (vv. 22–23).

The conflict is sharpened in chapters 19 and 20. Jeremiah performs the second sign in the valley of Hinnom, symbolising the lowest degree of Israel's apostasy, and the breaking of the flask signifies an irreparable destruction. Returning, Jeremiah, the LORD's man, stands in 'the court of the LORD's house', and repeats his message. This is the word of the LORD from Zion. Pashhur retorts with violence. The terrible ambivalence of the prophet's mediating position is expressed in the last and most bitter lament (20.7–18), leading up to the recognition that his birth was a curse. To understand this depth of bitterness, one has to understand the nature and role of an Israelite prophet, in a period of national crisis.

(2) A COLLECTION OF ORACLES ON KINGS AND PROPHETS MAINLY AFTER THE TIME OF JEHOIAKIM 21.1–24.10

Once again a collection of oracles is identified by the introductory formula (see introduction to chapters 7–20).

This is the word that came to Jeremiah from the LORD, and prefaced by a prose section in Deuteronomic style (21.1–10). In this case the prose passage relates to the second and finally destructive Babylonian attack on Jerusalem in the reign of Zedekiah, and summarises the final advice of the prophet before every forecast of doom, set out in the previous oracles, was fulfilled. From this we may deduce that the collection was made after this event. From the sort of material added we may infer the purpose of the collector—a scribe of the Jeremiah tradition.

The editor narrates first the request of Zedekiah for a word of the LORD and the unexpected answer that the LORD will be found destroying his own people. This is said in terms of the Deuteronomic curse upon Israel's disobedience. This then provides the framework for a series of oracles in judgment upon the kings of Judah whose task was to lead the people in righteousness. These are earlier oracles, probably separate from one another in time and circumstance, now conveniently set together under the title 'Concerning the royal house of Judah' (v. 21.11). 21.11–14 and 22.1–8 are addressed generally to the house of David; 22.9–12 concerns Jehoahaz; 22.13–23 concerns Jehoiakim; 22.24–5 concerns Jehoiachin. 23.1–7 is an oracle of hope looking beyond the 'shepherds' who have helped to create the present distresses to the shepherd of David's house who will execute justice and righteousness, and preside over a restored people. This passage is in prose and probably the collection is no older than this can be. In 23.9–40 a series of oracles against the prophets is added, probably because the prophets are the other major leaders who bear the greatest responsibility for guiding Judah to disaster. This is introduced under the title concerning the prophets (23.9).

The editor rounds off the collection by adding the vision of the baskets of figs (24.1–10). He thus reverts to the manner of his beginning in 21.1–10, both in form and content. The passage is in prose in the first person with characteristic Deuteronomic touches; and the conclusion, while offering a glimpse of hope to the exiles, reinforces the judgment on Zedekiah and the people shortly before the events of 587–6 B.C.

ON THE KINGS OF JUDAH 21.1–23.8

THE FATE OF JUDAH AND THE END OF THE MONARCHY 21.1–10

Like so many of the prose passages from chapter 7 onwards, this section tells of an event which evoked significant teaching of Jeremiah (see introduction to chapters 7–20). We saw reason for attributing these prophetic narratives to Baruch or at least a scribe in the Jeremiah tradition. It seemed probable that the characteristic style of Baruch was influenced by the Deuteronomic school in which he had been trained, and that he used a degree of freedom in the recollection and transmission of the message of Jeremiah. Here the event itself is uncomplicated. Zedekiah sent a man named Pashhur (probably quite unconnected with the 'Pashhur, son of Immer' of chapter 20) and the priest Zephaniah to ask Jeremiah, in the conventional way, for an oracle concerning the Babylonian invasion now in progress. Was there any hope of divine intervention on behalf of Judah? Jeremiah gave the required oracle, predicting that there would be total defeat, and that those who survived the siege, including Zedekiah, would be delivered into the utterly uncompassionate hand of Nebuchadrezzar. In Deuteronomic terms, he set before the people the way of life and the way of death and declared the way of life to be unreserved capitulation to the foreign enemy.

Inevitably the narrative invites comparison with 37.3–10 where also

Zedekiah sent a messenger to Jeremiah and Jeremiah's reply reaffirmed the total defeat of Judah at the hands of Babylon. Some scholars think that these are duplicate versions of the same event. They emphasis the Deuteronomic handling of 21.1–10 and the vagueness of the introduction. They conclude that 37.3–10 is closer to the historical facts. Other scholars refer the passages to quite separate occasions, even if not widely separated in time.

For reasons set out below, it is not plausible to regard 21.1–10 as Deuteronomic preaching or midrashic invention. And as soon as the passage is taken seriously as referring to an event in the life of Jeremiah, it is the contrasts with 37.3–10 that become impressive

(a) The messengers are different and are precisely identified in each case. It is quite arbitrary to suppose, as some commentators have done, that an editor derived the names of the two messengers from 38.1 and 37.3.

(b) The terms of the enquiry are different, in 21.1–10 seeking an oracle of hope, in 37.3–10 (as though having no further expectation of an oracle of hope) requesting Jeremiah's prophetic intercession.

(c) The answers, while restating the LORD's intention to destroy his people, vary in detail. In 21.1–10 the heart of the oracle is that the LORD's 'holy war' will be against, rather than for, his people and that the curse, promised in the Deuteronomic law upon disobedience, is about to be implemented upon Judah. In 37.3–10, Jeremiah gives no direct answer to the request for prayer, but refers to a temporary lifting of the siege of Jerusalem, when the Babylonian army heard that the Egyptian army had left Egypt for Palestine. He took the opportunity to declare the impotence of Egypt to change the purpose of the LORD, and added that nothing, not even the defeat of the Babylonian army, could now prevent the burning of Jerusalem. It therefore seems somewhat gratuitous to treat these passages as variants of the same traditions. There is no need, and the efforts to do so are not persuasive.

But the narrative inevitably invites comparison with some other passages, in particular 34.1–6 and 52.4–16. In the one Jeremiah predicted, and in the other it is narrated, that Zedekiah was indeed captured. His eyes were put out and his sons slain, but he was not himself put to the sword. This conflicts with the prediction of comprehensive slaughter in 21.7. The obvious conclusion is that the prediction of chapter 21 was made without knowledge of the actual course of events, that no subsequent effort was made to doctor it according to the events. Nor can it be regarded as a piece of writing composed after the event to look like a prediction. It is a primary witness to the view taken by Jeremiah as to the course of events.

That is not to deny that the passage shows some signs of compilation. Verses 1–6 are the base. Verse 7 is introduced with **Afterward**, which is a formula of transition and marks v.7 as an expansion. Verses 8–10 may well be a separate and independent prophecy. There is no doubt that at some stage Jeremiah recommended capitulation to the enemy and drew on himself the vituperation and hostility one would expect. See on 38.2–3. As in 38.2, so in 21.9 there is a breach in the otherwise universal prediction of destruction: some will save their lives as a prize of war. When this is placed in the context of 21.1–6, 7, it appears to be a contradiction. It is, however, entirely believable that in different contexts the prophet should utter both predictions. The one belongs to the expectation of invasion, the other to the moment of its execution.

The Deuteronomic style is striking. It is however by no means obvious that its author is to be sought outside what might be called the Jeremiah circle, for the following reasons.

(a) As we have observed again and again in the Deuteronomic prose, it retains features peculiar to the book of Jeremiah. Here in particular, we note the use of **Behold** with the participle in the first person (vv. 4, 8). Verse 8 is the more significant because this is the participial form of a statement otherwise close to Dt. 30.15, 19. Again, the threat **he shall not pity them, or spare them, or have compassion** (v. 7) is no doubt a use of the tradition relating to the 'ban', as in Dt. 13.8, 17, but it is closest to Jer. 13.14. Again, the warning that he who stays in the city **shall die by the sword, by famine, and by pestilence** (v. 9.) is comprehended in the great curse of Dt. 28, but it is characteristically explicit in the Jeremiah tradition and in the poetry, as well as in the prose (14.12; 22.7, 9; 24.10; 27.8, 13; 29.17, 18; 32.24, 36; 34.17; 38.2; 42.17, 22; 44.13). Again, **I have set my face against this city for evil and not for good,** (v. 10), is the theme of Dt. 28, and the evil is 'in accordance with all the curses of the covenant written in this book of the law' (Dt. 29.21, 27), but this way of expressing it as that of the Jeremiah tradition (Jer. 39.16, cf. 38.4; 44.11, 27).

(b) The expression **shall have his life as a prize of war** (v. 9) is peculiar to Jer. 38.2; 39.18; cf. 45.5. See on v. 9.

(c) Where expressions look like quotations from Dt., they are in the nature of clichés which remind the audience of the truths they know, by pounding repetition. Such are **with outstretched hand and strong arm, and in fury, and in great wrath** (v. 5). The first part occurs repetitively in Dt. 4.34; 5.15; 7.19; 11.2; 16.8 (and in Jer. 32.21); the second part in Dt. 29.27 (and in Jer. 32.27).

There can be little doubt that these Deuteronomic expressions are not simply the inevitable stylistic turns of phrase natural to the author. He is affirming two harsh truths suggested by the Deuteronomic tradition, and there is no convincing reason why Jeremiah should not have formulated his oracle in this way.

The first truth is that the great curse, promised as the inevitable result of disobedience (Dt. 28) is about to fall upon this people. The choice between the way of life and the way of death (Dt. 30) is no longer open in its full possibilities. The choice is now narrowed tragically to those who are survivors of the destruction of Jerusalem. This is an application of Deuteronomic teaching within a situation which is already tragic and largely beyond salvation. It derives its power and thrust from this ironic application, and loses it if it is thought of as subsequent preaching.

The second example of the application of Deuteronomic principles is the handling of the tradition of the holy war. It is the essence of this tradition that the LORD saves his people by many or by few, 'with outstretched hand and strong arm', and that all spoils of war are 'devoted' to him, or put to the ban (ḥērem). With unmistakeable intention, the prophet reverses this picture. The irony is intense. Taught to believe that his weapons will become the victorious implements of the LORD's saving acts, Zedekiah is now warned that they will be gathered uselessly into the city. Schooled in the tradition that the LORD fights the battles of his people, Zedekiah is now told that the LORD will fight against his people. Whereas all spoils of war were to be put to the ban, now Judah herself is to be 'devoted' without pity or compassion. This is a reversal of staggering proportions, and also derives its force from its application to the moment of tragedy. Cf. the way in which Jeremiah also appropriated to himself the language of the holy war in 1.17–19.

The announcement in v. 7 that the LORD will give king Zedekiah into the hand of their enemies (identified in MT as the king of Babylon) for further punishment, does not of itself imply the end of the monarchy as known in Judah, but there can be no doubt that the editor so understood it. He rests his hope in the emergence of 'a righteous Branch' (23.5) and in the closing prose oracle (24.8–10), he spells out the exemplary horror of the fate of Zedekiah and his entourage. At the same time, in the various oracles critical of the monarchy there is little directly reminiscent of the criticism implied in Dt. 17.14–20.

That Zedekiah is the centre of interest in the editor's mind is clear from the way he arranges his material and suggests that this king was still alive when the collection was made. What is certain is that the arrangement of the oracles makes sense, and there is no case for the mistaken confidence with which some scholars transpose the oracles. It is important to interpret the collection in its present order. A stylistic feature of this passage is a preference for synonyms or phrases arranged in two and threes. This is increased by the explanatory additions, identified by comparison with the shorter text of LXX. Allowing for these, examples are as follows:

1. with outstretched hand   and strong arm.
2. in anger, and in fury and in great wrath.
3. both man   and beast.
4. Zedekiah king of Judah,   his servants   and the people.
5. the pestilence   sword   and famine.
6. into the hand of their enemies   into the hand of those who seek their lives (LXX has 'into the hand of their enemies who seek their lives').
7. he shall not pity them   or spare them   or have compassion.

That some of these can be regarded as commonplace quotations cannot diminish the cumulative force of the list. Plainly it is found elsewhere in the prose tradition.

1. Pashhur the son of Malchiah: cf. 38.1. Nothing to do with the Pashhur who put Jeremiah in the stocks (chapter 20), but one of the *śārîm* who played an important part in the final events (chapters 36, 38).
   Zephaniah the priest: cf. 37.3. The messenger on another occasion also. See above.
   2. Inquire of the LORD for us: *dāraš* (seek) often used of consulting an oracle, cf. especially Jer. 37.7.
   Nebuchadrezzar King of Babylon is making war against us: i.e. the second invasion beginning in 589 B.C., cf. 2 Kg. 25.1.
   4. The Chaldeans: (Heb. *Kaśdîm*, originally Aramean (*kaldu*) probably detachments of the Babylonian army, perhaps related to the neo-Babylonian dynasty, who joined with the Medes to bring about the fall of the Assyrian empire. In the Jeremiah tradition they are referred to simply as the army of Nebuchadrezzar. The Heb. text is probably expanded and LXX may be basic: 'Thus says the LORD: Behold I will turn back the weapons of war with which you are fighting against the Chaldeans, who are besieging you outside the walls, into the midst of the city.'

5. with outstretched hand and strong arm: normally a formula suggestive of the Exodus, but here as elsewhere in prophecy separated from its original context. See above.

7. into the hand of Nebuchadrezzar king of Babylon: LXX omits. This is one of a number of identifying glosses, as in chapter 25 where the older spelling of the name is used. The glosses of chapters 27–29 have the later spelling. This therefore represents a very early stage of redaction.

8. the way of life and the way of death: The idea of the two ways of life is a theme of the wisdom schools which appears in Prov. and is taken up in the Community Rule (Qumran) and in the early Christian *Epistle of Barnabas* and the *Didache*. Its particular utilisation in Deut. (30.15–20) is its sharpest form and corresponds to the blessing and the curse, which is a pervasive contrast in all the Deuteronomic writings.

9. shall have his life as a prize of war: literally 'as a booty'. This expression, whose idiomatic force is uncertain, occurs also in 38.2; 39.18 and 45.5. These are its only occurrences, so that it may be said to be a feature of the prose tradition in Jeremiah. In each case its function is to suggest that escape from the Babylonian conquest of Judah is a most fortunate 'windfall'. See also on 39.18.

THE KING, GUARDIAN OF JUSTICE **21.11–14**

The superscription **And to the house of the King of Judah (say)** probably heads the collection of ten or eleven oracles from 21.11–23.8. Although the *RSV* rendering is permissible, it is probably better translated (omitting the copulative) 'Concerning' or 'on the house of David' and is parallel to the similar superscription in 23.9 'Concerning the prophets'. The fact that the superscription occurs here rather than before 21.2ff. could (but not necessarily) mean that the editor added his prose piece on Jeremiah's reply to Zedekiah to an already made collection. It certainly highlights the editor's intention to relate all Jeremiah's words on the kings to the fate of the last of the kings shortly before the fall of Jerusalem. All his oracles concerning the kings are here collected.

The editor starts with the most generally phrased of all these oracles, such as Jeremiah might have uttered at any time during his ministry. But since Jeremiah acknowledged that Josiah did in fact fulfil the demand here made, it is more likely that the oracle was uttered during the reign of one of his successors, before the political situation became desperate, i.e. before 598 B.C. The oracle is in verse. The only imaginative image occurs in v. 13, where a general warning is given that the secure and complacent will find punishment inescapable. Verses 11b–12 cannot be regarded as a Deuteronomic addition.

12. O house of David: a recognised way of referring to the royal house, cf. 2 Sam. 3.1, 6; 7.26, etc. The expression can refer to the line of kings, or as in Isa. 7.2, 13 to the living representative of the line. Here the imperative **hear** is plural, but this is in all probability the touch of the editor who thereby applies this oracle to all the kings subsequently named.

Execute justice in the mornings, and deliver from the hand of the oppressor him who has been robbed: thus Jeremiah demands of the king that he fulfil the responsibility placed upon him at his enthronement, to be the supreme judge, the guardian of righteousness, as is so powerfully stated in the royal psalm 72. Why 'in the morning'? It is possible to understand this distributively (cf. Ps. 73.14) and to translate with *NEB, REB* 'betimes'. More likely it refers to the custom of administering justice in the morning.

lest my wrath go forth like fire: it is possible that *yāṣā'* has the meaning 'shine forth', 'flash', 'blaze up' (*NEB, REB,* following G.R. Driver).

and burn with none to quench it: a commonplace expression of judgment in terms of fire-imagery (cf. Isa. 1.31). The commonplace character of the line is confirmed by the fact that it is repeated word for word in 4.4, q.v. No doubt Jeremiah himself repeated it with the regularity of a refrain.

13. O inhabitant of the valley, O rock of the plain: the objection that neither Jerusalem, nor the king's palace fit this description is wide of the mark. This is a proverb-like image and refers to the sense of security belonging to those who live in pleasant, civilized places. The 'plain' (*mîšôr*) is sometimes used of the tableland between the Arnon and Heshbon, and may mean 'plateau'. But it is also used in the Psalms of a place of safety and prosperity (Pss. 26.12; 27.11) or of integrity (143.10). Such is the complacency and confidence of those whom Jeremiah addresses that they believe they can never be disturbed. On the contrary, says Jeremiah, they will be disturbed by a punishing fire. This is the teaching that the divine judgment is inescapable (cf. Am. 5.19) and, in its criticism of a false sense of security, is in line with one of his most persistent and dominant themes. The metaphor is, like most proverb-like sayings, concrete and precise in its imagery, but of almost infinitely wide application. Here it is applied to the confidence of the kings and their capital. If this is the correct interpretation, then proposed emendations (conjectural and dubious) may be dismissed. Nor is there need to translate 'enthroned o'er the vale', though this is grammatically feasible.

14. I will punish you: Heb. *pāqaḏ*, lit. 'visit, as in Dt., but characteristic of Jeremiah.

I will kindle a fire in her forest: again a now somewhat stylised image of judgment, cf. Am. 1.14 and especially Isa. 9.17; 10.18; which shows that here also there is no need to see in the forest a direct reference to Jerusalem's splendid cedar buildings!

REINFORCEMENT OF THE PRECEDING ORACLE **22.1–9**

This prose section is a remarkable example of the literary art of the editor. Its pattern is exactly that of the preceding oracle, and at first it looks like an alternative prose version of the preceding poem. This tempts the thought that it is simply a phenomenon of transmission, i.e. the poem gives us the actual words of Jeremiah, the prose gives us a form of the message assumed in tradition. But the truth cannot be as simple as this. For one thing the section contains in vv. 6–7 a poetic oracle which makes a similar point to 21.13–14, and yet cannot be interpreted as an alternative form of the same oracle. For another, the prose seems to depend to some extent verbally on the poetic oracle and, both in its corresponding sections and where it amplifies the poetic oracle, it quotes passages mainly from the Jeremiah prose tradition. This is so intricate that it has the appearance of a literary mosaic and cannot be explained in terms of oral tradition. Nor can it be regarded as an alternative prose form of the same tradition, even if its literary character is acknowledged. The absence of any special heading can perhaps support the view that the editor of the collection constructed this passage, using the traditional poem in vv. 6–7 and his memory of Jeremiah's actual intervention, to supply reinforcement he deemed to be necessary to the complete expression of Jeremiah's attitude to the kingship. Literary constructions of this kind are not unique to Jeremiah and may certainly be discerned, e.g. in Isa. 10.16–19, 20–27; 11.10–16. It is probable therefore that this passage had no independent history before its incorporation into the present collection of oracles.

The evidence upon which this judgment is based may be set out in the table on p. 286.

Thus we have another impressive statement of the ideal of kingship. It is more than an ideal; it is a requirement. The kingship which does not guard and promote justice will be dispensed with. And this leadership determines the health of the community ('this city', v. 8).

	21.11–14	22.1–9
The address	v.11. 'O House of David'	v.2. 'O King of Judah, who sit on the throne of David' Amplified by (a) the command to go down to the house of the king. (b) 'your servants, and your people who enter these gates' (from 7.2; 17.20)
The command to guard justice	v.12a. 'Execute justice . . ., and deliver from the hand of the oppressor him who has been robbed'	v.3. 'Do justice and righteousness, and deliver', etc. Amplified by 'And do no wrong or violence to the alien, the fatherless, and the widow, nor shed innocent blood in this place' (from 7.5–6).
The punishment	v.12b. The image of fire.	v.7. The image of felling noble trees to be cast into fire.
Security no protection	v.13. The proverb-like image of the plain-dwellers.	vv.6–7. The quoted poem of Gilead and the cedars of Lebanon. Amplified by The reaction of the nations (from Dt. 29.23f.)

1. Go down to the house of the king: it is sometimes argued that the prophet must have been in the Temple precincts from which passage to the adjoining palace was to a lower level. But the verb seems to have been used with the same freedom with which we refer to the up line without implying that the way is up hill. In any case the introduction above would suggest that this opening is conventional.

2. the throne of David: an evocative image which is already attaching to itself some of the overtones of the messianic hope. Cf. 1 Sam. 3.10; 1 Kg. 2.12, 24, 45; Isa. 9.6; Jer. 22.30; 29.16; 36.30; Lk. 1.32. The expression links both the promise of 2 Sam. 7 and the hope of a righteous branch.

who enters these gates: as in 7.2, where the gates are those of the Temple and 17.20, where they are those of the city.

3a. virtually 21.12a. **3b.** cf. 7.6.

4. The condition as in 7.5; the promise more or less as in 17.25.

5. I swear by myself: cf. Gen. 22.15; Isa. 45.23; Jer. 4913. There is none other by whom the LORD may make solemn and binding promise. **this house shall become a desolation:** cf. 25.11; 44.22, where the expression is used of the land.

6. You are as Gilead to me: see on 8.22 and cf. 46.11; 51.8, where the balm or resin derived from the storax tree may suggest that the point of the poem lies in the valuable or majestic trees of Gilead and Lebanon. The cutting down of the cedars of Lebanon (as also the oaks of Bashan, cf. v. 20) is familiar Day of the LORD imagery (Isa. 2), suggesting the humbling of human pride and the tragic reversal of judgment (cf. also Isa. 10.34; Zech. 11.1, 2). On the other hand Gilead may stand in a more general way for the particularly well-favoured eastern territory of Israel where might be found 'from the earliest times to the Assyrian captivity, Hebrew communities, centres and rallying-places for Hebrew dynasties, Hebrew character and heroism, with prophecy, the distinctive glory of Hebrew life' (George Adam Smith, *The Historical Geography of the Holy Land* 10 1903, p.578).

Gilead and Lebanon are also linked in Zech. 10.10 as an overflow for the returned people to return from captivity. But here the meaning of the oracle concerns the judgment which shall be like the cutting down of mighty cedars. In 21.13 the meaning of the parallel image was that judgment was inescapable even for those who imagined themselves secure. Here the point is similar, the cedars being the symbol of human power and impregnability. The mingling of the images of felling trees and burning with fire is also found in Zech. 11.1–2.

7. I will prepare destroyers against you: lit. 'sanctify'. See on 6.4 and cf. 4.7.

8–9. An adaptation of Dt. 29.24–25, there applied to the land, here to the city, but with such fidelity to the words of Dt. that Moses' pronouncement of the effect of 'the curses written in this book' is cited and invoked. The same sort of appeal to Dt. 28 and 30, but also to 29 was noticed in 21.1–10, q.v. Rudolph's judgment that vv. 8–9 are a post-exilic, pedagogic addition which did not originally belong to the section is wide of the mark, and renders a satisfactory exposition impossible.

MOURNING FOR JEHOAHAZ **22.10–12**

There now follows a series of oracles about particular kings in chronological order—Jehoahaz, Jehoiakim and Jehoiachin and (in chapter 24) Zedekiah. It is not difficult to recognise the oracle concerning

Jehoahaz in the verse lines of v. 10, followed in v. 11 by an explanatory sentence in prose, identifying the king and reaffirming the prediction of permanent exile. This explanatory sentence is most probably provided by the editor and is not an alternative form of the tradition which he received.

The oracle of v. 10 is allusive. Its significance would be perceived only by those who were living through the tragic events leading up to and following the death of Josiah. 2 Kg. 23.29 is best understood as indicating that at Megiddo in 609 B.C. the Egyptian pharaoh Necho had somehow captured Josiah and then put him to death. The Israelite army capitulated in consequence. Josiah's eldest son, Jehoahaz, was then proclaimed king by the influential landed aristocracy (the ʿam-hāʾāreṣ), but reigned for only three months. Pharaoh Necho seized him at Riblah, put him in prison and then took him to Egypt where he died, (2 Kg. 23.30–35). It was at this juncture that Jeremiah uttered his oracle, i.e. while Jehoahaz was in captivity and not yet dead. An argument can be mounted that the king is Jehoiakim and the one who goes away Jehoiachin. But it is better to rely on the slender evidence we have (the prose commentator) than on pure speculation.

The importance of mourning rites in Israel is illustrated by the effect of Ezekiel's failure to weep for his wife (Ezek. 24.15–27). Thus he drew attention to another and a greater loss, the destruction of the sanctuary, which would leave the people unable to mourn or weep. In similar fashion, Jeremiah bade the people to stop their mourning for Josiah. This must have seemed crude advice, for the quality and achievement of Josiah was widely recognised, not least by Jeremiah himself (vv. 15–16), and his death was an unmitigated misfortune. But by this means Jeremiah turns attention on Jehoahaz. So long as he lives people remain complacent and hopeful of restoration. The command to **weep bitterly for him who goes away** (v. 10) is a command to treat him as though dead. His captivity has the finality of death. In his oracle (v. 10) Jeremiah did not actually speak of his death, and it was not to his purpose to do so. But the truth of the prediction was endorsed by his death, which no doubt took place sooner than Jeremiah expected and gave added power to the oracle. The point is registered by the editor in his prose comment (v. 12).

11. Shallum: i.e. the king's personal name, cf. 1 Chr. 3.15. Jehoahaz, meaning 'the LORD has seized (him)' was the name given him at his enthronement.

CONTEMPT FOR JEHOIAKIM 22.13–19

The 'woe' (*hôi*) of v. 13 and the 'therefore' (*lākēn*) of v. 18 are usually pointers to the occurrence of the primary prophetic form of speech. *hôi* introduces the criticism which provides the ground of judgment (sometimes called diatribe or invective or indictment or accusation or reproach); *lākēn* the threat or announcement of judgment, passed on the basis of the criticism and commonly introduced by the messenger formula 'thus says the LORD'. The combination occurs more than fifty times in the *OT*.

As might be expected in the book of Jeremiah, this 'therefore' occurs frequently; 'woe' is comparatively rare, cf. 22.18 and 23.1 in this collection and 30.7; 47.6; 48.1 (only the latter introducing a threat). The main conclusion to be drawn from these observations is that this rare reversion to a prophetic convention indicates the unity of the passage, despite the change in person. Verses 13–14 refer to the king in the third person; in vv. 15–17 he is addressed in the second person; vv. 18–19 revert to the third person. This has led some commentators to think in terms of 'additions'; but the power of the section lies in its completeness and the change in person is common enough in prophetic oracles.

The judgment on Jehoiakim supplements the information given in 2 Kg. 23.34–24.7 and there is no reason to doubt the accuracy of Jeremiah's observations. The criticisms have to do with Jehoiakim's social policy, and the punishment, linked by contrast with the fate of Jehoahaz, shows no awareness of the national peril soon to be suffered. For the first year or so of his reign Jehoakim was subservient to the Egyptians and ruled over the reduced kingdom they allowed him, rendering a heavy fine to Necho from money raised by taxation. But in 605 B.C. the Egyptians were defeated by Nebuchadrezzar, probably at or near Carchemish (Jer. 46.2, cf. 2 Kg. 24.7), and Jehoiakim came under Babylonian control. Thereafter the political situation was unremittingly dominant. It is altogether probable therefore that this oracle was uttered early in the reign of Jehoiakim during the precarious peace which he used for his own ends. Probably Jeremiah intervened as soon as the king had had time to demonstrate his intentions and his character.

Jeremiah's indictment was in terms of social justice. Jehoiakim set out to extend his palace, but with such ruthlessness and disregard of justice as to betray the principles on which the Hebrew monarchy was based. (See on 21.13–19; 22.1–9.) He did not pay his workmen; he made dishonest gain; he was unnecessarily and (for the times) blatantly extravagant and ostentatious. He who was the supreme court of appeal and guardian of justice both failed to protect the humble and poor and connived at the miscarriage of justice so that innocent blood was shed. In all this he was in glaring contrast to his father.

This indictment amounts to a remarkable criticism of a reigning king, comparable with Elijah's attack on Ahab. It is not surprising that when we have the narrative of Jehoiakim's dealings with Jeremiah (chapters 26 and 36) we are given stories of unrelenting hostility. The section also demands attention from the point of view of the underlying attitude it reveals to the Hebrew monarchy in principle. If some of the more extreme theories of divine or sacral kingship were true, it would be incredible if Jeremiah did not draw attention to these god-like pretensions, as Ezekiel did in respect of both the prince of Tyre (Ezek. 28.1–10) and the Egyptian Pharaoh (Ezek. 29.1–12). On the contrary Jeremiah refers with almost self-conscious 'democracy' to the way Jehoiakim makes his neighbour serve for nothing (v. 13). The king and his meanest subjects are, in the sight of the LORD, on the same footing. Whatever the implications of Pss. 2, 45 and Isa. 9, the utmost that can be said of the king is that he is first among equals and is subject and answerable to the same covenant law he is anointed to administer.

13. his upper rooms: it seems that Jehoiakim added a floor to his palace, cf. v. 14.

14. and cuts out windows for it: probably on the Egyptian pattern so that he could 'appear' before his subjects.

panelling it with cedar: cf. 1 Kg. 7.7; Hag. 1.14.

15. you compete in cedar: cf. 12.5. The universal weakness that provokes a man to do more splendidly than others. Does he think *this* makes him a splendid king?

Did not your father eat and drink and do justice and righteousness: appeal is often made to Mt. 11.19, as showing that the phrase 'eating and drinking' can mean simply the enjoyment of the good life. Jeremiah is then saying that Josiah ('your father') enjoyed a full life without either extravagance or neglect of his royal duties. Undeniably the line is susceptible of this interpretation. But Martin Buber correctly drew attention to the special significance of the phrase 'they beheld God, and ate and drank' (used absolutely) in Exod. 24.11 In Exod. this eating and drinking is part of the covenant making (cf. 2Kg. 23.3). Although Buber withdrew this suggestion in the German edition of his book *The Prophet of Faith*, it is one to which the reader should be open as at least a possibility.

The verse then leads aptly to the statement of the true knowledge of God.
16. Is not this to know me? This knowledge is not simply a matter
of entering into covenant worship and going to the sanctuary (cf. Hos.
6.6). It is demonstrated and expressed in the keeping of the terms of the
covenant and in particular in the performance of the vital, royal duty
which is essential to the covenant.

17. for shedding innocent blood: confirmation of 2 Kg. 24.4, and
see above.

18. LXX adds 'woe (*hôi*) to this man!' 'Ah (*hôi*) my brother!' or 'Ah
(*hôi*) my sister': that is, in all probability, an expression of grief uttered
by the mourners to one another. 'Ah (*hôi*) lord!' or 'Ah (*hôi*) his majesty!':
that is, concerning the king himself. That these expressions are quotations
of conventional forms of lamentation is confirmed by a Mesopotamian
text describing the New Year festival. A wailing woman would go round
the worshippers crying 'Ah, brother! Ah, brother!' The translation 'sister'
is open to doubt but no convincing alternative has been proposed. *NEB*,
REB has 'Alas, brother, dear brother'. The general sense is not affected.

19. With the burial of an ass he shall be buried: an ass would be
taken outside Jerusalem, thrown aside in some suitable place and left to
the birds of prey. Jeremiah means that the distresses of the times will
be such that the king himself will not receive proper burial. Perhaps also
he is implying that the people who have been exploited by him will show
their true regard for him in the manner of his burial. Such was the
importance attached to burial that this was a frightful punishment.

Was Jeremiah's prediction fulfilled? That he meant what he said is
confirmed by the reaffirmation of the prediction in 36.30. In 2 Kg. 24.6
it is stated that 'Jehoiakim slept with his fathers'; and the LXX text of
2 Chr. 36.8 adds 'and was buried in Ganoza 'i.e. the garden of Uzza)
with his fathers', i.e. no doubt somewhere in the grounds of the palace.
Scholars have speculated whether the body of Jehoiakim was given burial
but subsequently disinterred and thrown to the birds either by the
Babylonians or by his own outraged subjects.

The greater probability is that Jeremiah's prediction was not accurately
fulfilled. It is unlikely that any strong feeling later existed to protect the
reputation and memory of Jehoiakim. That being so, the note in 2 Chr.
36.8 probably registers local knowledge of his burial place. The truth is
that the editors of the *OT* were not too worried by the discrepancy. They
had Jeremiah's oracle and they had the tradition of Jehoiakim's burial
and it is the measure of their reverence for their material that they
manipulated neither. Jeremiah's oracle remained word of God. There

could be no doubt of the justice of the judgment or of Jeremiah's courage in making it. Such was the appropriate reversal of this man's megalomania. So much did the correctness of Jeremiah's judgment impress itself on succeeding generations, and so comprehensively were his historical predictions fulfilled in one way or another, that a discord of this kind could be received; and paradoxically it increases our trust in the tradition that it was thus received.

ZION'S DISMAY AT THE LOSS OF HER KINGS **22.20–23**

This poem has affinities with the oracles collected in chapters 2 and 3, belonging to the earliest period of Jeremiah's ministry. As here there is reference to **your lovers** (22.20), so there Jeremiah speaks of seeking lovers (2.33) and playing the harlot with many lovers (3.1). Indeed the image of adultery is a dominant one in the early chapters. As here the poet cites the obstinate response **I will not listen** (22.21), so there he envisages Israel's responses as 'I will not serve' (2.20), 'I am not defiled' (2.23), 'I have loved strangers, and after them I will go' (2.25), 'We will come no more to thee' (2.31), 'I have not sinned' (2.35). As here it is affirmed that Jerusalem has sinned **from your youth** (22.21), so there the LORD remembers 'the devotion of your youth' (2.2), quickly followed by infidelity.

Indeed the general theme is similar to the dominant theme of the earliest chapters. But the differences are decisive. Whereas in 2.36 Jeremiah predicts that Judah will be let down by those nations in whom she puts her trust, and in particular by Egypt, here the 'lovers' are **destroyed** (v. 20) and are about to go into captivity. Whereas in chapters 2 and 3 the 'lovers' are foreign gods (though no doubt involved in alliances with other nations), here the worship of foreign gods is not in mind. It is not impossible that an oracle, originally referring to foreign alliances, is here interpreted simply of Judah's kings. Indeed this poem seems capable of varied interpretation at two levels. The parallel passages in chapters 2–3 suggest the following. Israel (personified in the second person feminine singular) is to go up to the great vantage points from which the whole scene may be surveyed. She will see that the nations ('lovers') to whom she has looked for security have proved broken reeds. Verse 22 may be translated and is so rendered by *NEB, REB*—'the wind shall carry away all your friends', and they will go into captivity. Israel will be confounded and even the proud inhabitants of Lebanon will share the travail. But see below, on v. 22.

But as the poem is now placed in this collection concerning the

kings, it bears a more precise meaning. The woman is the
personification not of Israel but of Jerusalem, as is suggested by 22.1–8
and particularly v. 8 (though theologically they may be identical). The
'lovers' are nor foreign nations or gods, but Judah's kings. Verse 22
must be translated as the Massoretes have left it to us: **The wind
shall shepherd all your shepherds, and your lovers shall go into
captivity.** As elsewhere in Jer. (see on 3.15) and widely in the *OT*,
the shepherd is a familiar figure of the ruler and particularly of the
king. This then is a vivid example of the importance of attending to
the meaning attached to the passage by the editor who left it to us
in this position. Unquestionably this is the interpretation which the
poem should attract in this context.

20. Lebanon . . . Bashan . . . Abarim: i.e. the high mountains in the
north, north-east (including Hermon) and the south-east (including
Nebo). It was from Nebo that Moses surveyed the land he could not enter.

21. See general comment above.

22. The wind shall shepherd all your shepherds: by a simple change
of pointing, 'friends' (translated as 'lovers' in 3.1) may be read for
'shepherds', thus encouraging the translation of *NEB REB*: 'the wind
shall carry away all your friends', in parallelism with 'and your lovers
shall depart into exile'. But this ought not to be the preferred reading,
for the following reasons:

(1) It must always be remembered that the MT represents a long
tradition of reading and we are not at liberty to play with the massoretic
vocalisation unless there are strong supporting reasons.

(2) The Versions read 'shepherds' and reproduce the play on words.

(3) The emendation weakens the word-play.

(4) Most important of all, as shown above, the very point of the placing
of this poem in its present context, is the recognition that it is about
Judah's kings, considered as shepherds, a theme plainly in the editor's
mind, as indicated by the inclusion of 23.1–4. If then the parallelism of
this verse is to be pressed, then **your lovers** is another description of the
kings, suggesting the unhealthy, uncritical devotion Judah has for her
faithless and unworthy representatives.

23. O inhabitant of Lebanon, nested among the cedars: it is just
possible that the reference is to the proud inhabitants of a particularly
beautiful and untroubled area who will now share the confusion of Judah.
It is more probable that this is an image of Judah herself, likened to the
birds who nest in the lofty branches of these famous cedars and regard

themselves as safe as they are inaccessible. Jeremiah never ceased to attack a complacent and false sense of security, cf. 21.13; 22.6–7.

how will you groan when pangs come upon you: cf. 4.31; 6.24; 13.21.

JEHOIACHIN BROKEN AND THROWN AWAY **22.24–30**

This section consists of two oracles, the one in prose (vv. 24–27), the other poetry (vv. 28–30). Both concern Jehoiachin, who succeeded his father in 598 B.C. Jehoiakim showed himself ready to use any opportunity to extricate himself from Babylonian sovereignty. Accordingly Nebuchadrezzar resolved to teach him a lesson and besieged Jerusalem. Jehoiakim died the same year before the fall of the city, leaving the eighteen year old Jehoiachin to face a hopeless situation and certain defeat. He reigned only three months and was deported with his family and leading officials to Babylon. The first oracle seems to anticipate his fate, the second to presuppose it. But they are linked yet more closely. The first likens him to a signet ring pulled off ; so he will be thrown away (*hētaltî*); the second to a broken artefact no longer valued. So he and his family are hurled (*hûṭᵃlû*) and cast away. Both speak of his exile, the first affirming that he will never return, the second that there will be none to succeed him on the throne of David.

Despite similarities and a catchword, these oracles cannot be interpreted as duplicates. The prose version has its own characteristics and is no doubt based on a telling word of Jeremiah in that desperate situation. At the same time it bears the usual marks of free adaption. The Deuteronomic stamp is observable, particularly in the phrase **into another country** . . . But the same Deuteronomic echo is heard in the poetic oracle in **cast into a land which they do not know** (vv. 26, 28; cf. 11–12), cf. Dt. 29.27.

24. As I live, says the LORD: the familiar oath formula which lends ultimate solemnity to the prediction.

Coniah: a shortened form of Jeconiah; or perhaps his personal name which was expanded to Jeconiah to produce his throne name. It is possible that the name is an editorial addition to identify the king. The rest of the oracle is addressed to him directly.

the signet . . . on my right hand: this was a seal used for letters and official documents, a personal and valuable possession bearing the owner's characteristic mark, sometimes attached to a cord and worn round the neck, cf. Gen. 38.18; Ca. 8.6. There is no reason to suppose that this seal might not also take the form of a ring. It is significant that the image of the signet ring is also used by Haggai of Jehoiachin's uncle Zerubbabel

(Hag. 2.22). It stands for the indissoluble relationship between the LORD and his anointed king, a relationship which nevertheless the LORD will dissolve.

25. and give you into the hand of those who seek your life: cf. 21.7; 19.7; 34.20, 21; 44.30; 46.26, i.e. it features in the prose tradition. **into the hand of those of whom you are afraid:** in the Heb. an unusual expression also found in 39.17, probably intended to recall *māgôr* (20.3, 4).

even into the hand of Nebuchadrezzar king of Babylon and into the hands of the Chaldeans: the absence of this phrase from the LXX suggests that it is an identifying gloss. If so it is both typical and correct. **26. and the mother who bore you:** Nehushta, named in 2 Kg. 24.8 as the daughter of Elnathan of Jerusalem.

and there you shall die: exactly fulfilled.

27. they will long to return: literally 'will lift up their souls to'. Perhaps 'they cherish false hopes' (McKane). The same idiomatic expression occurs in 44.14. The idiom possibly goes back to the notion of craning the neck as a figure of intense longing, cf. v. 11.

28. Is this man Coniah a despised, broken pot?: The text is uncertain, since 'this man' is omitted by LXX and Old Latin; 'broken' (*māpûṣ*) is omitted by LXX and plausibly explained as a dittograph of 'no one cares for'. *'ên ḥēp̄eṣ bô*; 'pot' is omitted by LXX and Old Latin. This leaves 'Coniah is despised as a vessel no one cares for'. It is safe to leave out 'this man', but by no means certain that otherwise the Greek text is the best. The word *'eṣeb*, here translated 'pot' is difficult to explain, if it is an addition. It means 'a thing shaped' and is often used of an idol. It could mean 'pot' but it is not the word one would expect if Jeremiah were developing the image of a shattered pot. The *NEB, REB* 'puppet' is and interesting suggestion but hardly satisfactory, since it is an interpretation of the basic image. In all probability Coniah is likened to a piece of shaped workmanship (whether idol or pot) which is broken. It is of course possible that this question, together with the **why** that follows, is asked by the people who are shocked and desolated by the fate of Jehoiachin. Jeremiah quotes and formulates their incredulous heart-searching.

29. O land, land, land, hear the word of the LORD!: The threefold call is not without parallel. Cf. 7.4; Ezek. 21.17; Isa. 6.3; and suggests an incantatory or liturgical formula. Cf. from the Epic of Gilgamesh, 'Earth, earth, earth, Gilgamesh casts a spell on you'.

30. Write this man down as childless: According to 1 Chr. 3.17,

Jehoiachin had seven sons, and Babylonian cuneiform tablets, published in 1939, list the ration of oil allowed to *Iaukin*, king of *Iakudu* and his five sons. This would probably be in 592 B.C. (*ANET*, p.308). Perhaps Jehoiachin is to be counted as childless because none of his children will succeed to the throne. The oracle would gain in point and poignancy if, as is likely, at least one of Jehoiachin's sons had been born at the time of its utterance. Perhaps, but this interpretation suggests rationalisation. G.R. Driver thought the Heb. *ʿriri* could mean 'stripped of honour or rights' (followed by *NEB*, *REB*). This would make good sense.

who shall not succeed in his days: omitted by LXX which has 'cast out' for 'childless'. It looks as if the Greek text represents a tradition in which it was felt necessary to adjust the translation to the known fact that Jehoiachin was not childless. We may therefore accept MT (and *RSV*) as correct.

GOOD SHEPHERDS ON THE THRONE OF DAVID **23.1–8**

Not surprisingly, the final section on kingship is concerned with the future. It contains at least three separate oracles (some think four), and it is disputed whether they are to be regarded as registering the thought of Jeremiah. Some deny them all to Jeremiah; some only the idea of the ingathering of the scattered Israelites in vv. 3, 7–8. The first oracle (vv. 1–4) is in prose and seems to belong to the prose tradition. The second (vv. 5–6) is poetry. The third = 16.14–15, q.v.

All that we have learned of the mind and methods of the editor suggests that this section is carefully built up. As so often he starts with his own prose account of Jeremiah's teaching, remembered and expanded with his characteristic commonplaces. He includes an oracle whose poetic form gave it relative fixity, though it is adapted in slightly different form in 33.14–16 where the symbolic name (the LORD our righteousness) is applied to Jerusalem, not to the king. The absence of 33.14–26 from LXX suggests perhaps that this section (23.1–8) is its basic home. He concludes with another prose oracle which had been used elsewhere in the process of redaction. This latter oracle is a classical expression of the thought of the new Exodus as adapted to the Jeremiah tradition. Even if, therefore, it proves difficult to identify what in particular proceeds from the lips of Jeremiah, we may regard the whole section as a statement of the messianic hope as it assumed articulate form in the Jeremiah tradition.

There are however some grounds for detecting the mind of Jeremiah throughout the section. First, **the LORD (is) our righteousness** (23.6) is a variant of the name Zedekiah ('the LORD my righteousness') and this would gain in significance if, in some way, the prophecy were connected with this king. There are two possibilities. The first is that Jeremiah uttered this prophecy of Zedekiah before he was placed on the throne. This is the view of Klausner (*The Messianic Idea in Israel*, 1956, pp.104–105). Zedekiah was son of Josiah and brother of Jehoiakim, and therefore a possible claimant to the throne. Jeremiah exhibited none of the hostility towards him that comes out, both in his dealings with, and his oracles concerning, Jehoiakim and Jehoiachin. Chapters 37 and 38 reveal Zedekiah as fundamentally sympathetic to Jeremiah, but weak, and inhibited by his ministers and advisers. Jeremiah's oracle concerning his peaceful death is in marked contrast to 22.10–11, 18–19, 24–30. Jeremiah may be thought to have turned to the young Mattaniah as to one more worthy of Josiah and capable of exemplifying the principle of righteousness. 2 Kg. 24.17 says that Nebuchadrezzar gave Mattaniah the throne name Zedekiah. This however is a way of stating that he owed his throne to Nebuchadrezzar. Plainly this Jewish name was proposed by Jews.

Klausner's view is attractive but not probable. It conflicts with Jeremiah's repeated cry that he could find not one righteous man (e.g. chapter 5). Moreover, whatever private assurance Jeremiah may have wished to give to Zedekiah, this is not a private but a public oracle, part of the word of God to his people. It is altogether improbable that Jeremiah offered any oracles of hope and salvation to the people until the full judgment was seen to be inevitable and was accepted. Jeremiah spent his life fighting complacency and false security. Not until the final destruction of Jerusalem was imminent could he speak of salvation without misunderstanding, cf. chapter 32.

We turn therefore to the second possible view, which is that Jeremiah uttered this prophecy in connection with Zedekiah *after* he was enthroned and either at the end of his troubled reign or perhaps shortly after its end. Full weight should then be given to the expression **a righteous Branch** (23.5). Jeremiah has clearly seen that no descendent of Jehoiachin will sit upon the throne of David (22.24–30). Zedekiah is either about to go into captivity or has gone. At this point Jeremiah in his own way reaffirms the divine promise that 'there shall never fail you a man before me to sit upon the throne of Israel' (1 Kg. 8.25). This is the throne that would be established for ever (2 Sam. 7.13, 16; Isa. 9.7). The means by which this promise would be fulfilled was another branch of the Davidic tree (cf. Isa. 11.1). No name could be more fitting for this as yet unknown king than 'the LORD our righteousness'. As the editor passes from the consideration of Josiah, Jehoahaz, Jehoiakim and Jehoiachin to Zedekiah, he takes his readers away from the failures of history and the machinations of men to the ideal whose realisation can be attained only by the divine initiative. There may well be an implied contrast between the way in which Zedekiah owed his throne to the Babylonian conqueror and the LORD's initiative expressed in the emphatic first person: 'I will raise up for David a righteous Branch' and 'in his days Judah will be saved'. This interpretation seems more probable than the somewhat facile assumption that this is one among a number of anonymous post-exilic expressions of a future hope, borne of despair of reality and meditation upon the traditions.

As to the opening prose oracle concerning the shepherds, there is still less reason to deny this to Jeremiah who from the beginning used the word'shepherd' for rulers (2.8; 6.3; 10.21; 12.10), or at any rate, in this case, to the redactor's version of his teaching. The prose is that of the Jeremiah prose tradition (note the 'behold' with participle in v. 2); and there is play on the word *pāqaḏ* here translated 'attend' in v. 2 and 'be missing' in v. 4, cf. 11.22; 29.32; 46.25; 50.18. This verb, as S.R. Driver remarks, is more frequent in Jeremiah than in any other prophet.

The outstanding question is whether the prophecy of the ingathering in v. 3 is not a post-exilic insertion into the oracle about the shepherds. If it is an insertion, it is a remarkably tidy and apt one, for it supplies an element otherwise missing from the oracle. Given a future righteous king, there could only be a restored kingdom to rule over if there were some form of ingathering! Moreover the way this hope is related in v. 8 to Jeremiah's prophecies concerning the north, an essential and dominant theme in the earliest collection, strongly suggests that the idea of ingathering was not altogether outside Jeremiah's mind when he once directed it to the ultimate ends that lay beyond the terrors of judgment. As we shall see, it is implied also in the poetic oracle itself, vv. 5–6.

Altogether therefore these passages of the Jeremiah prose tradition may be understood to reveal the mind of the prophet. If they are the only substantial glimpse of his teaching on this subject, that is perhaps to be expected. The life and times of Jeremiah do not lend any probability to the view that he would have done more than touch on future hopes of this kind. That he did in principle look to the future becomes clear later and rests on broader grounds.

1. Woe *(hôi)* as in 22.13 and followed (as in 22.18) by 'therefore', but the expected forms are confused, and the indictment and threat of judgment come together after the 'therefore'. The old patterns have already dissolved and form-critical considerations have to be treated with common sense.

the shepherds: it is sometimes suggested that since Zedekiah tried to be friendly and true to Jeremiah, the 'shepherds' here are the ministers who surrounded him. Zedekiah was so weak that they were the rulers of the country. It is of course theoretically possible that Jeremiah first uttered this oracle in this sense. But there can be no doubt whatever that the editor who gave it its present form and included it in this section of kingship understood the 'shepherds' to be the last kings of Judah. And it is likely that he had a fair idea of the mind of Jeremiah.

2. your evil doings: a cliché of the prose tradition, cf. 4.4; 21.12; 23.22; 25.5; 26.3; 44.22; Dt. 28.20.

3. their fold: cf. Jer. 31.23, a word used by Jeremiah as a descriptive symbol of restored Israel.

they shall be fruitful and multiply: that which the LORD intended for all mankind will become true for God's people, cf. Gen. 1.22, 28.

they shall fear no more, nor be dismayed: cf. 30.10; 46.27, cf. Dt. 1.21; 31.8. No doubt originally this phrase belonged to the context of war.

neither shall any be missing: *pqd* in this sense also in 3.16. A play on its more usual use in the book of Jeremiah, as in v. 2, 'visit them' in the sense of 'care for them', and 'visit upon them' in the sense of punish.

5. Behold the days are coming: cf. 19.6; 23.7 = 16.14; 30.3; 31.31, 38; 33.14; 49.2; 51.47, 52. Undoubtedly this phrase can be used as a sort of editorial suture. But it seems to be used in the Jeremiah tradition to introduce oracles relating to the faith picture of the future. It is more than a suture; it is a mark of the vision of redemption.

a righteous Branch: the phrase could mean legitimate representative of the royal line. In a Phoenician inscription it seems to describe 'crown prince' or heir apparent of the king of Sidon. But even if it can bear this meaning in Heb., the context here suggests a stress on both words separately. The fact that Jeremiah has predicted that no son of Jehoiachin shall inherit the throne, means there must be another growth from the royal tree, or, as we should say, another 'branch'. The fact that Jehoiakim was condemned for not doing justice and righteousness, means that the prophet looks for a guardian and exemplification of righteousness. Crown prince—maybe—but a Branch who is the embodiment of righteousness. Cf. the use of this term in Zech. 3.8; 6.12.

and shall execute justice and righteousness in the land: as did Josiah, 22.16, cf. Isa. 42.4. This expression has a Babylonian equivalent, which is a recurring formula. But its meaning is really self-evident, and Jeremiah does no more than state that the king whom the LORD will provide will be faithful to every principle which the monarch was intended to reflect, as constantly rehearsed in prophecy and psalm.

6. In his days Judah will be saved: carefully avoiding saying that the king will himself save Judah.

and Israel will dwell securely: probably Judah and Israel are not here interchangeable terms but the mention of both serves to complete the picture of the restored People of God, over whom the king will reign, thus implying the ingathering of vv. 3, 7–8, and the unity of one people under one shepherd, cf. Ezek. 37.15–28.

this is the name by which he will be called: the giving of names was nearly always significant, and particularly so at a king's enthronement. But this is prophecy, and the giving of the name is tantamount to a prophetic sign, as notably in Third Isaiah, cf. Isa. 56.7; 58.12; 60.14, 17f; 61.6; 62.4, 12. This is the reason, in all probability, why the order of words is reversed. Zedekiah is 'my righteousness is the LORD'. Here Jeremiah says: 'The LORD is our righteousness', thus laying extra stress on the word 'LORD'. Paradoxically the king is the better embodiment of righteousness because he recognises that it is the LORD who is the only ground and giver of righteousness.

7–9. Substantially as in 16.14–15, except for the adaptation already noted. The LXX did not have this section at all in chapter 16 and placed it quite unsuitably at the end of chapter 23. If it is at home anywhere, it is in its present position where it fills out the implication of the poem (vv. 5–6) and amplifies v. 3, thus sketching in an essential element of 'the messianic age'. It opens with the 'therefore' of the threat but is in fact an oracle of salvation. What Jeremiah does is to provide a revised oath formula. We may assume that the formula **As the LORD lives who brought up the people of Israel out of the land of Egypt** was in familiar use. It was an oath of supreme solemnity because it appealed both to the LORD himself, beyond whom no appeal could be made, and to the greatest and exemplary act of redemption wrought by him, upon which the very national existence of Israel rested. The new oath therefore implied that the new act of redemption would be of such magnitude and significance that it would replace the Exodus from Egypt in the memories of the people. There would be a new tradition of salvation. The expression of a prediction in this novel and intriguing form is an example of the prophetic technique of communication.

descendants: lit. 'seed', cf. 2.21. Modern English translations disguise the theological use of this word in Gen. 11–50 and elsewhere in the *OT* to denote the people of Israel as the fulfilment of the divine promise to Abraham.

out of the north country: this more than anything else puts a Jeremianic stamp upon the prophecy. Jeremiah had employed every means in his early years to persuade the people that their punishment would be administered by a Foe from the North. Is it not appropriate that, if he envisaged salvation at all, he should see the captive peoples coming from the places of their captivity? Thus the promise to Abraham of seed and land would again be honoured. These glimpses of the new era of peace and justice are not wishful thinking or crystal ball gazing. They are compounded of the ancient promises and knowledge of the faithfulness of God, who was driven by the infidelity of his people to a temporary alienation, but is impelled by his own nature to fulfil the intention he had enshrined in the sacred traditions.

The question is often asked whether these prophecies are messianic. The question is not an unambiguous one because the concepts 'messiah' and 'messianic age' are multiplex. Certainly later messianic hopes grew out of the institution of the monarchy and were forged, as here, out of a profound attention to the character and promises of God. It is possible to affirm that this passage contains the main ideas that contributed towards the picture of the expected Messiah of David's line.

In him all the ideas of righteousness and wisdom expressed in the kingship psalms are embodied. He will come at an unspecified time in the future, in place of those kings who have betrayed both their commission and their country, and brought the monarchy to oblivion. He will bring salvation to Israel, i.e. he will remove every impediment which prevents them rising to their vocation as God's people, and he will unite the people who have been divided both by schism and captivity.

The new age will be ideal in all respects, and every glimpse of this ideal, whether it explicitly includes the figure of the king or not, contributes to the total kaleidoscopic vision of the age which can properly be called messianic. When for example, this visionary speaks of the gathered people being fruitful and multiplying, he picks up a memorable phrase used for God's purpose for mankind in creation and so hints at the idea of the end as a recapitulation of the beginning, the new age as paradise regained, a conception more poetically and graphically expressed in Isa. 11.6–9. He also utilises the image of the new exodus as the initiation of this age and stresses twice the theme of ingathering, so important in the Isaiah tradition, as in Isa. 11, 49 and 60.

It is precarious to theorize about dependence and borrowing. The idea of the branch seems to be a stereotype of the image created in Isa. 11.1. More certainly it lies behind the use of the term in Zechariah. The picture of the king as the symbol and exemplification of righteousness is as close to Isa. 9.1-6 and 11.1-5 as it is to the royal psalms. Without asserting precise borrowing, it is sufficient to say that there is a common movement of thought in the main prophetic traditions which provides a basic element of the *OT's* intuition of the future. That it so looks to the future with this hope, confidence and yearning is part of its secret.

ON THE PROPHETS 23.9–40

The redactor now introduces a brief collection of oracles on the prophets, with the same introductory formula (v. 9) as he used to preface the oracles concerning the kings (21.11). His intention was probably to link the prophets with the kings, as being the most powerfully influential and therefore responsible leaders in the community. There is no comparable collection of oracles on the priests. On the other hand the prophets receive further attention in the narrative concerning the false prophets in chapters 27–28. This suggests their dominating role. In the denunciation of prophets scattered about the earlier collections, they are usually linked with the priests (2.8; 4.9; 5.31; 6.13; 18.18; like vv. 9–12).

With the exception of 14.13–16 these oracles in chapter 23 are the only passages which deal with prophets exclusively. They do this without reference to particular situations or the historical judgment to fall on the nation. In this respect they are, so to speak, in the air and might belong to any period of Jeremiah's ministry earlier than the great crises. In contrast 14.13–16 arises, as we saw, out of the circumstances of a fast-day liturgy, when Jeremiah himself was probably regarded as a false prophet, is developed in prose of the Jeremiah tradition in terms of the Deuteronomic and Levitical traditions, and is related to the coming invasion. There is no sign of Deuteronomic vocabulary in 23.9–40. There are separate poems in vv. 9–12, 13–15, 16–22. Verses 23–40 are in prose, with poetic snatches which either occur as the prophet's feeling rises, or more probably represent basic, memorable sayings upon which the prose account is built. It contains the tradition of some arguments conducted by Jeremiah involving significant word-play. Although specifically Deuteronomic vocabulary is not noticeable, there are characteristic expressions of the Jeremiah prose tradition.

The prophets with whom Jeremiah came into conflict are difficult to identify with certainty. In the ninth century, communities of prophets were closely associated with Elijah and Elisha, and the opposition came from the prophets of Baal, brought into the establishment by Jezebel when she married Ahab from Tyre. There is evidence that prophets were closely associated with local sanctuaries, that they were subject to ecstasy and were increasingly distinguished from the outstanding individuals whose oracles have been preserved. Amos explicitly dissociated himself from them. It is clear that they provided an influential leadership particularly in Jerusalem (see on Jer. 18.18), and were regularly consulted. It is not altogether misleading to refer to them as cultic or institutional prophets. Their tendency was to uphold the establishment. They did not know how to react to the forthright independence of Amos, Hosea and the succession of Israel's uncompromising mentors.

At the same time Jeremiah's difficulties in distinguishing between true and false prophets show that there was no easy, external means of distinguishing between himself and the others. Certainly the prophets were closely associated with the priests, and 29.26 seems to imply that there was a supervisory priest at Jerusalem who had some responsibility over prophets. Jeremiah himself came of a family of priests. Nowhere does Jeremiah attempt to identify false prophets by means of their association with the cult, or with priests, or by means of their characteristic modes of oracular utterance, or by their dress or their lineage, or by their institutional status.

Indeed, it appears that from the standpoint of the people, there was no external distinction between the truth of Jeremiah and the falsehood of Hananiah. Both used the same language forms and used the same type of dramatic sign. This is confirmed in v. 16 where Jeremiah says that the prophets 'prophesy' and 'speak visions', in v. 25 where he speaks of their dreams, in v. 34 where they speak of 'the burden of the LORD' and above all in v. 31 where they 'use their tongues, and say "Says the LORD" '.

From this it appears that we should not read back into the situation the clear black and white distinction which history has bequeathed to us. For us the prophets are Jeremiah and the succession of which he was part, and our problem is to identify the prophets with whom he came into conflict. For the contemporaries of Jeremiah the prophets were the institutional prophets and their problem was to know what to make of the non-conforming, unpredictable, irrepressible Jeremiah. Jeremiah himself, in this section, shows that his quarrel was not with the prophets as an institution but with their abuse of their trust.

THEIR OFFENCE AGAINST THE LORD **23.9–12**

The first oracle is not precisely against the prophets but against prophets and priests, in the manner of previous denunciations (2.8; 4.9; 5.31; 6.13; 18.18). Its scope is wider than the oracles that follow, just as the opening prose passage 21.1–10 is more comprehensive in its scope than the particular oracles concerning kings in 21.11–22.30. But there the comparison ends. 21.1–10 is in the familiar prose style of the Jeremiah tradition. 23.9–12 is a poetic oracle. It is placed here probably because it starts with the prophets own inimitable inspiration and raises the awful question of what it means on the one hand to be burdened with the 'holy words' of God and on the other to be an official minister of God who betrays his commission. Where the true word of the LORD is received, it is intensely and uncomfortably disturbing, in contrast to the easy claims of false prophets, which are apparently compatible with profanity and immorality. By implication Jeremiah cries out that no one who wants comfort and security would choose to be a spokesman of the LORD. It is the true word of the LORD he speaks. It is against the LORD that the prophets and priests, his official representatives, have committed their offence.

9. My heart is broken within me, all my bones shake: the sense is clear enough to the English reader, because we also speak of the parts of the body in a highly metaphorical sense. But the Heb. has a more precise meaning, despite the fact that the physiological function of the heart was unknown. The heart includes what we would identify as the brain and denotes what we would call the centre of the personality. It therefore relates not only to emotional but also to volitional and intellectual activity. To say that the heart is broken is to say more than that one is inconsolably sad; it is to say that the personality is turned upside down. The same thing is said, but from a more external point of view, when it is added that the 'bones shake'. The bones provide the structure of a man and are thought to break up under the force of distress. Cursing words soak into the bones like oil (Ps. 109.18). Here they are said to 'quiver' (Heb. *rāhap*, used of the 'hovering' of the spirit over the waters at creation). For the defence of this interpretation, see A.R. Johnson, *The Vitality of the Individual in the Thought of Ancient Israel*, 1964, p.32, n.8. This is another way of describing the intensity of inspiration like that in 20.7–9 where also Jeremiah refers to 'a burning fire shut up in my bones' (see on 20.9) and cf. 4.19. Thus Jeremiah affirms the totally penetrating character of the word of God, which is 'living and active, sharper than any two-edged sword, piercing to the division of soul and spirit, of joints and marrow, and discerning the thoughts and intentions of the heart' (Hb. 4.12). To say also **I am like a drunken man, like a man overcome by wine** is to affirm the totally possessing power of the divine word. For an application of this language to the prophets and priests themselves, see Isa. 28.7–8; 29.9–10.

because of the LORD and because of his holy words: the idiomatic Heb., literally rendered, is 'because of the words of his holiness' i.e. stressing the origin of the disturbing probing, possessing word in the Holy God.

10. For the land is full of adulterers: Omitted by LXX but not necessarily intrusive. This can describe either widespread immorality (as in v. 14, cf. 5.7; 7.9) or the spiritual infidelity of apostasy (as in 3.8–9). For the same linking of adultery with lies, see 9.2, with the same double reference. Probably Jeremiah intended to leave the application open.

because of the curse the land mourns, and the pastures of the wilderness are dried up: LXX reads 'because of these'. the LXX translator, having a Heb. text before him without the later massoretic vocalisation, would have had no means apart from tradition of distinguishing between *'ālāh* (curse) and *'ēlleh* (these). But once again MT is probably correct. There is almost certainly a connection with Dt. 29.19 where *RSV* translates *'ālāh* as 'sworn covenant'. See further on vv. 15, 17. The curse is appropriately pictured in terms of drought and the desert, just as blessing is figured in terms of fruitfulness and vitality. It is not too much to say that these complementary images are commonplace throughout the Bible, and immediately understood. For the notion of the land mourning, cf. 4.28; 12.4; 14.2; and linked with the drying up of vegetation, cf. 12.4. This is not the romantic idea of the sympathy of nature, but an image of the connection between disobedience and its total destroying consequences. For a further application of the idea of the curse going over the land, see Zech. 5.1–4.

11. even in my house I have found their wickedness: hardly needs the historical confirmation of 2 Kg 23.7, since this is a recurring theme both in Jer. (e.g. especially vv. 11 and 30) and elsewhere (e.g. Ezek. 8).

12. Therefore: here the conventional introduction to the announcement of judgment. **The year of their punishment** (visitation) is a commonplace of the Jeremiah tradition (cf. 6.15; 8.12; 11.23; 46.21; 48.44; 49.8; 50.27, 31). The judgment is a typically ironic recoiling of evil upon their own heads, expressed in the most general terms. It is quite impossible to pinpoint this oracle to a particular time in Jeremiah's ministry.

THEIR OFFENCE AGAINST MORALITY **23.13–15**

This brief poetic piece now turns the searchlight on the prophets of Jerusalem, and achieves this the more effectively by comparing them with the prophets of the northern kingdom. Already a prose version of a related theme has been included in the first collection (see on 3.6–14 'a cautionary example'). There it was explicitly declared that Israel was less guilty than her sister Judah. Here the contrast is implied in the comparison, and probably in the words 'an unsavoury thing' (v. 13), used of the prophets of Judah. Judah recognises the justice of the judgment that fell upon Israel and the complicity of her prophets. She is blind to the far deeper guilt of her own prophets, whose profanity has infected the whole people. Jeremiah is concerned here, not so much in the first instance with their false advice (that is dealt with in the next oracle), as with their moral rottenness, though he seems to stress the connection between them. He makes the same indictment of the prophets Zedekiah and Ahab in 29.22–23.

The reason is plain, and clarifies the difference between the inspiration of the poet and that of a prophet. A poet is sensitive to the richness of human life, sees some aspect of it more profoundly than others and registers his discernment in words. It is not surprising that a man whose preoccupation is with the vitalities of human life should sometimes lead an unconventional, even an irregular life. A prophet is primarily sensitive to the world of the spirit and moral values, sees more deeply into this world than others and also registers his discernment in words. He exhibits a fundamental distortion of character and aim if his own life is at odds with the content of his inspiration. This is why Jeremiah's moral test is a correct one. Those who are prepared to undertake the burden of prophetic responsibility as representative of the eternal and holy God must be prepared for this searchlight of criticism.

13. an unsavoury thing: *tiplāh* literally 'tasteless', 'lacking salt', the adjective used in Lam. 2.14 of the lying words of the prophets. These prophets have rendered the discrimination of truth impossible. But plainly the word *tiplāh* is applicable to their total character. The indictment of the prophets of Israel is no doubt based on the tradition which Jeremiah has received. His knowledge of the oracles of Hosea alone would be sufficient to account for this stress on compromise with Baal worship.

The historical Deuteronomic traditions stress the same analysis of their guilt.

and led my people . . . astray: cf. Hos. 4.11–13; Isa. 3.12; 9.14–15.
14. a horrible thing: the use of the term *ša'arûrāh* in Jer. 5.30; 18.13; suggests that it is as strong a term as Jeremiah can find, indicating moral revulsion. Hos. 6.10 confirms this, and certainly the passage only makes sense if this implies an even stronger denunciation than *tiplāh*. In Jer. 29.17 it is used of the 'vile', uneatable figs, apparently intensifying the 'bad (*rā'ôt*) of 24.3. These prophets have rendered the discrimination of morality impossible. But this also is an offence against truth.

they commit adultery and walk in lies: cf. the same combination in 29.13. This neatly encapsulates the double error of the false prophets. Adultery of course may be a metaphor of apostasy. But in the light of 29.22–23 it may be taken literally. At any rate it retains the potentiality of both interpretations.

they strengthen the hands of evil-doers: cf. Ezek. 13.22 also of encouraging the wicked, in contrast to the more usual activity of assisting some good work as in Isa. 35.22; Job 4.3; Ezra 6.22; Neh. 2.18; 6.9.

all of them have become like Sodom to me . . . like Gomorrah: cf. Gen. 18.23–33 where the story presents Sodom and Gomorrah as types of the community which has ceased to be serviceable for the purposes for which it exists. Jeremiah is saying that the prophets are beyond redemption.

15. Therefore thus says the LORD: as in v. 12 the 'therefore' indicates the transition from the reproach or statement of the grounds of judgment to the threat or announcement of judgment, here with the stereotyped messenger formula. This combination is probably the most characteristic 'form' of prophetic utterance. 15ab virtually equals 9.15, where it became clear that it was part of a prose amplification of material from the Jeremiah tradition to answer the question of 9.12. This suggests that we have in this passage the tradition upon which the editor was dependent. Wormwood and poison feature together in parallelism in Am. 6.12 where they are a figure of injustice, and also in Lam. 3.19 and Dt. 29.17. Here the thought is of a sort of trial by ordeal. The judgment on the prophets will be like a poisoned meal from which they will not recover. They will, so to speak, consume their own wickedness and it will kill them.

ungodliness: 'profanity', that which implies the repudiation of the true religion and affronts the holiness of God.

THEIR OFFENCE AGAINST TRUTH **23.16–22**

This oracle focuses attention on the profound question of truth. What is the difference phenomenologically between a man who had a vision of God the other night and a man who said he had a vision of God the other night? There is no observable difference, and this constitutes the problem, which is a universal problem of human life, as pressing in the contemporary world as in the time of Jeremiah. The problem is faced again in the narrative of chapters 27—28 and some tests are proposed. But in the end Jeremiah has no infallible guide which can guarantee correct discrimination.

One thing however is clear, Jeremiah cannot surrender the conviction that the truth is here rather than there, however hard it may be to provide a principle of verification. He know that there is a distinction between the true and the false; and he must continue to bear witness to what has been given to him as the truth. The distinction between true and false prophecy is traced back to starting-points which are unseen and not open to detached inspection. In particular Jeremiah locates the impulse to false prophecy in the hearts of the prophets themselves; while true prophecy has a transcendental source in 'the council of the LORD' (v. 18). Jeremiah knows that no one can decide empirically whether an oracle proceeds from the mind of the prophet or from the innermost counsels of God himself. He believes it is given to true men to bear witness to the truth, and it is the total and complete harmony of the witness with the content of his testimony which gives ground for confidence.

16. the words of the prophets who prophesy to you: the relative clause is absent from the LXX and overloads the line. It is to be omitted if the poetic form is to be recovered.

they speak visions of their own minds: to speak a vision sounds superficially a contradiction in terms. But the Heb. *ḥāzôn* is not restricted to visual phenomena. It may denote the 'vision' of Mic. 3.5–7, and like the English word 'observation', it can be used of that which is spoken. It is used sometimes synonymously with 'word' to describe the divinatory function of the prophet, cf. 14.14; Ezek. 7.26; 12.21–28. The oracles of Amos are introduced as 'the word . . . which he saw' (*ḥāzāh*, i.e. 'observed', Am. 1.1, cf. also Isa. 2.1). In other words, this is part of the technical vocabulary of Heb. prophecy. On 'minds' (lit. 'hearts') see on v. 9.

17. 'It shall be well with you': Heb. *šālôm*. All the individuals who stood out from the groups of prophets from the time of David onwards, uttered message of warning, criticism or judgment. Conversely it was characteristic of the institutional prophets to speak comfortably of peace and salvation. See on 6.14; 8.11. So few were the exceptions to this rule that Jeremiah was able to point to it as a rough but not infallible guide to discriminating between true and false. See 28.8–9. But he did not exclude the possibility of true oracles of salvation.

every one who stubbornly follows his own heart: lit. 'goes in stubbornness of heart'. This expression is characteristic of the Jeremiah prose tradition (3.17; 7.24; 9.13; 11.8; 13.10; 16.;12; 18.12). It occurs only once in Dt. (29.19), but in a passage which has a number of other verbal and conceptual links with the Jeremiah tradition, and deals with any one, man, woman, family or tribe (not prophets only), who might say, 'I shall be safe' i.e. 'I shall have šālôm'. There is clear affinity between the two passages, not easy to explain. It is not possible to conclude that this is Deuteronomic language. It is characteristic vocabulary of the Jeremiah tradition with a Deuteronomic affiliation.

18. For who among them has stood in the council of the LORD: The idea of the 'council (sôḏ) of the LORD' is a colourful and recurring feature of Hebrew mythology. Here in his heavenly court the LORD makes his plans and sends out his messengers and servants to do his will. Around him are the 'sons of God', (in polytheistic systems 'gods'), later understood as angels (Zech. 1.7–17). They planned the creation of man (Gen. 1.26); they engage in worship and praise (Ps. 29); they send prophets to deliver the LORD's messages and perform his will, both the true prophets called to be his servants (Am. 3.7; Isa. 6) and the false prophets who are activated by lying spirits (1 Kg. 22.17–23). They discuss the situation on earth and plan the testing of chosen individuals (Job 1). A significant point about prophets is that they have been admitted to this council, and have been told the LORD's will, and appear as messengers to deliver it. The effect of the myth is to declare precisely that the prophets have not concocted their preaching from their own imaginations or dreamed it. They are simply messengers passing on a message from their master.

The words 'among them' are based on a questionable hypothetical addition to the Heb., which simply expresses the question: 'Who has stood in the council of the LORD?' If this were a rhetorical question requiring a negative answer, it would perhaps be difficult to accept, because Jeremiah clearly believes that true prophets have access to the LORD's council. Some scholars regard the verse as derived from v. 22, and to be omitted, particularly as vv. 19–20 are identical with 30.23–24, betraying editorial 'interference'. But all such manipulations are really unnecessary. What Jeremiah is saying is, that when you are facing the problem of true and false prophecy, this is the fundamental question to ask: 'Who has stood in the council of the LORD?' Does the message come from the prophet himself or from God? It is the transcendental source which makes prophecy. Otherwise it is nothing.

19–20. These verses are repeated in 30.23–24. Some scholars think they break the connection between vv. 18 and 21 and are intrusive. If so, it is as difficult to explain how such a verse should be introduced so clumsily. If on the other hand there is a reasonable explanation, it is more plausible to attribute the intention to the redactor than to subsequent dislocation. It is in fact probable that the editor deliberately drew on this section, as he built up the collection, in order to express the full weight of the divine judgment on those who falsely claim to stand in the council of the LORD. Unless the claim is true it is a morally dangerous claim to make. Alternatively the editor may have chosen to introduce a characteristic oracle of Jeremiah as an example of what the prophet who has stood in the council of the LORD says. No prophet of the establishment spoke like this. This editorial motive would explain why suddenly in a collection of oracles of rather general scope, there occurs the note of imminent judgment, suggesting perhaps the last year of Jehoiakim or the reign of Zedekiah. With the opening **Behold** Jeremiah introduces his own 'vision' of judgment anticipated, and not abating until the purpose of God is achieved. **The storm of the LORD** here and 30.23 is a figure of judgment; often it is a figure of epiphany as in Ezek. 1.4; Job 38.1; 40.6; Zech. 9.14.

20. In the latter days: i.e. the ultimate future from the perspective of the speaker, cf. 48.47; 49.39; Dt. 4.30; Isa. 2.2; Ezek. 38.16. The expression is used conventionally and is not to be pressed into the service of a precise eschatology. But it is more than a mere editorial suture. It is a marker' indicating finality either of salvation, as in Isa. 2, or of judgment, as here.

21. I did not send the prophets: The situation from the LORD's point of view. It is black and white. He did not send them. The fundamental question therefore about prophets is whether the LORD sent them or not. Our inclination is to probe into the complexity of motives and to discern a mixture of motives, so that the difference becomes one of degree rather than of true and false. There can be no retreat from this determination to understand. Yet the mythological

picture helps to make a distinction which is true to experience. Anyone
who claims to speak in any measure in God's name is a person who
listens rather than invents. His stance is that of one obedient to that
which is given, rather than one who speculates from his own imagination.
He is subject to a divine initiative. In this sense the biblical myth holds
together, in the unity of a single pictorial image, ideas and principles
which are lost in the subtle qualifications and relativities of a
psychological understanding.

**22. and they would have turned them from their evil way, and from
the evil of their doings:** both phrases are characteristic of the Jeremiah
prose tradition. For the former cf. 18.11; 35.15; and the latter, see on
23.2, and both together in 25.5; 26.3. This is perhaps best explained as
the handling of the poetical material by the redactor as he builds up the
material into the present collection. To what extent is this a test of truth?
If it is, Jeremiah was not judged to have passed it. The above discussion
has suggested that he knew of no such simple test. But these words, of
the tradition, should not be pressed in the manner of an advocate. The
true prophet proclaims God's word and his one aim is to turn his people
from the evil of their ways.

LYING DREAMS AND STOLEN WORDS **23.23–32**

The next two sections reveal such intricacy of pattern in the arrangement
of question and answer and in the repetition of significant words that
they suggest a background of disputation. It is not perhaps necessary to
presuppose an actual disputation, here recorded. Rather once thinks of
techniques of disputation providing the structure and model of Jeremiah's
encounter with his audience. The first of these sections may be set out
as follows:

I   The LORD's threefold rhetorical question (in verse):
      a. 'Am I a god at hand, $n^{e\flat}\bar{u}m$ $yhwh$ . . .' (v. 23)
      b. 'Can a man hide himself . . . and I not see, $n^{e\flat}\bar{u}m$ $yhwh$' (v. 24)
      c. 'Do I not fill heaven and earth? $n^{e\flat}\bar{u}m$ $yhwh$' (v. 24)

II   The LORD's answer (in prose):
      a. The dreams of the prophets (v. 25)
      b. The LORD's lament—How long? (vv. 26–27)
      c. The LORD's decision—in the manner of a judge (v. 28a)

III   The LORD's twofold clarifying question (in verse):
      a. 'What has straw in common with wheat? $n^{e\flat}\bar{u}m$ $yhwh$' (v. 28b)
      b. 'Is not my word like fire, $n^{e\flat}\bar{u}m$ $yhwh$ . . . ?' (v. 29)

IV   Threefold pronouncement of judgment (in prose):
   a. 'Behold, I am against the prophets, n^{e}'$\bar{u}m$ yhwh, who steal . . .' (v. 30)
   b. 'Behold, I am against the prophets, n^{e}'$\bar{u}m$ yhwh who use their tongues
       and say n^{e}'$\bar{u}m$ yhwh' (v. 31)
   c. 'Behold, I am against those who prophesy lying dreams, n^{e}'$\bar{u}m$ yhwh . . .
       n^{e}'$\bar{u}m$ yhwh' (v. 32)

Thus Jeremiah, on the basis of the all-seeing power of God, attacks the
pretension of the prophets to divination by dreams. The repeated n^{e}'$\bar{u}m$
yhwh (word of Yahweh), and especially v. 31, show that the utterance
of this phrase was a particularly significant way of claiming divine
inspiration, used by false prophets as by true. The attachment of the
phrase to all five questions and to the three statements of judgment in
unparalleled repetition suggests a particular intention. Jeremiah by this
means affirms that the true prophet alone can use this solemn expression.
In his view the others dare not let it pass their lips. In contrast, their
dreams, which they claimed to be divine communication by means of
the phrase n^{e}'$\bar{u}m$ yhwh, are but the figment of their scheming imaginations.
Jeremiah seems to regard dreams as wholly false prophetic pretensions.
He obviously did not make use of them himself. It is however doubtful
whether he would have regarded them as inherently incapable of becoming
the vehicle of truth. They are a feature of the E tradition in the Tetrateuch.
In Num. 12.6 it is said explicitly: 'If there is a prophet among you, I
the LORD make myself known to him in a vision, I speak with him in
a dream'. This is contrasted with the directness of communication with
Moses: 'With him I speak mouth to mouth, clearly'. See also 1 Sam.
28.6, 15; Zech. 10.2. Dreams continued to be of prophetic significance.
The visions of Zechariah, though apparently distinguished from dreams
(4.1), take place by night (1.8), and are certainly the stuff dreams are
made of. Joel in 2.28 so far approves of the prophetic use of dreams and
visions that he projects them into the future as the gift of all in the new
age of the spirit. The author of Dan. records visions which are probably
dreams. The dreams of the *NT* are revelatory (Mt. 1.20; 2,12, 13, 19,
22; 27.19; Ac. 11.5–10?) The dreams recorded by Jung in *Memories,
Dreams, Reflections* have much in common with the strange dreams of the
book of Daniel. It is however easy to see how dreams can become the
ready material of frauds and romantics. The realism of Jeremiah is
uncompromising. He may also be said to endorse a clear tradition (Num.
12.6) which rates the word above the dream.

23–24. Am I a God at hand, says the LORD, and not a God afar off?

LXX, Vulg. and translators dependent upon them, add a negative to the first part of this question, thus reversing the sense. But MT makes best sense in the context and is to be preferred. That this should be in the form of a question is demanded by the structure set out above. The second question, 'Can a man hide himself in secret places so that I can not see him?' (and the third) may be allowed to determine the interpretation of the first. There are those who think that God is one from whom it is easy to escape. They trivialise him and forget his all-embracing sovereignty. There is an area from which they dismiss him and assume their own dominion. This is not far from saying that they have domesticated God to their own requirements, putting themselves on easy terms with him and making themselves their own masters (a God at hand), repudiating his total and sovereign freedom (a God afar off). Imagery of this kind may suggest varieties of interpretation, and there is no reason to suppose that Jeremiah would have rejected either of the interpretations given above. Those commentators are wide of the mark who think these verses have nothing to do with the rest of the section.

25. lies (*šeqer*): a key word in the theology of the Jeremiah tradition. See on 3.10 and cf. 14.14.

26. How long? a traditional mark of the lament, cf. 4.14, 21; 12.4; 13.27; 31.22; 47.5.

the deceit of their own heart: this verse and v. 32 are close to 14.14, and it is prose of the Jeremiah tradition.

28. Let the prophet who has a dream tell the dream, but let him who has my word speak my word faithfully: this reads uncommonly like the decisive judgment pronounced at the end of an enquiry, or a disputation, after the pattern of a legal decision. Could it be that it was in these words that Jeremiah gave answer to those who enquired from him about the validity of dreams? If so, it would indicate vividly the difficulty Jeremiah faced. There is no empirical means of discrimination. True and false must therefore grow together like straw and wheat until they reveal their identity (cf. 28.9; Dt. 18.21). If this is the sense of the passage, Jeremiah is not admitting, as A.R. Johnson argues, that the authority of the dreamer is as valid as his own.

What has straw in common with wheat? a wisdom-type saying which suggests the radical difference between the two types of prophecy, cf. the parable of the wheat and tares (Mt. 13.14–30).

29. Is not my word like fire, says the LORD, and like a hammer which breaks the rock in pieces? Cf. v. 9, and 20.9 on the effect of the divine word on the prophet himself, and 5.14 for the fire imagery.

30. who steal my words from one another: cf. Mic. 3.5 for further evidence that prophets did a trade in oracles, exacted payment for their services, and even created trouble when they did not get the return they looked for! This verse suggests that, in order to satisfy their customers, they would filch oracular answers from one another, making out that they were directly from the LORD, thus proving that they had no true access to the divine council.

31. who use their tongues and say, Says the LORD: the verb 'say' is the denominative of the noun *n*ᵉ*ʾum*, and might be rendered 'they word the word of the LORD' or even 'they mouth, Mouth of the LORD'. The Heb. verb translated 'use' is lit. 'take'. The emphasis of the sentence may therefore be on the way these prophets rely upon their own tongue to mouth their own thoughts, in contrast to Jeremiah who is the mouthpiece of the LORD (1.9; 15.19). Alternatively Jeremiah may refer to a kind of incantation employed by these prophets, involving a particular use of the tongue. The Arabic word cognate to *naʾam* means 'groan, whisper'. The prophets may have spoken in low, humming tones like the Arab *Kahim*. The *n*ᵉ*ʾum yhwh* might then take its origin from the significant way in which these oracles were uttered. This is entirely conjectural. The evidence is confined to this verse, which supports the view but does not require it. The repetition of the formula in this section would have added point if such were the case. Verses 30–32 sum up the objection to the prophets as (a) their trafficking in oracles, (b) their use of *n*ᵉ*ʾum yhwh*, (c) their lying dreams. Plainly it is being treated as much more than a mere formula. On the other hand, the formula *n*ᵉ*ʾum yhwh* in the prophetic collections lost any ecstatic associations it once may have had, and became simply a mark of the prophetic oracle.

32. their recklessness: the noun occurs here only. Vulg. *in miraculis suis*. The verb occurs in Zeph. 3.4 also of prophets.

ON THE 'BURDEN' OF THE LORD **23.33–40**

This section deals with the activity of institutional prophets in relation to the use of the formula 'burden of the LORD' The argument would suggest that like *n*ᵉ*ʾum yhwh*, this had special force, suggesting the heavy responsibility of the prophetic word, like a burden on the shoulders of the prophet. If so, the evidence is confined to this passage (and perhaps 2 Kg. 9.25). Elsewhere the term is used almost exclusively as a stereotyped editorial heading for a certain number of oracles. It is relatively common in the first section of Isaiah in predominately late material (13.1; 14.28; 15.1; 17.1; 19.1; 21.1, 11, 13; 22.1; 23.1; 30.6) and then occurs sporadically (Ezek. 12.10; Nah. 1.1; Hab. 1.1; Zech. 9.1; 12.1; Prov. 31.1). Its primary meaning 'burden' gives a somewhat obvious opportunity for word-play.

The tendency among commentators is to regard v. 33 as an oracle of Jeremiah and the rest as the comment or elaboration of a learned scribe in the manner of the Talmud. Lindblom regards it as one of the longer glosses to be found in the Old Testament. These are not satisfactory explanations, because they fail to do justice to the prophetic nature of the section. The casuistic provisions are the formal clothing of prophetic demands, building a fence against the deceptions of false prophecy. This is more than scribal comment. Only a prophet has the right to order such a restriction in the name of the LORD. This must be the work of either Jeremiah himself or a prophet in the tradition. Verse 36 will be seen to be in the centre of the tradition of true prophecy. Verses 39–40 are a typical prophetic judgment. The verb 'punish' (pāqad) is so used elsewhere but more frequently in the Jeremiah tradition than anywhere else, c.f. vv. 2, 12.

33. When one of this people, or a prophet, or a priest asks you: In this verse the LORD directly addresses the prophet. It is possible that 'prophet' and 'priest' is added from v. 34, but they do no more than draw out something of the inclusive meaning of 'this people'.

What is the burden of the LORD?: We know that it was a regular procedure to consult prophets for divine oracles. This is evidence of the precise words sometimes used.

You are the burden of the LORD, and I will cast you off: the pun is as obvious in Heb. as it is in this English translation. This translation involves a universally accepted emendation of MT, supported by the LXX, Vulg. and Old Latin. It is perhaps significant that the only occurrence of the formula in Ezekiel (12.10) has similar word-play (whether one accepts MT or the text implied by LXX). Did Ezekiel employ it for the pun? This is a typical piece of prophetic technique, proceeding from known and acknowledged practice, by way of a verbal twist, to an unexpected and ironic statement of judgment. It is concluded with 'says the LORD' (nᵉ'ūm yhwh) the only occurrence of the term here, as contrasted with the repetition in the previous section, but, retaining the emphasis it receives in the previous section, suggesting the special weight and importance of this prophetic judgment. Let those who ask for a 'burden' remember that they themselves are the burden which the LORD is no longer prepared to carry.

34. Separated from v. 33 by *neʾūm yhwh*, this is an amplification of the fundamental judgment there laid down. The LORD speaks and declares a universal sanction on the utterance of the expression *maśśāʾ yhwh*. This is a way of saying that he will punish false prophets who characteristically cover their inventions with a varnish of divine endorsement using the formula as their credential. It has become a trademark to be avoided, a sign of bogus goods. But more than that, the question to the prophet shall no more be formulated in this way.

35. Thus shall you say, every one to his neighbour and every one to his brother, What has the LORD answered? or What has the LORD spoken? The permitted way of formulating the question is now made clear. Again the scope is widened. The question shall not be so asked even in the enquiries of familiar conversation. Thus it shall not be reduced to contempt by familiarity. Now the LORD is speaking through his prophet to the people, who are addressed in the second person plural. This no doubt is the sense in which v. 34 also should be understood.

36. But the burden of the LORD you shall mention no more, for the burden is every man's own word, and you pervert the words of the living God, the LORD God of hosts, our God: 'mention' – lit. 'remember'. This is a perfectly accurate translation of the Heb. and it is supported by the Versions. For all that it may not be correct. It looks as if the Versions translated literally and did not understand the more idiomatic 'for the burden is (restricted) to the man of his (the LORD's) word'. The *NEB* (rejected by *REB*!) paraphrases: 'that (the burden) is reserved for the man to whom he entrusts his message. If you do, you will make nonsense of the words of the living God'. This draws out what must surely be the sense of the whole section. The prophet is laying an embargo on the use of this formula, but he can hardly exclude its use where the LORD actually puts the burden of his word on his own man. At the same time this translation gives full value to the *waw* 'but', 'if you do' and the imperfect tense following it. The expression 'the living God' occurs rarely in the *OT* (see on 2.13), but it is nevertheless a key to Israel's profoundest understanding of God (see on 10.10). It is here, in the final touchstone of the difference between the true God and false, that the only valid means of discriminating between true prophecy and false is to be found. This verse has itself the unerring touch of true prophecy and is to be attributed not to a late, learned glossator but to Jeremiah himself or a successor in the tradition.

38–39. The announcement of divine judgment is introduced with a double **therefore** and the messenger formula, as improper from the pen of a glossator or scribe, as *maśśā'* from the lips of a false prophet.

behold, I will surely lift you up: further word-play, the verb *nāśā'* 'lift up' being the basis of the noun *maśśā'* 'burden'.

And the city: this touch suggests a mind preoccupied with the threat to and the destruction of Jerusalem. Otherwise one would expect 'land', as in the Deuteronomic tradition.

40. everlasting reproach and perpetual shame: 'reproach' and 'shame' are both words used in this sense in the psalms of lamentation, and both used elsewhere in the Jeremiah tradition. Cf. especially 'reproach' in 20.8 and the exact expressions: 'perpetual shame which shall not be forgotten' in 20.11.

In general this interpretation comes into direct conflict with generally accepted views of today, which may be summed up in words of Lindblom 'this is a specimen of Talmudic learning which has nothing at all to do with the prophecies of Jeremiah'. The unwritten implication of such views is that the section is unimportant and irrelevant for the interpretation of the book of Jeremiah. But if the comment above is correct, this section expresses and strengthens the fundamental insights of the Jeremiah tradition concerning the problem of false prophecy and, so far from being the literary convolution of the learned, is itself authentic prophecy and here recognised to be such.

THE VISION OF GOOD AND BAD **24.1–10**

At first sight the meaning of this vision is straightforward and its position here puzzling. Further scrutiny suggests a reason for its position but uncovers somewhat enigmatic features in the narrative.

The passage is placed here surely because it enables the editor to end the collection, chapters 21–24, on the same note that he began. In chapter 21 the theme of the kings is introduced by way of the specific enquiry made to Jeremiah concerning the Babylonian invasion in the reign of Zedekiah. This led to a collection of oracles concerning the kings, revealing the cumulative guilt inherited by Zedekiah. The section on prophets followed because they, more than any, bore responsibility of leadership with the kings, as mentors of the people. Chapter 24 forms a climax because it destroys the last complacent hope of the Jerusalem remnant that judgement has been completed in the exile of 597. The judgment yet to come focuses on the fate of Zedekiah. This suggests that the section and the editing of the collection as a whole belong to the last years of Zedekiah, between the first invasion and the second.

Formally the section has strong marks of the Jeremiah tradition.

Though the opening formula **The LORD showed me** (which in the Heb. comes first) has no parallel in Jeremiah, but introduces the visions of Amos (7.1, 4, 7; 8.1), the formal question and answer (v. 3, cf. Am. 7.8; 8.2) exactly conforms to the convention already noticed in Jer. 1.11, 13. There is, therefore, an intrinsic probability that the principle there elicited of the primacy of the word over the vision applies here also. As in 1.11, 13; the prophet recounts the vision in the first person. The collective *gālût* 'exiles' is found twice in Isa. but otherwise confined to Jer. (28.4; 29.22; 40.1). The phrase 'for good' is more common in Jer. (14.11; 21.10; 39.16; 44.27) than elsewhere. 'I will build . . . and not tear them down; I will plant them and not uproot them' (v. 6) is a clear echo of 1.10, q.v. The 'heart to know that I am the LORD' coupled with the covenant formula clearly anticipates the unique formulation of the new covenant in 31.31–34.

The sending of 'sword, famine and pestilence' is a commonplace of the prose tradition (v. 10, see on 14.12). And although v. 9 has the same form and says the same thing as Dt. 28.37, it is expressed with detailed variations. The word *zawᵃ'āh* 'horror' occurs (with spelling variations) in Dt. 28.25 but also in Jer. 15.4; 29.18; (34.17; *māšāl* 'byword' in Dt. 28.37; *qᵉlālāh* 'curse' in Jer. 25.18; 26.6; 42.18; 44.8, 12, 22; 49.13 but not in this sense in Dt.). *herpāh* 'reproach' occurs in Jer. 6.10; 20.8; 29.18; 42.18, 12; 49.13; 23.40, but not in Dt. The conclusion must be that there is some unexplained connection with Dt. 28 in v. 9, that even here the freedom of the Jeremiah tradition is exercised, but that elsewhere the Jeremiah tradition is dominant. In no sense can this section be ascribed to Deuteronomic origin. At most one can say that in a verse not germane to the central image of the section, there is evidence that the Jeremiah tradition shows familiarity with a specific element within Deut. and has made it its own.

The 'vision' often prompts questions about the baskets of figs, whether they contained first-fruits brought to the Temple, whether they were figs which Jeremiah happened to see, and induced the message. If, as seems probable, the same principle of interpretation applies to this as to the visions of the Almond Branch and the Boiling Pot in chapter 1, then such questions are unnecessary. The vision starts from the word concerning the good and the bad. It may be also that Graf Reventlow is correct in seeing these words as indicating, not in the first instance the character of the exiles and the remanent Jews respectively, but their fate. There is ultimate good for the exiles; there is further judgment (evil) for Jerusalem.

This accords with Jeremiah's use of these words elsewhere. Jeremiah is faced with a situation similar to that encountered by Ezekiel (chapter 11) when the exile of 597 B.C. took place. Those who escaped deportation and remained in Jerusalem came to believe that they now were the true Israel protected by God. The LORD had shown his disapproval of the exiles by removing them. Ezekiel dealt with the consequent demoralisation of the exiles (11.14–21), Jeremiah with the arrogant complacency of the men of Judah. Jeremiah proclaimed that a further judgment must fall upon Judah and that ultimate salvation lay with the exiles. It will be seen that when the chapter is read in the light of this explanation it comes alive. It may be therefore that the visions are mental pictures conjured up as a result of the primary message about the good and the evil, rather than photographs of actual baskets lying about in the Temple or in gardens.

Again when the chapter is thus interpreted the objections of inconsistency raised by some scholars do not seem valid. It is said that the hope of salvation for the exiles is inconsistent with the emphasis in chapter 5 on universal sinfulness. Notice that Jeremiah is not emphasising the moral qualities of the exiles; but in any case the emphasis on total doom comes into some conflict with any future hope at all. We have to come to terms with this. It is overwhelmingly likely that Jeremiah reacted to the two situations differently and let the apparent inconsistencies look after themselves. Once Jeremiah's situation and involvement are understood, the interpretation above seems intrinsically right.

Again, it is said that the form of the hope is in conflict with the prophecy of seventy years captivity in chapter 29, effectively removing any hope of return until after the death of any now living. But once more, Jeremiah is dealing there with a false impatience to return. Here he is dealing with the simple contrast between those in whom the future of the people of God lies and those in whom it does not. It would be unlike a prophet to obscure his message by qualifications appropriate to a different pastoral situation. Again, it is said that the contrast conflicts with the criticism of Jehoiachin in 22.24–30 (now in exile), and Zedekiah, who is regarded as weak and vacillating but not evil.

All these objections rest on a misunderstanding of the meaning of good and evil in this prophecy. Jeremiah is not handing out moral compliments and criticisms. He is dealing with the future as it is revealed to him and as it turned out to be. Thus the objections to the ascription of this passage to Jeremiah collapse. Not that it matters supremely by whom a prophecy is uttered, except that Deuteronomic prophecies after the event do not seem to have much significance, and where objections can be shown to be fragile, it is well to dismiss them. This is a section which seems to make powerful sense as the work of Jeremiah (even if amplified in the tradition), but appears diminished when ascribed to literary Deuteronomists. The clue is to discern the essential simplicity of the contrast. This is difficult for the modern commentator who is too often lost in a sea of detail and complexity.

1. The historical note seems to be a summary of 2 Kg. 24.10–15 with specific mention of **Jeconiah** (there called Jehoiachin), **the princes** and particularly the **craftsmen, and the smiths**.

the LORD showed me this vision: the word 'vision' is not present in the Heb. but is no doubt implied in 'showed me . . . Behold'. The expression is consistent with either the observation of actual baskets or the recollection of baskets suggested by the primary intuition of the divine word.

4. so I will regard as good: this suggests a moral judgment. But the Heb. is lit.: 'I will regard them for good', i.e. auspiciously. This is strictly parallel in meaning to v. 6. 'I will set my eyes on them for good', which the *NEB* correctly paraphrases, 'I will look upon them meaning to do them good'. Jeremiah is concerned primarily with their fate and not their quality. The primary meaning of good (salvation) and evil (judgment) in this context may be destroyed by too allegorical an interpretation of the details of the vision.

8. and those who dwell in the land of Egypt: it does not follow that this dates the passage to the aftermath of the destruction of Jerusalem in 586 when we know many Jews fled to Egypt. Pro-Egyptian Jews may well have been compelled to take refuge there at various times during the intrigues of the period, from the reign of Jehoiakim onwards.

C   CONCLUSION OF THE COMPLEX (1–25)

Chapter 25 is composed of three sections (a) verses 1–14, warning that the collected oracles of Jeremiah's twenty-three year ministry are to be fulfilled; (b) verses 15–29, the cup of wrath against the nations; (c) verses 30–38, a poetic oracle of judgment against the nations and their leaders. After v. 13, the LXX has the oracles against the nations, which in the Heb. Bible are arranged as chapters 46–51. The fact that differing and intelligible arrangements were possible after verse 13 is perhaps best

explained if we suppose that the collected oracles of Jeremiah at one stage
stopped there. Verses 1–13 (and 14) therefore provide the basic section
of chapter 25 and the two other sections may be regarded as subsequent
additions 'deposited' here for good editorial reasons. These reasons will
be suggested below.

JEREMIAH'S ORACLE ON HIS ORACLES 25.1–14

This section is crucial for the understanding of the structure of the book
of Jeremiah and has been so recognised by most commentators. The
related problems are: (a) the character and authorship of the prose; (b)
whether the section is intended to introduce or close a collection of oracles;
(c) its present and (putative) original relation to the preceding collections;
(d) its relation to chapter 36; (e) its relation to the LXX tradition.

The character of the prose is that which we have observed again and
again in this book. It cannot be described simply as Deuteronomic. There
is the observable covenant form, consisting of introduction (vv. 1–2); the
LORD's call to obedience (vv. 3–6); Israel's disobedience (v. 7);
consequent judgment (vv. 8–11), and certainly this same form can be
detected throughout the Deuteronomic literature, as well as in chapters
7, 11, 17, 34, 35, etc. of Jeremiah. But this says nothing about authorship,
since it has become an obvious and well understood stereotype. More
significant is the style and vocabulary, and while this has the usual echoes
of Deuteronomy, it is more characteristically the distinctive prose style
of the Jeremiah tradition. Thus

> 'I have spoken persistently to you' (v. 3) and 'the LORD persistently sent
> to you all his servants the prophets' (v. 4), see on 7.13, 25; and cf. 11.7; 26.5;
> 26.19; 32.33; 35.14; 44.4.
>
> 'You have neither listened, nor inclined your ears to hear' (v. 4), 7.24 etc.
> 'Turn now every one of you from his evil way, (v. 5), see on 18.11. 'and
> wrongdoings' (v. 5), see on 23.2, 22. These might even be called clichés of
> the prose tradition.
>
> 'dwell upon the land' (v. 5), cf. 23.8; 35.15. At this point one could expect
> the oath formula, referring to the oath made by the LORD to the forefathers,
> so beloved of Dt. (1.35; 6.10; 18.23; 7.13; 8.1; 9.5, 10, 11; 11.9, 21; 19.8;
> 26.3, 15; 28.11; 30.20; 31.7, and cf. Jer, 32.22), but as in 35.15 it does not
> occur.
>
> 'do not go after other gods' (v. 6), cf. 7.6, 9, 18; 11.10; 13.10; 16.13; 22.9;
> 19.13; 44.3, 5, 8, 15.

'or provoke me to anger with the work of your hands' (v. 6), cf. 7.18, 19;
8.19; 11.17; 32.20. 32; 44.3, 8. The idea of 'vexing' the LORD, which is
probably nearer to the sense of the Heb., is a commonplace of Dt. (4.25; 9.18;
31.24; 32.16, 21) and the Deuteronomic history, but the full expression (i.e.
'provoking him to anger through the work of your hands') occurs only in 31.29.

'Therefore . . . behold, I will send' (vv.8–9) – sentences of this type ('behold
with the participle) we have noticed again and again as characteristic of the
Jeremiah prose tradition.

'all the tribes (families of the north' (v. 9) links with 1.15 and may well be
a sign of the redactor's hand in both. The lament-type repetition of words
to denote 'a horror, a hissing, and an everlasting reproach' (v. 9) is in varying
combinations characteristic (cf. 2.15; 4.7; 18.16; 19.8; 25.9, 11, 18, 35; 29.18;
42.18; 44.12, 22; 46.19; 48.9; 49.13, 17; 50.3, 23; 51.29, 37, 41, 43. See note
on 19.8). And finally v. 10, 'the voice of mirth . . . bridegroom', etc. occurs
in 7.34; 16.9; 25.10; 33.11 and is characteristic.

This list is impressive and convincing. It is unacceptable to attribute this
prose to a Deuteronomist, let alone to a Levitical preacher, of the post-
exilic synagogue. This prose belongs to the distinctive Jeremiah tradition
and is to be attributed to Baruch or someone else in that tradition, who
was familiar with the words and the activity of Jeremiah. This is not to
claim that the passage contains the very words of the prophet. The
succession of stereotypes suggests that it is an editorial version. But it
does suggest that the passage has to be taken seriously as reflecting,
through the redactor, the prophetic intervention of Jeremiah himself.

This oracle is about the oracles of Jeremiah delivered over a period
of twenty-three years. Its centre of interest is not a narrative with prophetic
significance (like chapter 36), but the total impact of the whole of
Jeremiah's ministry to date. Each oracle had its own point, in its own
context. But in the year 604, Jeremiah was concerned with the cumulative
effect of his past prophecies in relation to the incomprehension of the
people and the judgment which was about to break. It is therefore
overwhelmingly probable that a redactor, understanding the nature of
the prophecy, would place it at the conclusion of a collection of Jeremiah's
oracles rather than at the beginning.

The fact that the MT and LXX agree in placing this passage here,
but disagree in what follows, suggests that it was arranged as the
conclusion to chapters 1–24. Indeed there can be no dispute that at some
stage in the transmission of the text, this was the editor's intention. At
this stage one may suppose that the fundamental deposit of the Jeremiah

tradition was contained in 1.1–25.14, and the rest of the tradition was
not yet determined in authoritative form. But two factors suggest that
25.1-1-4 has had a previous history. The first is that the date of this
passage is clearly recorded as the fourth year of Jehoiakim, whereas a
number of passages, mainly in chapters 21–24 clearly belong to the reign
of Zedekiah. The second is the relation of MT to the LXX version. MT
is slightly longer and contains the following expansions:

v. 1   'that was the first year of Nebuchadrezzar king of Babylon'.
v. 2   'Jeremiah the prophet'.
v. 3   'the word of the LORD has come to me' . . . 'but you have not listened'.
v. 9   'says the LORD, and for Nebuchadrezzar the king of Babylon, my servant' . . . 'these'.
v. 11 'for they shall serve among the nations seventy years' (LXX) becomes in MT: 'these nations shall serve the king of Babylon seventy years'.
v. 12 'the king of Babylon . . . the land of the Chaldeans, for their iniquity, says the LORD'.
v. 14 this whole verse is omitted by LXX.

This list contains all the references the passage has to Nebuchadrezzar
and the Babylonians. Moreover these are in the nature of identifying
glosses, such as are familiar in the Isaiah tradition (e.g. 7.8b, 17, 18,
20; 8.7b). Thus the LXX represents the older text only in the sense that
it has not been subject to these identifying glosses. Without these MT
and LXX represent the same text.

Elsewhere in the *OT* and without exception in the LXX, the later form
'Nebuchadnezzar' is found. In the MT of Jer. 27–29 there are eight
instances of this later spelling. Seven of them are omitted from the LXX
and provide a set of indications that these chapters were subject to the
influence of a special literary environment. Otherwise in MT from chapter
21 onwards the older spelling 'Nebuchadrezzar' is consistently used. In
about ten cases scattered about these chapters, including a number of
superscriptions, the LXX renders the MT 'Nebuchadrezzar' as
'Nebuchadnezzar'. In about twelve cases LXX omits altogether. It seems
to follow that the earliest form of the prose tradition has 'Nebuchadrezzar',
that the earliest glosses of this text, as in chapter 25, have
'Nebuchadrezzar' and that the glossing of chapters 27–29 represents a
somewhat later redaction, before the spelling 'Nebuchadnezzar' had
become virtually universal.

When these identifying glosses are removed, it becomes clear that the passage alludes in the same general terms to the same unspecified Foe from the North as chapters 1–6, and is patient therefore of a similar explanation. This becomes particularly clear in v. 9 which, without the gloss, reads: 'Behold, I will send for all the tribes of the north and bring them against this land'. Significantly also this wording is close to 1.15: 'I am calling all the tribes of the kingdoms of the north' which may well represent, as Janzen suggests, the conflation of two variant readings (see below). In those earlier years Jeremiah spoke of the enemy from the north without knowing specifically what that enemy would be. It was in the circumstances of 604 when Jeremiah's old oracles, long disbelieved and discounted, could clearly be seen to be on the point of fulfilment, that the reproduction of his old oracles had its point. At the same time the enemy could now be seen by everyone to be Babylon, and this identification is pointed up by a later glossator.

Thus behind this oracle lies the same set of circumstances and prophetic expedients as make sense of the related chapter 36. This gives some plausibility to the suggestion that this passage originally completed the Baruch Scroll, i.e. chapters 1–6. If this were so, then the features which relate the passage with chapter 1 would gain in significance. These are (a) the phrase 'all the tribes (families) of the north', cf. 1.15; (b) the phrase 'which Jeremiah prophesied against all the nations' (v. 13), cf. 1.5, 10; though as we shall see below, this phrase has additional forward looking significance; (c) we noticed a certain Deuteronomic element in chapter 1 and raised the question of Baruch's influence in the final form of that chapter. Or one might say chapter 1 shows the influence of the prose tradition which comes to complete self-expression in chapter 25; (d) 'the word of the LORD has come to *me*' (v. 3) echoes 1.7, 11, 13.

If then the substance of chapter 25.2–14 at one time completed the Baruch Scroll which was the nucleus upon which subsequent collections were deposited, it would be easy to understand how its concluding section would be placed always at the end when additional collections were inserted. For some reason this process ended when chapters 21–24 were added, and thereafter the passage remained as chapter 25. And since, on the whole, it is a different kind of material which follows chapter 25, this hypothesis receives some confirmation.

But the chapter with which 25 has the closest relationship is 36, which tells of Jeremiah's command to Baruch to write down his oracles 'from the day I spoke to you, from the day of Josiah, until today'. The relation between 25.1–14 and chapter 36 has some features in common with the relation between chapters 7 and 26, see on chapter 7. Chapters 26 and

36 are more concerned with the event; chapters 7 and 25 with the content of Jeremiah's message. All four passages belong to the prose tradition. None can claim to be photographic representations either of the event or of the message. It is therefore as useless and foolish to set chapter 25 *against* chapter 36 as to set 7 against 25. Chapter 25 expresses the *intention* behind the writing down of the oracles and the reading of them in chapter 36.

Thus 25.1–14 has the character of a representative summary of the prophet's ministry. It is unlikely that Jeremiah himself uttered a string of clichés of the prose tradition in precisely this form. Nevertheless this sermon sums up his prophetic intervention; his call to obedience in the manner of the prophetic succession; his direct accusation of disobedience; and his warning of the consequences. The judgment would include defeat by an invader from the north. Comparison with the Greek text enables us to see the beginning of a process that not only identifies the enemy, but expands the summary to include judgment on Babylon itself. The passage tells us how the Jeremiah tradition understood the gist of Jeremiah's message over a period of twenty-three years.

Further observation will be made concerning the probable redaction history of this section under v. 13 below.

1. The word that came to Jeremiah concerning all the people: The formula is the one which seems to be used to introduce supplementary collections, cf. 7.1; 11.1; 18.1; 21.1; 30.1. That the oracle should be directed to 'all the people' corresponds to the intention made clear in 36.3, 6. The high drama of Jeremiah's conflict with Jehoiakim was an incidental consequence of his causing the oracles to be read and is so presented in chapter 36. There is no hint in chapter 25 of the consequential events, because the accent here is on the content of the message.

in the fourth year of Jehoiakim the son of Josiah, king of Judah (that was the first year of Nebuchadrezzar king of Babylon): the fourth year of Jehoiakim was 605/604 B.C., and though Nebuchadrezzar (here correctly spelt) began his official reign in Nisan, April 604, his father had died in August 605. Chapter 36 also says that it was in the fourth year of Jehoiakim that Jeremiah was commanded to write down the oracles of the previous twenty-three years. But it was on a fast-day in the fifth year, in the nine month (i.e. Kislev, December 604) that Baruch read them (Jer. 36.9–10). If we are to take the dating precisely, it is suggested that this oracle to the people was delivered before the reading of the oracles in the Temple by Baruch. But of course we cannot know

how accurate the dating is, or how freely Baruch or another represented
the teaching of Jeremiah in this stereotyped language.

2. all the people of Judah and all the inhabitants of Jerusalem: a
well-worn expression which describes the people of God as they then
existed, and from which no conclusions can be drawn as to the way
Jeremiah delivered his message. See on 11.2

3. The chronology appears to be correct. Working back twenty-three
years from 604 gives 627, which was the thirteenth year of Josiah.

3–10. As shown above, these verses are composed of phrases
characteristic of the prose tradition in Jeremiah. At the same time they
are not an artificial assembly of borrowed sentences. The redactor is
expressing the known teaching of Jeremiah in the expressions that come
most naturally to him. And the content is intrinsically probable as the
substance of the oracle of Jeremiah, when he took the step of putting
together his oracles and drawing out the awesome meaning of his total
ministry. That which had been humanly so ineffective was now to be
validated by the LORD himself in the judgment of history.

9. against all these nations round about: LXX has 'all the nations
roundabout'; in v. 11, for **This whole land** it has 'the whole land'; and
for **these nations shall serve the king of Babylon** it reads 'they shall
serve among the nations'. Plainly the redactor or glossator of the MT
has been trying to be more precise and in all probability to relate this
text to the appended oracle in vv. 15–29 on the cup of wrath against the
nations. Probably this attention to the text was given at the same time
as the Foe from the North was identified by means of the identifying
glosses noticed above.

I will utterly destroy them: i.e. lit. treat them as *ḥērem*, the by this
time archaic institution by which every thing connected with a foreign
god was rendered harmless, usually by destruction. Cf. Dt. 2.34; 3.6;
7.2; 13.16; 20.17. The usage here is figurative, as also in Mic. 4.13; Mal.
4.6; Zech. 14.11.

10. See the discussion of the vocabulary and images above.

11. serve the king of Babylon seventy years: this is the first
formulation of the prediction that the exile would last seventy years (cf.
29.10), a prediction with a long tradition history to follow (cf. Zech. 1.12;
2 Chr. 36.21; Dan. 9.2). Both of the Jeremiah passages occur in the prose
tradition, and it is impossible to be quite sure whether this prophecy was
that of Jeremiah or one of his interpreters. As a prophecy after the event
it might refer to the period from 586 B.C. to the completion of the Second
Temple in 516 B.C. But if it were invented in the light of the events, it

would be odd if it did not refer to the effective end of the Babylonian captivity which must be associated with the rise of Cyrus less than fifty years after Nebuchadrezzar's capture of Jerusalem.

It is not an improbable prophecy on the lips of Jeremiah, if he was using the number seventy to refer to the normal length of a man's life (Ps. 9.10), indicating that no one now living could expect to return from exile. This becomes clearer in 29.10. That this was the true origin and context of the prophecy is perhaps confirmed by the fact that it was not precisely fulfilled, and caused much perplexity. Zechariah, prophesying about 519 B.C., could be excused for applying it to his situation. The author of Dan. however, by interpreting it of seventy 'weeks of years', i.e. as a period of 490 years, showed that he was unaware of an obvious and clear fulfilment of the prophecy which, so to speak, exhausted its significance and dispensed with it.

Altogether it is easier to suppose that this was originally a prophecy of Jeremiah which remained to tease subsequent generations who could not be satisfied except by exact fulfilment. And if the reference to Babylon is omitted and we read with LXX 'and they shall be slaves among the nations seventy years', then we may suppose that Jeremiah's prophecy of the duration of exile was originally as indefinite as his forecast of its place. Now that the motif of a seventy years' subjugation (of Babylon) has turned up in an inscription of Esarhaddon, we may assume that this expression was understood both in Babylon and Judah to denote a substantial but temporary period of subjugation.

12. Then after seventy years are completed, I will punish the king of Babylon and that nation, the land of the Chaldeans, for their iniquity: again without the identifying glosses, and according to the text of LXX, this prophecy is formulated with the kind of vagueness that we have previously encountered in Jeremiah's prediction of the Foe from the North. Thus it reads: 'Then after seventy years are completed, I will punish that nation'. The word 'punish' (*pāqaḏ*, lit. 'visit') is more frequent in this sense in Jer. than in any other part of the *OT*. See on 10.15; 11.22.

13. I will bring upon that land all the words which I have uttered against it, everything written in this book, which Jeremiah prophesied against all the nations: as it stands, in the final form of the text, the meaning of this verse is unambiguous. 'That land' is Babylon, as also is 'that nation' in v. 12. The sequence is entirely in keeping with well known prophetic principles. The LORD will bring a judgment upon his people by means of a foreign power, whose king, for this purpose is his 'servant' (v. 9, cf. Isa. 10.5–12). But in due course the ironic course of justice will turn full circle and the agent of judgment will himself become the object of judgment.

What then is 'written in this book' to support this confidence that Babylon will be punished within seventy years? Where are the oracles, now set down in writing, for all to inspect, to which appeal is now made? If as we have argued, this section as a whole came at the end of the collection of Jeremiah's oracles, one would expect to find such predictions in chapters 1–6 or at least in chapters 1–24. There is very little — only the rather general prophecies of 2.37; 12.17; the prediction of the punishment of the circumcised (which excludes Babylon) in 9.25, and a number of passages which imply more than they say, like 23.8. This is not enough. The 'book', for this purpose, must include at least the oracle on the cup of wrath (vv. 15–29) which includes 'all the kings of the north' and, as a climax, 'after them the king, of Babylon', and possibly it includes the oracles against Babylon in chapters 50–51; indeed it may be the book explicitly referred to in 51.60.

One expedient, which has respectable scholarly pedigree, is to change the 'that' to 'this', and to omit vv. 12 and 14 as subsequent additions made perhaps in the time of Zedekiah. Then 'I will bring upon this land all the words which I have uttered against it, everything written in this book' (omitting 'which Jeremiah prophesied against the nations') refers to the prophecies against Judah and the fulfilment of the oracles concerning the Foe from the North, exactly as in chapter 36. Then the verse can refer easily and naturally to Baruch's Scroll or to chapters 1–24. The trouble with this suggestion is that it involves a conjectural emendation of the text without support, and incapable of disproof of or verification. A strong argument against it is that the alternative hypothesis (below) corresponds more adequately to a satisfactory understanding of the redaction history of the text.

If we may assume that 'that land' is the correct reading, then the first thing to observe is that both this phrase and 'that nation' of v. 12 lack an explicit antecedent. Of course the implicit antecedent is 'the tribe of the north' (v. 9) identified by the glossator as Babylon. The likelihood therefore is that the whole of vv. 12–14 represent a suture, a build-up, on the basis of the narrative, appropriate to the fourth year of Jehoiakim. This build-up would be made at the earliest in the time of Zedekiah and might or might not be done at the same time as the identifying glosses were added. The teaching of Jeremiah, appropriate to the fourth year of Jehoiakim, ended with the threat of v. 11 that 'this whole land shall become a ruin and a waste and they shall serve among the nations seventy years' (LXX). At a certain stage (the fourth year of Zedekiah or later), the picture was broadened to include the judgment of Babylon (now identified). Now when this was done the material against Babylon (25.15–29; 50–51), already existed in the Jeremiah tradition. It was appropriate therefore to refer to the fulfilment of 'all the words which I have uttered against it, everything written in this book'.

But in expressing things like this, the redactor was not necessarily confining his reference to what followed. He looked both before and after. It was the context of the passage, i.e. the oracle on the collected oracles of 627–604, which made this comprehensive reference appropriate. The 'book' therefore is chapters 1–24 and whatever at this stage followed it, certainly 25.15–29, 50–51, maybe the whole tradition as we now have it. By adding 'which Jeremiah prophesied against all the nations' MT linked chapter 1 with later oracles against the nations, as we have seen.

All this is entirely in keeping with the movement of nucleus and deposit, which is the most probable model of the way the prophetic books were assembled. This is a significant example of the history of the transmission of the text, about which the last word has not yet been said. For a summary of the stages, see Introduction p. 33. In the LXX the verse ends: 'I will bring upon that land all the words which I have uttered against it, everything written in this book'. The words added by MT 'which Jeremiah prophesied against all the nations' are in LXX adapted clumsily to provide a heading for the first of the oracles against the nations – 'which Jeremiah prophesied against the nations – Elam'. This suggests that the MT form of v. 13 is primary, and the LXX arrangement of the oracles against the nations secondary

14. A general statement of the principle of judgment which means that the triumph of the foreign power will not be for ever unchecked. The minister of judgment will himself be subject to judgment in the ironic process that is characteristic of providence. Omitted by LXX.

THE CUP OF WRATH 25.15–29 (LXX 32.1–24)

This oracle must be of a visionary character. It is not possible to envisage any convincing situation in which Jeremiah might, for example, interpret a cup shared by foreign ambassadors as a sign of judgment on the countries. This is not an acted sign, but an appeal to the imagination. The effect of the oracle is dependent upon the imagery.

The imagery may be interpreted at several levels. At the simplest level the cup of the wine of wrath suggests the effect of wine causing men to 'stagger' and 'be crazed' (v. 16). Jeremiah had already used this metaphor to denote the power of the divine word possessing him (23.9). Even so would the divine judgment take hold of the nations and render them helpless.

But there are other levels of interpretation which cannot be obvious to the modern reader. Drink offerings were a part of the Temple ritual (Exod. 29.40–41; Num. 28.7). Pss. 11.6 and 16.5 suggest that drinking from a cup had some connection with the sacred lot. In the ceremony of ordeal (Num. 5.23–28) those who are guilty find the cup a curse; whereas the innocent are unscathed. Otherwise the ritual cup seems to be mainly associated with happiness and deliverance (Ps. 23.5), and in Ps. 116.13 is called 'the cup of salvation'. It may be therefore that Jeremiah achieved some shocked attention by harshly changing the familiar cup of salvation into the cup of wrath. We cannot of course be sure that Jeremiah was the first to speak in this way. Certainly it is in his time and later that all the references to the cup of wrath belong (Ezek. 23.33; Isa. 51.17, 22; Lam.4.21; Ps. 75.8, cf. also Jer. 49.12; 51.7; Hab. 2.16). One may say that in the *OT* drinking the cup becomes a well-understood figure of submitting to the divine judgment.

In vv. 15–16 the LORD commands the prophet to take the cup. In v. 17 he relates that he took the cup and made the nations drink it. In v. 27 are the words with which he commands the nations to drink. In vv. 28–29 the possibility that they refuse to drink is covered. This is a drink they cannot escape. There are signs of the familiar prose style of the Jeremiah tradition, betrayed in vv. 16, 27 'because of the sword which I am sending among them' (cf. 9.16; 24.10; 19.17, cf. 49.37); in v. 18 'to make them a desolation', and a waste, a hissing (and a curse)' cf. 19.8; 24.9; 25.9, 11; 26.6; 29.18; 42.18; 44.8, 12, 22 and Dt. 28.37; and in v. 29 'for behold I begin to work evil at the city over which my name is called', cf. 7.10, 11, 14, 30; 32.34; 34.15; 14.9; 15.16; I Kg. 8.43. The narrative is in the first person, cf. Jer. 1.4, 11, 13 (2.1; 3.6, 11), 11.6, 9; 13.1, 8; 14.11; 15.1; 16.1; 19.1. We have seen reason to ascribe this first person narrative to one close to Jeremiah. This narrative is best understood as expressing, with some stereotyped prose, the substance of an imaginative oracle made known at some stage by Jeremiah himself. Indeed these phrases are in some cases scarcely disguised amplifications.

On the other hand, the central section (vv. 18–26), has clearly been subject to development. It is simply a list of nations. Some scholars have questioned whether the original oracle contained the names of any nations.

This is unnecessary scepticism. Verse 17 seems to lead naturally into some sort of list of 'the nations to whom the LORD sent me'. Without a list of nations, there is a lacuna. However it is entirely probable that the list has been extended in the light of history. The LXX version (chapter 32) omits 'all the kings of the land of Uz' and 'all the kings of the land of the Philistines' (v. 20). It reads 'the kings of foreign tribes', though it specifies Ashkelon, Gaza and Ekron (v. 20); it omits 'all the kings of Arabia', though it includes Dedan, Tema and Buz and the tribes that dwell in the desert (vv. 23–24); above all it omits 'after them the king of Babylon shall drink' (v. 26). For 'all the kings of the north' in v. 26, LXX has 'east'. This is sufficient to prove that this list was at a certain stage a hunting-ground for identifications, no doubt relevant to later times. Was there a similar history of the adaptations of that text which is common to MT and LXX? In all probability yes. Certainly if Jeremiah himself included a list appropriate to his own time. It is possible that the formula 'all the kings of . . .' provides a key to one such subsequent adaptation. This phrase occurs somewhat erratically, and if all the nations thus introduced are omitted, the following list is left:

(1) Egypt in the south, with all the foreign people there settled
(2) The Philistine cities in the west. (The mention of Ekron is probably rhetorical since it had long lost its independence. Jos. 19.41–48.)
(3) Edom, Moab and Ammon in the south-east and east
(4) The north Arabian tribes

This is roughly the order of the oracles against the nations in MT save that Damascus comes in for the north Arabian tribes.

It makes good sense that Jeremiah should have seen these tribes and kingdoms sharing the judgment which was coming upon 'Jerusalem and the cities of Judah'. The motive of updating the list is perhaps most clearly shown in the phrase 'and a curse, *as at this day*' which, omitted in LXX, has been added by one to whom the prediction of the desolation and waste of Jerusalem is a present reality. It is not possible to write a clear history of the tradition of the text because it involves too much guesswork. But the evidence is to show that much happened to it between the utterances of Jeremiah and the final form of the text.

The most significant change is perhaps the last. Jeremiah no doubt was thinking of the judgment which was to be administered by Babylon on the nations surrounding Jerusalem. A redactor has included Babylon itself among those who are to drink the cup (cf. 25.12). Both are true.

We do not have to pronounce any form of the text unauthentic. We do need to have some idea how it grew into its present form and so to read it. Why and when this oracle was placed in its present position following verses 1–14 is suggested on pp. 33ff., 328, 333.

15. to me: absent from LXX and no doubt added to accord with 1.4, etc. But it is no more than the crossing of a t, since the first person is implied by the 'so I took the cup' of v. 17.

this cup of the wine of wrath: LXX has 'the cup of pure wine' cf. Ps. 75.8. Again MT is but giving the thing its appropriate name.

16. because of the sword: the poet does not need to give an explanation of his imagery, but the interpreter commonly does. It is significant that, as shown above, this sentence belongs to the prose tradition. On the sword in Jer. see 5.17; 14.12, 16; 15.2, 9; 18.21; 19.7; 21.7; 46.16; 50.16.

20. and all the foreign folk: cf. Exod. 12.38; Neh. 13.3; Ezek. 30.5; Jer. 50.37; PS. Sol. 17.15.

all the kings of the land of Uz: a possible motive for the addition of the gloss (absent from LXX) is furnished by Lam. 4.21, 'Rejoice and be glad, O daughter of Edom, dweller in the land of Uz; but to you also the cup shall pass; you shall become drunk and strip yourself bare!' cf. Job 1.1.

the remnant of Ashdod: according to Herodotus (II.157), besieged by Psammetichus I (663–609 B.C.) for twenty-nine years and rebuilt by Nehemiah (Neh. 13.23).

23. Dedan, Tema, Buz: north Arabian tribes. For Dedan, see Gen. 10.7; Jer. 49.8. For Tema, see Isa. 21.14; Job 6.19. Buz is otherwise unknown.

All who cut the corners of their hair: see on 9.25. Those who haunt the fringes of the desert? (So *NEB, REB*).

24. all the kings of Arabia: *ᵃrāḇ*, possibly a dittograph of *ʿereḇ* 'mixed tribe'.

25. Zimri: omitted by LXX and otherwise unknown. The change to z-m-k-i produces an atbash of Elam. This would then be a gloss on what follows. Atbash is a cipher by which the last letter of the Heb. stands for the first, the next to last for the second, and so on. There can hardly have been need to conceal the meaning; so that, if the hypothesis is true, it represents the work of a scribe who liked to mystify rather than an interpreter of the Jeremiah tradition. *NEB* reads Zamri.

Babylon: Heb. *šēšak*, another atbash.

26. And after them the King of Babylon shall drink: So the tradition comes round full circle. Babylon, which in the mind of Jeremiah, was to administer the drink, is itself to drink.

29. For behold, I begin to work evil at the city which is called by my name: this corresponds to the setting of Jerusalem at the head of the list in v. 18, which is often interpreted as a later insertion. It also suggests that the oracle in its first form was uttered by Jeremiah before the fall of Jerusalem. 'which is called by my name' is the familiar paraphrase of the English versions, but is more accurately translated 'over which my name is called'. The phase suggests the LORD's ownership and protection of his city. See S. R. Driver on Dt. 28.10.

We have seen reason to suppose that this section is the product of a prolonged redaction process. The remaining question is at what stage in this process was it added to 25.1–14 and for what reason? The probability is that it was added when 25.1–14 had itself reached the end of its main development and included v. 13 with its reference to the prophecies of Jeremiah 'against all the nations'. And in all likelihood this would be at the stage when 25.1–14 concluded chapters 1–24. For it was a nucleus of 25.1–14 which concluded chapters 1–6. Once v. 13 was included, it provided an admirable setting for the oracle on the cup of wrath to be drunk by the nations, and the concluding poems in vv. 30–38 telling of the LORD's sentence on the nations and their rulers. Such a rounding off of the section became the more suitable when it became obvious that other sections were to follow in the complete scroll of the Jeremiah tradition.

THE NATIONS AND THEIR LEADERS SENTENCED
25.30–38 (LXX 32.30–38)

This section probably divides at least into two poems, v. 31 ending with the cryptic $n^{e\ni}\bar{u}m$ *yhwh*, and v. 32 beginning with a new introductory formula.

Verses 30–32 contain a brief poem, picturing in traditional imagery the appearance of the LORD to enter into judgment with the nations and sentence them. This is to put into legal terms what has been said in the vivid image of drinking the cup of wrath. He comes with all the terror and overwhelming power associated with theophany.

30. The LORD will roar from on high, and from his holy habitation utter his voice: the pattern of this sentence is exactly that of Am. 1.2,

with which there must be some unexplained connection, cf. also Jl 3.16.
The difference is that in Am. the LORD roars 'from Zion' and utters
his voice 'from Jerusalem'. Jeremiah could not express the divine
intervention thus, for the LORD is to destroy Zion (**his fold**) and declare
his judgement over Jerusalem, as over all the nations of the earth. The
change is therefore necessary and deliberate. The word **roar** is used most
naturally of the roaring of a lion as in Jg. 14.5; Am. 3.4, 8; Ps. 104.21;
and often figuratively of invaders, as in Isa. 5.29. Here it may be that
the picture is of the thunder, itself a figure of the divine judge pronouncing
his terrible judgment from one end of the world to the other in the
vicissitudes of history. 'His holy habitation. . .on high' is no doubt
heaven. There is nothing in the theology of Jeremiah to support the idea
that the reference is to Sinai; much to point to the principle of the
unconditional divine sovereignty, cf. Dt. 26.15.

   and shout, like those who tread the grapes: a comparison of this passage
with Jer. 48.33; 51.14 and Isa. 16.9, 10 suggests that **shout** (*hêdād*) is a cry
of joy and triumph specially associated with trading grapes, and not simply
a shout of any kind. The similarity of the word with the name of the
Canaanite storm-god Hadad prompts the obvious solution that the cry is
derived from the old Canaanite religious customs which survived, despite
the opposition of the prophets. There is therefore a characteristic irony in
the idea that the *hêdād*-cry should register, not the joy of revellers but the
lion-like roar of historical judgment. Again the half-echo of the storm-god
subtly builds up the picture of the divine thunder to which the judgment
is likened. It is this image which lends individuality to a poem otherwise
composed of well-worn motifs. There is no doubt meant to be an analogy
between the treading of grapes and the flowing of blood, cf. Isa. 63.1.

   31. The LORD has an indictment against the nations: Heb. *rîb*,
cf. Hos. 4.1, and of his indictment against his own people, Hos. 12.3;
Mic. 6.2; Isa. 3.13.

   all flesh: i.e. all mankind, as in Isa. 66.13; Gen. 6.12. The expression
can also suggest the inherent weakness of men over against the power
(spirit) of God, as in Isa. 31.3. Cf. 12.12.

   The second poem also is introduced in vv. 32–33 with echoes of
Jeremiah's teaching recorded elsewhere. The heart of the poem is a call
to the shepherds, described uniquely as 'lords of the flock', to wail (vv.
34–35), leading into an anticipation of their cry when their peaceful folds
are devastated (vv. 36–38).

   32. Behold, evil is going forth: a characteristic affirmation in Jer.,
but most often referring to the foe from the north coming against Judah,

cf. 1.14; 2.3; 4.6; 6.1, 7, 19; 11.11; 18.11; 19.3, 15. The significant amplification here is that it will go **from nation to nation**, as though by a self-destructive intoxication, cf. the cup of wrath.
    a great tempest is stirring from the farthest parts of the earth: cf. 6.22 where it is a great nation that is stirring. The change is appropriate to the storm imagery which better describes the universal power of the LORD against the whole world.
    33. This verse is usually treated as a prose comment derived, pastiche fashion, from other parts of the book. But it is by no means certain that vv. 30–38 existed in any other form but this. The build-up is clear. And the word-play of 'those slain' (*ḥalᵉlê*) and 'wail' (hêlîlû) suggests that v. 33 is no subsequent insertion. The **slain:** whereas in 14.18, they will be in 'the field', here they shall extend from one end of the earth to the other, (cf. 12.12).
    They shall not be lamented, or gathered, or buried; they shall be dung on the surface of the ground; so in 8.2b of the kings of Judah, and in 16.4 of the children born in 'this place'. Here the phrase is used of the worldwide carnage of the nations.
    Thus phrases used elsewhere more narrowly are given a wider application.
    34. Wail, you shepherds, and cry; Jeremiah often referred to kings or rulers as 'shepherds'. Cf. 2.8; 6.3; 10.21; 12.10 and particularly see on 23.1-8.
    you lords of the flock: probably suggests majesty, dignity, nobility and is used of the LORD himself in Pss. 76.5; 93.4. It is used here to depict the highest royal dignity which is brought low, and the effect is heightened by threefold repetition. Are these shepherds the leaders of the nations or of Judah? If they are Judaean, then vv. 34–38 have to be interpreted independently and out of context. It has to be admitted that this is possible. But the editor had no doubt that this was to conclude a section of judgement on the nations and the shepherds are the kings of the nations. On the other hand v. 30 shows that Jerusalem -Judah was not excluded from this universal judgment.
    for the days of your slaughter have come: again the ironic reversal of judgment, for Jeremiah himself had been like a gentle lamb, led to the slaughter (11.19).
    and you shall fall like choice rams Heb. has a 'fine instrument'. The emendation, which is as appropriate to the context as the Heb. is not, is supported by LXX.
    35. nor escape for the lords of the flock: the Heb. *pᵉlêṭāh* is correctly translated 'escape', but elsewhere, with but one exception, it probably

has the sense of an escaped remnant. The thought may well be that in this judgment, there will be no remnant.

36. Hark, the cry of the shepherds: the poem passes from prediction to anticipation in words close to Zech. 11.3, which seems to be verbally dependent upon the Jeremiah tradition.

for the LORD is despoiling their pasture: the Heb. is *šōdēd* (destroying). The word gains significance from its special use by Jeremiah, referring to the instrument of judgment as 'the destroyer' (6.26) or 'the destroyer at noonday' (15.8). At the same time the word is specially frequent in the oracles against the nations, precisely in the sense here conveyed, in 47.4 of the destroyer of the Philistines, in 48.8 of the cities of Moab, in 48.18 of Moab, in 48.32 upon the vintage of Moab (a passage related to 25.30, q.v.), in 49.28 of the people of Qedem, in 51.48, 55.56 of Babylon (from the north). In a way perhaps impossible to capture in English translation, the word has been appropriated to describe the destroyer of the nations.

38. Like a lion: cf. the roaring of v. 30 and 4.7.

because of the sword of the oppressor: Heb. has 'because of the anger', but the emendation implied by *RSV* is almost certainly correct. It is supported by a number of MSS, by LXX, Old Latin, and Targ., and the phrase, to be translated as 'Because of the cruel sword', occurs in 46.16 and 50.16. (So most modern versions, but not *GNB*).

II PROPHETIC NARRATIVES AND SERMONS MAINLY OF THE TIME OF ZEDEKIAH INCLUDING THE ORACLES OF HOPE 26.1–35.19 (36.32)

This next block of oracles contains varied material. Some interpreters would regard chapters 26–44 (45) as a homogeneous collection. But there are good grounds for considering chapters 37–44 (45) as separate and independent, and delimiting the new section to chapters 26–35 (36). The two blocks are built up in quite different ways. Chapters 37–44 (45), as will be demonstrated in the appropriate place, tell the story of the fall of Jerusalem and of Jeremiah's experience during the event. It is a work of sustained narrative skill, designed to show the consequences of the calling of a prophet in that situation. The chapters are arranged on strict chronological lines and are similar to the prophetic narrative in Isa. 36–39 (2 Kg. 18–20). They are marked by a diminution of the number of phrases characteristic of the Jeremiah prose tradition, and there are sections (39.1–10; 40.7–41.15) in which the prophet does not figure at all.

In contrast, chapters 26–35 (36) is an example, worked out in detail below, of how thematic considerations determine the character of a traditional complex. Like previous collections it contains both poetry and prose, it lacks both chronological and thematic cohesion when considered as a whole, and yet it is possible to see how it has been built up step by step. The narrative element within it, both the story of Hananiah and of the symbolic purchase of the field, is more precisely geared to a didactic purpose, and chapters 26, 34 and 35 are more closely related to the prose discourses scattered through chapters 7–25.

All these considerations point towards the conclusion that when chapters 1–25 had reached substantially their present form, the next complex of traditions to be deposited in the collection was chapters 26–35 (36). Chapter 36 remains an enigma. From some points of view it might be regarded as a prelude to chapters 37–45. From others (which seem more cogent) it appears to be the concluding narrative of chapters 1–35 at that stage in the history of the redaction of the book, and it will be so interpreted here.

We turn now to examine in more detail the structure of chapters 26–35 (36.) It contains two easily identifiable sections. The first, chapters 27–29, is mainly concerned with Jeremiah's struggle with false prophets of hope and particularly his encounter with Hananiah, but also includes in 29.15–32 his dealings with false prophets in exile. The uniting theme is false prophecy, and there are precise indications that this formed a separate collection, noted on pp. 366ff. The second, chapters 30–31, is a collection of mainly poetical oracles on the future and has been called the 'book of consolation'. It is this second section, together with 27.22; 29.10–14; and chapters 32 and 33, which has led a number of interpreters to call the whole block 'oracles of salvation'. But this is an unsuitable description of the material as a whole, since it is inappropriate to chapters 27–29, 34 and 35. Either of these sections or both could have existed as independent tradition units before they were incorporated in the present block, but it is perhaps easier to imagine an earlier history of transmission for chapters 30–31 than for 27–29.

The placing of chapter 26 as a preface to chapters 27–29 suggests that the initial motive for setting down this tradition was to present the most vivid example of Jeremiah's encounter with false prophecy (Hananiah) in the context of the imminent fall of Jerusalem. It is true that a pattern can be discerned in both chapter 26 and 29, which focuses (a) on the divine word to Israel through the prophets, (b) Israel's rejection of that word, and (c) the consequential judgment. But this is so general and common a pattern (cf 25.1–11) that it gives no clue to the distinctiveness of the theme of these chapters. The further deduction that this is Deuteronomic preaching does not follow from the evidence. It is much more likely that Baruch or another scribe of the later circle of the Jeremiah tradition recognised in the dispute with Hananiah a significant drama which needed to be told and retold. Once a body of Jeremiah material was established, this material offered an irresistible claim to be added. Then other material was attracted to it, as by a magnet.

The second version of Jeremiah's preaching in the Temple in Chapter 26 (cf chapter 7.1–15), though out of place chronologically, provided a powerful introduction to the theme. For here above all was the occasion when Jeremiah escaped by a hair's breadth the appropriate capital punishment of a false prophet. Suitably the accent here is not on the content of the sermon, as in chapter 7, but on the bitterly hostile reaction of priests and prophets. Appeal is made by the *śārîm* to the example of Micah, who also prophesied the destruction of Jerusalem. But it is also narrated how Uriah, whose message was in tune with that of Jeremiah, was extradited from Egypt and put to death. Only the friendly protection of Ahikam guarded Jeremiah from a similar fate. It is difficult to imagine a more dramatically suitable lead into the story of Hananiah. The episode of the Temple sermon is here told from the point of view of the question of false prophecy. The accent is on the theme rather than on chronological sequence.

It is the vindication of Jeremiah as a true prophet in chapters 26–28 which provides the grounds for trusting him when he takes new and unprecedented steps in Chapter 29. This chapter opens with the account of the letter which Jeremiah wrote to the exiles in Babylon (vv. 1–14). This leads on to the problem of the false prophets in Babylon who gave contrary advice (vv. 15–25), and to the hostile action of Shelemiah (vv. 24–32). This continued preoccupation with false prophecy is the obvious link binding chapter 29 to chapters 27 and 28. On the other hand, Jeremiah's letter raises the issue of the future. In one sense Jeremiah is continuing his message of judgment over against those who say the exile will be short and the return to Judah prompt; Jeremiah states that the exile will exceed the lifetime of any one now living. (See on 25.11–12.) In another sense Jeremiah is implying a delayed salvation. Although the exile will be substantial, it will also be temporary. Though beyond the lifetime of the present exiles, there will be an end to the Babylonian subjugation.

If then the note of hope in 27.22 is a subsequent glossing of the text, it is but a drawing out the implication of Jeremiah's teaching. 29.10–14 also draws out the implications of hope and salvation, cf. also 29.32. It is this emphatic seizing upon the positive, hopeful implications of Jeremiah's message to the exiles (whether by Jeremiah himself or another) which now provides the most suitable launching-pad for the collection of oracles of salvation (chapters 30–31, the 'book of consolation'). Along with this goes the account of Jeremiah's purchase of family property, (chapter 32) a prophetic sign of salvation, and chapter 33 is a supplementary collection of oracles of salvation. Chapters 34 and 35 form an appendix containing a sermon on the breach of the law concerning the septennial release of slaves, and a pointer to the exemplary obedience of the Rechabites. The explicitly didactic character of both chapters marks them off from the narrative in the next block, where the didactic purpose is implicit.

Chapter 36 may be taken as the finale of the collection of the prophecies of Jeremiah at this stage in their development, the emphasis now being not on the chronology (the fourth year of Jehoiakim) but on the fact that the prophecies of the true prophet Jeremiah had survived as by fire, and that they contained not only the original scroll but many similar words that had been added to them. Chapter 36 thus performed a similar function to that which chapter 25 performed at a slightly earlier stage in the history of the transmission of these oracles, and such as chapter 45 was to perform a little later still. In this way the complex as a whole may be understood as another example of the redaction of prophetic traditions, and chapter 45 as an index to the growth of these traditions, upon the familiar principle of nucleus and deposit. It may be taken as confirmation of this hypothesis of the redaction process, that these chapters present a picture of the cumulative building up of the Jeremiah traditions, rather than the complicated knitting together of originally independent poetic, didactic and narrative traditions.

A   THE EXPOSURE OF FALSE PROPHECIES OF HOPE
26.1–29.32

RESPONSES TO JEREMIAH'S TEMPLE SPEECH **26.1–24 (LXX 33)**

This chapter demands to be interpreted independently of those that follow. Although it deals with the same theme as chapters 27–29, i.e. the problem of true and false prophecy, it is clearly divided from those chapters by its date–'the beginning of the reign of Jehoiakim'. Chapters 27–29, in

contrast, are headed 'the beginning of the reign of Zedekiah'. There is
also a cohesion in this chapter which is absent from the parallel chapter
7. Baruch's version of the Temple sermon in chapter 7 is confined to
vv. 1-15. The rest of that chapter is a series of three supplementary
accounts of related teaching.

Chapter 26, on the other hand, is less concerned with the content of
Jeremiah's sermon than with the way it divided his audience. It raised
in an exemplary way the question of the authenticity of Jeremiah's
prophecy. The priests, prophets and people judged that he was a false
prophet to be justly put to death according to Deuteronomic law. Only
a hint of the content of the speech is necessary for the narrative, in
particular, Jeremiah's abrasive and unforgettable allusion to the
destruction of Shiloh. The 'princes' or ministers, on the other hand, who
appeared to have sat as judges (v. 10) in the case which was formally
brought before them, delivered an unambiguous verdict that Jeremiah
had done nothing worthy of death. In fact, they pronounced Jeremiah
a true prophet in the words: 'he has spoken to us in the name of the LORD
our God' (v. 16). This verdict was supported by certain elders who found
in an oracle of Micah a precedent for an authentic prediction of the
destruction of Zion. Plainly there was a Gamaliel among them.

So far the narrative moves smoothly and unbrokenly. Verses 20-25
are also much to the point, illustrating how Jehoiakim carried to its
ultimate conclusion his hostility to the otherwise unknown Uriah. Uriah
uttered oracles similar to those of Jeremiah, but was extradited from Egypt
that he might be put to death. It is probable however that these verses
had an independent existence before they were quoted here, appropriate
as they are. For in this case 'all the princes' take the initiative against
Uriah, whereas in the previous verses the ministers supported Jeremiah
against the priests and prophets. Chapter 36 continues this favourable
view of the śārîm, who tended to be ready to listen to Jeremiah during
the reign of Jehoiakim. On the other hand, it is altogether probable that
37.15; 38.4, 25, 27 correctly record the enraged hostility of the 'princes'
when they had reason to suppose that Jeremiah was deserting to the
Babylonians during the siege of 586. No doubt it was in the light of this
change of sentiment that the account in vv. 20-23 was written. Perhaps
Uriah was unfortunate to lack a friend and champion among the 'princes',
who could sway the cabinet. Ahikam (v. 24) fulfilled this role for Jeremiah.
Was he the wise man of this crisis? It may also be significant that in vv.
20-23 the variations in LXX are proportionately more numerous than
in the rest of the chapter.

The style of the narrative is that of the Jeremiah prose tradition. In particular, the expressions: 'everyone turn from his evil way' (v. 3); 'because of their evil doings' (v. 3); 'my servants the prophets whom I send to your urgently' (v. 5); 'a curse for all the nations of the earth' (v. 6); 'the priests and the prophets and all the people' (v. 7); 'amend your ways and your doings' (v. 13, cf. 7.3); 'in truth' (v. 15); are commonplaces of this tradition.

Not only does this chapter betray the familiar signs of the prose tradition, but it also has the repeatedly noticed event character. The combination is best explained as the narration, in the well-worn phrases of the tradition, of an event remembered and handed down. Where in the narrative Jeremiah speaks, we do not therefore expect to hear his very words. But we do expect that the event is rooted in history and that this is a stereotyped version of Jeremiah's intervention. We accept the narrative as part of the Jeremiah tradition which has its characteristic mode of speech, but at the same time holds the memory of the activity of the prophet. We do not dissolve the event itself into pure invention.

In this respect we come into conflict with the interpretation of Carroll, who thinks the narrative is a 'a story constructed to make certain points and not an account of a historical incident in the life of Jeremiah'. The alternative is not between unhistorical didactic story and plain history, but between plain history and a version of the event told in conventional language to make certain points. Carroll critically analyses features of the story to show up contradictions in relation to Jehoiakim, the parties to the dispute and Uriah–concluding that the motif of the persecuted prophet is a dogma of a later time. This is to attribute to other scholars a literal approach to the narrative they do not hold. But Carroll is nothing if not consistent and extends this method of interpretation to the whole book and to Jeremiah himself. He must not complain if some of us find this a reduction to absurdity, incapable of supplying any reasonable explanation of the phenomenon of the Jeremiah tradition.

1. In the beginning of the reign of Jehoiakim: if the Heb. expression *rēšît mamlᵉkût* is equivalent to the Babylonian *res sarruti*, then it refers to the period between the death of his brother Jehoahaz in 609 B.C. and his own enthronement on the ensuing New Year's festival, i.e. Tishri (Oct) 608B.C.

2. Stand in the court of the LORD's house: i.e., at the gate between the inner and outer court, giving Jeremiah the maximum opportunity to be heard by the worshippers. Cf. 19.14.

3–6. The narrator sketches the substance of Jeremiah's sermon in stereotyped commonplaces until v. 6 and the reference to Shiloh, which focuses attention on the essential point of the sermon. It was this shift which seemed to contradict the comfortable Zion-theology and stirred up the passionate reaction of Jeremiah's opponents. The reference to **my law** in v. 4, as a criterion of judgment, is characteristic of the prose tradition, cf. 9.12; 16.11; 31.33; 32.23; 44.10, 23; but it recurs also in the poetry (6.19), and there is no reason to suppose that this is alien to the thought of Jeremiah. His constant stress on obedience implies the observance of the divine will. The figure of 'walking' in the law here and 9.12; 32.23; 44.10, 23 relates this obedience to the more comprehensive idea of a way of life, which is perhaps the central image of biblical ethics. There is little reason to suppose that Jeremiah refers precisely either to Deut. or to the law of Sinai. Cf. Isa 1.10.

6. Shiloh: see on 7.12-14. This of course links the two chapters together.

this city a curse: a threat of Deuteronomic retribution, not an act of cursing.

7. The priests and the prophets and all the people: this is the combination which seems to have generated the most hatred of Jeremiah and the greatest threat to his person and mission. From 5.30-31 we may infer that the prophets (LXX Pseudoprophetai) were the principal influence, understandably, since Jeremiah directly branded them as false prophets and their utterances as lies. The priests took the initiative for action and the people found the inquisition much to their liking.

8. You shall die: cf. 11.18–12.6. Their vendetta against Jeremiah had a legal justification which no doubt gave them a warm feeling of self-righteousness. Once they had persuaded themselves that Jeremiah was a false prophet, they were required by the Deutromonic law (Dt. 13) to put him to death. We do not know how far the provisions of this law were normally carried out. Deut. 13.9 suggests that the death penalty could be administered in an *ad hoc* manner. Probably, however, there were always precise legal conventions as to the way a verdict might be reached and the penalty administered. The evidence of Jer. 26 is that such a case had to be brought before what might be called the 'high court', i.e. the *śārîm* sitting in the gate. The phrase 'you shall die', if endorsed by the *śārîm* would have led to the official 'he shall die', as in Exod. 21–23.

9. And all the people gathered about Jeremiah: the Heb. verb *qhl*, while often referring to a gathering for religious purposes, may, according to context, take on hostile overtones. The hostile overtones are certainly present here. The people were threatening and ready to take the execution of Jeremiah into their own hands.

10. It is vain to ask whether the 'princes' were asked to set up judicial proceedings or whether they acted on their own volition. This kind of narrative is not concerned with veridical details. Nothing is known of **the New Gate.** But it is reasonably certain that to say **they took their seat in the entry** is to indicate that this was the hearing of a case in the accustomed and recognised manner. Jeremiah was accused and tried.

11. The presupposition of the case against him was not simply that he had prophesied against the city. There was no law against that. The presupposition was that to prophesy against the city in itself branded him as a false prophet. False prophecy was the capital offence. **This man deserves the sentence of death:** *mišpaṭ māweṯ* also probably a technical term of the judicial process. Cf. v. 16.

12–15. Jeremiah's defence is given in commonplaces of the prose tradition. The allusion to **innocent blood** in v. 15 is an illustration of what prophets meant when they accused their contemporaries that 'your hands are full of blood' (Isa. 1.15; 59.3; Jer. 2.34; 7.6; 19.4; 22.3, 17). It seems that to lose one's life as a result of the miscarriage of justice was one of the principal hazards of Israelite life.

16. Then the princes and all the people: we may take it that the verdict was that of the *śārîm*, and that the people played a supporting role. The tendency of the narrator is to add 'and all the people' somewhat indiscriminately cf. vv. 7,9. The clear verdict of acquittal **(This mean does not deserve the sentence of death,** cf. v. 11) is based on the judgment that Jeremiah **has spoken to us in the name of the LORD our God.** This is greatly to the credit of the authorities and has to be set against the impression given elsewhere of universal opposition. No doubt some of the support he received during the reign of Jehoiakim dissolved in the circumstances of extreme national peril encountered in the reign of Zedekiah. But the idea that no one but Baruch followed Jeremiah is not borne out by the facts.

17. certain of the elders: these were men with some kind of official position as leaders in the community. In Deut. they appear to have judicial functions. It is difficult to be more specific, except perhaps to notice that elders are present in all periods of Israel's history of which we have evidence, and act on behalf of the people in dealings with, for example, Moses or the contemporary king. There is a continuity in their role as leading inhabitants or representatives of a community (city or larger unit). This organisation persists even into exile, so that Jeremiah himself is understood to have sent his letter (29.1) 'to the elders of the exiles'. This means that Jeremiah's prophetic commission was recognised both by some of the *śārîm*, who held national office, and by elders who were representatives of the community. To this extent the impression Jeremiah gives elsewhere of total isolation has to be modified.

assembled people: Heb. *qahal*, i.e. the people of Israel as a worshipping 'congregation'. (LXX synagogue).

18. Micah of Moresheth: i.e. the Micah who, a hundred years earlier, had come from a village twenty five miles south-west of Jerusalem, and whose prophecy of the destruction of Jerusalem had lingered uncomfortably in both the prophetic and the popular memory. The quotation from Mic. 3.12, which is the only acknowledged quotation of a prophet in another prophetic book, is exact. Although this precision could be the result of subsequent correction, there is a presumption that the elders remembered correctly one of the most striking passages in that part of the book of Micah which is almost universally attributable to Micah himself. The prophecy measured up to Jeremiah's own test of validity, cf. 28.8–9. Micah's utterance was remarkable. In his own day it was all but fulfilled: in Jeremiah's day it was fulfilled tragically and completely. We have no knowledge of the precise timing of the prophecy. In a critical situation at the end of the eight century, (probably as much as twenty years later), Isaiah had confidently predicted that Jerusalem would not be taken by the Assyrians, and he proved right. The correctness of Isaiah's assessment and the influence of the Zion theology makes Micah's bold prediction of doom the more extraordinary.

19. The implication is that it was Hezekiah's response of faith, prayer and obedience which prevented the direst calamity falling upon Jerusalem in his own day. The righteousness of God was thus vindicated. For this reason the difference between the prophecies of Micah and Isaiah was not henceforth a problem, even on the basis of the old doctrine of retribution. Cf. Isa. 38.1–6.

But we are about to bring great evil upon ourselves: the observation that it is in the character of divine judgment for people to bring calamity upon themselves is a notable prophetic intuition, cf. 2.19; 5.25; 6.19; 7.19. There is something in the constitution of the universe which makes them draw upon their own heads the nemesis they dread. It seems that people weave such a net around themselves that they can only be freed by some destroying cataclysm which drives them back to simplicity and a new beginning. Hezekiah is implicity contrasted with Jehoiakim.

20–23. For the view that the section concerning Uriah was in some way independent of the rest of the chapter, see above. **20. Uriah, the son of Shemaiah from Kiriath-jearim:** nothing is otherwise nown of this Uriah. The attempt to identify him with 'the prophet' of the Lachish Ostraca is based on unsupported guesswork and involves such chronological difficulties that the theory may be pronounced, with D. Winton Thomas, as untenable. This is direct evidence of the activity of another prophet of the LORD, whose words were recognised to be **like those of Jeremiah.** Jeremiah was not entirely alone in his struggle with false prophets. The words **against the city,** absent in LXX, link the passage with the rest of the chapter, and particularly with the prophecy of Micah. They are no doubt a deliberate addition.

21. While the law of Dt. 13 required that a false prophet should be put to death, a true prophet reflected the holiness of the God in whose name he spoke, and was treated with the utmost reverence. There was therefore normally a profound reluctance to proceed against a prophet, reflected in the rareness of such an event. The only similar notice of the killing of a prophet is in 2 Chr. 24.10–22 which records the stoning of Zechariah, the son of Jehoida the priest, cf. Lk. 11.51; Mt. 23.35. Later tradition permitted accounts of prophetic martyrdoms to proliferate.

LXX omits 'with all his warriors' and 'he was afraid'. Plainly there were easy movements to and from Egypt, to which Judah was at this time vassal. But as this provided a natural refuge for Uriah, so it enabled Jehoiakim to have him extradited. Carroll argues that if Uriah really was executed, then Jeremiah himself would not have survived!

22. certain men: Heb. has 'men to Egypt', but this is not straight-forward and in any case is superfluous.

Elnathan the son of Achbor: occurs in 36.12, 25 as one of the *śārîm* who urged Jehoiakim not to burn the scroll. He is, therefore, a particular instance of the alienation of the *śārîm* from Jeremiah noticed above and implicit in the difference observed between vv. 1–19 and 20–23.

23. the burial place of the common people: cf. 2 Kg. 23.6. LXX has 'grave of his people'. suggesting the family grave, but this is the opposite of the true sense, as indicated by the verb.

24. Ahikam the son of Shaphan: according to 2 Kg. 22.12, 14 one of the leading men, close to Josiah, at the time of the discovery of the Deuteronomic scroll in the Temple, and the father of Gedaliah (2 Kg. 25.22). Clearly a very influential figure who championed Jeremiah when his colleagues turned against the prophet. The simple, unelaborated statement, provides an effective climax to the chapter. See also on 29.3.

Note on chapters 27–29 (LXX 34–36)

There are indications that these chapters once formed a separate collection of oracles. Their common theme is the falsehood of false prophecy illustrated by (a) Jeremiah's consistent advice to submit to Babylon, coupled with the warning not to trust the prophets (chapter 27), (b) his encounter with Hananiah (chapter 28) and (c) his conflict with prophets in exile (chapter 29). There are also some of those small linguistic variations which are the most convincing signs of a separate literary environment.

(a) The name of the Babylonian king is spelt 'Nebuchadnezzar' (27.6, 8, 20; 28.3, 11; 14; 29.1, 3) rather than 'Nebuchadrezzar' (with the exception of 29.21, where in any case it is absent in the LXX).

(b) In these chapters alone the name Jeremiah occurs in its shorter form (*yirmᵉyāh* rather than *yirmᵉyāhû*) (27.1; 28.5, 6, 10,11, 12, 15).

(c) In chapter 28 Jeremiah is referred to as 'Jeremiah the prophet' (vv. 5, 6, 11, 15) and his opponent as 'Hananiah the prophet' (vv. 1, 5, 10, 12, 17). Cf. also 29.1.29. This feature is however not unique to these two chapters, and does not of course occur in chapter 27, where Jeremiah speaks in the first person.

The natural deduction from the last observation would be that chapter 27 has some independence of chapters 28 and 29. At the same time it is securely linked to them by the theme of the yoke. Without chapter 27, chapter 28 would lack its essential presupposition and clue. In particular 28.10 presupposes 27.2. In chapters 27 and 28 a story unfolds from its beginning in the divine word that came to Jeremiah, instructing him to perform a prophetic sign, to its conclusion in the death of Hananiah. It may well be significant that the prophetic signs of Jeremiah are for the most part in the first person (cf. 13.1–11; 18.1–11; 19.1–13; 20.1–6 and note 1.4–19). We have already felt the need to hazard the guess that a special intimate of Jeremiah assumed the right to transmit his oracles in the first person. If this is so, then chapter 27 forms the nucleus and chapter 28 would be the completion of this tradition by a redactor who completes the story of chapter 27 and in chapter 29 adds complementary material. The differences are just sufficient to demand some such variety of origin; but the homogeneity of theme equally points to a single redactor who has stamped the whole with the singleness of his own purpose.

The proses is everywhere that of the Jeremiah prose tradition.

ORACLES TO NEIGHBOURING NATIONS, TO
ZEDEKIAH AND TO PRIESTS AND PEOPLE TO
ACCEPT THE YOKE OF BABYLON, WITH
WARNINGS AGAINST FALSE PROPHETS
27.1–22 (LXX 34.1–22)

We have seen reason to suppose that this chapter is basic to the
construction of chapters 27–29. Similar considerations suggest that, within
chapter 27, the fundamental unit upon which the rest is built is the
prophetic sign narrated in vv. 2–11. This contains the distinctively new
element in the chapter, the sign of the yoke. This sign, as it is narrated
with its introduction in the first person ('Thus the LORD said to me'),
is comparable to the first person sign-narratives in 13.1–11; 18.1–11;
19.1–13; 20.1–6, but its content is unique. In contrast, the oracle to
Zedekiah in vv. 12–15 is repetitive and stereotyped.

The oracle to priests and people in vv. 16–22 introduces the theme
of the return of the sacred vessels from Babylon. But important as this
theme is, it comes as an anti-climax to the sign of vv. 2–11, which is
one of the most courageous and outrageous acts of Jeremiah's ministry.
The sign of the yoke goes far beyond even the Temple sermon of chapter
26, foretelling the destruction of Jerusalem. It is consonant with the advice
he gave to king and people to fall away to the Babylonian army; it is
'weakening of the hands of the soldiers' (38.4). If this element of lese-
majesty had not existed in the teaching of Jeremiah, what later editor
would have attributed it to him? On the other hand the sacred vessels
are a simple symbol of the security of the priestly people and so, as P.R.
Ackroyd has shown, furnish a continuity theme. Verses 16–22 re-state,
in this form, that with the judgment, the centre of Judah's life will shift
to Babylon and its return must wait for the unknown future.

For reasons given below we cannot be sure of the provenance of this
theme. Altogether, it seems overwhelmingly probable that vv. 2–11 are
the basis of this chapter and that the rest is an editorial development of
it. What links the three sections is the urgent plea not to listen to the
false prophets. 'Do not listen to (the words of) your prophets (vv. 9, 14,
16) . . . for it is a lie which they are prophesying you' (vv. 10, 14, 16),
cf. 5.31; 14.14; 20.6; 23.25, 26; 29.9, 21. This thrice repeated
combination, linking three sections of the chapter together and indicating
probably the theme which the editor of chapters 26–29 has in mind, is
in this form, unique to the book of Jeremiah. (See Helga Weippert, op.cit.
pp. 110–121.)

As to the style of vv. 1–11, there is sufficient indication of the familiar prose tradition; that is to say, there are Deuteronomic echoes but rarely unambiguously Deuteronomic writing. There are elements not found in the Deuteronomic literature, and there are features otherwise only found in the Jeremiah prose tradition.

In v. 5 the phrase 'by my great power and my outstretched arm' is found in the Deuteronomic writings, and the latter half of it is a commonplace to describe the redemptive acts of Yahweh and particularly the Exodus (as in Jer. 32.21). But only here and in Jer. 32.17 is the phrase used of creation. 'I have made the earth . . . ' (cf. Gen 31.1; Neh. 9.6; Job 9.9; Prov. 8.26; 2 Chr. 2.11; Pss. 95.5; 146.6; etc) is not a phrase or a significant theological emphasis of the Deuteronomic writings. On the other hand 'to whomsoever it seems right to me' (of God) is a Deuteronomic commonplace.

In v. 6 'I have given all these lands into the hands of . . . ' is predominantly Deuteronomic. The infinitive 'to serve him' is otherwise used of the service or worship of God (Zeph. 3.9) but usually of false gods and although recurring in Dt. 28.14 and Jg. 2.19, is more characteristic of the Jeremiah prose tradition (11.10; 13.10; 25.6; 35.15).

In v. 8, 'I will punish (visit)' is characteristic of both the verse and the prose of Jeremiah (3.16; 5.9, 29; 6.15; 9.8, 24; 11.22; 13.21; 14.10; 15.3; 21.14; 23.2; 23.34; 25.12; 27.22; 29.10, 32; 32.5; 36.31; 44.13, 29; 46.25; 49.8; 49.19; 50.18, 31, 44; 51.27, 44, 47, 52). Moreover 'with the sword, with famine and with pestilence' is, as we have repeatedly noticed, a characteristic phrase of the Jeremiah prose tradition (see on 14.12, 13 and the introduction to Chapter 21), but not without appearance in the poetic sections.

The section on false prophets (vv. 9–11) has marked verbal and substantial connections with 14.11–16. We noted there the probability that Jeremiah encountered the problem of false prophecy early in his ministry, but that the account of his conflict was given the somewhat conventional style of the prose tradition. Exactly the same style occurs here. Notice particularly the characteristic 'it is a lie' (šeqer) in v. 10 14.11–16 also begins 'The LORD said to me', and the conclusions reached as to the authorship of that passage apply here also. The evidence suggests the authorship of a writer or teacher within the Jeremiah tradition and not simply a 'Deuteronomist'. To speak of such authorship is not to imply a biographical intention. These scribes were intent to convey the teaching of Jeremiah as much as any putative Deuteronomic preacher.

Verses 12–15 are phrased in exactly the same terms as 1–11 without

any significant variation. It looks as if the editor derived his phraseology
from the earlier account so as to emphasise that Jeremiah delivered the
same message to Zedekiah as to the five kings.

A judgment on the style of vv. 16–22 is complicated by the textual
problem (see below). If it is to be assumed that the LXX represents an
earlier stage of the text than MT, then it is to be observed that the shorter
text maintains contact with vv. 1–11. Indeed **do not listen to the words
of your prophets who are prophesying to you** (v. 16) echoes vv. 9, 14.;
for it is a lie they are prophesying to you (v. 17) echoes vv. 10, 14.

From the point of view of the content, the emphasis on the intercessory
function of prophecy is an emphasis found elsewhere both in the poetry
(4.10; 18.20) and in the prose tradition (7.16; 11.14; 14.11; 15.1;
37.1–10). On the other hand the longer text also maintains some contact
with vv. 1–11, particularly **serve the king of Babylon** echoes vv. 8, 11,
12, 14. Stylistically, therefore, vv. 16–22 exhibit no independent features
and this is consistent with the view that the chapter is built up on the
basis of vv. 1–11 and that the last section represents the last stage in the
process of redaction.

1. The superscription, being absent in LXX, may be supposed to be
an editorial addition, derived perhaps from 26.1. And that being so, the
date of these events would be as stated in 28.1, i.e. the fourth year of
Zedekiah 594–593B.C., 'in that same year'.

THE SIGN OF THE YOKE 27.2–11

If this is the basic tradition-unit of the chapter, comparable with the
narratives of other prophetic signs, it is reasonable to assume that we
are in touch with a sign performed by Jeremiah himself and not the
invention of a later mind. The temptation of the reader is then to ask
more questions than the text will confidently answer. Does the presence
in Jerusalem of the ambassadors of the five neighbouring states (v. 3)
indicate that they had come on a special mission to plot rebellion against
Nebuchadnezzar, or did they just happen to be there? The latter, in days
when there were no permanent embassies, is not likely.

It is therefore a fair guess that the ambassadors of Edom, Moab,
Ammon and the Phoenician cities had come to Jerusalem because it was
the convenient and obvious centre for planning concerted resistance to
Nebuchadnezzar. The Philistine cities were at this time vassals of Egypt.
And since Egypt was preoccupied with African problems, she may not
have wished to get involved with Assyria. This would explain the absence
of her ambassadors on this occasion. Nothing is known of the insurrection

except what can be precariously deduced from this passage, and nothing of its terms. No doubt the primary question to be faced was whether the time had come to declare independence of Babylon or not. This would make Jeremiah's message, carried back by the ambassadors to each of the kings, timely and apt.

It is however difficult to decide from the text exactly what Jeremiah did. That he wore a yoke, tied with thongs about his neck, is confirmed by 28.10. MT then says that he was ordered to send 'them' to the five kings **by the hand of the envoys.** RSV 'send word' is a conjecture, as is also *NEB* and *REB* 'give them the following message', encouraged by LXX's indecisive 'send' (without object). It may be that MT is to be taken seriously and means that Jeremiah sent representations of some sort (drawings or models). This would be entirely in keeping with the expedients which prophets adopted and the power with which signs were invested. However this may be, it was not simply a verbal message which Jeremiah was concerned to communicate, but a picture either mental or by representation of the yoke, as on some captive ox, declaring and anticipating the submission of the nations to the yoke of Babylon.

The message outlined in vv. 5–6 is a version, in the prose tradition, of what Jeremiah's followers understood his meaning to be. There is no reason to suppose that they seriously distorted it. It is close to the tradition of prophecy. Grounded in an uncompromising creation-faith, it sees Nebuchadnezzar as the Lord God's servant to carry out his will in judgment, just as Isaiah had seen the Assyrians as rod of the Lord's anger (Isa. 10.5). The dark prophecy of v. 7, predicting an ultimate nemesis for Babylon, is absent in the LXX, and, as commentators have freely pointed out, weakens the force of Jeremiah's message. It is unlikely that this was part of the message to the kings. On the other hand it is probable that Jeremiah envisaged an end to the hegemony of Babylon (see on 25.11 and cf. 29.10). Whoever added v. 7 was therefore completing a sequence of thought which was true to the total perspective of Jeremiah's prophecy, in accordance with the prophetic principle that he who is the instrument of judgment must himself face judgment.

9. your prophets, your diviners, your dreamers, your soothsayers or your sorcerers: the nearest comparable list is to be found in Dt. 18.10–11 which, however, is more comprehensive and associates these methods of divination with cultic enormities like passing children though the fire and necromancy. There they are denounced as Canaanite abominations. For discussion of the techniques implied in these terms, see S. R. Driver *Deuteronomy*, ICC (3rd ed. 1902). Here only the techniques

which may be regarded as those of divinatory prophecy are cited, though
it is clear that in Dt. also (18.15 ff.) the wider list of techniques is regarded
as in conflict with true prophecy. On dreams see notes of Jer. 23.25–32.
10. The threat of exile was an obvious and integral part of the judgment
Jeremiah predicted, and the prose tradition correctly indicates the
message.
11. Again this verse but draws out the full implication of the sign of
the yoke, and involves, from the point of view of the state, such an
undermining of the national will to resist the enemy, that its content,
if not the exact expression, can scarcely be attributed to any other than
the man whose courage was maintained by the certainty of divine
inspiration.

THE MESSAGE TO ZEDEKIAH **27.12–15**

The sign of the yoke was communicated to the five kings. It is
inconceivable that the same message should not have been delivered to
Zedekiah, and this section notes the fact. It is simply repetitive of the
language used in vv. 1–11, with the same warning about the prophets.
There is no new feature, nor any significant variation of vocabulary. Of
course the repetition serves to hammer home the message.
12. in like manner: lit. 'according to all these words'.
15. I have not sent them: this expression is found outside Jer. in 1
Kg. 22.12; Ezek. 13.2, 16; 38.17; 1 Sam. 19.20; but its use in close
connection with 'lies' (*šeqer*) is confined to the prose of Jer. 14.4; 29.9;
cf. also 23.32; 28.15; 29. 31; 43.2.

THE DESTINY OF THE TEMPLE VESSELS **27.16–22**

We have seen reason to suppose that usually the shorter LXX text
represents the earlier text. In chapter 25 the reasons for coming to this
conclusion were more cogent. In this section some commentators have,
on the contrary, seen the 'abridging tendency of LXX at work' and in
vv. 20–21 a case of homoeoteleuton. But the repetition of the word 'to
Babylon' does not necessarily indicate an omission in LXX, and the
reasons are not strong enough to overturn general probability. The fact
is that, as an earlier form of the tradition, LXX makes very good sense.
Moreover the narrative of chapter 28 presupposes this shorter from ,which
runs thus:

> Then I spoke to all these people and to the priests, saying, 'Thus says the
> LORD: Do not listen to the words of the prophets who are prophesying to

you, saying, "Behold, the vessels of the LORD's house will return from Babylon", for it is a lie which they are prophesying to you. If they are prophets, and if the word of the LORD is with them let them intercede with me. For thus says the LORD. As to the vessels which are left, which the king of Babylon did not take away, when he took Jeconiah into exile from Jerusalem, they shall go to Babylon. This is the very word of the LORD.'

Thus in its earlier form, this oracle was an oracle of doom conformable to, though not commensurate with, the uncompromising doom of vv. 2–11.

But this eases the historical question only in part. Could the false prophets actually have spoken thus, in the terms of the **the vessels of the LORD's house**? The problem is that in 2 Kg. 24.13, q.v., it is stated that all the vessels of gold in the temple were 'cut in pieces'. This seems to mean that they were converted into bullion, though it is not inconceivable that some of the more artistic pieces were carried to Babylon as prizes of war. 2 Kg 25.14 suggests that some minor gold and silver vessels were spared at this time, but were taken after the final assault on Jerusalem in 586B.C.. Here an explicit distinction is made between the large pieces of brass which were broken up (*šbr*, v. 13), the vessels of gold and silver which the captain 'took away as gold . . . as silver' (v. 15) and the small articles left over from 597 B.C. It appears clear therefore that not everything was broken up in 597 B.C., that some vessels remained until 586 and were taken intact to Babylon and to this extent, if this was a prophecy of Jeremiah, it was fulfilled. Jer. 52.17–23 is based on 2 Kg. 25.13–17.

Undeniably the point about the Temple vessels was that they furnished a symbol of continuity. It is however unwise to be too sceptical about the historical basis of this idea. Indeed if on the basis of 2 Chr. 36 and the book of Ezra (and Dan. 1; 5), it is argued that the contradictions best accord with a theological rather than a historical intention, this theological intention of signifying the essential continuity of the Holy People is hardly consistent with the shorter and earlier text of Jer. 27.16–21. Here it is the false prophets who reassure the people of continuity. Jeremiah declares only that the judgment which is as yet incomplete will be complete. He takes hold of a glimmer of hope held out before the people and extinguishes it. The symbol which false prophets exploited for their use Jeremiah turns upside down for his own. It becomes more and more difficult to interpret this passage (in its shorter form) as a prophecy after the event. It has the marks to authentic prophecy and of the grim uncompromisingness of Jeremiah himself.

But that in the light of events the passage has been expanded and transformed there can be no doubt. The expansions include:

(a) in v. 17, **Why should this city become a desolation?** (*ḥorbāh*, cf. 7.34, 22.5; 25.9, 11, i.e. the prose tradition.

(b) In v. 18, **that the vessels which are left in the house of the LORD, in the house of the king of Judah, and in Jerusalem may not go to Babylon:** this simply gives the content of the intercession in terms of v. 20.

(c) Verse 19 specifies the vessels in terms of 2 Kg 25.13 as used in Jer. 52.17.

(d) In v. 20 **and all the nobles of Judah and Jerusalem:** no doubt a filling-in of the picture from 2 Kg 24.14.

Verse 22 alone presents new material and transforms the oracle from one of uncompromising judgment to one of long term hope.

22. Until the day when I give attention to them: lit. 'the day of my visiting (*poqdi*) them'. This is of course the 'visitation' which is a characteristic usage both of the poetry and the prose of the Jeremiah tradition. The use of the infinitive with 'day' rather than the noun (*peqūdāh*) with 'time' (8.12; 10.15; 46.21; 50.27; 51.18) or 'year' (11.23; 23.2; 48.44) is unique to this verse.

In the great majority of cases in Jer. (more than thirty), the LORD's visitation is for judgment, and the word is almost a synonym for punishment (as in 27.8). But he may also 'visit' for salvation, as when Jeremiah prays that the LORD will visit him (15.15). Zedekiah will remain in Babylon 'until I visit him' (32.5) and significantly in this same complex (29.10) the LORD's visitation is associated with the end of the seventy years' captivity. It is not possible to regard this verse as alien to the later Jeremiah tradition. The idea of visitation for salvation thereafter has a long history, so that *episkeptein* in the LXX, where God is subject, may refer to his gracious condescension. This is the meaning in Ps. Sol. 10.5, 1.5–12; 5.16; 7.9; 8.2–3 and in the Benedictus. This transformation of the meaning of the earlier oracle must belong to the stage when chapter 29 also received additions of hope and chapters 27–29 were associated with 'the book of consolation' (chapters 30–31).

CONFLICT WITH A LEADING PROPHET OF THE ESTABLISHMENT
28.1–17 (LXX 35.1–17)

Two features of this chapter might at first encourage the view that it is independent of chapter 27. The first is that it has its own superscription, which is different in date from 27.1. The second is that while chapter

27 is in the first person, chapter 28 is a narrative in the third person. But we noticed that the superscription of chapter 27 is absent from LXX and appears to be an editorial touch to link the chapter with chapter 26, thus dating the event erroneously in the reign of Jehoiakim rather than in that of Zedekiah. Here the LXX version is shorter, but similar in form. It is likely even in its shorter form to be editorial and to say nothing about the original independence of the chapter. As to the change of person, this is capable of two equally plausible explanations. While it could indicate the separateness of the tradition, it could as easily point to a separate stage of editorial expansion. In view of the additional features of the chapter now to be described this would seem the more probable view.

Stronger far than those features which suggest separateness are the stylistic features which link this chapter with chapter 27.

(1) Whereas in chapter 27 the sign of the yoke (vv 2–11) and the oracle concerning the Temple vessels (vv. 16–22) are separate and distinguishable, chapter 28 presupposes both, and Hananiah combines both in his opening oracle: **I have broken the yoke of the king of Babylon. Within two years I will bring back to this place all the vessels of the LORD's house** (vv. 2–3).

(2) When in v. 10 the narrative relates that **the prophet Hananiah took the yoke-bars from the neck of Jeremiah . . . and broke them**, there has been no previous mention in this chapter of the sign enacted by Jeremiah. The narrative of chapter 28 thus presupposes (and fails to make sense without) the narrative of 27.2–7.

(3) There are verbal echoes which suggest that chapter 28 was composed in literary dependence upon chapter 27. Thus the 'yoke-bar' (Heb. singular *môṭāh*; LXX, Syr., plural) corresponds to 27.2. 'I have put upon the neck of all these nations an iron yoke of servitude to (lit: to serve) Nebuchadnezzar king of Babylon, and they shall serve him, for I have given to him even the beasts of the field' (28.14) echoes, and is in part identical with 27.6, 7, 8.

'Listen, Hananiah' (v. 15); contrast 'Do not listen to the prophet' (27.9, 14, 16, 17).

'Do not listen to the prophets; let the prophet listen.'

'The LORD has not sent you' (v. 15), cf. 27.10.

These correspondences, together with the entire absence of any special vocabulary, are best explained if we suppose that the story of Hananiah is told in direct relationship to the accounts either received by the author or also told by him in chapter 27. The reader's sense that these chapters belong together and should be read together thus receives some critical support.

There is every reason to suppose that the editor based his narrative on a dramatic event in the ministry of Jeremiah. Jeremiah's greatest battle, as Martin Buber observed, was with the false prophets of whom Hananiah was chief. The battle was, as it happened literally, to the death. It would have been easier for all, and in particular for the people witnessing the struggle, if it had been between a shining warrior of righteousness and a dragon of wickedness. Instead it was between the lonely, odd and partly discredited Jeremiah and the honoured leader of the established prophets. It is not said, probably because it could not be said, of Hananiah that he was immoral like the prophets of Jerusalem castigated in 23.14, or like the exiled prophets Ahab and Zedekiah in 29.23. He spoke the authoritative language of a prophet ('Thus says the LORD of hosts'), used the prophetic perfect to enforce the certainty of his prediction ('I have broken the yoke of the king of Babylon') and demonstrated his message with a prophetic sign. His very name meant 'Yahweh has been gracious'. He was so confident that he was prepared to speak of deliverance coming within a specified number of years (v. 11). It was precisely the exemplary character of Hananiah which makes this the classic confrontation of prophecy with prophecy.

In the nature of the case therefore, Jeremiah could not point to any external aspect of Hananiah's conduct or person as evidence of his falseness. This explains Jeremiah's ironic response: **Amen! May the LORD do so; may the LORD make the words which you have prophesied come true** (v. 6). Cf. Micaiah in I Kings 22.15. The irony is not diminished by the fact that Jeremiah would have *liked* this prophecy to come true. But it has become clear that, forbidden to pray for a redemption he desired, and interiorly compelled to announce a judgment he dreaded, Jeremiah was tortured and torn in two. At the same time he must have been very sure of himself to resist the blandishments of Hananiah when they coincided with the longings of one half of his own nature.

Interest now centres on the criteria used by Jeremiah to distinguish between true prophecy and false. He produces two: (a) *fidelity to the prophetic succession* -**The prophets who preceded you and me from ancient times prophesied war, famine, and pestilence against many countries and great kingdoms** (v. 8); and (b) *the test of fulfilment* -**As for the prophet who prophesies peace, when the word of that prophet comes to pass, then it will be known that the LORD has truly sent him**. The difficulty with the first is that there were genuine prophecies of salvation. Isaiah is a conspicuous example. Hence the need for the test of fulfilment. The difficulty with waiting for an outcome which may be years away is that it gives no guidance for the present. The difficulty with any appeal to a simple test of fulfilment is that a genuine prophet may find a particular prophecy turn out differently from his precise expectation and, on the other hand, a false prophet, like a fortune-teller, is likely to have sufficient success to hold the confidence of the people.

While therefore there is substance in Jeremiah's answer (and more to be said about it –see below), it provides no convincing answer to the onlookers, and leaves Hananiah free to perform what he imagines is the *coup de grâce*. This is (v. 10) his counter-sign. He breaks the yoke which Jeremiah wears before the people and so neutralises Jeremiah's prophecy. Jeremiah's words seem to the people as broken as the broken wood. But Hananiah intends more than a denial of Jeremiah's message and authenticity. He means to indicate that thus the power of Nebuchadnezzar will be broken. The difference between true and the false prophet is embodied in the direct conflict between the two signs, in which Hananiah has the last word. At this point Jeremiah has no further response to make. **Jeremiah the prophet went his way** (v. 11).

He does not, however, leave the broken yoke as the final sign. After and unspecified interval he is directed to speak to Hananiah again. The incident vividly shows how the prophet received the divine message in the solitude of seclusion, out of his intimacy with God, rather than in the activity of his engagement with people and his grappling with problems. From the detachment of withdrawal he comes forth with a new form of the reaffirmation of his message: **You have broken wooden bars, but I will make in their place bars of iron** (v. 13). There is no suggestion that Jeremiah now produced objects of iron to serve as a prophetic sign. He simply uttered the word and reaffirmed his prophecy of subjection to Nebuchadnezzar. His last shaft was a declaration that Hananiah spoke falsehood, together with a prediction of his death. In the LXX, which is likely to be closer to the first account than MT, the denouement is laconic. 'Behold I will remove you from the face of the earth. This very year you shall die. And he died in the seventh month'.

1. In that same year, at the beginning of the reign of Zedekiah: It is not likely that these events took place in the accession year of Zedekiah, but, as the LXX has it, 'in the fourth year of Zedekiah', i.e. 594–593B.C. It is clear that the datings of 26.1, and 28.1 are editorial and we have already seen that 26.1 is manifestly incorrect. It is probable that the present text is a conflation of two readings, (a) the LXX, which is correct, and (b) a simpler form of MT. 'in that same year' which has been expanded in the light of 27.1.

the prophet from Gibeon: Gibeon was evidently a proud city with a long history. Tradition held memories of a people friendly to Joshua so that there the sun stood still (Jos. 10.12–14), and of the divine promise of wisdom to Solomon vouchsafed in a dream. Archaeological investigations suggest that in the time of Jeremiah Gibeon was the centre of a considerable wine industry, contained some noble houses and was well protected against drought by an enormous cistern. It is now identified with the modern el-Jib, eight miles north and a little to the west of Jerusalem (see W. L. Reed in *Archaeology and Old Testament Study*, ed. by D. Winton Thomas, 1967, pp. 231–243). Hananiah of Gibeon was a successful prophet from a flourishing city. LXX pointedly refers to him as 'Hananiah the false prophet'.

spoke to me: the first person is probably an editorial assimilation to the previous chapter 27, since after v. 5 this chapter refers to Jeremiah in the third person.

3. which Nebuchadnezzar king of Babylon took away from this place and carried to Babylon: absent from LXX. The late spelling of Nebuchadnezzar, one of eight examples in chapters 27–29, indicates the hand of a later glossator, but he does no more than point the obvious.

I will bring back to this place: in Heb. the familiar participle of the prose tradition.

4. Jeconiah: i.e. Jehoiachin. See on 22.24. LXX omits **the son of Jehoiakim, king of Judah** which is an explanatory gloss characteristic of MT.

6. Amen cf. 11.5.

may the Lord make the words which you have prophesied come true: The expression, lit. 'make the words to stand', is used of a person carrying out a command, as in I Sam. 15.13; Jer. 35.16 (the Rechabites). In Dt. 9.5 it is used of the confirmation of the promise made to the patriarchs and in I Kg. 12.15 of the fulfilment of the prophetic word of Ahijah. Cf. I Sam. 1.23; 3.12; 2 Sam. 7.25; I Kg. 6.12. But it is not exclusively Deuteronomic, cf. Gen 26.3; Lev. 26.9; and may be said to be prophetic. the idea that the word or plan of the LORD 'stands' is pervasive in the Isaiah tradition, cf. Isa. 7.7; 8.10; 40.8; 46.10; and in 44.26 is the affirmation that it is the LORD 'who confirms (makes to stand) the word of his servant, and performs the counsel of his messengers'. Cf. Rom. 15.8.

8. famine, and pestilence: absent from LXX. Added no doubt to relate the expression to the characteristic formula of the Jeremiah tradition: 'sword, famine and pestilence'. The sense remains unchanged and makes the prophets of woe the norm. By and large it is true that they are the norm. Consider Samuel (and the house of Eli and Saul), Nathan (concerning David and Bathsheba) Gad (2 Sam. 24.11–17), Ahijah, the unnamed prophet in 1 Kg. 13, Elijah, Elisha, Micaiah ben Imlah, Amos, Micah, Nahum, Zephaniah. Until the events of the fall of Jerusalem and the Exile the prophets were monitors of judgment, first to individuals, particularly the kings, then to the nation. Isaiah prophesied of salvation in relation to particular crises, but witnessed the fall of the northern kingdom and was Judah's most probing critic.

10. the yoke-bars: Heb. *môṭāh* singular; plural in LXX and Syr., 27.2 and 28.13. A yoke was constructed of two parts. The singular may well refer to the part that was on Jeremiah's neck, and need not be corrected.

14. Nebuchadnezzar: absent from LXX. See on v. 3. For the theme, see on 27.5–6.

15. the LORD has not sent (*šālaḥ*) **you, and you have made these people trust** (*bāṭaḥ*) **in a lie** (*šeqer*): A repeated theme and characteristic language of the prose tradition. See on 14.13–16; 29.9. (Helga Weippert, op.cit., pp. 118–121.)

16. Behold, I will remove you from the face of the earth: the now familiar 'behold' with participle of the prose tradition. Cf. 'I will cast you (*šālak*) out of my sight' 7.15, cf. 2 Kg. 13.23, etc. Here the 'I will remove you' (*šālaḥ*) is perhaps suggested by the insistence that Hananiah has not been 'sent' by the LORD like a true prophet. Cf. Jer. 14.16 (Moses and Samuel). If this is so, it is difficult not to recognise further word-play in the contrast between Hananiah's prophecy that Nebuchadnezzar's yoke will be broken 'from (*mēʿal*) the next of all the nations', and his own fate removed 'from the face (*mēʿal pᵉnê*) of the earth'!

LEGITIMATE AND FALSE HOPES OF THE EXILES AND CONFLICT
WITH THEIR PROPHETS 29.1–32 (LXX 36.1–32)

This chapter completes the section on the problem of discerning between true and false prophets. Chapter 26 drew attention to the supreme issue between Jeremiah and the false prophets in the Temple sermon (of the time of Jehoiakim before the disaster of 597 B.C.). A comparison with 7.1–15 shows that in chapter 26 the principal interest is in the conflict to which this sermon gave rise. The resolution of this conflict requires the correct discrimination of true from false. In fact, Jeremiah's forthright utterance led to something like a trial. Those who were or had been on the side of truth are named: Micah of the eighth century who escaped death, the contemporary Uriah who did not, and Ahikam who supported Jeremiah.

In chapter 27 the sign of the yoke (of the time of Zedekiah after the disaster of 586 B.C.) is presented, and upon this basis the chapter is built up in three sections, so as to repeat the message to the neighbouring peoples, to Zedekiah and to priests and people. The third part introduces the theme of the Temple vessels which may or may not be original to the episode, but the mind of the author is shown in the warning, repeated in each of the three parts, not to listen to the false prophets. The story of Hananiah, Jeremiah's most considerable opponent, in chapter 28 is told in such a way as to presuppose the narrative of chapter 27. It is itself an unbroken narrative.

That Jeremiah is not condemned after the Temple sermon and that the validity of his vocation is sealed by the death of Hananiah, provides *prima facie* evidence for believing him to be trustworthy when in chapter 29 he both denounces false hopes and defines the hopes that are true. Chapter 29 is constructed on the basis of three events: (1) Jeremiah's advice to the exiles by letter, (2) his denunciation of the named prophets Ahab and Zedekiah, (which some think is part of the same letter) and (3) the correspondence involving Shemaiah.

All three events have to do with those who had been consigned to exile in Babylon after 586. All three have to do with false prophets who comfort the people with messages that there will be a speedy end to the exile and a return home. The total effect of the chapter is to destroy the complacent hope of an immediate reversal of fortune (vv. 5 ff., 21–23, 28, 32a), but to keep open an ultimate purpose of good which will be realised beyond the lifetime of anyone living (vv 10–14, 32b).

It is clear that a shorter text lies behind the present Massoretic text. The greater part of v. 14 and vv. 16–20 are absent from LXX. Some have agreed that a scribe omitted vv. 16–20 by homoioteleuton, since 'in Babylon' occurs both at the end of v. 15 and at the end of v. 20. It would however be too much of a coincidence that a scribe omitted the one passage that on other grounds betrays itself as an editorial addition. The reasons for assuming that LXX represents the earlier form of the Heb. text, before it received this redactoral touch on the basis of the tradition, are set out below.

Each section of the chapter bears marks of the prose tradition and looks like a version of the remembered words of Jeremiah in that tradition.

There is little reason for supposing that the very words of Jeremiah's letter have been quoted, although the rhetorical prose of vv. 5–7, with its parallelism and balance, is memorable. It quickly passes in v. 8 into a warning against the false prophets and their lies, phrased in the commonplaces of the prose tradition.

The continuation of vv. 10–14a referring to the seventy years' duration of the Exile is widely assumed to be prophecy after the event. It is however more convincingly interpreted as a prophecy of Jeremiah himself which created a certain degree of perplexity both then and later. See the full discussion on the related passage 25.11. It is then to be understood both as a reiteration of judgment upon the exiles, in the sense that it firmly repudiates all hopes of their return during their lifetime, *and* as a measured gleam of hope that, in God's own time, salvation lies on the yonder side of judgment. That there was a carefully limited degree of hope in the thought of Jeremiah is confirmed by a number of passages, not least by chapter 32. It is of course easy to understand how his followers and interpreters built on this hope in the light of further experience, and this would explain the introduction of the theme of the ingathering of the exiles in v. 14b, absent from the LXX.

The editorial unity of chapters 26–29 in general and chapter 29 in particular, is shown not only by the pervasive *theme* of false prophecy and the *prose* of the familiar prose tradition, but also in two more detailed features: (1) The common theme is more precisely registered by the repetition of the phrases–listening, sending, prophesying lies (in my name) and banishing–in 26.4, 5, 9, 12, 16; 27.9, 10, 14, 16, 17; 28.15; 29.8, 9, (19 and 21 absent from LXX), 31. (2) There is unparalleled *naming* of prophets, false prophets, and others: Micah, Uriah, Elnathan and Ahikam in chapter 26; Hananiah in chapter 28; Ahab, Zedekiah, Shemaiah and Zephaniah in chapter 29. This no doubt represents the desire to be circumstantial in what amounted to the continuing trial of Jeremiah as a prophet of the LORD. Jeremiah's greatest conflict was fought out, not only in his own consciousness, but in public contests witnessed by impressionable people whose basic optimism predisposed them to favour his opponents.

This optimism is the unexpressed presupposition of chapter 29. We are dealing with a period and a situation when the first attack on Jerusalem and the exile of Jehoiachin and the leaders in 597 had already vindicated the repeated prophecies of Jeremiah over a long period. No sooner had Zedekiah's regime settled down than the defeated peoples began to plan insurrection (chapter 27) and declined to acquiesce in submission to

Babylon. To Jeremiah submission was the corollary of the LORD's judgment and therefore to be accepted. Then even the exiles themselves began to hope for a quick end to their banishment, and in this were supported by prophets who encouraged them with oracles of salvation. Jeremiah believed that exile also had to be accepted. He betrays no vestigial feeling that a foreign country is necessarily an unclean country (cf. Am. 7.17; Hos. 9.3) or a place where the LORD cannot be worshipped, feelings that false prophets were no doubt happy to stir to life. On the contrary, in vv. 12–14a he affirms that relationship with God will be fully maintained in exile, without land or Temple or sacrifice, in the reciprocity of sincere prayer.

This note of acceptance of judgment is one of the most important contributions of the OT to the theology of politics and revolution. It does not mean abject acceptance of any tyranny. It does mean the submission to that condition which can be prophetically identified as divine judgment. No people is disposed to recognise submission as deserved chastisement, since submission runs directly against national and human pride and the optimism which accompanies it. To judge by their utterances, there are few theologians who, in their attitude to the revolutionary movements of the twentieth century, take account of this fundamental perception of Jeremiah. Carroll's interpretation of this as time-serving pusillanimity is turning truth on its head.

Along with the acceptance of exile goes the conviction that while this is the provisional design of providence, it is not the ultimate divine will. Introduction 29.1–3.

INTRODUCTION **29.1–3**

The letter is introduced with a somewhat emphatic amount of circumstantial reference in keeping with the motive we have discerned throughout chapters 26–29.

1. the words of the letter: there is no need to deny the full implication of 'words'. The redactor refers not to the 'story' of the letter (a possible meaning of the Heb.) but to its form, and this is probable even if he was not quoting the very words.

the elders of the exiles: Heb. has 'the remainder (*yeter*) of the elders' *RSV* has followed LXX. It is difficult either to understand or explain the addition of 'remainder'. There is no ground for transposing it before 'all the people' nor any evidence that the word could mean 'most distinguished' or 'chief'. Of the four occurrences of the word in MT only two (27.19; 52.15) are represented in LXX. 39.19 is part of a section not found in LXX, and 27.19, like 29.1, shows that MT seeks in some way to emphasise the location. Thus in 27.19 'the remainder of the vessels' is translated (LXX) 'the vessels remaining ' and glossed 'which are left in this city'. The sense of 29.1 may well therefore be: 'the remaining elders of the exile' and not be intended to distinguish between elders in general and elders in Babylon, but to emphasise that not all the elders were deported. On the role of elders as local representatives of the people, see 26.17.

whom Nebuchadnezzar had taken into exile from Jerusalem: a typical and correct gloss of MT absent from LXX. Verse 2 is often said to be an insertion derived from 2 Kg. 24.14–16, breaking the connection between vv. 1 and 3. The historical reference both here and in 24.1 is present in LXX and may be said to fit the circumstantial emphasis of the narrative. Note also the reference to the queen mother in 13.18. she was plainly a person of considerable influence.

3. Elasah the son of Shaphan: Shaphan (whose name probably means 'Rock-badger') may well have been the leading *šōper* in the discovery of the law-book and Josiah's reform (2 Kg 23). His son Ahikam (2 Kg. 22.12; Jer. 26.24) was both active in the events of 621 B.C. and a supporter of Jeremiah in his time of trial under Jehoiakim. If Elasah and the Gemariah of Jer. 36.12, 25, and Ahikam are brothers and Micaiah of Jer. 36.11ff. a grandson of the same Shaphan, then we have evidence of a remarkable family who were united in unwavering devotion to Jeremiah. They were all highly educated, belonging to the circles from whom |Israel's scholars were bred, and while it may be misleading to call them with Baruch, the nucleus of a 'school', it is clear that a group of men existed, competent and eager to defend the prophet and protect, transmit and interpret the tradition of his teaching.

Gemariah the son of Hilkiah: a different Gemariah from the brother referred to above. Jeremiah's father was named Hilkiah, as also was the high priest of the reform (2 Kg. 22). An identification is not likely with either.

JEREMIAH'S LETTER **29.4–9**

The main body of the letter in vv. 4–8 is in a rhythmical prose with an element of parallelism that can be discerned in English translation. It is introduced with a full cultic formula (v. 4) and it has a rounded completeness. It is as memorable in English as in Hebrew, and it is reasonable to suppose that those who preserved the teaching of Jeremiah remembered it!

To the modern reader the content sounds positive and reassuring. The exiles are to settle down and flourish. The advice to build houses implies a certain freedom and opportunity. The conditions were far from those of incarceration and the concentration camp. The position of their own elders (v. 1, cf. Ezek. 8.1; 14.1; 20.1) was one of delegated responsibility, and there were opportunities of development which the exiles came to exploit to the full. No doubt they developed new modes of worship which may or may not be the direct antecedents of the Synagogue. It is reasonable to suppose that this was the context of Second Isaiah's activity.

The advice to marry and multiply, together with the prospect of grandchildren, suggests no immediate chance of return. The advice to **seek the welfare** *šālôm* **of the city where I have sent you into exile** and, (another way of saying the same thing), to **pray to the LORD on its behalf** (v.7) was clean contrary to any thing which would have occurred naturally to a pious and faithful Jew. For him the worship of the LORD was inextricably bound up with the Temple and the Land, and this culturally conditioned reaction was reinforced by the conviction that the Land was one of the great gifts of the LORD to his chosen people. Indeed this was one of the central emphases of Deuteronomic teaching. Not only was the possession of the Land an article of faith (Dt. 26.5–10), but a foreign land was unclean. We may endorse the importance Volz put upon this passage as fundamental in Jewish thought for the development of a positive attitude to the nations in the LORD's providential purposes.

The immediate effect of Jeremiah's teaching was not therefore reassuring, but devastating. His letter counselled an acceptance which the exiles were not prepared to allow. This counsel he presents not as a nicely calculated judgment on what will serve the good of the greatest number, but as the LORD's will. Given a true prophet to whom the LORD's secret is revealed, then he may be expected to know what is right and what in fact will lead to the welfare of the people.

At this point the people were given conflicting advice, for there were prophets in exile who gave exactly the advice the people wanted to hear. Verse 8 follows naturally upon the content of the letter, and even if the expression is couched in the familiar language of the prose tradition, and may therefore be a secondary version of his teaching, it no doubt represents sufficiently well what Jeremiah wrote. Indeed it is not unlikely that the repetition **do not listen . . . for it is a lie which they are prophesying to you in my name** registers Jeremiah's unwearying repetition, in a conflict which lasted all his ministry, against false prophets in Jerusalem, in Babylon and in Egypt.

THE SEVENTY YEARS **29.10–14**

See the discussion above, and particularly, the comment on the related passage 25.11, for the view that this prediction is intrinsic to the forward vision of Jeremiah. Properly understood this also is not a kind of hope agreeable to the exiles, since it puts the possibility of return beyond their life time. If it gives 'a future and a hope' (v. 11, absent in LXX), the word 'future' (*'aḥªrît*) indicates 'the final period of the future so far as it falls within the range of the speaker's perspective' (S.R. Driver on Dt. 4.30, cf. Isa 2.1). Such a hope therefore embraces acceptance of the judgment of exile and repudiation of the false prophets. At the same time it reaffirms the divine promise to Abraham and the fathers, and the role of Israel as the elect people who have a service to perform within the LORD's plans.

10. I will fulfil to you my promise: literally 'my good word', which could mean 'fortune bringing word' (cf. Ps. 45.1) but LXX has simply 'establish my words' and the reference is probably to all those words of the LORD (held in the various traditions) which conveyed the hope of land and prosperity. See on 28.6.

11. I know the plans I have for you: a way of expressing the divine purpose and providence in history which is one of the distinctive contributions of the *OT* to religion.

In verses 11–14 the LXX is briefer:

> I will think out a plan for your good, not for evil
>   to give you these things;
> and you will pray to me and I will hear you,
> and you will seek me and find me, when you seek me
>   with all your heart,
> and I will reveal myself to you.

Here we touch the heart of religion, independent of cultural limitation. MT represents a text which has been expanded to emphasise a future and a hope (see above, and on 31.17 from which this could be derived), and in v. 14 to introduce the theme of the ingathering from exile (cf. Isa. 11; 49; 60) which is a vital component of that hope.

The basic text has the marks of the Jeremiah prose tradition. There is the familiar use of the word 'visit' (*pāqaḏ*) in v. 10 (see on 27.22). V. 11 is specially significant as supporting this affiliation in the light of Helga Weippert's discussion (op. cit. pp. 203–209). The grouping of 'good' and 'evil' meaning 'salvation' or 'judgment' (in this form) is found in the story of Micaiah (1 Kg. 22.8, 18), but otherwise mainly in Jeremiah (21.10; 38.4; 39.6; 44.27 cf. Am. 9.4) and may be said to be prophetic rather than Deuteronomic.

Verses 11–14a are as revolutionary as they are unobtrusive. Jeremiah is affirming that when the exiles settle down to accept their banishment, they will find that their relationship with the LORD can be maintained, despite the absence of the props normally considered indispensable. Without the land of promise, without the Temple and the sacrifices laid down by divine command, without prophets (for the prophets they acclaimed, v. 15, Jeremiah repudiated) they may still **pray to me . . . seek me and find me.** The Heb. words for 'seek' (*biqqēš* and *dāraš*) are used frequently of seeking guidance from a prophet or some other appointed means, or of attending the Temple. Jeremiah thus emphasises that this guidance and worship will be possible in the circumstances of exile, but in a simpler mode.

This emphasis is not unique to Jeremiah. Indeed it can be argued that Amos linked non-sacrificial worship with exile (Am. 5.25–27), and that in Hos., Isa. 56–66 and the Psalter the recognition of a non-sacrificial worship is associated with the destruction of the Israelite institutions. (See also on 7.22–23, and D. R. Jones, 'The Cessation of Sacrifice after the Destruction of the Temple in 586 B.C.', JTS. NS 14 (1963) 12–31.

On the other hand, the primacy of this personal relationship with God receives in Jeremiah an exemplary endorsement. It was precisely in the tragedies of history that the instrumental and secondary character of institutions was taught. Again and again it was taught also that when the restoration took place, then the institutions would resume their proper function (Pss. 51.20–21; 69.30–36; 102.14–17; Hos. 3.4–5). It is not surprising therefore that the editorial handling of the earlier text includes the theme of the ingathering and the return to the land and temple (v. 14). By putting the stress on the 'future' and the 'hope' and clothing this hope in the pattern of the ingathering, the editor has weakened the force of Jeremiah's insistence that, without any such hope for the exiles in their life time, intimacy between themselves and their God may be unimpaired.

The same thought is present in Dt. 4.29, where the language is closely similar. If this is part of the final framework of the Deuteronomic history to be dated after the release of Jehoiachin from prison, then it probably belongs to the period following Jeremiah's ministry and illustrates the mutual influence of the Jeremiah and Deuteronomic circles at this time.

Isa 55.1 and 65.1 show later prophetic handling of the same theme. The reason for supposing the Jeremiah passage in the LXX form to be primary is given below.

The most significant difference in the LXX version is 'I will reveal myself to you' for 'I will be found by you' (MT, v. 14). The Heb. underlying LXX was probably *ûniglēti* (niphal). This commends itself as the earlier reading for three reasons.

(1) It is a play on the word *gôlāh* 'exiles') which is derived from the same root. It is altogether in line with prophetic use of language that Jeremiah should thus memorably make the point that to be an exile is still to be a person to whom the LORD may reveal himself.

(2) The notion that the LORD reveals *himself* (Greek '*epiphanoumai*', English 'epiphany') may well have been found too strong in later circles who sought to mitigate the directness of the image.

(3) the Hebrew *wᵉnimṣe'tî lākem* 'I will be found by you' is an assimilation to Dt. 4.29, and more particularly Isa. 55.6, 65.1. The assimilation was easy to make since both verbs converge in the sense of 'discovered'.

All this makes it probable that LXX is here close to the teaching of Jeremiah, and justifies the comment of John Skinner: 'Where God is thus revealed in experience, there all the powers of religion are, and nothing essential can be added thereto. That is the core of Jeremiah's teaching in this passage; and it is by no means clear that any previous prophet or thinker could have given it as well as he' (*Prophecy and Religion*, p. 290).

EXTENDED REJOINDER TO THE BABYLONIAN PROPHETS **29.15-19** (absent from LXX)

This mosaic of commonplaces from the prose tradition is sparked off by the memory of the claim made by the exiles that **the LORD has raised up prophets for us in Babylon** (v. 15). This implies a judgment that Ahab, Zedekiah and others were true prophets whose acceptable message was to be believed. It is also implies both the falseness of Jeremiah and the view that, remaining in Jerusalem, he has no business to interfere with the exiles. The LORD's care for his people follows them to Babylon in the sense that he does not leave them without prophets. The passage that follows exemplifies the principle enunciated by Jeremiah in his confrontation with Hananiah, viz: fidelity to the prophetic succession, as also to the known teaching of Jeremiah himself.

In verses 16-19 there is not a single new or distinctive idea. A string of commonplaces of the prose tradition are exploited to express the essence of the prophet's attitude to false prophets in general and the prophets resident in Babylon in particular.

V. 17. has the familiar **Behold** with participle, and the threefold **sword, famine, and pestilence** (also in v. 18). The allusion to the **vile figs**, despite the adjective *šōʿārîm* which is a *hapax legomenon*, shows the author using a passage which is chronologically later than the letter of chapter 29 (see exposition of chapter 24).

V. 18. has **a horror** (cf. 24.9) . . . **a curse, a terror, a hissing, and a reproach among all the nations where I have driven them.** The same form of sentence, with a variety of nouns, occurs in Jer. 15.4; 24.9; 25.9, 11, 18; 26.6; 29.18; 42.18; 44.8, 12, 22; Dt. 28.25, 37; 2 Kg. 22.19. See comment on 24.9.

V. 19. has the idiomatic phrase concerning the persistence of the true prophets (rising early and sending) which is characteristic of the prose tradition.

All this suggests that LXX represents an earlier form of the text and the expansion in MT. is the result of *literary* activity. At the same time one must not rule out the possibility that Jeremiah's successors and followers reinforced his teaching by repeating it, and by doing so emphasised the divine authority of what they were saying. It is doubtful whether a rejoinder of this kind was necessary after the events of 586 B.C. had finally discredited the false prophets and vindicated Jeremiah.

THE FALSE PROPHETS AHAB AND ZEDEKIAH **29.20–23**

Nothing is otherwise know of these two characters. The phrase '**who are prophesying a lie to you in may name** (v. 21) is a commonplace of the prose tradition, based, as we have seen, on the teaching of Jeremiah, and indicates the milieu in which the story was preserved. It is of course possible that this is part of the letter which, in the tradition, has been interpolated, but if it is, it is a free version, as is shown by comparison with the rhetorical prose of vv. 5–7.

The charge levelled against these two men by Jeremiah was primarily a moral one. They had **committed adultery with their neighbours' wives** (v. 23). From the point of view of the Jewish community, this was pronounced a folly in Israel. The solemn designation (*nᵉbālāh*) seems to have been reserved specially for sexual offenses (Gen. 34.7; Jg. 20.6, 10; 2 Sam. 13.12; Dt. 22.21). Jg. 20 shows how this might involve a solemn act of Judgment by all Israel bearing witness to the covenant law. Dt. 22.21 is an example of how it was written into the law. But the punishment was inflicted by the Babylonian authorities and was extreme.

Burning for adultery is attested in Gen. 38.4 and Lev. 21.9, cf. also Jos. 7.15, 24; Job. 20.4; 30.7; 41.19, 25. Dan. 3 may be interpreted as reflecting a Babylonian use of burning as punishment, though otherwise the paucity of evidence would suggest that this form of punishment was rare. The account clearly suggests that it was intended to be exemplary, so that it became a curse: **The LORD make you like Zedekiah and Ahab** (v. 22).

The exemplary and extreme nature of the punishment requires explanation, and this has commonly been sought in the nature of the crime. The real crime, it is alleged, must have been political intrigue, connected of course with their predictions of return to Jerusalem. Against this is the fact that the narrative does not give this reason when it would have been easy enough to do so. The easiest solution is that when these prophets had been found guilty of public misdemeanour at an early stage of the exile, the Babylonian authorities decided upon an extreme punishment as a deterrent, particularly in the light of the freedom they allowed subject peoples in their midst.

There may be word-play in the narrative. The 'curse' ($q^e l\bar{a}l\bar{a}h$) echoes the name 'Kolaiah' ($q\hat{o}l\bar{a}y\bar{a}h$) and the verb 'roast' ($q\bar{a}lam$). This sort of thing often happened and Hebrew speakers and writers delighted to seize on it. But it does not follow that the story is therefore a fabrication, and that this is a cautionary tale about the fate of false prophets, as imaginary as that of Daniel in the fiery furnace. Once again we are not to be artificially impaled on the horns of a dilemma — between treating the letter as an exact document or as a later invention.

Jeremiah himself linked the immorality of these prophets with their prophetic lies. In this he was insisting on a total integrity which is the *sine qua non* of prophecy. There are disciplines in which it is possible to argue that what a man does with his life outside them is irrelevant. It is possible for a poet or an artist to be sensitive to the sensual aspect of existence to the extent that it enhances his poetry but encourages moral licence. It cannot be so with a prophet. His sensitivity is to the moral and spiritual order. To be true to spiritual truth at one level, but insensitive to moral purity at another, is for a prophet schizoid. The man who compromises with the one is apt to compromise with the other.

That is why Jeremiah links **adultery** (v. 23) with **lying words**, and names both as the cause of this prophetic failure. It is a matter of integrity at the deepest level, of sensitivity to divine truth both spiritual and moral. Therefore Jeremiah adds the LORD's final message: **I am the one who knows, and I am witness**. Cf. 11.20; 12.3; 42.5; Job 16.9.

SHEMAIAH **29.24–32**

The opposition to Jeremiah's letter to the exiles was concentrated in the
otherwise unknown figure of Shemaiah. Verse 31 may imply that he was
a prophet and, if so, it is fair to assume that he was entirely free of the
moral stigma that attached to Ahab and Zedekiah. The content of his
prophecy is not given, no doubt because it lacked distinctiveness. On
the other hand it is said of Pashhur the priest that he prophesied falsely
(see on 20.6), and it may be that Shemaiah belonged to priestly circles.
He buttressed with divine authority the view that the exile would be short.
His method was one familiar in the struggles for power in all ages. He
attempted to discredit Jeremiah in the eyes of authority and have him
suppressed. To this end he wrote to **Zephaniah** (v. 25), who is described
as 'the priest' and in 21.1 is linked with Pashhur, who had previously
put Jeremiah in the stocks (chapter 20). Zephaniah seems to have
succeeded Pashhur (at two removes) as some sort of overseer (*pāqîḏ*) with
disciplinary authority. His immediate predecessor was **Jehoida** (not of
course the Jehoida of 2 Kg. 11, 250 years earlier). According to Jer. 52.24
Zephaniah became 'the second priest', i.e. second to the chief priest, and
was executed after the invasion of 486 B.C..

Zephaniah was challenged to show his strength in the exercise of his
statutory duty, with the implication that he was weak if he failed to take
action. When it is said that he had **charge in the house of the LORD
over every madman who prophesies** (v. 26), clear evidence is thus
presented that prophets and priests were subject to the same jurisdiction.
Whether further deduction may be drawn, that there were 'cultic
prophets' officially attached to the Temple and part of the establishment,
is precarious. A. R. Johnson judiciously argued that the problem was
that of any person who caused a disturbance. (*The Cultic Prophet in Ancient
Israel*, 1962, pp. 62–63). What Zephaniah's attitude to Jeremiah was is
not made plain. He seems to have contented himself with reading the
letter to Jeremiah. If he had exercised discipline, as required, it is likely
that the narrator would have said so, and that Jeremiah's rejoinder also
would have been remembered, as in the case of Pashhur. In the light
of 37.3 it is probable that Zephaniah was inclined to be sympathetic to
Jeremiah.

Jeremiah's judgment upon Shemaiah is given in the commonplaces
of the prose tradition (vv. 30–32) and the hint of **the good that I will
do to my people**, which he will not see is the final hint of an ultimate
purpose of salvation which runs through this section (27.22, absent from

LXX; 29.10–14, the element of hope strengthened in MT.) It seems to have a basis in the thought of Jeremiah, to be extended in the tradition and to form a link in the redactoral process leading to the oracles of hope now to follow.

25. letters in your name: speculations about the number of letters are entirely out of place since LXX omits. LXX itself has: 'I have sent you in my name, and to Zephaniah the priest he said . . . ' (omitting 'to all the people who are in Jerusalem . . . and to all the priests'). It is clear that MT has embellished the earlier text but that the precise form of the earlier text is irrecoverable. Either this was a simple narrative: 'he sent letters in his name and to Zephaniah he said . . . ' (following Syr.); or perhaps MT happened to get it right and *RSV* may be allowed to stand.

26. to have charge: Heb. *p^eqidîm*, but all the versions have the singular. His office is the *pāqîd nāgîd* or chief overseer of 20.1.

every madman who prophesies: lit. 'every man (*'îš*) who is mad and prophesies', i.e. any individual who creates this sort of disturbance. The verbs are parallel—*m^ešuggā'* is to 'be frenzied or mad'. The Arabic suggests the cooing of pigeons and is used of the recital of rhythmical prose, as in the Koran. It is difficult in this context to avoid the suggestion that this is the characteristic behaviour of a certain kind of prophet who is now regarded with contempt, cf. 2 Kg. 9.11 where the prophet sent to Jehu is described as 'this mad fellow' (*m^ešuggā'*), and Hos. 9.7. On the other hand the word was used of madmen generally, cf. Dt. 28.34 and I Sam. 21.15 ff. (of David). The dividing line between inspiration and madness was clearly a fine one.

31–32. The language of the prose tradition. Note 'behold' with the participle *pōqēd*, which is characteristic.

32. shall not have any one living among these people to see the good: LXX 'and there shall not be one left among you'. MT is probably an assimilation to the context.

for he has talked rebellion against the LORD: absent from LXX, no doubt a gloss suggested to a scholarly redactor by Dt. 13.6.

B TRUE PROPHECIES OF HOPE
30.1–31.40 (LXX 37.1–38.40)

These prophecies of hope have already been editorially anticipated. In the section made up of chapters 26–35 (36), chapters 26–29 formed a sequence of prophetic narratives illustrating Jeremiah's struggle with false prophecy, both exposing their falsity and vindicating Jeremiah as a true prophet. Jeremiah's letter to the exiles (29.1–14) implied some future for Israel, though beyond the lifetime of anyone living. There can be little doubt that chapters 26–29 were subsequently subjected to glossing, to emphasise and develop this dimension of hope (27.22). The exact limits of glossing are impossible to determine. It seems probable that the shorter LXX text of 29.11–14, in the prose tradition, represented the thought of Jeremiah himself. This was redactorally expanded to include the post-exilic theme of the ingathering (29.14).

The context determines that in chapters 27–29 the return and restoration of the *southern kingdom* is envisaged. It looks as if chapters 30–31, with their preoccupation with the future, were added at the same time; that chapters 26–29 were presented in more or less their present form, and that the hopeful implications of Jeremiah's message to the exiles provided the link required to introduce the collection of oracles of salvation. Here the return and restoration of the *dispersed northerners* is included. It would, however, be premature to conclude that chapters 30–31 is therefore a collection of oracles all later than Jeremiah. It has the marks of a typical collection containing both Jeremiah oracles and material of the tradition.

There are features which suggest that chapters 30–31 formed, at some stage, an independent collection, or at least that they represent an independent effort to collect together material, held within the Jeremiah tradition, concerning the future. There is first the homogenous character of the subject matter, which has led to its being often labelled 'the book of consolation'. There is the predominantly northern affiliation of the oracles. And there is the special superscription of 30.1–2, which introduces the section as a 'book', together with the concluding 31.26. Moreover, there are two features which link this collection with the earlier collections identified as chapters 7–10; 11–13; 14–17; 18–20; 21–24.

(a) It has the introductory phrase 'the word that came to Jeremiah from the LORD' as in 7.1; 11.1; 14.1; 18.1 and 21.1, cf. also 32.1; 33.1; 34.1; 35.1; 36.1. We have seen reason to identify this phrase as the mark of the redactor of the prose tradition, a redactor who included poetic passages within the collections.

(b) It has, following the poetic passages which are concluded with the special note of 31.26, a set of three prose passages introduced with the phrase 'Behold the days are coming'. This occurs within the prose collections as follows:

7.7.32, to introduce judgment
9.25, to introduce judgment
16.14, redemption from the north -a new Exodus
19.6, as 7.32.
23.5, the Davidic Branch, and 23.7 as 16.14.
33.14, as 23.5

The phrase also occurs in the poems against the nations (48.12; 49.2; 51/47, 52). We may say that in the collections following Baruch's Scroll, up to and including chapters 31–32, this phrase marks the introduction within the prose tradition of passages referring to the ultimate future from the perspective of the sixth century.

Since the phrase also occurs in 30.3, following the introductory formula noticed above, the conclusion seems inescapable that we are confronting the same editorial activity that we have seen in the earlier collections, that 30.4–31.26 is a collection of poetic material incorporated by this redactor and that 31.27–40 is the same sort of prose reproduction of the Jeremiah tradition that we have seen hitherto. This means that it is not necessarily a late appendix added to a scroll which happened to have space at the end, but a substantial part of the prose tradition that should be interpreted accordingly.

Fourteen or fifteen oracles are here knit together in a carefully constructed collection. Whatever the earlier history of the oracles may be, this redactoral activity is subsequent to the prophetic utterance. This leaves open the question of the dates and provenance of the individual oracles. The investigation is one of great complexity. Some oracles clearly assume the form of the prose tradition. Some are introduced from other collections. Some seem more closely related to the oracles in chapters 1–6 than to any others and, with their preoccupation with Jacob/Israel, belong perhaps to the earliest period of Jeremiah's ministry. Stylistic considerations support the view that the collection contains oracles which are the work of Jeremiah himself.

There is one feature of the collection which suggests that it was largely compiled within the period of the life of Jeremiah or shortly afterwards. There is no suggestion that the judgment is in the past. Individual oracles (30.4–7, 11, 12–17, 23–24; 31.15–20) seem to be presented from within the experience of desolation, and the fact that 31.15–20 comes very near the end of the collection may indicate that the redactor himself worked from within the same experience. The conclusion that this is a late compilation is altogether too facile.

Each oracle will be examined separately, and views about authorship and date are plainly disputable. Whatever may be the truth about their derivation and the situation of the original composition and utterance, the final editor has left a powerful and unified message. He announces, in a prose introduction, that the LORD will restore the fortunes of Israel and Judah, and bring his people back to the land he promised to them (30.3). This will happen against a background of great terror and tribulation in which men will be helpless like women in childbirth, and the hopeless question will be asked: 'Can Judah be saved from this?' But such is the Day of the LORD (30.4–7); the LORD will break the yoke (cf. 27.2) of foreign subjugation, and Judah will enjoy freedom under her own Davidic king (30.8–9). (Set in this context, vv. 5–7 may well be interpreted in a sense different from their original meaning. But the theme of the yoke shows that the redactor has in mind the end of the southern kingdom in 586).

In 30.10–11 (which are derived from 46.27–28 and absent from LXX), Israel is bidden to have no fear, because the LORD will save them from their distant land of captivity, making an end of the imperial powers but dealing judiciously with Israel.

This judicious treatment of Israel is spelt out in 30.12–17. Israel should neither be surprised nor complain that she had undergone heavy punishment at the hand of a merciless enemy, so flagrant are her sins. Nevertheless the roles will be reversed. Her enemies will become captive: she, the outcast for whom no one cares, will be liberated and restored. Then (30.18–22) traditional pictures of the secure and prosperous community will be fulfilled. The city will be rebuilt, happiness will abound, children will flourish, they will have their own ruler, the covenant will be secure.

30.23–24 reasserts the weight of the divine judgment as already described in vv. 5–6 and justified in vv. 10–17. these verses are as plainly the object of editorial arrangement here as in 23.19–20, where they also appear, complete with the closing didactic comment: 'In the latter days you will understand this'. They speak as though from the experience of the Wrath itself, as also do vv. 5–6, 11, 12–17. This means that the redactor is no easy-going purveyor of salvation hopes when peace has followed the storm, but one who understands the word of salvation to be the obverse side of the word of doom. He works from this situation. It is unwise therefore to assign a late date to this collection, at any rate in its earliest form. It was made within hailing distance of the ministry of Jeremiah himself, and therefore reflects his own mind and teaching.

The essentials have been said. Now a group of oracles are added which, in one way or another, spell out some of the implications. First 31.2–6 addresses the people of the northern kingdom now dispersed. Verse 2 seems to refer to the redemption from Egypt, the wilderness wandering and the final entry into the promised land. This is expressed in terms of the divine 'grace' and 'everlasting love', which is the earnest of a new demonstration of God's faithfulness. He will once again build up his people Israel, and settle them fruitfully and joyfully upon the mountains of Samaria. And from their northern home they will make pilgrimage to Zion. The assumption is that Zion is the centre of worship and of unity for the restored people, both north and south.

The accomplishment of the divine grace for Israel is now anticipated with a song of thanksgiving *as though it has already occurred* (31.7–9). The remnant of Israel is envisaged as saved, in terms of the classical picture of the ingathering. The language is like that of Second and Third Isaiah, but presents features of the Jeremiah tradition. From the north, which had been the dread source of Israel's punishment, the whole people, including the incapacitated, will be led as the father's first-born. In verses 10–14, which may or may not be separate from verses 7–9, a second oracle in the Isaiah style expresses the same picture of the ingathering of Jacob/Israel in terms of redemption (*pdh, g'l*), and the vision again includes the picture of their united worship on the heights of Zion. The crops, the herds, the young men and girls and the priests will all fulfil their purpose, as sorrow gives way to gladness.

At this point the tone appears to change. But the dialogue that follows in vv. 15–20 enforces the same message in a different form. The dialogue form suggests an independent oracle, complete in itself. The picture is of Rachel, the ancestress of the northern kingdom, wailing at the loss of her children in the place associated with her. The LORD bids her cease weeping, and reassures her that her sons will return to their own land, and that there is an ultimate hope. He then recites the complaint that he has heard Ephraim making . . . that he has been chastised like an animal, and he wants to return to his God, that he is ashamed and repentant. And of Ephraim he then speaks as his 'darling child', for whom his heart yearns and on whom he will have mercy.

The oracle in 31.21–22 speaks of the 'highway' by which the virgin Israel (contrast the image of the son in v. 20) shall return to her cities. This takes up both the language of Jeremiah, describing Israel as a 'faithless daughter' and that of Second Isaiah concerning 'the way'. In a difficult verse it seems to say that so great a reversal of the natural course of things will be tantamount to a new creative act. The comparison with Second Isaiah suggests that the oracle may have referred originally to the return from Babylon. However this may be, in its present context it refers to the ingathering of the scattered people of the north, unless it is intended to anticipate the oracle of Judah in vv. 23–25.

31.23–25 is in prose, and, since it draws the basic collection to an end, may well be the work of the redactor. He speaks of the restoration of Judah and her cities in the stereotyped commonplaces of v. 23 and quotes what may well be a greeting formula used by pilgrims coming to Zion for the feasts (cf. 31.6, 12). There will be pastoral prosperity (vv. 24, 25).

Verse 26 is unlikely to be a gloss. More probably it is the concluding formula of the collection of poetic oracles, corresponding to the unusual introduction in 30.2. This is presented as a scroll of the night visions of Jeremiah, that look into the future with hope and reassurance and are therefore 'pleasant'.

The collection of poetic oracles was supplemented with some material of the prose tradition. Verses 27–28 reaffirm the complete reversal of fortune, which will take place in terms of a repeated image of the prose tradition, noted in the vocabulary of Jeremiah himself (indeed it is the transformation of the tragic terms of his call, cf. 1.10; 24.7; 42.10; 45.4). Verse 29 introduces the popular saying, which is developed in an exemplary way in Ezek. 18 to assert the inescapable moral responsibility of the individual. But here the force of the saying is changed by its context. The emphasis is on the release which redemption will bring from corporate responsibility of the sins of the fathers. In the new age there will no longer be a dead weight of the entail of the past, but with a new start, the individual will simply be responsible for his own transgression. This is spelled out in 31.31–34 where the new dispensation is summed up in the image of a new covenant. As the present generation will no longer be burdened by the consequences of the sins of the fathers, so a new covenant of the individual will be inaugurated. As each man will be responsible for himself, so each man will have the divine instruction inscribed in his heart; he will know the Lord for himself and experience the liberation of forgiveness.

31.35–37 states allusively the permanence of the divine provision for Israel. The promise of seed once made to Abraham, will be as unbreakable as the order of nature. Verse 35b = Isa. 51.15 and perhaps indicates the editorial origin of the passage. This is another way of speaking of the divine faithfulness, as in 31.3.

Finally 31.38–40 states with circumstantial detail that the city will be rebuilt (cf. 31.4), and ends with an echo of the theme of uprooting and overthrowing which springs from Jeremiah's call (cf. 31.28).

Three themes stand out in this medley of oracles and traditional material connected, some directly and some indirectly, with the ministry of Jeremiah. There is the affirmation of hope out of the midst of judgment and tribulation; there is the special interest in the northern people coupled with insistence on the centrality of Zion; there is the new start summed up in the concept of a new covenant.

THE SUPERSCRIPTION 30.1–2

The instruction to **write in a book all the words that I have spoken to you** (v. 2) is unique in Jeremiah as the introduction to a collection of oracles. Clearly it echoes the instruction in 36.1. Whether Jeremiah himself at some stage following the fall of Jerusalem arranged his oracles of salvation in a scroll on the pattern of his earlier collection of oracles of doom, whether Baruch took the task upon himself or whether it is the work of another, unknown redactor, it is impossible to determine. The subscription is however best explained if it formed the beginning of a separate scroll, and 31.26, with its suggestion that the visions of the future were night-vision (cf. Zech. 4.1) may well have closed the collection, before it was supplemented. Verse 26 is not well explained as a gloss. The view that 31.27–39 contain a sort of supplement to the collection may be regarded as confirmed by the threefold **Behold the days are coming** in vv. 27, 31, 38, which is a characteristic expression of the prose tradition. That material was deposited in this way on the basis of a nucleus is amply illustrated elsewhere in prophetic collections and particularly in Isaiah (e.g. the repeated 'in that day' in Isa. 7.18, 20, 21, 23). The collection bears the marks of redactoral activity, but because it emphasises hope out of tribulation and speaks from experience of the trials of judgment, it is unlikely to be later than the later period of Jeremiah's ministry or at the latest that of Second Isaiah.

THE HOPE IN A NUTSHELL 30.3

For behold, days are coming: a formula which is characteristic of the Jeremiah prose tradition (7.32; 9.25; 16.14; 19.6; 23.5, 7; 31.27, 31, 38; 33.14; 48.12; 49.2; 51.47, 52 and only elsewhere in Am. 4.2; 8.11; 9.13; 1 Sam. 2.31; 2 Kg. 20.17 = Isa 39.6). See note on 23.5. The whole verse reads like a redactoral summing up of the message of hope in terms of familiar commonplaces, and must surely be linked with the threefold repetitions of 31.27, 31 and 38. The phrase **restore the fortunes** occurs more frequently in Jeremiah than in any other author, but is widely scattered though prophecy and the Psalter. Its context may give it the more precise interpretation of the older English versions; i.e. 'turn again the captivity', a meaning supported also by general usage, whether the verb is derived from the root *šbh* or from the root *šûb*.

The land which I gave to their fathers and they shall take possession of it is a Deuteronomic commonplace taken up in the Jeremiah prose tradition (7.7, 14; 14.5, 10; 23.39; 24.10; 25.5; 31.32; 32.22; 34.13; 35.15). In the phrase **Israel and Judah** (vv. 3, 4), Judah is often regarded as an editorial intrusion, reinterpreting a collection of oracles referring originally to the northern kingdom alone. This is unlikely. Concern with the southern kingdom cannot be erased, and the redactor's intention appears to have been comprehensive from the start. See also on vv. 8–9, 10–17, and note the same order in 31.27.

CAN JACOB BE SAVED? **30.4–7**

This oracle no doubt comes first in order to set the scene. It is an oracle which belongs to a period of tribulation and hopelessness, appropriately in *qinah* rhythm. If **Jacob** (v. 7) is to be understood as referring to the northern kingdom alone, then an appropriate situation has to be sought within the period of Jeremiah's ministry. This is difficult. It is easier to suppose that the term 'Jacob' is here, as in Second Isaiah, a way of speaking of the people of God and that the identity of the people of God was at this juncture invested in the southern kingdom. The 'great' day of the Lord is then the fall of the southern kingdom and its aftermath: hence the extreme desolation of the people, the men being as helpless as women in childbirth. The climax of this oracle is then better understood as a question: 'Shall he be saved out of it?' When however the redactor introduced vv. 8–9, it became natural to turn the question into a statement 'yet he shall be saved out of it '.

6. can a man bear a child? The irony is as obvious as the similar impossible questions asked by Amos (6.12). The prophet's listeners contribute their own answer. The cry of terror and panic can only be interpreted as reaction to the horrors of the times. But also this is meant to emphasise that redemption is not within human resources. Only a new divine intervention of grace, like a new creation, can save God's people. Cf. 31.8, 22, 27.

like a woman in labour: absent in LXX. The metre is improved without this expression, but if it is a gloss, it is one which correctly points the meaning.

7. Alas! that day. The day of judgment is the day of the Lord, as in 17.16–18, where it is described as the day of disaster and the day of evil. It is the 'great' day in Zeph. 1.14–16 and Jl 2.11, 31.

SECOND REDACTORAL SUMMARY OF ISRAEL'S HOPE 30.8–9

Whatever may have been the original application of the preceding oracle, the redactor himself interpreted it to refer to the southern kingdom, understood as the remaining representative of Israel, the people of promise. He shows this by his explicit allusion here to Jeremiah's sign of the yoke (27.2, 28.10). The message which on the lips of Hananiah had been false prophecy, resisted by Jeremiah with all his power, is, in the totally new situation, true. Israel has worn the yoke of iron. The divine punishment is complete. The divine mercy will bring liberation. The redactor may be understood to be speaking consistently with the mind of Jeremiah. The notion that a prophet, whose message is predominantly one of doom, is psychologically incapable of responding to hope when the storm is over, is not one that bears inspection. Ezekiel provides the classical example of the prophet who speaks appropriately before and after judgment.

and David their king: this reference to the future king (messiah) of the house of David is here a part of the redactoral structure, but that Jeremiah himself, in a guarded way, was receptive to 'the permanent central features of Israel's messianic ideal' was argued in the note on 23.1–8 q.v. The redactor therefore, from the outset, believed the collected oracles of chapters 30 and 31 to refer to Judah as well as Israel, as he made clear in vv. 3 and 4.

9. and strangers shall no more make servants of them: i.e. the reversal of the warning that the people would serve strangers in a foreign land, as given in 5.19. This is a relatively common prophetic image of judgment, cf. Isa. 1.7 and its reversal in Isa. 61.5 (cf. Jl. 4.17); Ezek. 7.21; 11.9; 28.7, 10; 30.12.

ASSURANCE OF LIBERATION 30.10–11

This oracle is repeated in 46.27–28. It is often said to be close to the thought and language of Second Isaiah, and therefore a late insertion in the Jeremiah tradition. The resemblance is however, superficial and really ends with the exhortation to Jacob to have no fear. This solemnly worded assurance no doubt had its origin in the 'priestly oracle of salvation' (Begrich) whose context was Israel's worship; and this provided the model for the similarly worded messages of hope both in Second Isaiah (41.10, 14; 43.1, 5; 44.2) and here in Jer. This alone diminishes the likelihood of a dependence of the Jeremiah tradition on Second Isaiah or vice versa. In fact, the use of these synonyms for fear in v. 10 (*yr'* and *ḥtt* in absolute form; cf. Isa. 51.7) is not found in Second Isaiah, but it is a feature of the Deuteronomic history (Dt. 1.21; 31.8; Jos. 8.1; 10.25; I Sam. 17.11; cf. also Jer. 23.4; 46.27).

10. shall return and have quiet is a suggestive use of vocabulary characteristic of First Isaiah.

none shall make him afraid is a widespread commonplace (Lev. 26.6; Mic. 4.4; Zeph. 3.13; Ezek. 34.28; 39.26; Job 11.19; Isa. 17.2).

11. I am with you to save you: (cf. 1.8; 15.20) may be regarded as an expression of the Jeremiah tradition.

I will make a full end of all the nations echoes Is. 10.23; 28.22, but is also in 4.27 and 5.10 within the Baruch scroll.

I will chasten you in just measure: as in 10.24. It is possible however that there is here a play on a nuance of the verb *niqqāh* and that the *NEB* (not followed in *REB*) has correctly caught the meaning with its translation: 'though I punish you as you deserve, I will not sweep you clean away'. Undeniably this more aptly, in context, brings the oracle to a consistent conclusion. Thus the *idea* of the message of assurance, based on the priestly model, is shared with Second Isaiah, but, the *form* it assumes here has features characteristic of the Jeremiah tradition, and is somewhat eclectic,

I will by no means leave you unpunished is found in Jer. 25.29.

This oracle is absent from the equivalent chapter 37 in the LXX but present in chapter 26 (LXX, equivalent to MT 46.27-28). This renders improbable the theory that 5-7 and 10-11 were originally a unity which was broken by the insertion of vv. 8-9. No doubt this oracle was placed here by the redactor precisely because it presents so appropriate an answer to the question raised in v. 7, in the manner of a priest's answer to a worshipper's lament. At the same time it fills out some of the implications of the liberation promised in v. 8.

(1) The Lord will bring back his scattered people
(2) He will grant them security and peace

(3) He will bring judgment to bear upon the nations who have been the instrument of judgment

(4) Though he will spare his people he will temper mercy with justice so that they are appropriately chastened

This latter theme of the degree to which Israel's punishment is but the appropriate reward of her sin forms the transition to the next section.

HOPE TEMPERED 30.12–17

This oracle betrays its independence of what goes before and what follows by the use of the second person *feminine*. In vv. 10–11 Jacob/Israel is addressed; here Zion the mother. Significantly Zion is explicitly mentioned in v. 17. This is consistent with the purpose of the redactor, as made clear in vv. 8–9, to apply his material to the situation following the fall of Jerusalem. He is not concerned with the divided kingdoms of history, but with Israel/Zion considered as God's people.

Some scholars think that there is a fundamental inconsistency in the oracle, that vv. 10–15 expressing hopelessness are contradicted by vv. 16–17 offering restoration. Duhm sought to solve the problem by regarding vv. 10–15 as the original oracle (in the metre characteristic of Jeremiah), and vv. 16–17 as the work of a subsequent author who betrayed his hand both by the illogical **therefore** and by a difference of metre.

This view is improbable. We cannot rivet a metrical form on Jeremiah since we have no means of identifying all the processes to which his oracles were subject in the tradition. A better explanation lies in the recognition that, in this oracle, the Lord himself reminds his people of their condition in terms of their own lament. The 'therefore' in v. 16 marks the point where the Lord's answer is given. It has no intrinsic logical force. The answer corresponds both to the announcement of judgment in a prophetic oracle and to a priest's answer to a worshipper seeking divine reassurance. Verses 12–17 should therefore be interpreted as a unity, the precise original form of the oracle being hidden from us.

As a unity the passage illustrates in more detail the affirmation of v. 11 that, though the Lord will save his people, his mercy is judiciously tempered with appropriate chastisement. The Lord recognises the extreme gravity of Israel's brokenness, speaking of it explicitly as a discipline and no more than her sins have required. It is the Lord himself who has thus treated his people (v. 15); but by the same token, it is the Lord who will reverse the tragedy so that Israel's enemies will, in their turn, go into captivity, and Israel will be healed (v. 17) and be no more an object of mockery.

12. Your hurt is incurable, and your wound is grievous: Despite LXX, which had either a different or a defective text, this is likely to represent the correct text, the idiomatic, emphatic *lamed* (*lᵉśiḇᵉrēḵ*), which older scholars found perplexing, probably pointing to its authenticity. The translation 'incurable' perhaps goes beyond the meaning of *'ānûš*, which is 'dangerously ill'. Arguments about the sequence of thought should not therefore be based on the categorical negative 'incurable'. Jeremiah uses these phrases of his own suffering in 15.18, but the idea is more thoroughly developed here. Translate: 'You are ill to breaking-point'.

There is none to uphold your cause, no medicine for your wound, no healing for you: the legal picture is said to confuse the medical metaphor. Many scholars, followed by *NEB* and *REB* regard it as a gloss. But Heb. poetry of the highest quality passes quickly from one metaphor to another, and there is no adequate reason for altering the text. 'medicine–no healing for you' is found in 46.11. The use of part-phrases in different contexts is vividly illustrated in Ps. Sol. and raises no problem within the same book.

14. All your lovers: cf. 2.25, where those loved are 'strangers', 2.33, 3.1, and 22.10, 22. As in chapter 2, the lovers are the nations with which Judah has compromised herself, with inevitable apostasy (c.f. v. 16), expressing imaginatively what is stated in more straightforward terms in v. 11. The link is with early oracles whose theme has been seen to have a marked affiliation to that of Hosea.

the punishment of a merciless foe: the word *mûsar*, 'discipline', 'chastening', is much used in Jeremiah (cf. 2.30). Here it provides a catch-word, linking this oracle with the previous one ('I will chasten you' in v. 11).

16. This verse expresses in four associated images the prophetic principle that those nations that have been used by God to be the instruments of his judgment, eventually have to submit to the very punishment they have administered.

THE MESSIANIC HOPE 30.18–22

Something of the content of the future hope is presented in this oracle, addressed to Jacob. Some have thought this a continuation of vv. 10–11, vv. 12–17 being an intrusion. But this is both to misunderstand the way redactors worked and to ignore differences. In vv. 10–11 Jacob was addressed in the second person masculine. In vv. 12–17, Zion was addressed in the second person feminine. Here the Lord refers to Jacob in the third person singular in a way that may be interpreted collectively, and in v. 22 uses the second person plural. The oracle therefore stands independently, but is used by the redactor to open up the meaning of the promise made in v. 10.

'Jacob' stands for the holy people and in no way restricts the oracle to the northern kingdom. It is inconceivable that the Jeremiah tradition should have thought of the restoration of an independent ruler of the north. Nor is it necessary to deny the essential messianic character of the oracle. The 'prince' or 'ruler', though referred to in unusual terms (see below) is not different from the 'David their King' of v. 9. Just as features of the messianic age are described in prophecy sometimes without any reference to the messiah at all, so there is no absolute consistency in describing the future king.

The future hope includes these elements:

(a) The restoration of all the clans of the holy people
(b) The rebuilding of the city (cities) and the fine buildings now reduced to rubble
(c) A new era marked by thanksgiving and joy
(d) The LORD's people will be many and honoured
(e) The presence of children as in the past, and the renewal of the integrity of the whole congregation of Israel
(f) Israel will have her own ruler, and be no longer subject to an alien domination. This ruler will have access to the LORD, as Israel's own king should
(g) The covenant will be reaffirmed.

18. the tents of Jacob: an archaic figure for the clans of Jacob.

the city shall be rebuilt upon its mound: probably collective, and including Jerusalem. Similarly, the 'palace' refers to all the fine buildings which had been destroyed, but includes the pre-eminent mansion which is that of the king. The 'mound' is essentially a mound created by ruins, as is explicit in Jos. 8.28 and Jer. 49.2, cf. Dt. 13.17.

20. and their congregation shall be established before me: the word 'ēdâ may not be inaccurately translated 'community', in view of our narrowing of the meaning of the word 'congregation'. But it has special overtones. The congregation of Israel is the people conscious of being God's own people identifying themselves in worship and in fidelity to the covenant, witnessing to their God. See on 31.8. LXX translates 'witness'.

21. Their prince . . . ruler: these terms are, in themselves, capable of a variety of interpretations and do not necessarily refer to the king. Thus *'addîr* here translated 'prince', means 'majestic', 'great' and is used of the sea, of majestic trees (Isa. 10.34, Zech. 11.2), of nobles, nations, of Yahweh himself. (In Jer. 25.34, 36, the 'lords [*'addîrê*] of the flock' are kings). It is of course appropriate, in context, to use it of the ideal king. 'Ruler' (*mōšēl*) is similarly capable of the sort of versatile use the word has in English, but particularly appropriate of the king. In 22.30 and 33.26 it is used explicitly of the davidic king or messiah of the future. It is the context which is decisive. Here the underlying presupposition is that Israel is subject to foreign rulers. The time will come when she will have her own ruler, drawn from herself, in the way it should be. That the ruler's access to Yahweh is now made a feature of this hope, tells against the collective interpretation (LXX) of these terms and supports the royal interpretation. In Zech 4.1-6a, 10b-14 prince and high priest together are the attendant servants of Yahweh. Despite their need for prophetic warning, the kings had been in a special sense God's men (David, Solomon) with special functions in worship. The principle that only those explicitly permitted may draw near to Yahweh is laid down again and again (Exod. 19.12-13, 21-25, Num. 12) but the kings themselves must not overstep their limits (I Sam. 13.6-14; 2 Chr. 26.16-23). LXX seems to have misunderstood the verse.

22. Omitted by LXX and no doubt added appropriately from the prose tradition. See on 7.23. But also note 31.1, which is in LXX.

JUDGMENT REAFFIRMED **30.23-24**

This is the second passage in chapter 30 which occurs elsewhere in the book, in 23.19-20, q. v. It is a reaffirmation of judgment in the well known image of the storm. In neither place does it sit easily and must be regarded as owing its place to editorial arrangement. The redactor is acutely conscious that the preceding oracles of hope, however tempered, are being communicated in a period which seems to mock them. Nevertheless all is the design of God. In this context the 'intents of his mind' (v. 24) include the judgment on Israel's enemies, and that is, of course, a form of the hope.

23. Wrath has gone forth: This reads intrusively and clumsily in the Heb. By a simple change of pointing, adopted by *NEB* and *REB*, it is possible to read: 'See what a scorching wind has gone out from the LORD'. 'Wrath' would then be explained as a natural assimilation to 'the fierce anger of the LORD' in v. 24.

NOTE ON 31.1-26

Although reasons have been given for interpreting chapters 30–31 together, as presenting, in their present form a unified theme of hope, there are nonetheless grounds for discerning a special feature in 31.1-26. This is its explicit concern with the northern kingdom.

The earlier oracles of chapter 30 addressed to Jacob/Israel, may, in their earliest form, have concerned the northern kingdom, though this is by no means certain, since Israel, theologically, as in Second Isaiah, may refer to the whole People of God. It is however almost certain that under the hand of the redactor they are addressed to the southern kingdom as the surviving representative of the People of God.

In 31.1-26, on the other hand, there is no ambiguity: a series of oracles refer to the northern kingdom specifically (Ephraim in vv. 6, 9, 18, 20; Samaria in v. 5; Rachel in v. 15), and to the hope of a comprehensive ingathering. This confers a special character upon them. There is no adequate reason for denying that Jeremiah, in view of the place of his birth, entertained a hope for the restoration of his own people; nor need a wedge be driven between chapters 30 and 31. A redactor might be expected to regard these oracles as the further explication of the hope expressed in chapter 30, as expressing a hope beyond hope. Zion, as in second Isaiah, remains the centre of the restored Israel's life (31.6, and 12) and this, in the context now provided, becomes the meaning of the Judah oracle (31.23-25) with which the collection is brought to an end.

1. The new section 31.1-26 is introduced by a simple prose statement of the covenant relationship (present in LXX, unlike the corresponding 30.22).

THE RESTORATION OF THE NORTHERN PEOPLE 31.2-6

The main drift of this oracle is clear. Upon the basis of the favour and love (*heseḏ*) of the LORD, the northern people will be restored outwardly and inwardly. Outwardly, this restoration will be marked by rebuilding and the renewal of prosperity, symbolised by fruitful vineyards in the central region (Samaria). Inwardly, their fidelity to their God will be shown by their pilgrimages to Zion. Unreserved joy will accompany the new era.

There are considerations which suggest that this oracle belongs to the later Jeremiah tradition, perhaps in the period of Second Isaiah. Only here and in vv. 9, 18, 20, is the northern kingdom referred to as Ephraim, which seems to mark it off from other oracles of Jeremiah. Scholars have asked which period in the life of Jeremiah would best provide a background for such an oracle. Could it be the earliest period of his ministry or perhaps before the murder of Gedaliah? They have speculated whether the vision of pilgrims going to Zion may have been suggested by the sight of men travelling from Shechem, Shiloh, and Samaria to present offerings at the ruined Temple (after the murder of Gedaliah. — Jer. 41.5). But how is this consistent with his sustained polemic against the Temple? The very difficulty inherent in these speculations encourages the hypothesis that this is the work of the later tradition. And if this were so, it would only illustrate how the word of God, in its completeness, is spoken not to one man but to several, that the greatest prophet needs complementing if his message is not to be one sided.

But could this paradoxically be too easy a conclusion? What are we to make of the following features?

(a) the relation to Hosea. It is Hosea who characteristically refers to his people as Ephraim (no less than thirty four times); Hosea who sees the wilderness as a time of favour; Hosea who uses the language of love and devotion (ḥeseḏ). Indeed it is difficult not to discern a verbal relationship between v. 3 and Hos. 11.1, and 4. Some relationship between Jer. and Hos. is already clear (See on 2.2-3, 26-28; 31.9).
(b) the uniqueness of the LORD's declaration in v. 4.
(c) the obscurity of the text in v. 2.

The textual problem suggests that the redactor's hand has not been strong upon the oracle, and comparable difficulties in LXX suggest that the textual corruption goes back earlier than the separation of the two streams. The uniqueness of v. 4 restrains attribution to some later writer. And the close relationship to 2.2-3, q.v. associates the oracle with material unequivocally the work of the young prophet. At the very least it is wise to be open minded.

2. The people who survived the sword found grace in the wilderness: the expression 'found grace' is used five times in Exod. 31.12-17. The stress on the wilderness period as one of the promise of youth is confined to Hos. and Jer. (see on 2.2-3). But in the present context, the meaning is allusive. Is this a direct reference to survival from the sword of the Egyptians? Or does the prophet speak directly of the consequences of 586 as a new wilderness period? Or is the poetic allusiveness meant to embrace both?

When Israel sought for rest: the Heb. is obscure, but emendations to not yield a significantly different meaning. *NEB* draws out legitimately the implications of *ḥālôk*, translating: 'Israel journeyed to find rest'. *REB* changes this to 'The LORD went to give rest to Israel'. The thought is of the wilderness wandering leading to the land of promise. The idea of the 'rest' for the fulfilment of promise, (though other words are used, e.g. *mᵉnûḥāh* in Dt. 12.9; Ps. 95.11) is familiar in the *OT*, as also in the *NT* in Heb. 3; 4.

3. the LORD appeared to him from afar: as no doubt the LORD appeared to Moses. The theophany gives the greatest possible weight to the divine declaration that follows.

I have loved you with an everlasting love: this remarkably emphatic self-witness is unparalleled in this form. Nevertheless it brings to expression a principle which underlies much prophecy, viz. that the basis of the covenant is the divine love (cf. Dt. 7.7–11; Hos; Isa. 41.8; 49.14), and that this love is both of old and eternal (the Heb. bears both meanings). *REB* 'I have dearly loved you from old'.

therefore I have continued my faithfulness (*ḥeseḏ*) to you: the expression *mᵉšaktîk ḥāseḏ*, by reason of its construction, suggests Hos. 11.4, where both verb and noun occur. But the sense of Pss. 36.10 (cf. 109.12) is perhaps closer. See on Jer. 2.2.

4. The prediction of a time of joy reverses the gloomy predictions of 7.34; 16.9; 25.10. The stereotyped expressions of the prose tradition are not however reproduced in this poetic piece.

5. the planters shall plant, and shall enjoy the fruit: this much disputed line is perhaps best treated as a dependent clause as in the *NEB* and translated: '(vineyards) which those who planted them defiled'. The selecting of vineyards as symbol of the restoration of Israel's economic and agricultural life is specially apt in view of the prophetic description of Israel as the LORD's vineyard (Isa. 5.1–7; 4.14; Ezek. 19.10–14; Ps. 80). *REB* reverts to the translation favoured by *RSV* above.

6. Arise let us go up to Zion: The centrality of Zion as the rallying point of the returning exiles, the unifying focus of restored Israel as the spiritual magnet of the world, is a powerful theme of the Isaiah tradition (2.2–5; 42.6; 11.10–16; 12; 18.7; 24.21–25; 27.12–13; 33.17–22; 35, 49, 60). It is part of the Zion theology in all its forms, and a feature of Israel's worship (Pss. 46; 48; 122; Zech. 14.16–21). Is this part of the thinking of Jeremiah? (Cf. 50.4–5). The answer is that it could well be, and for three reasons.

First, because the Deuteronomic law required exclusive worship at the central sanctuary on Zion and, if our interpretation of 11.1–14 is correct,

Jeremiah championed the reform. Even if, as seems probable, he became disillusioned by the political exploitation of the reform, he may well have looked to a time when Zion would truly fulfil the divine intention. Such a hope could have been aroused in the latest period of his ministry, i.e. after the judgment.

Second, the centrality of Zion was a firm part of the prophetic tradition, so that even Amos, prophet of the north, acknowledged that the LORD roared from Zion and uttered his voice from Jerusalem (1.2). Third, the centrality of Zion is the unstated presupposition of the oracles on the Foe from the North (Jer. 4.6, 31; 6.2, 23; cf. 8.19; 9.19; 14.19; 30.17). It is just because Jeremiah shared the belief that Zion is central to the divine purpose that these oracles were so terrible, not only to his hearers but also to himself. It is therefore unwise to be dogmatically negative about the attribution of the thought of these oracles to Jeremiah. Particularly premature is the speculative but dogmatic scepticism of Carroll, who writes: 'The fictional Jeremiah created by the tradition is temperamentally incapable of uttering such images of love and merrymaking'.

THANKSGIVING TO ANTICIPATE THE INGATHERING **31.7-9**

The opening 'thus says the LORD' is the familiar introduction to prophecy. And prophecy this is. What has been implicit in vv. 2-6 is now made explicit. The restoration of the northern people involves the ingathering of those scattered in exile, and the LORD announces that he will bring back his people, even those who cannot make their own way, from the dreaded north and from 'the farthest parts of the earth'. The Father of Ephraim will re-establish his first born. This prophecy is set in a psalm context, but not in the conventional psalm pattern. The thanksgiving begins, like some hymns of descriptive praise in the Psalter, with a call to praise in the imperative. But, unlike these psalms, it then proceeds to describe a saving act of Yahweh. This is exactly the phenomenon that is found in Second Isaiah–(see C. Westermann, *Isaiah 40–66*, 1969, p. 102) — (Isa 42. 10–11; 44.23; 48.20; 49.13; 52.7–10, cf. also Isa. 12). It is the adaption of psalm language for prophetic purposes. Like the so-called prophetic perfect, the thanksgiving is in anticipation of the redemption the LORD will bring. It expresses supreme certainty.

The theme of ingathering is pervasive within the final form of the Jeremiah tradition (23.3; 29.14; 30.3; 32.37; 46.27). See on 23.1–8 for the view that it is not easy to dissociate some form of this hope from the horizon of the prophet. 29.14 may be regarded as the intervention of the redactor. Nowhere is there the sustained development of the idea of the ingathering that we find in Isa. 11, 49, and 60. This passage is the major treatment of it within the book of Jeremiah. For the development of the theme in Judaism, see J. Klausner, *The Messianic Idea in Israel*, 1956, part III, chapter VIII.

7. Sing aloud: the verb (*ronnû*) is used often in the Psalter, but, in combination with 'raise shouts' (*ṣahᵃlû*), is found in the similar psalm Isa. 12 and also in Isa. 24.14.

for Jacob, . . . for the chief of the nations: in the LXX 'for Jacob' is added to the introduction 'Thus says the LORD'. This may well be right, in which case translate: 'and raise shouts over the chief of the nations'. The discomfiture of the nations is the obverse side of Israel's vindication.

8. Behold, I will bring them from the north country: *hinᵉnî* with participle, a characteristic usage of the Jeremiah tradition. The description of the region where Israel was scattered as the 'north' is appropriate to describe the reversal of fortune. Judgment came from the north: now salvation.

among them the blind and the lame: LXX has 'at the feast of Passover'. This represents only a slight variation of the consonants with some repointing. But the phrase would be unique and it has every appearance of the late doctoring of a disturbed text. Moreover, the LXX rendering of 'the woman with child . . . ' does not inspire confidence that it understood the correct text. Indeed the addition of 'sons of Levi' to priests in 31.14, together with this 'feast of Passover' suggests that the LXX text has been subject to a very late orthodox editing. MT, despite the perhaps questionable *bām* 'among them', (cf. Isa. 6.12) is to be preferred. The mention of the blind, and particularly the lame, as being brought home by the miracle of the divine redemption is a familiar theme in the Isaiah tradition (Isa. 33.23; 35.5, 6; 42. 16; Mic. 4.7).

a great company: *qāhāl gāḏôl*, cf. 44.15, cf.the *qāhāl rāb* of Pss. 40, 10, 11. This is the word most characteristically used to describe Israel's existence as God's people. The LXX saw no special significance and translated 'a large crowd'.

9. and with consolations: In this case LXX is to be preferred. The Heb. 'supplication' can be explained as an assimilation to 3.21. Translate: 'I will comfort them and lead them back', cf. Isa. 40.1.

I will make them walk by brooks of water; in a straight path: a quiet combination of images which come to sustained and classical expression in the Isaiah tradition.

On the straight way, cf. Isa. 40.3–4; 35.8–10; 45.13. On the desert made fertile, cf. Isa. 35.1–2, 6–7; 41.18–20; 43.19–21; 51.3; 55.12–13. **in which they shall not stumble:** thus reversing the prophecies of 6.21 and 18.15, where the people stumbled because they had strayed into 'bypaths, not the highway'.

for I am a father to Israel and Ephraim is my first-born: this unqualified declaration of the divine fatherhood is the answer to the doubts expressed in 3.4, 19, 'I thought you would call me, My Father, and would not turn from following me', cf. also 2.27, and of course Hos. 11.1. This double relationship with the early chapters of Jer., where the Hosea affiliation is so marked, and with Hosea, cannot be a coincidence. Rudolph is surely correct that the description of Ephraim as the Lord's first born is made in contrast not to Judah, but to the nations, cf. Ps. 89.27 where the usage becomes clear. David is first-born in comparison with the kings of the earth and so cries 'Thou art my Father'.

THE RESTORATION PROCLAIMED TO THE WORLD **31.10–14**

Within the context of chapters 30–31, this oracle is simply variation on the same theme. The declaration that the LORD will father his scattered people (v. 10) has been made more fully in v. 8; that he has saved Jacob (v. 11) has been affirmed in v. 7; that subsequently Israel will make pilgrimage to Zion (v. 12) has been the theme of v. 6. The prospect of economic health (vv. 12–13) has been offered in v. 5. The note of rejoicing (v. 13) has been already struck in 30.19 and 31.4. What is fresh here is that all this is proclaimed to the world (v. 10) and the language is differently minted.

The echoes of Second Isaiah have been often noted. The rhetorical address to the nations is a characteristic of Second Isaiah; cf. Isa. 49.1 as one example among many, where also the address is to the 'coastlands'. The word here translated 'redeemed' (*g'l*) is a notable feature of Second Isaiah and does not otherwise occur in the poetical oracles of Jeremiah. The expression 'a watered garden' is otherwise found only in Isa. 58.11. Verse 13b echoes Isa. 35.

Even so, there are other features which suggest that this oracle is not borrowed from another tradition but belongs firmly to the Jeremiah tradition. First, the concentration of themes already expressed in these chapters, as noted above, suggests a primary relationship to this context; and second, this relationship is widened to the context of the earlier collections of Jeremiah's oracles of doom, when it is observed how the passage provides answers to the old warnings.

Thus the nations, who are now to hear the news of Israel's salvation, are those who had been explicitly warned of the coming instruments of judgment in Jerusalem (4.16). The LORD, who will now shepherd his flock, is he who had spoken of foreign rulers as shepherds (6.3; 12.10; 23.1) and promised his people that they would have good shepherds of their own (3.15, 23.1–4). Only, the prose tradition does not speak of the LORD himself as the shepherd. In this respect 31.10 is closer to Isa. 40.11. The 'grain, the wine and the oil' is a favourite expression of Dt., but also occurs significantly in Hos. 2.10, 24. The turning of mourning into joy reverses the considerable emphasis Jeremiah placed on mourning as a sign of the judgment (9.10–22; 14.1–10; 15.5–9; 22.10–12). See also, note on v. 13. Moreover, there are signs of the catchword principle making the immediate connection of this oracle with the preceding one ('gather' vv. 8, 10; 'sing aloud' vv. 7, 12; 'comfort' vv. 9 [emended], 13), cf. also 'dance' in vv. 4, 13. A reasonable conclusion would be that this is an oracle of the Jeremiah tradition, carefully introduced into this collection by the redactor, but one which owes something to the vocabulary and ethos of Second Isaiah.

11. ransomed: Heb. *pdh* cf. 15.21, where it is impossible to know whether we are dealing with the vocabulary of Jeremiah or of a successor in the tradition. The word is used in Isa. 35.10; 51.11; and Isa. 1.27, where also it appears to be part of exilic editing.

redeemed: Heb. *g'l*. See above. The two terms are here synonymous. they seem to be derived from different origins, *pdh* containing the idea of price, and expressing the idea of release through ransom; *g'l* having a legal background and expressing the responsibility of the next of kin, as in Ru. 3–4, Jer. 32.6–15. This background made it peculiarly suitable to use of the LORD himself in relation to Israel (Job 19.25; Second Isaiah *passim*). They are here essentially soteriological terms, expressing the idea of redemption in fulfilment of the LORD's purpose for his people. It is however too easy to conclude that this is a post-exilic usage, since the verbs are similarly used synonymously in Ps. 69.19 and Hos. 13.14. The date of both passages is disputed. The view of the present writer is that Ps. 69 belongs to the period of the monarchy and that the denial of Hos. 13.4 to Hosea creates rather than solves problems. If yet once again therefore the Jeremiah passage is influenced by Hosea (see also on v. 12), the reader will not be surprised.

12. the height of Zion: otherwise in 17.12, a disputed passage, q.v., which in my view cannot be denied to Jeremiah.

and they shall be radiant: the verb *nāhar* can mean either 'flow' or 'shine'. The meaning 'flow' would suit 'the goodness of the LORD' and echo Isa. 2 = Mic. 4.1. But the rest of the verse would then have to be a gloss, for which there is no independent evidence. The meaning 'be radiant' is sufficiently attested by Ps. 34.6 and particularly Isa. 60.5. It is therefore to be preferred.

the grain, the wine, and the oil: this combination is frequent in Dt. 7.13, etc. and occurs also in Hos. 2.10, 24. The relation of the book of Jeremiah to both Dt. and Hos. makes this particularly suggestive. See above.

13. the maidens rejoice in the dance: the word 'dance' here and in v. 4 occurs nowhere else in Jeremiah. It is found in Pss. 149.3 and 150.4, not at all in Isaiah. In Lam. 5.15, we have 'dancing' turned to mourning, and the reverse in Ps. 30.11: 'Thou hast turned for me my mourning into dancing' and this is what is being said here. There is no reason for thinking Ps. 30 to be a late psalm. This reinforces the judgment made in the general note to this section that this oracle is only superficially Deutero-Isaianic.

14. I will feast the soul of the priests with abundance: 'soul' (*nepeš*) here represents the whole person and has nothing to do with the spiritual welfare of the priests. Translate with *NEB* and *REB* 'I will satisfy the priests with the fat of the land'. 'Abundance' is more accurately 'fat', and particularly the fat of sacrifices. The more prosperous the land and the more secure Zion and its Temple, the more will the priests enjoy their legitimate portion of the beasts brought for sacrifice. The verse is not primarily about priests but about the restoration of worship, which their prosperity symbolises. Thus understood, this verse does not really qualify for dismissal as a gloss. LXX has it, though it omits 'fat' and adds 'priests sons of Levi'. 'Fat' is surely right, since it is parallel with 'goodness', and 'sons of Levi' is plainly a gloss and confirms the view that in this chapter LXX is not to be preferred to MT. See note on v. 8.

RACHEL'S GRIEF AND EPHRAIM'S REPENTANCE **31.15–20**

The next section betrays its separateness by its form. It is a dialogue. Rachel speaks first (v. 15). She is answered by the LORD directly in terms of her plaint (vv. 16–17). Ephraim then speaks (vv. 18–19), his repentance presented as a quotation by the LORD himself. But this does not in fact weaken the dialogue structure. The LORD concludes the dialogue (v. 20). There are no echoes of Second Isaiah as there are in the previous oracle. The northern kingdom is once again Ephraim, as in the previous oracles vv. 2–6 and 7–9, and the connections, both with

the early oracles of Jeremiah and with Hosea, are striking. These are
drawn out in the comments that follows. Note particularly the dialogue
of repentance in 3.21–4.4.

There are three strikingly new elements. First, the grief of Rachel,
mother of Joseph and Benjamin and ancestress of the northern people.
Accordingly to Gen. 35.16 and I Sam. 10.2, her grave was at Ephrath
on the northern border of Benjamin, very close to Anathoth. The
alternative tradition that it was a mile north of Bethlehem rests on a
palpable gloss in Gen. 35.19 and is to be rejected. This means of course
that Jeremiah may well have had a special youthful veneration for this
mother of Israel. However that may be, the cry of Rachel is imaginative,
powerful and evocative. The subsequent dialogue shows that her lost
children are the people scattered by the Assyrian invasion in the eighth
century, since the promise is twice affirmed that they will return from
the land of the enemy. It is not really convincing to speculate, as some
have done, that Jeremiah uttered the oracle at Ramah when, released
from a gang of prisoners, he watched some of his countrymen being
transported to Babylon. The present context is a safer guide to its
interpretation. This original and unforgettable image is not to be
attributed to subsequent preachers or redactors; it is the utterance of the
poet himself.

The second new element is equally compelling. The repentance of
Ephraim is imaginatively presented as though he were the prodigal son.
It is true that there has already been a dialogue of repentance in 3.21–4.4.
This also begins with a 'voice' weeping and pleading for Israel's sons.
There the voice is not specified, and the repentance is developed in prosaic
terms of the tradition. Here the poetic momentum is maintained and there
is no sign of later doctoring. There is no reason to suppose that this
corresponds to an act of contrition publicly confessed. Jeremiah projects
the confession in the form of prophecy. He was unlikely to have so
expressed himself if he was not aware that the contemporary
representatives of scattered Israel were in a chastened frame of mind.
On the other hand, he is basically expressing his understanding of the
indispensable condition of the LORD's merciful redemption and of the
emotive response of v. 20.

The third element is the LORD's unrestrained love of Ephraim (v.
20). For all the past faithlessness he remains his 'darling child'. This is
strongly reminiscent of Hos. 11.1, 3, 4.

'When Israel was a child, I loved him . . .
Yet it was I who taught Ephraim to walk,
I took them up in my arms;
but they did not know what I healed them.
I led them with cords of compassion,
with the bands of love.'

Both Hos. 11.1 13, 4 and this passage have a strongly emotional tone. This is the everlasting love of v. 3, and it is a permanent contribution to the religion of mankind.

15. A voice is heard in Ramah: see above. Cf. the voice in 3.21. This similarity is strengthened by the related reference to weeping. And the bitter (*tamʿrûrîm*) weeping answers to the bitter provocation of Hos. 12.15.

16. your work shall be rewarded: i.e. Rachel's labour is bringing up her children. Isa 1.2.

17. There is hope for your future: for the meaning of this see on 29.11 (cf. 23.20), a prose addition which may well be derived from this poetic original.

18. Thou hast chastened me and I was chastened: the Heb. is capable of several meanings, but this translation is to be preferred to the *NEB*'s effort to carry through consistently the analogy of the untamed calf— 'Thou has trained me to the yoke like an unbroken calf'. Full weight should surely be given to the parallelism:

Thou has chastened me that I might be chastened,
Restore me that I may turn back (to the LORD).

Then the meaning is: 'You have disciplined me that I might really learn discipline' (cf. Volz). The image of the untamed calf is then an added illustration.

19. after I was instructed: this is a not impossible rendering of the niph. of the Heb. verb *ydʿ*, since the niph. may sometimes serve as a passive of the hiph'il. But it is strained. This is an example where the otherwise well attested meaning of *ydʿ* as 'to be made quiet, submissive' is to be preferred. (D. Winton Thomas, *JTS* 35 (1934) 304 and supported by G. R. Driver and *NEB* 'now that I am tamed' and REB.) Verses 18–19 now have a nice poetical balance:

Thou has chastened me that I might learn to
be disciplined,
like an untrained calf;
Restore me that I may turn back,
for thou art the LORD my God,
For after I turned away I repented
and after I was reduced to submission, I smote
upon my thigh.

I smote upon my thigh: a sign of mourning, as in Ezek. 21.17. The *sense* is that of the frank paraphrase in *TEV*, 'we hung our heads in grief'. E. Lipinski notes that the same expression occurs in the Sumerian and Accadian versions of the Descent of Ishtar and is therefore attested in Mesopotamia. The same custom was found among the Greeks (as in Homer).

the disgrace of my youth: contrast 'devotion of your youth' in 2.2; 'the friend of my youth' in 3.4. In the parallel dialogue of repentance, Israel confesses: 'From our youth . . .'. Cf. also 22.21. Hos 2.15 significantly links this youth with her wilderness origins. She shall make a new beginning from the valley of Achor, 'and there she shall answer as in the days of her youth'. The links with the earliest collection of Jeremiah oracles and with Hosea are once again evident.

20. Is Ephraim my dear son? Cf. Hos 11.1. The word translated 'darling' suggests special delight, as in Isa. 5.7 and especially Prov. 8.31; Ps 119.24.

For as often as I speak against him: this is the normal meaning of the Heb. verb *dabbēr*. The existence of a homonym meaning 'turn aside', and in the hiph'il 'drive back' is however attested by Ps. Sol. 2.25, where the literal LXX translation makes no kind of sense. This *dābar* is no doubt related to the Accadian *dabaru* 'push back'. Follow therefore *NEB*, which renders: 'As often as I turn my back on him, I still remember him'. *REB* returns to the traditional translation.

RETURN, VIRGIN ISRAEL **31.21-22**

The separateness of this brief and tantalising oracle is shown by the address to the Virgin Israel in the second person feminine. In vv. 7-9, 15-20 the oracles have concerned Ephraim as the Lord's son, and in vv. 10-14 Israel is likewise in the third person masculine. This is then a reversion to the address of vv. 3-4. From the redactor's point of view it follows the previous oracles intelligibly. The LORD's message of salvation has been delivered to the scattered northern people; their repentance is assured. Now is the time for action.

The oracle takes up the theme of the highway central in the Isaianic tradition (Isa. 11.16; 19.23; 40.3; 49.11; 62.10; 35.8) and refers to it as though it is already a known image: 'Consider well the highway, the road by which you went'. The question 'How long will you waver?' suggests that the opportunity is already present and the response is half-hearted. Either this belongs to a period when the Babylonian grip was weakened, and groups of Israelites had the chance they were hesitant to take, or it belongs to the period of the more liberal Persian domination.

22. faithless: cf. 8.5 and the noun in 3, 6, 8, 11, 12, 22 and Hosea 14.5. The form here could very well be explained by the requirements of the pun as explained below.

a new thing: used of a new divine intervention in Isa. 42.9; 43.19 and corresponding to a new song, Isa. 42.10; Ps. 33.3; 40.3; 96.1; 98.1; 144.9; 149.1.

A woman protects a man: This last line is a crux. Carroll calls it 'perhaps the most incomprehensible saying in the whole book'. The LXX offers no help and gives no evidence that it was in touch with the correct text. Either the Massoretic version must be abandoned or an attempt must be made to interpret it as it stands. The following is a suggestion. The word for woman (*neqēbāh* in Gen. 1.27 and in Lev. suggests woman's sexuality as differentiated from man's (*zākār*). These two words are correctly translated male and female. The word used here for man (*geber*) is also used in Dt. to denote man as distinct from woman (e.g. Dt. 22.5 'A woman shall not wear anything that pertains to a man' (*geber*)). If there is a common feature, suggested by context, in the more than sixty occurrences of the word chiefly in poetic passages of the *OT*, it is summed up by BDB. thus: 'man as strong, distinguished from women, children and non-combatants whom he is to defend'. The verb (*tesōbēb*) in v. 22 is correctly translated 'protect' (lit. 'surround') and this plainly fits the sense. We may suppose therefore that the sense of the line is that the normal way of things is to be reversed. Normally 'a man protects a woman'. It requires a new initiative of God to bring about a situation in which 'a woman protects a man'. Appropriately the word *created* (*bārā'*) is the word used of the creation in Gen. 1 and associated exclusively with the divine creative act, including the making of male and female (Gen. 1.27). This reversal of roles has already been suggested in 30.6.

> Ask now and see, can a man bear a child?
> Why then do I see every man with his hands on
>   his loins like a woman in labour?

The collection begins with the picture of men, in the moment of judgment, weak as woman. It ends with the picture of the Virgin Israel strong to protect men. The word 'protect' (*tesōbeb*) looks like a pun on 'faithless' (*haššōbēbâ*) and reinforces the point of the contrast. Not only will Virgin Israel be a strong to protect men, but she that is faithless will be strong protectress. If it is now asked, what sort of protection does she give, it must be answered that this is surely an image of the role of the nation.

She that has been subject to the nations and under the protectorship of the great powers, will now herself become protector. and this is so great a reversal that nothing can bring it to pass save a creative act of the sovereign LORD.

A BLESSING ON ZION **31.23-26**

The redactor corrects the balance of the collection of oracles in chapter 31 by ending with an oracle on Judah. This section has something in common with later insertions in the book of Isaiah, which are marked sometimes by a remarkable universalism, yet looking to Zion as the centre of worship in the coming salvation, cf. Isa. 18.7; 19.23-24; 27.12-13. In the two latter passages the theme is the ingathering of dispersed Israel. Isa. 19.23 presents the image of the highway (cf. Jer. 31.21), and Isa. 19.24 has the LORD's blessing not only upon Israel, but also upon Egypt and Assyria. The blessing appears to be derived from the worship of the Temple (Pss. 128.5; 118.26; 115.12-15), an extension of the familiar priestly blessing to comprehend the destiny of Israel. This background of influence suggests that the 'holy hill' is to be understood as Zion, and is not a figure for the whole land. The passage begins in prose, but may well be quoting the blessing of v. 24 and a poetic line in v. 25.

25. Thus says the LORD of hosts, the God of Israel: hitherto this form of introduction has been mostly confined to the prose tradition (7.3, 21; 9.14; 11.3; 13.12; 16.9; 19.3, 15; 21.4; 23.2; 24.5; 25.15, 27; 27.4, 21; 28.2, 14; 29.4, 8, 21, 25; 30.2) and is rare in other prophets. It is editorial in 6.6, 9.

restore their fortunes: in this context the traditional translation of the English versions, 'turn their captivity', may well be right. See on 30.3.

O habitation of righteousness, O holy hill: the blessing will reflect the coming salvation when the character of Judah will have been changed, the whole land reflecting righteousness, and holiness proceeding from its sacred centre, cf. Ezek. 40-48. The meaning of righteousness here will not be different from the prophetic designation of the Davidic branch in 23.5-6. It may indicate the saving activity of the LORD, but this shades into the more familiar idea of rightness in conduct and relationship. There is therefore no need to contrast this passage with the description of Jerusalem in Isa. 1.21-26 as the 'city of righteousness'. In 2.3 an early oracle of Jeremiah speaks of Israel in her unspoiled youth being 'holy to the LORD'; and in 25.30, an oracle of the tradition, the LORD utters his voice from his 'holy habitation'. This is not necessarily a narrow priestly conception and it cannot be said therefore that this verse, which has all the appearance of being quoted, is intrinsically foreign to the Jeremiah tradition in its final form.

the farmers: no longer ashamed as in 14.4.

25. This line has both parallelism and chiasmus and appears therefore, in a prose passage, to be a poetic fragment (3 + 3) quoted.

languishing: cf. 31.12 'they shall languish no more'. The earlier hint is expanded.

26. Thereupon I awoke and looked, and my sleep was pleasant to me: this could be the end of the short section vv. 23–26. In that case, the author of this 'dream' of the blessedness of Zion is indicating the visionlike character of his hope. Or it could be the end of the whole original collection of oracles on the future in chapters 30–31. This is more likely. First, because the section has an unusual beginning (30.1) 'Write in a book all the words that I have spoken to you'. And second, because the separate character of what follows is shown by the threefold 'Behold, the days are coming . . . in vv. 27, 31, 38. The suggestion that this is a quotation from an otherwise unknown song, solves nothing; or that it is a gloss, seems flippant. That the description of inspiration can take odd forms is shown by Eze. 3.1–3, where Ezekiel eats the scroll 'and it was in my mouth as sweet as honey'. Since we are told that the visions of Zechariah came to the prophet by night (Zech. 1.8) and yet seem to be distinguished from a dream (4.1), and contain intellectual symbolism, it may be thought wise to interpret this verse of the process of prophetic inspiration. Just as the angel's interpretation of Zechariah's vision begins when he has 'waked me, like a man that is wakened out of his sleep' (Zech 4.1), so the discussion of the meaning of these oracles begins when what has been *given* is set down in writing for us to read.

THE COMMUNITY OF THE NEW COVENANT **31.27–40**

One of the most momentous passages of the book of Jeremiah is embedded in a section of the prose tradition. There are three parts, each introduced with 'Behold, the days are coming', as also is the prose introduction to chapters 30–31 in 30.3. And since this phrase occurs up to this point within the prose passages (see introduction to chapters 30–31), this is one among other reasons for supposing that the same circles which were responsible for the editing of the earlier complexes of tradition were also responsible for this one. It follows that unless there are strong arguments to the contrary, we are dealing with the transmission of the message of Jeremiah as presented within the tradition, rather than with the direct memory of his oracles, which are usually, of course, in poetic form. The arrangement here equally strongly suggests that we do not have simply a late appendix to the 'book of consolation', but the prose framework within which the poetic collection was set.

(a) 31.27–30

The theme of this section is the new, creative intervention of the LORD which will restore the People of God. This will reverse the process of destruction involved in judgment, and means that Israel will be released from the inhibiting effects of the entail of the past. This is not, however, a straightforward piece of prose. It begins in v. 27 with what appears to be quotation. **I will sow the house of Israel and the house of Judah with the seed of a man and the seed of beast** has the allusiveness and the teasing obscurity of a long remembered prophetic utterance. It is a way of describing the new prosperity of all Israel, that will come by the divine initiative. After the decimations of the period of judgment, men and beast will be renewed to inhabit the restored land. This is in accordance with the original purpose of God for his people, but in present circumstances it is tantamount to a new creation, cf. 31.22 and 30.10 where 'offspring' corresponds to the same Heb. word. The word 'seed' marks a fundamental theme in the Pentateuch. Abraham's 'seed' are the children of promise (Gen. 12.17, translated 'descendants', 13.15, 16; 16.10; etc.; Dt. 11.9; Isa. 54.3). In Isa 66.22 the permanence of the 'seed' is part of 'the new heavens and the new earth'. Cf. the Magnificat (Lk. 1.55). Undeniably this utterance is full of overtones and was no doubt understood so to be.

Verse 28 will contain a second quotation, if the exposition of 1.10 is correct. The prose tradition has taken hold of a fundamental statement of Jeremiah's call vision and used it from time to time. In 18.7, 9 both the negative and positive aspects are used to interpret the prophetic sign of the potter and his work. In 24.6 this positive aspect is related to the parable of the good figs. In 42.10 it is related to Jeremiah's advice to remain in the land following the murder of Gedaliah. In 45.4 the negative aspect is related to the work of Baruch.

Hitherto the work of Jeremiah has been unrelenting, **to pluck up and to break down, to overthrow and destroy**. Now the time has come **to build and to plant**. The allusion to the call narrative becomes emphatic with the words **I will watch over them**, echoing the pun on the almond branch and its interpretation in 1.12. The LORD is indeed watching over his word to perform it. This part of the LORD's word has waited a long time for fulfilment, but it is coming as surely as the preceding destruction was irreversible.

Verse 29 contains a third quotation, this time of a popular proverb, dealt with at length by Ezekiel (chapter 18). The evidence of both prophets is that the proverb was widely uttered and used as complaint against God's justice. This is explicit in Ezek. 18.25. In Ezek. the proverb was exploited to shrug off responsibility, and Ezekiel answered, pastorally, by driving home the responsibility of the present generation and of every individual. In Jer. 31 the context suggests a related but different nuance. The situation is the present consequence of judgment, the entail of which seems inescapable and to make restoration impossible. The proverb is quoted to demonstrate the hopelessness of a tragedy brought about by past generations. The prophet here also answers by stressing the responsibility of the present generation, but primarily he is concerned to counter a popular objection to his insistence that a new beginning is, by God's grace, possible. The proverb is, of course, but the onesided interpretation of the orthodox teaching that God visits the sins of the fathers on the children to the third and fourth generation. (Exod. 20.5; 34.7; Num. 14.18; Pss. 79.8; 109.14). In God's new initiative the future will no longer be burdened by the past.

(b) 31.31–37
This section is in two originally distinct parts. Verses 31–34 is the prophecy of the new covenant in prose. Verses 35–37 is a poem beginning on the pattern of a participial hymn of praise, similar in form to the hymnal additions to the book of Amos. Its purpose, in the present context, is to affirm that the new order of redemption for Israel will be as certain and indestructible as the fixed order of nature.

The new covenant 31.31–34
This is presented in prose of the tradition. This renders it intrinsically improbable that the passage can be a late contribution of a learned scribe for whom the new covenant is the dispensation in which all Israel will be learned scribes knowing the Torah by heart! (Duhm). Nor is this the most natural meaning of the words, which set the personal knowledge of God and forgiveness as the climax. It is difficult to image a learned scribe writing so ambiguously that the comparatively banal should be capable of so revolutionary a meaning. Duhm turned gold into sand. Carroll calls it 'minor and prosaic'.

Previous investigation of the prose tradition would suggest that this must be an interpretation or version of Jeremiah's known teaching, put in its present form by Baruch or another of those who came to constitute the circle of followers. That may be so here. In that case the teaching is Jeremiah's; the precise wording is not. Such a conclusion would not be in the least disturbing. All that is important is that the divine truth should be communicated through Jeremiah *and* those activated by him, not that we should be assured of Jeremiah's authorship even of so great a passage.

But there is here another consideration. This piece of prose, with echoes of Dt. and Hos., has a perfection of form which perhaps may be thought to befit its content. It flows in Heb. as it does in English translation. The 'not like . . . But this' is emphatic and compelling. And when the point of the essence of the new covenant is reached, the high prose merges into poetry, so that the phrase 'I will put my law within them and I will write it upon their hearts' is marked by both parallelism and chiasmus. This seems to be the appropriate language for the proclamation of the new order.

Is this then the prose form of something Jeremiah may have uttered in poetic form? On the contrary, might not prose be the appropriate form for this announcement, giving something more precise and less allusive than the suggestive and often obscure imagery of poetry? Does the very memorability of *this* prose not point to the conclusion that this is the original? And if this is so, could any other than the prophet himself, authenticated as a prophet by his call, be the author of so bold a revision of the *OT* covenant? Would a secretary, or a disciple, or a later student of the prophecies, or even a preacher of the Jeremiah tradition have the authority or indeed the presumption or even the effrontery to set himself up to speak a word like this word?

For consider what the prophet has done. He has proclaimed a *new* covenant. Ezekiel also looked for a 'covenant of peace' (Ezek. 34.24; 36.26–28), as the security and guarantee of the new messianic era. He also looked back to the covenant which Israel had broken (*hāpēr*, Ezek. 16.59, cf. Jer. 31.32) 'yet I will remember my covenant with you in the days of your youth, and I will establish with you an everlasting covenant' (Ezek 16.60). This presupposed a new heart and a new spirit (Ezek. 36.25–27), and would ensure a paradisal state in which neither nations nor beasts would destroy (Ezek. 34.25–31) and there would be the blessing of prosperity.

What distinguishes Jeremiah's new covenant is its explicit relation to the Torah. He is not of course proclaiming a new Torah. But his boldness lies in explicitly contrasting the new covenant with the old in relation to the Torah. And by the old covenant he means specifically the covenant made with Israel through Moses after the Exodus, involving the promulgation of Torah as the terms of the covenant. In what way will the old covenant be superseded? Not in terms of the content of the Torah, but in the way Israel receives it. Hitherto it had been an external requirement, capable of being codified and fundamentally broken. Henceforth it would be **within them** and written **upon their hearts** (31.33).

To suppose that this means it will be known by heart and that every Israelite will be a learned scribe, is absurdly unimaginative. As well ask what is the literal meaning of the circumcision of the heart (Dt. 10.16; 30.6), which enables one to love the LORD. And Jeremiah shared this reinterpretation of circumcision (4.4, q.v.) with Dt. Plainly this is Jeremiah's way of speaking of an inward disposition, which means that the substance of the Torah (the divine instruction) is received and honoured to become the motive power of mind and will. The knowledge of the Torah and its fulfilment are one.

According to chapter 11 Jeremiah had, in his early days, espoused and preached the Deuteronomic reformation, and held up before the people the Deuteronomic law which was referred to in the tradition as 'the words of this covenant' (11.3). He had seen it exploited (8.8) and turned into a lie. But he understood the witness within the present book to a Torah which is not so much an alien and final demand as an inward and healing succour (Dt. 30.11-14). This is part of the mutual relationship of Dt. and Jer. which is impossible further to probe. It is the defining of the new divine dispensation in terms of a new and deeper appropriation of the divine instruction (Torah) which has made this passage central to the Christian Bible and given a name to the New Testament.

This inwardness of the saving Torah means the knowledge of God, and it is based on forgiveness. Jeremiah's well documented acquaintance with Hos. makes it no surprise that he sees the new dispensation as a time when the knowledge of God will have become universal. Later, Joel was to look to the coming of the Spirit as the means of opening up intimacy with God, previously confined to prophets and visionaries, to sons and daughters, old men and young men, menservants and maidservants (Jl. 2.28-29). Essentially Joel was anticipated by Jeremiah, who saw the time when the people of God would not be divided between teachers who knew God and others who did not, but all would have that knowledge of God which Jeremiah and Hosea understood as the purpose of human life (Hos. 4.1, 6; 5.4; 6.6; 8.2; cf. Jer. 2.8; 4.22; 9.3, 6, 23-24; 22.16. 24.7 is particularly germane). And of course, such a new covenant will not be broken, because God's people will no more have the disposition to break it.

31. a new covenant: cf. 'the LORD has created a new thing' (v. 22, qv.) The redactor no doubt saw this as a catchword corresponding to the essential unity of the theme, which is the restoration of God's people as a fresh act of creation.

house of Israel and the house of Judah: cf. 30.3; 31.27. If, as some critics claim, Judah is an addition, it is but pointing the true meaning of Israel as a theological term for the whole people of God.

32. which I made with their fathers: cf. Dt. 5.2. 'The LORD our God made a covenant with us in Horeb'. This involved statutes and ordinances 'which I speak in your hearing this day', i.e. it must include the substance of Dt. 5.3: 'Not with our fathers did the LORD make this covenant, but with *us*'. Jeremiah takes the more revolutionary step by speaking of a new covenant — 'not like the covenant which I made . . . But this is the covenant which I *will* make'. This contrast draws out the dimension of Jeremiah's creativity. Cf. also Jer. 11.3, 'Cursed be the man who does not heed the words of this covenant which I commanded your fathers' and 31.34. Again the contrast demonstrates the profundity of the new covenant in which the divine instruction (Torah) will have been received inwardly and personally. No anathema will therefore be necessary.

though I was their husband: LXX implies a different verb, though it is not obvious what. The proposed emendations are not convincing, particularly as MT makes good sense and links both with 3.14 'for I am your master', and with the martial imagery of Hos.

34. each man teach his neighbour: in contrast to Dt. 5.1, see above. **I will forgive their iniquity:** contrast the time to come when it will be offered and received (33.8; 36.3).

(ii) The reliability of God 31.35–37
This is the ground of confidence that he will restore his people and establish a covenant which shall not be broken.

What follows is an independent poem, yet highly appropriate to its context. The catchword 'seed' (vv. 36, 37 translated 'descendants') links it with v. 27, and signals the theme. The original promise to Abraham (see on v. 27) is to be re-established by a new creative act, and the guarantee that this will be so lies in the God of creation himself. He who sows the seed of man and of beast will make the seed of Israel to flourish forever. At the same time the contrast between the old covenant which was broken, and the new, which is based on an inner apprehension of the divine Torah, presupposes that the new covenant will not be broken. And the guarantee again is to be found in God.

Verse 35 is in the form of a participial hymn of praise and ends with the refrain **the LORD of hosts is his name** that is so marked in Am. 4.13; 5.8–9; 9.5–6. See also on 10.12–16. Here the familiar form of the doxology is used, not as the solemn prelude to judgment, but as the equally solemn introduction to the divine announcement of the indestructibility of the kingdom of God. Thus v. 35 is in effect a particularly striking and even momentous way of introducing the divine assurance. The allusion to the fixed order of nature is of course particularly apt, since this is the sign of the unchanging purpose of God. LXX places v. 35 after v. 37 and thereby destroys its point. MT is to be preferred

THE REBUILDING OF ZION **31.38–40**

The third section introduced by 'Behold, the days are coming' descends once more to prose, and prosaically suggests topographical details of the rebuilt city. Yet the passage has its surprises and its force. Its conclusion, **It shall not be uprooted or overthrown any more for ever** (v. 40) shows that the author had the promise 'to build and to plant' of v. 28 in mind, and applied the promise of the preceding poem to the building of Zion. Jerusalem, the holy city, would thenceforth be eternal. The redactor no doubt also saw this as a response to the promises of 30.18 and 31.4. Cf. also 33.4–9 and 3.17.

38. the tower of Hananel, in the north-east, probably built in the time of Manasseh (2 Ch. 33.14), and mentioned also in Zech. 14.10.

the Corner Gate: also in Zech 14.10. Might well be the Valley Gate of Neh. 2.15, cf. 2 Kg. 14.13. Towards the West.

39. And the measuring line shall go out farther, straight: For the same imagery, but without the topographical detail, see Zech. 2.1–5. A simple emendation from *negdô* to *negbâ* would give 'to the south' instead of 'straight', and this would give an indication of the position of Gareb and Goah, which are otherwise unknown. But the emendation is without authority.

40. of the dead bodies and the ashes: these words are omitted in LXX. It is perhaps plausible to guess that they were added to contrast with the Molech cult in the 'valley of Hinnom' — named the Valley of Slaughter — (7.31–33; 19.6) situated west, south-west and south of old Jerusalem.

the brook Kidron: the wady of nearly three miles bounding Jerusalem from the east towards the south. Hinnom runs into it from the west. It could be significant that it was in the valley of Kidron that, as part of the Deuteronomic reformation, Josiah commanded Hilkiah to burn the symbols of the Baal cult, casting their dust over the common graves which were situated there. If this were so, it would add to the force of the reversal. All this region is to become holy to the LORD.

the Horse Gate: (cf. Neh. 3.28; 2 Kg. 11.16), probably on the east side of the court of Solomon's palace where it joined the precincts of the Temple.

It is the measure of the new creative act of restoration that regions fatally corrupted by extremes of apostasy should not be permanently alienated. Every vestige of the past will be cleansed. This is a specific aspect of the promises of vv. 29–30, 34. Again, that Jerusalem will become sacred to the LORD is the recovery of the original condition and purpose of Israel, expressed in one of the earliest oracles of Jeremiah. 'Israel was holy to the LORD' (2.3) and will become so again and for ever.

It is possible to evaluate these prophecies as matter of fact predictions which have never been fulfilled and never will be, or as waiting still to be fulfilled by Jews who return to their ancient homeland. Most will then regard them as expendable elements of the *OT*. There is, on the other hand, a different approach to the future hopes of the *OT*. They are eschatology in the sense that the last things, in the general perspective of the *OT*, remain on the historical plain but project the promises of God and the hopes of Israel on to an ultimate screen, where the divine purpose is seen to be fulfilled. The essentials of this eschatology are a combination of insight into the divine mind, together with a robust faith that what God wills he will also bring to pass in his own time.

This is no different in principle from the eschatological dimension of the kingdom of God. In the light of the *NT* two adjustments have to be made. The historical perspective has to be extended beyond history. The true fulfilment can only be in the deeper and more mysterious form of the Jerusalem that is above (Gal. 4.26; Heb. 11.10, 16; Rev. 21.2; and especially Rev. 21.15–27, which may be regarded as the reinterpretation of this hope, appropriate to the *NT*). But also the national limitation has to be exploded. The new Israel embraces Jew and Gentile. The essential principle behind the concept Israel is not the narrow one of race but the potentially universal one of election to be the People (and Servant) of God. This accords with the basis of the prophet's confidence that the fulfilment of the future is the recovery of the purpose of God in creation. Thus understood, these idealistic pictures of the future become influential visions, clothing aspirations and hopes in concrete images, ever recalling us to the divine purpose as we face the ebb and flow, caused by the vicissitudes of history and the changing faith and faithlessness of men and women in succeeding generations.

C PROSE SERMONS
32.1–35.19 (36.32) (LXX 39–43.32)

The collection of poems in chapters 30–31 is now followed by a collection of powerful, didactic sermons. Chapters 30–31, like earlier collections, showed evidence that it was put in its present form by a redactor of the prose tradition, who introduced it and concluded it with prose. The theme of hope was linked to 27.22 and 29.10–14. This same theme provided the appropriate springboard for chapters 32 and 33, both concerned with the future. Chapters 34 and 35 have the same sermon character, but revert to the theme of judgment. Chapter 36 concludes the collection, and indeed probably concludes the whole of chapters 1–35 when the larger complex had reached this stage of compilation (see p. 35).

These prose sermons, for the most part, betray the same characteristics of the prose tradition that we have observed throughout the collection. In particular, they have the same combination of striking Deuteronomic vocabulary with phrases unique to the Jeremiah prose tradition (see comments below). In the judgment chapters there is the same rhythm of warning, rejection and judgment. There is the same introductory formula: 'The word that came to Jeremiah from the LORD', cf. 7.1; 11.1; 18.1; 21.1; 30.1. This formula occurs in 32.1; 33.1; 34.1; 35.1; 36.1. And there is the same inclination to link the message with an event in the life of Jeremiah, or to present it with a certain event character. This became clear in chapters 7,11,14, 18, 19, 20. Here each sermon is dated. Chapters 32, 33, 34, belong to the time of Zedekiah. Chapters 32 and 33 are linked to Jeremiah's imprisonment. Chapter 32 gives the narrative of the buying of the field at Anathoth. Chapter 33 develops associated themes. Chapter 34 is linked with Jeremiah's prophecy to Zedekiah that Jerusalem was to be given into the hand of the Babylonians and Zedekiah himself captured, together with his denunciation of those who perfidiously released and rescinded the release of slaves. Chapter 35 goes back to the time of Jehoiakim and proceeds from Jeremiah's meeting with the Rechabites. Chapter 36 is the dramatic story of the writing and rewriting of the scroll of his oracles.

At the same time the sermon is everything. This section is not primarily narrative, as in chapters 37–45. Chapter 32 declares that even within the hopelessness of judgment now inescapably being fulfilled, hope is created by the will and power of God. Chapter 33 develops a series of more detailed aspects of this hope. Chapter 34 draws out the consequences of moral turpitude and unscrupulousness and shows how the destruction of Jerusalem and of the land was a just judgment. Chapter 35 sets up the Rechabites as a model example of obedience and fidelity. The example was the more powerful since Jeremiah showed no disposition to follow their way of life. Chapter 36 appears to tell a straight narrative of the way Jeremiah's oracles were put together and transmitted. But reflection shows that the theme is really the fate of the word of God in the hands of a ruthless king, how this word encountered rejection and entailed judgment.

The strong similarity of this prose, both in the form and theology, with the earlier examples of the prose tradition, suggests that it is from the same circles. If Baruch was the author of some of the prose, it does not follow that he was the author of all. The passage on the Levites in 33.17–22 is certainly late. It is unlikely that Baruch wrote the account of his own part in the buying of the land in chapter 32, or in the production of the scroll in chapter 36. Moreover, we are dealing with the particular version, within the Jeremiah tradition circles, of a style which was the intellectual style of the period. What we can affirm with confidence is that we have here the sermons of those who stood in the tradition of Jeremiah, faithful to his teaching, and believed they were expressing the force of his message in the new circumstances of their time. Thus interpreted these sermons may be used as indirect witness to the life and teaching of Jeremiah but direct witness to the word of God.

A PROPHETIC SIGN OF HOPE 32.1–44

THE CIRCUMSTANCES 32.1–5

The preacher who interprets the words and deeds of Jeremiah to his contemporaries betrays his interest by giving close circumstantial details of the situation within which Jeremiah gave his prophetic sign. In vv. 1–5 he uses material from the historical narrative (chapter 37), sketching the picture in the most general terms without pedantic accuracy. For example, strictly speaking it was not Zedekiah who imprisoned Jeremiah but the king's ministers (37.14–15). At the same time the weak king could not shuffle off royal responsibility (38.5, 24–26) and the account does not mislead.

The preacher's intention is revealed by the order of events. He states that Jeremiah was 'shut up in the court of the guard' (v. 2), *before* he gives the reason, and Jeremiah's crucial utterance is even then presented as quoted by the king. It is important to observe the inverted commas in *RSV*. It may well be that this somewhat involuted style of narration is deliberate, and is designed to emphasise Jeremiah's utter powerlessness. The prophet of the LORD is imprisoned because he has proclaimed his country's powerlessness to evade the Babylonian judgment. He is himself a sign of the inescapability of judgment. And yet, it is from this improvised prison (in the house of Jonathan, 37.15) that he voices a hope and recognises in the errand of his cousin a sign of the LORD's positive intention for his people. From his own position of weakness he declares this hope to be founded on the power of God. Twice, as he appeals to the power of the Creator, he stresses that nothing is too hard for Him (vv. 17, 27 cf. 33.2). The contrast is between the sovereign God of the universe and his spokesman in prison.

1. the tenth year of Zedekiah: i.e. 588–587 B.C.. The eighteenth year of Nebuchadnezzar appears to be about a year later, but the discrepancy is slight and understandable.

2. Cf. chapters 37 and 38.

the prophet was shut up in the court of the guard: according to 37.15 he was imprisoned in the house of Jonathan the secretary; in 38.6 in the cistern of Malchiah. In each case he was committed to the court of the guard as a more tolerable place of detention (37.21; 38.13, 28). See introduction to chapters 37–45.

3–5. This may be understood to give the gist of Jeremiah's terrible prophecy to the well-intentioned but weak Zedekiah. Cf. 34.2–5 which is virtually the same version. There is fuller detail in chapters 37 and 38. See comment on 21.1–7 for the view that not one but several enquiries were made of Jeremiah at this time (see also note on v. 39).

3. Behold, I am giving this city: the familiar 'behold' with participle of the prose tradition.

5. until I visit him: the various nuances of the word 'visit' leave this ambiguous. The LORD's visitation may mean punishment, as often in the prose tradition (9.24; 11.22; 13.21; 8.12; 10.15), but also in the earlier poetic oracles (5.9, 29. See note on 5.9). Or it may mean salvation, as in the prose of 27.22 and 29.10 (see note on 27.22), but also in the poetry of 15.15. 29.10 might suggest that the meaning here is that Zedekiah will ultimately be brought back to Jerusalem, but the word is used there of the restoration in the context of the completion of the seventy years. That puts the event outside the range of any adult now living. Rashi's suggestion, derived from Num. 16.29, was that this is the visitation of death. At least this fits in with the prediction that Zedekiah would die

in peace, 34.4-5. Or it may be that the precise meaning of 'visit' is left open: 'There he shall remain until I decide what his future shall be'.
the Chaldeans: see on 21.4.

JEREMIAH REDEEMS THE FAMILY PROPERTY **32.6–15**

There follows a succinct account of the transaction in which Jeremiah recognised a sign from the LORD. Indeed, the word of the LORD, introduced in v. 6, follows on from v. 1. Verses 2–5 are a sort of parenthesis to explain the circumstances of the prophet, but the importance of these verses for the rest of the chapter is yet to be unfolded.

The story of the buying of the field illustrates uniquely and vividly two aspects of Hebrew custom.

(1) It illustrates the duty of redemption g^e'*ullāh* which is the social background to the theological idea of the redeemer (Job 19.25) and of redemption (Jer. 31.11, qv.). This duty is laid down in Lev. 25.25, cf. also Ru. 3–4. Hanamel's son must therefore have been compelled by poverty or debt to sell family land at Anathoth. Jeremiah, his cousin, must have been next of kin, with the duty (if he could afford it) and the opportunity to buy it for himself, and so keep it in the family.

(2) The story also illustrates how commercial dealings were carried through. The money transaction was witnessed and made permanent by means of a legal deed of sale. There was a sealed deed and an open copy of it. If these were like the deeds found at Elephantine (E.G. Kraeling, *The Brooklyn Museum Aramic Papyri* (1953), pp. 51 ff; George E. Mendenhall, *BA 17.2* (1954) p 43; G. E. Wright, *Biblical Archaeology* (1951), p 206 for photographs), there was one scroll divided into two parts. It was bound with papyrus string, the string passing through a hole in the middle of the scroll. The one half was rolled to the middle and sealed before witnesses so that there was some guarantee against subsequent alterations. The other half was left open so that it could be inspected. Verses 10, 11, 12, 14 seem to indicate that these two parts were one scroll. The deed was then placed by Baruch in a clay pot (v. 14) 'that they may last for a long time'. How effective a method of preservation this was is shown by the way the Elephantine and the Qumran scrolls have survived. This is the twofold light shed on Hebrew social and commercial custom.

The accent of the narrative however lies elsewhere. It is from beginning to end prophecy. Jeremiah receives advance intimation that his cousin will visit him and offer him the right of redemption. 'The word of the LORD came to me: Behold, Hanamel will come to you . . .'. Hanamel's coming is then told with the observation that it was 'in accordance with the word of the LORD'. And when he had delivered his errand, Jeremiah concluded: 'Then I knew that this was the word of the LORD'. Thus with repeated emphasis the reader is prepared to receive the event as a prophetic sign.

When then the deed of sale was duly signed, Jeremiah instructed Baruch, 'Thus says the LORD of hosts, the God of Israel: Take these deeds . . .' and he drew out the prophetic meaning with the same messenger formula of prophecy (vv. 14–15). No doubt the heavy emphasis was required. For the episode occurs when Jeremiah's most terrible prophecies had partly taken place (597 B.C.) and the rest were about to be fulfilled (586). From every point of view this seemed to be the least appropriate time to be buying property, and indeed contrary to any reasonable inference to be drawn from his previous utterances. When the people were optimistic, Jeremiah thundered doom. When the doom broke upon them and their pessimism was complete, he enacted a sign of hope. Such is the contrariness of a prophet.

We may properly suppose that the witnesses were intended to be witnesses not only of the commercial contract but also of the prophecy. This comes out clearly in V. 25: 'Yet, thou O Lord God, hast said to me, "Buy the field for money and get witnesses" — though the city is given into the hands of the Chaldeans'. The purpose of the witnesses was that, when the prophecy was fulfilled, they might confirm that this was the LORD's word and his word would be acknowledged to be true. The same function of witnesses, and for the same prophetic purpose, is to be discerned in Isa 8.1–4, and also in Is. 8.16, where Isaiah's prophecies concerning the Syro-Ephraimite crisis are to be bound and sealed in presumably the same way, and where Isaiah's disciples are the witnesses.

There seems to have been a precision and a permanence associated with that which was written, giving a strong motive for transposing prophecy from the oral to the written mode. This no doubt is why Jehoiakim had cut up Jeremiah's first scroll and burned it (36.23). He thought thus to destroy the prophecy. The written witness of Jeremiah's transaction had similar sort of significance as a permanent sign of the message of hope in the days of hopelessness. All this shows how vital and substantial an element in Jeremiah's prophetic ministry was the delivery of this signal of hope, remembered and reaffirmed by those who followed him. And it was done while he was in prison! The whole prophecy is contained in v. 15. The rest is circumstance, but such as to provide a divine sign and to impress the truth upon a scarcely comprehending people. Thus understood, this hope is seen to be a major feature of the ministry of Jeremiah.

7. Hanamel the son of Shallum your uncle: the name may be a variation of Hananel, cf. Zech. 14.10. If it means 'God is gracious', that is a coincidence, and it is unlikely that the name has symbolic significance for the sign.

Anathoth: see on 1.1. How sacred were the rights of family property in old Israel is shown most vividly by the story of Naboth in 1 Kg. 21.

9. seventeen shekels of silver: no doubt related to the market price; but we do not have objective standards by which to judge.

12. Baruch: In each case where Jeremiah is known to have taken steps to give permanence to his prophetic witness, Baruch is involved. Cf. chapter 36. And what Baruch is instructed to do in vv. 13–14 is specific divine command.

14. Take: In Heb. an infinitive absolute, as in the command to Isaiah (8.16); cf. 2 Kg. 3.16. This seems to lend an enigmatic character to the oracle.

A QUESTION TO THE LORD **32.16–25**

The interpretation of the prophetic sign is given in the form of a prayer (vv. 16–25), together with its answer which is developed in the rest of the chapter. The prayer has the outward structure of prayer, but is a scarcely disguised way of putting the question to the LORD: 'In all these circumstances, how can there by any hope at all?' Thus the prayer begins with the expression 'Ah Lord God' which occurs in the call-vision of Jeremiah and also in 4.10 and 14.13, similarly in Ezek., perhaps more flexibly in the Deuteronomic History (Jos. 7.7; Jg. 6.22; 11.35; 2 Kg. 3.10), but never in the Psalter. It echoes the doxology of 31.35, but not so as to introduce a hymn of declaratory praise; rather to express faith in the God of creation, as the context of what follows.

The prayer quotes the most characteristic and most often repeated epitome of the nature of the LORD as God of both grace and judgment (v. 18), and then summarises the history of Israel: redeemed from Egypt, endowed with the land of promise, given the Torah, constantly disobedient and therefore deserving the evil that has come upon them. This leads up to a description of their present plight. The siege mounds are erected, the city is given into the hands of the Chaldeans. All this is a brief summary of what is now Gen. to 2 Kg.

The argument has mounted and the tension has been created. All that now has to be said is the bare statement; 'Yet thou O Lord God hast said to me, "Buy the field . . ."." The bare statement is of course the question, 'Why?' If logic is pressed, this means that in buying the field, Jeremiah was obeying the divine instruction, without himself knowing the reason why. Subsequently he asked the question and was given the reason. This is of course possible. It is more likely that the question and answer is a device of the preacher to enable him to develop the interpretation. Certainly he has built up an eloquent case of cumulative force. If *this* is Israel's story and this the divine intervention, all consistent and making sense, what is the point of the buying of the field, an expedient which presumably Jeremiah would not have carried out had not the LORD so instructed him? Thus the paradox of Jeremiah's situation, expressed in vv. 1-5, is subsumed in the paradox of Israel's destiny.

The prayer has been written in prose of the tradition. It reads at first like a mosaic of passages, partly from the existing Jeremiah tradition, partly from Dt. The echoes are listed with comments that follow. But it is no more literary compilation. It has the impact of a preacher eloquently enforcing a striking point.

17. Ah Lord God!: an expression which seems to belong to prophecy, particularly to Jeremiah and Ezekiel, not to the psalmists. See above.

by the great power and outstretched arm: The only other example of the use of this expression to describe creation is in 27.5, a prose passage of the same tradition. In passages describing creation, God 'stretches out the heavens' as in the similar 10.12 (= 51.15), which also shows signs of belonging to the Jeremiah tradition, but not directly the work of the prophet. (cf. also Ps. 104.2; Isa. 40.22; 42.5; 44.24; 45.12; 51.13). The outstretched arm is normally the power that sent back the waters of the Red sea and brought the Israelites out of Egypt. Thus v. 21 is the conventional picture, as frequently in Dt. but also in Jer. 21.5. **Nothing is too hard for thee:** the main lesson drawn from creation. Cf. v. 27.

18. Who showest steadfast love to thousands, but dost requite the guilt of fathers to their children after them: the form is the participial hymn of praise. The content is a version of one of the most important concentrated summaries of the character of God to be found in the *OT*, and it cannot be attributed to Dt. In Exod. 34.6-7 (J) it is presented as a divine revelation. It is not unlikely that this classical expression represents the traditional ground of an affirmation repeated in the cult. If it were a cultic formula, that would explain why it is so much quoted, cf. Exod. 20.5-6 = Dt. 5.9-10; Num. 14.18. The most memorable version of it is as found in Neh. 9.17 Nah. 1.3; Jl 2.13; Jon. 4.2; Pss.

86.15; 103.8; 145.8. The repetition 'is an eloquent testimony to the centrality of this understanding of God's person' (Childs). **steadfast love:** *ḥeseḏ*. See on 2.2. Piety to God, grace to men, kindness of one man to another, variously translated 'love', 'loving-kindness', 'mercy', 'devotion'. Usage shows that it carries the idea of a settled purpose and commitment and is appropriate to a covenant relationship. **mighty God:** *gibbôr*. For the thinking of the *OT*, the image of God as a warrior did not seem inappropriate, cf. Ps. 24.8; Dt. 10.17; Isa. 10.21 (and used of the royal child in Isa 9.6). Here, as in Neh. 9.32, it may be thought to be alien to the cultic formula. But undeniably it fits its new context, where the preacher is intent to emphasise both the power and the justice of God's dealings with the world and with Israel. Probably here the preacher's touch.

whose name is the LORD of hosts: the refrain as in 31.35, qv. But here we do not have the sense of a quoted doxology. Rather is it used to touch up the cultic formula in its new creation context.

19. great in counsel: The unusual expression is 'great in devotion' (*ḥeseḏ*) as in Exod. 34.6; Mic. 14.18; Neh. 9.17; Jl 2.13; Jon. 4.2; Pss. 86.5, 15; 103.8, 145.8. The variation is in keeping with Jer. 10.12.

rewarding every man according to his ways and according to the fruit of his doings: identical with 17.10b, a wisdom poem, qv. 'I the LORD search the mind and try the heart' (17.10a) corresponds to **whose eyes are open to all the ways of men,** cf. 16.17. Again the preacher is calling on material from the Jeremiah tradition.

20–23. These verses are a conglomerate of Deuteronomic phrases adapted to their present purpose.

20. who hast shown signs and wonders in the land of Egypt: cf. particularly Dt. 6.22; 26.8; but also 4.34; 7.19; 34.11; and Pss. 78.43; 105.27; 135.9; Neh. 9.10.

and to this day: is also a Deuteronomic emphasis cf. Dt. 2.30; 4.20, 38; 6.24; 8.18; 29.28, but the particular connection here is unique. That it has become a part of the Jeremiah tradition is shown by Jer. 11.5; 44.6, 22, 23.

and among all mankind: deliberately broadens the perspective. Verse 21 corresponds most closely to Dt. 26.8 and v. 22 to Dt. 26.9, 15.

22. a land flowing with milk and honey: a standard description of the promised land in Dt. (6.3; 11.9; etc.) but going back to the pentateuchal source J. (Exod. 3.8, 17; 13.5; 33.3; Num. 13.27, etc). Corresponds to 11.5. It is an indication that the preacher lives at a distance from these traditions that he is primarily concerned with the destruction of the city.

23. They did not obey thy voice: is frequent in Dt., but is already a commonplace in Jer. Dt. usually has 'walk in the way of Yahweh'. The Jeremiah tradition prefers 'walk in the Torah' (9.13; 26.4; 44.10, 23) as here. **made all this evil come upon them:** in this form here only. This verse sums up the theme of the Deuteronomic history. **24. Behold, the siege mounds:** these are ramps built up against the wall to enable the battering rams to advance. From behind the shields, the archers would give covering fire. Such is the picture suggested by reliefs of Sennacherib's siege of Lachish. **because of sword and famine and pestilence:** better with *NEB, REB* 'the victim of the sword', etc. On these three standard punishments see on 14.12, characteristic of the Jeremiah tradition. **What thou didst speak has come to pass, and behold, thou seest it:** so the sermon, in the form of dialogue with the LORD, is brought down to the realities of the present. All is what might have been expected, in accordance with the will of the LORD, his design for his people, his character and his power to carry out his will. Why then buy the field? The crunch question is in v. 25.

THE LORD'S ANSWER **32.26–44**

It is probable that an earlier form of this sermon in dialogue form lacked vv. 26–35. The key is in v. 36 which directly takes up v. 24–'the city is given into the hands of the Chaldeans' and expounds the meaning of the hope implied in v. 25. In contrast v. 28–'Behold, I am giving this city into the hands of the Chaldeans' echoes the prediction of v. 3 which is now being fulfilled, and back pedals to expound Israel's crimes which have entailed the punishment. Another preacher has 'improved' the earlier sermon. But he belongs to the same tradition, and his exposition has the effect of giving substance to the accusation of disobedience in v. 23 in terms which have already become familiar in the prose tradition.

It is not of course to be supposed that this sermon, like the others, was delivered in the form in which it has come down to us. We may fairly assume that the preachers knew no such inhibitions. But when it came to the business of committing the sermons to the written tradition, they gave the substance in the well known and easily remembered phrases that are used again and again. This literary character of the final form of essentially oral rhetoric is clearly revealed in vv. 26–35 and results in its some what mosaic character. Thus vv. 28, 29, 34–35 are virtually

repeated elsewhere, as shown in the comments below; while the rest of
the sermon is paralleled in the prose tradition.

(a) The tally of Israel's sins 32.26–35
The essence of the analysis of Israel's sin is like that which forms the
basis of all the Deuteronomic writings, Hosea and the other eighth century
prophets. It is apostasy, faithlessness to the LORD, who has revealed
his will specially to his own people. Of this apostasy, the worship of Baal
in v. 29, and the child sacrifice to Molech in v. 35, are the symbol, because
they are the extreme. See on 7.31. In fact Israel and Judah have done
evil 'from their youth' (a touch which corresponds to a characteristic
emphasis of the poetic oracles), turning their back on the LORD, despite
his constant warnings though his own prophetic spokesmen.

26. Behold, I am the LORD the God of all flesh: The first part of
the LORD's answer, analysing Israel's disobedience, is introduced
solemnly and impressively by means of the self-predication formula: 'I
am Yahweh'. The origins of this is uncertain. Its use in Exod. 20.2
suggests that it is a formula employed to introduce, in the most solemn
manner, a divine law. Its frequent use in the Holiness Code (Lev. 17–26),
which in Lev. 25.38 is close to Exod. 20.2, seems to emphasise the
separateness which is enforced in the demand for holiness, cf. Lev. 18.2–4.
At the same time its use in the Babylonian cult is as an introduction to
oracles obtained by divination. Thus the woman Baia of Arbela spoke
to Esarhaddon: 'I am Ishtar of Arbela. I have turned Ashur's favour unto
you . . . I am the god Nabu, lord of the tablet stylus, praise me' (ANET.,
p. 450). In another text, the formula is associated, as so often in Second
Isaiah, with creation. 'I am Ishtar, the goddess of the evening . . . who
opens the shutters of the resplendent heavens, this is my glory'. Cf. Isa.
42.5, 8, 'Thus says God, Yahweh, who created the heavens . . . I am
Yahweh, that is my name, my glory I give to no other, nor my praise
to graven images'. It is tempting to see a conscious contrast with the claims
of other gods, particularly if the queen of heaven (Jer. 7.18, qv., 44.15–19)
is to be identified with Ishtar. Whether this is so or not, the formula
inevitably becomes a declaration of Yahweh's uniqueness and sole
godhead, as in Isa. 45.5; Dt. 32.39. Whatever its origin, it becomes a
'monotheistic formula'. Here in Jer. 32.26–27, several of these strands
are present. It is the introduction to an oracle, and the addition of the
words **the God of all flesh** shows that the monotheistic claim is being
made. 'All flesh' is a way of referring to mankind as a whole (Dt. 5.26;
Pss. 65.3; 145.21) or even to all creatures, men and animals (Gen. 6.17;

9.16; Job 34.15) cf. already Jer. 12.12; 25.31. The nearest parallel is the expression 'God of the spirits of all flesh' (probably P, in Num. 16.22, 27). There is thus no evidence of direct dependence. The presumption is that the expression is at home in the exilic period, and there is no reason to deny it to the prose traditionist of the school of Jeremiah. There is undeniably something portentous about it. The preacher thus declares that the ending of the history of the chosen people was totally within the purpose of the sovereign God of creation.

is anything too hard for me? the preacher picks up the theme of the primary sermon in v. 17.

28–29a. The familiar 'Behold' with the participle introduces the prediction of the fall of Jerusalem in terms repeated in 34.2; 37.8; 38.18; cf. 21.4–10. The preacher's real interest here is in what follows, viz. the reasons for the disaster.

29b the houses on whose roofs incense has been offered to Baal and drink offerings have been poured out to other gods: this, with the substitution of Baal for ' the host of heaven', is virtually identical with 19.13. See comment *there*.

to provoke me to anger: here and in vv. 30, 32, a commonplace of the Deuteronomic tradition . See introductory comment to 25.1–14.

30. evil in my sight: cf. 7.30; 8.10, Dt. 4.4; 9.18; etc.

from their youth: cf. 3.24, and especially the confession of v. 3.25, and 31.19. Cf. also 2.2; 3.4.

my anger and my wrath: cf. 7.20; 42.18 (Dt. 9.19; 29.22).

32. cf. 7.11, 12, 17. **their kings and their princes, etc.:** cf. the poetic oracle 2.26, qv.

33. They have turned to me their back and not their face: cf. 2.27. In view of the link between v. 32 and 2.26, it seems that here we have an example of the way the redactor of the sermon uses the poetic tradition, as well as the clichés of the prose tradition. This phrase is peculiar to Jeremiah.

though I have taught them persistently: literally 'rising up early and teaching . . . '. This expression, 7.13; 25.3; 35.14 (speaking); 7.25; 25.4; 26.5; 29.19; 35.5, 44.4 (sending); 11.7 (warning) is again peculiar to the Jeremiah tradition (except 2 Chr. 36.15). See on 7.13.

to receive instruction: again a characteristic expression of Jer., cf. 5.3; 7.28; 17.23; 35.13 and, confirming the argument above that there is some dependence on the poetic oracle in chapter 2; also 2.30.

34–35. This is a slightly pointed version of 7.30–31, cf. also 19.5. That a Molech sacrifice is involved is made explicit, and the addition of **to**

cause Judah to sin (v. 35) weaves the passage into the theme of the sermon.

35. nor did it enter into my mind: also an expression characteristic of the Jeremiah tradition, cf. 3.16; 7.31; 19.5; 44.21.

Thus the evidence is overwhelming that the person who set down the substance of the sermon in writing was heavily dependent upon the existing vocabulary and expressions of the tradition which he was transmitting. This tradition can only be called the work of disciples of Jeremiah, demonstrating the validity of their prophetic claim. The LORD had spoken. All the horrendous events were in his power and by his design, no more than just retribution visited upon a people whose inner rottenness was now analysed and disclosed.

(b) The greater good 32.36–44

As there is a powerful contrast between the power of God and the powerlessness of the prophet, so there is now a contrast between the dispensation of judgment and the dispensation of grace. The sermon of vv. 26–35 seems to have been inserted precisely to highlight this contrast, by underlining the sin and wrath of judgment, before the interpretation of the sign is continued in vv. 36-44, drawing out the full dimensions of the divine purpose of restoration and grace.

Thus v. 36 takes up again the theme of v. 24, and the answer to the question implied in v. 25 is now given. There will be an ingathering of the scattered peoples (v. 37), a new and enduring covenant (v. 40), a 'planting' of people in the land (v. 41) and the freedom to buy fields in the exilic and post-exilic territory of Judah (v. 44). The expression 'the places about Jerusalem' (v. 44) means the region of Jerusalem and is not intended to exclude the city itself. It is nevertheless significant that there is no specific reference to the rebuilding of the city, in view of the heavy emphasis on its destruction (vv. 3, 24, 28, 29, 31, 34, 36) and especially the introduction of the oracle in v. 36 as 'concerning the city'. This lacuna is to some extent filled in chapter 33.4–9, leaving the impression that in vv. 36–44 there is a distinct limitation of the details of the future hope, appropriate to the very earliest interpretations of the sign of the buying of the field at Anathoth.

37. The familiar **'Behold'** with participle. The theme of the ingathering is firmly present in the poetic oracles of 31.8, 10, and repetitively in the prose tradition (23.3; 29.14, where it is an expansion of the basic text). See notes on 31.7–9.

in my anger and my wrath and in great indignation: partially in verse 31. The full phrase in 21.5 and Dt. 29.27.

dwell in safety: a commonplace to describe the freedom of the new age, to be found with significant semantic variations in Dt. 12.10, (33.12), as also in Jer. 23.6; 33.16, but too common to be labelled Deuteronomic.

38-40. A reaffirmation of the new covenant. That this is is not a primary statement seems to follow from a comparison with 31.33-34. The latter is marked by artistry, balance, simplicity and memorability. In contrast the Heb. of this passage is involved and laboured. It reaffirms an essential point of 31.31-34, but does not spell out its full implication. What it does say is an implication of the meaning of both the ingathering of v. 36 and also of the planting of v. 41. That is to say, it is part of the build-up of the sermon. It does not stand as an independent statement or proclamation like 31.31-34.

38. This is the commonplace statement of the covenant relationship also quoted in 31.33.

39. I will give them one heart and one way: 'heart' is the inner disposition; 'way' is the way of life centred on obedience to the divine instruction (i.e. the Torah). The repetition of the word 'one' creates a problem. There is no parallel to this in the prose of Jeremiah and the only comparable passage is in Ezek. 11.19. In both texts, the LXX reads 'another', involving the change of a single letter, while some MSS and Syr read 'new' implying a more substantial change in the Heb. The reading 'new' in Ezek. 11.19 may be explained as an assimilation to Ezek. 18.31 and 36.26. Probably 'one' is to be retained as the more difficult text.

The sense will not be altogether different from the corrections, but the emphasis must then be on the unity of the people of God in the re-established covenant relationship. As they are gathered together physically as one people, so they will be spiritually one people. As they have finally given up the worship of other gods and rejected the way of life that goes with that worship (vv. 29-30, 35-35), so their worship will no longer be divided and their response no longer compromised. The Deuteronomic idea of the two ways (Dt. 30.15-20) was known within the Jeremiah tradition and probably taken up by Jeremiah himself. See on 21.1-10, also relating Jeremiah's dealings with Zedekiah. 21.8 is explicit. What is now being affirmed is that when the people of God are inwardly faithful, there will then be only one way. The way of death will no longer be a possibility, the way of life a certainty. Divided in themselves, they perish. *REB* has 'I shall give them singleness of heart and one way of life'.

fear me forever: in view of the exhortation not to fear, which is a characteristic of the oracle of salvation, it must be insisted that the word 'fear' does not have the overtones of our English usage. It means 'awe', the fundamental religious disposition which is the beginning of wisdom. Jeremiah understood the relationship of love (31.3). Yet, even if love casts out fear, there is a reverence, which is the proper response of the creature to the Creator, and which will never be superseded.

40. An everlasting covenant: this statement follows from the affirmation that there will be one heart and one way, and when it is further said **I will put the fear of me in their hearts**, the essential inwardness of 31.31–34 is being restated. There the formulation is more precise. The Torah itself will be inwardly received. Here the quality of the relationship is described, without specifying its content. It amounts to the same thing. The new covenant will never be broken because God's people, renewed at the spring of thought and action, will never break their obligation. The truth which stands out from both passages is that the new era of peace and life cannot be secured without a fundamental change in the human personality; and this change, only God can give. (See on 31.31–34, and cf. Ezek. 34.24, 36.26–28).

41. I will plant them in this land: the imagery is, of course, appropriate to the interpretation of the sign of buying the field. But principally it links with the terms of the call vision in 1.10. (cf. 31.28). As there will henceforth be no danger of the way of death, so there will be no danger of plucking up and breaking down, if the heart of the people remains secure in the LORD.

The LORD's pleasure in the fulfilment of his purpose is expressed in language unrestrainedly anthropomorphic, and has to be decoded accordingly.

42–44. The sermon now refers explicitly to the sign of the buying of the field which it purports to interpret. Verse 42 also makes explicit the tension and contrast which has been built up. The place where fields shall be bought are specified in a list which begins with Benjamin (where Jeremiah bought his own ancestral property) and includes the territory of Judah as it was limited in the exilic and post-exilic period. This list itself became a way of referring to the dimensions of restored Judah, as is shown by its use in 17.26 and 33.13. In the light of Jeremiah's strong concern with the northern people, manifest particularly within the poetic oracles of chapters 30 and 31, and present even in his earliest oracles, this limitation appears odd, if not contradictory. This makes it the more significant that v. 43 effectively brings to a conclusion, in echoing terms, the substance of Jeremiah's prayer in v. 25. Verse 44 is therefore best regarded as expansion of the prose tradition, which, by what it omits, fails to do justice to the full scope of the theology of Jeremiah.

THEMES OF THE FUTURE HOPE 33.1–26 (LXX 40.1–13)

The editor supplements the prose sermon of chapter 32 with a section which extends the interpretation there given of the hope of restoration. Verse 1 no doubt corresponds to his assumption that the substance of the sermon comes from the imprisoned Jeremiah. *We* must regard it as a palpable device to link the material together, as indeed it belongs together. Thus **a second time** really means a supplementary sermon from the tradition.

Startlingly, LXX does not have vv. 14-26, the longest single passage which LXX lacks. There is no obvious reason why LXX should have deliberately omitted it. The conclusion must therefore be that it is a relatively late addition to MT. The content supports this. There are quotations or echoes of passages already in the tradition, while the linking of the Levites so closely with the Messiah in vv. 17-21 may well be thought to point to a date later than the rest of the material. This is the only mention of the Levites in Jer., but by no means the only mention of Messiah. It is the beginning of a long Jewish tradition of the place of the Levites in the future hope. Though it found a place in the Jeremiah tradition, it can hardly be attributed to the prophet himself, and must represent a late stage in the formation of the tradition.

THE RESTORATION OF THE CITY 33.1–13

The prose sermon of vv. 1-13 is therefore an earlier production of the prose tradition than vv. 14-26. But vv. 1–13 themselves show evidence of feeding on that tradition. Even the linguistic signs of the familiar prose style (eg. v. 11a, cf. 7.13; 16.9) look, in the light of the whole, to be quotations. Indeed this is a remarkable example of what might be called derivative inspiration. Its source is not direct communication of God's word, but the tradition of that word already received and here revitalised. In the mind of the editor this still permits the headings 'the word of the LORD came to Jeremiah' and 'thus says the LORD', since the ultimate source is one. The way the preacher uses the tradition before him may be demonstrated as follows;

(a) The sermon begins with a doxology (v. 2), with the familiar participal description and refrain. The text is disturbed, but the form is clear. Similarly use of this kind of doxology is found in 31.35, (qv.), and 32.18.

(b) The call and answer theme of v. 3 is the reversal of 23.35, 37.

(c) The city. Attention was focused in chapter 32 on the city (vv. 3, 24–25, 28, 31), yet when the answering oracle was proposed (v. 36–'concerning this city'), nothing was said about its rebuilding except by implication. This omission is here rectified, especially in 33.6–9. In v. 11 the restoration of the Temple is envisaged. The rectifying of this omission is no doubt the main point of this supplementary sermon.

(d) The siege mounds of v. 4 are mentioned here and in 32.24, but nowhere else in Jeremiah.

(e) The reference to dead bodies in v. 5 lacks immediate background: but this is supplied in 31.40.

(f) 'In my anger and my wrath' echoes 32.31.

(g) 'Health and healing' (v. 6) draws out 30.17.

(h) The forgiveness of v. 8 echoes 31.34.

(i) 'A name, a praise and a glory' is virtually identical with 13.11. In 13.11 it said that this was the LORD's purpose in making his people, but like the waistcloth they have become good for nothing. Here the hope of the fulfilment of that original purpose comes to expression.

(j) 'Waste, without man or beast' takes up the concluding verse (32.43) of the basic interpretation of the sign of the field.

(k) Verse 11a is a characteristic refrain of the Jeremiah prose tradition (see 7.34; 16.9; 25.10).

(l) The picture of worshippers bringing thank offerings to the Temple adds to the poetic 30.19 and gives it more precision. It also amplifies 31.6.

(m) The shepherds as a sign of pastoral peace, implicit in 31.12, are here made explicit.

(n) Verse 13 repeats 32.44b, qv.

This is a remarkable list and suggests a close and detailed attention to the literary formulation of the tradition. And yet with all this dependence upon the tradition, especially on that part represented in chapters 30–32, by focusing on the rebuilding of the city, it says something vital to the total picture of the future hope. In view of the place of the symbol of the City in the apocalyptic visions of the *NT* and of the Fathers, it may be regarded as authoratative in its own right.

2. who made the earth, the LORD who formed it to establish it: 'the earth' is supplied from LXX, no doubt a correct interpretation of the Heb. 'it'. The antecedent is also missing in v. 5. Two such undefined references in the same context are unlikely to be a coincidence, and suggest that the text, as it came into the hands of the editor, was either defective or derived from a context which provided the clues.

3. tell you great and hidden things which you have not known:
this meaning of the Heb. *ûbᵉṣūrôt* (hidden) is unique, but the idea is
present in the closely related Isa. 48.6. Some MSS assimilate the one
to the other. We have seen reason to suppose that these verses represent
a late stage in the Jeremiah prose tradition, though not as late as vv.
14–26. There is simply not the evidence to enable a precise dating. What
is certain is that we have here the signs of a change in the conception
of prophecy, such as is studied in John Barton's *Oracles of God* (London,
1986). The prophets themselves, and Jeremiah in particular, initiated
a 'living and continuous flow of trradition'. In the period of Judaism and
early Christianity, they have become a closed treasury of secrets. To
prophesy then was to claim to be able to communicate fresh truth which
would otherwise remain unknown. Barton correctly concludes that it was
in 'the "tunnel" period between the activity of named prophets and the
emergence of finished books bearing their names' that 'the shift in
perception must have begun to take place'. Here is a pointer to that
change. In Isa. 48.6 the sense is subtly different. There the hidden and
new things are the redeeming events about to happen, which are the
fulfilment of the divine plan obscured by the national disasters of the past,
but anticipated in prophecy.

4. the houses of the kings of Judah: i.e. the royal palace which was
a collection of buildings.

**which were torn down to make a defence against the siege mounds
and before the sword:** this is a defensible translation, but creates
problems of interpretation. Why single out the houses destroyed by the
defenders? Would the royal palace be thus destroyed? Better follow *NEB*
which has 'concerning the houses in this city . . . which are to be razed
to the ground, concerning siege-ramp and sword'.

5. The Chaldeans are coming: the Heb. has 'they are coming' and
this is followed, apparently ungrammatically, by the Chaldeans with the
ʾet, the sign of the accusative. This *ʾet* is however used so often to mark
an identifying gloss (27.8; e.g. Isa. 7.17, etc) that this commends itself
as the solution here. The text reads '*they* are coming in to fight . . .'.
The antecedent is missing (see introductory note above) and a glossator
made the right identification by adding 'i.e. the Chaldeans'. This found
its way into the permanent text. This view is supported by the theory
of P. P. Saydon (VT 14 (1964) 192–210) that *ʾet* may be properly
regarded as a particle of determination or emphasis.

6. and reveal to them abundance of prosperity and security: the
form of expression is unique in the Jeremiah tradition. The word

ᵃṭereṭ, translated 'abundance', is uncertain. 'Abundance' is possible but not supported by the Versions. Vulg. shows that *ᵃṭereṭ* was in its Heb. text but it did not know this meaning. LXX probably had a defective text and made the best of it. *NEB* resorts to an unacknowledged emendation which is an unsupported guess. A well attested Heb. word *ᵃṭereṭ*, meaning 'crown', would have sounded similar, and perhaps this offers the least questionable solution– 'and disclosed to them the crown, i.e. the perfection of prosperity and security'.

9. And this city shall be to me a name of joy: the Heb. has 'it', correctly identified as 'this city'. This is the third time an antecedent is not clearly given in this passage. 'Joy' is probably a gloss, since the 'to me' suggests that the name means 'reputation'. Cf. *NEB* and *REB* 'this city will win me a name'. And cf. 13.11.

10. This verse demonstrates the prolixity of the prose, referring back to what may be regarded as the final verse (32.43) of the basic interpretation of the sign of buying the field.

11. The psalm refrain is no doubt a direct quotation from the familiar thank-offering psalms, sun in the Temple when the cult was in operation. In fact it is a slightly 'improved' version of Ps. 136. 1, and the refrain is there repeated with each verse. This throws light on the original use of Ps. 136.

13. See on 32.44. This again shows that the preacher's horizon was limited (despite v. 7) to the restoration of Judah.

pass under the hands of the one who counts them: cf. Lev. 27.32; Ezek. 20.37; where, in each case, the same image is differently used.

PRIESTS AND KINGS IN AN UNBREAKABLE COVENANT **33.14–26**

At some stage this passage, absent from LXX (see above) was appended to the prose sermons of 31–33.13, in order to complete the picture of the future hope. It was natural enough to reintroduce the messianic hope, already present in the prose tradition (see on 23.5–6). What is quite new is to link the promise of an unfailing royal line with that of the Levitical priests. The main thrust of the passage seems to be in the repeated emphasis that the promise concerning both is unbreakable.

14–16. This is almost identical with 23.5–6 and introduced with the same **Behold, the days are coming** characteristic of the prose tradition. But there are some variations. 'He shall reign as king and deal wisely' is here omitted, and 'in his days' is changed to **in those days**. The effect of these changes is to direct attention away from an individual king to the line of kings, and this seems to be the way the word 'branch' is understood. This therefore is a reaffirmation of the promise of an unfailing Davidic line, as classically expressed in 2 Sam. 7.13, 16. **Jerusalem will dwell securely** (v. 16) replaces 'Israel' in 23.6, and this corresponds to the exclusive concern with Judah-Jerusalem in this comparatively late period of the prose tradition (cf. 31.38–40; 32.44; 33.12) But perhaps the most revealing change is the addition of the words **I will fulfil the promise I made to the house of Israel and the house of Judah** (v. 14). This is a characteristic Deuteronomic formula (cf. 1 Kg. 2.4; 8.25; 9.5; where also the reference is to the Nathan prophecy). It shows the preacher dealing with 'scripture' that has come down to him, reaffirming it and interpreting it. The interpretation follows.

17–18. The phrase **David shall never lack a man to sit on the throne of the house of Israel** (v. 17) follows the Deuteronomic formula in each case in 1 Kg. 2.4; 8.25; 9.5. It is here quoted precisely. This highlights the more emphatically the association of the Levites with the Davidic house in the same formula. For the reference to the Levites is not an exact quotation, nor is there any obvious older passage which might, so to speak, provide 'scriptural' authority. The nearest parallels are the references to the covenant with Levi in Neh. 13.29 and Mal. 2.4.

The phrase **the Levitical priests** (v. 18) is Deuteronomic (see Dt. 10. 8–9) and refers to the Levites as a whole, both those who, after the Deuteronomic reformation, found the opportunity to discharge their priesthood, and those who remained potentially priests. The great argument as to whether the priesthood should be exclusively Zadokite, or widened to include those Levites who could lay claim to descent from Aaron (see Num. 25.12f.), was yet to break out. That this argument should follow, and be settled in favour of the Aaronites, shows that this passage is unlikely to be later than the fifth century and might well be late sixth.

In other words, though it is a late phase of the prose tradition, perhaps the latest, it provides no evidence for a redaction beyond the sixth/fifth century and remains within the mainstream of the Jeremiah tradition. Indeed it is not difficult to discern a polemical intention behind the claim that the Levitical succession is divinely secured. As against the claim of the Zadokites (in Ezekiel circles) and the eventually victorious Aaronites (in the prose tradition), both of whom existed even in the pre-exilic period, this sounds like a resounding challenge. And since the Aaronites were within the wider family of Levites, the putative divine promise cannot be said to have been altogether falsified.

This polemical intention may also be suggested by the restriction here of the function of the Levites to the service of the altar, since it was this which was in dispute. Notably the Blessing of Moses (Dt. 33.8–10), a document of the pre-exilic period, widens this function to include teaching and divination; the service of the altar, coming last, seems to be subsidiary. And in Mal. 2.6–7 it is the teaching office of the Levite which is exalted. There is no reason to deny that this wider function was assumed in this passage; but undeniably the concentration on the sacrifical function suggests that it should be read in the light of the contemporary struggle for power.

19–22. Here the main concern of the preacher comes to the fore. He emphasises with all the force at his disposal that the divine assurance of vv. 17–18 is as secure as day and night. The negative argument is the same as that in the poem in 31.35–37 and is no doubt suggested by it. In 31.35–37, however, the application is to Israel as a people; here the argument is directed to the houses of David and Levi. As unbreakable as the covenant with Noah (Gen. 8.22; 9.8–17) will be the covenant with David and with the Levitical priests. The same Heb. word *prr* is used for 'breaking' a covenant as in 31.22 and it may be that a contrast is intended, as in 31.35–37. This covenant is therefore regarded as an aspect of the new covenant of 31.31.

The expression **As the host of heaven cannot be numbered and the sands of the sea cannot be measured** (v. 22) echoes the promise to the patriarchs (Gen. 15.5; 22.17; 26.4; Exod. 32.13, cf. Dt. 1.10; 10.22; 28.62). In every case it refers to the people of Israel as a whole. Plainly it is rhetorical exaggeration to use the expression of the house of David and of the priests, and this throws light on the preacher's method as he applies the traditional language to his own concern.

23.26. The final section of the appended sermon (vv. 14–26) is at first perplexing. It does not follow the previous sections logically. The application of the analogy of the Noachian covenant to the Davidic and Levitical covenants was at least intelligible. Here **the two families** (v. 24), which in context might have been thought to refer to the royal priestly families, must, on the contrary, refer to the northern and southern kingdoms. And in v. 26 David is linked not with Levi but with Jacob. Levi is not mentioned.

But if one looks for a new element in the passage, it is to be found in the quotation of a complaint of the people in v. 24; and it is this which determines the rest of the passage. It is best therefore to regard it as an independent element, appended at the end and deliberately adapted to what precedes. The complain of the people is **The LORD has rejected the two families which he chose**, and is correctly marked in *RSV* with inverted commas. The fate of Israel and Judah was the more perplexing to many, just because they believed so implicitly that the LORD had elected them. The preacher understands that the LORD put this in a question of Jeremiah–'Have you not observed?' and then, the LORD still speaking, adds: **Thus they have despised my people so that they are no longer a nation in their sight.** 'They' are the other nations, those who traditionally mocked stricken Israel (cf. Pss. 2.1–3; 44.13–16; 74.18, 23 etc.), and this is the proof that the 'two families' are not David and Levi, but Israel and Judah, cf. Isa. 8.14; Ezek. 37.15ff. The argument of v. 19 is now repeated, but the application is the one that seemed to be suggested by v. 22, viz. to the whole people of God.

26. **Descendants of Jacob,** lit. 'the seed of Jacob', relates this application once again to the promises to the patriarchs (sse on vv. 19–22 above), within which the promises to David are subsumed. Thus the complaint of the people provides a sort of sounding board for the repetition of the theme that the covenant of God with his people stands, and in the future will be as secure as the universe itself.

THE 'RELEASE' OF SLAVES AND THE RELEASE OF JUDGMENT
34.1–22 (LXX 41.1–22)

The previous prose sermons in chapters 32 and 33 have centred on the hope of restoration after judgment, and, in this respect, followed appropriately the poetic collection of chapters 30–31, which was probably added to chapters 26–29 at the same time as the dimension of hope in these chapters was pointed by deft glossing. Chapters 34 and 35 break the sequence and revert to the warning of judgment to come. Yet chapters 34 and 35 have the same prose character as 32 and 33, and it is this which explains their present position. They belong to the same circle of preachers in the Jeremiah tradition. The sermonic character of chapter 34 is paramount. The prose sermon finds its place in the collection of prose sermons even if, from the point of view of subject matter, it appears to revert to earlier themes.

This explains the repetition of the judgment on Zedekiah (vv. 1–5) which has already been stated in part in 32.1–5. Just as the historical context was important there for the sermon, so it is vital here, though for quite different reasons.

Those who treasured the tradition remembered how Jeremiah had predicted that Zedekiah would be captured but not killed; 'until I visit him', was the way it was expressed in 32.5; 'You shall not die by the sword. You shall die in peace' is the expression in 34.5. In both passages it is enigmatically predicted that Zedekiah will 'see the king of Babylon eye to eye and speak with him face to face'. In 34.5 it is added that it will be possible to honour Zedekiah with customary mourning rites. But in neither passage is it stated or hinted that, though the prediction will be fulfilled, it has a darker side, that Zedekiah's sons will be put to death before his eyes and then his own eyes put out (39.6–7).

It is in the highest degree unlikely that the sermon was preached in ignorance of this terrible sequel, since we are dealing with the sermons of followers of Jeremiah who are preaching on his words and deeds. This has two consequences: (1) It means that the preacher remembered the prediction of Jeremiah to Zedekiah, as it was, without improving it in the light of the sequel. And (2) it means, in all probability, that the preacher knew, as he spoke, that his hearers were well aware of the full story. The question then arose, why was the event, in respect of Zedekiah, more horrifying than Jeremiah anticipated? The answer is given in vv. 8 ff.

Verses 8 ff. must therefore be read not only in the light of the historical context (vv 1–5) but also the knowledge that the fate of Zedekiah was more severe than the prophecy of vv. 3–5 foreshadowed. The section then becomes the more significant as it is seen to offer an explanation. In brief, the explanation is that the repudiation of the proclamation of release of slaves (vv. 8–11) was evidence of such infidelity (vv. 15–16) that the 'release' of the LORD's anger without inhibition was inevitable (vv. 17–22).

It is clear that the proclamation of release of slaves owed nothing to Jeremiah. It was entirely the initiative of the king and his advisers. We may suppose that they thought, by an act of virtue, to influence the divine mercy and obtain a stay of execution. They therefore entered into a solemn covenant, Zedekiah and the people, before the LORD (v. 15) in the Temple. The covenant-making involved the cutting of a calf in two (v. 18) and walking between the parts (v. 19), thus calling a curse upon themselves if they broke the covenant. The slaying of the calf does not seem to have been a sacrifice in the technical sense. This ritual of covenant-making was known not only in the *OT* (cf. Gen. 15.7–20), but to other peoples as well. On the slaying of an ass at Mari, see M. Noth's essay 'Old Testament Covenant making in the light of a text from Mari', in *The Laws in the Pentateuch and Other Essays*, ET, 1966. On covenant making in connection with a treaty between Bar-gaya of Katak and Mati-el of Arpad in the mid eighth century, see *Near Eastern Religious Texts relating to the Old Testament*, ed. Walter Beyerlin, 1978, p. 260. Here the comparison is remarkable. For Mati-el is threatened, if he breaks the covenant:-. 'And as the man of wax is blinded, so will Mati-el be blinded.

And as this calf is cut up, so will Mati-el be cut up, and so will his nobles be cut up.' Cf. v. 19.

The substance of the covenant was the release of slaves. It looks as though Zedekiah proposed the reactivation of an institution that had fallen into abeyance (v. 14), was nevertheless endorsed by the Deuteronomic law, but not put into practice. **The proclamation of liberty** ($d^e r \hat{o} r$), v. 9, is based originally upon the slave law in the Covenant Code, probably antedating the monarchy. Here (Exod. 21.2–11) the law concerns a 'Hebrew slave' at a time when the term 'Hebrew' indicated an inferior social class of persons who had sold themselves into slavery. The rule is that such a slave, under the conditions specified, shall serve for six years and then be **free** ($hop\check{s}\hat{\imath}$) vv. 9, 10, 11, 14, 16) i.e. no longer a slave, but still below the status of a citizen. The slave could however, if he wished, elect to remain his master's slave for life.

The law of Hammurabi concerns itself with a seignior who, because of debt, may have sold the services of his wife or children. In this case the service shall last for only three years. The word $d^e r \hat{o} r$, 'release', appears to be a feudal word, found also in Accadian, meaning 'freeing from burdens'.

The Deuteronomic law (Dt. 15.12–18) takes up the slave law of Exod. 21 and modifies it to include the Hebrew woman as well as the man, but also to make it clear that a 'Hebrew' means every fellow Israelite. Dt. also includes this release of slaves within a more general release of property which is to take place every seven years on the basis of a fixed cycle. Thus Dt. 15 is introduced: 'At the end of every seven years you shall grant a release ($\check{s}^e mitt\bar{a}h$). And this is the manner of the release . . .'

That some account of the older law was taken is shown by the incident of the woman of Shunem in 2 Kg. 8.1–6. After a famine of seven years which led her to leave her patrimony, the king restored it to her on her return. It may well be that the more formalised and fixed period of law of Dt. was rarely, if ever, carried into effect. Balancing the ideal with the realistic, the priestly law of Lev. 25 prescribed a jubilee year. 'You shall hallow the fiftieth year, and proclaim liberty ($d^e r \hat{o} r$) throughout the land to all its inhabitants; it shall be a jubilee for you, when each of you shall return to his property and each of you shall return to his family' (Lev. 25.10). A man who sells himself because of his poverty shall not be a slave, but a 'a hired servant' ($\check{s}\bar{a}k\hat{\imath}r$) and a 'sojourner' ($t\hat{o}\check{s}\bar{a}\underline{b}$) and shall be released at jubilee.

It seems probable therefore that Zedekiah seized on a Deuteronomic provision which had not been implemented, and thought that by obeying it he might avert the doom ahead. If some or most of the slaves were agricultural workers, it is probable that their occupation was in any case interrupted by the Babylonia invasion. But the principle remained. According to v. 13 Jeremiah referred specifically to the covenant 'I made . . . with your fathers when I brought them out of the land of Egypt'. But despite the reference to Egypt, which might suggest that he had the Covenant Code formulation in mind, there can be no doubt that, as in Jer. 11, he relies on the Deuteronomic formulation (see note on v. 13). This is clear from a comparison of Jer. 34.14 with Dt. 15.12 and 15.1. For the Jeremiah tradition the Deuteronomic Law was part of the basic covenant provision.

As to the circumstances which led to the repudiation of the solemn covenant and the taking back of the slaves, we can only guess (see on v. 6 below). Verse 22 suggests that there was a temporary lull in the siege of Jerusalem, so that the invaders withdrew and encouraged a false sense of relief in the besieged. They thought there was no longer urgent need to propitiate the LORD and ignored both the divine law and the solemn covenant they had recently made. Jeremiah's response was to reassert the judgment with typical prophetic word-play. **Behold, I proclaim to you liberty** ($d^{e}r\hat{o}r$) **to the sword, to pestilence, and to famine** (v. 17) and to warn them that they themselves would suffer the fate of the calf they had used for their oath taking; see also on v. 18 below. The fate of Zedekiah and his ministers would be total submission to the Babylonians, and no distinction is now made between Zedekiah and his ministers. Altogether this is one of the most calculated and time-serving acts of public disobedience recorded in the *QT*. If we read between the lines, we may suppose that Zedekiah did not have authority to carry through what he initiated. Here as elsewhere he was well-intentioned but weak. Here as always this was not enough, and could not avert either the fall of his people or his own sad destiny.

5. As spices were burned for your fathers: the Heb. is 'like the burnings for your fathers, so men shall burn (*NEB* and *REB* 'kindle fires') for you'. Josephus mentions spices for the funeral of Herod the Great, but no fires. 2 Chr. 16.14 relates that the bier for Asa was filled with spices and adds 'they made a very great fire in his honour'. Conversely 2 Chr. 21.19 says of Jehoram: 'his people made no fire in his honour'. It seems therefore that the burning is not one of aromatic herbs but a special fire which was regarded as an honour.

7. against Jerusalem and against all the cities of Judah that were left, Lachish and Azekah: The situation here presupposed is an advanced stage of the second siege of Jerusalem. Apart from Jerusalem itself, only two fortresses remained Lachish (Tell ed-Duweir) and Azekah (Tell Zakariyeh). These were situated in hill country. The year is 588 B.C. and the crisis has external witness in the Ostraca of Lachish, inscribed potsherds found in 1935 and 1938 in the ruins of the gate tower of Tell ed-Duweir. (See *DOTT*, pp. 212–217; *ANET*, pp. 321–322). These are letters from various outposts received by Yaosh, the military governor of Lachish. Ostracon IV may well mark the precise moment of the fall of Azekah. It reads: '(my lord) will know that we are watching for the signals of Lachish, according to all the signs which my lord had given, for we cannot see Azekah'. In Ostracon VI the complaint is made that there were those 'who weaken the hands of the land and the city'. Jeremiah is not named, but the cap fits. According to Jer. 38.4 the ministers said to Zedekiah: 'Let this man be put to death, for he is weakening the hands of the soldiers . . . and of all the people'. In Ostracon III it is said that 'The commander of the army, Konjahu, son of Elnathan, has gone down on his way to Egypt, and Hodawjahu, son of Ahijahu, and his men he has sent to obtain . . .'. The Ostracon is tantalisingly defective at this point. But it is difficult not to associate this mission with the effort to obtain Egyptian aid. According to Jer. 37.5 the Egyptian army did make an invasion which caused the Babylonians to lift the siege of Jerusalem temporarily. This may well be the historical episode which provides the background to the repudiation of the recently made covenant and so to this sermon.

9. that everyone should set free his Hebrew slaves, male and female, so that no one should enslave a Jew, his brother: In the light of the general exposition above, the wording here will be seen to be significant. The older law specified the Hebrew man, and this may well in the pre-monarchical period have carried a special, and a pejorative meaning. In Dt. the Hebrew was any Israelite, male or female. Here all ambiguity is overcome by further definition. A Hebrew man or woman is a fellow Judaean.

13. I made a covenant with your fathers when I brought them out of the land of Egypt, out of the house of bondage: The nearest parallel to the whole sentence is in Jer. 11.3–4 which however has 'iron furnace' for house of bondage'. House of bondage' in apposition to Egypt, occurs in both versions of the Ten Commandments (Exod 20.2; Dt. 5.6 and frequently in the Deuteronomic literature–Dt. 6.12; 7.8; 8..14; 13.5, 10; Jos. 24.17; Jg. 6.8; cf. Mic. 6.4). 'Iron furnace' also occurs in Dt. 4.20; 1 Kg. 8.15. The Deuteronomic Law is presented as delivered by Moses on the basis of the redemption from Egypt and before entrance into the

Promised Land. Jeremiah accepted it as such. The reason for supposing that it is the Deuteronomic form of the slave law to which Jeremiah refers is given above. The Deuteronomic interpretations of 11.3–4 and 34.8–14 confirm one another.

14. At the end of six years: The Hebrew reads 'seven' years. *RSV* here follows LXX which reads 'six', no doubt understanding that the seventh year was the sabbath year. *NEB* and *REB* think the Heb. may be translated 'within seven years', but not apparently in Dt. 15.1! It appears that Dt. envisaged the general release taking place by the end of the seventh year.

15–16. You . . . repented . . . you turned round: the same verb in Heb. constitutes a word-play characteristic of this sermon. See on v. 18. The irony is that their 'turning' was the wrong way.

17. to the sword, to pestilence, and to famine: A standard expression of the prose tradition, occurring eighteen times. See on 14.12.

a horror to all the kingdoms of the earth: See on 15.1–4. The relation to Dt. 28.2 is close, because there the horror is that 'your dead body shall be food for all the birds of the air, and for beasts of the earth'. And this is exactly the fate which the preacher sees about to come on the leaders and people of Judah (v. 20). This is the curse of the Deuteronomic Law which he sees about to be fulfilled.

18. the men who transgressed my covenant: The word-play is subtle and cannot be reproduced in translation—ʿābar 'transgressed', and thus used widely, but notably in the Deuteronomic writings, is also the verb used for 'passing through' the parts of the victim (Gen. 15.7; Jer. 34.15, 19). Combined with the word-play on repentance, on the proclamation of release (see above), and on the slaughtered calf, this reinforces powerfully the ironic modes of judgment and illustrates the skill of the preacher.

THE RECHABITES: A MODEL OF FIDELITY **35.1–19 (LXX 42.1–19)**

The last of the prose sermons in the collection 32–35 reverts to the time of Jehoiakim. The Rechabites are used as a model in a highly didactic passage. The sermon character of the chapter is no doubt sufficient explanation of its place here. Some have emphasised the positive future promised to the Rechabites (v. 19) as a reason for the association of this chapter with oracles concerning the future. Similarly they have suggested that the future offered to Zedekiah in 34.5 explains the position of chapter 34.

In the case of chapter 34 the exposition above has proposed a different interpretation and does not permit the fragmentation of the chapter. In chapter 35 there is undeniably a conditional hope. If Israel were to be obedient like the Rechabites, her future would be secure. But Jeremiah had long ceased to reckon on repentance. He could no longer even intercede to avert the judgment. And what is more, the preacher in the Jeremiah tradition was in the position to know that Jeremiah was right. Israel's disobedience was to bring upon her the inevitable doom. The Rechabites' zeal for the LORD only throws Israel's incurable obstinacy into greater relief. This chapter is about unrelieved judgment. At the same time chapters 34 and 35 are a foil to one another in that the one presents an example of cynical disobedience and the other of fanatical obedience.

Two literary features of the chapter should be noted.

(a) In the basic narrative (vv. 1–11) which tells of Jeremiah's dealings with the Rechabites, the story is told in the first person. This corresponds with 1; 11; 13.1–11; 14.11–14; 15.1; 16.1–4; 17.19; 18.1–11, all prose passages. The most natural explanation is that the preachers of the tradition had access to Jeremiah's own witness to his prophetic activity. Thereafter Jeremiah is referred to in the third person (vv. 12, 18) and although it is conceivable that the prophet himself drew out the lesson of the Rechabites, it is clear that the version we have is that of his successors.

(b) The prose is more obviously than in chapters 32–34 the prose of the tradition. This is not so much in the narrative of vv. 1–11 where the new character of the event naturally determines the vocabulary, but in the didactic exposition (vv. 12–19). Here the familiar clichés of the prose tradition abound, notably in vv. 13, 14, 15, 17, (see below)

All this points to a close association with an event of Jeremiah's life of the kind we have noticed to be characteristic of the prose tradition. See particularly the introduction to chapters 7–20, where it was argued that Baruch may well have been responsible for introducing his own version of much of Jeremiah's teaching, especially when it springs from an event in his ministry.

Jeremiah is commanded by the LORD to go to the Rechabites, as he had been commanded to go to the potter (chapter 18). The whole episode is thus a prophecy. He took Jaazaniah and his family into a room in the Temple made available to him by a sympathetic 'man of God'. His intention was no doubt to give the ensuing test maximum publicity and a setting which gave it representative status. He put wine before them and invited them to drink. They declined on the basis of their principles.

The wine test in no way means that the Rechabites were in the modern sense teetotallers. Their protest was not against a single social problem, but against a type of civilisation which they regarded as fatal to Yahwism. They represented the desert traditions of Israel's youth. Jonadab, son of Rechab, their founder, appeared in the ninth century to support Jehu's revolution (2 Kg. 10.15–17) to extirpate the apostatising dynasty of Ahab. The narrative emphasises that he was heart and soul with Jehu, and approved his bloody deeds as evidence of his zeal for the LORD. But it is here in Jeremiah that we learn more detail of the principles for which the followers of Jonadab stood. Not only did they reject the fruit of the wine and therefore plant no vineyards, but they would not sow crops or build houses. They continued to live in tents. This no doubt represented the kind of life lived by Israel in the wilderness, before her settlement in Canaan and subsequent corruption by Canaanite religion and civilisation.

It is possible that the name Rechab was given to a movement with a longer history, since in I Chr. 2.55 the clan of the Rechabites is connected with the Kenites, but of this we know nothing. The similarity with the Nazarites is only partial. The Rechabite vow was more comprehensive and binding upon the whole clan. The threat that Yahwism would be submerged by the Canaanite environment was great in the ninth and eight centuries, not least because Israel took over much that was good in almost every aspect of settled life. It was easy for the common people to attribute the crops to Baal, even while they paid lip-service to their ancestral deity.

It is perhaps no accident that Elijah, that prophet of antique simplicity, 'wore' a garment of haircloth, with a girdle about his loins and came from the semi-desert region where the wilderness traditions were alive. His journey to Horeb signified a return to the ancestral traditions. Hosea saw the period of the wilderness as the time of youth and innocence. (Hos. 2.14–15). Jeremiah shared Hosea's vision, as in 2.2. 'I remember the devotion of your youth, your love as a bride, how you followed me in the wilderness, *in a land not sown*'. The Rechabites took this prophetic insight to an extreme. They wished to freeze Israel's development, to accept the promise of the land, but to live as those still travelling to it. They were as fanatical and uncompromising as contemporary Muslims in the Near East.

It is clear that Jeremiah did not himself accept their way. If he lived in Jerusalem, he inhabited a house. He made use of the Temple. He owned property and understood the necessary steps to secure it as divine guidance. There is no evidence that he rejected wine in the same way that he felt bound to reject marriage. What impressed him about the Rechabites was their consistency and fidelity. They were uncompromisingly obedient, and it was the quality of their obedience alone to which he appealed (v. 16) and which he contrasted with Israel's disobedience, despite the constant succession of prophets to guide and warn (vv. 14–15). It was precisely because Jeremiah did not accept all the Rechabite principles that his appeal to their example was telling and unforgettable.

2. the house of Rechabites, i.e. the clan or community. It is not clear whether Rechab was the farther of Jonadab (2 Kg. 10.15–17) or simply the eponymous ancestor of the clan. The latter is more likely.

3. Jaazaniah the son of Jeremiah, son of Habazziniah: The name provides, so to speak, circumstantial evidence, and there is no reason to doubt the accuracy of the tradition. Jaazaniah has the function of a witness (cf. Jer. 32.12; Isa. 8.2) to the truth which he is to exemplify.

4. the chamber of the sons of Hanan the son of Igdaliah, the man of God: The circumstantial detail is deliberate, and is made even more precise in the rest of the verse. There were a number of rooms in the Temple, some for store, some for meeting, some for individuals, and the whole was supervised (Neh. 13.4–5). In this case, the room seems to have been allotted to one Hanan ben Igdaliah and his disciples.

That he is described as 'man of God' suggests that he was a prophet, since the term is used of Samuel, Shemaiah, Elijah, Elisha and some unnamed prophets. The title seems to come into use in the north in the ninth century, and to be used retrospectively of Moses and David. It is used in the Deuteronomic history and by the Chronicler. There seems therefore every reason to assume that the meaning is not different here. Whether this is evidence of what have come to be called cultic prophets is perhaps less certain. The conclusion of A. R. Johnson was that 'the reference is to a particular school or guild of prophets forming part of the temple personnel. It was doubtless in such circles that the various prophetic compositions were preserved' (*The Cultic Prophet in Ancient Israel*, 1962, p. 62). Here we have one of these prophets who had such sympathy with Jeremiah that he was prepared publicly to support him.

6. Jonadab . . . our father: The Rechabites had been true to the principles of their founding father from the middle of the ninth century to the end of the seventh. Thus the strength of their commitment is emphasised.

7. that you may live many days in the land where you sojourn:
The motive clause happens to be attached to the commandment to honour
father and mother (Exod. 20.1). No doubt part of the preacher's development of his theme. The 'sojourner' or 'resident alien' was normally a
foreigner, about whom, because they had no rights, the prophets showed
special concern. The Rechabites were native Israelites who adopted the
'nomadic' form of existence on principle. Their existence in the land was
not so much a settlement as a sojourning and their customs expressed this.

11. Here the Rechabites feel the need to defend their presence in the
city of Jerusalem, lest they appear to have deviated from their principles.
They had fled behind the city walls simply and only to find protection
from the invading armies.

the army of the Chaldeans and the army of the Syrians: This is the
main clue to the date of Jeremiah's encounter with the Rechabites. No
doubt the source of the reference to the Aramaean cooperation in the
invasion is the narrative of 2 Kg. 24.1–7. 'The LORD sent against him
raiding parties of Chaldeans and Aramaeans'. The term 'Chaldean' is
not unambiguous and may well here refer to the nomadic *Kaldu* who were
part of the ethnic group of Aramaeans, stationed in Syria and under the
command of Nebuchadnezzaar.

The difficulty is to know what year this was, since we do not know
from which year Jehoiakim paid tribute and which year, three years later,
he ceased to pay tribute. Josephus puts it at 601 B.C. (*Ant* X 6.1). The
most probably hypothesis is that Jehoiakim's submission followed the
defeat of the Egyptians at Carchemish in 605 B.C.. Ashkelon fell in 604
and Judah surrendered at this time. Then Jehoiakim's rebellion would
be triggered by the defeat of the Babylonians in their Egyptian campaign
of 601/600. It is clear from the Wiseman Chronicle that Nebuchadnezzar
undertook regular campaigns in Syria and Palestine from 605 onwards.
No certain synchronisation is possible, but sometime between 601 and
598 would seem probable.

12–19 As the preacher now relates Jeremiah's interpretation of the
event, he at once resorts to the well known commonplaces of the tradition.
They are as follows:-

13. men of Judah and the inhabitants of Jerusalem: see on 11.2
receive instruction see on 7.28

14. I have spoken to you persistently . . . cf. 7.13; 25.3

15. sending them persistently cf. 7.25; 25.4; 26.5; 29.19; 44.4. Note
both forms of the expression (lit. 'rising up' and saying or sending) in
25.3–4. See on 7.13, 25.

Turn now every one of you from his evil way: cf. 18.11; 25.5; 26.3; 36.3; 7.

amend your doings: cf. 2.33; 7.3; 18.11; 26.13.

do not go after other gods to serve them: cf. 7.6, 9; 11.10; 13.10; 16.11; 25.6. See on 7.6.

you shall dwell in the land which I gave to you and your fathers: cf. 16.15; 24.10; 25.5.

But you did not incline your ear: cf. 7.24, 26; 11.8; 17.23; 25.4; 34.14; 45.5. This expression is not found in Dt.

17. Behold, I am bringing . . . evil: cf. 5.15; 6.19; 11.11; 19.3, 15; 39.16; 45.5, (49.5).

I have spoken to them and they have not listened, I have called them, and they have not answered: cf. 7.13, 27; 11.11, 14; 33.3.

This is strong evidence of a common pool of language, characteristic of the Jeremiah tradition. Particularly significant is the relation to chapters 7, 11 and 25. The events are different, but when it comes to enforcing the message, the preacher uses identical phrases, and makes no effort to achieve originality or even variation. The well-worn phrases are adequate pointer to Jeremiah's teaching and that is enough.

19. Jonadab the son of Rechab shall never lack a man to stand before me: cf. the promise made concerning the house of David in 33.17 and the Levites in 33.18. The expression 'stand before me' is used in 15.1, 19; 18.20 of the prophetic intercession of Moses, Samuel and Jeremiah himself. The meaning here must be of a more general service of the LORD. There is little evidence that the promise was directly fulfilled. The 'Malchijah the son of Rechab' referred to in Neh. 3.14 is otherwise unknown, and, if he was a Rechabite was plainly compromising his principles by rebuilding the Dung Gate. Guignebert saw the Rechabites as precursors of Essene asceticism, but Martin Hengel can see no connection (*Judaism and Hellenism* I, 1974, p. 243).

THE WORD OF GOD WRITTEN AND INDESTRUCTIBLE
36.1–32 (LXX 43.1–32)

This vivid narrative provides a link in the long process which led ultimately to the production of the written Bible and the Canon of Scripture. It implies that for twenty-three years Jeremiah has uttered his oracles without writing them down. In this respect he is both a man of his age and consistent with his prophetic predecessors. They were primarily orators, appearing before their people to warn, plead, denounce, teach and guide. This is why their oracles were predominantly in verse, enabling them to be suggestive, allusive, colourful, enigmatic and above all memorable. The prophets used the clever devices of the orator, from the pun to the enacted sign, to bring their message home to ears not altogether disposed to hear. Their difficulty was that many delighted in their art but dismissed the content.

To read them with the presuppositions of a book civilisation is anachronistic. The prophets represent the high point of a different kind of culture which was in no way inferior. The point was made trenchantly by W. Robertson Smith (*The Prophets of Israel*), 1897, p. 126).

'At the Courts of the Caliphs and their Emirs the rude Arabs of the desert were wont to appear without any feeling of awkwardness, and to surprise the courtiers by the finish of their impromptu verses, the fluent eloquence of their oratory, and the range of subjects on which they could speak with knowledge and discrimination. Among the Hebrews, as in the Arabian desert, knowledge and oratory were not affairs of professional education, or dependent for their cultivation on wealth and social status. The sum of book learning was small; men of all ranks mingled with that Oriental freedom which is so foreign to our habits; shrewd observation, a memory retentive of traditional lore, and the faculty of original reflection took the place of laborious study as the ground of acknowledged intellectual pre-eminence. In Hebrew, the best writing is an unaffected transcript of the best speaking.

By the time of Jeremiah the professional, scribal type of production had also been developed, and resulted in the prose version of the tradition. The poetry and the prose are side by side, enabling a peculiarly effective discrimination to be made.

It is not, however, necessary or plausible to suppose that Jeremiah dictated every word of his orations. His purpose was not simply to give permanence to his oracles, but to speak a new and powerful word in the special circumstances of the year 604 B.C. Allowing for perhaps a long period of relative silence in those twenty-three years, Jeremiah will without doubt have spoken at length. On the other hand the transcript of his dictated oracles was read three times in one day, first to the people, next to the ministers and finally to the king. Jeremiah will therefore have remembered the salient verses and sometimes the telling phrase, often providing a *concentrate* of what he once developed without inhibition. And since the substance of his early warnings was judgment in the form of invasion by an unspecified Foe from the North, it is not difficult to see the main point of his present action. The warning that had been ignored could now be seen to be to the point. The foe that had been dismissed because it was unspecified could now be identified. The word of the Lord might be unconscionably slow in coming to fulfilment, but it must catch up with Israel in the end. Its very slowness made the present danger seem all the more terrifying. It was inescapable and could now be seen to be so. This is the point of giving the permanence of writing to old oracles and it is the reason that the effect of reading the transcript rather than uttering it from memory was new and traumatic. In other words, the writing down of the oracles was itself a prophetic sign, like the many other prophetic signs which Jeremiah performed. This interpretation finds striking confirmation in the parallel chapter 25 (qv.).

The perception that this event is a prophetic sign, performed under the direct command of the Lord, determines the place of this chapter in its present context. As a narrative it could belong with chapters 37–45 and some have so linked it. This is, however, only superficially plausible, since the chapters 37–45 have their own character as an account of the final downfall of the kingdom of Judah, alternative to 2 Kg., and demonstrating the part of the prophet Jeremiah in these events. Thus chapter 37 opens in the annalistic style of 2 Kg. and is concerned with events from the time of Zedekiah until shortly after 586 B.C. In contrast, chapter 36 is concerned with an event in the fourth year of Jehoiakim and focuses on, so to speak, the history of the word of God. This links it with the other prophetic signs in the Jeremiah tradition. It has already been observed that many of the prose sermons are built on an event or sign in the life of Jeremiah and that these are significant in the prose framework of the accumulating tradition complexes. Chapters 7, 11, 14, 17, 18, 19, 20, 24, 25, are examples. Cf. also 32. Finally convincing is the observation that chapter 36 is related closely to chapter 25, as chapter 26 is related to chapter 7.

The two passages have complementary intentions. Chapter 25 is an oracle on Jeremiah's oracles to date; it is concerned with content and intention and is didactic in the manner of the preachers of the tradition. Chapter 36 is a detailed narrative with a powerful prophetic significance, in which the message speaks for itself because it is the story of the reception of God's word. Each is concerned with the same event. See introduction to chapter 25. And just as chapter 25 is properly to be understood as concluding a collection of oracles and may once have concluded the Baruch Scroll (chapters 1–6), ultimately sealing chapters 1–24; so chapter 36 is best understood as concluding chapters 30–35 and probably the whole collection to date, i.e. 1–35.

This judgment is in no way weakened by the evident relationship of this narrative to the story of the discovery of the Law-book in 2 Kg. 22. It seems clear that the narrator wished to contrast the truculent Jehoiakim with his pious father Josiah. That Jeremiah keenly felt this contrast is shown by Jer. 22.13–17. It is here spelt out with sufficient precision to suggest that the narrator was well acquainted with the story of the finding of the Law-book. And since the Jeremiah tradition owes much to the Deuteronomic schools in any case, its scholars coming from the same educational stables, there is nothing strange or unexpected in this influence. The finding of the scroll of the Law in the Temple, and the reading of Baruch's scroll in the Temple, are clearly compared. Each scroll requires a judgment to be made of its authenticity as God's word. In 2 Kg. 22.9 the secretary, one of the *śārîm* or ministers, reads first and then shows the scroll to the king; in Jer. 36 the *śārîm* hear the reading and then send the scroll to the king.

The reaction of the king is in each case crucial. Acceptance by Josiah and rejection by Jehoiakim is made explicit in contrasting sentences. 'And when the king heard the words of the book of the law, he rent his clothes' (2 Kg. 22.11). 'Yet neither the king, nor any of his servants who heard all these words was afraid, nor did they rend their garments' (Jer. 36.24). Just as Huldah the prophetess responded with an oracle (2 Kg. 22.14–20) so also Jeremiah, hearing that the king had burned the scroll, ordered a fresh copy to be made and completed the prophetic significance of the event by adding an oracle concerning Jehoiakim.

The differences are many, but the correspondence of pattern suggests that the narrator, knowing the story of Josiah, was intent to make a detailed contrast between Josiah and Jehoiakim, first suggested by Jeremiah himself, and corresponding to the facts of history. The notion that the story of chapter 36 is a complete invention, based on the narrative of 2 Kg. 22, runs counter to the understanding of the narrative element in the prose tradition of Jeremiah, presented in this commentary. It is a gratuitous theory with which the trained historian will have little sympathy, for it proceeds from a failure of discrimination.

If, as we have argued in the introduction, and suggested as a clue to chapter 25, the collected oracles dictated to Baruch are substantially, (not identically), chapters 1–6, then those chapters take on a new dimension. The individual oracles, about thirty-two of them, have their own context. But as they are now presented, they are alive with the dangers and uncertainties of the year 604 and assume new homogeneity. Thus chapter 2, a collection of nine oracles, presents a certain underlying unity of theme–the case against God's people, their persistent infidelity and disobedience, with the legal metaphor obtruding in vv. 9 and 29. 'Therefore I will bring a charge against you'. 'Why argue your case with me?'*NEB*. The idea of accusation and defence runs through the whole. One senses the increase of tension as Jeremiah piles oracle upon oracle. No doubt he communicated the *substance* of this teaching, but we can be fairly sure that these verses never assumed precisely this form until he dictated them to Baruch. Baruch himself may have influenced the expression here and there, particularly when he wrote them out a second time. Similarly in 3.1–4.4 there is a unity of purpose dictated by the new situation. Divorce is now inescapable. The brazenness of Israel's worship and behaviour is stressed and likened to the infidelity of an harlot. Judah is warned to ponder the tragic example of her sister Israel. The section ends in 3.19–4.4 with a dialogue of repentance, in which the LORD sums up the conditions of avoiding the full force of the divine judgment. When the full force of the divine judgment could be thought to be on the point of erupting it is not difficult to feel again the power of these oracles, and the dismay of those who witnessed the recital in 604 B.C.

The final section 4.5–6.30 contains the oracles on the Foe from the North, and so, presenting unrelenting judgment about to fall in the realities of contemporary events, provides a climax and finale for the preceding sections and for the scroll as a whole. The section ends with the paradoxical assertion that the work of Jeremiah as an assayer or refiner of the people has been ineffective. Paradoxical because it highlights the effectiveness of the divine word which cannot now be resisted. The Foe from the North, once teasing, uncertain, enigmatic, and therefore capable of being ignored, is now unmistakenly identified. There was no need to gloss these poems further. They were and are unresistably terrifying. All comes together in a unity which is not that of a modern writer. But it is intelligible and compelling on its own terms.

Such we believe was the text which Jeremiah dictated and Baruch wrote down. The prophetic sign for the year 604 B.C. lay in the permanent fixation, by means of writing, of the old oracles. The king himself perhaps obscurely recognised this. It may be that his view of the scroll was influenced by semi-magical ideas of its inherent power, and that by destroying it he sought to neutralise the word of God. He was not far from the truth. This word did have inherent power, but it could not be neutralised. And once, for this particular purpose, the oracles were written, and so became a permanent witness to the prophet's teaching, a powerful impetus was given to the continuation of the process. A similar motive may be discerned in the first steps to commit the oracles of Isaiah to writing. Thereafter those who were faithful to the prophet's teaching and counted themselves as his disciples undertook the double role of both preaching his word and preserving the tradition. The process did not cease until the book was complete in the form we have it, and indeed, modern attempts to reestablish the text and expound its meaning are contemporary forms of the same activity, by the same spirit.

The style befits the fast moving narrative and lacks the long didactic sermons which characterise many of the prose sections of the book. In this chapter 25 is a strong contrast. But where it is appropriate to spell out the judgment or to give an oracle, the prose has the familiar phrases of the tradition, as particularly in vv 3, 7, 30–31.

36.1–3

1. In the fourth year of Jehoiakim: i.e. 605/604 B.C. Jeremiah dictated his oracles in the period of the great crisis. The international scene was changing, dramatic and menacing. After the demise of the Assyrian empire, there followed a period in which Egypt and Babylon struggled for control of the all important region of Syria. The first move was in favour of Babylon, and was the result of the emergence as a major figure of the crown prince Nebuchadnezzar. Nabopolassar, now old and sick, entrusted his armies to his son, who decisively defeated the Egyptian garrison at Carchemish in May–June 605 B.C. The Babylonian Chronicle records: 'He accomplished their defeat and (beat them) into non-existence' (Wiseman, *Chronicles of Chaldean Kings* 1961, p. 67). It is also recorded that 'at that time Nebuchadnezzar conquered the whole area of the Hatti country'; i.e. the whole of Syria and Palestine. Nebuchadnezzar succeeded his father in September 605 B.C. He spent the first six months of his reign in Syria on an expedition which was unopposed. The Babylonian Chronicle says that 'all the Kings of Hatti appeared before him and rendered heavy tribute'. It is difficult to suppose that Jehoiakim was not among those who made their submission (cf. Kg. 24.1).

The extreme peril of the situation is illustrated by the fate of Ashkelon which refused submission and drew upon itself the full destructive might of Nebuchadnezzar's army. He marched against it in December 604 (if the defective text may be so read) and though the campaign was long, the city was captured and plundered, its king and leading citizens taken to captivity in Babylon (Wiseman p. 69). If an Aramaic letter from King Adon to a Pharaoh may be identified as an appeal from Ashkelon for Egyptian aid, then we have a pathetic illustration of the political game played at this time. He says that the Babylonian troops have advanced as far as Aphek' and have begun to . . . ' (how we would value the complete text!) He says that 'if the king of Babylon takes it (Ashkelon?), he will set up a governor in the land, and . . . '. The uncertainties of identification (see E. Vogt, *'Die Neubabylonische Chronik über die Schlact bei Karkemisch und die Einnahm von Jerusalem'* VT *Suppl.* (1957), 67–96) in no way diminish the importance of this text as illustrating the principal alternative to submission to Babylon, a recourse which was never far from the mind of Jehoiakim and to which he eventually succumbed. It may be supposed that Jeremiah's dictation was carried out while Babylonian troop movements could be observed, while Babylonian garrisons were present in the main cities, and before the miserable fate of Ashkelon could be held up as an example. Jehoiakim's submission meanwhile gave a false sense of peace and security. But by the time the scroll was actually read (December) Ashkelon had been assaulted. This must have contributed to the consternation.

2. Take a scroll and write on it: cf. the similar command to Isaiah in 8.1. There also the writing down of a name on a placard was a prophetic sign, performed under the specific command of the LORD. Cf. chapter 25.3 where the thirteenth year of Josiah is mentioned and the period of prophetic activity determined as twenty-three years q.v.

against Israel and Judah: LXX has Jerusalem and Judah, but the unusual order tells against this reading.

3. As soon as the narrator departs from the story to reinforce the divine intention, he summarises the main purport of the prose sermons in familiar phrases of the tradition.

THE WRITING OF THE SCROLL **36.4–8**

5. I am debarred from going to the house of the LORD: The Hebrew *'āṣûr* translated 'debarred' is capable of several interpretations. In 33.1 and 39.15 it indicates arrest, but clearly here Jeremiah had not been arrested. Many have thought that Jeremiah was under a ceremonial taboo: 'I am restrained from entering the sanctuary by ceremonial impurity'. It could of course be that the Temple authorities had banned Jeremiah from entering. It seems probable that *'āṣûr* is a technical term used to indicate exclusion, for whatever reason, from the Temple. But the real reason for Jeremiah's exclusion has to do with the prophetic sign to be enacted. It is the LORD himself who restrains Jeremiah from entering the Temple, even if he uses intermediate means. It is essential that Jeremiah himself does not read his own oracles and distances himself from them because they are now to take on independent life as God's word to his people. It is this which Jehoiakim tries to destroy. As long as the oracles are an intrinsic part of a discredited Jeremiah, he has little to worry about. But when they stand over against him, witness to the divine word he wishes to ignore, then he tries to obliterate them, lest they become a standing rebuke like Joshua's stone at Shechem: 'if you renounce your God, it shall be a witness against you' (Jos. 24.26–27 *NEB*).

6. and on a fast day in the hearing of all the people of the LORD's house: The regular pre-exilic fast day was probably part of the great autumn festival; it is unlikely that the Day of Atonement (Lev. 23.26–27) was a complete Levitical innovation. This occurred in the month Tishri (October). But fasts were called in situations of need, and particularly in times of national crisis. Jer. 14.1–10 refers to fasting and lamentation called in time of drought. The people assembled in the Temple tore their clothes (Isa. 32.11; Mic. 1.8; Jl 2.13); wore sackcloth (2 Kg. 6.30; Isa. 22.12; 58.5; Jer. 4.8), disfigured themselves and rolled in the dust (Ps. 44.25; Mic. 1.10).

It has long been held that many of the laments in the Psalter were composed for exactly such occasions, and often an oracular response was awaited. This sort of reconstruction provides an apt context for the reading of the scroll. Jeremiah had long anticipated such a lament in terms which were part of the reading and indeed its very climax (6.26):

> O daughter of my people, gird on sackcloth,
>   and roll in ashes;
> Make mourning as for an only son,
>   most bitter lamentation;
> For suddenly the destroyer will come upon us.

But instead of the comfortable prediction of deliverance given by a priest or an institutional prophet, came the bleak reading of the oracles, old oracles, which appeared to be on the point of gruesome and inescapable fulfilment.

7. As in v. 3 the narrator resorts to the clichés of the prose tradition.

8. The repetition nicely rounds off the first part of the narrative and a new stage begins.

THE READING BEFORE THE PEOPLE **36.9–10**

9. In the fifth year of Jehoiakim . . . in the ninth month: i.e. Kislev or December 604 B.C., which fell in the fifth year of the king's reign.

The delay is no doubt simply that Baruch waited until a fast was called. To say that **all the people in Jerusalem and all the people who came from . . . Judah to Jerusalem, proclaimed a fast** is of course shorthand for 'observed a fast called by the authorities'.

10. in the chamber of Gemariah, the son of Shaphan the secretary: The name of Shaphan keeps appearing. If it is the same Shaphan who is referred to in 26.24, then another son, Ahikam, (2 Kg. 22.12–14), had actively supported Jeremiah at the beginning of the reign of Jehoiakim, when the prophet's accusers sought the death penalty (609–608 B.C.). Another son, Elasah, assisted in taking Jeremiah's letter to Babylon (29.3). Micah (36.11) and Gedaliah the governor after 586 B.C. were grandsons. Shaphan himself was the secretary who presented to Josiah the Law-book found in 621 B.C. and seems to have been involved in the consequential reform. Jeremiah had the support of this family through three generations.

which was in the upper court, at the entry of the New Gate: cf. 26.10. Nothing is known of this gate, but it is reasonable to guess that the room provided the facility for addressing a maximum crowd of people below.

THE READING BEFORE THE CABINET **36.11–19**

12. Shaphan's grandson now goes to the palace, to the secretary's room, where the cabinet was in session. He reports the content of the scroll. Four of the śārîm are named. Nothing is known of **Delaiah** or of **Zedekiah**. Gemariah had put his room in the Temple at Jeremiah's disposal and the messenger was his son. Elnathan was one of the ministers whom Jehoiakim had sent to Egypt to extradite Uriah, who was then executed (26.2–23). Since, in 36–25, he is linked with Delaiah in attempting to dissuade Jehoiakim from burning the scroll, it is difficult to think of him as ruthlessly anti-prophetic. His father had been actively involved in the finding and identification of the Law-book (2 Kg. 22.12). Elnathan's daughter had married Jehoiakim (2 Kg. 24.8). Either he was forced into an intolerable conflict of loyalties, or he came to modify his opposition to prophetic interference in the affairs of state. In any case the circumstantial details are of importance in judging the character of the narrative. It is gratuitous to suppose that these names are incorrect.

14. Hearing the content of the scroll, the ministers wish to check it accurately and send for Baruch who reads it at length. As we have already seen, it is the reading of the written scroll which is of the essence of the sign. Unwittingly the śārîm are cooperating with Jeremiah in the fulfilment of his purpose. And the point is enforced in vv. 17–18.

16. When they heard all the words, they turned to one another in fear: What kind of fear is this? The Heb. verb. *pḥd* often indicates a sort of religious dread, and some interpreters think the ministers thus showed a profound awe for the word of God. On the other hand the verb is patient of the more usual nuances associated with the English word fear. Accordingly, it is possible that the fear of the ministers concerned either the historical consequences of the oracles (which they believed), or their predictable effect on the morale of the population, which they regarded as deplorable. The only substantial clue lies in the use of the same verb *pḥd* in 36.24, where the king and his servants are said to have shown no fear. It is not plausible to argue that the ministers in v. 16 are the same as those in v. 24, since a different word ('servants') is used in v. 24 (W. McKane, *Prophets and Wise Men*, 1965, pp. 118–126). We may therefore conclude that a deliberate contrast is intended between Jehoiakim who did not fear and the ministers who did. The fear may thus be comprehensive. Jehoiakim showed no awe of the scroll as God's word, nor did he therefore fear the consequences. In contrast the ministers, however much they criticised Jeremiah for weakening morale, could not eradicate from their minds the fear which Jeremiah's oracles were intended to arouse. This put them on the horns of a dilemma. The conflict between the word of God spoken by Jeremiah (which they respected) and the proper reasonable demands of statesmanship in national emergency (which they entirely recognised) created intolerable tension. This tension they were unable to resolve, like so many statesmen from that day to this.

17. The question is answered by a repetition of the description of Jeremiah's dictation of his oracles. The very repetition draws attention to the central point of the scroll, but the form of the Hebrew sentence re-enforces it. Literally it runs: 'How did you write all these words from his mouth?' And Baruch answered, 'From his mouth he read to me all these words, while I wrote them on the scroll in ink'. Thus the order emphasises that the oracles proceeded from the mouth which the LORD had touched (1.9); and the order also emphasises that the spoken oracles have now been transcribed into the permanence of ink. The ink used will have been a mixture of carbon, with a solution of gum or olive oil. 'Analysis of one of the letters from Lachish has suggested a mixture of iron in the form of oak-galls or copperas and carbon'. (G. R. Driver, *Semitic Writing*, 1948, p. 86.)

19. The ministers apparently know the sort of reception Jehoiakim will give to the scroll. They temporarily resolve their conflict by advising Baruch and Jeremiah to go into hiding. Their action clearly distances them from the king and the 'servants' of v. 24, both in their attitude to Jeremiah and their respect for his words.

THE READING BEFORE THE KING **36.20–26**

20. Again the contents of the scroll are reported, perhaps in the hope that the king will not demand to see the scroll itself. Since the point of the sign lies in the written witness to old oracles, a verbal report must soften the impact. But ironically Jehoiakim himself orders the scroll to be brought, and thus himself ensures that the sign will be fully enacted. **Elishama the secretary:** amongst the leaders named in v. 12. Otherwise nothing is known of him.

21. and all the princes who stood beside the king: thus completing the picture. The ministers have of course already heard the oracle and have come to the palace to report.

22. the ninth month: i.e. Kislev (December)

23. For the deeper meaning of Jehoiakim's burning of the scroll, see the general exposition above. The king's deliberate action, three or four columns a time, suggests brazen and confident resistance to the oracles. He seeks appropriately to reverse the sign, as Hananiah thought to reverse another sign by breaking the wooden yoke (28.10). It is not a good idea to burn books, as fanatical censors have liked to.

24. Yet neither the king, nor any of his servants who heard all these words, was afraid, nor did they rend their garments: Thus the king is explicitly contrasted with Josiah (2 Kg. 22.11), in respect of tearing his clothes, but also, it must be insisted, with at least some of his ministers standing by. For the same Heb. verb *phd* is used as in v. 16. The ministers showed fear, the king did not. Plainly the narrator wished to present Jehioakim as one who scornfully dismissed the sign and felt nothing of the emotion that was created by respecting the sign. Plainly the ministers respected the sign and felt the dread it entailed, whether this fear was of the scroll itself as God's word, or of the threats it contained, or of the consequences for morale, or a combination of all. Some have argued that this interpretation is made unconvincing by the words 'nor any of his servants'. These, it is said, cannot be a different group of *śārîm* from those of vv 11 ff. Two factors may be significant:

(1) They are not explicit said to be the *śārîm*, but 'servants'. And though the ministers are in a real sense servants of the king, the sudden use of the word 'servants' (whereas throughout the narrative otherwise, as also in chapter 26, the *śārîm* are spoken of), suggests that a distinction is being made. It would indeed be appropriate to refer to those who support the

king to the hilt, or those who have a special place, as his servants. The term 'servants' is more comprehensive than *śārîm* cf. 37.2. *NEB, REB* has 'courtiers'.

(2) If such a distinction is probable, this adds weight to the view that the LXX text is here correct in omitting the word 'all'. Read for 'nor any of his servants', 'nor his servants' (v. 24). This is in any case the more probable text, since the addition of 'all' can be so easily explained as suggested by the repeated and emphatic 'all' in vv. 12, 14, 21. This does not mean that the ministers were without their misgivings concerning the political action implied by the oracles of Jeremiah. And when Jeremiah spelt out this advice, some of the princes wanted him put to death (38.4), though in this case the leading ministers are different (38.1). Likewise in v. 26 those commanded to seize Baruch and Jeremiah are not among the *śārîm* named earlier. But they are without question Jehoiakim's trusted servants. The inner conflicts of the *śārîm* must have been intense, and it is tension and conflict which provide the clue to the problem of this chapter.

25. Elnathan and Gemariah, among the leaders according to v. 12 (Gemariah also providing the room v. 10), **urged** (translated 'interceded' in Isa. 53.12) or entreated the king not to do this thing. Explicitly Jehoiakim acts against the advice of his leading ministers. This confirms the interpretation of v. 24 above.

26. but the LORD hid them. The conclusion of this part of the story is laconic like the conclusion of the story of Hananiah in 28.17. LXX has 'they hid themselves', probably the earlier text.

THE REWRITING OF THE SCROLL **36.27–32**

27–28. The rewriting is also a direct divine command in the same terms as were expressed in v. 2.

29. The prophetic sign is accompanied by a new oracle directed to Jehoiakim. The reason given for the judgment against Jehoiakim is that in burning the scroll, he resisted the divine word. The crucial point is summed up in the question: **Why have you written in it that the king of Babylon will certainly come and destroy this land?** As we have seen (see exposition of chapters 25 and 36), Jeremiah had spoken of a Foe from the North, and only in the present crisis could the destroyer be clearly identified. This may be taken as a confirmation of the hypothesis.

his dead body shall be cast out to the heat by day and the frost by night: as in the oracle concerning Jehoiakim in 22: (18–19).

30. the throne of David: cf. 13.13; 17.25; but especially 22.2, 4, 30.

31. And I will punish him: the Heb. is the verb *pqd*, well used in the prose tradition; as also is the expression **the inhabitants of Jerusalem and . . . the men of Judah.**

32. The narrative is completed with a simple statement which by repetition, emphasises the completion of the LORD's purpose. It performs a narrative function similar to v. 8. This highlights the addition: **and many similar words were added to them.** The argument that this is a circumstantial clause 'describing in more detail the conditions under which the roll was reproduced' (E. Nielson, *Oral Tradition*, 1954, p. 78), will not do, and flies against the simple meaning of the text. The scroll has been produced by direct command of the LORD, Jeremiah dictating 'all the words' to Baruch. The niphal 'there were added' leaves the subject of the additions indefinite. The fact is that the precisely motivated prophetic sign led to a process. Once the scroll of Jeremiah's oracles was in writing, there was an irresistible tendency to collect other oracles, and the movement to produce new collections went on. Such collections we have identified in chapters, 7–10, 11–13, 14–17, 18–20, 21–24, 26–35, 37–44. At certain stages a 'final' section was added to the existing collection of collections, as chapters 25, 36 and 45. All the narrator does is to indicate the beginning of this process. Exactly what had been added when he wrote we cannot know.

III   JEREMIAH AND THE FALL OF JERUSALEM
37.1–44.30 (45.5) (LXX 44.1–51)

THE THEME

These chapters, perhaps more than any other single block in the book of Jeremiah, need to be read consecutively and as a whole. The narrator has stamped them with a single, powerful theme. That is not to say that he wrote them in the manner of a modern author. There are clear signs of the already existing material he had to hand. But he wove this material into a homogeneous narrative whose primary purpose is betrayed most clearly in his exhortatory additions. The historical limits of his narrative are the eve of the siege of 586 B.C. and the flight to Egypt following the murder of Gedaliah. The theme is the effort made by Jeremiah to persuade king, ministers and people to accept the divine judgment which he had faithfully predicted.

Acceptance of the divine judgment takes different forms as the historical situation changes. (1) The first and basic form is applied to the dilemma of the Jews facing the Babylonian invasion. In appropriate ways the same divine judgment has to be accepted; (2) when Gedaliah is appointed governor, (3) again when Gedaliah is killed, and (4) yet again when the Jews under Johanan have settled in Egypt. This is the main theme of chapters 37–45, not the narration of the historical events themselves, still less the personal part and sufferings of Jeremiah.

Zedekiah is to recognise that, though the siege has been temporarily lifted (37.5), the Babylonian army will return. There is no point in intercession as requested by Zedekiah (37.3). Jeremiah is accused of desertion and imprisoned. Zedekiah, in two minds, has him released (37.21). He is kindly disposed to the prophet but exemplifies the weakness of the well-meaning. Nothing but total obedience to the divine will will suffice.

The logic of accepting the divine will is to submit to the Babylonians. The prophet does not shrink from his own logic (38.2–3). In a state of war, this means, from the point of view of the authorities, nothing less than treachery; so the ministers call for his death (38.4). This is the impossible position in which the LORD's spokesman is inevitably placed when the way of life and the way of death are allowed to proceed to ultimate collision. Jeremiah is imprisoned and rescued by an Ethopian eunuch. The Jews themselves have proved faithless. The form of a sustained conversation with Zedekiah in 38.7–26, provides the framework for a renewed prediction of final destruction, and further insight into the divided loyalties of the king. He will not abandon Jeremiah, but equally, lacks the courage to accept his message. He is inhibited by fear of his strong-minded ministers (38.5, 19, 25).

The king's repeated vacillation cannot avert the destruction of Jerusalem (39.1–3). The consequences for his family and himself (39.4–10) are in keeping with the enigmatic predictions made by Jeremiah. Zedekiah suffers the fate of the half-believer who in the time of trial lacks the courage to stand. Jeremiah himself is well treated by the Babylonians and given into the hands of Gedaliah. The Gedaliah tradition (40.7–41.18) which lacks any mention of Jeremiah, is however, carefully introduced by means of a didactic passage in which the LORD speaks through the Babylonian captain Nebuzaradan. Jeremiah elects to link with the remanent Jews rather than go to Babylon. The way of life now means supporting the Babylonian nominee Gedaliah.

40.7–41.18 illustrates how the Jews began to follow the example of Jeremiah, but were thrown off course by crisis. Gedaliah speaks Jeremiah's word (40.9–10), so there is no need for the prophet's intervention. But when Gedaliah is murdered by Ishmael, on the orders of the king of Ammon, all the old confusions re-appear. No doubt the

Ammonites despised every submission to Babylon. Whatever the reason, the assassination led to further murders of supporters of Gedaliah. The new leader was Johanan who, with his captains and the people, took up a position near Bethlehem. The question then arose, should they stay or should they go to Egypt? The choice earlier presented by Jeremiah now takes a new form. The importance of this choice is that it is the last such choice, and the narrator highlights the climax in a sustained piece of his own composition (42.1–43.7). He enforces the point with the well-worn phrases of the prose tradition. First they ask Jeremiah to intercede for them and find out the LORD's will (42.2–3). Jeremiah promises to seek the divine will and to keep nothing back (42.4). The people promise to obey, whether they like God's answer or no (42.4–5). Next, as befits so crucial a decision, there is a ten day's delay before Jeremiah receives the LORD's word (42.7). The people assemble. Jeremiah restates the two ways. If they will remain in the land and serve the king of Babylon, all will be well (42.8–12). But if they go to Egypt, then the doom will catch up with them in the end (42.13–17).

The exhortation not to go to Egypt is repeated with a reminder of their previous undertaking to obey the divine word (42.18–22). The preacher has come to his climax and seems to fight for the positive response of his hearers.

The reaction is consistent with all previous reactions. Jeremiah is branded a liar (43.2); the same word that the prophet used of false prophets (*šeqer*), now thrown in his face. Baruch and Jeremiah are played off against one another (43.3). 'So Johanan the son of Kareah and all the commanders of the forces and all the people did not obey the word of the LORD, to remain in the land of Judah' (43.4). They added to their disobedience by forcing Jeremiah and Baruch to go with them (43.5–7).

Finally 43.8–44.30 records Jeremiah's prophetic activity in Egypt. The symbolic act of 43.8–13 anticipates the long arm and irresistable power of the nation from which the Jews thought to escape. Chapter 44, again in the familiar phrases of the prose tradition, shows the preacher reminding his hearers that what has happened is divine judgment according to the word of the prophets, and taunting them for their renewed apostasy. They are accused of forgetting (43.9–10, cf. Dt. 6.12; 8.11; 18, 19 etc.). The prophecy of judgment is therefore reinforced (44.11–14). The response of the people, so far from penitence, is one of deeply obstinate resistance. They turn Jeremiah's argument on its head. It was not neglect of Yahweh but of the queen of heaven which has caused all this (44.15–20). Jeremiah can only state the opposite (45.21–23). As when he dealt with Hananiah, there is no external proof of true and false prophecy. 'Then confirm your vows and perform your vows!', he concludes (44.25). But the LORD nevertheless is watching (cf. 1.12) over them for evil (44.27).

The section is concluded by the short chapter (45) on Baruch, referring back to chapter 36 and therefore suitable at the end (45.1). The cry of pain (45.3) is appropriate, as one reviews the unrelenting conflict between the prophet and a people, whose disobedience persists even through the completion of judgment, and feeds on every new situation. The final reference to the call-vision (45.4) reaffirms the prospect of destruction. Baruch can hope for nothing for himself, only survival. Here without a vestige of hope, the curtain drops.

All this adds up to an impressive interpretation of a critical historical event, as no modern historian would presume to write it. The theme is the divine will expressed through Jeremiah, resisted at every stage by the people who are intended to be the LORD's people. It seems to come to a climax in the sermon before the flight to Egypt. A succession of scholars have understood particularly chapters 38–39 and 42–44 as details in the personal life of Jeremiah and the whole section as part of a biography of Jeremiah, perhaps written by Baruch. Some have spoken of a sort of passion-narrative spot-lighting the prophet's sufferings in the final period of Judah's collapse. If the exposition above is correct, these notions of biography or passion narrative are wide of the mark and deflect the reader from the real point of the narrative. For reasons set out below, it is highly improbable that this was written by Baruch, though not improbable that the later preachers used traditions handed on by him.

THE SOURCES

That the narrator used substantial sources is clear from two facts — first, the occurrence of passages from the Deuteronomic history and second, the existence of duplicate accounts.

(A) THE DEUTERONOMIC HISTORY

The Deuteronomic history seems to have provided the starting point and to some extent the framework. 2 Kg. 24 raises problems of its own. It is by no means clear where the first edition of the Deuteronomic history ended. Some think it ended at 2 Kg. 23.25 and that the material with

which we are concerned is an appendix written by a contemporary. The
existence of fuller information concerning Gedaliah in Jer. 40.7–41.18
than in 2 Kg. 25.22–26 and the overlapping Jer. 52, are complicating
factors. But these uncertainties need not inhibit provisional conclusions
about the relationship between the Jer. passages and 2 Kg.

It seems quite clear that the Jeremiah tradition is dependent upon the
Deuteronomic history rather than the reverse. This is shown first by the
annalistic introduction of 37.1 which summarises the fuller 2 Kg. 24.17,
refers to Jehoiakim as Coniah, a form of Jeconiah found otherwise only
in Jer. 22.24, 28 and then, in place of the stereotyped judgment of the
Deuteronomic historian (2 Kg. 24.18–20), provides an appraisal of the
king in relation to the prophetic activity of Jeremiah. This opening verse
furnishes a preface to two versions of Jeremiah's imprisonment (chapters
38, 39). These duplicates suggest alternative oral traditions rather than
a longer text from which the Deuteronomic historian took selections.

At 39.1–2, the narrator apparently uses the Deuteronomic history, this
time quoting 2 Kg. 25.1–4a and abridging it to his purpose. This passage
may however be a slightly later insertion. A problem is created by the
detached phrase, at the end of 38.28, 'and it happened when Jerusalem
was taken'. It is not in the LXX and it is omitted by *NEB* and *REB*,
while *RSV* transfers it to the beginning of v. 3. Verses 4–13 are also absent
from LXX, vv. 4–10 being taken from 2 Kg. 46–12 and vv. 11–13 added
for the narrator's own purpose. The best explanation of these omissions
and borrowings seems to be as follows.

The original narrator wrote thus:

38.28 And it happened when Jerusalem was taken,

39.3   all the princes of the king of Babylon came and sat in the middle gate:
       Nergal-sharezer, Samgar-nebo, Sarsechim the Rabsaris, Nergal-
       sharezer the Rabmag, with all the rest of the officers of the king of
       Babylon . . .

39.14 They sent and took Jeremiah from the court of the guard. They
       entrusted him to Gedaliah the son of Ahikam, son of Shaphan, that
       he should take him home. So he dwelt among the people.

This makes good sense. The taking of Jerusalem is mentioned without
detail, to lead to the moment when the victorious officers sat in the Middle
Gate (where the judges would normally meet to dispense justice and where
conquerors established their authority; see Jer. 1.15) to make the necessary
administrative decisions. Among those decisions was one concerning

Jeremiah, and this is all that concerns the narrator. It is assumed that the reader knows the importance of Gedaliah as the man whom Nebuchadrezzar had made governor (40.5; 2 Kg. 25.22). A subsequent editor has wished to define the time 'when Jerusalem was taken', and he has done this simply by quoting from 2 Kg 5.1–4a.

> In the ninth year of Zedekiah the king of Judah, in the tenth month, Nebuchadrezzar king of Babylon and all his army came against Jerusalem and besieged it; in the eleventh year of Zedekiah, in the fourth month, on the ninth day of the month, a breach was made in the city.

His purpose, to give the exact time of the fall of Jerusalem, explains why he omits from 2 Kg. 25.1–4a the references to the siege works and to the famine. And this strengthens the view that Jer. 39.1–2 is dependent upon 2 Kg. 25 rather than the reverse. This addition was made in the version which was eventually available to the LXX translator.

Verses 4–13, on the other hand, must have been added from 2 Kg. 25.4b–12 by a second editor and did not occur in the tradition available to the LXX translator. The motive for adding this passage would be partly to complete the account from 2 Kg. 25.1–4a, but mainly to show how Jeremiah's double prediction had been fulfilled. In both chapters 37 and 38 he has insisted that both city and king will be taken. The addition to vv. 1–2 told of the fall of the city. The addition of vv. 4–10 told of the fate of Zedekiah.

Some think that the LXX translator omitted the passage by the scribal error known as homoeoteleuton. The translator's eye passed from the names in v. 3, to the repetition 'Nergal-sharezer the Rabmag and all the . . . officers of the king of Babylon' in v. 13 and omitted what lay between. In that case MT is the original text and the LXX an unfortunate mutilation. Against this are the following considerations.

(1) Whereas the shorter text makes good sense, the longer text does not to the same degree. Was it really the sight of the officers which sent Zedekiah and his men fleeing? Did they wait until all the fighting was over and the administration was taking over? It is inherently more probable that, as 2 Kg. 25.4 tells, they fled as soon as they saw that the city was breached.

(2) Jer. 39.4 ('When Zedekiah . . . and all the soldiers saw them ') looks and reads like the narrator's connecting link.

(3) It is easy to explain the insertion of vv. 4–13. The redactor reads

the introduction from 2 Kg. 25.1–4a but thinks that more of the same
source is appropriate. His motive is to show how Jeremiah's predictions
concerning Zedekiah (32.4–5; 34.3–4; 37.18; 39.16) have so far been
fulfilled. Jer. 39.11, 12 are an additional tradition which associates
Nebuzaradan, the captain of the guard, with the kindly treatment of
Jeremiah, and so enables the redactor to harmonise the passage with
chapter 40. Once Nebuzaradan is introduced he has to be added to the
names in v. 13.

(4) The absence of a verb in 2 Kg. 25.4 may be deliberate. But even
if it has to be supplied (and the verb 'fled' is present in 52.7) this is not
an argument for the priority of MT. since both texts are defective and
can be used to correct one another.

(5) The text of 52.7–16 is almost identical with 2 Kg. 25.4b–12. In
contrast the abbreviations and adaptations of Jer. 39.4–13 are of a piece
with the careful way in which the passage is knit into its context in vv.
4 and 13.

(6) This conclusion accords with the observed tendency for the shorter
LXX text to provide the basic text. It remains true however that each
example has to be examined on its own merits.

So far then we note that the Deuteronomic history was used freely to
provide the background to two stories of Jeremiah's imprisonment, and
more closely to provide the occasions of Jeremiah's association with
Gedaliah.

The narrator seems to be acquainted with the brief notice concerning
Gedaliah in 2 Kg. 25.22–26. Jer. 40.5 sums up, allusively, what is stated
directly in 2 Kg. 25.22. The assembly of the captains with Gedaliah at
Mizpah, noticed in 2 Kg 25.23–24, is taken up in Jer. 40.7–9 and the
verbal relationship is such as to indicate direct quotation. The additions
of the Jeremiah text (the sons of Ephai and details of those who had been
committed to Gedaliah) together with the expansion of Gedaliah's speech
in v. 10, suggest that the narrator is expanding the somewhat meagre
material of the Deuteronomic history to his purpose. Jer. 41.1–3 seems
likewise to be an expansion of 2 Kg. 25.25. Particularly the addition of
a dependent clause, separating the two objects in vv. 2–3 (as compared
with 2 Kg. 25.25), amounts to a demonstration.

> 'and struck down Gedaliah, the son of Ahikam,
> son of Shaphan, with the sword, and killed him
> *whom the king of Babylon had appointed governor*
> *in the land* and all the Jews who were with him'

Likewise the account of the escape to Egypt seems to betray acquaintance with 2 Kg 25.26. Cf. particularly Jer. 42.16, 18. Thereafter there is nothing in 2 Kg. to use. The section on the Temple vessels is quoted in Jer. 52, but is plainly irrelevant here, and the section on the release of Jehoiakim from prison is not to the narrator's purpose. He pursues the theme, outlined above, with discipline and determination, and uses only that which serves his theological ends.

The individual comparisons all make best sense on the basis of the hypothesis that the narrator and some later editors used the appendix to the Deuteronomic history. When they are considered cumulatively the case is overwhelming.

(B) DUPLICATE ACCOUNTS

The main problem here is the relation of chapter 37 to chapter 38. In chapter 37 Zedekiah sends Jehucal and Zephaniah to Jeremiah to ask for his intercession. The answer is a reinforcement of Jeremiah's uncompromising message of doom on the city. Jeremiah's attempt to go to his patrimony is interpreted as desertion. The śārîm are enraged, beat him and put him in prison in the house of Jonathan. Zedekiah sends for him and asks for a word from the LORD. Jeremiah says Zedekiah will be given into the hand of the king of Babylon, and pleads not be returned to the dungeon. Zedekiah instead sends him to the court of the guard, where he remains until Jerusalem falls.

In chapter 38, a group of the śārîm hear that Jeremiah has been preaching submission to Babylon. They pronounce him worthy of death, and consign him to the waterles cistern of Malchiah, from which, with the agreement of Zedekiah, he is rescued by an Ethiopian eunuch. Zedekiah sends for him and asks for a word of the LORD. Jeremiah repeats that salvation lies in submission. The alternative is the destruction of the city and capture for Zedekiah. He sets out the consequences of disobedience in the form of a vision. He sees the women of the royal house being led out to the king of Babylon, making lament as they go. This is the way of death. Finally it is arranged that, when the śārîm question him, he shall answer that he has been pleading with the king not to send him back to the prison in the house of Jonathan. He is sent to the court of the guard where he remains until Jerusalem falls. 21.1–7 seems to reflect part of the same event.

Many interpreters have presented these chapters as accounts of separate and consecutive incidents. But the natural desire to rationalise must give way to the force of the evidence. The differences between the two accounts should not be underestimated. The story in chapter 37 of Jeremiah's arrest as he was going to Anathoth has no parallel in chapter 38. Chapter 38 is the more vivid story by reason of the intervetion of Ebed-melech the Ethiopian (vv. 7–13), and the introduction of the lament of the royal harem in a vision of the fate of king and city (vv. 21–23. But apart from these features the correspondence is striking. The following elements are common to both accounts:

(1) The *śārîm* hear of Jeremiah's preaching, and cast him into a prison which is of such a kind that, if he is allowed to remain there, he will die.

(2) Zedekiah has him released and questions him secretly.

(3) Jeremiah's oracle is in each case twofold: Zedekiah will survive; Jerusalem will fall.

(4) Jeremiah pleads not to be returned to his former cell and is committed to the court of the guard.

(5) There he remains until the fall of the city.

In addition, the preaching activity to *all the people* in 38.1–3, affecting the morale of the soldiers, implies that Jeremiah was at liberty, as is stated in 37.4. If the stories are consecutive, he was in detention. The narrator really betrays his case when, in 37.20, he had Jeremiah pleading not to be sent back to **the house of Jonathan**, whereas the prison in the second account is **the cistern of Malchiah** (38.6). Both accounts leave him in the court of the guard until the fall of the city; the bread in fact ran out (37.21) shortly before the capitulation. If the second account provides a greater exhortatory element in the interview with Zedekiah, that in any case must be regarded as owing much to the licence of the narrator who is using these stories in the interests of his theme.

All in all, there can be no reasonable doubt that these stories are duplicate traditions of the same event, each however providing something which the other omits. And if this is so, some time has to be allowed between the event and the present account in writing, during which the parallel traditions were established. It is probable also that Baruch can have had nothing to do with the final form, since a participant in the events (43.6) would have put the record straight.

There seems to be a parallel tradition also of the assignment of Jeremiah to Gedaliah.

(1) In chapter 39, according to the basic text (LXX), the officers who presided over the temporary administration, after the fall of the city and government, took Jeremiah from the court of the guard and entrusted

him to Gedaliah (39.3, 14). The account ends: 'So he dwelt among the people' (39.14).

(2) In chapter 40 Jeremiah had been brought, with other capitives, to Ramah. There Nebuzaradan, captain of the guard, gave him the choice of going to Babylon or returning to Gedaliah. He chose to go to Gedaliah (40.5, 6). The account ends: 'Jeremiah . . . dwelt with him among the people who were left in the land' (40.6). Again there can be no reasonable doubt that these are parallel traditions of the same event. This is confirmed by the scarcely disquised expedient of the final editor who added 39.9–12 to the excerpt from 2 Kg, thus introducing Nebuzaradan to an account from which he was puzzlingly absent. And of course, as we have seen, he added Nebuzaradan to the list of captains (39.13, cf. 39.3) as he was then bound to do.

The existence of these doublets, with the historical problems they raise, may have the effect of drawing the mind of the reader back to the purpose of the narrator. This purpose is to some extent independent of the detailed problems of historicity. On the other hand, when a narrator has admitted duplicate traditions into his account, without ironing out the differences, we have a much stronger historical witness to the events which gave rise to the traditions. We know, beyond all reasonable doubt, that Jeremiah was imprisoned for sedition, that he was in danger of his life, that he had secret conversations with Zedekiah and renewed his oracles concerning both the king and his kingdom, that the king had him transferred to less lethal conditions where he remained until the fall of the city. We know also that the Babylonian authorities, apparently aware of the importance of Jeremiah, allowed him to remain with Gedaliah, thus exemplifying in his person the message which he had so persistently reinforced.

FIRST ACCOUNT OF JEREMIAH'S MESSAGE FROM PRISON
37.1–21 (LXX 44.1–21)

1–2. See on the sources above section (A) pp. 451f.

2. **the people of the land:** In some contexts, this is a technical term denoting the landed classes. Here however it is probably intended to be comprehensive.

3. **Jehucal the son of Shelemiah, and Zephaniah the priest.** The participation of these characters in the events of this time is confirmed by the naming of Jehucal (the same as Jucal) in 38.1 and Zephaniah in 21.1.

The names are remembered, but there is confusion about who did what. **Pray for us:** Jeremiah had been commanded not to pray for his people. See on 7.16; 11.14; 14.11. Here the prayer is for an oracle; cf. 38.14, though the technical form of such a request is as in 21.2; 37.7.

5. The army of Pharaoh had come out of Egypt: i.e. 588 B.C. This is our only information about the Egyptian campaign. Unfortunately the Babylonian Chronicle stops at the year 594/3 B.C. But such a campaign is intrinsically probable, particularly as the last encounter between the Babylonians and the Egyptians in 601 B.C. had been indecisive, cf. 34.21. The memory of a Babylonian withdrawal seems to have been a strong one. It encouraged a sense of relief, even euphoria, and by the same token, not only the taking back of the released slaves (see chapter 34, and particularly on 34.6) but also the discrediting of Jeremiah. Hence the oracle that follows.

THE DIVINE MESSAGE IN ITS FIRST FORM (FIRST ACCOUNT)

7–10 The oracle reiterates the prediction consistently made by Jeremiah (21.4–7; 32.3, 24; 34.22). It comes to a climax in a piece of hyperbole not characteristic of the prosaic preachers, no doubt a memorable shaft of the prophet himself (v. 10). This is the first, in chapters 37–45, of a series of adaptations of the divine word to the current situation, in this case to the mood of relaxation created by the Babylonian withdrawal.

12. to the land of Benjamin to receive his portion there among the people: i.e. (*NEB*) to take possession of his patrimony. This must be the prelude to the event narrated in chapter 32, unless there are confusions we cannot solve. For at this time he was freely going in and out among the people (v. 4), 'for he had not yet been put in prison', whereas in chapter 32 he was 'shut up in the court of the guard', cf. 37.21; 38.13, 28. Are we to suppose that it was because Jeremiah was prevented from going to Anathoth that Hanamel visited him in prison (32.8)?

13. When he was at the Benjamin Gate cf. 20.2; 38.7; Zech. 14.10, but not in 17.19, q.v. The sentry believes Jeremiah is deserting to the Babylonians, not simply because he is leaving Jerusalem, but because he had actively recommended this course of action (21.9; 38.2). Jeremiah therefore practically courts misunderstanding.

15. It is, however, the attitude of the *śārîm* or ministers which is decisive. It is possible that the ministers named in chapter 36, influential in the time of Jehoiakim, had been taken to Babylon in the deportation of 597 B.C. Those named in 38.1 are different and, for whatever reason, there is a new group who are set in opposition to Jeremiah. At the same time we may well suppose that, in the new circumstances, Jeremiah lost most of the support he had. There were few, if any, who distinguished between his advice and treachery. Hence the anger of the *śārîm*, the beating and the imprisonment.

in the house of Jonathan the secretary: According to this account, the secretary's house was used as a prison because it had a vaulted cell underneath (see v. 16). In the parallel account, Jeremiah is put in the 'cistern of Malchiah' (38.6), but there seems to be an effort of harmonisation in 38.26. Common to both traditions is the judgment that, if Jeremiah is left there, he will die. (37.20; 38.10)

16. The dungeon cells: lit. 'into the house of the pit, into the vault', i.e. into a vaulted cell. The LXX did not understand the term for 'vault'.

ZEDEKIAH'S SECRET MEETING **17–21**

This also is a motif which recurs in chapter 38 in much greater detail. Both accounts concur in presenting Zedekiah as well-meaning but weak, as supporting Jeremiah privately but hesitating in public, as torn between political expedience and his basic respect for God's word spoken by the prophet, as divided between a religious dread of the prophet and a human fear of his own headstrong ministers.

In this account the intervention of the Ethiopian eunuch is absent. The omission does not, however, create a conflict. The purpose of the secret meeting is to complete the oracle of vv. 7–10. The king sends for Jeremiah as in 38.14, and seeks an oracle. The oracle, as stated in v. 17, is brief and lacks both the detail of 21.7 and the alternative presented in 38.17–23. In both accounts the announcement of the impending destruction of the city is complemented by the announcement of the capture of the king. And this completes the divine message in its first form.

19. An indication that the Babylonian advance had discredited the establishment prophets. The disputes represented in 23.9–40; 28–29 were not now the issue.

21. the court of the guard: cf. 38.5, 13, 28; 32.2 locates this court in the environs of the royal palace, cf. Neh. 3.25, and according to chapter 32 it entailed enough freedom to enable Jeremiah to receive visitors. It was a place of detention. The note that Jeremiah was given bread until the bread failed, means that his detention lasted until the fall of the city. See 52.6. 38.9b is probably exaggeration. Jeremiah's release would be to no purpose if there was nothing to eat.

SECOND ACCOUNT OF JEREMIAH'S MESSAGE FROM PRISON
38.1-28 (LXX 45.1-28)

1-6. The alternative account of Jeremiah's imprisonment leaves the initiative with certain named ministers. These verses may be regarded as an expanded tradition of 37.15.

1. Shephatiah: otherwise unknown. **Gedaliah the son of Pashhur:** again unknown, though his father may be the Pashhur also listed. **Jucal:** the Jehucal of 37.3. The variant, thus preserved together with other circumstantial variations, probably indicates that the two accounts had already reached fixed form before they were used, and to some extent, harmonized by the narrator.

Pashur the son of Malchiah: omitted by LXX. If the tradition is correct, he is the Pashur named in the parallel 21.1. Another Pashur 'the priest', had beaten Jeremiah and put him in the stocks, probably at an earlier stage in the reign of Jehoiakim (20.1-6). We cannot know if they were related.

THE DIVINE MESSAGE IN ITS FIRST FORM (SECOND ACCOUNT)

2-3. The ministers are well aware of the terms of Jeremiah's oracle. To demonstrate this, the narrator quotes exactly from 21.9, 10, where the options are set out explicitly as the way of life and the way of death. To omit these verses as a gloss, on the grounds that they are practically identical with 21.9, 10 is not only arbitrary, but also a failure to understand the mind and method of the narrator. It is important to understand that, in the final conflict, the ministers are under no illusions as to the word of God spoken by Jeremiah the prophet. They themselves, in this account, state the divine message in its first and basic form.

2. his life as a prize of war: see on 39.18.

4. Let this man be put to death, for he is weakening the hands of the soldiers: Here the combination of Jeremiah's own pathetic dilemma and the problem of the relativities of politics come to their breaking point. Who cannot have sympathy with those who bear responsibility for the safety of the realm? Once military resistance has begun, it is all or nothing. There is no practical difference between obedience to the divine word and treason; only the all important difference of motive.

The question is whether Jeremiah's word is really and in all respects the word of God. How is it possible to know that he is not deceived like the prophets he himself accuses? We are dealing here not with a modern pacifist, but with a prophet. He has consistently and by many means sought to show that the contemporary events are the drama in which the LORD is acting to bring judgment upon his faithless people. The Babylonian invader is the LORD's instrument. To resist him is to resist the LORD. The situation is therefore totally different from that faced by Isaiah during the Syro-Ephraimite crisis or the invasion of Sennacherib, and the message is therefore different. But what is common is the prophet's understanding of what the LORD wills at that time and in those circumstances.

All therefore depends on whether the prophet is a true prophet or not. The ministers react from the standpoint of those who have to make practical decisions in relation to all the human and political factors. Jeremiah is doing what no citizen can be allowed to do. He is undermining morale, and this is for evil, not for good. As we have already noticed (see on 34.7) the seventh of the ostraka from Lachish refers to those 'who weaken the hands of the land and of the city' and could very well refer to Jeremiah. At the same time there were those who deserted to the Babylonians for the wrong motives (38.19), who may be the subjects of this notice. They made the standpoint of Jeremiah all the more difficult to distinguish.

5. The weakness of Zedekiah is a motif in both accounts. Cf. 38.19 24-26.

6. The question whether the circumstantial detail of Jeremiah's plight in the cistern of Malchiah is part of the embellishing process of oral tradition, or whether it is a more accurate version of the alternative account in 37.15, 16, is one that cannot be answered.

THE ETHIOPIAN EUNUCH **38.7–13**

The effect of these verses is to supply a prod to Zedekiah, so that he may send for Jeremiah and question him (37.17, cf. 38.14). There is no parallel to it in the alternative account, nor does the incident conflict with the previous account. What does the story do? It illustrates, of course, with special vividness, the nature of Jeremiah's incarceration. It makes clear that Zedekiah's pusillanimity was such that he did not have the strength of will to take the initiative himself. Or at the very least it supplies the means of acquainting the king with the full danger of the prophet's plight.

Does it also suggest that Jeremiah was now abandoned by all his own countrymen? That no one would help him now, lest he also be tainted with suspicion of treason? That priest, Levite and king were passing by on the other side and the Ethiopian alone provided a Samaritan's assistance? Whatever the explanation, there is no obvious theological motive or narrative motif. To label it 'historical fantasy' (Carroll), a bit of variety typical of the art of the storyteller, is an unconvincing resort to a meagre rationale. The best explanation is that the story was founded in history, however it was subjected to the storyteller's art. See also 39.15–18.

7. The Ethiopian, a eunuch: he is said to be 'in the king's house' and has knowledge of the storehouse and its contents (v. 11). The Heb. *sārîs* commonly means an eunuch in the accepted sense, and is understood to be an incomplete human being (Dt. 23.1) who shall not enter the assembly and cannot be a priest (Lev. 21.10; 22.24). Isa 56.4 modified this rigour. In employing eunuchs, Judah was imitating the great courts, who used them as guardians of the harem. However, the frequent employment of the *sārîs*, particularly in military command, suggests an additional use of the word, which may justify the *AV* translation 'officer' or 'chamberlain'. Cf. the term 'Rabsaris' in 39.3. However, in this story we may be sure the term is used in the accepted sense of the word 'eunuch' and that it highlights the prophet's predicament. He who bears the word of the LORD is deserted on all sides and left to die. But the LORD delivers his man by means of one who is both outside the community of the chosen people and an emasculated human being. The LXX lacks the words 'a man who was a eunuch'. If MT has introduced a gloss, it is no doubt one which correctly describes the Ethiopian.

10. Take three men with you: Heb. has 'thirty' and the emendation is commmonly made on the basis of the evidence of one MS. But 'thirty' is probably correct and is an example of the exaggeration that sometimes creeps into narrative tradition, cf. 2 Kg. 5.5, 26; 8.9.

ZEDEKIAH'S SECRET MEETING **38.14–28**

This passage corresponds to 37.17–20. The narrator now brings the collated accounts to a climax by representing the first form of the divine message with suspense and dramatic accompaniment. This message is dynamite. Zedekiah knows that Jeremiah will not weaken it or compromise. He therefore arranges to meet him secretly. No doubt **the third entrance of the temple** (v.14) in some way assisted to maintain the secrecy. The conversation in vv. 14–16, and especially the solemn oath formula of v. 16, suggest to the reader the explosive nature of the prophetic message, and vv. 24–27 confirm this. If the *śārîm* make enquiries about Jeremiah's conversation with the king, he is simply to answer that he requested not to be returned to the dungeon. The hand of the narrator is here betrayed by the fact that he now reverts to the house of Jonathan and ignores the cistern of Malchiah! The answer entirely satisfies the *śārîm*, and indeed has the advantage of being both convincing and true (37.20; 31.15).

All this is the setting for the message, which is of such a kind that it might indeed have led Zedekiah to put Jeremiah to death, and certainly would provide the *śārîm* to put him to death, and must therefore be clothed in secrecy. Actually, of course, the message (vv. 17–25) is only an amplification of the divine message in its basic form, such as had been proclaimed openly both to the people and to the king. Surrender to the Babylonians is the only condition of life for king and city. The message of 21.1–10; 32.1–5, 26–29; 34.1–5, implied in chapters 36 and 38, 1–6, is rammed home, now with the particular exhortation to surrender, and in terms of the alternative ways of life and of death.

19. I am afraid of the Jews who have deserted to the Chaldeans: this suggests that bitter disputes had taken place. The fact that Zedekiah, who must have cast his lot with those who chose resistance, feared their reprisals, probably indicates that they were not the kind of men who were following the advice of Jeremiah, but in a real sense defectors. This made Jeremiah's position all the more difficult to explain to those who jumped to conclusions. See on 37.11–15.

21. This is the vision which the LORD has shown to me: the Heb. has *dābār* 'word', but the word of God clothes itself in a picture of what shall happen, and the paraphrase is not inaccurate, cf. Am. 1.1. For the combination of 'the LORD showed me' and 'behold. see Am. 7.1, 4, 7; 8.1; Jer. 24.1. Cf. also Num. 23.3; 2 Kg. 8.13; Ezek. 11.25; Zech. 1.20; 3.1. The form of the vision-report seems to correspond to a pattern which has become accepted in prophetic circles. What Jeremiah sees is a picture of the royal harem, and indeed all the women, being led out to hear their fate from the Babylonian command, and making lament as they go. Their lament is in the familiar qinah rhythm (3.2) of the Hebrew lament (see on 9.17–19) and is intended to anticipate the humiliation of Zedekiah.

22. Your trusted friends have deceived you and prevailed against you: the idiomatic Heb. expression is lit. 'Men of your peace' cf. Obad. 7. Zedekiah is like the victim envisaged in Ps. 41.10. Jeremiah had already experienced this personal betrayal and expressed it in one of his own laments. See 20.10. The picture of Zedekiah already gained, as a well-intentioned man who cannot stand against his more powerful lieutenants, is confirmed. As so often, the weak are too trusting in those near at hand. It would have taken immense strength of character to trust the prophet Jeremiah to the point of obeying his direction.

now that your feet are sunk in the mire: while this may have an overtone, alluding to Jeremiah's own peril in the cistern of Malchiah (38.6) the principal allusion no doubt is to a familiar motif of the Hebrew lament. (Cf. for example, Pss. 69.1-2, 15; 40.2; Jon. 2.3-10) To die or to approach death is to sink to the waters of the underworld, indeed to fall into a cistern (Pss. 30.3; 88.3) or well (Ps. 69.15). The brevity of the lament and its poetic form are deliberate. They are intended to suggest allusions which prose cannot achieve.

24-28 The final section ties up the loose ends of the narrative and brings it to an artistic conclusion. The narrator does not need to state what was Zedekiah's final reaction to Jeremiah's message. That is sufficiently implied in the events which follows.

FIRST ACCOUNT OF THE ENTRUSTING OF JEREMIAH TO GEDALIAH
39.1-18 (LXX 46)

The structure of this chapter has been discussed in the introduction to chapters 37-45-section on 'The Sources'. The fall of Jerusalem is briefly narrated without comment. The purpose of the narrator is not to preach on this event, but to pass to its aftermath and the new situation in which the word of the LORD by the mouth of Jeremiah is presented. The chapter provides a means of transition to the Gedaliah tradition.

1-2. The notice of the fall of Jerusalem is taken verbatim from 2 Kg. 25.1-4a to define the exact time of the event. It glosses the detached sentence at the end of 38.28, transposed by *RSV* to the beginning of v. 3. See introduction above.

The ninth year of Zedekiah . . . in the tenth month . . . in the eleventh year . . . in the fourth month. Reckoning from his official accession at the New Year Festival in 596, these dates would be December 588 and June-July 586.

3. The list of officers is plainly intended to be the same list as appears in v. 13. The confusions appear to be caused by the hazards of textual transmission. There is only one Nergal Sharezer, and he comes from Sinmagir (corrupted to Samgar). He thus appears in an official list of Nebuchadrezzar's officers. Then Nebo Sarsechim may be understood as a corruption of Nebushazban the *sar sārîs* (a variant form of rabsaris, v. 13). The list should therefore be:

Nergal-Sharezer from Sinmagir, the Rabmag
Nebushazban the Rabsaris   (cf. v. 13)

It is probable that Nergal Sharezer is to be identified with Neriglissar (Nergal–shar–usur), who married a daughter of Nebuchadrezzar, and in 559 seized the throne on the death of Amel-Marduk (the Evil-Merodach of Jer. 52.31). The Rabmag was some sort of commander officer. *NEB*, *REB*, have 'commander of the frontier troops'. The Rabsaris was also a high official, and certainly not 'chief eunuch' as the name might seem to indicate. See on 38.7.

4–10. Absent from LXX and introduced from 2 Kg. 25.4b–12, both to complete the quotation and to show how Jeremiah's double prediction of the fall of the city and king (chapters 37 and 38) was fulfilled. With the phrase **when Zedekiah king of Judah and all the soldiers saw them**, the passage is connected with v. 3 by means of a palpable suture.

4. 2 Kg. 25.4 adds 'though the Chaldeans were around the city'. The omission is immaterial.

5. 2 Kg. 25.5 adds 'and all his army was scattered from him'. Again the omission is immaterial. Here the Jer. text adds 'in the land of Hamath', possibly a gloss from 2 Kg. 23.33 to explain the situation of Riblah near to Qadesh on the Orontes, and a natural choice of headquarters for an invading army. What had already been explained in the narrative of 2 Kg. needed explanation in Jer. 39.

6. The Jeremiah text also adds 'and the king of Babylon slew all the nobles of Judah', perhaps to indicate that, whereas the nobles of Jehoiakim had been taken into captivity (27.20), those of Zedekiah were not eligible for similar concession.

8. The text seems defective, since it would seem odd to omit the burning of the 'house of the LORD' (cf. 2 Kg. 25.9 and Jer. 52.13); unless of course, the 'house of the king' was understood to include the Temple.

9. Nebuzaradan, the captain of the guard: the expression in Accadian seems to mean lit. 'chief cook', but had clearly changed its meaning (like Rab-saris), The *RSV* translation may be regarded as a fair equivalent. The repetition ('the rest of the people who were left in the city' and the 'rest of the people who were left') is either to be explained as dittography and the second sentence omitted; or, the second sentence is to be corrected from 2 Kg. 25.11 to 'together with the rest of the multitude'. *NEB*, *REB* prefer the second solution and translate: 'and any remaining artisans'.

10. Varies 2 Kg. 25.12 without changing the meaning, except to emphasise the complete poverty of those left in the land. **11.-13.** These verses are also absent from LXX. Verse 13, at least, became necessary as soon as vv. 4–10 had been interposed to break the connection between v. 3 and v. 14. It is probable that the opportunity was then taken to harmonise with the tradition of chapter 40, where it is Nebuzaradan who permitted Jeremiah to go to Gedaliah. Once Nebuzaradan was introduced in vv. 11–12, then it was necessary to add his name to v. 13. We are being told that a particular directive came from Nebuchadrezzar himself, through his chief-lieutenant, for the special care of Jeremiah.

12. But deal with him as he tells you: the narrator wishes to emphasise that it was by Jeremiah's own volition that he stayed in the land. Chapter 40 presents the choice more graphically. Although Jeremiah had insisted on submission to Babylon, this had nothing to do with desertion, only with complete obedience to the will of God.

14. Gedaliah the son of Ahikam, the son of Shaphan: Only in parenthesis in 40.5 is it noted that Gedaliah was appointed governor of Judah, cf. 2 Kg. 25.22. Ahikam had supported Jeremiah against those who would have put him to death (26.24). See on 36.10 for the friendly influence of the family of Shaphan. In chapter 40 Gedaliah speaks as the mouth of Jeremiah. A clay seal impression found at Lachish reads 'Belonging to Gedaliah who is over the house'. Was this the same man? **take him home:** lit. 'to the house'. Omitted by LXX. The absence of further definition is puzzling. Bright thinks this might be a technical term for release from prison.

THE SALVATION OF EBED MELECH 39.15-18

Some scholars transpose this section, thinking it more appropriate to follow 38.28a or 38.13 or (as an appendix) 40.6. The fact is that it cannot be closely welded into the main theme of chapters 37–45. Wherever it occurs, it is an aside, noticing the destiny of one who is on the side of the angels. The editor no doubt had his own reasons, and it is better left where it is. See 38.7-13.

That this is an independent pericope is shown by its formal likeness to chapter 45. Both concern individuals who stand by Jeremiah and, by the same token, obey the will of God while others disobey. Both have to do with their providential salvation in the day of the judgment of Judah. Both are introduced by an identification of the occasion: 'while he was shut up in the court of the guard' (39.15) and 'when he wrote these words in a book at the dictation of Jeremiah' (45.1). Both curiously have a sentence, difficult in Heb., absent in the LXX, and adding little to the sense (39.16; 45.4). This suggests perhaps the vicissitudes of independent transmission.

Both set this individual salvation within a prophecy of judgment, beginning with 'Behold', and continuing with a participle (*ḥinnî mēbî*) 'bringing', in the one case 'my words' (39.16), in the other' 'evil' (45.5). Both describe the individual as a 'prize of war' (see below). And both elaborate this final expression of the main point of the oracle. The formal likeness is therefore impressive. There must have been something very special about the quality of obedience and fidelity, exemplified by Ebed-melech and Baruch, which singled them out for these oracles of salvation. From the point of view of the editor, they are the only illustrations available to him of positive response to the choice Jeremiah has consistently presented to Judah through these years.

15. while he was shut up in the court of the guard: It will be remembered that Jeremiah was in improved conditions, with a measure of liberty. This was a form of detention which made contact with the Ethiopian servant possible.

16. Go, and say to Ebed-melech: the infinitive absolute 'go' is a pleonasm which has no significance in itself except to introduce the main verb and give it emphasis.

they shall be accomplished before you on that day: absent from LXX. Lit. 'they shall be before you . . .'. The subject is the 'words' which are to be fulfilled. The repetition of **on that day** perhaps strengthens the view that this a gloss meant to suggest that the Ethiopian, having so responded to Jeremiah, will remain under God's word through the tribulations to come.

17. the men of whom you are afraid: cf. Zedekiah in 38.19. Those who did not toe the line lived in personal danger.

18. you shall have your life as a prize of war: lit. 'as a booty'. This is an idiomatic expression whose precise meaning is not obvious. It occurs in 21.9; 38.2 and 45.5. In each case it refers to escape in the Babylonian conquest of Judah. LXX translates *heurema*, a word which suggests an unexpected gain or windfall. What is certain is that it does not indicate a joyous and rich salvation. Ebed-melech will be among the things that are not destroyed in the general carnage and pillage. He will be, so to speak, up for booty. But at the very least this means that he will be alive.

SECOND ACCOUNT OF THE ENTRUSTING OF JEREMIAH TO GEDALIAH
40.1-6 (LXX 47.1-6)

This account has every appearance of a free narrative based upon a
tradition that it was Nebuzaradan who entrusted Jeremiah into the hands
of Gedaliah at Ramah. In this respect it differs from the first account
which named Nergal-Sharezer and Nebushazban, and was doctored to
include Nebuzaradan (39.11–13), who arranged the matter in Jerusalem.
The narrator thus sets the event in context (v. 1) and then freely uses
Nebuzaradan as the LORD's spokesman (vv. 2–5). He acknowledges
that the destruction of Jerusalem is the fulfilment of the will of Judah's
God, in accordance with prophecy (vv. 2–3). Judah is in this predicament
because of disobedience to her God (v. 3). Jeremiah is given the choice
of going to Babylon or staying with Gedaliah (vv. 4–5). This is not the
same as the choice between the way of life and the way of death, though
staying in the land will finally dispose of the suspicion that Jeremiah is
a deserter. For Jeremiah it is the LORD's will that he stay, in order that
he may continue to try to guide the people in the choices that remain.
Gedaliah in particular needs his support, as he himself attempts to follow
the right way.

1. The word that came to Jeremiah from the LORD: Some interpreters
are troubled because strictly no oracle to Jeremiah follows. It is, however,
most unlikely that anything is missing. In the subsequent narratives the
mouths of others than Jeremiah are used to express the divine will or to
echo it. Here a word of the LORD is echoed *in the words of Nebuzaradan*.
Whether the narrator realised the theological implications of this is not
clear. It remains significant that he should write thus. If the Assyrian could
be recognised as the LORD's instrument to punish (Isa. 10.5), (and
Nebuchadrezzar in Jer. 25.9), it was only logical that Cyrus should be
recognised as the LORD's instrument to save (he is called 'messiah' in
Isa. 45.1), and a short step to recognising that such a servant may speak
in the LORD's name. The formula is as in 7.1; 11.1; 18.1; 21.1; 30.1;
32.1; 34.1; 35.1. It has been used to introduce new complexes of tradition,
but also to introduce short sections. Rudolph thinks it breaks the flow of
a Baruch narrative. But we have not been able to discern a connected
narrative in chapters 37–39 or to attribute them directly to Baruch. The
formula is best understood as a conventional mode of introducing a notice
of the time of the event to be described, and in a comprehensive way to
refer to the word of God which emerges from the event.

Ramah: In the first account Zedekiah and his company are brought to distant Riblah. Ramah is near at hand, a few miles due north of Jerusalem. Accordingly to Isa. 10.24 it was bear Gibeah, Saul's home town in Benjamin, and on the route of the Assyrian's invasion. Accordingly it fits that it should have been the route of the Babylonian army's return with the captives. Tradition placed Rachel's tomb here. See Jer. 31.15.

2. The Babylonian captain speaks like a prophet, and indeed in the prose of the Jeremiah tradition, drawing the lesson which Jeremiah does not need to draw, because the events speak for themselves.

this place: see the discussion on p. 147.

4. The reader is to understand that Jeremiah was wholly free to go into the relative security of Babylon, if he wished, with the leaders, the wealthy and the notable people of Judah. We are to understand that only the poor were left (39.10)

See, the whole land is before you: These were the words of Abraham to Lot (Gen. 13.4). Jeremiah, that his ministry may continue, elects to support Gedaliah. The sentence is absent in LXX and reads like an embellishment.

5. If you remain: the Heb. here is corrupt, but it is part of the text absent from LXX. It looks as if an addition has been made to the basic text which was not clearly written. At all events, there is little point in trying to restore it. Read, with LXX 'If it seems good to you to come with me to Babylon, come, and I will look after you well. If not, stay. Return to Gedaliah . . .'

Gedaliah: see on 39.14. The dependent clause **whom the king of Babylon appointed governor** appears to allude to the statement in 2 Kg. 25.22. The succeeding verses are then quoted in 40.7–9. This is a good example of the way the narrator uses the Deuteronomic history by allusion, by quotation, by amplification from other sources and by free interpretation.

gave him an allowance of food and a present: the instinct of the story-teller takes over!

6. And dwelt with him among the people: So the second account ends like the first. Jeremiah remains with the poorest of the land, the vinedressers and the ploughmen, and with Gedaliah on whom their peace now depends.

The Choice for Judah under Gedaliah
40.7–41.18 (LXX 47.7–48.18)

It is often raised as a problem that Jeremiah does not figure in 40.7–41.18. Those who understand the surrounding chapters as the work of Baruch, in particular find it difficult to attribute these chapters to the same author. Certainly this tells against any interpretation of these chapters as a personal history of Jeremiah. But in the context of the overall theme of the narrator (who is not Baruch), the problem vanishes. For not only does Gedaliah appear as the *alter ego* of Jeremiah (40.9–10), but also the story of the killing of Gedaliah has to be told as a response to Gedaliah's counsel, leading to a crucial choice for which the advice of Jeremiah is sought (42.1–21).

Gedaliah's counsel in 40.9–10 is similar to that given by Jeremiah to the Babylonian exiles (29.5–7), and the natural consequence of Jeremiah's decision to remain with the poor remanant Jews. We may infer that most Jews were now ready to accept the situation, including the leader Johanan, and that a good harvest reinforced their decision. The tragedy was that a new crisis was precipitated, not by their disobedience but by outside interference. The king of Ammon evidently wished to compel Judah to support him in his own anti-Babylonian policy, and found a willing instrument of his purpose in Ishmael ben Nethaniah of the Judean royal house. Ishmael sought to kill all followers of Gedaliah, whom no doubt he regarded as an upstart, and at once civil war broke out. Ishmael was defeated but escaped. Realising that this must entail Babylonian reprisals, Johanan and his followers met together near Bethlehem with the intention of fleeing to Egypt (41.18). Thus the transition is made to the next choice which lay before the Jews (42.1–21, 43.7) in which an oracle is sought, is given and rejected.

From this point of view the narrative flows dramatically. The unity of the narrative is created by the narrator. We have already seen that, for the story of Gedaliah, he is partly dependent upon 2 Kg. 25, which he uses in very much the same way as he used earlier passages. At the same time there is available to him much more information about Gedaliah and the assassination. The circumstantial detail of 40.7–41.10, and to some extent 41.11–18, justifies the designation of the substance of this material as 'the Gedaliah tradition'. Thereafter in 42.1–43.7 the narrator uses great freedom in pursuing his main theme.

7-9. From 2 Kg. 25.23–24, 2 Kg. 25.22 having been used in v. 5. There are additions. MT adds 'in the open country' in v. 7 and 'had committed

to him men, women and children, those of the poorest in the land who had
not been taken into exile to Babylon'. This re-emphasises 39.10 (= 2 Kg.
25.12). MT has 'Johanan and Jonathan the sons of Kareah' but in this
case LXX and 2 Kg. 25.23 probably have the correct text which has been
followed by *RSV*. MT adds 'the sons of Ephai' in v. 8, but in this case
probably supplies the missing antecedent of 'the Netophathite'. MT
expands the speech of Gedaliah in v. 10. This verse has no parallel in 2 Kg.

8. Mizpah i.e. Tell-en-Nasbeh of Benjamin, about eight miles north
of Jerusalem. Whereas archaeological research has confirmed the tradition
of the total destruction of the towns of Judah in 588–586, Mizpah,
according to the same evidence, escaped. It was in a commanding
position, on the line of communications between Judah and the north,
and now replaced Jerusalem as the centre of government. Still more
remarkable is the discovery of an agate seal from a tomb at Mizpah with
the words 'Belonging to Jaazaniah the servant of the king'. Since the
chronology is right it is tempting to identify this Jaazaniah (so 2 Kg. 25.23,
for Jezaniah) with the leader listed here. (See Archaeology and Old
Testament Study, ed. D. Winton Thomas, 1967, p. 336).

The divine message in its second form 40.9–10
Here Jeremiah does not need to advise what to do, since Gedaliah speaks
for him. Cf. Jeremiah's comparable advice to the exiles in 29.5–7. This
is the logical conclusion of Jeremiah's counsel to submit, cf. 21.8–9; 38.17.
Gedaliah was, from another point of view, wearing the mantle of the house
of Shaphan, consistent supporters of Jeremiah. The divine instruction
before the fall of Jerusalem was to submit to the Babylonian invader.
Now in its second form it is to accept the new situation and seek the peace
of the land.

your cities that you have taken: indicates a speedy return to those
cities which were abandoned by the Babylonians and where life was
possible.

11–12. Reveals that, as would be expected, many had fled to nearby
Moab, Ammon and Edom. But now the stand of Gedaliah in his new
capital spread new hope and the harvest confirmed confidence.

THE MURDER OF GEDALIAH **40.13–41.3**

This is a version, with more circumstantial detail, of 2 Kg. 25.25. 41.1a,
23 is a quotation, which has been overlaid with some repetition, and
amplified with the addition of 'As they ate bread together at Mizpah'
and 'whom the king of Babylon had appointed governor in the land'.

The latter in particular overloads the structure of the object clause and betrays itself as an addition. The passage shows how the Jews, through no direct fault of their own, find their new desire to make the best of defeat overthrown by foreign influence, coupled with the duplicity of a member of Gedaliah's inner circle (40.8). Nothing is known of **Baalis the king of the Ammonites**, but it is clear that his country, together with Moab and Edom, had earlier planned resistance to Nebuchadrezzar, and so became the object of Jeremiah's prophetic intervention (27.1–11). Cf. also the anti-Babylonian stance of the Ammonites implied in Ezek. 21.18–21, 28–32. Gedaliah is represented as another well-meaning man, who brushes aside Johanan's warning that there is a plot to assassinate him. Johanan's emphatic support of Gedaliah and his policy is shown by his willingness to anticipate events by killing Ishmael (40.15).

The narrator highlights the nature of the treachery by adding to his source that Ishmael struck while the leaders were at table together, thus breaking the sacred law of hospitality.

41.1. In the seventh month: i.e. Tishri (October). The narrator understands that this is three months after the fall of Jerusalem (cf. 39.2). Thereafter the day was observed as a fast-day, one of the four commemorating the fall of Judah (Zech 7.5; 8.19).

of the royal family: i.e. in some way belonging to the Davidic house. No such claim is made for Gedaliah, and it is reasonable therefore to guess that personal motives entered into his calculations.

2. whom the king of Babylon had appointed governor in the land: This is added by the narrator to the bare information of 2 Kg. 28.25, and with the emphasis on the fact that Ishmael slew **the Chaldean soldiers who happened to be there**, shows his intention to demonstrate the full implications of Ishmael's rebellion. He was unleashing an inevitable Babylonian retaliation, but, more important, resisting the will of the LORD as made clear by Jeremiah and Gedaliah.

THE EIGHTY PILGRIMS FROM SAMARIA **41.4–10**

It is not immediately apparent that this narrative contributes materially to the theme of these chapters, except to emphasise the ruthlessness of Ishmael. This may be paradoxically a ground of trust in the basic historicity of the narrative. The editor has the Gedaliah tradition before him and includes this passage because it is part of his source and because it rounds off the story. On the other hand a more substantial reason might lie in a comparison of the conduct of Ishmael with that of Jehu. Jehu had not been content to kill Jehoram whom he replaced as a result of the prophet-inspired revolution. He also killed Ahaziah king of Judah, Jezebel, the queen mother, and the whole family of Ahab, seventy strong. Gratuitously he massacred the southern royal family also and the leading worshippers of Baal. For this ruthless extravagance, Jehu came under severe prophetic criticism, particularly from Hosea (1.4). Ishmael is thus shown to act in the spirit of Jehu and to carry the same judgment.

Historically the narrative is of considerable significance. It tells of eighty pilgrims, in deep mourning, on their way from the former central sanctuaries of the north and from Samaria, to worship at Jerusalem. They had not heard of the death of Gedaliah (v. 4), but they must have known of the destruction of the Jerusalem sanctuary. They bear witness to the effectiveness of Josiah's reformation and the continuing centrality of the Jerusalem Temple, which was the exclusive sanctuary. Its destruction might have been exploited as an excuse for reverting to the local sanctuaries. Though there were those who offered sacrifice, they seem to have been a corrupt section of the people who brazenly opted for extreme Canaanite practices (Isa. 57.3–13, 65.3–7, 66.17). These pious men on the contrary were intent to go to Zion. The 'seventh month' was the month of the New Year festival (Tabernacles) and it may be they wished to do all that could be done in the new circumstances at the greatest feast of the year. Their appearance (v. 5) suggests that, if this were so, they were in effect turning the feast into a fast.

A long succession of scholars have interpreted this passage as evidence that, though the Temple buildings were in ruins, the external altar continued to be used for sacrificial worship. This is improbable (D. R. Jones, 'The Cessation of Sacrifice after the destruction of the Temple in 586 B.C.', *JTS NS XIV* (1963), 14 ff.). The eighty brought cereal offerings and incense, the very two offerings permitted to the Jews at Elephantine, when they sought to rebuild their temple after its destruction in 410 B.C. They agreed with the Jerusalem authorities that 'no sheep, or goat are offered there as burnt offering, but (only) incense, cereal offering'. These two items were the essence of non-bloody sacrifice. The most probable hypotheses therefore is that the destruction of the Temple brought the full sacrificial cult, including the feast of Tabernacles, to a halt. These eighty men were making a special pilgrimage of a penitential kind, bringing with them such offerings as were permitted in the new circumstances. They exemplify the sentiment which led to the establishment of the four new fast days (Zech. 8.18–19), the one in the seventh month being a commemoration of the murder of Gedaliah.

5. to present at the temple of the LORD: in the hands of the redactor, this cannot mean any other sanctuary than the exclusive Temple in Jerusalem. Lit: 'Yahweh's House'. The suggestion that the eighty were looking for the new house of Yahweh in Mizpah is eccentric.

6. Ishmael's weeping, a sign of intensive mourning, is of course part of the deception.

8. Personal advantage to Ishmael alone saves the lives of ten men who can offer stores of food. Hebrew narrative delights in the sub-plot, cf. the four lepers in 2 Kg. 7.3–15.

9. The large cistern which king Asa had made: the translation follows the LXX. MT has 'by the hand of Gedaliah, which is plainly untrue. But it is easy to explain this error as a corruption of the Hebrew text. The building of the cistern is no doubt comprehended in the reference to Asa's fortifications described in 1 Kg. 15.22.

10. The fact that when these prisoners were rescued Jeremiah was among them (42.2), suggests that he is to be included here. It is reasonable to guess that Baruch was among them too. This verse also provides evidence that the women of the court had not been deported to Babylon, but committed to the care of Nebuzaradan.

JOHANAN DEFEATS ISHMAEL AND PREPARES TO GO TO EGYPT **41.11–18**

The prompt action of Johanan leads to the speedy dissolution of Ishmael's rebellion. He escapes to Ammon whose king had inspired the revolution. In the end no more than eight men support him. But Johanan does not judge his loyalist success sufficient guarantee against Babylonian reprisals for the murder of Gedaliah. He therefore moves south and takes up a station near to Bethlehem, intending to go to Egypt. Thus the story prepares the setting for the next great choice which faces the people of God. Obedience to the divine will, as interpreted by the prophet Jeremiah, will be tested by their response to the question, should they stay or should they go to Egypt.

12. the great pool which is in Gibeon: (cf. 2 Sam 2.13) among the major archaeological discoveries at the modern el-Jib (see plate IX in *Archaeology and Modern Study*, ed. D. Winton Thomas). This is six miles north-west of Jerusalem, a border town of Benjamin. Like Mizpah it was strategically important. The pool was the source of the town's water supply. Some have argued that this identification favours the view that Mizpah is the modern Nebi Samwil rather than Tell-en-Nasbeh (see on 40.8). It is argued that if Ishmael were fleeing from Mizpah to Ammon, Gibeon would be in the wrong direction. But the text does not say that, at this stage, Ishmael was on his way to Ammon, only that Johanan caught up with him at Gibeon. In the circumstances of war there could be any number of reasons for going in one direction rather than in another.

17. Geruth Chimham: otherwise unknown.

THE CHOICE FOR JUDAH AFTER THE MURDER OF GEDALIAH
42.1–43.7

The divine message in its third form

Throughout this narrative the message of Jeremiah is consistent. It amounts to a resolute submission to the divine judgment. The first form of this message, appropriate to the moment, was: Submit to the Babylonian invader. King and people would not do this and suffered the consequences. The second form was: Seek the peace of the land under Gedaliah. The people were disposed to accept this counsel, but thrown by foreign interference. The third form, after the death of Gedaliah was: Stay in Judah; do not flee to Egypt. It is this advice which now forms the substance of a sustained piece of writing by the narrator.

There is no clear indication of the use of sources, no duplicate accounts put together as in chapters 37–41. It is as though the narrator gives free rein to his pen, straining in his repetitive manner to express the force of Jeremiah's rejected message. The vocabulary and style is that of the Jeremiah prose tradition, i.e. it has marked signs of Deuteronomic influence, but it is not simply Deuteronomic. It is the distinctive style of the book of Jeremiah, and may therefore be regarded as the style of a disciple, though there is no means of knowing how near he was in time to Jeremiah himself. The disciple is intent to show how right Jeremiah was in the face of opposition.

The links with the prose tradition are many. In v. 2 Jeremiah is asked to exercise his prophetic vocation in prayer, as negatively or positively, in 7.16; 11.14; 18.20; 21.2; 27.18; 37.17. The expression 'let our supplication come before you' is found in 36.7; 37.20 and 38.26, and 'pray to the LORD for us' in 7.16; 11.14; 14.11; 32.16; 29.7; 37.3; 42.20. The description of the audience 'from the least to the greatest' is found in the poetic piece 8.10 but also in 44.12 and, perhaps significantly in the appendix to 2 Kg. 25.26, which we have seen to be used by the narrator. The use of the term 'remnant' (v. 2) for survivors after judgment is found in 8.3; 24.8 and then consistently in this section–40.11, 15; 41.10, 16; 42.2, 15, 19; 43.5; 44.12, 14, 28. It occurs in the poetry (6.9; 15.9; 31.7) and there is no reason to deny the idea to Jeremiah, but clearly it has become the pointer to an accepted theme in these latter chapters.

The familiar 'behold' with a participle of the prose tradition occurs in
v. 4. The idea of the LORD as a true and faithful witness (v. 5) is unique
(cf. Prov. 14.5, 25).

The influence of Deuteronomy may be seen in the repeated demand
for obedience to the voice of the LORD, with consequences for good or
for evil, together with the emphasis on 'this day' (vv. 19, 21), but of course
these are commonplaces. The latter is in the call narrative (1.10) which
clearly furnishes the vocabulary of building and planting in v. 10 (cf.
18.7; 24.7; 31.28; 45.4). The enigmatic character of 1.10 is here dissolved,
as the phrases are used to express a clear and unambiguous hope of
salvation. The particular form of the sentence, i.e. strengthening the
positive idea by the negation of its opposite, is a characteristic device of
the Jeremiah tradition (cf. 4.22; 7.24; 24.6; 39.16; 44.27) and is not
common elsewhere. The salvation vocabulary of v. 10: 'I am with you
to save' is a formula already well-known in Israel and attested in Sumerian
texts.

The punishment in terms of sword, pestilence and famine (vv. 16, 17,
22) is again characteristic of this book (5.12; 11.22; 14.12, 13, 15, 16,
18; 16.4; 18.21; 21.7, 9; 24.10; 27.8, 13; 29.17, 18; 32.24, 36; 34.17;
38.2; 44.12, 13, 18, 27). It occurs both in the poetry and the prose and
may be regarded as an emphasis of the prophet which is exploited in the
prose tradition. The pouring out of the Lord's wrath (v. 18) is a phrase
of the tradition (7.20; 44.6) and the description of Judah as 'an execration,
a horror, a curse and a taunt' is related to 24.9, 29.18 and 44.12. See
notes on 24.9 and 29.18. The expression 'know for a certainty' (vv. 19,
22) occurs sporadically in the Deuteronomic history, but also in 26.15.
The theme of false prophecy as a lie ($\check{s}eqer$) in 43.2 is a feature of the prose
tradition, but no doubt based on Jeremiah's own use of the word to denote
the people's false sense of security and false worship. See on 3.10.

All this points to the conclusion that this prose is the literary vehicle
of a man closely involved in the Jeremiah tradition and, as we shall see,
intent to defend his master to the utmost. But while he uses commonplaces
of the tradition to express the prophet's teaching and, particularly in vv.
18–22, allows his knowledge of subsequent events to influence the manner
of his narration, probably also attributing to Jeremiah a simplistic scheme
which does no justice to the subtlety, suggestiveness and force of his poetic
oracles, there is at the same time no reason to doubt that he has adequately
captured the gist of the prophet's message in the successive crises of this
period. The notion that he has invented everything is gratuitous, and
a sad indication of the poverty of some contemporary criticism. On the

contrary he knew what it meant to be (in his own words) 'a true and faithfully witness' (42.5) and laboured in his own way to express what he understood to be the word of God by the mouth of the prophet.

The choice which Jeremiah now puts before the people is the more important because it is effectively the last. Accordingly the narrator draws out the critical nature of the situation in a piece of unbroken composition (42.1–43.7) built up in the following way.

(1) The leaders and people ask Jeremiah to intercede for them, as they may expect a true prophet to do, in order that they may receive divine guidance in their dilemma (42.2–3). The dilemma was clearly created by those who were pressing to escape to Egypt.

(2) Jeremiah agrees to do so, and emphasises that when he has received that guidance he will deliver it whole and keep nothing back (42.4).

(3) Leaders and people then solemnly undertake, the LORD himself being their witness, to follow that guidance, whether they like it or not (42.5–6).

(4) As is appropriate for so crucial a prophecy, there is a delay of ten days before Jeremiah receives the message. There is nothing hurried or facile about this prophecy. Jeremiah does not command it. He has to wait the LORD's pleasure. It is the LORD's message, not Jeremiah's, and comes in his time (42.7).

(5) The message itself is the third form of the divine message given in the succeeding crises, viz. to accept the divine judgment. Acceptance of that judgment now means remaining in the land, having no fear of the Babylonian overlord (42.8–12).

(6) The alternative of course is to go to Egypt in the belief that this will guarantee peace and provision. This is what the people want to do, the advice they want to hear. But there will be no escaping the divine judgment by running away. Sword, famine and pestilence (symbols of judgment) will pursue and overtake them (42.3–17).

(7) As now the narrator warms to his theme and emphasises the fate that lies before those who reject the divine message (42.18), he forgets to keep himself in the situation of the hour, and assumes the sequel (which of course he knows well). Thus he ascribes to Jeremiah the knowledge that leaders and people have already rejected the message. Jeremiah reiterates that he had been asked to pray for guidance, but the people have disobeyed and must endure the consequences (42.20–22).

It is of course probable that Jeremiah knew what the reaction to his message would be, but improbable that he said so when he uttered it! The emphasis on the full weight of judgment in terms of sword, famine and pestilence makes it most unlikely that the narrator totally invented the narrative or indeed wrote very long after the event, since there is no evidence that anything like this was the actual fate of those who fled to

Egypt. In Jeremiah's prophetic vocabulary, sword, famine and judgment were a symbol of judgment and it is not unlikely therefore that he used this symbol. By the Deuteronomic test of fulfilment, and in the light of the literal misunderstanding of the symbol, Jeremiah was proved wrong. It is however true that Nebuchadrezzar's long arm reached Egypt in 568 B.C. See further on 43.8–13.

(8) Jeremiah was then accused of being a false prophet and uttering a 'lie', the very word he had so often used himself. Baruch must have been a strong-minded and influential person, since he is accused of being the *eminence grise* behind Jeremiah. It may well be that the lesser man was inclined to be more dogmatic, and that the gentler personality of Jeremiah was used as a reason for accusing him of weakness (43.1–3).

(9) So Johanan led the flight to Egypt, taking with him, it is claimed, everyone whom Nebuzaradan had committed to Gedaliah, together with some others, and compelling Jeremiah and Baruch to accompany them (43.4–7).

42.10. **If you will remain in this land:** the corrected Heb. text is emphatic, 'If you will indeed remain'. As it stands MT witnesses to a time when the text was edited in exile: 'if returning you remain . . . '. A similar allusion to exile may be discerned in v. 12, where **let you remain in your own land** may be referred to those who were preparing or were already on the move to go to Egypt. In the tradition, on the other hand, it came to presuppose exile.

43.5–6. The list of those who went to Egypt is entirely credible. Johanan, the leader with his officers; those who, having fled to Moab Ammon and Edom, had returned to Mizpah with Gedaliah (40.11), together with the others who had rallied to Gedaliah. **the princesses** lit. 'daughters of the king', had not therefore been taken to Babylon. Significantly there is no mention of royal sons.

Tahpanhes: cf. 2.16, on the eastern border of Egypt on the delta.

THE CHOICE FOR THE JEWS IN EGYPT
43.8–44.30 (LXX 50.8–51.30)

Once in Egypt, Jeremiah continues to reaffirm his demand for utter obedience to the LORD's will, now in relation to a reawakening of syncretistic worship. That the Jews in Egypt should turn to the kind of worship which it was the whole purpose of Josiah's reformation to obliterate, is altogether probable. It was in disobedience to the declared will of the LORD that they had come at all. One act of defiance commonly leads to another and then to a settled disposition. The argument was plausible. When the queen of heaven had been acknowledged in the reign of Manasseh, there had been peace. (44.16–17). Josiah himself had perished violently. And since the reformation, all the greatest disasters had occurred. Moreover the people did not believe they were rejecting Yahweh, only propitiating his most powerful support. The women took the lead, as is shown in the narrative (vv. 15, 19, 24). There is something to be said for Skinner's view (*Prophecy and Religion* p. 334) that the women, who kept this long memory, were themselves from the leading families, and that the princesses may well have played their part, though there is no doubt of the popularity of the cult and its widespread use.

Once again the narrator freely employs his somewhat repetitive eloquence, though he may have used a more precise tradition in 43.8–13, while some think that 44.28–30 may be an appendix subsequently added. There is the same blend of Deuteronomic influence, more pronounced in the denunciation of false worship, with a style and vocabulary characteristic of the tradition and similar to chapter 42 in particular. Thus the prophetic sign in 43.8–13 is interpreted in terms of pestilence, captivity and sword, while sword famine and pestilence reappear in 44.12–13, 18, 27. See on chapter 42. It also has the characteristic messenger formula–'thus says Yahweh of hosts the god of Israel' which is more frequent in Jeremiah than in any other prophet and recurs in 44.2, 7, 11, 25. In 44.4 the prophets of the past are described in the way peculiar to the prose tradition; see on 7.13. The 'wrath and anger' of v. 6 echoes 42.18. The phrase 'the cities of Judah and the streets of Jerusalem' in vv. 6, 9, is paralleled in 7.17, 34; 11.6; 33.10 (cf. also 5.1; 11.13; 14.16) and is not common elsewhere. The prospect of becoming 'an execration, a horror a curse, and a taunt' v. 12 (cf. vv. 8, 22) echoes 42.18 and the tradition. The use of the verb 'to visit' of punishment, as in vv. 13, 29, is a marked characteristic of the tradition. see on 11.22. The phrase of v. 21 'did it not come into his mind'? literally, 'come up upon the heart', is found in 3.16; 7.31; 19.5; 32.35 and is otherwise rare. Verse 27 is a striking proof of the position here maintained that this prose is not primarily Deuteronomic but the prose exclusively of the Jeremiah tradition. The 'Behold, I am watching over them . . .' (v. 27) as pointedly plays on the theme of the almond branch in 1.11–12 as 42.10 played on 1.10; while the phrase 'for evil and not for good' is yet another example of the device whereby the positive idea is strengthened by the negation of its opposite (cf. 39.16 and 42.10 q.v.) The linguistic evidence strengthens the case for regarding this section as a further free piece of writing by the narrator. Nor are the repetitions and convolutions evidence of literary patching and subsequent additions, but characteristic of his preaching style.

But as in chapter 42, the conclusion that this is a sustained piece of writing by a disciple does not carry with it the conclusion that all is invention. The phrases are stock phrases and there is no means of sifting out the prophet's very words. But that the narrator correctly conveyed the substance of Jeremiah's preaching in Egypt there can scarcely be a doubt. For a later Deuteronomic preacher, speaking in the light of events, must needs have presented his historical predictions with some show of relation to the facts. In this case Jeremiah's dire predictions were not fulfilled. According to the narrator, the disobedient fugitives to Egypt would not escape the full force of divine judgment. Except for a few fugitives they would all be consumed; none would escape (44.12, 27). Nebuchadrezzar will conquer Egypt, destroying its temples and its people (43.11–13) and Pharaoh Hophra will suffer a fate like that of Zedekiah (44.30). In fact Nebuchadrezzar appears to have subdued Egypt in 568), but in such a way as to secure co-operative relationship, until the Persians took over; not was the religion of Yahweh extinguished in Egypt (v. 25), for the Jews, under divine providence, were able so to establish themselves in Egypt as to make a distinct Alexandrian contribution to their tradition. Philo reckoned that in his day there were a million Jews there, and they enjoyed a real degree of self-government with religious freedom. It is difficult to imagine these chapters being written any later than about 570. It is permissible to suppose that Jeremiah himself was not long dead and that his followers were preaching in his name, giving the substance of what they believed to be his message.

THE SIGN OF THE STONE BEFORE THE GOVERNMENT BUILDING 43.8–13

This prophetic sign is of the type that Jeremiah had been wont to enact and is to be compared with the sign of the waistcloth in 13.1–11. Cf. 18.1–12; 19.1–13 and 20.1–6. There are some ambiguities. It is not clear to us what exactly Jeremiah did with the large stones because the Hebrew words, translated in *RSV* 'the mortar in the pavement', are obscure. *bammeleṭ bammalbēn* look like doublets and the LXX has only one equivalent, which appears to be an attempt at a generalisation: 'in the area in front of the door'. The rendering 'secretly' by other Greek versions is improbable since the point of the sign is that it should be seen. In Talmudic times *meleṭ* and *malbēn* were related architectural terms. Probably therefore the narrator used a single architectural term *meleṭ* which, because it was obscure, was then glossed by the related term *malbēn* which still had some currency (2 Sam. 12.31; Nah. 3.14). We are left to guess that the account probably refers to a brick terrace.

The stones which Jeremiah hides are intended symbolically to mark the place where Nebuchadrezzar will establish his sovereignty over Egypt. Jeremiah had already used this image in the elucidation of the vision of the boiling pot (1.15), as indicating the way the northern enemy would demonstrate its conquest of Jerusalem. This was to be at the entrance of the gates, cf. also 39.3. Strictly, or course, Pharaoh had no 'house' in the border town of Tahpanhes, but there was no doubt a government building. The meaning of the symbolism is not obscured by uncertainty over the Heb. word translated 'royal canopy'. Some think this is a carpet. Either way it adds colour to the parallel 'throne', which is the essential point.

The prediction was partially fulfilled when, according to a fragmentary inscription (Pritchard, *ANET*, p. 308, Wiseman, *Chronicles*, p. 94), (in) 'the 37th year Nebuchadrezzar king of Babylon mar(ched against) Egypt to deliver a battle . . .' Nothing is known about the outcome of the battle. The date is 568 and the Pharaoh Amasis. It is reasonable to assume that Nebuchadrezzar successfully established his authority. In view of the subsequent satisfactory relations between Babylon and Egypt, it may be assumed that the Babylonian hegemony was administered with discretion and that, subsequently, the dreadful threats of vv. 11–13, apart from the inevitable casualties of invasion, must have looked like a palpable exaggeration. We have already seen that these elements of exaggeration are in the style of the prose tradition, and must antedate the events to which they may be taken to refer.

12. as a shepherd cleans his cloak of vermin: in the Heb., literally, 'as a shepherd wraps himself in his cloak, so he will wrap himself in the land of Egypt'. The translation 'de-louse' is dependent upon the LXX and is precarious, presupposing an otherwise unknown homonym, i.e. a word of the same sound but quite different meaning. The well attested literal translation above in fact makes good sense and suggests a picture of the Babylonian king claiming Egypt as his personal possession

JEREMIAH'S PREACHING IN EGYPT 44.1–30

The story of Jeremiah's preaching in Egypt is, as argued above, in the style of the prose tradition. Is it a sustained piece of composition like chapter 42? The style is all of a piece. Some scholars discern signs of division. They point to v. 1 as indicating a wide dispersion of Jews in Migdol, Tahpanhes, Memphis and Pathros, i.e. from the north to the south. In v. 15 there appears to be a large gathering, providing Jeremiah with an audience in Pathros. By v. 19 it is the women who are replying to the prophet. But such considerations point not to subsequent expansion of a supposed nucleus, but to the freedom with which the narrator builds up his case. Still less is there any substantial reason for distinguishing between elements of a historical narrative and a Deuteronomic preaching source. The exact historical events we have no means of re-establishing and apart from some small additions suggested by their absence in the LXX, the purpose of the narrator is to be discovered in the whole. He means his message to be received by all the Jews in Egypt, and they are now widely scattered. They include not only the new fugitives but some who have been long settled (cf. 24.8). In vv. 1–10 he sets the whole sermon in the wider context of Israel's rejection of the prophets whom the LORD has sent to her. Verses 11–13 re-state the punishment. All this transfers to *this* situation the essential points which the prose tradition has re-affirmed for *every* situation, and nothing is new.

Verses 15–23 set within this general theme the particular problem of the fugitive Jews gathered in Pathros, i.e. a large district of upper Egypt. This is sufficiently unexpected to suggest that this was an area where some of the Jews had settled and that it was here that Jeremiah encountered them. Can there be a connection between these Jews and the later military colony at Elephantine, who worshipped Yahweh's consort Anath, and referred to her without so much as batting an eyelid? At all events the object of their worship is the queen of heaven. See on 7.18.

The response of Jeremiah to the women who claim virtuously that they will perform their vows is, **Then confirm your vows and perform your vows!** (v. 25). He has come to the end of the possibilities of persuasion, as he earlier came to the end of his conflict with the prophets, and as he had also come to the end of the possibilities of intercession. One is reminded particularly of his dealings with Hananiah. He envisages the end of the religion of Yahweh in Egypt (v. 25).

28. those who escape: this appears odd, following the explicit statement 'until there is an end of them'. So also the ruthless judgment of v. 14 is modified by 'except some fugitives'. Here some interpreters detect the interfering hand of a later contributor. That is possible; but it is more probable that this is the idiom of the narrator, in whose mind the straggling exception in no way weakens the affirmation of total judgment.

30. Behold, I will give Pharaoh Hophra into the hand of his enemies: this, in v. 29, is designated a sign of the long arm of the LORD in judgment. A future event is to be the sign of the judgment to follow.

This is strictly without analogy in prophecy. The birth of Immanuel in Isa. 7 is not parallel, since the prophet's sign is firm and established. Here the fulfilment of prophecy is the sign of the fulfilment of prophecy. There is of course no reason to doubt that the fate of Hophra was pointed to as the first fruits of the judgment predicted by Jeremiah. The two verses look like an appendix. Hophra (otherwise known as Apries) reigned from 588–569. The reference in the same verse to Zedekiah is to the purpose, since Hophra had given assistance to Zedekiah when he rebelled against Babylon, sending an army to relieve Jerusalem, according to 37.5, not apparently without some success. But when towards the end of his reign he sent Amasis to control a military revolt, Amasis was proclaimed king. After a short period of co-regency Hophra was put to death. The turn of Amasis (now Ahmose II) to receive Nebuchadrezzar's discipline came, as we have seen, in 568/7.

THE FATE OF A FAITHFUL DISCIPLE 45.1–5 (LXX 51.31–35)

The remarkable similarity between this passage and the passage in 39.15–18 on the fate of the Ethiopian Ebed Melech has been spelled out in the comment on 39.15–18, q.v. It must be significant that both are to be found within the section chapters 37–45. Both on the other hand have an independent character and are not knit separately into the narratives of which they now form part. In the theme of the narrator their function seems clear. 39.15–18 presented the modified judgment (amounting to salvation) which was to be expected by the only individual uncompromisingly faithful to Jeremiah in the crisis of the reign of Zedekiah. Chapter 45 now presents the modified judgment to be expected by Jeremiah's faithful amanuensis and disciple Baruch. Despite the date of v. 1, the effect of the oracle in its present position is to qualify the out and out doom predicted for the Jewish community in Egypt. Baruch will not die. On the other hand he will experience the force of the Babylonian invasion and become a prize of war. He will have existence but not freedom. His survival will be, so to speak, a windfall. So much is clear.

The passage does however raise problems. The date. Suddenly at the end of a section entirely devoted to the fate of Zedekiah and the flight to Egypt, we have a passage reverting to the fourth year of Jehoiakim. It is of course possible that this is editorial, but difficult to imagine an editor introducing the earlier date if the oracle was in fact delivered in Egypt. It is therefore more probable that this independent oracle carried with it the date presented. It would then pre-date the Ebed Melech oracle and form the pattern on which it was based. If that is so, then the point of the oracle in its present position would be twofold. First the reference to 'the writing of these words in a book' seemed to come well at the end of a collection of oracles, just as chapters 25 and 36 had performed this function. Second, the oracle provided the only sort of hint of salvation possible in the otherwise uncompromising promise of judgment. Moreover the last words took on telling significance when repeated in Egypt–'in all places to which you may go'–amounting to a vindication of the prophecy.

4. That is the whole land: is almost certainly a gloss. It is absent from the LXX and the final *hi'* of the Heb. is the mark of the identifying gloss as in Isa. 9.14, etc. This then leaves a plain reference to the terms of the call-vision. See also on 42.10.

5. and do you seek great things for yourself: there is a natural tendency to read into this question possibilities of ambition in the character of Baruch. It is clear that he was more than an amanuensis, and there is a hint of leadership in the accusation of 43.3. Certainly the references to Baruch are such as to make it a reasonable assumption that he played a leading part in the establishment of the prose tradition of the oracles of Jeremiah, as also in the transmission of his poetic oracles. See on chapter 36. But here the truth may be simpler. What triggered off this oracle was apparently Baruch's own lament that the pressures involved in assisting Jeremiah had become unendurable. He was protesting at sharing Jeremiah's vocation of suffering. It was in this context that Jeremiah told him that he could not be an exception to the general doom. When everything was being dissolved, he could not be exempt. There is no escaping the Cross. 'Great things for yourself' is probably a way of describing such exemption. The only qualification of this judgment is that he will live as a 'prize of war'. See on 39.18.

So the main body of the transmitted oracles and prose tradition of Jeremiah ends. Mowinckel saw in the deliberate placing of an oracle of the time of Jehoiakim at the very end, confirmatory evidence that 'Baruch has been the literary and spiritual heir to the preaching of Jeremiah and the one who has taken care of the spiritual remains of the prophet, the founder and carrier-on of the tradition about him, 'the author' of the book of Jeremiah' (*Prophecy and Tradition*, p. 61). If this falls short of demonstration, the pointers are nevertheless in this direction and there are no others.

IV   THE LORD'S SOVEREIGNTY OVER THE NATIONS
46.1–51.64

These chapters compete for the reputation of being the most puzzling in the book of Jeremiah, and no confident conclusions can be expected in respect of date, authorship, purpose or the history of transmission. The basis for the view here presented is to be found in the commentary on chapter 25. In the Greek version these oracles, in a different order, are placed to follow 25.1–13, and some scholars think this was the original place for them. But this is by no means to be taken for granted. We showed reason for supposing that 25.1–14 is itself the end of a complicated history of transmission and that the link to connect that chapter with these oracles is likely to be an editorial provision. We noted also that the Cup of Wrath oracle in 25.15–29, also subject to subsequent expansion, presents in its earliest form an order of the foreign nations which corresponds to the order preferred by the Hebrew tradition. The basic form of 25.1–14 we saw to be a conclusion to a complex of oracles, possibly at one time concluding the Baruch scroll of chapters 1–6, finally concluding the deposit of chapters 1–24. The overwhelming probability therefore is that the oracles against the foreign nations were a separate complex of the tradition which had not assumed a final resting place in either the earlier form of MT or that of the LXX.

Undeniably the oracle on the Cup of Wrath follows well upon 25.1–14. Moreover in the LXX there seems to be a palpable editorial manipulation to make a neat connection between 25.13 and the opening of the oracle against Elam. Verse 13 in MT is 'I will bring upon that land all the words which I have uttered against it, everything written in this book, which Jeremiah prophesied against the nations'. The latter phrase in LXX is divided to introduce the first oracle, and becomes 'what things Jeremiah prophesied against the nations -Elam'. Then, following the oracle against Babylon which ends in 31.44 (LXX), the editor has added: 'which things Jeremiah prophesied against all the nations', so leading back to the Cup of Wrath oracle. Thus, there seems no doubt that the LXX editor introduced this complex of oracles against the nations into a position which they did not hold in the MS as it came to him. The editor of MT preferred to present the close and natural link of 25.1–14 with the Cup of Wrath oracle and placed the complex at the end of his collection. This may be regarded as not unsuitable, having regard to the independent character of the oracles. They are strictly like nothing else in the book. In one respect the LXX may well preserve the order of the oracles when they existed independently. It presents the oracles against Moab last, and the literary build-up of this chapter (Heb. 48) makes it intrinsically probable that it was compiled last.

The oracles against the nations are therefore to be regarded as a separate collection within the book of Jeremiah, despite links with the tradition, which will be noted below. They raise many of the problems already posed in the prophetic collections, particularly by Am. 1-2, Isa. 13-23 and Ezek. 25-32. Indeed the phenomenon of the prophecy against a foreign nation is encountered much earlier in the utterances of the Moabite prophet Balaam concerning the coming rise of Israel to greatness (Num. 23-24) and again outside Israel, in a prophet's revelation to Zimri-lim of Mari of the demise of Hammurabi of Babylon. This prophecy belongs to the earlier part of the second millennium. Moreover, in Egypt we encounter the so-called 'execration texts', curses pronounced on foreign enemies accompanied by a sign of their destruction (e.g. the smashing of a pot). If there is a magical conception underlying this custom, the idea is suppressed in Israel. But what this shows is that the oracle against the foreign nation is not a late deviant or a sporadic outburst in Israel, but an integral element of prophecy with which we have to come to terms.

Discussion about its place in the life of Israel must be speculative. The Holy War tradition is an obvious suggestion, The very idea behind it is the war against the enemies of the LORD himself, which he will win by many or by few. It belongs essentially to the period of the conquest, though there are some who think it was revived by Josiah, thus explaining the place of this ideology in the book of Deuteronomy. But unquestionably its main thrust is pre-monarchical and its subsequent history is a matter of influence. Ideas and vocabulary from this ideology are to be found in the Deuteronomic history, in prophecy and in certain psalms like Ps. 44. Some attribute the concept of the Day of the LORD in Amos and Isaiah to this background. But it will be quickly seen that this background is restrictive and can only apply to such denunciations of enemies as are relevant to particular wars, and at such times as the holy war tradition was alive and operative. Clements has correctly observed that these oracles cannot consistently be regarded as 'directed at Israel's enemies with a view to providing assurance for Israel'. They are neither to be regarded comprehensively as threats nor as veiled assurances. (See further Clements, *Prophecy and Tradition*, pp. 58-72.)

In the case of the oracles against the nations in the book of Jeremiah, it is necessary of course to clarify why such questions have to be asked at all. Is it not sufficient to accept the superscriptions and ascribe them to Jeremiah himself? Jeremiah had been called explicitly to be a prophet to the nations (1.5) and exercised his ministry at a time when Judah was so embroiled in international events that no parochial ministry could be of any significance. The early Foe from the North oracles in chapters 1–6 are all addressed to Judah and do not raise the same problem. There is some evidence (chapter 27) that Jeremiah may have used the occasion of the presence in Jerusalem of ambassadors from Edom, Moab, Ammon, Tyre and Sidon, to send a message to these nations, comparable to that which he delivered to Zedekiah. There is a suggestion that this message was accompanied by a sign, but no hint that he uttered anything comparable to the oracles in chapters 47–49. A straightforward message which an ambassador might carry, is one thing; a colourful, powerful, condemnatory prophecy is quite another.

By and large these oracles must have been addressed to the Jews. They reflect the prophetic conviction, from the time of Amos, that the LORD is lord of the nations and not of Israel only, that none ultimately escapes the divine judgment, that those who have gloated over Judah's fall will themselves stumble and fall, that the LORD is not mocked and the whole world is in his hand. There is therefore no *a priori* reason why Jeremiah should not have exercised his ministry as a prophet to the nations by uttering some or part of the oracles collected in his name. It is however, virtually certain that he is not responsible for the final collection, particularly since some seem to be built up as mosaics of his and other known teaching. Each part must therefore be examined and judged separately. The question then arises, why was it that the prophetic circles (those of Isaiah as well) particularly developed this kind of oracle in poetic form? Where and how did they declaim them? Why did they do this just at the period when Judah was smallest, powerless and utterly at the mercy of foreign powers? Was this one of the ways in which the faith was kept alive that Yahweh had suffered no defeat in the defeat of his people but remained lord of all the earth?

Examination of the oracles shows that while they all have certain characteristics which link them firmly with the Jeremiah tradition, they also have characteristics which link them with one another and prove them a unique type of prophecy. As the collection proceeds the delineation of particular oracles becomes more difficult, because there are signs of the literary mosaic and of careful redaction. The oracles against Babylon in chapters 50–51 are many oracles, gathered in no significant order. But the first two oracles against Egypt in 46.3–12, and 14–24, appear to have retained a poetic form and completeness which encourages some preliminary deductions about their structure and purpose. The following elements are common to the early oracles of this collection.

(1) A rhetorical introduction. In both poems this is expressed by a series of *imperatives*. 46.3–4 (seven) 46.14 (four). Cf. Jl. 3.9–14 (fifteen).

(2) A description of defeat, in both poems expressed in terms of *stumbling* (*kšl*) and *falling* (*npl*), 46.6, 12 and 46.16. Cf. 50.32; 48.32, 44; 49.21, 26.

(3) The source of judgment is *the north*. In 46.6, 10 the battle takes place in the north. In 46.20, 24 the instrument of judgment is from the north, and this is the case elsewhere. Cf. 47.2; 50.3, 9, 41; 51.48.

(4) The day is *the day of the LORD* 46.10; 46.21. Cf. 47.4; 48.44; 49.2, 8, 26; 50.4, 20, 27; 51.17, 33.

(5) The exercise of judgment is by *the sword* 46.10; 46.16. Cf. 47.6; 48.10; 49.37; 50.16; and this theme is highlighted by the song of the sword in 50.35–38.

(6) The result for the enemies is *shame* 46.12; 46.24. Cf. 47.5 (baldness); 48.2, 20, 37; 50.12, 47.

It is interesting to compare this structure with that of, for example, Isa. 13. That also begins with imperatives (v. 2); sees the instrument of Wrath coming 'from a distant land' (v. 5); centres on the day of the LORD (vv. 6, 13); the sword is the instrument of judgment (v. 15); and the shame is expressed in terms of the overturning of Babylon's pride (vv. 19–20) like Sodom and Gomorrah, cf. 50.39. Other motifs are: dismay like a woman in childbirth (Isa. 13.8), as in Jer. 48.41; 49.22, 24; 50.43; cf. Ps. 48.6; destruction and the destroyer (Isa. 13.6; 16.4; cf. Jer. 47.4; 48.8, 15; 49.10); the putting down of the pride of the arrogant (v. 11) as in Jer. 46.7–8; 48.11, 14, 26, 29, 42; 49.4, 7; 50.29; subject peoples turning back to their own land (v. 14) cf. Jer. 46.21. It is perhaps a pointer to a somewhat restricted vocabulary that the Heb. word *hipnû* is repeated (Isa. 13.14; Jer. 46.5; 46.21; 48.39; 49.24; 50.16).

At the same time, throughout the Jeremiah poems against the nations there are phrases characteristic of the Jeremiah tradition. The most striking examples are: 'terror on every side' 46.5 cf. 49.29 and 6.25; 20.3, 4, 10; 'the time of visitation' 46.21 cf. 48.44 = 11.23; 49.8; 50.27, 31; 51.17 cf also the familiar *hinnê* with participle in 46.25; 50.18 cf. also 6.15; 11.22; 23.2; 27.22; 29.32; 44.29; the presentation of the enemy as a derision and a horror, 48.39; 49.13; 50.23; 51.41, 43. Add to these considerations the quotations from other parts of Jer.–e.g. 46.11 = 30.13; 46.27–28 = 30.10–11; 48.34–44 is a mosaic; 50.41–42 = 6.22–24;

51.15–19 = 10.12–16. (Note also 48.32–33 is equivalent to Isa. 16.9–10. See further, below.)

The following conclusions may be drawn. These oracles, though independent, belong to the Jeremiah tradition, and it is a fair guess that the author of them is a prophet or prophets in that tradition.

At the same time *the restricted interest of the oracles, the recurring and limited themes, the circumscribed pool of vocabulary, suggest that they were composed for a single type of occasion which itself determined the similarities.* It is possible to hazard a guess as to what that occasion was, and to locate it in the feast of Tabernacles. Dogmatic confidence is out of place, for there is no way of avoiding a hypothetical proposal as to the place and purpose of the oracles, itself based on a hypothesis. But there are strong pointers.

The feast of Tabernacles or Tents or Booths, was the third of the great pilgrimage feasts, held on the 15th of the month Tishri, five days after the Day of Atonement (Dt. 16; Lev. 23). In the earlier calendars of Exod. 23.16 and 34.22, it is called Ingathering. As such, according to the Gezer calendar of the time of David and Saul, it opened the year. Thereafter it certainly marked the turn of the year, the culminating vintage festival, lavish, joyful and the most widely observed. It became known as 'the feast of Yahweh' (Lev. 23.39; Ezek. 45.25; 1 Kg. 8.2, 65). Josephus called it 'the holiest and greatest of Hebrew feasts' cf. also Jn 7.2. In the post-exilic period it seems to have been divided into three, that part of it which looks forward to the new year becoming the ecclesiastical New Year's Day of Tishri 1. For our purposes it is sufficient to say that Tabernacles was not in itself the New Year Festival, but looking both backwards as Harvest Home and forwards, it embraced features of the New Year Festival, later separated to make a distinctive feast. We do not know how or when these transitions were made.

These observations have importance when we come to establish the connection of kingship with this feast. In Zech. 14.16 it said that those who survive of the nations that attack Jerusalem on the Day of the Lord, 'shall go up year after year to worship the King, the LORD of hosts, and to keep the feast of booths'. And upon those who do not respond, the rain will not fall. In the impressive closing rites (according to later Jewish sources) seventy bullocks were sacrificed as burnt offerings, and the explanation given that these were on behalf of the seventy heathen nations. And a characteristic feature of the New Year rite, which had come to be regarded as an annual judgment of mankind, was the three benedictions, of which the first (Malkuyoth) celebrates in selected passages

(Exod. 15.8; Num. 23.21; Dt. 33.5; Ps. 22.29; Ps. 93.1; Ps. 24.7-10; Isa. 44.6; Obad. 21; Zech. 14.9) the sovereignty of Yahweh over all the world, and ends with a vision of the future universal range of the kingdom.

It is reasonable to deduce that these features preserve in the post-exilic period an earlier, intimate connection of 'the feast' both with the monarchy and with the kingship of Yahweh. Here, it is fair to assume, in the pre-exilic feast of Tabernacles, was the context of the psalms which celebrate the kingship of Yahweh. It can be no accident that these psalms, together with the so-called royal and Zion psalms are those which celebrate or anticipate the triumph of Yahweh over the nations which threaten Zion and its king. (2, 18, 46, 47, 48, 68, 72, 76, 93, 97, 98). Notice also the power of Yahweh as the giver of rain in Pss. 29, 46, 68, 93. Further see A. R. Johnson, *Sacral Kingship in Ancient Israel*, pp. 57 ff. and *passim*, who argues for the view that the old agricultural feast was transformed by the influences of the Jebusite cult from the time of David.

The great day of the feast is in a special sense the LORD's day, attracting to itself the ideology of the Holy War. Here Israel receives the promise that, though the nations band themselves against the LORD's people, he will intervene to save them. This is in a nutshell what is sometimes called the Zion theology, compounded of a variety of old influences. The psalms which support this thesis betray signs of being cultic rather than historical pieces, and demand some such explanation. The theme determines the manner of the telling of Sennacherib's invasion (2 Kg. 18-19 = Isa 36-37). It is palpably determinative in the mind of the editor of the oracles of Isaiah, especially in 10.4-12.6. And it gives rise to the eschatological picture in the so-called apocalyptic passages in Jl. 3, Zech. 12 and 14 and Ezek. 38-39. It influences those oracles against the nations which are really salvation oracles for Judah, but cannot explain all. It is probable also that the feast of Tabernacles in its time-honoured character as Ingathering provided the occasion for the post-exilic proclamation of the ingathering of the LORD's dispersed people. But that is another matter.

What we may imagine to have happened is this. The feast of Tabernacles, when the monarchy had perished, provided the occasion when the theme of the kingship of Yahweh over all nations was kept alive, cf. particularly the independent section of Ob., vv. 15-21 ending 'and dominion (*melûkâh*) shall belong to the LORD'. This was the more striking when Judah was small, demoralised and powerless, still more when her people were in exile (Jer. 46.14).

In two ways prophets can have intervened. It may be that the establishment (cultic?) prophets had a place in the feast when they were expected to declare the sovereignty of Yahweh in a tangible way by showing how he would chastise the recalcitrant nations, especially how he would turn the tables on those who assisted in the judgment on the LORD's people but exceeded their commission.

Or it may be that either establishment prophets or prophets of the tradition of Isaiah, Jeremiah and Ezekiel used the occasion, because at no other time could they find 'the congregation of Israel' so conveniently gathered together. This might well be true in exile. See on 46.14. With some freedom they latched on to themes of the festival to trigger their message. The single underlying theme of their message was the sovereignty of Yahweh and this comprehends those oracles which imply the salvation of Judah and those which do not. This, combined with the freedom of the prophet, gives sufficient background for all the oracles against the nations without exception.

This hypothesis makes it unlikely that Isaiah, Jeremiah or Ezekiel were the actual authors of these oracles, but in view of the demise of prophecy and the absence of signs of the Persian dominion, it is also unlikely that they are to be dated after the fall of Babylon. They are a *genre* and a tradition which belong to the period between the fall of Jerusalem and the rise of Persia. The same prophets of the Jeremiah tradition may well be responsible for the Lamentations, thus explaining their traditional association with Jeremiah.

THE LORD'S SOVEREIGNTY OVER EGYPT
46.1–28 (LXX 26.2–28)

46.1. The superscription defines the whole collection of oracles against the nations.

THE FIRST POEM 46.2–12

Verse 2 is a superscription for the first oracle only. It is grammatically clumsy and best understood as either a conflation of two headings or containing a subsequent expansion. The note concerning the defeat of Pharaoh Neco by Nebuchadrezzar at Carchemish in 605 B.C. is confirmed by the Wiseman Chronicle. Nabopolassar was now old and ill, and handed over the command of the army to Nebuchadrezzar, who was crown prince. The Egyptians had crossed the Euphrates in 609. They moved south-west to take Syria-Palestine and then back again. The Chronicle tells us that Nebuchadrezzar

marched to Carchemish which is on the banks of the Euphrates and crossed
the river against the Egyptian army which lay in Carchemish . . . fought with
each other and the Egyptian army withdrew before him. He accomplished
their defeat and to non-existence (beat?) them. As for the rest of the Egyptian
army which had escaped from the defeat (so quickly that) no weapon had
reached them, in the district of Hamath the Babylonian troops overtook and
defeated them so that not a single man (escaped) to his own country (pp.
68–69).

Despite the defeat inflicted on Nebuchadrezzar by the Egyptians in their
own country at the beginning of 600, Carchemish still marks the end of
the power of Egypt as capable of world dominion. Some interpreters think
it is this which may be the real theme of vv. 2–12 (note especially v. 8).
They judge that this poem comes unquestionably from Jeremiah himself
and that it is of very high poetic quality. At the very least we must insist
that this judgment is over-confident and that the considerations expounded
above point in a different direction.

The poem is the first of a collection which is marked by dependence
upon known passages in the Jeremiah tradition, reaching a climax in
48.32–47, which is nothing less than a mosaic of quotations. It is of course
not impossible that an original piece should form the nucleus of a
secondary collection, but the signs are otherwise.

The first theme describing preparations for battle (vv. 3–5) ends with
'terror on every side, says the LORD' which is already a slogan in the
tradition. It occurs in one of the Foe from the North poems (6.25), is
applied as a symbolic name to Pashhur (20.3), and is perhaps significantly
part of the oracle against Kedar in 49.29.

The use of the term 'north' in this poem is quite different from its use
in Jeremiah's early ministry where it is undefined and ominous. In v.
6 it is not the origin of judgment for Judah but the place of judgment
for Egypt. The same is true of v. 10 (unless it is here a gloss). And since
the word does not here carry its striking dramatic overtones, it is surprising
that the geographical location is not defined more accurately. Altogether
this would be an extraordinary use of the term by Jeremiah at the very
time when he was pre-occupied with the identity of the Foe from the North
as the Babylonian conqueror. The phrase 'that the day is the day of the
LORD God of hosts' (v. 10), as identified with a particular event, is
unique and looks like the result of reflection. The phrase 'the LORD
God of hosts holds a sacrifice' occurs in this form in Isa. 34.6, and the
idea in Ezek. 39.17, 19 and Zeph 1.7, 8. The reference to balm in Gilead
(v. 11) is surely derived from 8.22 where the point is clear. Once the

vivid picture has been created it can then have an extended application.
Natural of Judah in 8.22, it is somewhat strained of Egypt. The latter
part of v. 11 is directly quoted from 30.13.

Some scholars have denied this oracle to Jeremiah simply on the ground
of the violent spirit of vengeance expressed in vv. 10–11. This is
unacceptable criticism. It is incorrect to apply post-Christian standards
of sensitivity to the prophet. What is more to the point is that if this oracle
were delivered by Jeremiah in 605 it would represent deviation from the
thrust of his main message of that period. This is clear in the use of the
term 'north' as described above, but more generally in the implications
of the whole passage. Nowhere in the main tradition of his work, both
prose and poetry, is there any such preoccupation with Egypt except to
insist that along with other nations they must drink the cup of judgment
(25.19). This tallies with the general observation made on these poems
as a collection.

Conclusions thus reached may then answer the problem of the tenses
in this poem. Is the perfect tense to be interpreted descriptively or
prophetically? If it is the familiar prophetic perfect, then the oracle predicts
the fall of Egypt at Carchemish with a precision unusual in prophecy.
The 'Why have I seen it?' of v. 5 will then indicate a prophetic vision
of the event. If the perfect is descriptive, then the poem will be a picture
of the event composed subsequently. The above considerations,
particularly the use of the term 'north' differently from in the remaining
oracles, make this latter conclusion much the more probable.

If then this poem was composed after the event, what was its point
and purpose? Clements points out that in a number of oracles against
the nations there appears as a recurring theme the idea of their *hubris*
or proud claim to independent world domination, in ignorance of the
real sovereignty of Yahweh. This is found in Isa. 10.7–10 of Assyria,
14.12–21 of Babylon, 16.6 of Moab and 23.6–12 of Tyre. It is most
emphatic in Ezek. 28.1–14 of Tyre, and Ezek. 31 and 32 of Egypt. The
same theme is explicit in Jer. 48.28–33 of Moab and it is present in vv.
7 and 8 of this oracle. It is fair to conclude that the deeper theme of this
prophecy against Egypt is the world sovereignty of Yahweh, that the
nearest parallels are in comparable oracles against the nations, and that
the author must have been a poet in the Jeremiah tradition circle, who
provided a contribution and a theological assertion which would otherwise
be lacking.

As to the circumstances in which such an oracle might be uttered, see
pp. 488ff. It is not unlikely that the poem is in three stanzas, vv. 3–6,

7-10 and 11-12; 'in the north by the river Euphrates' is a sort of refrain repeated in vv. 6, 10; while 'stumbled and fallen' occurs in vv. 6 and 12. English translation disguises the significant repetition of 'go up' in vv. 4 ('mount'), 7 (rising'), 8 ('rise') and 9 ('advance'). 'warrior' occurs in vv. 5, 6, 9, 12. 'Earth in vv. 8, 10 ('country'), 12. These repetitions are by no means banal, and have the effect of intensifying the vividness of the language.

3-6. These verses are a vivid description of the call to war. The seven imperatives are rhetorical. **Why have I seen it?** may be taken as indication of the visionary character of the poem (omitted by LXX, probably by an oversight). This accords with the argument set out above, that this cannot be Jeremiah's description of, say, the battle of Carchemish. It is also improbable that it is someone else's description, introduced into the Jeremiah corpus. This poem, as we have seen, belongs firmly to the Jeremiah tradition. But the visionary description may well be influenced by the memory of Egypt's venture into Mesopotamia. That was a model of Egypt's fateful march to destruction. The victor is not named, but the location of the battle **in the north by the river Euphrates**, clearly identifies Babylon, but gives a different nuance to the term 'north' from that characteristic of Jeremiah.

stumbled and fallen: falls short of the fivefold build-up of synonyms in Isa. 8.15, but has the same effect as providing a minor climax. The pair is a characteristic of the collection of poems.

7-10. This stanza begins with an ironic description of Egypt, in terms of the well-known cosmic mythology of chaos. The waters of the Nile are set against the waters of Euphrates. It is ironic because Egypt is thus described as having world-shaking ambitions. These are destined for complete reversal, (cf. Am. 9.5).

9. The **men of Ethiopia and Put . . . men of Lud:** are either mercenaries or auxiliaries, parallel to the 'hired soldiers' of v. 21. Put is probably along the coast of E. Africa; Lud, perhaps (with a slight change) the Libyans who figure with Put in Nah. 3.9. Ethiopia is, of course, south of Egypt.

In v. 10 the real victor is identified. Egypt believes she is marching to defeat Babylon, which is not mentioned. But she is delivering herself into the hands of the LORD. The Day of the LORD, the day of the great feast, the day of Yahweh's victory in holy war, subsequently given eschatological overtones, is here identified as Babylon's victory over Egypt. The old vocabulary is used — 'God of hosts', 'the day of vengeance', but its new context is determined by a belief that Yahweh is sovereign LORD of the whole world. This is the answer to Egypt's pretension to **cover the earth** (v. 8).

10. The sword shall devour and be sated: a motif of the oracles against the nations. Here the personification is marked and the symbolism clear.

The stanza reaches its climax in the picture of the LORD holding a sacrifice **in the north country by the river Euphrates**. This image expresses a philosophy of history. This is the real meaning of the climactic collision course marked out for themselves by the most powerful nations of the earth. The bloody ritual of ancient sacrifices says it all. The phrase 'the LORD holds a sacrifice' is formal. It is used of Edom in Isa. 34.6.

11–12. There is no healing for Egypt. For the association of Gilead with healing, see 8.22. Though *shame* is indeed a motif in all these oracles, the word *qᵉlônēk* should probably correspond to the LXX *phonen sov* 'your cry', thus completing the parallelism. This can be achieved either by emendation to *qôlēk* or by guessing at the existence of a meaning found in late Heb. The stumbled and fallen of the last line rounds off the whole poem with the same word-pairing that completed the first stanza (v. 6).

THE SECOND POEM **46.13–24**

The second oracle is in some ways related to the first despite differences. It has its own superscription (v. 13) which sets it in the context of Nebuchadrezzar's invasion of Egypt. There is no record of Nebuchadrezzar having defeated Egypt on her own soil. In 600 B.C. Nebuchadrezzar's invasion was a failure and his forces were defeated. He mounted a campaign against Amasis in 568/7 B.C. but the fragment which gives us the information tells us nothing of the result. The first clear notice of a defeat is that inflicted by the Persian Cambyses on Psammetichus III in 525 B.C. The superscription does not therefore seem to be a valid historical comment.

It is therefore perhaps significant that the poem itself contains no clear historical identification of the conqueror, referring only to a 'gadfly from the north' in v. 20 and to 'a people from the north' in v. 24. Supposing then that the superscription is a later attempt at historical identification, other possibilities are opened up for the interpretation of the poem.

Again in this oracle there are some signs of dependence upon the Jeremiah tradition. In this case the term 'north' is used as in the early oracles of Jeremiah himself; as signifying an as yet unidentified agent of the divine judgment *from the north*.

Given the context proposed for these oracles, it is possible to expound 46.14–24 as follows. The imperative **declare in Egypt, and proclaim in Migdol; proclaim in Memphis and Tahpannes** (v. 14) is the prophet's way of expressing his own commission. These are the places where, after the initial journey to Tahpanhes (43.7), the Jews of the Egyptian dispersion were to be found (44.1). But see note below. There is evidence that Jews in Egypt were able to carry on their traditional worship, though it is unlikely that temples could be built and sacrifice offered as at Elephantine in the fifth century. No doubt in some way the harvest element of Tabernacles was observed.

What the prophets emphasised was the associated theme of Yahweh's world sovereignty, now profoundly relevant. He was sovereign over the very people who held them in their hand. Their own native worship will avail the Egyptians nothing (v. 15). Those from other countries who served the Egyptians would decide to return to their own people (v. 16), including the mercenaries (v. 21) who are named in the previous oracle (v. 9). Pharaoh becomes despised as one who makes loud pretensions but cannot deliver (v. 17). This, together with the image of the **beautiful heifer** of v. 20 suggest the familiar theme of the pride (*hubris*) which is to be brought low. The imagery of the felling of trees in v. 23 is the now commonplaced imagery of the Day of the LORD (cf. Isa. 2) which is **the day of their calamity** (v. 21) further describe, as so often in the Jeremiah tradition, as the 'day of visitation'. Egypt's shame will be encompassed by an unspecified foe from the north (v. 24).

The theme of the sovereignty of Yahweh is all pervasive, but comes to expression in v. 15, where it is Yahweh who humbled Egypt and her gods, but above all in the oath formula of v. 18: 'As I live, says the King, whose name is the LORD of hosts'. Yahweh is the true and only King. The oracle is about his sovereignty in Egypt.

14. It may be that the occurrence of the verbs 'declare', 'proclaim' and 'say' in 4.5 indicates some relation of these poems to the original Foe from the North poems.

Migdol, etc: see on 44.1. LXX omits Egypt and Tahpanhes. It is of course possible that MT is an expansion based on 44.1.

15. Why has Apis fled?: a universally accepted, because convincing emendation, making sense of scarcely intelligible Hebrew, from the LXX. Apis was the sacred bull of Memphis, son or incarnation of the God Ptah.

16. stumbled and fell: the Heb. is a quarry for hypothetical emendation. But cf. vv. 6 and 12.

17. Noisy one who lets the hour go by: The giving of symbolic names was a prophetic ploy practised by Hosea, Isaiah and Second Isaiah. Pharaoh seems to have been a fair target, Isaiah of Jerusalem calling him 'Rahab who sits still'. *NEB REB*, have 'King Bombast, who missed his moment'.

18. like Tabor . . . and like Carmel: this is an image which would have little point except to a Jew who remembered these mountains, not particularly lofty, but in their own context imposing and awesome.

22. She makes a sound like a serpent gliding away: The LXX has 'like a serpent hissing (*šōrēq*)', preferred by many commentators. But the best explanation is that this is an elaboration of the metaphor. MT is to be preferred. Nor need the metaphor of the serpent be sustained, as though the foresters are attacking the snake. Various metaphors are used — the serpent, the felling of trees, the locusts — without any attempt to weave them into a single picture.

25–26. The redactor adds a prose comment in the manner of the prose tradition–**Behold I am bringing punishment** ('visit upon'– *pôqēḏ*) cf. 11.22; 23.2; 29.32; 50.18.

Amon of Thebes: Amun or Amunre was the high god of the capital of upper Egypt. The queen was regarded as in some sense the early consort of Amun so that the Pharaoh was physically his son. Verse 26 is missing in LXX.

26. Afterward Egypt shall be inhabited: at some stage of redaction (after LXX), the ultimate salvation of the nations was envisaged, cf. 48.47 (Moab); 49.6 (Ammon); 49.39 (Elam). For this universalist spirit see also Isa. 19.16–25. All are absent from LXX which here represents an earlier text. It should not occasion surprise that this note should be introduced subsequently. It is the inner logic of the teaching on the sovereignty of Yahweh and it took time to work it out. The reference to Nebuchadrezzar, being a post-LXX attempt at identification, should be ignored.

27–28. A redactor has also added these verses which occur at 30.10–11. So completing the eschatological hope for God's people.

THE LORD'S SOVEREIGNTY OVER THE PHILISTINES
47.1–7 (LXX 29.1–32)

1. The superscriptions must be regarded as an editor's vain attempt to find a historical fulfilment for the prophecy. The LXX, which renders 'Philistines' as 'the foreign tribes', does not have **before the Pharaoh smote Gaza**, which must be regarded as post LXX editorial identification (cf. Nebuchadrezzar in 46.26). There is no record of a conquest of Gaza

by the Egyptians in the seventh to sixth centuries. They sought to expand
into Philistia under Psammatichus I. Some have seen in an obscure notice
of Herodotus (ii. 159) indication that Necho II took Gaza in the time
of Josiah, but this is entirely uncertain. At most we can suppose that an
editor is aware of an Egyptian conquest of Gaza, which is the only such
conquest he knows. For a conquest by Gaza by Egypt would have to refer
either to the opposition put up by Gaza to Cambyses in 525 B.C. or to
the siege of Gaza by Alexander the Great in 332. The expedient to which
this editor was driven is of course shown by the plain fact that the poem
itself speaks, like the other poems, of a foe from the north. In the period
of Jeremiah the only conquerors can be the Babylonians. According to
the Wiseman Chronicle, Nebuchadrezzar took Askelon in 604 B.C. 'He
marched to the city of Askelon and captured it in the month Kislev. He
captured its king and plundered it and carried off . . . he turned the city
into a mound and heaps of ruins' (Wiseman, p. 69).

In the ration-tablets which mention Jehoiachin of Judah, there are also
the sons of the kings of Askelon and the kings of Gaza and Ashdod.
Thereafter the records are silent. This poem must therefore be interpreted
entirely independently of its misleading superscription. Like the oracles
with which it is associated, it is a declaration of the sovereignty of Yahweh
over these alien peoples who, in their city states, had succeeded in
preserving some independence, despite the vicissitudes of the eighth to
the fifth centuries. The traditional enemies of Yahweh retained something
of this character, refused to be assimilated and became therefore the object
of prophecy (cf. Isa. 14.28–32: Zech. 9.5–8). That the Philistines are
the traditional enemies of Yahweh in the period of the holy wars and
the early monarchy is no doubt the real reason they are singled out for
this 'prophetic' treatment.

The oracle (vv. 2–7) conforms perfectly to the stereotypes which we
have observed to be characteristic of the oracles against the nations. The
rhetorical introduction likens the northern conqueror to **an overflowing
torrent** (v. 2) cf. 46.7 of the Nile and Isa 8.7–8 of Assyria. Indeed this
looks like the application of a slogan derived from the much more fully
developed image in Isa. 8. the **Waters** from **the north** once again suggest
the waters of chaos, and therefore reversion to chaos (see on 46.7–8).
The advance of an irresistible army is described in v. 3, cf. 46.9; Isa.
5.26–28, and this leads, as in 46.10, directly to the declaration that
Yahweh's **day** will destroy these peoples. The explanatory $k\hat{\imath}$ 'for' in v.
4 matches the explanatory $k\hat{\imath}$ in 46.10. And the personification of the sword
in v. 6 develops the theme of 46.10. And of course the word $\check{s}dd$ (destroy)

in v. 4 is to be repeated in succeeding oracles (48.8, 15; 49.10, etc). It is therefore permissible to imagine a prophet of the school of Jeremiah using the opportunities afforded by the major feast of the year to declare the divine sovereignty over Israel's hereditary enemies.

4. to cut off from Tyre and Sidon every helper that remains: In Isa. 23.1–18 (unless of course this refers to Sidon only), and Ezek. 28.26–28, Tyre receives individual attention. Here the Phoenician cities are mentioned because they have supported the Philistine bid to preserve their independence. This is inherently probable. The very fact that Nebuchadrezzar besieged Tyre after the fall of Jerusalem, makes it likely that this oracle was composed when Tyre had settled down and reconstructed its life.

Caphtor: i.e. Crete and the islands from which the Philistines had originally migrated (cf. Am. 9.7).

5. baldness: may be a sign of mourning as in Isa 15.2; Ezek. 27.31 and Jer. 48.37, but also a sign of shame, cf. Isa. 3.24, a feature of these oracles.

O remnant of the Anakim: this represents an attempt by the LXX to make sense of unintelligible Hebrew 'O remnant of their valley' in the light of the tradition that remnants of the giant Anakim once remained in Gaza, Gath and Ashdod (Jos. 11.22). What is wanted to complete the balance of v. 5 is the name of a town. It could be Ashkelon or Ashdod, but the disturbance of the text is too complete to permit a confident emendation.

THE LORD'S SOVEREIGNTY OVER MOAB **48.1–47 (LXX 31.1–40)**

This chapter is a collection of several poems which have been subjected to a complicated editorial process. Some features of the previous oracles against Egypt and the Philistines re-occur, e.g. the emphasis on shame (vv. 1, 20, 39), on pride (vv. 2, 7, 29–30, 42), on the sword (v. 2), on the destroyer (vv. 8, 15, 18). These are the signs which link the poems with the Jeremiah tradition, like the form of v. 12 ('Behold the days are coming . . .), the use of passages from elsewhere in Jeremiah (see on vv. 7, 44) and the phrase 'a woman in her pangs' which uses a verb entirely restricted to Jeremiah (v. 41, cf. 49.22, 4.31). There are also signs that the great feast which we have found to be the most plausible suggestion for the context and occasion of these oracles may be also the context here. Verse 15 has: **says the King, whose name is the LORD of hosts,** cf. 46.18. Here also the real theme is the sovereignty of Israel's

God over other peoples. And vv. 32–34 may well play on the popular shouts of the vintage festival.

On the other hand there are differences.

(1) This is a *collection* of material rather than an oracle or oracles with an easily discernable form. It is difficult to distinguish the basic oracles from the subsequent elaboration, and there is nothing like the structure set out on p. 487 The signs of compilation are overwhelming, not only in the quotations (see below) but also for example in the tell-tale fact that Moab is feminine in vv. 1–10 but masculine in v. 11.

(2) An unusual number of place names occur.

(3) There is no mention of a foe from the north.

(4) The theme of the Day of the LORD is implicit only, and is brought to explicit expression in the editorial v. 44.

(5) The theme of mourning and lamentation is sufficiently pronounced (vv. 5, 17, 31, 37) to suggest that this has something to do with the purposes of the oracles.

(6) There is remarkable use of 'scriptural' passages. In particular the oracle against Moab in Isa 15–16 is rewoven into a new mosaic in vv. 29–39. Isa. 24.17–18 is quoted in vv. 43–44 and Numbers 21.27–30 in vv. 45–46. Because so much is quoted, the dependence must be this way round.

Nor is it so easy to regard all the material as prophecy. The emphatic declaration that Moab **is no more** (v. 2), **is destroyed** (vv. 4, 18, 39) together with the calls to mourning, suggest a disaster which has happened, but may be prophetic vision and the tenses prophetic perfects. the reader is left wondering. In the first poem (vv. 1–10), one would have to conclude at the very least that the historical defeat is incomplete and is about to be completed (v. 8). Elsewhere the prophetic element is more pronounced. Verses 12 looks forward to judgment. Verse 16 says the calamity of Moab is **near at hand**. Verse 35 is predictive and so are vv. 40–44, ending with the warning of the familiar 'year of visitation' (cf. 11.23; 23.12). Perhaps a firm basis is supplied by v. 11. This seems to betray a knowledge that Moab has hitherto escaped serious defeat and has become correspondingly complacent. No doubt complacency fed the pride which is so emphatically described in vv. 29–30, 42.

If the oracle in vv. 1–10 is descriptive, it is impossible to discover a historical episode which answers to it. Not much is known of the origins of the Moabites. They were eastern neighbours of the Israelites as long as their settlement in Canaan. A convenient summary of their history is provided by J. R. Bartlett in *Peoples of Old Testament Times*, ed. D. J.

Wiseman (1973). The stele of Moab's king Mesha, of c. 853 B.C. shows
that this people, who had once been subjugated by David, were now
reasonably prosperous by reason of sheep-farming, spoke the same
language as the Hebrews and worshipped Chemoth with many of the
same attributes that were thought appropriate to Yahweh. We find them
paying tribute to the Assyrian Tiglath–Pileser III in 734 B.C. They seem
to have come under pressure from the tribal peoples in North Arabia
at the end of the eighth century and avoided trouble in the seventh by
continuing to pay tribute to Assyria. A note in 2 Kg. 24.2 gives
information that in the time of Jehoiakim, 'the LORD sent against him
. . . bands of the Syrians, and bands of Moabites, and bands of the
Ammonites, and sent them against Judah to destroy it'.

It is after this that the evidence mounts of a feeling in Judea of hostility
to Moab. Some scholars deduce from the oracles against Moab that there
must have been a Babylonian conquest of Moab, and locate this in the
course of Nebuchadrezzar's invasion of Egypt in 582 B.C. as reported
by Josephus. But this is to beg the question of the character of the oracles,
as to whether they are descriptive or predictive or a combination of both.
There is no independent evidence of a conquest of Moab at this time.
It is perhaps significant that in the time of Nehemiah, the Ammonites
are linked not with the Moabites but with Arabians (Neh. 4.7). Was it
a Babylonian conquest which left the country prey to the Arab tribes from
the east and south? We do not have the means of knowing. But see W.
F. Albright, *JBL* 61 (19), p. 119.

A reasonable conclusion may be the following. Chapter 48 may,in
parts, be interpreted as showing knowledge of a conquest of Moab, but
the absence of any reference to a foe from the north makes it precarious
to assume that this is the Babylonian. It certainly, in other parts, looks
forward to a judgment on Moab. There may therefore have been some
subjection of Moab or perhaps pressure from Arab tribes, which was
interpreted as an anticipation of the judgment to come. Or else the whole
is predictive, bringing Moab within the orbit of the judgment that is to
fall on all Judah's neighbours, thus demonstrating the sovereignty of
Judah's God over all peoples.

THE FIRST POEM **48.1–10**

This seems to be a complete poem. Verse 11 introduces a new theme.
It has the following elements:
(a) A declaration of Moab's destruction (vv. 1–4). The enemy is pictured
as planning her final destruction from Heshbon. They cry goes up, 'Moab

is destroyed' (v. 4). There is repeated emphasis on destruction: *šdd* in vv. 1, 3, 8; *šbr* in vv. 3, 4, 5.

(b) Lamentation (v. 5).

(c) The summons to flee (verse 6)– including their god Chemosh, priests and princes.

(d) A solemn curse on the invader if he is slack in performing what is 'the work of the LORD' (v. 10).

If v. 10 is a prose addition to a poem which ends at v. 9, then the uncertainties outlined above remain. My own view is that one should expect a solemn curse to have the distinct, but nicely balanced form of v. 10. In that case the view that the poem is visionary and anticipatory receives confirmation. The future judgment is described imaginatively as having happened, such is the certainty of its execution. And the curse is uttered on the invader if he is dilatory in the use of his sword. For he is to do the LORD's work.

1. Nebo: the name both of the mountain which was the traditional vantage point from which Moses viewed the Promised Land (Dt. 34.1) and the place of his death, and of a nearby town. Once in Israelite hands, it was conquered by Mesha, cf. Isa. 15.2.

Kiriathaim: was also in the disputed area between Reuben and Moab, and also occurs in the Moabite Stone.

The destruction (*šūdādāh*) of Nebo and the shaming (*hōḇîšāh*) of Kiriathaim are motifs of the collection. On the destroyer (*šōḏēḏ*) see v. 8.

2. In Heshbon they planned: the word-play cannot be reproduced in translation. The village, two miles above the Jordan, was also formerly in Reubenite territory, but later firmly Moabite (cf. Isa. 15.4; 16.8).

You also, O Madmen, shall be brought to silence: also word play. The initial *mem* could well be a dittograph from the final *mem* of the preceding word; in which case the village could be Dimon (cf. Isa. 15.9), or the Dibon referred to in Num. 21, 26, 30. This village was also taken by Mesha and figures on the stele, cf. also Isa. 15.2 and Jer. 48.18, 22.

the sword: another motif of the collection.

3. Horonaim: vv. 5, 34, and Isa. 15.5. Also on the Moabite stone.

4. a cry is heard as far as Zoar: one of the cities of the plain (Gen. 18–19), located north or south of the Dead Sea. So the LXX, which makes good sense. Hebrew 'her little ones make a cry heard' is less convincing.

5. The ascent of Luhith: so also Isa. 15.5. Otherwise unknown. This verse is either a free or a corrupt version of Isa. 15.5, though the end of Isa. 15.5 itself required emendation. the LXX has difficulty with both passages, but seems to have the variants in the text it uses. Altogether the *RSV* translation is as good a solution as is at present available.

6. Be like a wild ass in the desert: *NEB* thinks 'sand grouse'. This is the reading of LXX. Or possible the Heb. means 'juniper' as in 17.6 and is a play on the name of the Moabite village Aroer (v. 19), which is also the least unconvincing solution to the last word of Isa 15.5. No certainty is possible. *REB* abandons all these for 'one destitute'. The imperative is of course rhetorical as so often in these poems.

7. Chemosh: the religion of Moab was fundamentally Canaanite, which makes all the more significant similarities in the cult of its chief god, Chemosh, as compared with that of Yahweh. Solomon is said to have built up a high place for Chemosh east of Jerusalem, no doubt to cement a political alliance (1 Kg. 11.7, 33). The ideology of the holy war and particularly the idea of the ban was current in Moab. What was holy to Chemosh was put to the ban in Israel and vice versa. Verse 7 is an adaptation of 49.3c. The profounder dimension of the religion of Israel is revealed by the assumption that Moab's fault is to have **trusted in your strongholds and your treasures** (cf. Ezek. 28.4–7).

8. The destroyer: see p. 487 and cf. 6.26 in particular. This is a theme of this chapter, but no further definition is given, suggesting that the author of the oracle did not know who the destroyer was to be. This is another theme of the collection (cf. vv. 18, 32, 51.48, 12.12). The origin of the idea may well be found in the 'destroyer at noonday' of 15.8. It is taken up by Jeremiah in the original Foe from the North oracles (6.21) and then used in this and other oracles against the nations. The destroyer is a 'great power'–but that power is an instrument of the LORD.

9. Give wings to Moab: this is an unlikely rendering. LXX has 'give signs to Moab', which supports the suggestion that the word *ṣîṣ* may, with the *NEB REB*, be translated 'a warning flash', on the basis of an Arabic cognate. Others have seen behind the LXX the Heb. word for 'signpost', monument or gravestone as in 2 Kg 23.7. This is better than 'salt' which some have derived from Ugaritic (cf. Jg. 9.45). Read either 'she shall surely surrender', which is the meaning of the Heb.; or with a slight change, 'she shall be laid in ruins'.

10. For the significance of the curse as determining the interpretation of the poem, see above. That the execution of the destruction of Moab is the LORD's work (cf. 50.25) is presented in an over-simplified way. But that a judgment is worked out in the tragedies and vicissitudes of history is part of the insight into history which is Israel's gift to the thought of mankind.

A FRAGMENT COMPLETED **48.11–13**

This verse (11) unambiguously belongs to a period when Moab has suffered no overwhelming national reverse. Reading between the lines one would suppose that Judah has so suffered.

and has settled on his lees: This expression has become proverbial in English and means 'making the best of a bad job, settling down on what is left, having squandered the main part of one's fortune'. But that is not the meaning here. The idea is of wine that is matured by resting undisturbed (BDB) on the lees. Even so Moab has got away with it. She has been undisturbed as the great disturbances have passed her by. Two imaginative and telling metaphors are used: (a) Being emptied, like the content of a jar from one to another, suggests the traumas of defeat, exile and captivity; and indeed this is the explanation given. Moab has been able to remain untouched in her own land. (b) Accordingly she has suffered no fundamental personal change; she has not lost her sense of taste or smell. That is to say, she has retained her natural vitality.

Now the prophet of Jeremiah's school sees fit to complete this fragment with a threat of judgment (v. 12) beginning in the familiar style of the tradition. Moab's consequent complacency is to be destroyed. The metaphor of the jars is developed. The LORD will send 'tilters' i.e. the jars will be emptied as Judah's jar has been emptied, the wine no longer left to mature, but shaken up and poured out.

Finally in v. 13, the metaphors are pointed in the most obvious manner. **Moab shall be ashamed of Chemosh**: this represents the reversal of Moab's pride. The comparison with Israel — **as the house of Israel was ashamed of Bethel, their confidence** — raises problems. The parallel suggests that Bethel here is not a place but the name of a deity worshipped in Israel. But the alleged example of such usage in the Elephantine Papyri is not certain. Moreover the absence of any such usage in the *OT* tradition of Bethel weakens the force of the passage. It must be an appeal to the familiar. It is much more probable that Bethel here stands for El-Bethel and the cult denounced so fiercely by Amos (3.14; 4.4; 5.5) and Hosea (4.15; 5.8), as the centre both of Jeroboam I's illegitimate worship and of the very symbol of Canaanite Yahwism. For the word 'confidence' used of Israel's syncretistic worship in Jeremiah's own poetry, see 2.37.

Thus the oracle appears to be a construction, by a member of the Jeremiah tradition, on the basis of a fragment. This does not mean that its existence is only literary. So constructed the oracle would have been as effective as any other, uttered either during or on the occasion of the feast, when the sovereignty of Yahweh over the nations was celebrated.

THE THIRD POEM **48.14–28**

It is not easy to be sure of the limits of this poem. Verse 29 may provide a firm beginning to a new section, since here the literary mosaic begins with a verse by verse dependence on other material, until the end of the chapter. If this is so vv. 14–28 may be regarded as a single piece, having something in common, structurally, with vv. 11–13. Both begin with the complacency of Moab (vv. 11, 14). Both announce a judgment that is to come (vv. 12, 16). Both have a vivid image of the process of judgment (v. 12: emptying and smashing his jars; v. 26: being drunk on the wine of wrath). Both relate the outcome to the experience of Israel (vv. 13, 27). The middle section is more developed than in vv. 11–13, and v. 12 looks like a prose amplification. It is therefore reasonable to conclude that this oracle was composed for the same purpose as vv. 11–13 (see above). The association with the Feast and the theme of Yahweh's sovereignty come to expression in v. 15: **says the King, whose name is the LORD of hosts.** That this is omitted by LXX does not alter the argument. Once again there is no indication of who the Destroyer is or from whence he is expected to come. See on v. 8. The best guess is again that Moab had been subjected to raids (v. 18), and perhaps constant pressure from Arab tribes, and this was interpreted as an anticipation of Moab's final downfall. If this were so the author of the oracle was not far off the mark!

The element of anticipatory mourning is strong in this poem, not only in the call to mourning (vv. 17, 20) but also in the use of *'êkāh* (vv. 14, 17) the characteristic opening of the elegy (Isa. 1.21; Lam. 1.1; 2.1; 4.1).

18. Dibon: see on v. 2. **parched ground:** does not require emendation.

19. Aroer: See on v. 6. A frontier town on the north bank of the Arnon. Once Reubenite, but Mesha had it in his possession and fortified it. See his stele.

20. the Arnon: the northern boundary of Moab, flowing westward into the Dead Sea. Mesha built a road by it. See the stele.

21–24. These verses have the appearance of a prose expansion. They simply complete the tally of threatened or stricken villages or towns. Jahzah (or Jahaz), Mephaath and Kiriathaim were formerly in Reubenite territory. Jahaz, Dibon, Nebo, Beth-diblathaim, Kiriathaim and Kerioth figure in Mesha's stele. Bozrah is otherwise known as Edomite. See on 49.13. Was there a Moabite Bozrah?

26. The recurring theme of *hubris*.

shall wallow in his vomit: rather 'overflow with his own vomit', i.e. of course, bring it up.

27. you wagged your head: often the verb used in parallel with a verb of mourning and indicates an attitude of grief. But here the prophet describes the mocking attitude (cf. 18.16) of Moab as, so far exempt from disaster, she gloated over the demise of her neighbour. Edom is denounced for the same attribute in Ps. 137.7. By the irony of judgment, Moab shall herself become a derision.

THE FOURTH POEM **48.29–47**

There is no clear indication where this poem begins. the rhetorical call of v. 28 would be in keeping with this type of oracle, as in 46.3 14. What is certain is that the quotation from, or use of, other oracles begins at v. 29 and continues to the end of the chapter. This is unlike anything else in the oracles against the nations, except the oracles against Edom in 49.7–22. The learned author could be continuing previously existing material and building on it, in which case he is essentially an editor, or this could be his method of composition. In the latter case the poem stands on its own from vv. 29–47 and should be read accordingly. Since the poem, despite its eclectic origin, has a shape and a point, this is the most likely hypothesis. It is not simply editorial addition, but a poetic piece in its own right, derived in the main from other poems, but newly minted in the style of what has been called 'the learned psalmography (Mowinckel).

The use of other passages may be analysed as follows:

29a = Isa. 16.6a

29b = Isa. 16.6b modified by the addition of 'the haughtiness of his heart'.

30 absorbs Isaiah's 'insolence' into a new sentence, beginning 'I know . . .' and adding 'says the LORD' which is absent in the LXX, and 'his deeds are false'.

31 then moves back to Isa. 16.7, changing to the first person and replacing 'raisin-cakes of Kir-hareseth' with 'men'. The clear rhythms of Isa. 16.7 are so disturbed that it is now difficult to discern a clear poetic pattern. The line is overloaded.

32a omitting Isa. 16.8, modifies Isa. 16.9a.

32b reorders the words of Isa. 16.8cd, and in so doing changes the picture questionably. The vine stretching from the wilderness to the Dead Sea, becomes one stretching over to the sea as far as the sea of Jazer. All through these verses Isa. 16 is plainly the original, which is being reordered.

32c is Isa. 16.9c with the change of *qāṣîr* (harvest) to the more precise *bāṣîr* (vintage) and *hêdād* (shout) (taken up in v. 33) to *šōdēd* characteristic of these oracles (47.4; 48.8, 18; 49.28; 51.48, 53, 55, 56 and cf. 6.26; Isa. 16.4).

33a is Isa 16.10a with palpable patching–'and from the land of Moab' replacing 16.10b.

33b changes Isa. 16.10b, extending the play on *hêdād* (the harvest shout). On the relation of this to Hadad, see note below. The author seems to wish to rub this word in !

34 reverts to Isa. 15.4a, 5a and 6a, suitably contracted.

35 is a free rendering of Jer. 16.12 in prose of the tradition, and as such points to the author's mind and purpose (see also vv. 38b, 39, 42, 44c).

36a is a free rendering of Isa 16.11 overloading the original rhythm.

36b is Isa. 15.7 but changes an absolute to a construct inexplicably and, leaving out the poetical completion, ends lamely 'have perished'.

37a is Isa. 15.2c, but 37b and 38a is a free rendering of 15.3.

38b like 35 is the writer's own words in the prose tradition–'for I have broken Moab like a vessel for which no one cares, says the LORD', picking up a phrase of 22.28.

39 is a sort of reinforcement of v. 20 using the word *hipnāh* which is a verb of no special significance but a characteristic of the poems (see p. 487).

There is no further use of Isaiah 15 and 16.

40 is, with slight variation, 49.22a.

41a takes up v.1 (i.e. the first poem against Moab) and

41b completes the quotation of 49.22, including the expression 'a woman in her travail' which in this form *mᵉṣērāh* is unique to Jeremiah (cf. 4.31).

42 seems to be of fresh mintage and therefore another clue to the mind of the author.

43–44 quotes a telling passage from Isa. 24.17–18 to describe the inescapability of judgment (cf. the same truth by means of a different image in Am. 5.19).

44c again reveals the characteristic vocabulary of the tradition, introducing the theme of the 'year of visitation', which is a vital motif of all these poems. For the phrase itself cf. 11.23 (of Anathoth) and 23.12 (of the prophets).

Finally the last section 48.45–47, absent in LXX, is derived from the poem in Num. 21.27–29. Here alteration is essential to adapt a ballad which belongs to an earlier and quite different historical situation. See comment below.

45b is doctored from Num. 21.29a or from a text underlying the present corrupt text.

47 is clearly editorial, but completes the theme of the sovereignty of Yahweh. His design looks beyond the destruction of Moab to an ultimate salvation, as also for Ammon 49.6 and Elam 49.39.

This analysis leads to the following conclusions.

(1) The nature of the literary relationships is such that this poem is dependent upon Isa. 15–16, Num. 21 and the Jeremiah tradition. The dependence cannot be the other way round. The poet is essentially learned, a student of previous traditions, who adapts them to a new purpose.

(2) Isa. 15 and 16 are comparatively straightforward laments over the doom of Moab. Here the lament element is extrapolated and becomes part of an oracle which, like the previous oracles, both celebrates some sort of disaster (the destroyer has fallen, vv. 32, 39) and looks forward to a completion of the judgment (vv. 35, 40–44).

(3) The overarching purpose of the poem is, like that of the previous oracles, the demonstration and celebration of the sovereignty of Yahweh. This becomes crystal clear in the passages which are either the author's own or derived from the Jeremiah tradition:

> For (*kî*) I have broken Moab like a vessel for which no one cares, says the LORD (v. 38b).

> Moab shall be destroyed and be no longer a people, because (*kî*) he magnified himself against the LORD (v. 42).

> For (*kî*) I will bring these things upon Moab in the year of their punishment says the LORD (v. 44b).

The repeated *kî* in these passages is significant as pointing to underlying motive, with which the author is concerned.

(4) Despite the intensely eclectic nature of the passage, it comes out as an oracle against Moab with many of the features of the other oracles. It is not therefore to be regarded as simply a literary mosaic, but as a poetic oracle.

> Moab's pride (*hubris*) is the basic reason for her fall (vv. 29–30, cf. 46.8; 48.7, 11)

> The lament is both actual and anticipatory (vv. 32–33, 36–39, cf. 48.5, 17, 20)

> Moab has suffered a beginning of her judgment (v. 32, cf. 48.1, 4 [Moab is destroyed], 20, 21)

but the final day is to come (vv. 40–44, cf. 48.8.12).

The context is once again most plausibly the vintage festival. Hence the special emphasis on the vintage shouts of rejoicing (vv. 32–33, cf. the king in 48.15)

(5) Nevertheless the dependent character of the oracle demands some explanation. It means that the author, though certainly in the Jeremiah tradition, is different from the author of the other Moab poems. He represents a tendency which is seen in the late psalm tradition, coming to fruition in the Psalms of Solomon and the Hodayoth. On the other hand this cannot be of such a late date, since the text of Scripture is not so fixed and authoritative that it may not be changed. This is particularly true of the use made of the ballad from Num. 21. If that ballad itself was being sung in the late sixth century, before its incorporation in the Pentateuch, that would provide the most probable date for this composition.

31. Kir-heres: also Kir-hareseth, one of the principal cities of Moab, cf. 2 Kg. 3.25; Isa 15.1; 16.7, 11.

32. Jazer: according to Num. 21.32 a former Amorite town taken by Israel and one of the levitical cities (Jos. 21.39). The image in Isa. 16.8 suggests that it was known for its vineyards. It lay on the border with Ammon and was in Ammonite hands when taken by Judas Maccabeus (1 Macc. 5.8).

more than for Jazer: better 'fountain of Jazer'.

Sibmah: masc. form 'Sebam', Num. 32.3, which indicates that it was then Reubenite.

the destroyer has fallen: the alteration is entirely in line with the author's purpose. He mans 'destroyer'. Isa. 16.9 has 'the vintage shout (*hêdād*) is hushed'. But now the word *hêdād* is repeated in the next verse.

33. The underlying Isa. 16.10c is changed so that the word *hêdād* occurs three times, as though reinforcing it and playing on it. Is there a play on the Canaanite storm and weather god Hadad, who was expected to guarantee the rain? On the connection between the feast of Tabernacles and the guaranteeing of rain, see Zech. 14.16–18 (A. R. Johnson, *Sacral Kingship*, pp. 57 ff.), cf. Jer. 3.2–3. The vintage cry *hêdād* may well be derived from this source and represent a relic of the old Canaanite religion. Such a play on words might explain the otherwise puzzling Hebrew, literally 'one does not treat them with hedad; hedad is not hedad'.

34. Heshbon: see on v. 2.

Elealeh: also once Reubenite (Num. 32.3, 37); a mile or so north of
Heshbon.

Eglath-Shelishiyah: otherwise unknown.

the waters of Nimrim: cf. Isa. 15.6, otherwise unknown, thought to
be near the southern end of the Dead Sea.

37. mourning customs.

45–46. The heart of the ballad quoted in Num. 21.27–29, celebrating
the destruction of the people of Chemosh, is very much to the author's
purpose. But in Num. the historical context is quite different. According
to the introduction, v. 26, Heshbon was the capital of the Amorite king
Sihon, and had been taken by the Israelites. The call was therefore to
Israel (the 'we' of 21.30) to rebuild Heshbon:

> Come to Heshbon, let it built,
> let the city of Sihon be established

The ballad however sings of the previous victory of Sihon over Moab.

> For fire went forth from Heshbon,
> flame from the city of Sihon.

To the author of Jer. 48.29–47 this is irrelevant. He therefore changes
the beginning radically:

> In the shadow of Heshbon
> fugitives stop without strength,
> for a fire has gone forth from Heshbon,
> a flame from the house of Sihon'.

The reference to Sihon is rhetorical, and of course in v. 46 the reference
to a captivity 'to an Ammonite king, Sihon' (Num. 21.29) is omitted.
One may say that the specifics of Num. 21 are omitted so that the song
may have a quite general application to the discomfiture of Moab.

THE LORD'S SOVEREIGNTY OVER AMMON **49.1–6 (LXX 30.17–21)**

For so short a poem, this one is remarkably full of commonplaces from
the tradition. Verse 2 'Therefore behold the days are coming . . . ' 'The
battle cry' may well be derived from 4.19 (cf. 20.16). In v. 3 'for Ai is

laid waste' may conceal a reference to the destroyer, as commonly in these oracles, cf. esp. 48.8.

'For Milcom shall go into exile, etc' has the same form as 48.7b. In v. 4 the trusting in treasures is as in 48.7a.

Verse 5 is now a familiar stereotype of the tradition: 'Behold' with the participle–'I am bringing upon you'. And 'everyman straight before him' is a positive expression of the negative 46.5; 47.3. The most striking syntax of the tradition is in v. 1. See below. This traditional element is too pervasive to permit the hazardous enterprise of stripping it away in order to identify a basic poem which has been editorially amplified. There are textual problems which are probably insoluble, but the poem has to be interpreted more or less as it stands. It is the work of a prophet in the tradition.

All these poems have as their spoken or unspoken theme the sovereignty of Israel's God. Hitherto, however, Israel herself has figured only incidentally, as in 48.13 and 27 where the experience of Moab is incidentally related to that of Israel. Here in 49.1–6, Israel is both the starting point and the theme. The judgment on Ammon will be strict retribution for her exploitation of Israel's weakness (vv 1–3).

At the same time there is a quite different type of introduction: a question (cf. 49.7) rather than rhetoric, no description of defeat, other than commonplaces, no hint as to the source of judgment, no explicit reference to the Day of the LORD, no reference to the sword as the instrument of judgment, no emphasis on resulting shame.

The theme is straightforward. The dispossessor of Israel will be dispossessed (vv. 1–2, cf. Ob. 17). There will be lamentation in Ammon as she and her god go into captivity. This will be the result of the dread that is inspired by Yahweh. In v. 6 the salvation of Ammon is envisaged, like that of Moab (48.47) but, as there, the passage is lacking in LXX. There is no new or distinctive contribution. If the poem belongs to the same liturgical background as those with which it is associated, then the reference to **Milcom** (LXX), the national deity of the Ammonites, is ironic. The Heb. reads 'their king' and the possibility must be considered that this was the original reading and intention. At the feast which celebrated the universal kingship of Yahweh, the eclipse of 'their king' is celebrated with obvious irony. The LXX contains an accurate identification of the god, but at the same time a weakening of the force of the poem, and modern translations, including *NEB.*, *REB*, *TEV.*, The Jerusalem Bible, as well as *RSV.*, have missed the point in following LXX. See RVm.

1. The poem is built on a verse in the form of a question. The structure of this question is quite distinctive in the Hebrew: the sign of the interrogative *h*, followed by *ʾim* (or) and then by *maddûaʿ* (why). This type of sentence is found mainly in the poetry of Jeremiah but also in the prose tradition. Its effect, as S. R. Driver saw, is to express 'mingled pathos and surprise' (cf. 2.14, 31; 8.4f., 19, 22; 14.19; 22.28).

Milcom: i.e. the LXX reading. Hebrew has *malkām* 'their king' and this should be kept. See above. But the Ammonite god is accurately identified as Milcom, for whom, as a political gesture, Solomon had established a sanctuary on the mount of Olives (1 Kg. 11.5, 33). It was destroyed by Josiah (2 Kg. 23.13). The name is of course derived from the Semitic *melek*, a king, cf. the Tyrian Melkart.

Gad: LXX has Gilead. But Gad may be the correct reading, as being the east Jordan tribe which was closely associated with Reuben. It is remarkable how many of the towns named in chapter 48 as Moabite were formerly Reubenite. By the same token it is most probable that Gad, which is mentioned in the Moabite stone, and ultimately absorbed Reuben, was subject to this kind of pressure from further east. According to Num. 32.5, Gilead was divided between Gad and Reuben after the 'conquest'. Gilead is mentioned in 2 Kg. 15.29 as one of the regions taken by Tiglath Pileser III in 733, whose people were taken captive to Assyria. If this verse refers to a historical event, it could be to this one, when the opening was created for neighbouring Ammon to exploit. Whether this is correct or not, the reference is to some episode of this kind. Historically Ammon took advantage of Israel's weakness, was employed evidently by Nebuchadrezzar, with the Syrians and Moabites, to harass Judah in the time of Jehoiakim (2 Kg. 24.2), was responsible through her king Baalis for the murder of Gedaliah, and opposed, by every means possible to them, the rebuilding of the walls of Jerusalem by Nehemiah (Neh. 2. 10, 19; 4.3, 7). But the dispossessor was himself dispossessed by Nabatean Arabs in the fourth century.

2. the battle cry: cf. 4.19 (20.16).

Rabbah: the capital city on the site of the modern Amman, capital of the kingdom of the Jordan.

a desolate mound: the expression used of Ai in Jos. 8.28, which may well explain the reference to Ai in v. 3.

3. Ai is laid waste: this cannot be the Ai of Joshua's campaign. That was situated east of Bethel. If is of course possible that there was a wholly distinct Ai in Ammon, but it is otherwise without confirmation, and more likely that the text has been disturbed. It is an attractive conjecture that the Heb. should read *šōdēd ʿalāh* for *šuddⁱdāh ʿay*, as in 48.18, 'the destroyer has come up'. If an editor was confronted with missing letters, he might well be led by v. 3 to supply the reference to Ai. Alternatively omit Ai and translate: 'Wail, O Heshbon for she (Moab) is destroyed'. The tense would be appropriate in a dirge, whether it is descriptive or prophetic, and this is supported by LXX.

run to and fro among the hedges: no doubt the hedges or fences refer to sheep-pens, and the 'run to and fro' indicates panic, as in Jer. 5.1. The Ammonites will be like their own frightened sheep. This makes sense. The alteration of a single letter would produce 'with gashes' (cf. 48.37), cf. Targum, 'and score your body with gashes (*NEB REB*). This is appropriate, but unnecessary if the Heb. text yields good sense.

The form of 3c is that of 48.7b.

4. Why do you boast of your valleys: Hebrew adds 'Your valley flows'. LXX has 'why do you boast in the plains of the Anakim' (see on 47.5). Dahood suggests a Ugaritic cognate meaning 'strength'. 'Why do you boast in your strength–your ebbing strength?' conflated with 'Why boast? Your strength has ebbed'. But the homonym is questionable and needs the support of other convincing instances. If *RSV* is correct in omitting *zāb ʿimqēk* as a gloss of the form *z bⁱimqēk* – and this is plausible–, then its translation may yet be the best solution. In this desert region, Ammon's boast was indeed in the valleys. This is the word used by the inhabitants of the high plateaux as they looked down into the more fertile broad valleys.

5. terror: *paḥaḏ*, the vocabulary and ideology of the holy war, cf. Exod. 15.16; 1 Sam. 11.7; Dt. 2.25.

THE LORD'S SOVEREIGNTY OVER EDOM **49.7–22 (LXX 30.1–16)**

Much of what was said in the introduction to 48.29–47 applies also to this poem. It appears to be a poem in its own right, not simply a collection of quotations. But it is a poem composed largely by quotation, partly Obadiah and partly from passages in the Jeremiah tradition. The motive of the poet is betrayed most clearly in those passages, which so far as we can tell, are his own writing. These include particularly vv. 12, 13, 20, which are probably in prose.

These prose passages are a feature of the collection from this point to the end of chapter 51. How are they to be explained? The most plausible explanation is that they are the work of the final editor who received the poetic oracles into the collection. This was probably towards the end of the sixth century. It is then an open question whether this person was responsible for the completing of the poetic pieces into their present form, or whether vv. 7–12 and 14–16 were oracles which he received and wove into their new context.

The use of other passages may be analysed as follows: Verse 7 begins in the form of question which is in part the author's own formulation and in part a loose re-writing of Ob. 8b. The question, as a suggestive opening of the oracle, is perhaps significant, since this is also the form of the oracle in 49.1 (see notes there).

Verse 8a = 49.30 with the substitution of Dedan for Hazor. This suggests it is a kind of refrain, applicable to various foreign peoples.

Verse 8b strikes a familiar note of the Jeremiah tradition, referring to the Day of the LORD in terms of 'the calamity of Esau' (cf. 'the day of their calamity' Jer. 18.17) and 'the time when I punish him', i.e. literally 'the time of his visitation', cf. 46.21c. Indeed the whole line = 46.21c and suggests a refrain of the tradition. Contrast 'the day of his calamity' in Ob. 13 which is a reference to the fall of Jerusalem.

Verse 9 virtually = Ob. 5 but reverses the order of reference to thieves and grape-gatherers.

Verse 10a: The passive sentence of Ob. 6 is changed into direct Yahweh speech and 'I have uncovered his hiding-places' is a free rendering of Ob.

Verse 10b has no parallel in Ob. and significantly introduces the word *šūdad* (destroyed) which is a feature of these oracles.

Verse 11 has no parallel.

Verses 12–13 appear to be a prose intrusion. The association of drinking the cup with the threat that they **shall not go unpunished** links it firmly with Jer. 25.28–29. The oath that Bozrah shall become **a horror, a taunt, a waste, and a curse** is a familiar theme of the national laments, but also much used in the Jeremiah tradition (cf. 24.9; 25.18; 26.6; 42.18; 44.8, 12, 22).

Verses 14–16 are from Ob. 1–4.

Verse 14a = Ob. 1b.

Verse 14b amplifies Ob. 1c.

Verse 15 virtually = Ob. 2a.

Verse 16 virtually = Ob. 3. Curiously the text of 16a seems less satisfactory than Ob, but that of 16b more so. Verse 16c is a shorter form of Ob. 4.

But then there is the invariable reversion to the Jeremiah tradition.

Verse 17 applies to Edom the prose threat of 19.8.

Verses 18–21 are the threat of 50.40–45 omitting verses 41–43 (which are equivalent to 6.22–24).

Verse 21 starts from the form of 50.46 but develops independently. It would appear that this material was applicable to any nation and the proper names could be supplied as appropriate. *RSV* prints as prose, but the persistent parallelism points to poetry as in *NEB* and *REB*.

Verse 22 applies the image of the eagle, used in 48.40 of Moab, now to Edom, and concludes with the image of the woman in childbirth as in 48.41b.

This, then is another remarkable example of the building of a new oracle from existing material. The exact form of this existing material, as the author used it, it is impossible to know with confidence. The traditional Jeremiah prose tradition seems to have provided a vocabulary and phraseology which could be called upon when required: it does not follow that the author quoted directly from the chapters of the book of Jeremiah as it now comes to us. As to the book of Obadiah, this is itself an unsolved problem. It seems to contain two separate sections, vv. 1–14 and 15–21. The Jeremiah author uses the first section. There is no evidence of any awareness or use of the second section. The theme of drinking in Ob. 16 is one that is dominant in the Jeremiah tradition, but as it is used in Jer. 49.12, it owes nothing to Ob. and everything to Jer. 25.28–29. The author seems to have had Ob. 1–14 before him and not the subsequent verses. Or of course both Obadiah and the Jeremiah tradition may have used an underlying tradition, either written or oral.

At the same time he uses Ob. 1–14 in a significant way. For vv. 11–14 refer unmistakenly to the way Edom took advantage of Judah's humiliation after the destruction of 586 B.C. These verses date the section of Ob. The Jeremiah author betrays no awareness of this situation and is not interested to quote these verses of Ob. What he quotes offers no evidence for a dating of his work. He has simply comprehended Edom in the judgment that is to come upon all the nations. Since there is hardly a word of original composition, we may suppose that the author was not so much a prophet, waiting upon inspiration, as a learned psalm compiler filling a gap. Why should not both types produce material for the annual feast when Yahweh's sovereignty over the nations was celebrated?

The author did his work of compilation competently and the result is as consistent an oracle as many an original composition. It begins, like 49.1 with a question (v. 7), and announces the 'time of visitation' for Esau (v. 8). This is to come, but characteristically has in part already come (v. 10). Edom is to drink the cup of wrath (v. 12, cf. 25.15–29). That which is high shall be brought low (v. 16), the proud humbled, in the tragic reversal which is the essence of the Day of the LORD, and Edom, whose wisdom has vanished, will become an object of taunt and derision (vv. 17–22).

7. Is wisdom no more in Teman? Teman was a tribe and district of Edom. In Gen. 36.11, 15, Teman is the eldest son of Esau: he therefore represents Edom, as in Am. 1.12. The territory was south-east of Moab. Job's 'friend' Eliphaz was said to be a Temanite, which suggests that the association of Edom with wisdom (cf. Bar. 3.22) should be taken seriously. This is not the court wisdom of Egypt, but a tribal wisdom; and while too much should not be made of it, it is entirely reasonable that some peoples, as well as individuals, should acquire reputations for their receptivity to wisdom traditions. It was no doubt somewhere in the region of Edom and north Arabia that the story (but not the book) of Job originated.

8. Dedan: a north Arabian people who must have bordered Edom on the south-east cf. Ezek. 25.13.

9. grape-gatherers: see on verse 13.

10. I have stripped Esau bare: This seems to refer to an event that has happened, or at least a process of destruction that is going on. It cannot, for the reasons given above, be explained by the Babylonian conquest of 586 B.C.. Yet the word šūdad (destroyed), suggestive of the 'destroyer' (a theme of these oracles) must indicate a pretty comprehensive disaster. This must probably be interpreted of the weakening of Edom which took place in the latter part of the sixth century, when Arabian tribes forced them to abandon many of their towns. It was probably at this time that many Edomites were forced to settle in southern Judah, as attested in later Jewish literature (1 Mac. 5.65; Josephus Ant. xiii 91.15.4). Ezek 25.12 ff. witnesses to the downfall of Edom from Tema to Dedan.

11. your fatherless children . . . your widows: the singling out of orphans and windows for special care is a feature of the Old Testament, found in Dt. 10.18 and Ps. 68.5, and highlighted, as a test of faithfulness to the LORD, by Isaiah in 1.17. The orphans and widows of a foreign nation, like the 'sojourners', are said to be the objects of the LORD's concern. In the disaster to come, they are to be left to his care. See also on 7.6.

12. drink the cup: This prose passage must be a deliberate expedient to link the fate of Edom with the Cup of Wrath, as in 25.28–29.

13. Bozrah: chief city of Edom. Heb. *boṣrāh*. It is difficult not to suppose that the word 'grape gatherers' in v. 9 (Heb. *bōṣᵉrîm*) is intended as word play on Bozrah.

16. The horror you inspire has deceived you, and the pride of your heart: The Heb. here is a problem. The word *tipleṣeṭ* is not in the equivalent Ob. text. It is, in this form a *hapax legomenon* (i.e. a form not otherwise found in the Hebrew Old Testament) and does not appear to by syntactically easy. In view of 1 Kg. 15.3 it is not impossible that this is a pejorative term, like *bōṣeṭ* (shame), used of the Edomite god. Note the theme of *hubris*, as in the case of Moab.

19. Behold, a lion coming up from the jungle of the Jordan: cf. 12.5; 50.44. This is an image of the Jeremiah tradition, probably borrowed in Zech. 11.3.

20. Therefore hear the plan which the LORD has made . . . and the purposes which he has formed: The announcement of judgment begins with the familiar 'therefore', and uses two words which are integral to the tradition. 'Plan' (Heb. *ᶜēṣāh*) and 'purposes' (Heb. *maḥšᵉbôṭ*) both describe the divine action as purposive design worked out in the events of history. The LORD is himself 'great in counsel' (*ᶜēṣāh*, 32.19). His plans are against his own people (18.11; 19.7), but also for their welfare (29.11), and of course against the predatory nations (49.20; 50.45). This is the material of a philosophy of history. The conception is pervasive in the tradition, a consequence of the divine sovereignty celebrated in the oracles against the nations, an insight of prophecy.

21. The Red Sea: i.e. the Sea of Reeds.

THE LORD'S SOVEREIGNTY OVER DAMASCUS
49.23–27 (LXX 30.29–33)

There are puzzling features about this short oracle. Damascus does not figure in the list of nations in Jer. 25.20–26. It is unlikely therefore that the addition of an oracle against Damascus was simply a literary requirement. It is more likely that some historical episode involving the weakening of Damascus (v. 24) sparked off the oracle. But it is unlikely that this episode was a dramatic event standing out in historical memory. For the main humiliation of Syria, and Damascus its capital, had taken place in the eighth century when Tiglath-Pileser III had annexed it to the Assyrian Empire, and divided it into provinces. This was the end of a proud nation which had been 'a major catalyst of civilisation in the ancient Near East'. Something of the kind may have been anticipated by Amos (1.3–5). Isa. 17.1–3 may well refer to it. And yet, all through this period Damascus itself was never destroyed.

The probability is that there was some movement of predatory tribes, or perhaps the Persian threat itself (see below), at the end of the sixth century, which threatened Damascus and brought it to attention. This would then explain the reference to Hamath and Arpath. Hamath was a city on the Orontes, once capital of the kingdom of Hamath, forming in the time of Solomon the border with Israel. It also was conquered by Tiglath Pileser III. It was a proud place in antiquity (Am. 6.2) and an area to which Israelite captives were taken (Isa. 11.11). That it still figured before the Israelite mind as a symbol of Aramaean power to be tamed is shown by Zech. 9.1–2. Arpath was still further in the north, formerly the capital of a petty Aramaean state. The character of the oracle does not support the view that this is an old anonymous oracle of the eighth century reapplied to Damascus. There is not a hint of the tortuous circumstances of the Syro-Ephraimite crisis. Rather does it appear that Hamath and Arpad are plucked out of history to symbolise the extent of the Aramaean kingdoms. And if the 'evil tidings' is of a movement from the north, then Hamath and Arpad would hear it first. It is possible that the events are those which lie behind the Babylonian oracles, and the reference is to the period of total disturbance leading to the rise of Cyrus, when Persian power had extended to the west coast of Asia Minor. If the oracle referred to the approach of Nebuchadrezzar, then one would expect some of the language expressions used of the Foe from the North to be used. There is not a sign of it.

The oracle itself is made up of commonplaces. Hamath and Arpad are 'shamed' (*bôšāh*). To say 'they are troubled like the sea which cannot be quiet' precisely describes the sixth century situation described above. The word 'turned' (*hipnᵉṭāh* v.24) is a solitary sign that the vocabulary is that of the oracles against the nations. But the rest of the oracle is a construction lacking any poetic inventiveness. Verse 24b, absent in LXX, echoes Jer. 6.24; 13.21; and 22.23; cf. 50.43. The thought, differently expressed, is characteristic of these oracles, cf. 48.41; 49.22; 50.43. Verse 26a exactly occurs in 50.30, applied to Babylon. Verse 27 is exactly quoted from the Damascus oracle in Am. 1.4 except that 'Damascus' is submitted for 'the house of Hazael'. It is to be observed that this verse occurs elsewhere in the Jeremiah tradition and is therefore a mark of that tradition. Cf. 17.27; 21.14; 50.32. In v. 24 the word panic (Hebrew *reṭeṭ*) is a *hapax legomenon*, and looks like an Aramaic loan-word. Otherwise the one outstanding note is the description of Damascus in v. 25 as 'the

famous city' (lit: city of praise or joyful song (*REB*)) 'the joyful city',
cf. of Babylon in 51.41 and Moab in 48.2. The Heb. has 'How the famous
city is *not* forsaken'. This is unlikely to be the emphatic *lamed*. Perhaps
a mischievous scribe, failing to see the irony, wished to deny the apparent
praise of Damascus by introducing the negative; or it may be a recognition
that Damascus had survived.

27 Benhadad: the name of the kings in Damascus in the ninth to eighth
centuries, and symbol of the dynasty. Most appropriate of course in the
time of Amos from whom this verse is quoted.

THE LORD'S SOVEREIGNTY OVER ARAB TRIBES
49.28–33 (LXX 30.23–28)

Kedar and Hazor are representative of the Arab tribes who inhabited
the desert in the east of Palestine. Hazor is not the old Canaanite city.
the word Hazor is clearly related to *ḥāzēr* 'unwalled village' and it may
well be that the Arab villagers had given their name to a district. This
oracle is unique in relating the judgment to the invasion of
Nebuchadrezzar (v. 30); and no doubt this suggested the title of v. 28.
There is verisimilitude, for Nebuchadrezzar is known to have raided the
desert, collecting spoil from the Arab tribes, during his march into Syria
in 599 B.C. (See Wiseman, pp. 31–32).

It is however improbable that the identification is correct and more
likely that the oracle, like those with which it is associated, belongs to
the late period of the Babylonian supremacy. The reason is the character
of the oracle. It is intensely eclectic and since this is the character of the
oracle, the overwhelming probability is that its author is dependent on
the related passages, rather than the other way round. This includes a
substantial quotation from Ezek. At the same time there is adequate
evidence that the author belongs firmly in the Jeremiah tradition. Thus:

Verse 28: the oracle begins with the rhetorical imperative addressed
to the instrument of the LORD's judgment and includes the verb *šdd*,
characteristic of these oracles.

Verse 29: the cry **Terror on every side** is a slogan of both Jeremiah
himself and the tradition. See on 6.25.

Verse 30a: is the formula of v. 8, there applied to Dedan.   Verse
30b: is the formula of v. 20, there applied to the plan of the LORD
Himself against Edom, and in 50.40 to Babylon.

Verses 31, 32a: appears to be an adaptation of Ezek. 38.11–12a. The
eclectic character of the whole oracle makes it improbable that the formula

is original to Jeremiah. This is not to say that the Ezek. passage was the original. It may be that there was a stock of material which both authors or editors used.

Verse 32b: has two expressions of the Jeremiah tradition

(a) 'those who cut the corners of their hair' cf. 9.25, q.v., and 25.23. Not found outside the book of Jeremiah. The *NEB* and *REB* translates 'fringes of the desert', but in the light of the tradition this is questionable.

(b) 'their calamity', cf. 18.17; 46.21; 48.16; 49.8. The use of the word calamity (*'êd*) is the third verbal connection with the Edom oracle.

Verse 33: the expression 'a haunt of jackals' is characteristic of the Jeremiah tradition, cf. 9.10; 10.22; 51.37. In 9.10 and 10.22 it has waste (*š^emāmāh*) in parallelism.

Verse 33b: is the formula of v. 18b, giving a fourth connection with the Edom oracle. Cf. also 50.40.

The evidence thus supports the description of this passage above as eclectic. The predominant debt is to the Jeremiah tradition, with a specially close relation to the Edom oracle, and a single debt to material of the Ezekiel tradition. the result is a simple statement of the LORD's judgment on the Arab tribes, without any of the strong characteristics of the early oracles against Egypt and Moab. The learned psalmography has taken over, nevertheless producing a straightforward prediction of judgment to come on the Arab tribes.

28. the people of the east: *b^enê qedem* was a specific geographical term, as in Gen. 29.1; Num. 23.7; Jg. 6.3, 33, referring to the territory of Arab bedouin tribes. Cf. the land of *Qdmy* in the 'Story of Sinuhe'1970 B.C. This was east of Palestine, and in course of time the term became more general to indicate the region of the east.

THE LORD'S SOVEREIGNTY OVER ELAM **49.34–39** (LXX **25.14–20**)

Elam is specified in 25.25 along with 'all the kings of Media'. It may be that both are part of the amplification of the text, q.v. Clearly at some stage events of history suggested the inclusion of Elam in the list of nations under judgment.

Elam, with Susa its capital, lay to the east of Babylon and the lower Tigris. It was conquered by the Assryians in the seventh century and some wish to relate this oracle to the period of Assyrian decline and an engagement between the Elamites and Nebuchadrezzar in 596 B.C. This depends on an unverifiable reading of the Wiseman Chronicles (p. 72). But even if this could be shown to be a probable reading it remains unlikely that the heading of v. 34 is correct in attributing the oracle to the beginning of the reign of Zedekiah. The association with the Medes (25.25) suggests the very period to which also Isa. 21.2 probably refers, viz. *c.* 540 B.C. when Elam was occupied by the Aryan tribes, the Medes from the north and the Persians from the south. This is the period to which the other oracles, in which this one is set, belong. And the character of the oracle suggests that it is a composition of this period, meant to be related to the Babylonian oracles which follow.

The oracle begins with *hin^enî* and the participle and thus betrays its relation to the Jeremiah tradition. Thereafter the oracle is straightforward prediction in the form of a series of seven divine 'I's. Verse 37c introduces the theme of the sword. Verse 38 refers to the throne of Yahweh and the overthrow of the Elamite king, thus latching on to what we have suggested is a late amplification in 25.25.

Verse 39 is a conventional prophecy of salvation as in the case of Egypt (46.26), Moab (48.47) and Ammon (49.6). Rietzschel sought a significant event in the history of Elam which could be regarded as a sign of salvation and found such in the decision of Darius to rebuilt his capital in Susa about 494 B.C. This is precarious. If such an event is a necessary assumption at all, then the general assistance afforded by Elam to the downfall of Babylon is a more probable guess.

The oracle is, as a whole, conventional and lacking in poetic distinction, which is no doubt why some commentators, including *RSV* (but *NEB* and *REB* have got the poetic structure right), have regarded it as prose. It is a series of clichés, marked out and enhanced only by the seven divine 'I's and by a somewhat stronger statement of the part of Yahweh in this judgment. The calamity which he will bring is a result of his 'fierce anger' (v. 37, cf. 51.45) and the establishment of his sovereignty is expressed in v. 38 explicitly for the first time since 46.18 and 48.15.

THE LORD'S SOVEREIGNTY OVER BABYLON
50.1–51.64 (LXX 27.1–28.64)

These chapters contain a series of short oracles probably unconnected with one another. Their precise identification is often uncertain. Rudolph calculated fifteen, but this must remain arguable. Others have maintained a variety of numbers from three to fifty! In both date and character, they stand independent of the oracles in chapters 46–49. Chapter 46 (Egypt) belongs to the period of enforced settlement in Egypt at an unspecified juncture after the fall of Jerusalem. Chapters 47 and 48 are best interpreted also of this period; the learned literary character of 48.14–28, 29–47, suggests that the Jeremiah tradition is already established. Similarly the oracle on Edom in 49.7–22 has this learned and mosaic character. Where historical events are alluded to, they are not to be precisely identified; but it is at least plausible to see all these oracles as belonging to the middle of the sixth century. In the case of 49.34–39 (Elam), it is probable that this oracle came chronologically last and was appended last. It belongs to the period immediately before the fall of Babylon, i.e. in the decade before 540 B.C. In none of them is the fall of Babylon referred to or expected.

In contrast, the theme of all the oracles in chapters 50–51 is the fall of Babylon and the consequent return of Israel/Judah. Either the fall of Babylon is celebrated as a *fait accompli*; or its destruction is awaited as an imminent event. The two are not incompatible, since Babylon capitulated without bloodshed to the Persians. The story of Cyrus' entry into Persia so contradicts the picture presented by these oracles that it is difficult to suppose they were uttered in the light of the event. Indeed the Persians are not mentioned; only the Medes (51.11, 28; Isa. 13.17). Cyrus defeated the Median king Astyages in 550, and this suggests the oracles belong to the earlier part of the decade before the final emergence of Cyrus as the successor to the world emperors. The date of these oracles thus roughly coincides with that of the ministry of Second Isaiah, shortly before and after 538 B.C., perhaps earlier. No dependence on Second Isaiah can be demonstrated.

The literary character of these oracles confirms the contrast. In the main the reader is conscious of repetition and restriction of theme. The formal character of the oracles against Egypt has been lost, and the themes there identified are here sporadic. 'The proud one shall stumble and fall' (50.32). The Foe from the North occurs in 50.3, 9, 41; 51.48; the day of the LORD in 50.4, 20, 27; 51.6, 33. The sword features in 50.16 but is mainly concentrated in the song of the sword in 50.35–38. Shame results in 50.12, 47. The pains of childbirth are referred to in 50.43; *hubris* in 50.29. And the verb *yipnû* occurs in 50.16. This is sufficient to indicate a fund of ideas and vocabulary common to the oracles against the nations; insufficient to counter the impression that the oracles in chapters 50–51 are more precise in their historical reference and more restricted in their linguistic resource.

The oracles concerning Babylon are laced with passages which speak of the restoration of Israel/Judah. It is a characteristic of the undeniably poetic oracles on Babylon that they express her downfall as the work or

vengeance or wrath of Yahweh, and in the repetitions and explicitness
of this theme, these oracles are markedly different from chapters 46–49,
where the sovereignty of Yahweh is always the underlying presupposition,
but the theme is never expounded (note 50.13, 15, 24–25; 51.1–10, 11,
12, 29, 44, 45, 49–51). The day of Yahweh is a day of vengeance in 46.10
and the restoration of Israel is proclaimed in 46.27–28 with a qualification
in v. 28. But the early oracles of chapter 50 are interspersed with passages
entirely given to this theme, and their prose or semi-poetical character
suggests that this arrangement is a phenomenon of redaction. Vocabulary
of the prose tradition is comparatively rare, e.g. 'the day of visitation'
50.27, 31; 51.17, but the conclusion that chapters 50–51 represent the
end result of a careful process of redaction is inescapable. The process
is that of nucleus and deposit. The nucleus is the collection of poetic
oracles. The deposit includes both the high prose and the mosaics of the
learned tradition. The build up is particularly clear in chapter 50.

50.2–3	Announcement that Babylon is taken
4–7	(prose?) prediction of the restoration of Israel/Judah.
8–16	The LORD commands flight from Babylon.
17–20	(prose?) Israel's restoration.
21–32	The LORD commands the destruction of Babylon
33–34	(prose?) Israel's redeemer (gō'el).
35–38.	The song of the Sword
39–46	An eclectic mosaic built partly on Isa. 13.9–20 and partly on earlier oracles in Jer. 49.18–21; 6.22-24

The contrasts of vv. 2–34 are analysed in the comment on verses 4–7.
The conclusion must be that there is careful compilation based on a
significant pattern in the assembling of the material. The editor could
of course be responsible for the mosaic character of some of the individual
pieces, though we do not have sufficient evidence to be confident. After
v. 34 there seems to be a much more haphazard addition of material.
The Song of the Sword is distinctive enough, but vv. 39–46 are a mosaic
of a particularly derivative kind, and include straight quotation on a
substantial scale.

In chapter 51 it is less clear how to make the distinctions.

51.1-4	The LORD will stir up the destroyer.
5	Does this verse, which expresses the redemption of Israel/Judah, conclude the oracle, or is it an addition? The only reason for the latter is the analogy of chapter 50. The former is more likely. This

chapter thus begins with oracles which predict the fall of Babylon, but end with the assurance of Israel's redemption.

6–9(10) Flee from Babylon. Verse 10–this is Israel's vindication.

(11)12–14 Address to the nations.

15–19 A song of the creator quoted from the tradition (10.12–16), designed to give assurance that he who predicts these things also has the power to fulfil them. The introduction of this song may be thought to be in principle like the insertion of the song of the sword in chapter 50.

20-23(24) The LORD's hammer. In this case v. 24 looks like a prose addition relating the fall of Babylon to the salvation of Israel.

25–26 The destroying mountain.

27–33 The Medes are introduced for the first time as the agent of the LORD's purpose against Babylon.

34–40 Complaint of Zion is answered by the LORD.

41–46 Lament over Babylon.

The collection ends (47–58) with two passages each introduced by 'Therefore, behold, the days are coming' (vv. 46, 52).

59–62 is editorial.

It appears then that these oracles give clear signals that they belong to the period which narrowly preceded and covered the fall of Babylon. From the literary point of view, they have points in common with the oracles against the nations in chapters 46–49, but on the whole betray a concentrated and restricted concern with the fall of Babylon and the restoration of the Jews, reflected in the vocabulary and ideas, and rendering them a type of their own. The same sort of mind may be detected in the way the oracles are transmitted, in both the addition of material which stresses its purpose, and the occasional production of mosaics composed of traditional, mainly but not exclusively Jeremianic, material. This is a powerful argument for the existence of traditionalists who mainly, but not exclusively, used material of the Jeremiah tradition for new purposes, but sometimes composed their own, new pieces.

The prophets of the Jeremiah tradition were content that all this oracular material should bear the name of Jeremiah. They were not concerned to promote their own authorship, only to continue his work for their own time. it was inevitable that in important respects their theological assertions should be such that Jeremiah could not have uttered them in his own day. For example, Babylon is no longer the instrument of judgment but the object of judgment (50.3, 9, 18, and *passim*); the Foe from the North is no longer to be identified with Babylon, but it is the scourge of Babylon (50.9, 41; 51. 11, 28); it is Babylon that has

sinned against the LORD (50. 14. 24; 51.5), and the profanation of the
Temple is part of the ground of judgment (50.28; 51.51); Israel's relative
innocence under oppression is stressed (50.33; 51.5, 10, 24, 24–37). The
LORD's vengeance is no longer the punishment of Israel but her
restoration. All this is the difference between prophecy pre-Israel's
judgment and prophecy post–judgment.

In what circumstances may we suppose these prophecies were uttered?
No other hypothesis rivals the suggestion set out on pp. 488ff. These
Babylonian oracles lack the tell-tale reference to the kingship of Yahweh
(except in 52.57). On the other hand his sovereignty is everywhere
presupposed, and the feast provides both the audience and the tradition
of oracular utterances against the nations. Differences of time and place
may be expected to have influenced the style of the oracles. The
likelihood'is that the oracles against Egypt were spoken in Egypt. These
Babylonian oracles (unlike the earlier oracles of Second Isaiah) were
probably spoken in Jerusalem (50.4–5, 28, 44; 51.10, 51), and the
dominating conviction of the prophets who were responsible for them
was that the all powerful Creator was even now restoring the balance
of his perfect justice. As a result retribution is about to fall on Babylon;
the spoiler is to be spoiled. And vindication is to follow for Israel 'the
tribe of his inheritance'. If the prophets were establishment prophets,
this would explain why the oracles lack the qualifications and indeed
the profundity characteristic of the oracles of Second Isaiah whose
message is otherwise similar.

Fulfilment took some time to occur. After Cyrus Babylon continued
to be inhabited. But the appearance of the Parthians in 124 B.C.
diminished the importance of the city. The last mention of Babylon is
on a tablet of 10 B.C. By that time the prophecies of Isa. 13.19–22 and
these Babylonian oracles of the Jeremiah tradition had been uncannily
fulfilled. Babylon the great was mounds and ruins.

50.1 Superscription, plainly editorial. Lit: 'by the hand of Yahweh',
an expression otherwise used only in the narrative of 37.2 and the LXX
46.13, cf. Hag. 1.1, 3; 2.1; Mal. 1.1, cf. 46.1. LXX has: 'the word of
the LORD which he spoke against Babylon'. MT must be regarded as
an expanded form. (See Janzen, *op.cit.* pp. 112–114.)

ANNOUNCEMENT THAT BABYLON IS FALLEN **50.2–3**

Probably to be interpreted as a speech of the LORD to his prophet,
commanding him to circulate the news of Babylon's humiliation. The
opening oracle says all. This is rhetorical. The setting up of a banner

is here little more than a decorative touch. The original point of the
banner, or flag, is either (a) to signal the nations to battle (cf. 4.21; Isa.
5.26) and to be a symbol of battle, cf. 4.6; 51.12; or (b) to provide a
rallying sign for the exiles (Isa. 11.10, 12; 49.22; 62.10). Here the main
point of the symbolism is lost.

2. Bel: equivalent to the Heb. *ba'al* and a way of referring to the
Babylonian god Merodach, which is probably Marduk with the vowels
of *ᵃdonay* (cf. Jehovah). Marduk was the city god of Babylon and head
of the pantheon.

Her images are put to shame: a theme which receives full treatment
in Second Isaiah especially Isa. 44.9-20; 46.5-7. Absent in LXX. MT
shows its mind by using a word for 'idols' that suggests dung.

3. out of the north: there is no reason to suppose that the prophet
knows precisely who the instrument of judgment is. The expression is
eschatological and ominous. Jeremiah himself had not always known that,
in his day, the Foe from the North would turn out to be Babylon. The
later prophets knew that it was Babylon. There is therefore a heavy irony
intended.

make her land a desolation, and none shall dwell in it: although
not exclusive to the tradition, this phrase has become a mark of that
tradition (2.15; 4.7; 5.30; 18.16; 19.8; 25.9, 11, 18, 38; 29.18; 44.12,
22; 46.19; 48.9, esp. in these oracles 51.29, 37, 41, 43).

THE RESTORATION OF ISRAEL **50.4-7**

It must be possible that vv. 4-7 are to be identified as a separate oracle.
The centre of attention changes suddenly from the destruction of Babylon
to the restoration of Israel; and the prevailing view is that there is also
a change from verse to prose. The latter view is not certain. At least one
must admit that it is at times a highly rhythmical prose, at times
indistinguishable from verse. But the homogeneity of theme cannot be
questioned. The overtones are gentle and sympathetic. Israel is **my people**
(v. 6). They have been the victims alike of leaders who have led them
astray, and enemies who have regarded themselves as innocent and Israel
as guilty. Now God's people are to return to Zion their true home. Their
weeping is no longer that of lamentation in disaster, but the sign of a
true and godly penitence.

This is however another consideration. Some think that vv. 4 and 20,
which have the same introductory formula and a continuation of the same
theme, constitute (in the now fashionable jargon) an *inclusio*, and that
therefore vv. 4-20 are to be taken as the unit. This also is over-

simplification. The more probable solution is that we have here an example of careful editing. We are offered a study in contrast and dialectic, in shade and light, judgment and salvation; which may be set out thus:

Babylon is taken (vv 2–3):	Israel shall be restored (vv 4–7).
Babylon has sinned against Yahweh and shall experience his wrath (vv. 8–16):	Restored Israel will be sinless (vv. 17–20).
Babylon's judgment is the LORD's work (vv. 21–27):	This is vengeance for his temple (v. 28).
Babylon has defied the LORD but the Day has come (vv. 29–32):	The LORD is Israel's redeemer (vv. 33–34).

The rest of the chapter contains further oracles descriptive of Babylon's downfall. These contrasts are so striking, and in themselves eloquent, that it is better not to dissolve them by attending exclusively to the separated oracles. The chapter should be read as the editor has left it to us, but with the understanding made possible by the above analysis.

4. In those days in that time, says the LORD: This double introductory phrase occurs otherwise only in v. 20, and in 33.15 where it prefaces the prediction of the new David, the righteous branch, and the salvation of Judah/Jerusalem. 33.15 occurs in a section absent from LXX and may be regarded as a late addition to the MT tradition. This confirms the view taken above that vv. 4–7 are an editorial expansion of the Babylonian oracles.

says the LORD: absent from LXX as also 8.17; 9.2, 21; 23.11, 12, 14, 31, 32 (bis); 25.9, 29; 29.11; 31.16; 32.30; 48.25; 49.16, 31, 38; 51.25. This is an editorial tendency to heighten the solemnity.

weeping as they come: i.e. they will go to Zion for the prescribed fasts.

5. They shall ask the way to Zion: The highway to Zion is a characteristic theme of Second Isaiah (40.3; 51.11; of the Return). In Isa. 35.10 the scope is extended to comprehend the return of all Jews from the Diaspora. In 62.10–11 the idea is probably that of the pilgrimage of worshippers to Zion as the centre of worship. It is this latter idea which seems to be expressed in this verse.

Come, let us join ourselves to the LORD in an everlasting covenant: picking up the theme of 32.40 and therefore a theme of the tradition,

but also found in the Pentateuchal traditions (Gen. 9.16; 17.7, 13, 19;
Isa. 55.3; Ezek. 16.60; 37.26; Isa. 61.8).

6. lost sheep . . . their shepherds: symbol of rulers as in 2.8; 3.15;
25.35; 34.4, 16, cf. Ezek. 3.15–18 a late passage that expresses the
theology of this period. Note particularly the similarity between v. 5 and
Ezek. 3.18.

from mountain to hill: a natural image of the wanderings of lost sheep,
but no doubt intended to suggest the illegitimate cults in the high places,
cf. 3.6. This is the apostasy which constitutes forgetting their **fold**. In
contrast (v. 7) the LORD himself is their **true habitation**, a phrase used
in 31.23 which appears to be a blessing derived from the temple worship.

7. This verse illustrates the change that had taken place in the theology
of the tradition. The implication is the guilt of the nations, who are no
longer justified by Israel's guilt, and the relative innocence of Israel, who
can confidently hope for restoration. And because the LORD was **the
hope of their fathers** (cf. 14.8; 17.13) they can expect him to be their
defender now, so fulfilling the promises made to the fathers. It was the
great problem of the sixth century that these promises seemed to be
repudiated. Now, after the punishment of judgment, they could be taken
up again.

THE LORD'S VENGEANCE ON BABYLON **50.8–16**

This oracle has a superficial appearance of poetic originality. In fact it
is derivative and composed of borrowed ideas and phrases. 'Behold I am
stirring up . . . ' (v. 9) is a commonplace, as in 51.1, 11 and Isa. 13.17.
'Does not return empty-handed' (v. 9) is verbally close to Isa. 55.11.
Even the image of the wanton heifer and the neighing stallions is a
variation of the idea in 2.23–24 and 5.8. Verse 13 is composed from
vocabulary common to 49.17 and 19.8. Verse 16b is borrowed from Isa.
13.14, and since in these oracles there are other borrowings from chapters
13–14 of Isaiah, this must be regarded as no insignificant oddity.

Perhaps this derivative character highlights the fresh emphasis of the
oracle when compared with the previous oracles against the nations. This
is the tremendous, hammer-like, theological emphasis on the wrath or
vengeance of Yahweh. The idea is present in 46.10 and 47.4, but now
becomes dominant. Thus the assertion of v. 13 'because of the wrath
of the LORD' is reaffirmed in v. 15: 'this is the vengeance of the LORD',
cf. vv. 25, 28, 29, 31–32, 34, 45; 51.1, 5, 6, 7, 10, 11, 12, 24, 29, 36,
44, 45, 47, 52. Babylon 'has sinned against the LORD'.

There is some relation to the earlier oracles against the nations. Note the imperatives; the north (v. 9); the shame (v. 12); the sword of the oppressor (v. 16); the term *yipnû* in v. 16 quoted from Isa. 13.14.

In the most explicit way Babylon the great is drawn into the mesh of the LORD's sovereign purpose. Her downfall is the expression of his wrath. Her conduct is sin against his will and purpose. The exact retribution is the working out of his 'vengeance'.

8. Flee from the midst of Babylon: a rhetorical imperative (cf. Isa. 48.20), uttered no doubt in Jerusalem, but addressed to the Jews in Babylon. There were other captive nations in Babylon, released by Cyrus. Were these the sheep, and Israel, at the head of them, the goats? A reversal, of course, of the normal distinction!

9. a company of great nations, from the north country: an expression of deliberate vagueness, born of lack of knowledge as to who the Foe from the North would turn out to be.

like a skilled warrior: 'skilled' represents the reading of LXX and Syriac and makes better sense than the alternative 'that make childless'.

11. O plunders of my heritage: the vicissitudes of history have changed the situation in which Jeremiah and Judah could expect only judgment in the form of destruction.

13. This quotation from 19.8 is in the idiom of the oracles against the nations, cf. the taunt against Babylon in Isa. 14.4ff.

14. for she has sinned against the LORD: omitted in LXX but a correct gloss in this context . As Israel is once again the LORD's heritage, so Babylon's fault is identified as a sin against a god she does not know or recognise. Such is the nature of Yahweh's sovereignty and such also the prophetic understanding of history.

15. do to her as she has done: cf. v. 29, an instance of exact retribution, which becomes a dominant theme of the learned psalmography represented by the Psalms of Solomon and the Qumran Psalms.

16. everyone shall flee to his own land: cf. 46.16, and Isa. 13.14.

THE HISTORICAL RESTORATION OF ISRAEL **50.17-20**

As the prose (?) passage (vv. 4–7) on the restoration of Israel followed the first oracle against Babylon, so this prose (?) section follows the second poetic oracle. It is concerned with the same theme — the restoration of Israel, but it is more explicit about the meaning of restoration and the spiritual condition of Israel.

(1) Whereas in v. 6 Israel is lost sheep in the sense that she has lost her spiritual

direction, and the shepherds are her own rulers who have misdirected the sheep, here Israel is lost in the sense that she is scattered in exile. Restoration is specifically the return of her lands and pastures.

(2) Because the theme is restoration from exile the situation of Israel can be looked at historically, Once Assyria was the hostile power, now Babylon. Assyria's punishment and downfall followed. So also will that of Babylon.

(3) Whereas in v. 7 the nations justified their destruction of Israel on the score of Israel's sin, now the innocence of Israel will be clear for all to see (v. 20). It will be founded on the forgiveness of the righteous remnant.

This theme, which is scarcely that of Jeremiah himself, is nevertheless founded in the Jeremiah tradition:

'Behold I am bringing punishment . . . as I punished–cf. 11.22; 23.2; 29.32; 46.25.
'In those days and in that time', cf. v. 4, q.v., and 33.15.
'I will pardon', cf. 5.1, 7; 31.34; 36.3.

The places named — Carmel, Bashan and Gilead — represent the most fruitful parts of the land.

Thus this short prose passage contains the summary of a comprehensive theological position. The Lord of history will restore his exiled people, showing that his sovereignty covers the historical changes in the world empires. He will give them the land that flowed with milk and honey, specifically indicating the regions that are naturally prosperous. And this outward prosperity will be matched by an inner innocence, the quality of the remnant through whom the divine purpose will be realised. There will be no remnant of Babylon.

THE LORD'S WORK IN BABYLON 50.21–32

Some commentators are inclined to divide this section further, but perhaps over confidently. It must be possible that a putative original oracle, uttered by a prophet, is contained within the final form; if so, we have no means of identifying it. The traditionalists have been at work expanding it into its present form and it is that form with which we must come to terms.

There is no substantial new feature to the section, only a variation of imagery.

There are rhetorical imperatives in vv. 21, 26, 27, 29, characteristic of the genre. The lament form of v. 23, with the effect of a taunt song (cf. v. 13; Isa. 14.6) may well be suggested by Isa. 14, in view of the relation of Isa. 13–14 demonstrated by the use of the phrase 'weapons of his wrath' in v. 25 (cf. Isa. 13.5). This is significant because of sporadic dependence upon Isa. 13–14 elsewhere in these poems. More striking however is the use of phrases from the Jeremiah tradition, particularly 'great destruction' which is taken from Jeremiah's Foe from the North oracles (4.6 and 6.1), and 'time of their punishment' or 'time of visitation' (v. 27), which is a well-worn phrase of the tradition (6.15; 49.8; 8.2; 10.15 = 51.18; 46.21; 51.27, cf. 'year of visitation', 11.23; 23.12; 48.44). 'Their day' in v. 27 and 'your day' in v. 31 are a palpable reference to the Day of the LORD. In v. 32 'the proud one shall stumble and fall' reveals a tell-tale linguistic feature of the genre; and the rest of this verse, though less obviously a quotation from Am. 1.4 than in the oracle against Damascus (49.23–27), is manifestly related to 49.27. This has become a mark of the tradition (cf. 17.27; 21.14). Moreover v. 30 is identical with 49.26, there applied to Damascus. This illustrates the restricted nature of ideas and vocabulary within these poems.

What stands out in this poem, as in the previous one (vv. 8–16), is the theological emphasis on the wrath of Yahweh. What is to happen to Babylon is by the command of the LORD (v. 21). They are to be utterly destroyed (v. 21) in the traditional sense of 'put to the ban' (Jg. 6.21–24). Babylon does not know (v. 24) the true instigator of her downfall. This perception is in keeping with the prophetic philosophy of history, as particularly exemplified by the Isaiah tradition. When Assyria destroyed the nations, he did not know he was the rod of the LORD's anger (Isa. 10.5–7). Cyrus did not know in whose service he was acting (Isa. 45.4). This unknown prophet applies the lesson. The real reason for the fall of Babylon is that 'you strove against the LORD', cf. v. 29. This, combined with the description of the fall of 'the proud one' in verse 32 is the *hubris* which we have already observed in the oracles against Egypt and Moab, and found to be a feature of the genre. The instruments of destruction are the LORD's armoury (v. 25) 'the weapons of his wrath' (cf. Isa. 13.5) and the events that are to follow are the 'work' that the Lord Yahweh of hosts has to do (v. 25, cf. 51.10, 12 29). This use of the word *me'lā'kāh* to describe judgment is unique. It is used of creation in Gen. 2.2, 3 which may help to explain why the redactors introduced a song of creation in 51.15–19. The returning exiles will 'declare in Zion the vengeance of the LORD' (v. 28). In v. 29 there is the insistence that retribution must be complete and exact as in verse 15 q.v.

21. Merathaim . . . Pekod: these are districts of Babylon, *nar marratu* designating the region of the mouth of the Tigris and Euphrates, and *Puqudu* a tribe of east Babylonia (cf. Ezek. 23.23). There is no evidence that either was normally used for Babylon as a whole. The reason for their use here is probably word play in Hebrew. Merathaim, in dual form, may well have suggested 'double rebellion' from the Heb. *m'rî*, and Pekod is either an imperative or an infinitive from the verb 'visit' or 'punish'. The LXX translator seems to have had this text before him, but to have been able to make very little of it. Presumably his *pikros* is an attempt to render Merathaim as an adverb. This is the first of a series of indications that this particular prophet has an ear for language. He likes the memorable phrase (in Hebrew) 'great destruction' in v. 22; the resonant title for Babylon, 'hammer of the whole earth' in v. 23, cf. 51.20–23; the lament form in v. 23; the 'weapons of his wrath' derived from Isa. 13.5; the 'work' for Yahweh to do in v. 25; he likens the Babylonians to bulls going down to be slaughtered (v. 27); and in v. 31 he manages to savour the irony of the proud one stumbling and falling, with none to raise him up.

destroy after them: omit 'after them', with LXX and Syriac, as dittography.

23. hammer of the whole earth: probably derived from the independent poem in 51.20–23, though the word for 'hammer' is different.

26. let nothing be left to her: i.e. let there not be a remnant, in contrast to Israel whose remnant shall inherit the land (v. 20, cf. v. 29).

28. vengeance for his temple: this phrase, absent from LXX, is no doubt an addition, amplifying the idea and particularising it. It is in keeping with the Jeremiah tradition of the period; history having run to the very opposite of the situation which Jeremiah faced in his temple sermon, cf. 51.11.

29. the Holy One of Israel: here and 51.5. This is not a sign of dependence upon second Isaiah, since the phrase is common to the whole Isaianic corpus. Its combination of the universal and the particular provides an aura of profound reverence, and therefore throws the pride of the Babylonian into greater relief.

30. = 49.26.

32. The proud one: in Heb. 'pride', cf. 49.16.

stumble and fall: see on 46.12.

THE RESTORER OF ISRAEL **50.33–34**

A third time the oracle against Babylon is followed by a brief passage proclaiming the restoration of Israel. This time the emphasis is on Yahweh Sabaoth the Redeemer (cf. Isa. 47.4), whose power is such that he can put the strongest earthly power in his place. The author enjoys word play: 'he will surely plead their cause', involving threefold repetition of the word *rîḇ*, amounting to alliteration (see on 51.36); and 'rest to the earth, but unrest to the inhabitants of Babylon', involving two similar verbs *hirgîaʿ* and *hirgîz* (cf. Isa. 14.16). It is also possible that 'they refuse to let them go' intentionally echoes the story of the Exodus and Pharaoh's refusal to release the Israelites. Both verbs are the same in Exod. 7.14; 9.2. It is not necessary to suppose that the text was in front of him. The phrase 'he refused to let them go' was a resonant one in the storyteller's articulation. A new Exodus was about to take place. The contrast of the last lines is the contrast and dialectic of the whole chapter in a nutshell.

THE SONG OF THE SWORD 50.35–38

Up to this point the redactor has collected or compiled oracles against Babylon, and carefully balanced them with passages on the restoration of Israel. Now he introduces an independent song, and thereafter brings this first complex of Babylonian oracles to an end with material drawn from the tradition. This is a familiar process of redaction. (See p. 285.)

The Song of the Sword is a simple sixfold repetition, possibly but not certainly, with variant word play in v. 38. Formally it resembles the repetition in the oracle against Elam (49.35–38), with its seven divine 'I's', one of which was: 'I will send the sword after them'. The sword is a constant symbol of battle in the oracles against the nations (see p. 487). It is not surprising therefore that a poem should be devoted to it. The author of the poem against the Philistines broke out into a similar rhetorical extravagance, but on a more modest scale (47.6–7), with the prose tradition in 25.20 links the cup of staggering with the sword as a sign of judgment.

36. upon the diviners: the Heb. *baddîm* means boasters, idle talkers (cf. 48.30). Here and In Isa. 44.25 a meaning like 'diviners' is required by the context. It is this which has tempted commentators to conjecture that this was a pejorative way of referring to the *barim* or *baru*-priests of Babylon. They were well-known as prognosticators. *NEB*, *REB* have 'false prophets'.

37. her horses and her chariots: an amplication absent from LXX, overloading the line, but not inappropriate.

the foreign troops: lit. mixed peoples, here mercenaries in the Babylonian army.

38. a drought upon her waters: *RSV* has here adopted a conjectural emendation based upon the Syriac and Vulgate. It involves a simple change of vocalisation. But it is more plausible to keep 'sword', symbol of battle and invasion, which play havoc with the lifegiving canals. LXX suggests that at some period the text was disturbed.

mad over idols: this also gave some trouble to translators. LXX has 'islands', Vulg. 'in portentis'. The Heb. term means objects of fright or horror. The probability is that it is used pejoratively of the Babylonian gods, and that *NEB, REB* get the sense with 'dreaded gods' or 'dire portents'.

A MOSAIC OF ORACLES AGAINST BABYLON **50.39–46**

The remaining part of this complex is a mosaic of material orchestrated by the redactor to reinforce the themes already expressed. What has been said about other nations must be true all the more of Babylon.

(a) 50.39–40
Verse 39b = Isa. 13.20, equivalent to Jer. 49.17
Verse 40 = Isa. 13.19. = Jer. 49.18.
The wild beasts, ostriches and hyenas all figure in Isa. 13.21, 22. All in all, vv. 39 and 40 are no more than an insignificant rearrangement of Isa. 13.19–22, such as to show that the redactor had the language of the text clearly in his mind.

The identification of the animals is uncertain. *NEB, REB* have marmots for wildbeasts, jackals for ostriches and desert-owls for hyenas, and may be said to have the better of the argument.

Sodom and Gomorrah (cf. Gen. 19); provides an image of total destruction where no mitigation of judgment can be justified.

(b) 50.41.43 = 6.22–24
This is a straight quotation and adaption from Jeremiah's final Foe from the North oracle. This referred to as an as yet unknown power coming against Zion. Herein lies the irony of history. The force of the oracle is precisely that Jeremiah's terrible oracle against Zion can now be directed against Babylon.

(c) 50.44–46 = 49.19–21
Finally this passage is close to the oracle against Edom. Since the Edom oracle (49.18) also takes from Isa. 13 the Sodom and Gomorrah reference, it is likely that both are versions of a common passage and both have been subject to redaction. See on Chapter 49 where the conclusion was

that this material could be applied to any nation and required only the substitution of the right names. Here the framework is used, with small variations, and the Foe from the North oracle inserted.

44. a lion coming up from the jungle of the Jordan: a sign that the prophet uttered his oracles in Jerusalem. The imagery would not have the same power to people who had been long exiled in Egypt or Babylon. **who is like me? who will summon me?** the theme of the incomparable power of Yahweh, brought to full expression by Second Isaiah, cf. v. 34. **Shepherd:** i.e. the ruler as in v. 6, q.v.

46. among the nations: now thought to echo v. 2 and so to constitute an *inclusio*, i.e. a phrase which brings the passage to a literary conclusion, linking the beginning and the end. But in v. 2 the call is by the announcer of doom. Here it is Babylon's cry of desolation. The echo is more likely to be accidental.

THE DESTROYER OF BABYLON **51.1–5**

After the typical resort to previous known teaching at the end of chapter 51, the redactor begins a new collection of poetic oracles against Babylon, together with other relevant material. At once the use of imaginative imagery is increased to reinforce the same, unvarying declaration of doom for Babylon. A destroying wind; winnowing; the paralysis of her soldiers — these occur in the first few verses. But the relation to the previous complex is most clearly shown in v. 5. The fall of Babylon means the salvation of Israel, and the real offence of Babylon is to have sinned against the Holy One of Israel (cf. 50.29, q.v.). Indeed the problems of v. 5 raise the question whether it has been introduced by the redactor to create the same balance that we have noticed in chapter 50. Whether original to the poem or added is however of no great moment. This is no more than conjecture as to how the text reached its present form.

1. the spirit of a destroyer: so the Heb, may be translated. The 'destroyer' is the *mašîṭ*, used of the demon from whom the Israelites were protected by means of the Passover (Exod. 12.23), but also by Jeremiah of the Foe from the North (4.7 'destroyer of the nations'), cf. 'the destroying mountain' in 51.25.

In the oracles against the nations in chapters 46–49, the alternative word *šôdēd* is used (47.4; 48.8, 15; 49.10, cf. Isa. 16.4; 21.2). This also goes back to Jeremiah's early oracles (6.26). This is a contributory piece of literary evidence indicating the independence of the Babylonian complex.

It is possible to translate 'a destroying wind' as favoured by *NEB* and

REB. If this is right, it simply means that the Destroyer is described by means of an appropriate image. The parallel opening verse of the third oracle (v. 10) suggests that *RSV* is correct.

Chaldea: the Heb. is *lēb qāmāy*, meaning, if anything, 'the heart of those who rise up against me'. This is an *atbash* (see on 25.25) for Kasdim = Chaldea. Since there is an area called Kambul, some have thought the present text is a confusion of this proper name. The *NEB* has fallen for this arbitrary solution; but not *REB*. Much more likely is the solution above. The later scribes loved to play with names and numbers and saw significance in the resulting Hebrew expression, however far-fetched. Some see evidence of magic, but that too is a view that lacks cogency.

2. the day of trouble: cf. 17.17, 18; more often in the early tradition 'time of trouble'. The word *rā'āh* 'trouble' or 'evil' is used more frequently in the Jeremiah tradition than any other, a sign of its grim preoccupation.

3. Let not the archer bend his bow: an attempt to make sense of a disturbed Heb. text. There is obvious dittography which makes it look related, in its present form, to 48.33. But the context hardly supports this.

5. Israel and Judah have not been forsaken: At first sight this appears to be complacent. Certainly it is difficult to image it on the lips of Jeremiah. But these passages belong to the yonder side of Israel/Judah's judgment. The hope which Jeremiah entertained has matured, and his successors take it up.

the land of Chaldeans: Heb. has 'their land'. The gloss is surely correct and in keeping with a major theme of these oracles that Babylon is guilty before the Holy One of Israel.

guilt: Heb. *'āšām*, chosen here, as in Isa. 53, because it carries the notion of a satisfaction to justice.

THE GOLDEN CUP IS BROKEN **51.6–10**

In this poem the main images are of Babylon as a cup in the LORD's hand, and of the medicine that cannot heal her. The image of the cup is an extension of the dominating theme in chapter 25. There the cup of wrath is administered by the prophet to the nations, all of whom must drink it. In the final form of the chapter Babylon is among those that must drink. Here Babylon is the golden cup. That is, Babylon has been the instrument of judgment making the other nations drink, and indeed 'making all the earth drunken'. And now this cup is broken (v. 8). This is an imaginative way of putting the familiar prophetic theme that the agent of the LORD's judgment must itself face judgment.

But unmistakably the closer interest of the prophet is in the implication of this for Zion. The fall of Babylon is the salvation of Israel. It is the vengeance of Israel's god, expressed this time at the beginning of the oracle. **Our vindication** (v. 10, see below) is to be declared in Zion. This amplifies 50.28, where the purpose of Israel's escape from Babylon is to proclaim in Zion the retribution of Yahweh. Here too (v. 6) the oracle begins with an exhortation to flee from Babylon. It is possible that v. 10 contains a hint of the liturgical context in which the oracle was uttered. **Let us declare in Zion** (v. 10) is Heb. *sappēr*, which often denotes the spoken part in 'myth and ritual'. So Isa. 52.15 and Pss. 44.1; 48.13. Thus the oracle ends with the same concentration on Israel's salvation as the previous one (v. 5) a balance which the redactor has written into the structure of chapter 50.

6. Flee from the midst of Babylon: cf. 50.8, q.v., 28; Isa. 48.20.

the time of the LORD's vengeance: cf. 50.15; 46.10; cf. the time of punishment 50.27, 31; 51.18; 46.21; 48.44; 49.8, i.e. of course, the Day of the LORD.

the requital he is rendering her: picked up in v. 56. See on 50.15.

8. balm: cf. 8.22; 46.11. There was no healing medicine for Judah; then none for Egypt; now none for Babylon.

9. each to his own country: see on 50.16.

10. our vindication: Heb. *ṣᵉdākāh*, righteousness or justification. This is part of the linguistic background to *NT* and Christian doctrine.

the work of Yahweh: a theme of these oracles, cf. 50.25, 45; 51.12, 29. If it is correctly argued that this verse interrupts the strophic construction of the oracle, it is a redactor's touch in line with the fundamental purpose of the Babylonian oracles.

THE FALL OF BABYLON THE PLAN OF THE LORD **51.11–14**

In this oracle the redactor's touch is more precisely identifiable in the prose additions of vv. 11bc and 12c. The one repeats the insistence of 50.28 and comparable passages that the fall of Babylon is the consequence of the LORD's vengeance. The other sees the LORD fulfilling prophecy. What is left, when these passages are removed, is a vivid poetic piece composed of staccato blows in stark simplicity.

Sharpen the arrows,   fill the quivers;
On the walls of Babylon raise the flag,   mount a guard;
Post watchmen,   prepare an ambush;

> You that dwell by many waters,   full of treasures,
> Your end has come   you are to be cut to size.
> The LORD of hosts has sworn by himself,
>   Though I filled you with inhabitants like locusts,
>   Over you shall be cried the vintage cry of triumph.

The redactor, by means of his additions, has transformed the oracle into something different, which has its own validity. So no doubt it was used.

11. The rhetorical call to take up arms is paralleled in 46.3; 50.29, 42.

Take up the shields: the noun elsewhere is some form of shield. But the verb is literally 'fill', hence LXX 'fill the quivers', so *REB*.

The LORD has stirred up the spirit of the kings of the Medes: everywhere else the destroyer of Babylon is unidentified, cf. 51.1, 'Behold I will stir up the spirit of a destroyer'. And of course, most often the foe is simply said to be from the north. Here we have a redactor's addition, probably dependent upon Isa. 13.17, or at least belonging to the same period. There is no mention of the Persians who, under Cyrus, overthrew Babylon without bloodshed. The Median King Astyages was either conquered or captured about 550 B.C. and Media lost its independence at that time. Although the Greeks referred to the Medes and Persians as Medes, it is probable that this redactor belongs to the period when the Medes were feared, and before the rise of Cyrus, i.e. about 550.

the vengeance for his temple: cf. 50.28. LXX has 'for his people', but 'temple' requires the change only of a single letter. We may assume that the redactor of the Heb. text intended this total change in the spirit and letter of the prophecy of Jeremiah (see esp. chapter 7).

12. For the LORD has both planned and done what he spoke: cf. 50.25 and 51.10, 29, a preoccupation with prophecy and fulfilment as characteristic of the redactor as of the Deuteronomic tradition.

13. your end: cf. Am. 8.2.

the thread of your life is cut: this is an attempt to draw out the metaphor, but probably beyond the evidence. *NEB, REB* 'your destiny is certain' is equally questionable. The Heb. is literally 'the cubit or measure of your cutting off' and this is almost exactly equivalent to the English expression 'cut to size'.

14. A particularly solemn form of divine oath, cf. 22.5; 44.26; 49.13.

Surely I will fill you with men: the translation above may be preferred, cf. *NEB*.

the shout of victory: i.e. the *hêdād* shout. for the probable background, see on 25.30 and 48.33. This may be simply a sign of rejoicing as at the vintage festival, cf. Isa. 16.10; 48.33, in which case judgment means silence. Or it may be a sign of the divine vintager treading the grapes of wrath, cf. 25.30. This may well be another indication of the liturgical context in the vintage festival.

THE SONG OF THE CREATOR 51.15–19

This is identical to 10.12–16, where also the chapter is the end result of a complicated process of transmission and a redactor is responsible for placing the psalm of praise in its present position. For detailed comment see on 10.12–16.

Here the question arises, why the redactor wishes to place the psalm here. The answer must be derived from the content. He wishes to say that the LORD, who has a work to do and a plan to fulfil, has the power to accomplish his plan. He is creator of the world and the power by which the world continues. In contrast man is nothing. At the same time, the universal creator has by no means abandoned his purpose to work through his chosen people 'the portion of Jacob . . . Israel . . . the tribe of his inheritance' (v. 19). This theme, in the idiom of Second Isaiah, nevertheless belongs to the Jeremiah tradition, as is shown by the tell-tale vocabulary in v. 17 'his images are lies (šeqer)' and v. 18, 'the time of their punishment (pᵉqūdāh)'.

THE LORD'S BATTLEAXE 51.20–23 (24)

The redactor now introduces an independent poem, without troubling to indicate the identity of the hammer or battle-axe. In 50.23 the hammer of the whole earth (paṭṭîš) is clearly Babylon and no one can reasonably doubt that Babylon is addressed here. The absence of identification is evidence of the independence of the poem. The poem has a simple repetitive basis, like the oracle against Elam (49.35–38: sevenfold) and the Song of the Sword (50.35–38: sixfold). Here there is ninefold repetition of the verb nippaṣtî 'I break in pieces', following the use of the verbal noun mappēṣ for hammer or, better, battle-axe. 'You are my hammer, with you I hammer the nations', etc. These three poems reveal an inclination to introduce pounding repetition to express inexorable judgment. Again the existence of these three poems within the collection of oracles against the nations is further evidence of their cohesion. What particular role these poems had in their liturgical context we can hardly guess. Was a sword and a battle-axe used to enforce the point?

The tenses suggest that Babylon is continuing to perform this function, even if the writing is on the wall.

23. governors and commanders: both terms (*peḥāh* and *sāgān*) are Assyrian loan words and belong to the period of Israel's subservience to the world empires. They are used together also in Ezek. 23.6, 12, 23. Not surprisingly both are used predominantly in the literature of the exilic and post-exilic period, cf. v. 28.

24. Here the redactor adds his characteristic emphasis, as throughout this collection,declaring that Babylon is no longer the instrument of judgment, but the guilty one to be punished for her treatment of Zion. The interesting new feature is the insistence that this will be done **before your very eyes.** The writer is conscious of history breaking up in his own day. This is the decade before Cyrus took Babylon.

The redactor's insertion is no doubt intended to lead, as it does, into the next oracle.

THE DESTROYING MOUNTAIN **51.25–26**

The LORD is the speaker, using an image which is suggestive but not immediately clear. A mountain was not the most obvious image for Babylon, which lay by the Euphrates in the flat plain of Sinar, dependent upon canals. The hill 'Babil' was in no sense a destroying mountain. This title is therefore symbolic, not descriptive, and it must be the application of the idea of the mountain of the gods (*sāpōn*) in a hostile sense to Babylon (see on 1.13). It is of course possible that this oracle referred originally to the unspecified Foe from the North, and was subsequently applied to Babylon. This would explain why Babylon is not mentioned in the independent oracle itself.

The emphasis is on the word 'destroying', an emphasis further enforced by the addition of 'which destroys the whole earth' (absent in LXX), no doubt suggested by one of the original Jeremiah Foe from the North oracles (4.7). A mountain does not itself destroy, unless it is a volcano. We have here to come to terms with a common feature of Hebrew prophetic poetry. Individual items of intense significance are put together, even if they do not constitute composite sense (cf. Ezek. 1; Isa. 53 and 54).

Even so the development of this image in v. 25 defies explanation. What does it mean to add that the mountain (or Babylon) shall be rolled down from the crags and made a burnt mountain? Here it is possible that editors have failed to understand the force of the Heb. *gilgaltîkā*. It may be taken as a denominative from *gal* 'mound' or 'heap of ruins' (cf. v. 37 = 9.10). The meaning then is: 'I will turn it into a heap'. A scribe, knowing the more familiar meaning 'roll down', has added 'from the crags'. A 'burnt mountain' may mean a defunct volcano, no longer a threat to anyone. Or it could mean a live volcano. This mountain is burning itself out and is no use for man or beast. In contrast to Isaiah's prediction of the rebuilding of Zion (28.16, using the same vocabulary) Babylon shall not be rebuilt, but remain a heap of ruins for ever. The oracle should then run:

> Behold, I am against you, O destroying mountain.
> I will stretch out my hand against you,
> and turn you into a heap of ruins,
> and make you (as waste as) a volcano.

BABYLON'S FALL IS IMMINENT 51.27–33

Immediately in this oracle, the sense of urgency is intensified. Things have been happening on the world stage which suggest that Babylon's destruction is imminent. This impression would be confirmed even if the introduction of specific names in vv. 27, 28, were judged to be a gloss. Rudolph is surely right that these oracles are not normally precise. They are general in expression, elusive and ominous, applicable to the specific situation when it arises. The repetition of 'prepare the nations for war against her' in v. 28, suggests the activity of a redactor, applying the oracle to his time when the Medes were still the new threat to world stability (see on v. 11). Ararat, Minni and Ashkenaz in v. 27 are Armenian districts in the hands of the Medes, and metrically superfluous. We conclude that this oracle was taken up and given this application before the rise of Cyrus. Subsequently the LXX translator did not understand that Minni was a proper noun. All three names occur in cuneiform texts.

27. The rhetorical imperatives are commonplaces of the genre and already employed by Jeremiah (4.5–8).

   a standard: here the image is part of the panoply of war, cf. v. 12 and 4.6, 12.

   blow the trumpet (ram's horn): its traditional purpose is to summon to war (Jg. 3.27; 6.34; 1 Sam. 13.3). It was also used in the temple to summon to worship (Num. 10.10; cf. Ps. 81.3). Appropriately therefore it might herald the Day of the LORD (Jl 2.1, 15). This overtone is surely present here (cf. 4.5; 6.17; 7.22).

   prepare the nations: literally 'sanctify'. The preparation for war in the name of Yahweh involved sacrifice. Here also the term had a cultic use (cf. Jl. 1.14) and peculiar appropriateness for those who were to do the LORD's work (v. 29), cf. 6.4; 22.7.

a marshal: an Akkadian word for a high military commander (cf. Nah. 3.17).

like bristling locusts: cf. v. 14. Whether this describes the habit of locusts unsheathing their wings is dubious. The word for 'bristling' is unique in the Heb. OT.

28. their governors and deputies: probably derived from v. 23 q.v.

29. the LORD's purposes: cf. 50.45; 51.12.

to make the land of Babylon a desolation: see on 50.3, a phrase which has become the mark of the Jeremiah tradition.

30. they have become women: cf. 50.37.

32. bulwarks the Heb. normally means 'marshes' or perhaps 'reeds', but clearly something more appropriate must be hazarded. This is a conjectural emendation from Arabic.

33. As in verse 14, q.v., the use of the harvest metaphor may suggest the liturgical context of the oracle. The attempt to link the metaphor of harvest here with that of the winnowers in v. 2 as if it created an *inclusio*, i.e. discerning a deliberate literary structure by linking the beginning (verse 2) with the end (verse 33), is particularly unconvincing.

ISRAEL'S PLEA, THE LORD'S ANSWER **51.34–40**

This oracle takes the form of a rhetorical liturgy. Verses 34–35 are Israel's lament on account of her extreme humiliation at the hands of Nebuchadrezzar. This lament uses the image of an empty jar (cf. 14.3). The absence of water of course spells death. And, perhaps to us incongruously, this is set alongside the image of the dragon who has swallowed Israel up and spewed her out. There then follows an uninhibited cry for blood vengeance, cf. Ps. 137.7–9. In vv. 36ff the LORD answers with total reassurance. It is repeated that Babylon shall become a ruin (cf. vv 25–26, 29), her sea dried up (v. 38). The lion-like roaring of her soldiers will not now be that of destroyers (4.7; 50.44) but of the hunted. They will drink the drink that consigns them to oblivion (v. 39) and be brought to sacrifice (v. 40, cf. 46.10–11).

As so often with passages that are rich in imagery, difficulties with the Hebrew increase.

34. crushed me: literally 'confused me', perhaps here 'exhausted me'. *NEB* and *REB*, 'sucked me dry'.

a monster: i.e. dragon, in Isa. 27.1; Job 3.8, 7.12; named Leviathan, (cf. Pss. 74.13; 104.26). This is no doubt an allusion to the near eastern creation myth which involved a combat in which the dragon was killed and the earth created. He represented the power of darkness and constituted a perpetual threat of reversion to chaos (cf. the engulfing sea in v. 43).

with my delicacies: requiring simple emendation, the noun is suggestive of the garden of Eden.

rinsed me out: this literal translation does not yield good sense. Better 'spewed me up' with *NEB* and *REB*.

35. and to my kinsmen: Heb. 'my flesh'. LXX has 'affliction'. Many emend the text. All, including *RSV*, are evasions, for 'my flesh' is parallel to 'my blood' in the next line. What Babylon has done to the flesh and blood of Israel will be visited upon her. Jerusalem chants a curse upon Babylon.

36. I will plead your cause: cf. 50.34, but also an expression favoured in the Jeremiah tradition, cf. 2.9, 29; 11.20 = 20.12 (linked with vengeance); 12.1.

I will dry up her sea: a commonplace in the prophets, and derived from the drying up of the Red Sea, but not literally applicable to Babylon. This suggests that the poet had little idea of what Babylon was like. See also on 51.25–26.

37. and Babylon shall become a heap of ruins: the exact expression is used of Jerusalem in 9.10, but here applied to Babylon. This is the more normal way of expressing the threat of v. 25.

a horror and a hissing, without inhabitant: a commonplace. See on 50.3; 51.29.

39. The idea of making drunk with the contents of the cup of wrath is taken up in 51.7. Babylon who made 'all the earth drunken' is to be subject to her own treatment. Repeated in v. 57.

THE PRAISE OF THE WHOLE EARTH 51.41–45 (46)

As almost without exception, in the build up of complexes of oracles, the redactor places derivative material at the end. It is impossible not to be impressed by the mosaic character of this passage, though it usually falls short of direct quotation. It is followed by two tell-tale introductions: 'therefore, behold the days are coming'(vv. 47, 52).

Not a single idea is new, though the result is an oracle which can justifiably stand beside the others as performing the function of oracles against the nations.

Thus the lament form, with repeated 'how', of verse 41 is exactly that of 50.23, with the substitution of 'praise' for 'hammer'. The expressive

'land of drought and desert' (v. 43) is that of 50.12, inappropriate after
the prediction that the sea will cover her (v. 42). The rest of v. 43 we
have noticed to be a repeated commonplace. The 'I will punish' (*pākaḏ*)
of v. 44 is a characteristic of the Jeremiah tradition, repeated here in vv.
47, 52, and the idea of 'taking out of his mouth what he has swallowed'
picks up the essence of vv. 34, 35 without reference to the dragon which
makes the image intelligible. 'The nations shall no longer flow to him'
is an idea applied to Zion in the eighth century messianic prophecy of
Isa. 2.1–2 = Mic. 4.1–2. The falling of the walls of Babylon has been
featured in 50.15 and will be repeated in 51.58. The imperative to flee
from the midst of Babylon occurs in 50.8 and 51.6. The expression 'let
every man save his life' occurs in 48.6 and 51.6, and the 'fierce anger
of the LORD' in 4.8, 26; 12.13 and 25.37, 38. Verse 46 seems to be
a suture in rhythmical prose designed to link this oracle with the final
sections.

The evidence is thus irresistible that a prophet or perhaps the redactor
has composed this piece of familiar commonplaces and expressions. If
so, he has nevertheless contrived to import a sense of urgency and
imminence. In prophetic mode, he sees the future as already unfolded
and combines the two major themes of the whole collection, the fall of
Babylon and the salvation of Israel ('my people' v. 45), with the triumph
of Yahweh's wrath.

41. Babylon: Heb. *šēšaḵ*, another *atbash*. See on 51.1 and 25.25.

42. The sea has come up: the contradiction in the images has been
noticed above. But not improbably the 'sea' is another way of referring
to the chaos monster, as in Job 3.8 ('sea' for 'day'), cf. Dan. 7.3 where
the four great beasts came up out of the sea, and Ps. 40.2 where rescue
from the sea is a figure of redemption, cf. the song of Jonah and cf. verse
55.

44. Bel: See on 50.2.

the wall of Babylon: a familiar symbol of civic and national pride (1.7,
14; 7.7; 39.8; 50.15, 44; 52.14), but it is doubtful whether the author
knew much of the superb splendour of Babylon (see André Parrot, *Babylon
and the Old Testament*, 1958).

46. In the Hebrew, this verse begins 'and lest'. It may be thought
unwise to omit a particle which was intended by the redactor to connect
this verse with the preceding verse. He writes at a time when rumour
followed rumour of violent disturbance on the international scene.

Verses 44b–49a are lacking in LXX, but this is best explained as

haplography by reason of an oversight. A copyist has let his eye follow
on from 'the wall of Babylon has fallen' in verse 44 to 'as for Babylon
has fallen . . .' in verse 49.

TWO FINAL ORACLES **51.47–58**

Each is introduced by the formula: 'therefore behold the days are coming',
each threatens Babylonian images at the start (vv. 47, 52), and there is
a recognisable common pattern.

> Punishment of idols (vv. 47a, 52a)
> The land full of wounded and slain (vv. 47b, 53)
> The destroyers (*šôd^edîm*) shall come (vv. 48, 53)
> Retribution for Israel (vv. 49, and 55, 56)

Thereafter the oracles go their own ways. There are new features, but
also some use of features of the earlier oracles against the nations, notably
the shame which Babylon shall experience (v. 47) in return for the shame
Israel has experienced (v. 51); the sword, symbol of destruction (v. 50);
the designation of the enemy from the north as the 'destroyers' (vv. 48,
53, 55, 56, cf. 47.4; 48.8, 18, 32); the explicit reference to the north (v.
48); and the renewed designation of Yahweh as 'the king, whose name
is the LORD of hosts' (v. 57), perhaps again suggestive of the liturgical
background of the oracles. See p. 488ff. There is also clear indication
of dependence upon the Jeremiah tradition and particularly on the
Babylonian oracles.

48. The exultation of the heavens and the earth is a new feature which
is designed to emphasis the universal repercussions of Babylon's fall, cf.
Isa. 44.23.

destroyers: *šôd^edîm*. See on 47.4; 48.8, 18, 32; and cf. 6.26 and 23.36.

49. This is an expression of the theme of exact retribution, cf. verse
5b and see on 50.15, 29.

50. Remember the LORD from afar: an exhortation to Jews in
captivity to turn to Jerusalem as the eternal centre of their religion, cf.
Dan. 9.20.

aliens have come into the holy places of the LORD's house: this
was true in the time of Nebuchadrezzar's invasion, and again of Antiochus
Epiphanes and of Pompey as witnessed by the second Psalm of Solomon.
It never ceased to be a horrifying profanation.

52. execute judgment: i.e. 'visit' Heb. *pākad* as in v. 47, a favourite
expression of the tradition.

55. stilling her mighty voice: a fresh feature in a collection of commonplaces.

like many waters: Heb. *mayîm rabbîm*, associated with *š^e'ôn*, here 'noise', perhaps 'roaring' (Ps. 40.3 but especially Isa. 17.13) as description of cosmic waters. See on v. 42.

56. For the LORD is a God of recompense, he will surely requite: a theme of the Babylonian oracles, cf. v. 6 and see on 50.15.

57. I will make drunk: see on v. 39 which must be the background to this verse, since it continues with the same **sleep a perpetual sleep and not wake.**

her governors and **commanders:** as in v. 23.

says the king: See 46.18; 48.15 and p. 488 for a conjecture as to the liturgical context of these oracles.

58. only for fire: this is a dubious sense, here and in Hab. 2.13, where the last line of this verse also occurs, but interchanged as though quoted from memory (Rudolph). The parallelism demands 'a mere nothing' as in *NEB* and *REB*. This may be obtained by emendation, either the attested *šāw'* or, by revocalisation, the conjectural *'ōš*. Or can 'fire' stand for the result of fire, viz. 'ashes'?

CONCLUDING PROSE NARRATIVE **51.59–64**

The final editor has taken a piece of the prose tradition and so placed it that it labels all the Babylonian oracles (chapters 50–51) as the work of Jeremiah himself. He believes them to have been uttered before Zedekiah went to Babylon. The date would be 599 B.C. Jeremiah, it is claimed, wrote them out and ordered one Seraiah the quartermaster, who must have been a brother of Baruch (see 31.12), to take the book to Babylon and read it to the exiled Jews to whom Jeremiah had already written a letter of prophetic advice (chapter 29). He was then to perform a prophetic sign. The book was to be tied to a stone and dropped in the Euphrates as a prophetic indication that Babylon itself must sink and perish.

In no way as it possible to come to terms with a course of historical events thus interpreted. The Babylonian oracles belong to the decade before the rise of Cyrus. But it is unlikely that the redactor wrote this passage and invented the tale; more likely that he took a passage, suitable for his purposes, from the old prose tradition. This means that the redactor lived far enough from the time of Jeremiah and from the Babylonian oracles to be able to associate the one with the other. What links this passage with the prose tradition is the circumstantial detail, particularly the mention of Seraiah and the description of the prophetic sign. Hitherto we have had reason to suppose that the prose tradition was in touch with events and did not freely invent the circumstantial detail. This does not mean necessarily that the passage should be attributed to Baruch; the prose tradition has several authors. Seraiah was evidently his brother and Baruch was responsible for an edition of Jeremiah's oracles and for other like material. The author was an editor in the tradition.

Assuming then that this is a passage which belongs to the prose tradition, we can agree with Rudolph that chronologically it falls between chapter 29 and 34.2–7. We cannot however be confident that Zedekiah went to Babylon himself. For 'with Zedekiah' in v. 59, LXX reads 'from Zedekiah'. But either he went to Babylon with Seraiah or he sent Seraiah to make peace. It may be that the vicious treatment handed out to Zedekiah later was because he was thought to have ratted on the agreement then made. It is plausible that Jeremiah, who had previously collected his oracles concerning the Foe from the North, should also collect his much shorter oracles concerning Babylon. There is no doubt that he did predict an end of the Babylonian exile and it is probable that he envisaged the fall of Babylon. But whatever the content, it merited the description: 'all the evil that should come upon Babylon'. The further amplification: 'all these words that are written concerning Babylon' has the tell-tale ʾẹt of a gloss, and looks like a touch of the redactor to make the passage suitable to its new purpose.

There is no case, as in 13.1–7, for supposing that here also Jeremiah designated a Palestinian wady as Euphrates for the purpose of the sign. There were now Jews in or near Babylon who would witness the sign and whom Jeremiah was concerned to influence. Moreover the narrative of what was done in Babylon, witnessed to by Seraiah on his return, would have a powerful effect in Jerusalem. We may suppose therefore that Jeremiah actually instructed Seraiah to tie the document to the stone and sink it in the Euphrates. This is not magic. It is a sign of what the LORD intended to do. Undeniably however the superstitious would be encouraged to think of it magically, rather than as the word of the LORD which will not return to him void. Modern commentators must make the distinction!

64. After 'upon her' Heb. adds 'and they shall weary themselves', but no sense can be made of it.

Thus far are the words of Jeremiah: no doubt the redactor's final touch.

Prophecy Fulfilled 52.1–34

In the finished book of Jeremiah, this passage, derived from the Deuteronomic history in 2 Kg. 25, appears odd. The story of Jeremiah's prophetic activity, as recorded in the book, goes beyond the reign of Zedekiah to Gedaliah and further still. The collection of oracles includes those against the nations, and in particular the Babylonian oracles, which belong to the decade before the rise of Cyrus. But the excerpt from 2 Kg. is almost entirely concerned with events during the reign of Zedekiah. This concern seems to have radiated backwards to the final section of chapter 51 (vv. 59–64). Indeed, it has been stressed in the comment on that chapter that the redactor, living sufficiently distant from the period of the Babylonian oracles, attributed them to Jeremiah in the time of Zedekiah. From his point of view therefore there was nothing incongruous in placing this limited historical tradition at the end of the prophetic collection.

But he had deeper reasons which retain their validity. The book of Jeremiah is predominantly prophecy. For the most part Jeremiah's work is theme and variations on the judgment that is to fall on the people of God at the hands of the Babylonians. In restricted measure he allowed himself to look beyond judgment to ultimate salvation. The effect of this historical appendix is to show how completely the prophecy of Jeremiah was fulfilled and, in the last section of Jehoiachin's release, how even the prophecy of hope received at least an anticipatory fulfilment. The redactor's self discipline is exemplary. He does not attempt to gild the lily. He simply quotes the final section, probably an appendix, of the Deuteronomic history, as though to say, 'Draw your own conclusions. The facts speak for themselves.'

When a long passage is quoted without any substantial doctoring, as this one is, the purpose of the redactor is revealed as much by what he excludes as by what he includes. Here comparison has to be made also with chapter 39, and is best displayed in a table.

A. Deut[c] formula for Zedekiah	2 Kg. 24.18–20b	Jer. 52.1–3b (vv. 2–3 om. LXX)	cf. 37.1–2
B. Siege of Jerusalem	2 Kg. 24.20c–25.4a	Jer. 52.3c–7a	39.1–2 om. 'And Zedekiah rebelled . . .'
C. Fall of Jerusalem	2 Kg. 25.4b–12	Jer. 52.7b–16 (v. 15 om. LXX)	39.4–10 (abbreviated om. LXX. LXX has v. 3, not in 2 Kg.).

D. Temple vessels	2 Kg. 25.13–17	Jer. 52.17–23	
E. Leaders killed at Riblah	2 Kg. 25.18–21	Jer. 52.24–27	
F. Numbers of the exiled	cf. 2 Kg. 24.14, 16	Jer. 52.28–30 (om. LXX)	
G. Gedaliah	2 Kg. 25.22–26		cf. 39.11–14; chs 40–41
H. Release of Jehoiachin	2 Kg. 25.27–29	Jer. 52.31–34	

In the case of chapter 39, we have already seen reason to conclude that a first redactor knew the Deuteronomic history and used it, but sparingly and with freedom (see on 39.1–2). A second redactor, at a time unknown, built on 39.1–2, which is an abridged quotation from 2 Kg. 25.1–4a, and added vv. 4–10 from 2 Kg. 25.4b–12, together with vv. 11–13, which are his own writing. This conclusion is derived from the fact that verses 4–13 are not present in LXX.

A similar phenomenon of redaction can be observed in Jer. 52. Verses 2–3, 15 and 28–30 are not present in the LXX, together with a few other, less significant touches. Verses 28–30 is the section giving the numbers of the exiled, which is also in this form, absent in the Deuteronomic history. We conclude that there was a first redaction which quoted 2 Kg. 24.18–25.29 more or less as it is known to us. The only substantial change was the omission of the standard Deuteronomic judgment on Zedekiah. Where this might have been quoted in 37.1–2, the redactor substituted a judgment based on Zedekiah's relation to Jeremiah. The omission in chapter 52 would seem to have been appropriate, in view of Zedekiah's admiration for Jeremiah. He was not wicked but weak. A second redactor, no doubt much more distant from the events, introduced the Deuteronomic judgment, together with the section on the numbers of the exiled (52.28–30). Thus in both chapters 39 and 52 two layers of redaction are disclosed, before the text reached its present form.

Three subsections require particular comment. Since the redactor was quite ready to omit a passage if he though fit (the Gedaliah section in 2 Kg. 25.22–26), it is proper to ask why he should include section D on the Temple vessels (Jer. 51.17–23). This is plain contrary to the profounder concerns of Jeremiah himself who envisaged the destruction of the Temple, whereas the fate of the Temple vessels constitutes what P. R. Ackroyd has called a 'continuity theme'. Despite the suggestion that the gold vessels were converted into bullion, the overall and deliberate impression is one of conservation. When the Temple was restored, the vessels could be returned in some form or other (cf. Ezra. 8.24–30). It is the dominance of this theme which makes it difficult to know exactly what was destroyed and what was not. It is however clear that the later men of the Jeremiah tradition were profoundly concerned with the future of the Temple, and regarded its destruction not as just punishment but as an outrage meriting retribution (see especially the sometimes editorial touches of the Babylonian oracles 50.28; 51.11, 24, 51; but also visionary hopes of 17.26; 33.17). This section is thus a symbol of a preoccupation, long after the death of Jeremiah, with the restoration of the Temple, and is intended to show that the dismantling of the Temple vessels was done in such a way, that by the divine providence, they could be restored to their sacred purpose. In 27.16–22 the prediction is on the lips of the false prophets! See notes there.

Section F, the numbers of the exiled (Jer. 52.28–30) is, as we have seen, a late addition to the chapter. Did the redactor have access to new and reliable information? The modesty of the numbers suggests that he did– 3,023 in 597 B.C., 832 in 587 B.C. and 745 in 582 B.C. i.e. 4,600 in all. These figures do not tally with those of 2 Kg. 24.14, 16 (10,000 and 8,000). Various explanations are offered, as that these numbers may be the total of adult males, or that they may be the total of prisoners who survived to reach Babylonia. It is unlikely, in view of the relative lateness of this passage, that Jer. 52.28–30 formed the basis for the construction of the number 10,000 in 2 Kg. 24. We have no means of telling how reliable the figures are. It seems clear from much indirect evidence that substantial numbers were left in Palestine and that the Babylonian exile did not leave the land utterly depopulated. It was the upper classes who were severely punished.

Section G. The brief mention of Gedaliah in 2 Kg. 25.22–26 is omitted entirely. In contrast, the Gedaliah tradition in 39.11–14 (in which Jeremiah is entrusted to Gedaliah) and chapters 40–41 (in which there is no mention of Jeremiah) is substantial. There is in fact no mention of Jeremiah throughout the quotation from the Deuteronomic history, and this confirms the view that the purpose of the redactor is to focus attention on the fate of Jerusalem and the hope of the future, not on the person of Jeremiah.

Section H. The release of Jehoiachin (52.31–34) = 2 Kg. 25.27–29) provides a glimmer of hope and is quoted to demonstrate this. It happened in 561 B.C. and no other event had this positive symbolic force before the rise of Cyrus, save more general disturbances on the world scene.

Amel-Merodach was Nebuchadrezzar's successor and reigned only from 562 to 560. Jehoiachin must have been interned for thirty-six years. This is one of the few events about which there is some independent archaeological evidence. In a Babylonian inscription discovered at the site of ancient Babylon, stored underground, not far from the Ishtar gate, there is explicit reference to Ya'ukinu king of the land of Yahudi, and a list of the rations apportioned to him and his five sons from the royal storehouse (*DOTT* 84–86). It appears that Jehoiachin continued to be regarded as the *de jure* king of Judah, whatever the exact status of Zedekiah may have been in *Judaea*.

4. in the ninth year:589 B.C.. LXX has 'tenth'.

5. the eleventh year of Zedekiah: 587 B.C.

12. in the fifth month: August.

the nineteenth year of Nebuchadrezzar: i.e. 587 B.C.

Nebuzaradan the captain of the guard: see on 39.9.

14. broke down all the walls: just as this was the first thing to do to make Jerusalem powerless, so it was the first part of the city to repair in order to restore its independence. Hence the paramount importance of the rebuilding of the walls in the work of Nehemiah.

15. of the poorest of the people: absent in LXX and 2 Kg.

17–23. Most of the vessels listed here correspond to the inventory in 1 Kg. 7. Additional to 2 Kg. 25 are the 'twelve bronze bulls which were under the stands' (it is LXX which supplies 'the sea', as in *RSV* (cf. 2 Kg. 16.17). The originals had been given as tribute to Assyria, but it is unlikely that they were not replaced. This and other additions to 2. Kg. 25, as for example v. 23, suggest considerable interest in precise detail. The height of the pillars (eighteen cubits in v. 21) is inherently more probable than the figure given by LXX and 2 Chr. 3.15 (thirty-five cubits and too high to go in the Temple!). **on the sides** in v. 23 is an attempt to render the puzzling Hebrew *rûḥāh* 'windward'. *NEB, REB* hazard 'exposed to view'.

24–27. The list of those whom Nebuzaradan took to Riblah and whom Nebuchadrezzar put to death. The specific way in which the list is presented suggests that the Babylonian commander took a deliberate step to remove the effective leadership. Anyone else who was any good was removed to Babylon, leaving as was said in v. 16, 'the poorest of the land to be vinedressers and ploughmen'.

24. Seraiah the chief priest: of a distinguished high-priestly family, grandson of Hilkiah (1 Chr. 6.13–15; 2 Kg. 22.4ff) and father of

Jehozadak who was taken into exile, whose son Joshua assisted Zerabbabel
to rebuild the Temple (Ezr. 5.2, cf. Hag.; Zech. 6.11).
Zephaniah: cf. Jer. 29. 24–29; 37.3.
three keepers of the threshold: high cultic officials with disciplinary
functions cf. 35.4.
from the city he took: absent in LXX
25. an officer: *sārîs*, cf. 29.2; 34.19; 41.16. But see on 38.7. Literally
'eunuch', but here no doubt correctly translated to denote one who had
some sort of administrative responsibility for the forces. The word 'in
command of' (Heb. *pāqîd* 'overseer'), much used in the Jeremiah
tradition, suggests general oversight.
   seven men of the king's council: 2 Kg. 25.19 has 'five'. Literally
'those who see the king's face' i.e. with right of access to the king or 'in
the king's personal service'.
   the secretary of the commander of the army: *NEB REB*, have
adjutant general and omit 'commander of the army' as a gloss. No doubt
some sort of chief of staff. He is said to have mustered 'the people of
the land'.
   sixty men of the people of the land: this expression has two meanings,
according to context. Either it can denote the common people generally,
or it can denote the landed gentry, i.e. the freemen of Judah, who based
their proud claims on kinship and tradition rather than the royal favour.
It was this group which had put Josiah on the throne (2 Kg. 21.24). They
tended to be distinguished from the inhabitants of Jerusalem. In this single
context, it is really impossible that both meanings should be intended.
NEB REB, opt for the common meaning: 'whose duty was to muster the
people for war, and sixty men of the people who were still there'. This
fails to do justice to the wider context of vv. 24–27 where the intention
is to list the influential. It is wiser therefore to interpret the secretary as
head of this powerful group of the gentry or freemen of Judah, and the
sixty as an indication of their number. The attempt was made by the
Babylonians to wipe them out. See also on 1.19.
   27. smote them: i.e. flogged them *REB*
   28–30. See above. Section F.
   31–34. See above. Section G.
   31. Evil-Merodach: i.e. Amel-Marduk. The Heb. *ᵛwîl* is no doubt
an intentional and pejorative play on words, meaning 'idiot'.

It appears therefore that the Babylonian conqueror dealt a double blow
to the reeling Jewish community. Any who might have become the basis

of further resistance were summarily executed. Those of the rest who were judged worth taking into captivity to serve the Babylonians were taken. This ignores the phrase 'the poorest of the people' in v. 15 (absent in LXX) and stresses the word 'artisans' which probably means 'skilled workers'. This policy completed the plan initiated with the exile of Jehoiachin, and can be detected beneath the exaggerations of 2 Kg. 24.14–16. Those left were labourers. Archaeology confirms the impression of large scale destruction of Judaen cities.

Even so not every glimmer of creative activity was suppressed. The production of the Deuteronomic history (some scholars think this was produced in Babylonia, but the evidence for a Palestinian origin may be judged stronger), the laments collected in Lamentations and probably Third Isaiah, show that there was a cultural and religious continuity centred on the ruined Temple. But the men of the Jeremiah tradition, despite Jeremiah's own exile in Egypt, saw the future with the Babylonian captives, a community which later enjoyed relative freedom, as shown particularly by Ezekiel. This accounts for the fruitfulness of their long-term contribution both in prophecy and in the adaptation of the legal and cultic traditions, to establish the vision of a new national structure for the people of God. The release of Jehoiachin from prison was understood to be the sign of the beginning of the fulfilment of this dream. As it has been said, a scion of David's house was alive and well.

INDEX